Management for Professionals

More information about this series at http://www.springer.com/series/10101

Bernd Stauss • Wolfgang Seidel

Effective Complaint Management

The Business Case for Customer
Satisfaction

Second Edition

Springer

Bernd Stauss
Catholic University of Eichstätt-Ingolstadt
Ingolstadt, Germany

Wolfgang Seidel
servmark consultancy
Ingolstadt and Munich, Germany

Originally published in English with the title 'Complaint Management: The Heart of CRM', Thompson Learning (Cengage), 2004

ISSN 2192-8096 ISSN 2192-810X (electronic)
Management for Professionals
ISBN 978-3-319-98704-0 ISBN 978-3-319-98705-7 (eBook)
https://doi.org/10.1007/978-3-319-98705-7

Library of Congress Control Number: 2018957270

Illustrations by Reinhold Löffler

This Springer imprint is published by the registered company Springer Nature Switzerland AG
The registered company address is: Gewerbestrasse 11, 6330 Cham, Switzerland

Preface

You all know me. I'm the one who never complains, no matter what kind of service I get.

I'll go into a bank and wait quietly while the tellers gossip and never bother to ask if anyone has attended to me. Sometimes someone that came after I did gets attended to before me, but I don't complain, I just wait.

And when an arrogant saleswoman gets upset in a shop because I only want to look around for a moment, I remain as polite as possible. I don't believe rudeness in return is the answer.

I never nag. I never criticize. And I wouldn't dream of making a scene in public. No, I'm the nice customer.

And I'll tell you who else I am. When I get pushed too far, I just take my business down the street to places where they're smart enough to hire and train people who appreciate nice customers. And the world is filled with nice customers, just like me, who can put anyone out of business.

I laugh when I see you frantically spending your money on expensive advertising to get me back, when you could have kept me with a few kind words, a smile, and some good service.

Source: Anonymous

These nice customers are the majority. Even if they are annoyed, they don't make trouble; they stay polite and silent, but they just go away and are lost forever. In times of fierce global competition, companies can less and less afford this silent loss of customers. Therefore, they have to strive uncompromisingly for customer satisfaction. However, if customers are dissatisfied for some reason, companies have to encourage these customers to address their complaint directly to the company, and they have to install a professional complaint management system to permanently restore customer satisfaction.

Currently, many companies lack a sufficient understanding that complaints offer the greatest opportunity for achieving customer loyalty, for reducing failure costs, and for improving product and service quality. Although most top managers publicly commit themselves to the goal of customer satisfaction, many customers going to the company with a problem experience that this is just "lip service." They receive no, belated, or inappropriate answers. Moreover, the information contained in complaints is hardly ever used for quality improvements and product innovations. Dissatisfied customers who are now additionally disappointed by the company's reaction to their complaint will definitely change the provider and engage in negative word-of-mouth communication. On the other hand, it has been verified in many cases that complainants who were satisfied with the company's reaction to their complaint show an extraordinarily high level of satisfaction and loyalty. Therefore, investments made in complaint management are investments in customer retention and a precondition for enduring market success.

This book is designed for managers who want to make optimum use of the opportunities offered by complaints. It provides insights into the behavior of dissatisfied customers, clarifies which goals can be achieved with the help of a proactive complaint management system, and points out concretely how to fulfill the operational asks.

The consequences for the organizational framework and the human resource management of a proactive complaint management system will be presented, as well as opportunities to handle complaints with the help of software tools.

This book is based on a long-term cooperation, which allows for a permanent exchange of research findings and experiences from practice. On the one hand, complaint management has been a research focus of many years for Bernd Stauss. In a number of empirical studies and theoretical contributions, he has dealt with the complaint behavior of customers and all relevant aspects of complaint management in large-scale companies. On the other hand, the book benefits from many years of consulting practice of Wolfgang Seidel. His consulting firm servmark focuses on complaint management problems and gives advice to internationally operating, large-scale German companies such as Allianz Group, Deutsche Post World Net, and Volkswagen AG.

Due to this unique combination of competencies, the German version of this book has earned the position of a standard work, and we are very grateful that the English version of the book is now available in its second edition.

We would like to cordially invite you, the readers of our book, to a constant dialog. We very much appreciate all of your comments, suggestions, and—of course—complaints.

Ingolstadt, Germany   Bernd Stauss
Ingolstadt and Munich, Germany   Wolfgang Seidel

Contents

Complaint Management in a Customer-Oriented Firm

© Springer Nature Switzerland AG 2019
B. Stauss, W. Seidel, *Effective Complaint Management*, Management for Professionals,
https://doi.org/10.1007/978-3-319-98705-7_1

Issues Raised
- Why is complaint management of strategic corporate importance?
- What role does complaint management play in customer relationship management?
- What relations exist between customer relationship management, customer care and complaint management?
- How important is complaint management in quality management?

1.1   Complaints as a Challenge to the Firm

Everyone in business *hates complaints*. Employees who come into contact with customers dread situations in which they might be abused by angry customers. Employees from all levels of decision-making authority feel that they are being criticized unjustly. They are also annoyed because they have to put time into handling customers' problems that they had not planned for, so that their own schedules are then thrown into disarray. Members of top management find themselves more and more confronted with the fact that customer address their complaints directly to them and also expect a personal answer. Indeed, top management's time has already been allotted for handling strategic problems. Moreover, members of top management do not see it as part of their responsibilities to grapple with the detailed problems of unknown customers. As a rule, therefore, they tend merely to give instructions that a solution should be found. Complaints are then passed down through the hierarchy, although the primary goal of complaint processing is usually to fend off customer concerns as much as possible and/or to find someone to blame within the firm.

Accordingly, many firms still *make it difficult for their customers to register complaints with them*. Neither product packaging nor homepages or advertisements give any indication as to whom dissatisfied customers can turn. If the customers do manage to contact the firm successfully—for example, by phone—they are often unable to find anyone who will take responsibility. It is not uncommon for them to be transferred a number of times to new, unaccountable or incompetent employee counterparts, without getting any closer to solving their problem. Such experiences can result in negative consequences for customers. They make an internal decision to sever the business relationship and choose a competing product the next time they make a purchase. For the firm, then, future potential business is permanently lost. In especially serious cases, the customers turn their case over to their attorney or they turn to the media. Based on these actions, firms are then forced to react. Usually, though, it does not matter how this turns out: the *"opponent" customer* usually is not won back, and the costs of complaint processing and problem-solving for the firm are higher than they would have been had the firm reacted earlier.

The *barriers* erected by firms to deter dissatisfied customers from complaining frequently have an even more direct effect: customers shy away from the exasperation and effort that accompany the search for a responsible contact person and do not complain but instead switch immediately to the competition. Since firms often know nothing about this or only find out indirectly and with a comprehensible time delay, they often come to incorrect conclusions. They refer to *low rates of complaints* and to the high level of satisfaction that is reflected in the corresponding results from customer surveys. They thus falsely equate low rates of complaints with customer satisfaction and overlook the fact that in these customer satisfaction surveys, they only poll customers who have not yet switched at the time of the survey.

On the basis of this faulty assessment, firms often see no need for action; and even when they do perceive one, goal-oriented activities remain undone because many firms have not yet recognized that dealing with complaints is a *top-level management task*. There are even quite a few executives who prefer to ban the terms "complaint" or "complaint management" in order to avoid the negative connotations associated with them. However, this is a short-sighted view.

The brief description of the often bad experiences that customers and companies have in the case of complaints demonstrates the *complex management tasks* that have to be solved. Internal communication and operating processes for complaint handling and problem-solving must be set up and monitored. Employees must be informed and trained on how to behave toward dissatisfied customers. The information contained in the complaints needs to be evaluated and included in decision-making processes. Individual and organizational competencies have to be defined, and the human resources, as well as the organizational and technological framework conditions must have an appropriate design to ensure that this responsibility is actually taken.

The list of important management tasks could easily be extended and specified in more detail. However, the relevance of complaint management does not stem from the complexity of the task, but from its *strategic importance in the context of a customer-oriented corporate policy.*

In a tightening buyer's market with an increasing level of international competition, almost all firms have increased their efforts to become more market-oriented and get greater access to their customers in recent years. These days, it is difficult to find top managers who do not declare their public support for customer satisfaction as the primary corporate goal. Proclamations like these remain merely *lip service*, however, as long as they have no effects on the experiences of dissatisfied customers. If firms are actually striving for customer satisfaction, then the minimal requirements for management include avoiding customer dissatisfaction as much as possible and, when it is already present, to put all their efforts into eliminating it. Customers cannot make their discontent any more clear to the firm than they can in complaints, and firms cannot express the fact that they are not interested in customer satisfaction any more clearly than by their disinterested or cool reactions to complaints. Or conversely: anyone who has recognized customer orientation as a prerequisite for the long-term survival of the firm and takes customer satisfaction seriously as a maxim will regard complaints not primarily as a problem to be warded off, but rather as an *opportunity*, and complaint management as the core of a customer-oriented corporate strategy.

1.2   The Strategic Relevance of Complaint Management

Complaint management involves a complex area of action. It includes the planning, conduct and monitoring of all measures taken by a company in connection with complaints. In strategic terms, complaint management is of outstanding importance in two respects. On the one hand, annoyed customers will be satisfied and kept loyal, so that positive effects for the company's economic success will be achieved. In this respect, complaint management includes a great *strategic potential for customer relationship management*. On the other hand, it is responsible for the collection and use of the information contained in complaints for the improvement of products and processes, resulting in a high *strategic potential for quality management*.

1.2.1   Complaint Management Within the Framework of Customer Relationship Management (CRM)

1.2.1.1 The Understanding of Customer Relationship Management

The term *customer relationship management* is associated with different conceptual ideas that can be roughly assigned to the two approaches "contact optimization" or "relationship development".

CRM as contact optimization represents an optimization focused on customer value and the integration of all customer-related processes in marketing, sales and service. It is based on the pooling and use of all customer data in one database as well as on the synchronization of all customer-related communication.

CRM as relationship development often uses the same technology; however, this is not the focus. Instead, the its main purpose is to build up a relationship that is considered important by customers. The aim is to establish a relationship of trust between provider and customer, leading to a commitment in the sense of an emotional bond and to loyal b*ehavior*. Trust and loyalty can, however, be neither forced nor bought; they must be won based on positive experiences. Only when customers actually learn via the various situations of the business relationship that the firm is behaving in a customer-oriented manner and thus has earned their trust can it be expected that the customers will hold on to the business relationship of their own. This understanding of relationship development forms the basis for the following discussion and characterizes the future use of the term "CRM".

A conscious turning away from the traditional perspective of conventional (transaction) marketing is also associated with placing the emphasis on the customer relationship. This conventional type of marketing was primarily focused on the acquisition of new customers and the execution of isolated individual transactions. The fundamental basis for the move toward *relationship orientation* is the knowledge that winning new customers is associated with extraordinarily high investments in mature markets with minimal growth rates and that the loss of customers weakens the firm itself on the one hand, and strengthens competitors on the other. For this reason, what is important is not simply to win the customers over in the pre-purchase phase, but rather to accompany them through all the purchase and use phases and to bind them for as long a time as possible by offering solutions to problems that are tuned to their various needs.

1.2.1.2 The Concept of the Customer Relationship Life Cycle

The conceptual basis for CRM is the *customer relationship life cycle* (Stauss 2011). This life cycle is a matter of an ideal typical depiction of the progression of a business relationship from the initiation through to the termination. It is assumed here that a business relationship—like a personal relationship—goes through different phases that are associated respectively with varied rates of growth in the intensity of the relationship and requires phase-specific customer relationship management tasks. Figure 1.1 shows a simple variant of such a progression. The intensity of the relationship is expressed via the value of the customer—for instance, through the individual customer's contribution to the profit margin.

The observation regarding the customer relationship life cycle brings to the fore the fact that *three groups of customers* can be differentiated with respect to the business relationship, each of which presents management with a completely different set of challenges. *Potential ("not yet") customers* are addressed by *acquisition management, current customers* make up the target group of *retention management*, and the activities of *regain management* are directed toward *lost ("not anymore") customers.*

The goal of *acquisition management* is to arouse interest in potential customers during the initiation phase and to induce leads to make an initial purchase. With the help of *retention management*, firms strive to bind the (attractive) customers that they already have in an ongoing and sustainable manner and to make sure that the respective business potential continues to grow (Baran and Galka 2017). *Regain management* is aimed at winning back attractive customers who have explicitly announced their intention to break off the business relationship or have actually terminated it (Stauss and Friege 1999; Bose and Bansal 2001; Griffin and Lowenstein 2001).

Complaint management deals with the current customers, namely those in the endangerment phase that is particularly highlighted in Fig. 1.1, during which there is a risk that customers will terminate the business relationship due to their dissatisfaction. Thus, complaint management is primarily intended to prevent the migration of dissatisfied customers, and represents the core of any customer retention management.

1.2.1.3 Retention Management as Core of CRM

In view of largely saturated markets, the goal of customer retention has become increasingly important over the years. Companies strive for sustainable growth of sales and profit by strengthening the relationship with existing customers and by extending the duration of the customer life cycle. Here, two fundamentally different

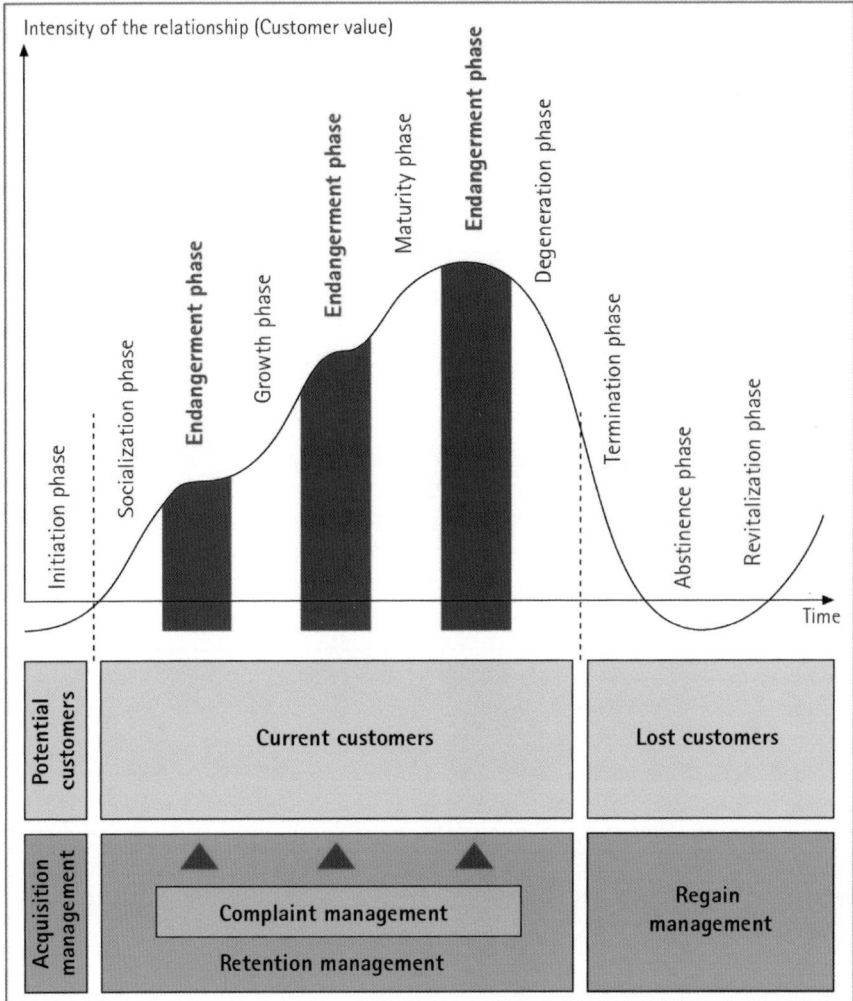

Fig. 1.1 Customer relationship life cycle (based on Stauss 2011, p. 434)

strategies can be chosen: growth due to the greatest possible increase of customer satisfaction (satisfaction maximizing strategy) or growth by avoiding and eliminating customer dissatisfaction (dissatisfaction minimizing strategy). In theory and practice, the satisfaction maximizing strategy is given great attention. In comparison, the importance of the dissatisfaction minimizing strategy, which is primarily pursued with the help of complaint management, is often underestimated. However, a closer look at the economic effects of both strategy options often shows that this prioritization is not justified. In many cases the dissatisfaction minimizing strategy proves to be the far more profitable option.

1.2.1.4 Satisfaction Maximizing Strategy: Usually Chosen, But Problematic

The central starting point of the satisfaction maximizing strategy is the exploitation of the sales potential of current customers by increasing their buying intensity and the initiation of additional purchases (cross-selling). This is achieved by satisfaction-enhancing measures—in particular by the granting of price advantages and other benefits in the context of loyalty programs or bonus and discount systems (Butscher 2016).

The satisfaction maximizing strategy is based on the assumption of a specific impact chain which is uncritically taken as real. According to this assumption, customer satisfaction leads to trust and commitment on the psychological level, which induces the customers to behave loyally, reflected by repurchases and recommendations. In this understanding, customer satisfaction leads to high customer loyalty and economic growth. It is self-evident that satisfied customers tend to behave more loyally than dissatisfied ones, but there is no guarantee that satisfaction always leads to customer loyalty. Managers who conclude from high satisfaction scores that their customers will be loyal in future are often deceiving themselves. Then they have fallen into one of the traps of the satisfaction maximizing strategy.

The Satisfaction Trap

The term "satisfaction trap" was coined by the American business author Frederick Reichheld (1996), when he observed that in the American automotive industry, companies such as General Motors could point to constantly rising satisfaction scores, while they lost market share and profits at the same time. The results of empirical studies in this industry show that 90% of the customers claim to be satisfied or very satisfied, but only 40% come back and buy again. This phenomenon has increased even more in recent years. Many companies are faced with the seemingly paradoxical situation that the usual satisfaction surveys indicate high customer satisfaction, while at the same time they suffer massive customer losses. There are several reasons for this. Even satisfied customers defect, for example, if their needs and circumstances change. Surveys of lost customers also show that the extent of customer churn due to dissatisfaction is usually much higher than could have been expected according to the results of the satisfaction survey (see *Spotlight 1.1*).

> Spotlight 1.1
> **Loss of Customers in Spite of High Customer Satisfaction and Repurchase Intention**
>   Many companies suffer severe customer losses in spite of high levels of customer satisfaction or even repurchase intention. Here are two real-life examples from companies in the financial services industry: the annual customer satisfaction survey of an insurance company shows excellent global satisfaction scores—58% of the customers are convinced (completely

(continued)

satisfied/very satisfied), another 38% are satisfied, only 4% are disappointed (less satisfied/dissatisfied). The customer satisfaction rate amounts to 96%; the repurchase intention rate is 91%. Nevertheless, the churn rate is 10%, meaning that one in 10 contracts was terminated. The total number of terminations amounts to approximately 300,000 policies with a premium volume of around 40 million €. This is equivalent to 1200 contract cancellations with a premium volume loss of 160,000 € per day!

A similar picture shows the analysis of customer satisfaction scores and the number of customer losses of a building society. The results of the satisfaction survey for the last financial year are as follows: 51% convinced customers, 45% satisfied and 4% disappointed customers (customer satisfaction rate 96%). In addition, 82% of the customers state they would be willing to repurchase the service. Despite this proof of high customer satisfaction and repurchase intention, the company has suffered huge customer losses. Approximately 100,000 customers have migrated over the last four fiscal years. This means about 400 lost customers per working day or a two-digit million Euro loss of EBIT (earnings before interest and taxes) over the period under review (see Fig. 1.2).

The examples are not individual cases. Therefore, high customer satisfaction scores cannot be regarded as meaningful indicators for customer loyalty. Many managers have reason to reconsider their efforts to increase satisfaction scores (satisfaction maximizing strategy), to focus instead on the actual customer losses, and primarily to avoid customer churn due to dissatisfaction (dissatisfaction minimizing strategy).

Source: servmark (2012)

When companies can no longer overlook the discrepancy between the results of satisfaction surveys and customer losses, they usually react in three ways. They modify the measurement, increase their efforts to maximize satisfaction and try to compensate for the loss of customers by the acquisition of new customers. In these ways they run the risk of falling into three other traps: the intention trap, the delight trap and the new acquisition trap.

The Intention Trap

Recognizing the low significance of high satisfaction scores for future customer loyalty, many companies have started to ask the customers not only about their satisfaction but also about their planned future behavior. Particularly, they collect data on the intention to remain a customer in future (*rebuy intention*) and/or their intention to recommend the product or company to others (*recommendation intention*). Special attention has been given to the Net Promoter Score (NPS) concept, which uses the likelihood to recommend as a single indicator (Reichheld 2006, 2011). However, even these measurement approaches cannot be regarded as reliable predictors of customers' future loyalty behavior (Keiningham et al. 2007).

Insurance company

Customer satisfaction

convinced	satisfied	disappointed
🙂	😐	🙁
58 %	38 %	4 %

Satisfaction rate 96 %

Contract losses

Rate   10 %

Premiums / year
40 Mio. €

Repurchase intention

yes, for sure	probably yes	no
43 %	48 %	9 %

Repurchase intention rate 91 %

Contracts / year
300,000

Building society

Customer satisfaction

convinced	satisfied	disappointed
🙂	😐	🙁
51 %	45 %	4 %

Satisfaction rate 96 %

Customer losses

Customers / year
100,000

Repurchase intention

definitely yes	probably yes	maybe	probably no	definitely no
36 %	46 %	14 %	3 %	1 %

Repurchase intention rate 82 %

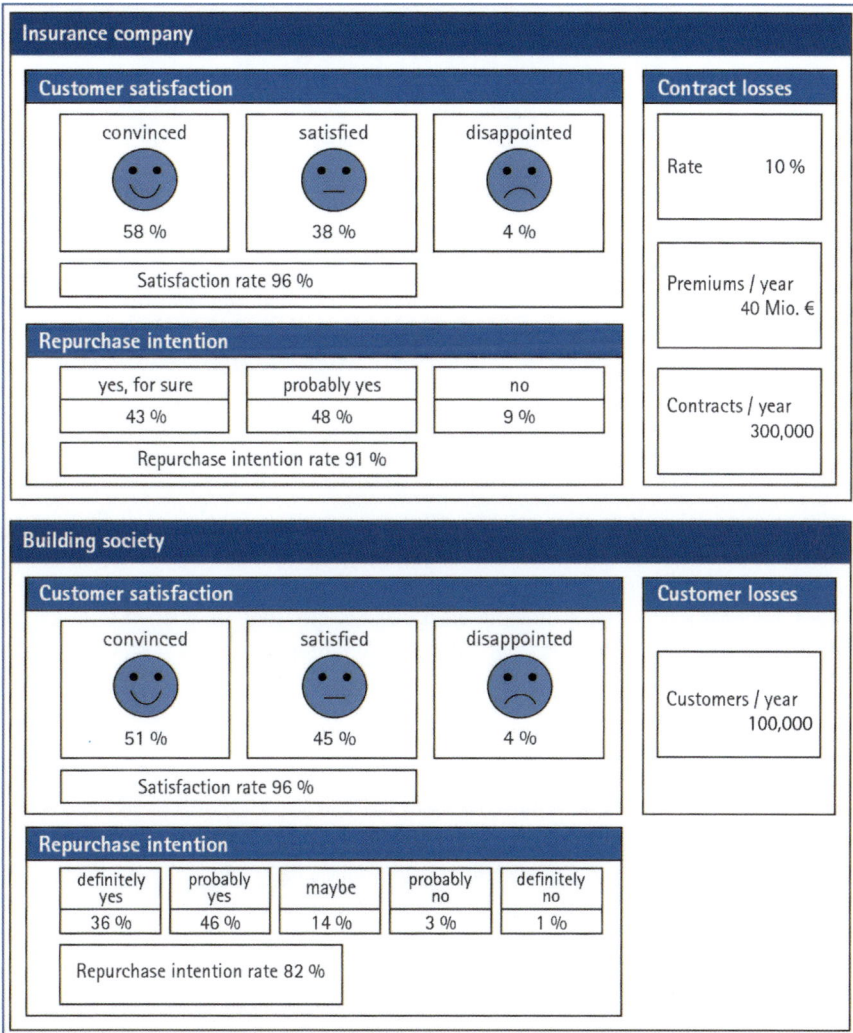

Fig. 1.2 Customer satisfaction—repurchase intention—customer losses

Statements of today about behavior intentions should not be equated with the actual behavior tomorrow. The customers' likelihood to recommend says little about whether they will still be customers in future.

The Delight Trap
Empirical studies show that the desired high binding effect occurs only when customers are extremely satisfied. Only completely satisfied customers remain loyal and act as "apostles" (Heskett et al. 1994, p. 166). Accordingly, companies

must not only satisfy their customers but *delight* them (Keiningham and Vavra 2001; Chiturri et al. 2008). However, if companies accept this request uncritically, they may fall into another economic trap. By no means all products and services are suitable for putting customers in the highly emotional state of delight. It is also necessary to consider that *basic quality attributes* have a much higher behavioral effect than *delight attributes*. For customers, the reliable and effective fulfillment of the core tasks is far more important than a surprising additional benefit. Accordingly, satisfaction with delight attributes cannot compensate for dissatisfaction with basic attributes or prevent migration.

From an economic point of view, it must also be noted that measures to delight customers not only involve considerable costs, but also increase the *aspiration level of customers* again and again. A satisfaction maximizing strategy focused on the delight goal requires the permanent exceeding of the expectations of increasingly demanding customers. But this is only justified if the measures generate additional revenue due to increased customer loyalty which exceeds the increased costs. The investments to increase the satisfaction of already satisfied customers must also be more profitable than potential investments to prevent the migration of dissatisfied customers. In their study on 'Return on Quality', for example, Rust et al. (1995, p. 66) found that delighted customers articulated a high rebuy intention; but "the biggest benefits are derived from converting customers from dissatisfied to satisfied, which is probably accomplished by solving or avoiding problems".

The New Acquisition Trap

If companies continue to massively lose customers despite the application of loyalty measurement and delight activities, they normally reinforce their efforts to *acquire new customers* in order to at least retain their customer base. Accordingly, they increase their advertising and marketing budgets and customers are lured away from competitors by expensive special benefits (Ratcliff 2014). However, in many cases this approach proves to be a strategic failure because the acquisition of new customers is associated with high costs, and the expensively acquired new customers often migrate before they became profitable. Moreover, since the advantages are only granted to new customers, this is de facto the abandonment of the customer retention strategy: current and previously satisfied customers are disadvantaged, become dissatisfied and are pushed to migrate in order to gain the new customer benefits from another company. Only a few companies have a realistic idea of the extent to which this kind of new customer acquisition promotes the migration of existing customers.

The description of the satisfaction, intent, delight and new acquisition trap does not in any way imply that efforts to increase customer satisfaction, loyalty, positive word-of-mouth communication or new customer acquisition are problematic per se. The primary aim is to recognize and consider the risks, but above all to change the ranking of the strategic options: *priority shouldn't be granted* to the satisfaction maximizing strategy but *to the dissatisfaction minimizing strategy*.

1.2.1.5 Dissatisfaction Minimizing Strategy: Often Neglected, But Primary

The second strategic option of customer retention management follows a different path. *Prevention and dealing with customer dissatisfaction* has priority here; the effort to make already satisfied customers even happier is secondary. A number of arguments support this option.

For many companies, the increasing *churn*—the loss of customers to another company—is one of the most serious management problems (Shewan 2017). In industries with contractual business relationships, churn rates—the proportion of customers who leave during a given time period—range from 20% to more than 60% (Neslin et al. 2006; Hughes 2007). In this situation, for companies it is of less interest what their remaining customers are satisfied with, but *why customers migrate* and to what extent these losses are avoidable. Therefore, it is necessary to precisely record and analyze the customers' dissatisfaction. Dissatisfaction is one of the main reasons customers abandon their loyalty to the company and are susceptible to offers from competitors:

- High levels of dissatisfaction do not arise because of the absence of additional benefits, but because of *deficiencies of the core service*, the non-fulfillment of basic needs. In these cases a risk of customer losses exists. Thus, it is essential to discover the quality defects perceived by customers and to eliminate them.
- Customer dissatisfaction caused by product or service deficiencies increases massively if companies do not react to the customers' complaint or answer inappropriately. The resulting *'double' dissatisfaction* often leads to immediate customer migration.
- The dissatisfaction minimizing strategy has a defensive orientation, because it aims to avoid customer churn. Nevertheless, it can be described as a growth strategy. It secures the *'lost growth'* due to customer losses, which would otherwise have to be compensated for by new customers (see *Spotlight 1.2*).
- Moreover, minimizing dissatisfaction often proves to be *the most profitable option* for retention management. For example, Reichheld and Sasser (1990) found in their empirical studies that reducing defections by 5% boosted profits by 25–85%. In this respect, it seems economically rational to give the number one priority to the minimizing dissatisfaction strategy: to prevent dissatisfaction by careful quality assurance and to reduce dissatisfaction by professional complaint management.

Spotlight 1.2
Avoidable Customer Losses Due to Dissatisfaction

Customer losses must be investigated systematically with regard to their causes and their preventability. Basically, five types of lost customers can be distinguished from each other (Stauss and Friege 1999; Seidel 2010):

(continued)

Spotlight 1.2 (continued)

- *Intentionally pushed-away customers:* this segment comprises customers with whom it is not profitable for companies to continue the relationship because they render a negative profit contribution.
- *Driven-away customers:* these customers are lost because the company's performance does not meet the customers' expectations or the company ignores their requirements.
- *Pulled-away customers:* competitors pull the customer to their side by offering a better product, service or price.
- *Bought-away customers:* this customer group does not primarily switch to a competitor because of a superior offer but because of 'bribes' such as exclusive benefits for new customers.
- *Moved-away customers:* they drift away as a result of changing needs due to the customers' age, their position in the family life cycle, or a new life style.

The loss of intentionally pushed-away customers and moved-away customers is unavoidable. Bought-away customers are usually not profitable, because they take any chance to defect. But driven-away customers and pulled-away customers represent the potential of generally *avoidable customer losses*.

A valid survey of customers who cancelled their insurance contracts shows the magnitude of the various types of lost customers and the extent of avoidable customer losses (servmark 2010). About 10% of these customers were intentionally pushed-away, mainly due to debt problems. Approximately 15% of the terminations were carried out by moved-away customers who did not own the insured object any longer. Thus 25% of customer losses seem to have been inevitable.

The vast *majority* of—65% of the churn—are classified as *avoidable*: 37% of the lost customers belonged to the pulled-away segment, while 28% were driven-away customers. Taking a closer look only at the driven-away customers, the extent of the avoidable economic loss is evident: approximately 82,000 contracts (a premium volume of around 11.8 million €) were cancelled by this group.

The growth potential of avoidable customer losses is illustrated in the growth balance (Fig. 1.3):

- The company achieved a *gross growth* of 7.2%.
- However, the contract losses (*lost growth*) amounted to 8.6% this year, of which 3.8% can be classified as inevitable, 4.8% as avoidable.
- As a result, the portfolio of contracts declined by approximately 1.4% (*negative net growth*).

Without avoidable lost growth, the company would not only have avoided a negative net growth but achieved a positive net growth.

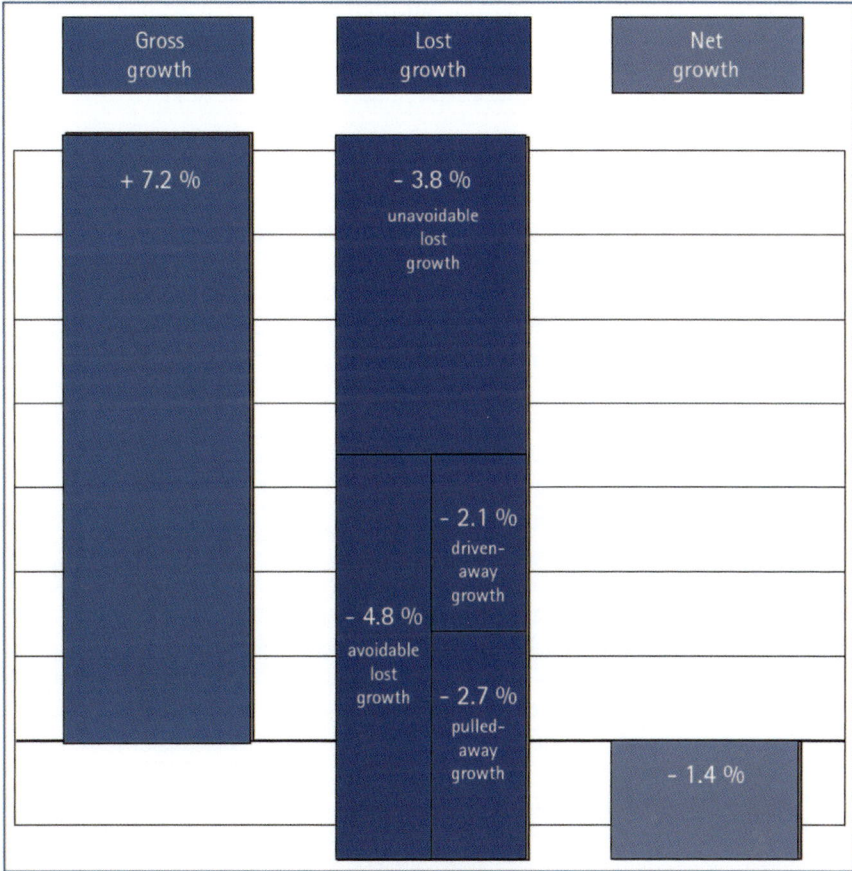

Fig. 1.3 Growth balance

Complaint management is important to avoid lost growth. However, two conditions must be met. Firstly, the annoyed customers must articulate their dissatisfaction in a complaint to the company. Secondly, complaint management must succeed in turning customers' dissatisfaction into satisfaction. Both conditions are often not met. For example, only 7% of the customers who cancelled their contracts with the insurance company concerned had complained about their experienced problem before migrating. And only 2% of the complainants were 'completely satisfied' or 'very satisfied', while 29% indicated they were "satisfied" with the complaint handling. In contrast, more than two-thirds (68%) of them were disappointed (servmark 2010). These results underscore the need to ask annoyed customers to articulate a complaint, and they show very clearly how strongly an unsatisfactory complaint response can trigger churn.

1.2.1.6 Complaint Management: Minimizing Dissatisfaction— Preventing Customer Migration—Retaining Customers

Complaint management is the key starting point to reducing dissatisfaction, because it provides the two decisive answers to the central question of an efficient customer retention strategy: "*What must be done to maximize customer loyalty in the sense of the prevention of customer losses?*":

- Complaining customers are very dissatisfied customers. They represent directly *endangered sales and contribution margin potentials*. In this respect, they are also the primary target group of any customer retention strategy. Complainants find themselves in a problem situation and are in urgent need of a solution. If companies offer this solution, they show that not only the customers, but they, too, have entered into a relationship and take responsibility. This is an excellent basis for gaining the customers' trust and commitment and thus creating the precondition that complainants will continue to be customers, despite the perceived problem. This customer loyalty effect of complaint management is achieved by activities that are part of the direct complaint management process (see Chap. 4).
- Complaints contain *concrete information on quality deficiencies* that are perceived by customers as serious. This information can immediately be used for quality improvements, which ensures that those problems that currently cause dissatisfaction and customer losses will not occur in the future. The package of measures that has to be applied for this purpose will be characterized in Chap. 4 as an indirect complaint management process.

Therefore, if companies primarily want to avoid the loss of customers, *complaint management has the key role*.

Figure 1.4 gives on overview of the two strategy options 'maximizing satisfaction' and 'minimizing dissatisfaction' and shows the necessary change of perspective.

1.2.1.7 Complaint Management and Customer Care

In many firms, complaint management tasks are taken over by departments that are then designated "Customer Care". For this reason, it is frequently unclear whether these terms have the same meaning. Similar confusion arises with respect to the relationship between customer care and customer relationship management, as these departments usually do their work using CRM software and follow its understanding of relationship management. In order to ensure clarity in this confusion of terms, first at all a distinction must be made between the fields of activity on the one hand and the organizational units on the other hand.

Fields of Activity in CRM, Customer Care and Complaint Management

In terms of the *breadth of the field of activity*, customer relationship management, customer care and complaint management can be differentiated by the type and extent of the respective tasks that must be accomplished.

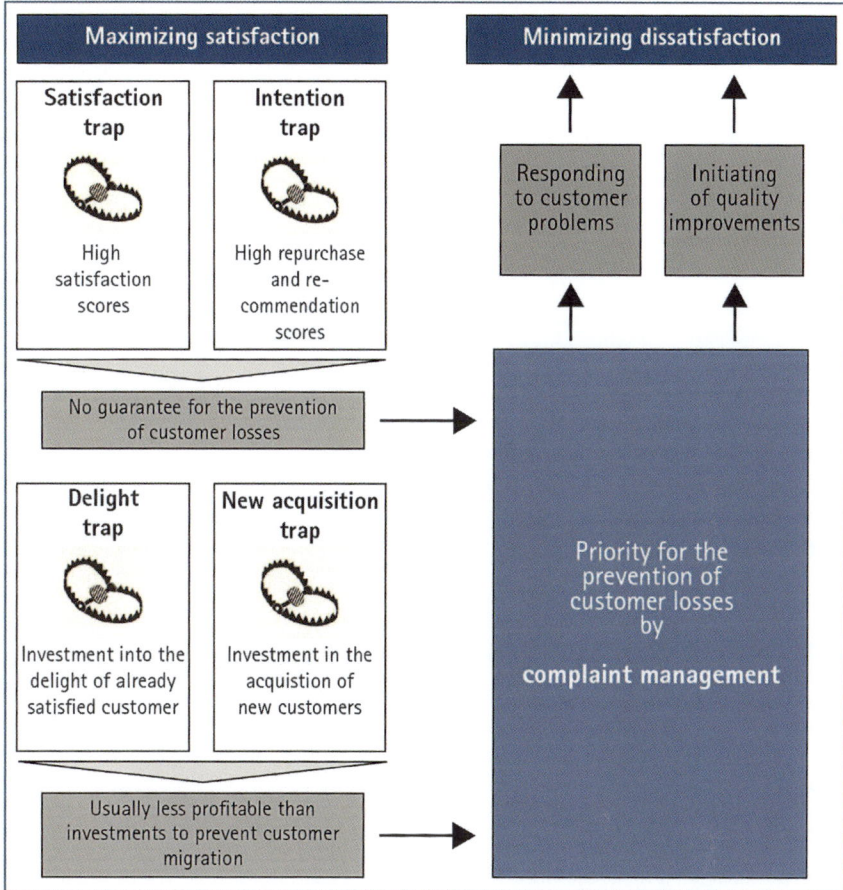

Fig. 1.4 Strategy options maximizing satisfaction versus minimizing dissatisfaction

Customer relationship management is the totality of corporate measures for the systematic initiation, development, maintenance and safeguarding, and even the termination and re-initiation of customer relationships, if necessary. Customer *retention management* stands at the center of the spectrum of activity.

Complaint management is a part of retention management. The target groups of its activities are those customers who have come to the firm with a complaint because they are dissatisfied.

Complaint management thus communicates solely with the group of customers who have a complaint. The central core is *inbound communication*. The active contacting of customers by the firm – *outbound communication*—takes place only insofar as it is useful in satisfying the complainant. This applies, for example, to telephone inquiries and to intermediate and final replies, as well as to follow-up actions and contacts.

Thus, it becomes clear that complaint management is not responsible for all forms of customer-initiated communication. Customers do not come to the firm only with complaints, but also with other articulations, including primarily orders, terminations, notices of amendment, praise, requests, ideas and suggestions for improvement. *Orders*, understood as a declaration of intentions to complete a sales contract, and *terminations*, understood as a declaration of intention to terminate a contractual relationship, constitute legally binding and purchase-relevant declarations on the part of the customer. In a *notice of amendment*, customers inform the firm of changes in their personal circumstances that are relevant to the business relationship. As far as *praise* is concerned, customers express their satisfaction with the firm's products, services and course of action, all of their own accord. In addition, it regularly happens that they ask for information that is important to them when they make *enquiries* or approach the firm with *ideas* for specific possibilities for improvement. *Junk contacts* that do not enable the organization to make a useful answer must be differentiated from these other forms of dialog. This type of contact includes statements that do not contain a recognizable concern or that do contain provocations, slander or threats. A response is largely unnecessary, or these statements constitute cases for the legal department. Table 1.1 gives an overview of the various forms of customer-initiated communication.

Table 1.1 Customer-initiated forms of communication (customer concerns)

▪ **Orders** or purchases are customer statements in which they make legally-binding declarations of their intentions to complete a sales contract. ▪ In **terminations** they express the fact that they would like to suspend the delivery of certain benefits or terminate a current contract. ▪ With a **notice of amendment** the customers inform the firm as to changes in their personal circumstances (marital status, address, bank account information). ▪ **Praise** is an expression of the customers' satisfaction with or enthusiasm for the firm's products, services and processes, as well as the behavior of its employees, all of their own accord. ▪ **Complaints** are articulations of customer dissatisfaction. ▪ In **enquiries** the customers ask for information although their information needs can be related to quite different issues. Substantial contents of enquiries are for example:	– General information about the firm and important corporate decisions (enterprise size, total assets, merger decisions, etc.) – Specific information about the range of products and services (assortment of goods, product attributes, availability, price, usage instructions, financial or health effects of consumptions, etc.) – Information about business transactions (volume of transaction, financing modalities, date of delivery) – Information about customer status (category of discount, obtained value in frequent-user-programs) ▪ With **ideas and suggestions for improvement**, customers provide the firm with specific indications as to how to improve their products, services and processes, without associating their expressions of dissatisfaction with the present state of the firm. ▪ Customer articulations that do not enable the organization to make a useful answer (provocations, slander, etc.) are designated as **molestations**.

The *planned handling of all these customer concerns* constitutes the functional area of *customer care* that includes complaint management as a central element. What customer care and complaint management have in common is the *inbound perspective*. Dominant is here a concentration on communication initiated by the customer and the condition that they seek to achieve customer commitment, not through the marketing of products and services, but through the resolution of concerns that are brought forward by customers. Customer care does, however, have a more extensive spectrum of tasks than does complaint management, by virtue of its inclusion of all forms of articulations.

With respect to customer relationship management, customer care is particular section. In addition to the primarily inbound-oriented activities of customer care, CRM encompasses *all the outbound measures initiated by the firm* that are necessary for the consolidation, strengthening, stabilizing, safeguarding or—in extreme cases—for the dissolution of the business relationship. Here once again, the focus is not on sales-oriented but rather on firm-oriented actions that aid in the building and further development of individual customer relationships. Such actions guarantee that specific attention is paid to the customers, that they are specifically informed and that their voice will be heard. Figure 1.5 summarizes these connections.

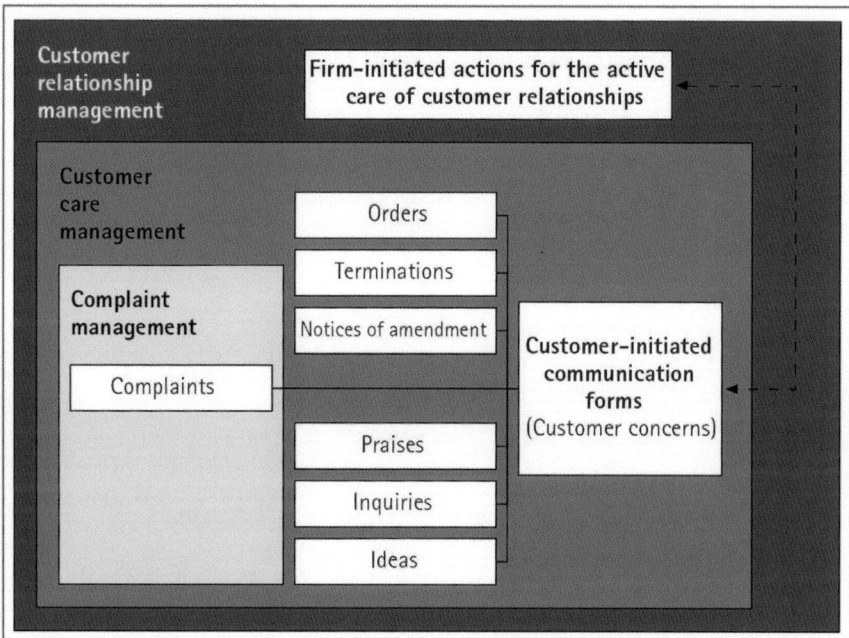

Fig. 1.5 CRM—customer care management—complaint management

Organizational Solution for CRM, Customer Care and Complaint Management
The question of how the tasks of CRM, customer care and complaint management should be *organizationally* assigned is completely independent of the terminological differentiations. For example, it might be very useful to combine all complaint-related tasks in a specific complaint management department or to bundle the entire customer-initiated communication in a customer care unit (see Sect. 15.2). It is also possible that operational units—such as a customer interaction center—will not only be responsible for the primarily inbound-related activities of customer care, but will also undertake outbound activities within the scope of marketing and sales measures.

1.2.2   The Role of Complaint Management in Quality Management

Complaint management aids in the stabilization of endangered customer relationships and is consequently a fundamental element of the type of relationship management that is oriented toward external customers. But this in no way means that stabilization represents the only goal of complaint management. The analysis of complaints is an important basis for continual quality improvement initiatives, meaning that complaint management is also a *fundamental starting point for quality management* (Brown et al. 1996; Linder et al. 2014; Bulsara and Thakkar 2016). In this respect, it seems only natural, that complaint management is an integral component of all the relevant quality management concepts.

1.2.2.1 Complaint Management Within the Framework of ISO 9001
A *customer-oriented understanding* is characteristic of the ISO 9001 "Quality Management–Requirements". As is stated in the introduction, this standard promotes the "development, implementation and improvement of the effectiveness of a quality management system, to enhance customer satisfaction by meeting customer requirements" (ISO 2015, p. vii).

This will be achieved by a process approach on the basis of the co-called PDCA (Plan-Do-Check-Act) cycle (see Fig. 1.6), which underlines the customer focus. The requirements of the customers are the primary starting point of the planning process, and the products and services as output of the value-added process are evaluated by the customer. Their satisfaction is the key measure of the organization's performance.

Complaint management holds a *place of central importance*, both in the determination of customer requirements and in the measurement of customer satisfaction. With regard to the requirements, it is necessary to identify information about customer expectations and their articulated wishes for corrections and new features, and to include this in the product planning process. In reference to the evaluation of products and services, complaints provide unambiguous evidence of the fact that customer expectations were not fulfilled. Since complaints also contain concrete descriptions of problems and suggestions for solutions, they often furnish much more valuable clues for the formulation of improvement possibilities than do the

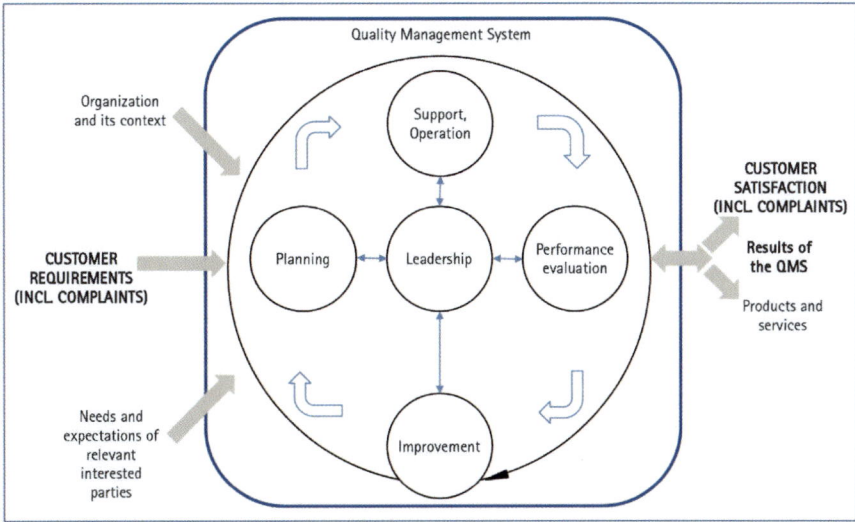

Fig. 1.6 Process approach of the ISO 9001 quality management system (Source: based on ISO 2015, p. 19; Reference to complaints added)

results of customer satisfaction surveys, which are mostly presented as relatively abstract average scaled values.

The further *explanations within the norm* substantiate the ideas of customer orientation and underscore the importance of complaints and complaint management. For example, with respect to customer communication it is required to obtain "customer feedback relating to products and services including complaints" (ISO 2015, p. 10). And when a nonconformity occurs "including any arising from complaints" the organization shall review and analyze the problem, determine the causes and implement corrective actions (ISO 2015, p. 19).

1.2.2.2 Complaint Management According to the Standard ISO 10002:2014

Since the year 2005 there has been an international standard for complaint management entitled "Quality management—Customer satisfaction—Guidelines for complaints handling in organizations" (ISO 2014). It is a separate standard that supports the objective of the international standards 9001 ("Quality Management Systems—Requirements") and 9004 ("Managing for the sustained success of an organization—A quality management approach" (ISO 2014, 02). It represents "guidance on the design and implementation of an effective and efficient complaints-handling process for all types of commercial or non-commercial activities" (ISO 2014, 01), without the intention to provide a specific certification of the complaint management. The process described in the standard promotes customer satisfaction and loyalty and improves a company's competitiveness by:

- providing a complainant with access to a responsive complaint-handling process
- enhancing the company's ability to resolve complaints in a consistent, systematic, and responsive manner
- helping to identify and eliminate causes of complaints
- supporting the personnel in improving their customer-oriented skills and
- providing a basis of continual review and analysis of the complaint-handling process (ISO 2014, 0.1).

The ISO 10002-2014 comprises eight sections, in which fundamental terms are defined, guiding principles are formulated, requirements on the organizational framework are specified and relevant tasks concerning complaint-handling, the use of complaint information and the continual improvement of the complaint management system are described. This is complemented by an informative annex, including concrete hints and recommendations by presenting, for example, special forms that may help complainants to provide the relevant information or aid the company to follow up on a complaint.

This standard provides a useful introduction to the topic. This is particularly helpful for small businesses with a limited number of customers and for all those who are dealing with this issue for the first time. However, the presentation is usually very brief and formulated on a general level with low requirements for the quality of the execution of tasks. In addition, several important aspects are ignored. Thus, the ISO 10002:2014 can be interpreted only as a minimum standard, and is not sufficient for companies striving for an excellent complaint management system.

1.2.2.3 Complaint Management Within the Business Excellence Frameworks

Much earlier even than the quality management system that complies with the ISO 9001 norms, the *Total Quality Management concept* emphasized the customer as the orientation factor of a quality-driven company. The fundamental goal of Total Quality Management (TQM) consists of bringing the firm into line with the expectations of customers and thereby increasing its competitiveness, so that an especially high degree of customer satisfaction and commitment is achieved as a result of superior quality.

TQM Awards such as the Baldrige Award or its European counterpart, the EFQM model, have for years been viewed as the most consistent conceptual realizations of the Total Quality Management approach. This view continues to be applicable, even though the notion of quality in these concepts has been widely replaced by "Business Excellence" in the meantime.

The *Baldrige Excellence Framework* demonstrates that quality is not an isolated phenomenon, but rather can only be implemented within the framework of a corporate-wide concept that encompasses all functions and areas. The seven criteria for performance excellence make this clear (see Fig. 1.7): "Leadership", "Strategy" and "Customers" represent the leadership triad and stress the responsibility of senior

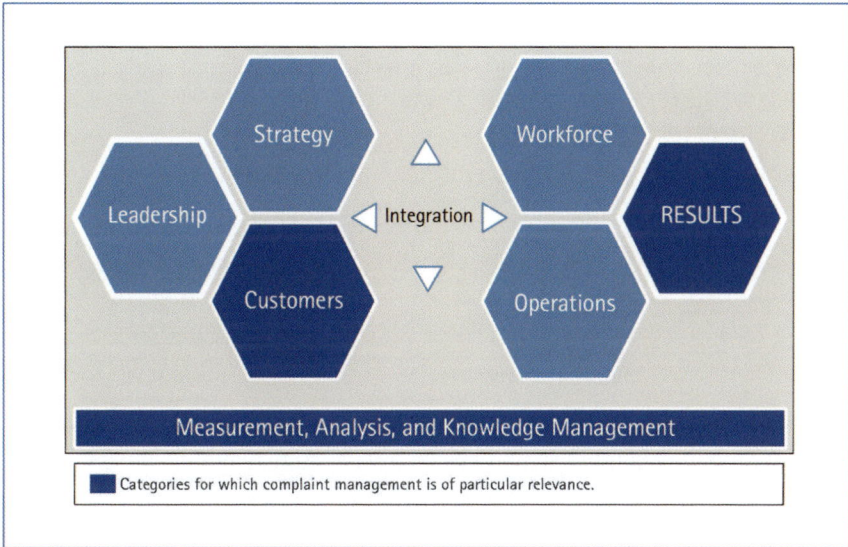

Fig. 1.7 Relevance of complaint management in the performance system of the Baldrige Excellence Framework (NIST 2017b, p. 1)

leaders for the company's direction and success. "Workforce", "Operations" and "Results" represent the results triad, demonstrating that employees and key processes accomplish the work of the organization that yields the business results. "Measurement, Analysis and Knowledge Management" serve as the information foundation for the performance management system. The word 'integration' in the center demonstrates that all elements of the model are interrelated (NIST 2017b, p. 1).

The *importance of complaint management* in the context of the Baldrige Model is high. Complaints are already addressed in the core values, because reducing complaints is viewed as an important part of customer-focused excellence. Added to this is the statement that "success in recovering from defects, service errors, and mistakes is crucial for retaining customers and engaging them for the long term" (NIST 2017b, p. 41).

The careful handling of customer complaints is of special importance for the criteria "Consumers", "Measurement, Analysis, and Knowledge Management", and "Results". In the section "Voice of the Customers" of the *"Customers"* category, companies have to describe how they listen to customers and determine their satisfaction and dissatisfaction. Here, complaint data that affect customers' purchasing decisions is explicitly mentioned. In the section "Customer Engagement" the companies are asked, inter alia, how they manage complaints, and the Baldrige Commentary explains the objective: "Complaint aggregation, analysis, and root cause determination should lead to effective elimination of the causes of complaints and to the setting of priorities for process and product improvements" (NIST 2017a). Under the criterion *"Measurement, Analysis, and Knowledge Management"* it is

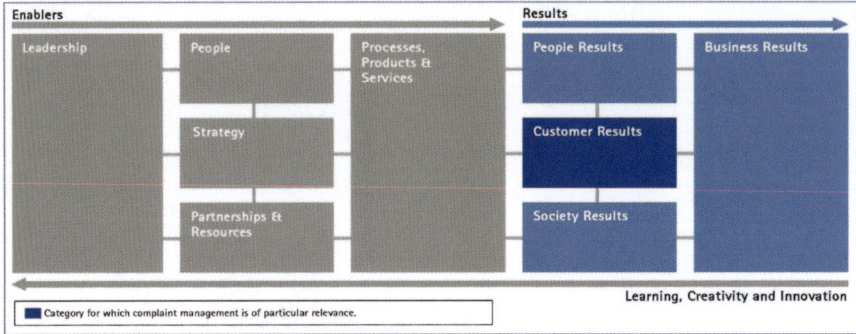

Fig. 1.8 Relevance of complaint management in the EFQM Excellence Model (EFQM 2012, p. 7)

required, among other things, to describe how voice-of-the-customer data "including aggregated data on complaints" is selected to build a customer focus culture (NIST 2017b, p. 16). Under the sub-category "Customer Results", the organization has to provide information on the current levels and trends of customer satisfaction and dissatisfaction, and the Baldrige Criteria Commentary lists here complaints, complaint management, effective complaint resolution, and warranty claims as relevant data (NIST 2017a).

The European counterpart to the Baldrige Excellence Framework is the *EFQM Excellence Model*. It is based on nine criteria, which build an integrated system: "Leadership", "People", "Strategy", and "Partnership & Resources" are 'enabler criteria' which cover what the company does; "People Results", "Customer Results", "Society Results" and "Business Results" are 'results criteria' covering what the company achieves (see Fig. 1.8).

Complaints as an indicator of quality problems and as customer input for improvement processes also play a role in this model. 'Adding Value for Customers' belongs to the fundamental concepts; and one of the maxims here is: excellent organizations continually "monitor and review the experiences and perceptions of their customers and respond appropriately to any feedback" (EFQM 2012, p. 9). Explicitly mentioned are complaints in the category *"Customer Results"*. Here complaints are listed as sources of insights into the customers' perspective of the organization and complaint management as a measure to monitor, understand and improve the company's performance (EFQM 2012, p. 35).

Fundamentally, critical customer feedback affects all model elements. Executives need to take customer concerns seriously; strategic decisions should be based on the knowledge of customer needs and requirements; employees have to understand the customers' perspective; partnerships, resources and processes have to be managed to create optimum value for customers, and all result categories are strongly influenced by how well these requirements are fulfilled. This underlines the strategic importance of complaint management.

> **Chapter 1 in Brief**
> - Complaint management is of strategic relevance in customer relationship management.
> - It has the dissatisfied customers as the target group and serves to stabilize customer relationships which are endangered due to dissatisfaction.
> - Therefore, complaint management is the core of a customer retention strategy, which aims at the prevention of customer losses by minimizing dissatisfaction (dissatisfaction minimizing strategy).
> - Customer care is responsible for inbound communication within the framework of customer relationship management and customer retention management. Complaint management as the most important part of customer care handles the communication with dissatisfied customers.
> - Complaints contain relevant information about quality defects perceived by the customers and their unfulfilled expectations. Thus, complaint management is of strategic relevance in quality management, too.

References

Baran RJ, Galka RJ (2017) Customer relationship management, 2nd edn. Routledge, New York

Bose K, Bansal HS (2001) Regain management: issues and strategies. In: Sheth JN, Parvatiyar A, Shainesh G (eds) Customer relationship management: emerging concepts, tools, and applications. McGraw-Hill Education, New Delhi, pp 63–70

Brown SW et al (1996) Service recovery: its value and limitations as a retail strategy. Int J Serv Ind Manag 7(5):32–44

Bulsara M, Thakkar H (2016) Customer feedback-based product improvement: a case study. Productivity 56(4):107–115

Butscher SA (2016) Customer loyalty programmes and clubs, 2nd edn. Routledge, London

Chiturri R et al (2008) Delight by design: the role of hedonic versus utilitarian benefits. J Mark 72(3):48–63

EFQM (2012) EFQM excellence model 2013. Kindle Edition

Griffin J, Lowenstein MW (2001) Customer winback. Jossey Bass, San Francisco

Heskett JL et al (1994) Putting the service-profit chain to work. Harv Bus Rev 72(2):164–174

Hughes AM (2007) Churn reduction in the telecom industry. DMN News, 24 Jan. http://www.dmnews.com/dataanalytics/churn-reduction-in-the-telecom-industry/article/94238/. Accessed 27 Aug 2017

ISO (2014) ISO 1002:2014 (E), quality management—customer satisfaction—guidelines for complaints handling in organizations, 2nd edn. ISO, Geneva

ISO (2015) ISO 9001:2015 (E), quality management systems—requirements, 5th edn. ISO, Geneva

Keiningham T, Vavra T (2001) The customer delight principle: exceeding customers' expectations for bottom-line success. McGraw-Hill, New York

Keiningham TL et al (2007) The value of different customer satisfaction and loyalty metrics in predicting customer retention, recommendation, and share-of-wallet. Manag Serv Qual 17(4):361–384

Linder A et al (2014) Technical complaint management from a quality perspective. Total Qual Manag Bus Excel 25(7/8):865–875

Neslin SA et al (2006) Defection detection: measuring and understanding the predictive accuracy of customer churn models. J Mark Res 43(2):204–211

NIST (2017a) Baldrige criteria commentary. https://www.nist.gov/baldrige/baldrige-criteria-com mentary. Accessed 20 Sept 2017

NIST (2017b) Baldrige excellence framework. A system approach to improving your organization's performance. NIST, Gaithersburg

Ratcliff C (2014) Marketers more focused on acquisition than retention. Econsultancy Blog, August 20. https://econsultancy.com/blog/65339-marketers-more-focused-on-acquisition-than-reten tion. Accessed 28 Aug 2017

Reichheld FF (1996) Learning from customer defections. Harv Bus Rev 74(2):56–69

Reichheld FF (2006) The ultimate question: driving good profits and true growth. Harvard Business School, Boston

Reichheld FF (2011) The ultimate question 2.0: how net promoter companies thrive in a customer driven world. Harvard Business Review, Boston

Reichheld FF, Sasser WE Jr (1990) Zero defections: quality comes to services. Harv Bus Rev 68 (4):105–111

Rust R et al (1995) Return on quality (ROQ): making service quality financially accountable. J Mark 59(2):58–70

Seidel W (2010) Customers-at-Risk-Management. Der Befreiungsschlag aus der Wachstumsfalle. In: Gouthier M et al (eds) Service excellence als Impulsgeber. Gabler, Wiesbaden, pp 527–547

Servmark (2010) Interne Versicherungsstudie. München

Servmark (2012) Interne Bausparkassenstudie. München

Shewan D (2017) How to calculate (and lower) your churn rate. WordStream, 27 May. http://www. wordstream.com/blog/ws/2014/05/12/customer-churn. Accessed 30 Aug 2017

Stauss B (2011) Der Kundenbeziehungs-Lebenszyklus. In: Hippner H et al (eds) Grundlagen des CRM, Strategie, Geschäftsprozesse und IT-Unterstützung, 3rd edn. Gabler, Wiesbaden, pp 319–341

Stauss B, Friege C (1999) Regaining service customers, cost and benefits of regain management. J Serv Res 1(4):347–361

Complaints

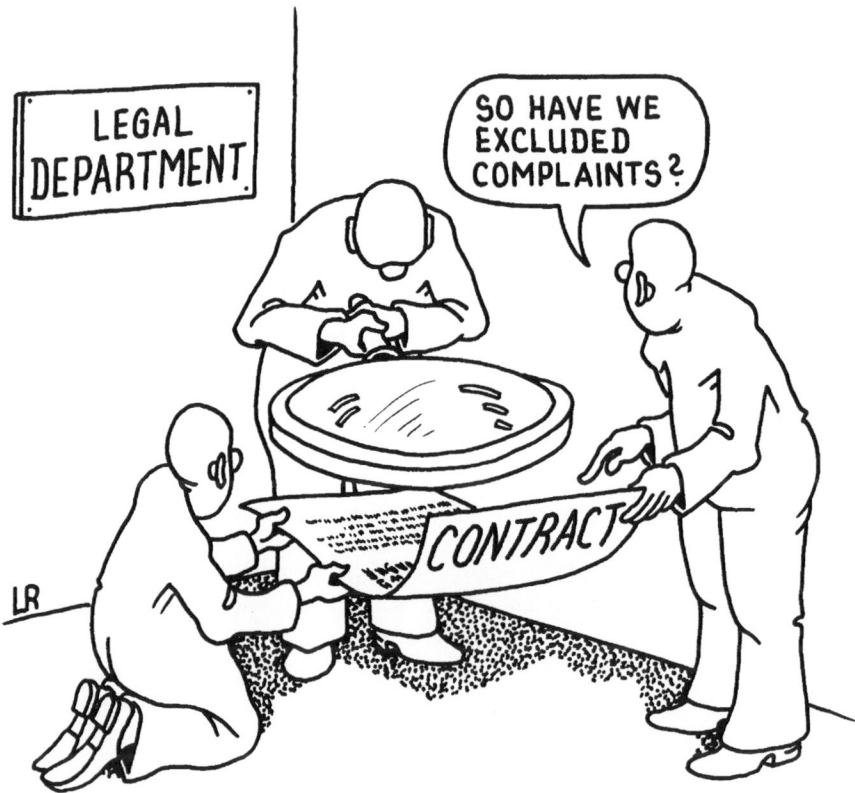

© Springer Nature Switzerland AG 2019

B. Stauss, W. Seidel, *Effective Complaint Management*, Management for Professionals,

https://doi.org/10.1007/978-3-319-98705-7_2

Issues Raised
- How should the term 'complaint' be understood?
- What distinguishes a complaint from a claim?
- Why is having a small number of complaints not a meaningful indicator of customer satisfaction?
- Why do complaints not only entail costs, but also offer opportunities for revenues and profits?

2.1 Definition and Types of Complaints

What are complaints? At first glance, this question seems strange, since customers often use the expression "complaint" in their letters or begin a conversation with the sentence, "I want to make a complaint." However, customers often avoid this expression, cloak their criticism in a polite request or even emphasize that they don't actually want to complain, but do expect that a repetition of the incident in question will be avoided in the future. Sometimes demands are also made on the company by people who are neither current nor potential customers. Thus, it is clearly necessary to clarify the *concept of complaints*.

Basically, the following understanding is to be assumed:

Complaints are expressions of dissatisfaction

This is a relatively broad conceptual understanding, which includes a differentiation of various types of complaints:

- Complaints are a matter of *expressions*, that is, verbal or written statements.
- From these statements emerges the fact that the complainant is *dissatisfied*. This is not, however, dependent on whether the customer uses the expression "complaint". The extent of dissatisfaction is also unimportant. All statements that show that the performance or the behavior of the firm does not fully comply with the customers' expectations are complaints as defined here.
- Complaints may be brought not only by potential, current or lost *customers*, but also by members of other *interest groups*, who for example lament damage to the environment from ecologically harmful production processes. Moreover, criticism is not expressed only by *individuals* but also by *institutions*—for example, associations or media—who demand a general solution for problems, independent of a specific individual case.
- As a rule, it is a question of statements that place the affected party in direct opposition *to the firm itself*. Dissatisfied customers can, however, choose an *indirect* path, in that they turn to a *third-party institution* (for instance, arbitrators,

administrative bodies or media) as an "advocate" of their interests. In such cases, the third-party institution approaches the firm in the customers' name or informs the public. An indirect complaint also exists, if the dissatisfaction is published in social media, but is not directly addressed to the company but to other users.

• The dissatisfaction of the affected person does not necessarily have to be related to product deficiencies or other aspects of the *market offering* (such as price). The *social-political behavior* of the firm can be a further object of complaints.

A complaint is brought forth intentionally, meaning that the customers demonstrate a particular intent in their articulation. In many cases, they turn to the firm in the post-purchase phase because they believe that they have not received the expected level of performance from them: an auto repair did not yield the desired result or furniture that was delivered shows signs of being damaged. Accordingly, the customers want either an improved or a completely new performance, the partial or complete restitution of the purchase price or compensation for consequential damages. If the customers understand this demand as a claim against the firm that they can establish via the legal process, then we can speak of *claims*. In practice, "complaints" and "claims" are often not differentiated. It is useful, however, to make this distinction in order to demarcate the special case of legally relevant complaints. In this sense, the concept of "claims" characterizes a subset of complaints in which customers in the post-purchase phase explicitly or implicitly connect complaints about the product or service with a lawful demand that can be established legally if necessary.

In this general sense, complaints are thus intentional expressions of dissatisfaction by interested parties or institutions with respect to some aspect of corporate behavior. The following considerations will be based on this broad understanding, even if the focus is on certain types of complaints. The analysis focuses on complaints that are articulated by *customers* directly to the company (*direct customer complaints*). With respect to the content complaints are discussed that relate to any aspect of the market offer, be it the product or service or any element of the marketing mix (*offer-related complaints*). This applies regardless of the motives and behavior intentions of the customers. All offer-related complaints are taken into consideration, regardless of whether the customers only want to draw the company's attention to a problem, have hope for a specific reaction of the company or are convinced that they can uphold their interests by legal means (*claims*). Thus, the explanations in this book will based on the following definition of *customer complaints*:

> In customer complaints, potential, current or lost customers express their dissatisfaction with any aspect of the market offer directly to the company.

Figure 2.1 shows an overview of the conceptual determination and the delimitation based on points of emphasis.

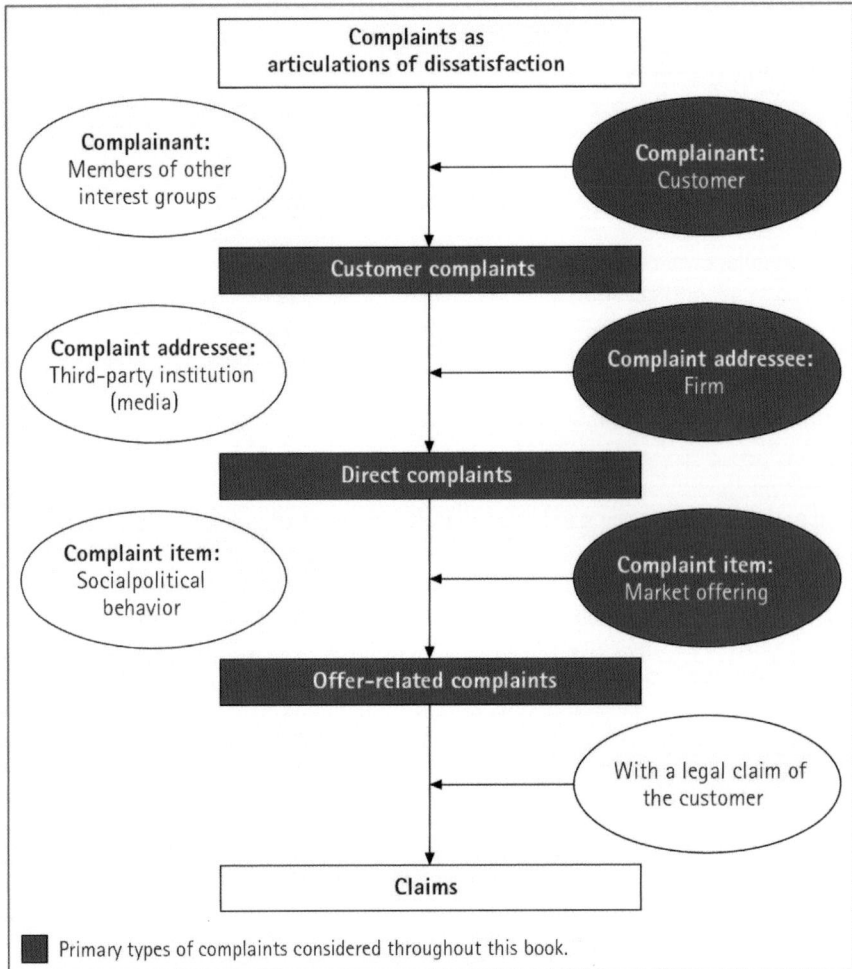

Fig. 2.1 Types of complaints

Spotlight 2.1 shows starting points, how the general complaint definition can be concretized company-specifically.

Spotlight 2.1
Company-Specific Concretization of the Complaint Definition
  In practice, there is often a debate about whether a customer concern is really a complaint or not. If employees have different opinions in this respect, they also categorize differently and initiate different processes. Deviating reactions and biased analytical results are the consequences. In order to

(continued)

Spotlight 2.1 (continued)

prevent these problems, it is necessary to ensure a uniform understanding and acceptance of the general definition of complaints and to concretize this understanding company-specifically.

To decide whether the customer articulation is a complaint, it is advisable to watch out for certain words and phrases that can be taken as indicators of dissatisfaction. These include:

- *Direct expressions of dissatisfaction by using words such as 'complaint' or 'criticism':* "Herewith I complain; I would like to express my dissatisfaction; I have to make the critical remark. . ."
- *Negative emotions:* "I am dissatisfied, disappointed, upset, angry, outraged..."
- *Accusation of mistreatment:* "fraud, deception, rip-off, bamboozle..."
- *Note of an error:* "wrong delivery, incorrect information and advice, product does not work, is defective, is damaged..."
- *Lack of service quality:* "late, rude, incompetent, unreliable, dirty..."
- *Direct description of unfulfilled expectations:* "does not meet my expectations, is different from description, does not fit..."
- *Indirect description of unfulfilled expectations:* "it's a pity that the product is not in stock; unfortunately, I got no callback..."
- *Insufficient response to a complaint:* "no answer, no response, did not react..."
- *Descriptions of the consequences of the problem:* "lost a lot of time, had to contact different departments to get a replacement...."
- *Demands:* "I want my money back, a new product, compensation..."
- *Termination of loyalty:* "you won't see me here again; I will cancel, switch to your competitor..."
- *Announcement to contact superior instances:* "I'll turn to the chief executive, supervisory board..."
- *Announcement of the involvement of third-party institutions:* "I'll turn to a consumer organization, ombudsman, regulatory authority, media..."
- *Announcement of legal action:* "I'll hire a lawyer, sue you, will go to court..."
- *Threats:* "you will regret this..."

The best way to proceed on a company-specific level is to conduct training workshops with employees of the complaint management department to identify complaints. The participants receive a sample of real customer concerns and are asked to determine the complaints and to assign the remaining articulations to other categories (orders, cancellations, notices of amendment, praise, enquiries, ideas). The cases with different assignments are analyzed carefully together and then assigned to the correct category.

(continued)

Spotlight 2.1 (continued)

Since new problems arise over time, different aspects are discussed and new formulations are used, the terminology must be adjusted again and again. The workshops also have to be repeated regularly and should also be used for the training of new employees. The effectiveness of the training is reflected in the extent to which the documentation of complaint information is correct, which must be checked within the framework of the task controlling (see Sect. 11.2).

2.2   True and False Regarding Complaints

In corporate practice, very definite judgments about complaints abound that are by no means firmly based on information. Many times, it is a question of *prejudices* that seem to be plausible at first glance. If someone is serious about active complaint management, however, it has to be differentiated between what is true and what is false regarding complaints and also make sure that prejudices in the firm are dismantled.

In the following discussion, several of the especially long-lived and stubborn prejudices will be repeated, and commentary that contradicts them will be introduced.

Prejudice 1

"Our customers are satisfied. The *low number of incoming complaints* proves it!"

Comment 1

"Wrong! Low complaint numbers are *not a meaningful indicator of customer satisfaction!*"

Many firms are convinced that complaint management is not a matter of urgent concern for them, since they receive comparatively few complaints. They infer from the low number of complaints that customers are satisfied. This conclusion is false. The bulk of dissatisfied customers do not complain. Whether a customer complains or not also depends on a multitude of factors that are, in part, substantially influenced by the firm. Low numbers of complaints can be the result of higher *barriers to complaints* or *resigned customer behavior*. Furthermore, in many firms very critical expressions by customers are not viewed or documented as complaints at all—for example, because they are *given orally*. Typical examples of this include auto mechanics and grocery stores. Complaints are integrated in the context of the normal course of business processes and customer conversations and overwhelmingly taken care of in conversations with customer contact personnel. Only a fraction of the customers who remain dissatisfied after such contacts complain in writing to management. Concluding based on this small number of complaints that customers are satisfied cannot be justified.

Prejudice 2
"The number of complaints should be *minimized!*"

Comment 2
"Wrong! The number of dissatisfied customers should be minimized. The percentage of dissatisfied customers who complain should be *maximized!*"

In many firms, the goal of minimizing the number of complaints is used as a pretext. In view of the fact that the number of complaints can be reduced without changing the level of customer dissatisfaction, this goal is pointless. The first priority must be to *minimize customer dissatisfaction*. The prerequisite for this is, however, that the firm be informed as comprehensively as possible as to the type and extent of customer dissatisfaction. The firm must therefore pursue an *active policy* that leads customers to turn to the firm with complaints, rather than saying nothing or going over to the competition. Accordingly, the path to a customer-oriented corporate culture mostly leads via an *increased number of complaints*. A long-term reduction in the number of complaints can only be achieved when the proportion of customers who complain is maximized.

Prejudice 3
"Customers who complain are *adversaries!*"

Comment 3
"Wrong! Customers who complain are *partners!*"

Customers who complain are often immediately categorized negatively. They are considered to be malicious, to be opponents. Accordingly, the firm assumes a *position of self-defensive* right away, and the basic corporate attitude is oriented toward defense if not toward counter-attack. This attitude is wrong. It does not take into account that the complainants are current (and possibly future) customers who have a right to bring forth their views, wishes and demands. The fact that they express their opinion toward the firm is often an expression of their interest in the firm in that they allow a *possibility of later improvement*. Customers who complain are not opponents, but rather partners in the effort toward continuous improvements in processes and products (Larivet and Brouard 2010).

Prejudice 4
"The majority of customers who complain are *either grumblers or grousers*!"

Comment 4
"Wrong! The vast majority of customers are *not grumblers or grousers*!"

Even among firms that basically accept the value of customer complaints, there is a widespread view that a large percentage of complaints are made by grumblers and grousers. Accordingly, the demand for complaint stimulation encounters a great deal of skepticism because it is feared that the proportion of those who would inundate the firm with *unwarranted complaints*, behave in an impudent manner and make unfounded demands would thereby increase. Indeed, it is difficult to come by reliable numbers because *no generally accepted definition* of a "grouser" exists and because it is the firm itself that makes the corresponding categorization in each specific case. But much speaks for the fact that the vast majority of customers are not grousers. Therefore, a complaint should not be regarded as an inadmissible grumbling, but as a legitimate customer concern. However, in order to increase the certainty that customers do not gain unjustified advantages, complaints should be analyzed carefully to identify 'professional complainants'.

Prejudice 5
"Complaints only lead to greater *costs*!"

Comment 5
"Wrong! Complaints are not associated solely with costs, but instead provide *opportunities for higher revenue and profits*! Ignoring complaints, on the other hand, only leads to greater costs, never to higher revenue!"

Complaints are also perceived by firms as threats because they are exclusively regarded as a *cost factor*. As a matter of fact, costs are generated during the processing of complaints just as they are when customer demands (product returns, reimbursements, etc.) are fulfilled. Indeed, these costs must be examined in relation to the *benefits that can be achieved*. The critical information that is contained in complaints gives firms the chance to identify and remove errors—that is, constantly to improve themselves and thereby to reduce costs. Since customers express their criticism with regard to the firm and do not immediately migrate to the competition, the firm still has the chance to keep the dissatisfied customer. "Any problem that employees who are close to the customer can discover and resolve is a chance to go beyond duty and win a customer for life" (Hart et al. 1990, p. 149). The costs of processing complaints are thus *investments in future business*.

Whoever wants to implement complaint management will be confronted with prejudices such as these. In order to refute them, one must have a sound basis of information. Internal sources can provide this. For example, data from the customer satisfaction surveys allow an estimation of how many customers had cause for complaint within a certain period. By comparing this figure with the number of complaints documented in the company, it usually becomes clear that the number of registered complaints is not a meaningful indicator of customer satisfaction. A survey among lost customers makes it possible to determine how many customers migrated due to dissatisfaction without articulating a complaint. If the number of these 'driven-away customers' is multiplied by the average value of their purchases, it soon becomes apparent what opportunities complaints provide to improve revenues and profits.

Chapter 2 in Brief

- Customer articulations are complaints whenever they contain an expression of dissatisfaction making clear that expectations have not been met.
- Claims represent a subset of complaints in which customers in the after sales phase make legal demands on a contractual basis.
- Low complaint numbers are not a meaningful indicator of customer satisfaction, because the majority of dissatisfied customers do not complain and many critical customer statements are not registered as complaints in companies.
- Complaints do not only entail costs but also offer opportunities for cost reductions, sales and profit growth through the prevention of customer churn and the use of complaint information.

References

Larivet S, Brouard F (2010) Complaints are a firm's best friend. J Strat Mark 18(7):537–551
Hart CW et al (1990) The profitable art of service recovery. Harv Bus Rev 68(4):148–156

© Springer Nature Switzerland AG 2019
B. Stauss, W. Seidel, *Effective Complaint Management*, Management for Professionals,
https://doi.org/10.1007/978-3-319-98705-7_3

Issues Raised
- What causes customer dissatisfaction?
- What advantages does the complaint analysis offer compared to the usual customer satisfaction measurement?
- Why don't many customers complain?
- What do complainants expect and what makes them satisfied or dissatisfied?
- How does complaint (dis)satisfaction affect the further behavior of customers?

Whoever wants to avoid dissatisfaction or placate dissatisfied customers must know how (dis)satisfaction arises, what keeps customers from complaining and which aspects of the firm's reaction to a complaint delight and bind customers.

3.1   Origin and Measurement of Customer Satisfaction

3.1.1   The Origin of Customer Dissatisfaction

How the customers judge products or services with which they have had prior experiences is reflected in their satisfaction or dissatisfaction. (Dis)satisfaction is, therefore, the result of an ex-post-assessment and implies a *concrete, self-aware consumption experience*.

The process of assessment is usually described in reference to the "*disconfirmation paradigm*" (Oliver 2015), according to which satisfaction or dissatisfaction arises as a consequence of a perceived *discrepancy between expected and experienced performance*. Customers develop more or less concrete *expectations* regarding offerings available in the market. These expectations are formed depending on respective *needs* and are greatly influenced by the *experiences* the customers have had in the past with the same or similar products. Furthermore, information is a factor that fundamentally influences expectations; to be specific, both information that customers receive via *word-of-mouth communication* in their social sphere and information that the firm itself disseminates through the media in the context of *provider communication* (for example, direct advertising) (Berry and Parasuraman 1991).

During the process of using or consuming consumer goods or of the utilization of services, the customers experience the actual performance level of the goods and compare the *perceived performance* with their *expectations* in a complex weighing process. *Satisfaction* occurs when the performance substantially exceeds the customers' expectations, while *dissatisfaction* arises when the performance falls decisively short of their expectations. The fulfillment of their expectations merely leads to a feeling of *indifference* (see Fig. 3.1).

This understanding of the satisfaction construct provides an important indication for an *explanation of complaint behavior*. Customers complain because their

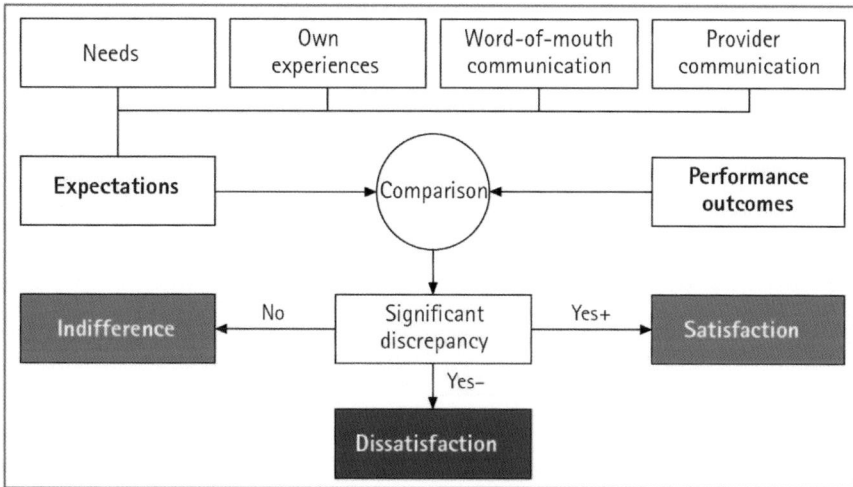

Fig. 3.1 Origin of satisfaction/dissatisfaction

expectations were violated to a great extent. It is this violation of *minimum expectations* that triggers such great irritation and leads to considerable endangerment of the business relationship.

3.1.2   Customer Satisfaction Measurement Compared to Complaint Analysis

3.1.2.1 Attribute-Based Measurement of Customer Satisfaction

To measure customer satisfaction a broad range of methods is available. Many companies conduct regular surveys using standardized questionnaires. This is by far the dominant type of satisfaction assessment and it takes place within a conceptual framework which is called the *attribute-based approach*. It is based on the assumption that the customers relate their expectations and perceptions to individual *quality attributes* and that their global satisfaction with a product or service results from their respective evaluations. Accordingly, in surveys customers are asked to indicate the degree of satisfaction with each quality attribute on a scale. Sometimes they are also asked to note on a second scale how relevant they consider the individual attributes. Thus, average values for both satisfaction and perceived importance of each quality attribute can be calculated and used as the basis for decisions on quality improvement measures.

These traditional attribute-based satisfaction surveys have a number of remarkable *advantages*. The methods are proven and provide *representative results*. They also allow companies to *compare* the current satisfaction scores with those of recent years and to gain insights into *satisfaction development*. It is possible, too, to compare the survey results of various corporate units (departments, plants, branches) and the company's values with those of competitors. Therefore, it makes sense to *monitor* customer satisfaction by surveys on a continual basis.

However, the attribute-based methods also have significant *disadvantages*. Information obtained with their help often gives only an *incomplete and abstract picture* of customer satisfaction, so that their contribution to concrete measures to enhance customer loyalty and improve quality is limited. The analysis of the satisfaction data gives average values, for example, an average satisfaction score of 2.3 on a five-point scale. In comparison with previous period scores, it is possible to determine whether customer satisfaction has increased or decreased. But poorer satisfaction scores with respect to individual quality attributes only signal that the customers have experienced problems, but *not which problems*. Lower values with regard to 'politeness' or 'competence' do not give any indication of which employee behavior is interpreted as impolite or incompetent. Furthermore, a questionnaire can cover only *part of the quality experience*. This applies first for reasons of quantity, because customers cannot be expected to fill in questionnaires several pages long. Secondly, the concrete customer experience in its complexity can often not be expressed in the form of attributes. Therefore, the attribute-based assessment needs to be supplemented by the use of incident-based methods.

3.1.2.2 Incident-Based Measurement of Customer Satisfaction

The informational deficiency of the attribute-based approach has led to the development of incident-based measurement methods. They are based on the concept of episodic information processing and assume that satisfaction is a result of *incidents* experienced regarding products or services. Accordingly, they assume that market offerings are not perceived and stored in memory as a sum of 'attributes' rather than as incidents integrated into a concrete local and temporal context. Of crucial importance are *'critical incidents'*, which customers perceive as exceptionally positive or negative. Customers keep these incidents in memory, talk about them with others and consider them when they are deciding about a renewed purchase. Therefore, it is essential for companies to gain insight into these critical incidents experienced by their customers. One way of doing this is to apply the *'critical incident technique'* by asking customers in oral interviews to describe in detail their particularly positive and negative experiences (Stauss and Hentschel 1992; Stauss 1993; Gremler 2004).

3.1.2.3 Complaint Analysis as an Approach for the Incident-Based Measurement of Customer Satisfaction

An obvious and easily applicable approach for the incident-based assessment of customer dissatisfaction is to evaluate the *negative critical incidents contained in customer complaints*. The information gathered in this way is, as compared with data from attribute-based surveys—particularly *relevant, current, concrete and cost-effective*.

The *relevance of complaint information* arises from the significance of the reported incidents for the customers. Only because customers evaluate these problems as serious, do they incur the material and psychological costs associated with a complaint. It is this subjective significance of the complaint incident and its negative assessment by the customer that make complaint information relevant for companies. While the usually very positive results of customer satisfaction surveys suggest that customers experience only few problems, complaints show the existence and nature of customer problems and also the corporate need for action.

Complaints also contain *current* information because consumers normally contact the company soon after the problem rises. In contrast, customer satisfaction surveys are usually conducted at longer intervals. This approach is of dubious value, because the length of the past period increases the difficulty of describing the former psychological situation correctly, particularly, because the previously perceived satisfaction is highly distorted through new product experiences and information as well as through mental reassessment processes.

In addition, complaint information is *very concrete*. Customers describe the incident experienced in detail. So they state precisely, for example, which employee behavior they interpret as an expression of rudeness or lack of advisory competence. This information is immediately usable by companies for corrective and innovative measures.

Companies receive this relevant, current and specific information about customer dissatisfaction in a *cost-effective* manner, as it is provided at the initiative and expense of the customer—in contrast to market research data.

3.2 Customer Satisfaction and Complaint Behavior

In many cases that are not especially aggravating, customers will tend to try to rid themselves quickly of the uncomfortable feeling they have when they are disappointed in their expectations and experience dissatisfaction. They are then engaging in a *process of dismantling their psychological dissonance* in that they, for instance, belatedly reduce the expectations they originally had or correct their original negative impression in a more positive direction. If this kind of belated harmonization of expectation and perception is unsuccessful, the customers face the question of how they should then behave.

3.2.1 Behavioral Alternatives of Dissatisfied Customers

In principle, *various ways of behaving* are available to the customers, although it is certainly also possible that they may resort to several activities at the same time (see Fig. 3.2). They may:

- *switch* in the sense of changing brands or of exiting the market
- engage in *negative word-of-mouth communication*
- remain *inactive* despite dissatisfaction or
- *complain* to the firm or to a third-party institution.

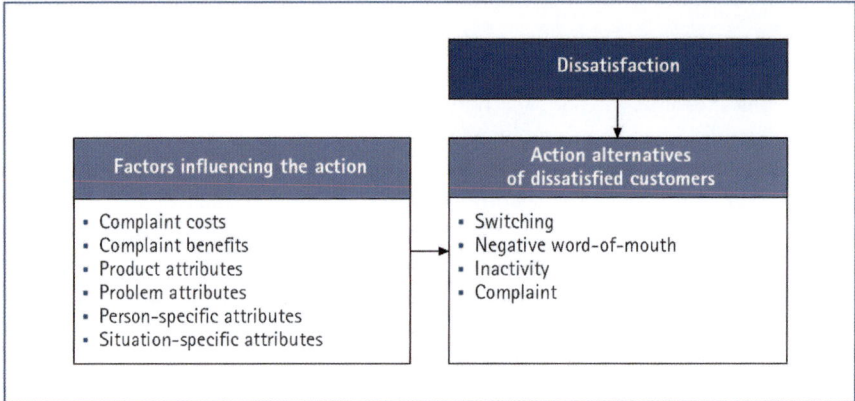

Fig. 3.2 Methods of dealing with dissatisfaction and their influencing factors

In many cases, customers *switch immediately* because they view an argument with the firm as time-consuming, irksome and/or futile. This switch is commonly accompanied by *negative word-of-mouth communication*, in which the customers recount their negative experiences within their social spheres—that is, to family members or among friends or acquaintances. This kind of word-of-mouth communication is particularly effective. Since the persons telling the story experienced the event themselves and are not pursuing selfish goals in their depiction of that event, the content of the word-of-mouth communication seems *more believable and convincing* by far than any type of paid communication methods the provider might employ (Herr et al. 1991; Gremler et al. 2001).

Some customers do not change their behavior despite being dissatisfied, thus making them appear to be *inactive*. They do not switch because, for example, to them the inconveniences associated with the change (such as closing one bank account and opening a new one) seem at first to be too great. They also do not engage in negative word-of-mouth communication to any appreciable degree. These customers should, however, *in no way continue to be regarded as loyal customers*. When other negative incidents arise or when a competitor makes an appeal to these customers, they will quickly decide to make a change.

3.2.2 A Majority of Dissatisfied Customers Do Not Complain

Some of the dissatisfied customers will certainly complain. The question then becomes, *under what conditions* do customers choose this alternative? Complaint research has been occupied with this question for years and can provide some important answers (among others, Singh and Pandya 1991; Singh and Widing 1991; Stephens and Gwinner 1998).

Social networks	94.6 %
Electricity companies	83.8 %
DIY stores	78.8 %
Post office branches	77.1 %
Banks/Saving banks	76.3 %
Hearing care professionals	76.1 %
Airlines	75.8 %
Food markets	73.1 %

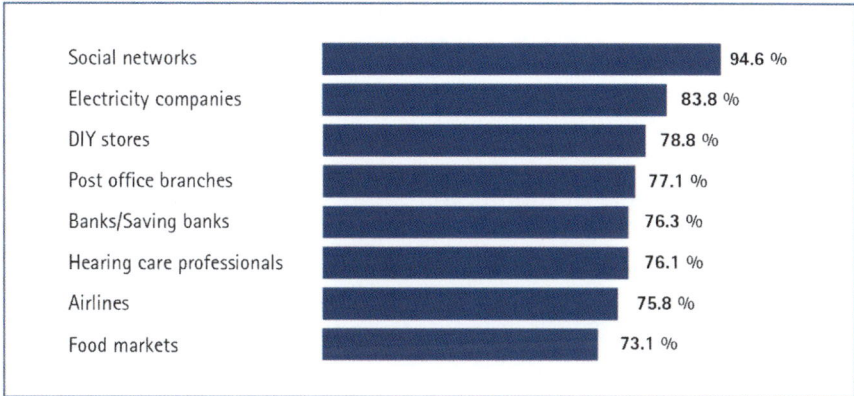

Fig. 3.3 Non-articulation rate of disappointed customers (Source: Servicebarometer 2016)

A fundamental result of this research is the insight that the bulk of the dissatisfied customers do not approach the firm with complaints. For every articulated complaint, there is a far greater number of *"unvoiced complaints"*. According to the findings of Goodman et al. (2000), one can proceed under the rough assumption that regardless of industry, approximately *50–80% of dissatisfied customers* forego the chance to bring their irritation to the attention of a customer contact employee or to a decentralized or centralized location of the firm. The national German customer satisfaction survey "Kundenmonitor" shows, too, that the proportion of non-complainants is extremely high and even exceeds 90% in some industries (Servicebarometer 2016; see Fig. 3.3).

Given this data, it is obvious that the number of complaints registered in the firm represents merely the *tip of a dissatisfaction iceberg*.

This phenomenon becomes even clearer when customers are not only asked to indicate the degree of their satisfaction, but also to state whether they were *annoyed* about an aspect of the product or service in a defined period of time (such as a year) and, therefore, in fact have had a cause for a complaint. Usually it turns out that even customers who are still satisfied with the relationship, experience negative incidents and only a few of them complain (Stauss and Seidel 2005).

The fact that only a portion of dissatisfied and annoyed customers complain is of *significant economic importance*. Firstly, a large number of these 'non-complainants' migrate immediately without the company having a chance to save the relationship through restoration of customer satisfaction. Secondly, focusing only on the number of complaints registered in the company results in a distorted picture and an underestimation of the negative customer experiences. These effects are especially problematic because empirical studies show that non-complainants have a particularly high tendency to churn. A comparison of two studies about the non-complaining behavior of customers of an insurance company confirms this. While a survey among current customers found that 55% of the annoyed customers did not complain, a survey among annoyed customers who had already terminated the relationship showed that 86% had quit without first complaining (Stauss and Seidel 2006).

3.2.3   Determinants of Complaint Behavior

When dissatisfied customers are queried about the reasons for their complaint passivity, they often give answers that provide information about the fundamental *dimensions of influence of their behavior*. Table 3.1 shows a compilation of these answers.

As the result of systematic analyses of answers such as these, empirical complaint research shows that it is primarily the following aspects that influence the decision to complain, meaning that they should be regarded as determinants of complaint behavior: complaint costs, complaint benefits, product attributes, problem attributes and attributes specific to the person and to the situation (see also Fig. 3.2).

Complaint Costs   Obviously, customers carry out an *internal cost-benefit analysis*, based on which they make the decision of whether to complain or not. In the context of this calculation, the costs of the complaint itself play an important role (Bearden and Mason 1984; Ross and Oliver 1984). Customers associate complaints with time and costs, and frequently with exasperating arguments, with frustration, anxiety, or stress as well (Oliver 2015). These *material and immaterial costs* to the customer are basically determined by the firm. If they refuse their customers information about where and how they can complain, firms increase customers' complaint costs. In addition, if they put up barriers to customers' obtaining restitution by demanding that they return an opened package, for example, the costs are increased yet again (Kendall and Russ 1975). If they make it uncomfortable or embarrassing for the customers to make their complaint, their immaterial costs increase. Firms can

Table 3.1   Customers' reasons for not complaining in spite of dissatisfaction (Source: Barlow and Møller 2008, pp. 75–76)

• "No one would listen to me anyway."
• "They told me I'd had to write a letter. Who's got time for that?"
• "I didn't know who to talk to."
• "I would have had to wait a long time for a reply."
• "I was partially responsible."
• "I wasn't sure how to talk about this situation. It was too personal."
• "The last time I complained, nothing happened."
• "It wasn't worthwhile."
• "The person I wanted to complain about might have lost her job."
• "I had a problem last week; they would think I am picky or a whiner."

consequently influence the probability of a customer complaint in the case of dissatisfaction by varying the complaint costs.

Complaint Benefits The costs must be compared to the benefits of the complaint. This comparison is primarily dependent upon the *subjective value of the solution* to the problem that the customer expects from the provider. The value is, however, weighed against the *probability that the complaint will be successful* (Jacoby and Jaccard 1981; Richins 1983). Most customers complain only if they believe there is a realistic chance that the firm is prepared to make restitution. Someone who has no hope of a positive reaction will refrain from making a complaint. Firms can influence the perception customers have that a complaint will be successful, specifically by the extent to which customer orientation is practiced and communicated. Paradoxically, the more coldly and inflexibly they conduct themselves with regard to customers, the fewer firms will have to reckon with complaints.

Product Attributes The *relevance of the consumer experience* is the foremost product attribute that influences the probability of complaints (Bearden and Oliver 1985; Richins and Verhage 1985). Making complaints is complicated and burdensome. The customers will only put up with the process when they view the damages they have suffered as being substantial, which is always the case with goods that they deem to be especially important because of their high purchase price or their prestige value, for instance.

Problem Attributes Not all the problems perceived by customers are equally likely to become the subject of their complaints. Customers are most apt to choose this approach when the problem at hand can be manifestly proven—that is, it is a *clear-cut problem* that can be somewhat objectively described and leaves little room for subjective evaluation. If the circumstances cannot be proven or if the incident could be interpreted differently by different people, customers are less likely to take the risk of complaining (especially in writing) (Best 1981). Quality attributes—which, like lack of friendliness, for instance, are evaluated subjectively—are considerably less often the object of complaints than verifiable circumstances (such as a malfunctioning product), even if the degree of dissatisfaction experienced is the same.

The *unambiguousness of causal attribution* figures prominently as a problem attribute. Complaints are more likely to be considered as a reaction by dissatisfied customers the more unambiguously the cause of their dissatisfaction can be attributed to the provider. If the customers are firmly convinced that the provider carries sole "responsibility" for the problem that has occurred, they are more likely to complain than they would be in cases in which they consider themselves to partly responsible also (Richins 1983; Folkes 1984). This explains the comparatively low volume of complaints about certain service problems. Many services are produced in an interaction between the customers and the employees of the provider. The customers are co-producers in the service provision process; they have to provide, for example, accurate information about their wishes and expectations. If the customers are not satisfied with the service result (e.g. the hairstyle), it is possible that they are at least partly blame themselves for the failure. If they have the impression that they did not articulate their wishes clearly enough, a complaint is unlikely.

Clear evidence of the effect that problem attributes have on complaint behavior can be found in a *study on complaint behavior* that was carried out in the furniture industry. An almost equal percentage of customers were upset about the problems of "incomprehensible assembly instructions" (18.5%) or "defective parts" (20.2%). Indeed, while 17.4% of customers complained because of the missing parts, the corresponding figure for those who complained because of the assembly instructions amounted to just 1.9% (Dobberstein 2001). The incomprehensibility of the instructions is difficult to prove objectively, a subsequent change is hardly likely and it is conceivable that the customers also consider themselves partly responsible for the lack of understanding.

Person-Specific Attributes Person-specific attributes are also clearly jointly responsible for whether a dissatisfied customer complains or not. The influence of *socio-demographic attributes* (like age, gender, education), *psychographic attributes* (like product knowledge, self-confidence, complaint experience) and *behavioral attributes* (like communicative and interactional behavior) were investigated in various empirical studies. The results are not consistent (Gyong Kim et al. 2010); however, one can make the general statement that the typical complainant tends to be a young, highly educated male with an average to high income level (Morganosky and Buckley 1987). In addition, complainants appear to be distinguishable from non-complainants in that they have a higher level of self-confidence (Bolfing 1989), in particular, they do believe that they are able to manage the complaining situation effectively (East 2000; Susskind 2000).

Situation-Specific Attributes Last but not least, the conditions of the situation are another factor that have an influence on whether a customer complains. Perceived *time pressure* can thus induce customers to refrain from making a complaint, or customers may regard themselves as compelled to express their complaints in an especially dramatic manner due to *comments from escorts* or the *observation of the incident by a third party*.

In order to assess the company-specific relevance of the influencing factors, it is advisable to ask customers, in a customer satisfaction survey, about their reasons for not complaining despite their annoyance. The percentage distribution of the responses provides valuable insights into customer expectations and perceptions as well as opportunities for companies to influence them. For example, a survey of annoyed customers of a financial service provider showed that almost 40% considered the effort of a complaint to be too high. Another 34% did not complain because they did not see any chance of success, 9.4% migrated directly to competitors and 7.5% terminated the relationship because they could not reach a contact person (see Table 3.2).

These findings of complaint behavior research are of extreme practical importance for complaint management. They demonstrate first and foremost that complaint information cannot provide a complete overview of problems as they are perceived by customers. The analyses of the determinants of complaint behavior also

Table 3.2 No complaint despite annoyance (servmark 2012)

Pos.	Complaint barrier	%
1.	Effort too great	39.6 %
2.	No chance of success	34.0 %
3.	Migrated to the competition	9.4 %
4.	No contact person reached	7.5 %
5.	Problem solved otherwise	3.8 %
6.	Customers feel themselves responsible for the problem	3.8 %
7.	Other	1.9 %
Σ	**Total**	**100.0 %**

provide information as to the fact that *complaint information should not be seen as being representative* because it is highly probable that specific problems of certain customer groups are under- or overrepresented. For this reason, the analysis of complaint information must always be *complemented* by the use of other methods to detect problems. Furthermore, the results described point out possible actions that can be considered as part of a firm's complaint policy, since some determinants can be *influenced through corporate measures*. It is possible, for example, to erect or dismantle barriers to complaints and in this way to have an influence on the costs to the customers and on their assessment of whether the complaint will be successful.

3.3 Complaint Satisfaction and Its Influence on Customer Behavior

3.3.1 The Origin of Complaint Satisfaction

If dissatisfied customers choose the alternative of complaining, they again have certain expectations with respect to the firm's answer and the targeted solution. This *complaint expectation* then becomes the standard on the basis of which the customers assess their *actual experience* with the firm's reaction (perceived answer to the complaint). If their expectations are exceeded, complaint satisfaction is the result; if they are fulfilled, indifference is the result; otherwise, complaint dissatisfaction occurs (McCollough et al. 2000; Gruber 2011; see Fig. 3.4).

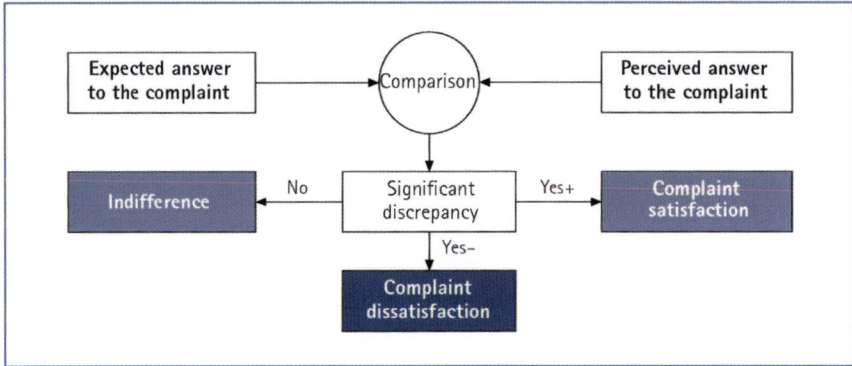

Fig. 3.4 Origin of complaint satisfaction/dissatisfaction

3.3.2 Dimensions of Complaint Satisfaction

Knowing *which aspects of the firm's reaction the complainants are rating* and how important these aspects are in the formation of complaint satisfaction or dissatisfaction is of great importance in the specific development of complaint management.

Complaint satisfaction research has increasingly taken up this question (Tax et al. 1998; Boshoff 1999; Smith et al. 1999; Buttle and Burton 2002; Davidow 2003). The dimensions and attributes of complaint satisfaction named in the various studies vary in the details but are basically consistent. The complainants' expectations and perceptions refer to the outcome achieved, the interaction with the company as well as to the complaint handling process. Accordingly, it is appropriate to distinguish between complaint outcome satisfaction, complaint interaction satisfaction and complaint process satisfaction. Eight attributes of complaint satisfaction can be assigned to these three dimensions).

*   *Complaint outcome satisfaction:* satisfaction of the complainant with the company's response.
    *   *Appropriateness/fairness of outcome:* appropriateness of the solution to the problem; fairness of the restitution offered.
*   *Complaint interaction satisfaction:* satisfaction of the complainant with the interaction that takes place during the acceptance and processing of the complaint.
    *   *Friendliness/politeness:* courteousness with which the complainant is treated; polite conversational tone/style of language;
    *   *Empathy/understanding:* readiness to see things from the customer's perspective; understanding of the customer's irritation; individualized handling of the case;
    *   *Effort/helpfulness:* recognizable effort to solve the problem in accordance with the wishes of the customer;

- *Activity/initiative:* actively seeking contact with the customer; inquiring about the desired solution; notification of delays;
- *Reliability:* adherence to promises with respect to content and time.
- *Complaint process satisfaction:* satisfaction of the complainant with aspects of the complaint-processing procedure.
  - *Accessibility:* ease with which a corporate contact person can be found for a customer's problem; knowledge of where complaints should be addressed;
  - *Reaction speed:* promptness with which an acknowledgment arrives; promptness of reaction to further inquiries from customers; promptness with which the case is solved.

As an alternative to the consistently satisfaction-oriented approach several researchers have proposed a justice-theoretical concept (Tax et al. 1998; Pizzutti and Fernandes 2010; Homburg et al. 2010). They distinguish the following three dimensions of justice and investigate their impact on the overall complaint satisfaction:

- *Distributive justice.* This refers to the outcome of the company's decision, the perceived adequacy and fairness of the solution offered.
- *Interactional justice.* This relates to the interpersonal behavior, such as honesty, politeness and empathy of the staff.
- *Procedural justice.* This involves the complaint handling process, i.e. the accessibility, response speed or flexibility.

It is obvious that satisfaction-oriented and justice-theoretical perspectives have strong similarities. Dimensions and attributes correspond to a large extent (see Fig. 3.5).

Both perspectives also underline the fact that complaint satisfaction is not solely influenced by the solution the firm offers, but rather by the *total experience of the complaint situation.*

3.3.3 Retention Effect of Complaint Satisfaction

The results of studies in complaint behavior research consistently demonstrate that complaint satisfaction or dissatisfaction has an *extraordinary degree of influence* on the attitude toward or the satisfaction with the business relationship, as well as on the purchase and communication behavior of the complainant (Maxham III 2001; Durvasula et al. 2000; Stauss 2006).

At the *psychological level*, complaint dissatisfaction increases the already existing dissatisfaction of the customer with the relationship to the company. This leads to a loss of trust and growing doubts about the reliability and integrity of the company and to a weakening of emotional loyalty in the sense of commitment (Smith and Bolton 1998; Her Astuti et al. 2011). At the behavioral level, complaint dissatisfaction leads to the intention to reduce rebuys in future, to terminate the relationship and to engage in negative word-of-mouth communication—or in a

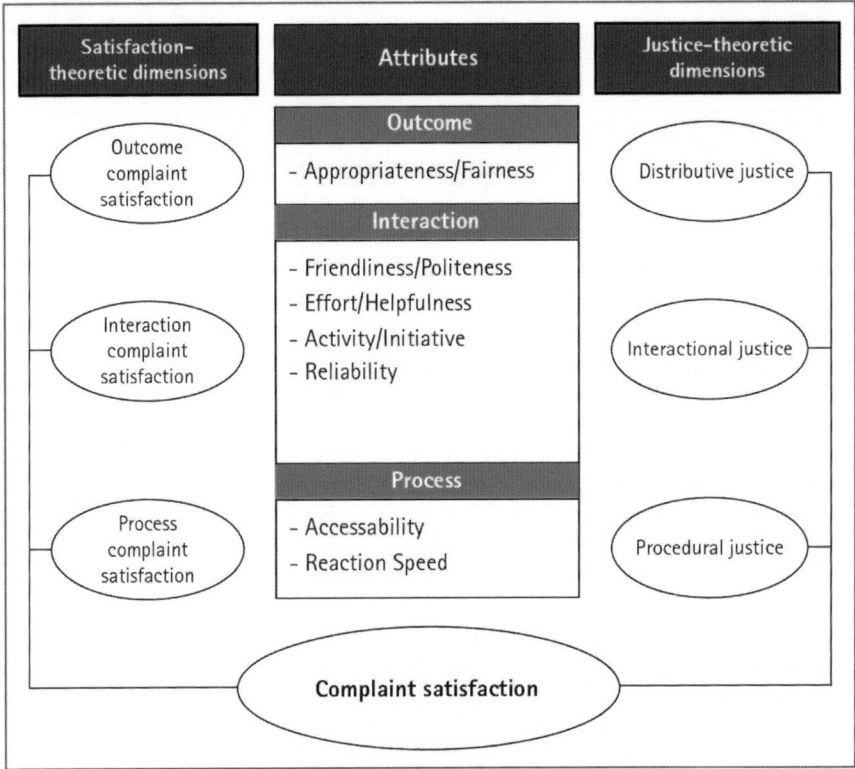

Fig. 3.5 Dimensions and attributes of complaint satisfaction

corresponding actual behavior. This means that negative complaint experiences increase the likelihood of customer churn (Hoffman and Kelley 2000). Customers who react especially strongly are those who have been very loyal in the past and are now particularly disappointed by the negative complaint experience and feel cheated (Grégoire et al. 2009, 2011).

In contrast, the chain of effects for complaint satisfaction is as follows: in psychological terms, customers who are satisfied with the complaint response, recover their satisfaction with the relationship and their commitment and trust increase. This leads to an increased readiness on the customers' part to express themselves positively within their social spheres with respect to the product and the firm (positive word-of-mouth communication) and to hold onto the business relationship (repeat purchase) (see Fig. 3.6).

The *effect of complaint (dis)satisfaction on the customer's global satisfaction* provide impressive confirmation of the results of the German "Customer Monitor" (Servicebarometer 2006), which records the satisfaction and the complaint satisfaction of German customers in a variety of industries on a yearly basis. As Fig. 3.7 from the do-it-yourself store industry shows, the average value of customer

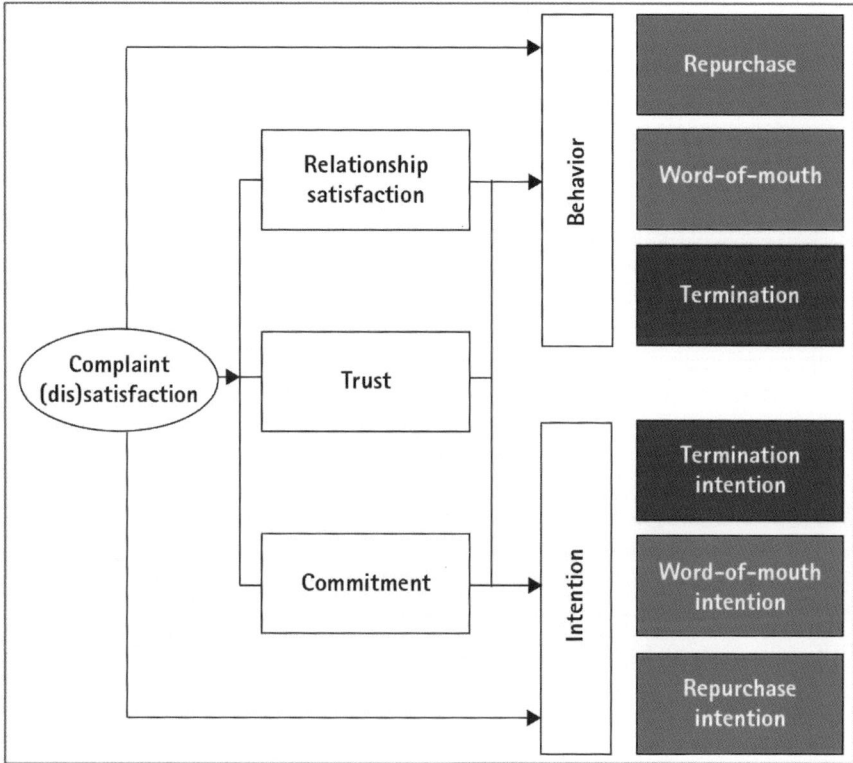

Fig. 3.6 Effects of complaint (dis)satisfaction (Stauss 2017, p. 377)

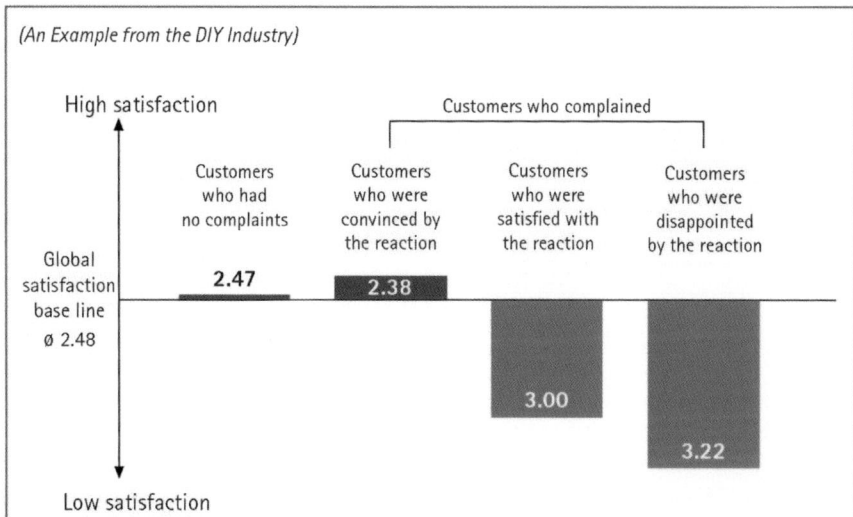

Fig. 3.7 The influence of complaint satisfaction on global satisfaction. An example from the DIY industry (Source: Servicebarometer 2006)

satisfaction in this industry is 2.48 on a 5-point-scale (1 = completely satisfied). For those customers, who didn't have a complaint, the satisfaction value is slightly better (2.47), whereas customers, who complained and weren't satisfied with the company's reaction show a satisfaction value way below average (3.22) and the satisfaction value of complainants, who were just satisfied is below average, too (3.00). In contrast, the satisfaction of those complainants, who were convinced by the company's reaction, is especially positive. The corresponding satisfaction value (2.38) is even better than that of those customers, who didn't have a complaint. This so-called "recovery paradox" is also confirmed in other empirical studies (Michel 2001; Magnini et al. 2007).

With regard to the *communication behavior* of the complainant, many studies confirm the fact that complaint experiences are made the subject of word-of-mouth communication. Positive as well as negative experiences are repeated on a large scale and thus have an effect far above and beyond the case itself (Maxham III 2001; Maxham and Netemeyer 2002). It has been proven again and again that the incidents that lead to *complaint dissatisfaction* are communicated considerably more often than are positive experiences. A study conducted by TARP for Coca-Cola showed that satisfied complainants told an average of 4–5 people about their positive experience, while dissatisfied customers told an average of 9–10 people about their negative experience (TARP 1979, p. 11). Sweeney et al. (2005) found in their study that negative word-of-mouth communication was twice as effective as positive in terms of purchase rates.

Not only does complaint satisfaction or dissatisfaction influence communication behavior, but also the *intention to make a repeat purchase* and the *actual repeat purchase behavior* (Liu et al. 2000; Miller et al. 2000). In their study Hansen and Jeschke (2000) came to the conclusion that satisfied complainants are characterized by a particularly high level of brand loyalty. An internal investigation of the car manufacturer Volkswagen AG showed that 54–70% of satisfied complainants became regular customers and that this proportion increased to 95% if the company reacted very quickly (Bunk 1993). TARP studies prove the 'recovery paradox' which says that the loyalty of satisfied customers can be even greater than the loyalty of customers who have experienced no problem whatsoever with the product or the firm (TARP 1979; Adamson 1993). Goodwin and Ross (1990) point to the fact that catalog customers whose complaints were solved in a timely manner were more profitable than customers who had no complaint whatsoever.

In view of these consistent findings concerning the contribution that complaint management makes to customer retention and thus to the achievement of fiscal goals, it is astonishing that not all firms draw the appropriate conclusions, thereby leaving substantial possibilities for *customer retention unexploited*. Empirical studies reveal that many complaining customers not even get an answer to their complaints. A survey among consumers who complained to a Better Business Bureau reveals a large proportion of cases in which consumers reported that companies did not offer any type of option to potentially resolve their complaints. In the home construction industry, for example, two-thirds of the consumers reported that the companies offered nothing to resolve their complaints (Fisher et al. 1999). In Germany, too,

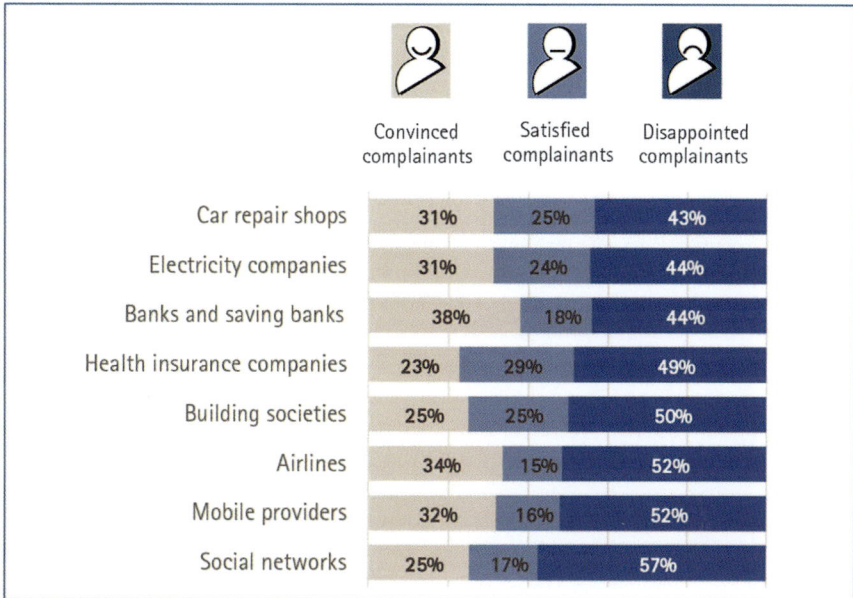

	Convinced complainants	Satisfied complainants	Disappointed complainants
Car repair shops	31%	25%	43%
Electricity companies	31%	24%	44%
Banks and saving banks	38%	18%	44%
Health insurance companies	23%	29%	49%
Building societies	25%	25%	50%
Airlines	34%	15%	52%
Mobile providers	32%	16%	52%
Social networks	25%	17%	57%

Fig. 3.8 The unexploited retention potential of complaint management—selected industries in Germany 2016 (Servicebarometer 2016)

complaint satisfaction remains at a relatively low level. According to the findings of the national customer satisfaction survey, some industries disappoint more than 40% or even 50% of their complainants (Servicebarometer 2016). Figure 3.8 shows this and makes clear what unexploited customer retention potential still exists.

Anyone who fails to stabilize otherwise endangered business relationships through the use of professional complaint management is foregoing potentially significant economic success. Specific possibilities for how firms can estimate the extent of this economic potential will be pointed out later. First of all, however, the conceptual foundations of professional complaint management will be described.

Chapter 3 in Brief
- Dissatisfaction arises if the perceived performance falls short of the customer's expectations.
- Complaints provide companies with more relevant, more current, more concrete and more cost-effective information about customer dissatisfaction than satisfaction surveys.
- The majority of dissatisfied customers do not complain. This non-complaining behavior can particularly be expected if customers

(continued)

judge the costs of complaining to be higher than the attainable benefits or see little chance of success.

- Complainants have expectations regarding the outcome of the complaint response, the interaction with the company as well as the complaint handling process. Complaint (dis)satisfaction arises when these expectations are (not) met.
- Complaint dissatisfaction is a major reason for customer migration and negative word-of-mouth communication; complaint satisfaction stabilizes the customer relationship and promotes positive word-of-mouth communication.

References

Adamson C (1993) Evolving complaint procedures. Manag Serv Qual 3(1):439–444

Barlow J, Møller C (2008) A complaint is a gift. Berrett-Koehler, San Francisco

Bearden WO, Mason JB (1984) An investigation of influences on consumer complaint reports. In: Kinnear TC (ed) Advances in consumer research, vol 11. Association for Consumer Research, Provo, pp 490–495

Bearden WO, Oliver RL (1985) The role of public and private complaining in satisfaction with problem resolution. J Cons Aff 19(2):222–240

Berry LL, Parasuraman A (1991) Marketing services, competing through quality. The Free Press, New York

Best A (1981) When consumers complain. Columbia University Press, New York

Bolfing CP (1989) How do customers express dissatisfaction and what can service marketers do about it? J Serv Mark 3(2):5–23

Boshoff C (1999) An instrument to measure satisfaction with transaction-specific service recovery. J Serv Res 1(3):236–249

Bunk B (1993) Retention Marketing: Das Geschäft mit dem Ärger. Absatzwirtschaft 36(9):65–69

Buttle F, Burton J (2002) Does service failure influence customer loyalty? J Cons Behav 1(3):217–227

Davidow M (2003) Organizational responses to customer complaints: what works and what doesn't. J Serv Res 5(3):225–250

Dobberstein T (2001) Beschwerde- und Reklamationsmanagement, Analyse und Maßnahmen dargestellt am Beispiel des Möbelhandels. In: Müller-Hagedorn L (ed) Kundenbindung im Handel, 2nd edn. Deutscher Fachverlag, Frankfurt, pp 289–320

Durvasula S et al (2000) Business-to-business marketing: service recovery and customer satisfaction issues with ocean shipping lines. Eur J Mark 34(3/4):433–446

East R (2000) Complaining as planned behaviour. Psychol Mark 17(12):1077–1095

Fisher JE et al (1999) Dissatisfied consumers who complain to the better business bureau. J Cons Mark 16(6):576–591

Folkes VS (1984) Consumer reactions to product failure: an attributional approach. J Cons Res 10(4):398–409

Goodman JA et al (2000) Turning CFOs into quality champions. Qual Prog 33(3):47–54

Goodwin C, Ross I (1990) Consumer evaluations of responses to complaints: what's fair and why. J Cons Mark 7(2):39–47

Grégoire Y et al (2009) When customer love turns into lasting hate: the effects of relationship strength and time on customer revenge and avoidance. J Mark 73(6):18–32

Grégoire Y et al (2011) When your best customers become your worst enemies, does time really heal all wounds? Gfk-Market Intell Rev 3(1):26–35

Gremler DD (2004) The critical incident technique in service research. J Serv Res 7(1):65–89

Gremler DD et al (2001) Generating positive word-of-mouth communication through customer-employee relationships. Int J Serv Ind Manag 12(1):44–59

Gruber T (2011) I want to believe they really care: how complaining customers want to be treated by frontline employees. J Serv Manag 22(1):85–110

Gyong Kim M et al (2010) The relationship between consumer complaining behavior and service recovery: an integrative review. Int J Contem Hosp Manag 22(7):975–991

Hansen U, Jeschke K (2000) Beschwerdemanagement für Dienstleistungsunternehmen—Beispiel eines Kfz-Handels. In: Bruhn M, Stauss B (eds) Dienstleistungsqualität, 3rd edn. Gabler, Wiesbaden, pp 433–459

Her Astuti P et al (2011) The evaluation of customer complaint handling with justice dimensions, effect on trust and commitment with prior experiences as moderating effect. Interdis J Contem Res Bus 2(11):228–237

Herr PM et al (1991) Effects of word-of-mouth and product-attribute information on persuasion: an accessibility-diagnosticity perspective. J Cons Res 17(4):454–462

Hoffman KD, Kelley SW (2000) Perceived justice needs and recovery evaluations: a contingency approach. Eur J Mark 24(3/4):418–432

Homburg C et al (2010) On the importance of complaint handling design, a multi-level analysis of the impact in specific complaint situations. J Acad Mark Sci 38(3):265–287

Jacoby J, Jaccard JJ (1981) The sources, meaning, and validity of consumer complaining behavior: a psychological analysis. J Retail 57(1):4–24

Kendall CL, Russ FA (1975) Warranty and complaint policies: an opportunity for marketing management. J Mark 39(2):36–43

Liu BSC et al (2000) After-service response in service quality assessment: a real-time updating model approach. J Serv Mark 14(2):160–177

Magnini VP et al (2007) The service recovery paradox: justifiable theory or smoldering myth? J Serv Mark 21(3):213–225

Maxham JG III (2001) Service recovery's influence on consumer satisfaction, positive word-of-mouth, and purchase intentions. J Bus Res 54(1):11–24

Maxham JG, Netemeyer RG (2002) A longitudinal study of complaining customers' evaluations of multiple service failures and recovery efforts. J Mark 66(4):57–71

McCollough MA et al (2000) An empirical investigation of customer satisfaction after service failure and recovery. J Serv Res 3(2):121–137

Michel S (2001) Analyzing service failures and recoveries: a process approach. J Serv Ind Manag 12(1):20–33

Miller JL et al (2000) Service recovery: a framework and empirical investigation. J Oper Manag 18 (4):387–400

Morganosky MA, Buckley HM (1987) Complaint behavior: analysis by demographics, lifestyle, and consumer values. In: Wallendorf M, Anderson P (eds) Advances in consumer research 14. Association for Consumer Research, Provo, UT, pp 223–226

Oliver RL (2015) Satisfaction: a behavioural perspective on the consumer, 2nd edn. Routledge, London

Pizzutti C, Fernandes D (2010) Effect of recovery efforts on consumer trust and loyalty in e-tail, a contingency model. Int J Electron Comm 14(4):127–160

Richins M (1983) Negative word-of mouth by dissatisfied consumers: a pilot study. J Mark 47 (4):68–78

Richins ML, Verhage BJ (1985) Seeking redress for consumer dissatisfaction: the role of attitudes and situational factors. J Cons Policy 17(1):29–44

Ross I, Oliver RL (1984) The accuracy of unsolicited consumer communications as indicators of "true" consumer satisfaction/dissatisfaction. In: Kinnear TC (ed) Advances in consumer research, vol 11. Association for Consumer Research, Provo, pp 504–508

Servicebarometer (2006) Kundenmonitor Deutschland 2006. Servicebarometer, München

Servicebarometer (2016) Kundenmonitor Deutschland 2016. Servicebarometer, München

Servmark (2012) Interne Bankstudie. Servmark, München

Singh J, Pandya S (1991) Exploring the effects of consumers' dissatisfaction level on complaint behaviours. Eur J Mark 25(9):7–21

Singh J, Widing RE (1991) What occurs once consumers complain? A theoretical model for understanding satisfaction/dissatisfaction outcomes of complaint responses. Eur J Mark 25 (5):30–46

Smith AK, Bolton RN (1998) An experimental investigation of customer reactions to service failure and recovery encounters—paradox or peril? J Serv Res 1(1):65–81

Smith AK et al (1999) A model of customer satisfaction with service encounters involving failure and recovery. J Mark Res 36(3):356–372

Stauss B (1993) Using the critical incident technique in measuring and managing service quality. In: Scheuing E, Christopher W (eds) The service quality handbook. American Marketing Association, New York, pp 408–427

Stauss B (2006) Beschwerdemanagement als Instrument der Kundenbindung. In: Hinterhuber HH, Matzler K (eds) Kundenorientierte Unternehmensführung, 4th edn. Gabler, Wiesbaden, pp 315–334

Stauss B (2017) Vermeidung von Kundenverlusten durch Beschwerdemanagement. In: Bruhn M, Homburg C (eds) Handbuch Kundenbindungsmanagement, 9th edn. Springer Gabler, Wiesbaden, pp 365–388

Stauss B, Hentschel B (1992) Attribute-based versus incident-based measurement of service quality: results of an empirical study in the German car service industry. In: Kunst P, Lemmink J (eds) Quality management in services. Van Gorcum, Assen, pp 59–78

Stauss B, Seidel W (2005) Non-complaining behavior of lost service customers. In: Paper presented at the 4th Servsig research conference, National University of Singapore, Singapore, 2–4 Jun 2005

Stauss B, Seidel W (2006) Evidenz-Controlling im Beschwerdemanagement—Ein Ansatz zur Abschätzung des "Verärgerungs-Eisbergs". In: Bruhn M, Stauss B (eds) Dienstleistungscontrolling—Forum Dienstleistungsmanagement. Gabler, Wiesbaden, pp 89–111

Stephens N, Gwinner KP (1998) Why don't some people complain? A cognitive-emotive process model of consumer complaint behavior. J Acad Mark Sci 26(3):172–189

Susskind AM (2000) Efficacy and outcome expectations related to customer complaints about service experiences. Commun Res 27(3):353–378

Sweeney JV et al (2005) The differences between positive and negative word-of-mouth—Emotion as a differentiator? In: Proceedings of the ANZMAC 2005 conference: broadening the boundaries. University of Western Australia, Perth, pp 331–337

TARP (1979) Consumer complaint handling in America: final report. White House Office of Consumer Affairs, Washington

Tax SS et al (1998) Customer evaluations of service complaint experiences: implications for relationship marketing. J Mark 62(2):60–76

© Springer Nature Switzerland AG 2019

B. Stauss, W. Seidel, *Effective Complaint Management*, Management for Professionals,
https://doi.org/10.1007/978-3-319-98705-7_4

Issues Raised
- What are the essential goals of complaint management?
- Which key performance indicators are useful for target-oriented complaint management?
- What are the main tasks of complaint management?
- Which frameworks are relevant and how should they be designed in order to ensure the best possible fulfillment of the complaint management tasks?

4.1   Goals of Complaint Management

Complaint management encompasses the planning, execution and controlling of all the measures taken by a firm in connection with the complaints it receives.

The *overall goal of complaint management* lies in increasing the *profitability and competitiveness* of the firm by restoring customer satisfaction, minimizing the negative effects of customer dissatisfaction on the firm and using the indications of operational weaknesses and of market opportunities that are contained in complaints (Brown et al. 1996; Tax and Brown 1998; Johnston and Mehra 2002; Davidow 2003; Stauss and Seidel 2010). This overall goal can be broken down in sub-goals that can be assigned to the areas of customer relationship management and quality management. Furthermore, there is the requirement of a productive task fulfillment (see Table 4.1).

Table 4.1 Goals of complaint management

Overall goal	• Increase of profitability and competitiveness
Customer relationship related sub-goals	• Stabilization of jeopardized customer relationsips through the establishment of (complaint) satisfaction • Increase in purchase intensity and purchase frequency, as well as promotion of cross-buying behavior • Implementing and clarifying of a customer-oriented corporate strategy • Creation of additional promotional effects via word-of-mouth communication
Quality-related sub-goals	• Improvement of the quality of products and services via the use of information that is contained in complaints • Avoidance of external failure costs • Avoidance of internal failure costs
Productivity-related sub-goal	• Efficient task fulfillment

4.1.1 Customer Relationship-Related Sub-goals

Stabilization of Endangered Customer Relationships by Restoring Satisfaction Complaint management is an essential part of retention management and "targets the re-stabilization of customer relationships that have been jeopardized as a result of dissatisfaction" (Stauss and Seidel 2012, p. 209). This customer relationship-related sub-goal is based on research findings that complaint satisfaction can be achieved through the fast und unbureaucratic handling of complaints (Smith and Bolton 1998; Durvasula et al. 2000; Stauss 2002). Complaint satisfaction leads to a significant improvement in global customer satisfaction, to customer loyalty and thus to securing of sales and profits (Stauss and Seidel 2012, p. 209).

Increase in Purchase Intensity and Purchase Frequency, as Well as Promotion of Cross-Buying Behavior A satisfying complaint handling should increase the commitment of the customers and their willingness to engage in intensified purchases from the firm. This phenomenon may occur in that they engage in multiple purchases, they increase their purchase frequency or they expand their purchasing of other products and services.

Creation of Additional Promotional Effects Via Word-of-Mouth Communication Complaint management should help to avoid negative word-of-mouth communication and stimulate positive ones. Both consumer problems articulated in complaints and the complaint experiences that follow are discussed within the customer's social sphere. Thus, "this personal communication is an important variable that influences the attitudes of other consumers toward the firm or the product (multiplication effect)" (Stauss and Seidel 2010, p. 416) and their buying behavior.

4.1.2 Quality-Related Sub-goals

Use of Information Contained in Complaints to Improve the Quality of Products and Services Complaints contain valuable information about problems customers experience with products, services or corporate behavior. This information is relevant for quality management, "as it provides an indication of the adequacy of fixed quality levels and adherence to quality standards. Furthermore, the information offers an abundance of insights into user expectations" (Stauss and Seidel 2010, p. 416) that when used in the development of product modifications and innovations can ensure future sales potential (La and Kandampully 2004; Vos et al. 2008).

Avoidance of External Failure Costs Problems that become the subject of complaints commonly lead to the occurrence of instances in which warranties and guarantees, legal processes or conflicts with third-party institutions (e.g., media, arbitrators, attorneys), are invoked. Warranty costs can be lowered, guarantee claims reduced and costs of conflicts prevented through a systematic analysis of complaint information with reference to product deficiencies.

Avoidance of Internal Failure Costs Complaints not only contain indications of product deficiencies, but also point to process flaws. An appropriate use of this information can lead to a more productive designing of internal processes and an avoidance of mistakes and redundancies.

4.1.3   Productivity-Related Sub-goal

Efficient Task Fulfillment In order to achieve the customer relationship-related and quality-related sub-goals, resources must be used economically. Therefore, the sub-goal of efficient task fulfillment must be taken into account in all measures.

4.2   Key Performance Indicators of Complaint Management

The verbally formulated objectives need to be concretized in several steps for systematic control of complaint management and examination of the achievement of the targets. This is done by defining pre-economic targets and key performance indicators for each of them. These indicators must have a direct positive effect on economic targets (such as revenues or costs), so that the orientation to the overall goal of complaint management—the increase of profitability and competitiveness— is ensured. The result is *the complaint management target chain*, which schematically illustrates the target relationships.

The *customer relationship-related sub-goals* can be achieved through the following pre-economic targets: increase of the complaint articulation of dissatisfied customers, increase of the registration of articulated customer complaints, increase of complaint satisfaction, reinforcement of positive word-of-mouth communication and promoting the repurchasing behavior of complainants.

To what extent these targets are achieved can be determined using the following *key performance indicators*:

- *Articulation rate/Non-articulation rate* (Target: increase of the complaint articulation of dissatisfied customers)
- *Registration rate/ Non-registration rate* (Target: increase of the registration of articulated customer complaints)
- *Proportion of convinced/disappointed complainants* (Target: increase of complaint satisfaction)
- *Recommendation rate/warning rate* (Target: reinforcement of positive word-of-mouth communication)
- *Repurchase rate/churn rate* (Target: promotion of the repurchase behavior of complainants).

The *quality-related sub-goals* can be specified by the following pre-economic targets: reduction of defects, reduction of customer annoyance about problems with products or services, reduction of warranty and guarantee claims.

The corresponding key performance indicators are as follows:

- *Defect rate* (Target: reduction of product defects)
- *Annoyance rate* (Target: reduction of customer annoyance
- *Warranty rate* (Target: reduction of warranty claims)
- *Guarantee rate* (Target: reduction of guarantee claims).

The *productivity-related sub-goal* can be expressed by the pre-economic target of an increase of the efficiency of the complaint management processes. The most relevant key performance indicator is

- *Employee productivity:* the number of complaints processed per employee or time unit (Target: increase of efficiency).

Table 4.2 gives an overview of the goals of complaint management, the related pre-economic targets and the key performance indicators.

If the sub-goals of complaint management are achieved, the *following economic effects* are produced:

1. The fundamental *customer relationship-related sub-goal* is the prevention of customer losses, i.e. the securing of revenues and contribution margins of customers who would have migrated if there were no complaint management (*retention benefit*). Furthermore, revenue gains are achieved by positive word-of-mouth communication of satisfied complainants (*communication benefit*).
2. The *quality-related sub-goals* are focused on the use of complaint information for quality improvements, which is primarily reflected in the reduction of failure costs (*information benefit*).
3. The achievement of *productivity-related sub-goal* leads directly to a *reduction of complaint management costs*.

Overall, an increase of the economic targets leads to an increase of the *profitability of complaint management,* which in turn contributes to the achievement of the global corporate goal of *improving the company's competitiveness.*

Figure 4.1 shows the complaint management target chain with its components.

In the context of complaint management controlling (Chap. 11) it will be described precisely how the key performance indicators and economic targets can be measured.

Table 4.2 Key performance indicators of complaint management

Goals of complaint management	Pre-economic targets	Key performance indicators
Customer relationship-related sub-goals	Increase of the complaint articulation of dissatisfied customers	Articulation rate / Non-articulation rate
	Increase of the registry of articulated customer complaints	Registration rate/ Non-registration rate
	Increase of complaint satisfaction	Share of convinced/ disappointed complainants
	Reinforcement of positive word-of-mouth communication	Recommendation rate/ Warning rate
	Promotion of the repurchase behavior of complainants	Repurchase rate/ Churn rate
Quality-related sub-goals	Reduction of product defects	Defect rate
	Reduction of customer annoyance	Annoyance rate
	Reduction of warranty claims	Warranty rate
	Reduction of guarantee claims	Guarantee rate
Productivity-related sub-goal	Increase of efficiency of the complaint management processes	Employee productivity

4.3   Fundamental Tasks of Complaint Management

The goals of complaint management can only be achieved if a series of *fundamental tasks* that can either be assigned to a direct or to an indirect complaint management process are accomplished.

"*Direct*" means that the task fulfillment requires a direct contact with the complainant. This contact situation reflects the "*moment of truth*" in the complaint management process. How the complainants experience the fulfillment of the tasks determines whether they will continue to be customers of the company in the future. The tasks of direct complaint management are therefore primarily aimed at achieving customer relationship-related goals.

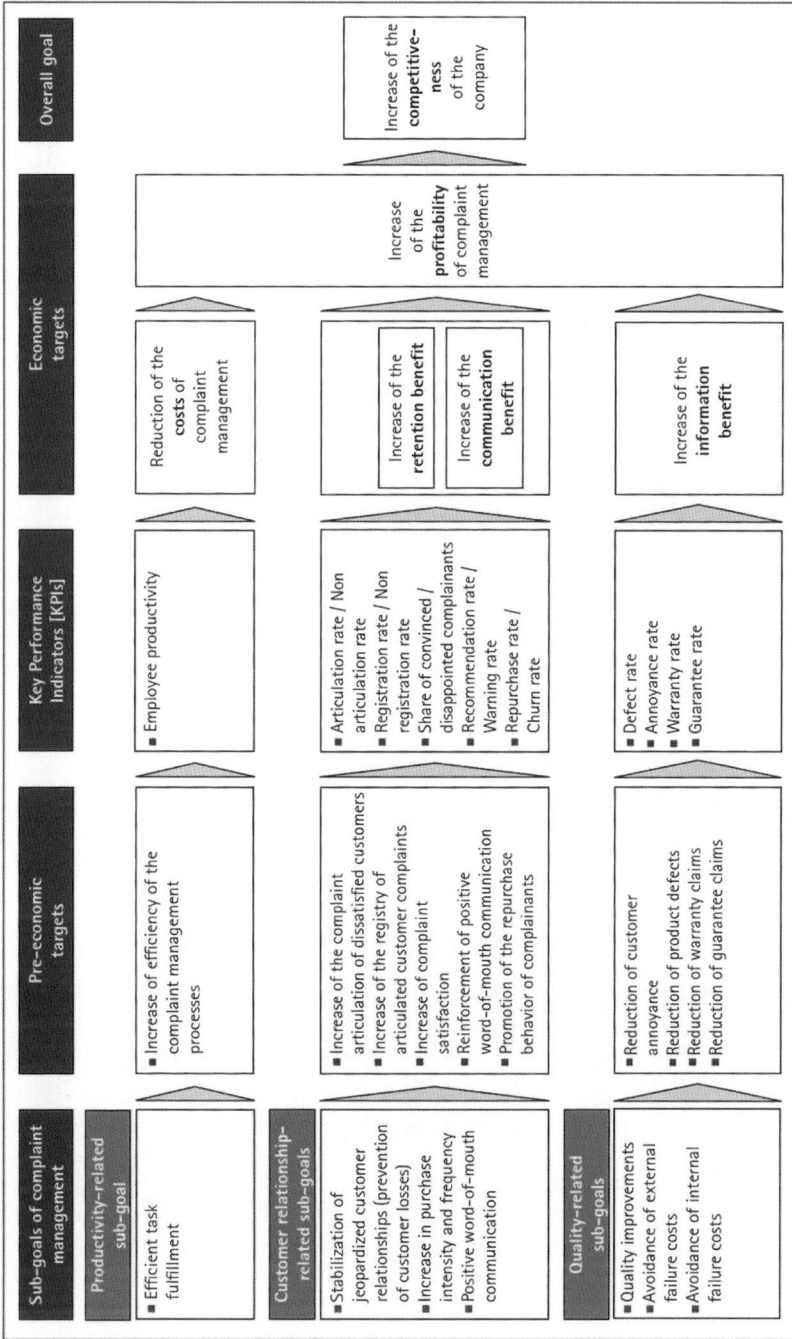

Fig. 4.1 Target chain of complaint management

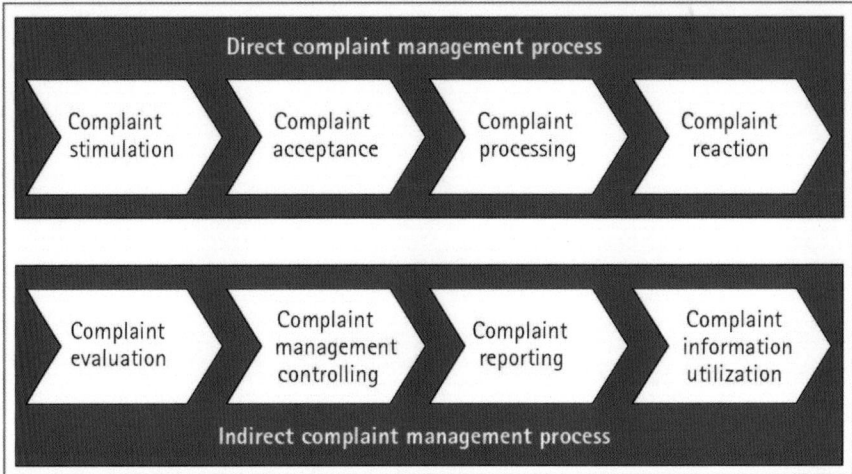

Fig. 4.2 Direct and indirect complaint management process

The complaint management tasks are known as *indirect*, when the customer is *not directly involved*. They enable the in-house learning process through evaluation, communication and use of the complaints and therefore primarily serve the quality-related goals of complaint management. Figure 4.2 gives an overview of the tasks of the *entire complaint management process*.

4.3.1 Tasks of the Direct Complaint Management Process

Relevant to the direct complaint management process are complaint stimulation, complaint acceptance, complaint processing and complaint reaction.

Since the majority of dissatisfied customers do not complain, but migrate immediately (Chebat et al. 2005), by *complaint stimulation* these customers should be encouraged to bring their perceived problems to the attention of the firm. There are three main sub-tasks that must be tackled here. Firstly, a decision about the *complaint channel* must be made—that is, the questions must be answered as to which method (verbal, telephone, written or electronic) customers should use in making their complaints and to which business location they should bring those complaints. Secondly, *active communication* of the complaint channels must take place so that the highest possible percentage of dissatisfied customers chooses to react with a complaint and select the proper complaint channel. Thirdly, *accessibility* of the business locations accepting complaints must be assured in that the capacity required within the context of gradual complaint stimulation is provided.

The *complaint acceptance* phase primarily affects the organization of the complaint input and the documentation of the complaint information. As far as complaints made in person and by telephone are concerned, the customers experience important aspects of the corporate reaction to their concerns during the initial contact with the firm. In the case of written complaints, by contrast, the initial contact with the complainants takes place in the form of intermediate replies or final answers. How the customers perceive the firm's reaction plays a decisive role in whether their dissatisfaction is reduced or increased even further. For this reason, it is important to *organize the receipt of complaints* so that clear lines of responsibility are drawn and the employees who will receive the complaints are prepared for what they will encounter.

With respect to the *documentation of the complaint*, what is important is to record the problem brought forward by the customer in a thorough, rapid and structured manner. Here decisions must be made as to the *contents of the documentation*, the categorization of those contents and the form that the documentation will take. Basic contents of the documentation include the informational content of the complaint (information on the complainant, the problem itself and the object of the complaint), as well as the complaint handling information (information on the complaint acceptance, complaint processing and complaint reaction). A useful *scheme of categorization* is required for the systematic documentation of complaint information. With respect to the *form of documentation*, firms may use standardized forms and/or fill-in-the-blanks forms in complaint management software programs. The process of documentation may also be at least partially transferred to customers, insofar as they are requested to describe their complaints on a structured opinion card or to enter them on a specific complaint page on the Internet.

What is most important within the scope of duties in *complaint processing* is the systematic design of complaint settlement. The first step is to identify and model the different *types of complaint processing procedures*. Next, it must be determined who is *responsible* at each level: for the entire complaint management process, this is the "process owner"; for the processing of an individual case, the "complaint owner"; and for the individual steps of the processing procedure, the "task owner". Processing deadlines for the various processes and sub-steps must also be established. A *system of reminders and escalations* that is developed according to these deadlines aids in monitoring adherence to them. Furthermore, rules and forms for *internal communication* of the locations that participate in the processing of a complaint must be stipulated. Finally, all the processing steps with their contents, the locations that carried them out and the deadlines must be chronologically documented for each individual complaint case in a *complaint history*.

In the area of *complaint reaction*, it is worthwhile to define fundamental guidelines and rules of behavior, so that the target goals of achieving a calming of the situation and of finding a satisfying solution are not threatened. In defining these *rules and guidelines*, it is necessary to make a distinction depending on the way in which customer criticism is articulated. Another key sub-task in the context of complaint processing is the decision as to which *solution* should be offered to the customers in view of their complaint. Financial (discounts, money back, compensation for damages), tangible (exchange, repair, another product, gift), or intangible offers of compensation (apology, information) are the principal types considered. In order to make a decision that is suitable for the customers as well as for the problem, informational prerequisites must be either satisfied or established. Included among these are the availability of *detailed data about the complainants*, their affiliation with certain customer groups and their economic value to the firm. Within the scope of activity of complaint reaction are also contained decisions about the *extent of and time frame for the communication* that takes place after the complaint input. On the one hand, it is important to determine which acknowledgments (e.g., confirmation of receipt and intermediate replies) will take place and in which form (verbally, by telephone, in writing); on the other hand, clear-cut standards for the maximum period of time in which these communications are to occur must also be set.

4.3.2 Tasks of the Indirect Complaint Management Process

Once the complaint reaction phase has been reached, the direct complaint management process is completed. Complaint analysis, complaint management controlling, complaint reporting and utilization of complaint information constitute the *indirect complaint management process*, which is handled in the absence of customer contact.

Complaints contain specific indications of organizational weaknesses in the planning, production and marketing of products and services, as well as evidence of changes in customer preferences or market opportunities. For this reason, the information contained in complaints must be analyzed. Here two tasks are of particular importance: first, in the context of *complaint evaluation* the extent and distribution of the volume of complaints have to be monitored. Second, a ranking of the problems perceived by customers has to be created to derive priorities for corrective actions and improvements.

The scope of responsibilities in the category of *complaint management controlling* encompasses three important subareas: evidence controlling, task controlling and cost-benefit controlling.

The central concern of *evidence controlling* is ascertaining to what extent complaint management is in a position to reveal the degree of dissatisfaction present among the customers of the firm, which appears in the form of complaints—that is, to make this dissatisfaction evident to management. To this end, the volume of non-articulated complaints of dissatisfied customers has to be determined. In addition, the volume of complaints that are articulated but not registered (hidden) must be evaluated.

Task controlling is concerned with monitoring the extent to which the tasks of complaint management are being successfully accomplished. Here, *quality indicators and quality standards* must be formulated with reference to all the subtasks, and these indicators and standards must be continually reviewed as to compliance and suitability. Objective standards can only be determined for some of the quality indicators (for example, time targets to ensure rapid complaint processing). In other cases, the solution is to use satisfaction values as standards and to revise them in reference to complaint satisfaction surveys. Moreover, *productivity indicators and productivity standards* that reveal the efficiency of task fulfillment should be fixed. The firm-relevant quality and productivity standards should then be collected in a *Complaint Management Index (CMI)* according to their respective level of importance. This CMI should be seen as the central aggregate control benchmark of task controlling.

The function of *cost-benefit controlling* is to estimate the cost and benefit effects of a particular system of complaint management. In *cost controlling*, the costs that arise during the acceptance, processing and reaction phases, as well as those that emerge in the context of the indirect complaint management process, must be calculated. *Benefit controlling* quantifies the various benefit dimensions of complaint management (retention, communication and information benefits). The economic efficiency and the *return on complaint management* can be computed by comparing the cost effects with the benefit effects.

The information from the complaint analysis and from complaint management controlling must be made accessible to the various internal target groups. Hence decisions must be made with respect to *complaint reporting* as to which analyses should be disseminated or provided on demand, at which time intervals and for which internal customer segments (management, quality control, marketing, etc.).

A key goal of complaint management lies in providing a substantial contribution to a quality management system, as complaint management ensures that the information gathered from complaints will be actively utilized in the development of measures of improvement. The achievement of this goal requires not only regular complaint reporting, but also a systematic *utilization of complaint information* through the application of specific management measures and instruments. Among these is the application of quality planning techniques in the development of solutions to problems, the inclusion of complaint information in the work of quality improvement teams, the exploitation of complainants' idea potential and the integration of complaint information in a customer knowledge management system.

4.4   Internal Framework Factors of Complaint Management

Optimal fulfillment of tasks is only possible if the *internal framework conditions* are appropriately designed. Systematic and carefully coordinated management of human resources and of organizational and information technological aspects is required.

The behavior of employees is often decisive for the complainant's satisfaction and thus for the success of complaint management. Therefore, the design of the *human resources* represents a particularly important area of action. First, the necessary *employee skills* must be defined (service orientation as the basic motivation, social competence, emotional competence as well as professional and methodological competence). Second, it is necessary to ensure by measures of *personnel-oriented internal marketing* that the qualifications of the employees are available and promoted. These measures include instruments for the targeted recruitment of appropriate employees, employee communication and training, tailored incentive systems, measures for avoiding burnout effects and the transfer of competencies and decision-making scope to employees (empowerment). In addition, these measures must be supported by the provision of an appropriate technological *infrastructure* and a firmly established *customer-oriented corporate culture*.

The establishment of active complaint management involves a number of *organizational issues*. With respect to the company's *organizational structure*, decisions must be made about the degree of centralization or decentralization. A second problem concerns the *internal distribution of functions* of a complaint management area. In particular, the relationship between the units for the operational complaint processing and the strategically-oriented head of complaint management must be clarified. With regard to the integration of the complaint management department into the corporate organizational structure, the questions must be answered of how the complaint management process is linked to other business processes, which influence rights should be granted to the department, and what type of institutional and hierarchical position (staff unit or line function) seems sensible. The question of *outsourcing* complaint management must also be clarified. This question has to be answered in a differentiated manner with regard to strategic-conceptual and operational tasks.

In addition to the HR and organizational aspects, *technological aspects* are also of particular importance. Complaint management processes cannot be efficiently implemented without the use of software programs, especially in the event of large numbers of complaints. Therefore, an important management task is to select the appropriate software. This includes answering the question of whether a *special complaint-management software* or an *integrative CRM solution* should be implemented. Another relevant information technology consideration is to determine the type and scope of integration of *intranet and Internet* into the task fulfillment and to build up the appropriate hardware and software infrastructure.

Figure 4.3 shows the overall concept of complaint management with the direct and indirect complaint management processes and the framework factors. It also

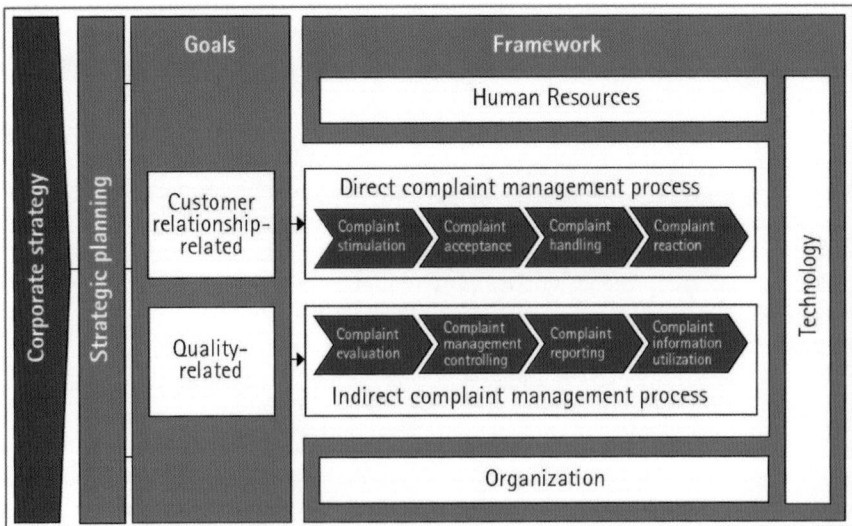

Fig. 4.3 The complaint management concept

illustrates clearly that the tasks and framework conditions must be shaped in a target-oriented way. The direct complaint management process should be oriented to the customer relationship-related goals, while the indirect complaint management process is oriented to the quality-related goals. The fundamental decisions about the whole process must be made within the context of *strategic planning* in accordance with the basic business strategy.

Chapter 4 in Brief

- The overall goal of complaint management is to increase the company's competitiveness and profit.
- Primary sub-goals with respect to customer relationships are to prevent customer churn and to achieve positive effects on revenues, corporate image and word-of-mouth communication.
- To what extent these customer relationship-related targets are achieved, can be determined using the following key performance indicators: articulation rate/non-articulation rate, registration rate/non-registration rate, proportion of convinced/disappointed complainants, recommendation rate/ warning rate and repurchase rate/churn rate.
- With regard to quality management, complaint management aims to improve the product quality and to reduce failure costs by the use of the information contained in complaints.
- The quality-related relevant key performance indicators are: defect rate, annoyance rate, warranty rate and guarantee rate.
- Regarding the complaint management tasks, a distinction must be made between the direct and the indirect complaint management processes.
- The tasks of the direct complaint management process include direct customer contacts and primarily serve the customer relationship-related sub-goals: complaint stimulation, complaint acceptance, complaint processing and complaint reaction.
- Tasks that can be completed without customer contact belong to the indirect complaint management process and aim to achieve the quality-related sub-goals: complaint evaluation, complaint-management controlling, complaint reporting and utilization of complaint information.
- Optimal fulfillment of the tasks requires an appropriate design of the human resources, as well as the organizational and technological framework conditions.

References

Brown SW et al (1996) Service recovery: its value and limitations as a retail strategy. Int J Serv Ind Manag 7(5):32–44

Chebat J-C et al (2005) Silent voice—why some dissatisfied consumers fail to complain. J Serv Res 7(4):328–342

Davidow M (2003) Organizational responses to customer complaints: what works and what doesn't. J Serv Res 5(3):225–250

Durvasula S et al (2000) Business-to-business marketing: service recovery and customer satisfaction issues with ocean shipping lines. Eur J Mark 34(3/4):433–446

Johnston R, Mehra S (2002) Best-practice complaint management. Acad Manag Exec 16 (4):145–154

La KV, Kandampully J (2004) Market orientated learning and customer value enhancement through service recovery management. Manag Serv Qual 14(5):390–401

Smith AK, Bolton RN (1998) An experimental investigation of customer reactions to service failure and recovery encounters—paradox or peril? J Serv Res 1(1):65–81

Stauss B (2002) The dimensions of complaint satisfaction: process and outcome complaint satisfaction versus cold fact and warm act complaint satisfaction. Manag Serv Qual 12(3):173–183

Stauss B, Seidel W (2010) Complaint management. In: Salvendy G, Karwowski W (eds) Introduction to service engineering. Wiley, Hoboken, pp 414–432

Stauss B, Seidel W (2012) Complaint management in retailing. In: Kandampully J (ed) Service management, the new paradigm in retailing. Springer, New York, pp 207–230

Tax SS, Brown SW (1998) Recovering and learning from service failure. Sloan Manag Rev 40 (1):75–88

Vos JFJ et al (2008) How organisations can learn from complaints. TQM J 20(1):8–17

Strategic Planning of Complaint Management

5

© Springer Nature Switzerland AG 2019

B. Stauss, W. Seidel, *Effective Complaint Management*, Management for Professionals,
https://doi.org/10.1007/978-3-319-98705-7_5

Issues Raised
- Why is strategic planning for complaint management necessary?
- What are the steps of the strategic planning process?
- Which aspects should be examined in the context of the strategic state analysis?
- Which basic strategy options are available?
- How can the appropriate strategy option be selected?

5.1   Strategic Potential and Need for Strategic Planning

Complaint management has high strategic potential for both customer relationship management and quality management. However, the results of empirical studies suggest that complaint management often does *not succeed*, or only to a limited extent, *in exploiting this strategic potential*. On the other hand, the complainants' satisfaction with the company's response is often low and information from complaints is rarely used systematically for quality improvements.

A clear diagnosis of the *causes* of this situation does not exist so far. Probably several factors work together. There is much to suggest that the strategic relevance of complaint management is underestimated by the top management, but also by those responsible for customer relation and quality management. Even today, complaint management is still regarded in many companies primarily as an organizational unit for the operational customer dialog, while its contribution to the added value of the company is fully recognized only in exceptional cases. As a consequence, a complaint management department is hardly involved in strategic decisions, although it has relevant, current, and detailed customer knowledge and could therefore provide particularly significant input.

However, complaint management should not lament the ignorance of the top management and the executives of other divisions and functional areas. Instead, it should consider what it can do itself to achieve a *better exploitation of its strategic potential*. Here are three starting points:

- Firstly, *the operational tasks* must be performed so professionally that customer satisfaction is achieved and an internal demand for information services is stimulated. This requires a coherent and systematic use of specific instruments. How this can be done, is the essential subject of this book.
- Secondly, it is necessary to prove internally its own *contribution to the company's value creation*. Since cost accounting usually captures only the costs of complaint management, but not its economic benefits, complaint management must make efforts to prove its profitability. Chapter 11 (Complaint-management controlling) provides appropriate approaches in detail.

- Thirdly, the managers engaged in the complaint management function must develop the strategic potential by thinking and acting strategically. This includes the use of strategic planning tools for the functional area of complaint management.

5.2   The Strategic Planning Process for Complaint Management

Strategic planning encompasses a systematic process for the foundation, formulation, evaluation and selection of strategies, i.e. the formation of basic regulations of a medium- or long-term basic nature with a structurally determining character. This planning process typically comprises *three steps* (Mende 2006): strategic state analysis, development of strategy options and strategy evaluation and selection.

5.2.1   Strategic State Analysis

In a first step, a thorough strategic analysis of the initial situation must be carried out. The managers of the complaint management function must identify the essential external requirements and the relevant internal influencing factors (environment analysis). Secondly, it is important to investigate the functional area of complaint management itself in detail with regard to the range of services, the performance quality and the existing internal framework conditions and restriction on actions (functional area analysis), see Fig. 5.1.

5.2.1.1   Environment Analysis

Within the framework of the environment analysis, two fields of investigation must be distinguished: the external environment of the company (macro environment) on the one hand and the internal functional environment of complaint management (micro environment) on the other. They are discussed separately below.

Analysis of the External Environment of the Company (Macro Environment)

The analysis of the *macro environment* focuses primarily on the investigation of the main external target group, the complaining customers. In addition, the complaint management activities of other companies must be observed as well as all external factors that may affect the complaint management.

The *complainants* are the key target group of the direct complaint management process. The primary goal of complaint management, to satisfy the dissatisfied customers and to retain them, can only be achieved if the essential requirements of the complainants are known. It is therefore necessary to find out what expectations the complainants have regarding the company's response, what issues determine their complaint satisfaction and how customer churn can be avoided. Only on the basis of this knowledge strategic options for action can be planned.

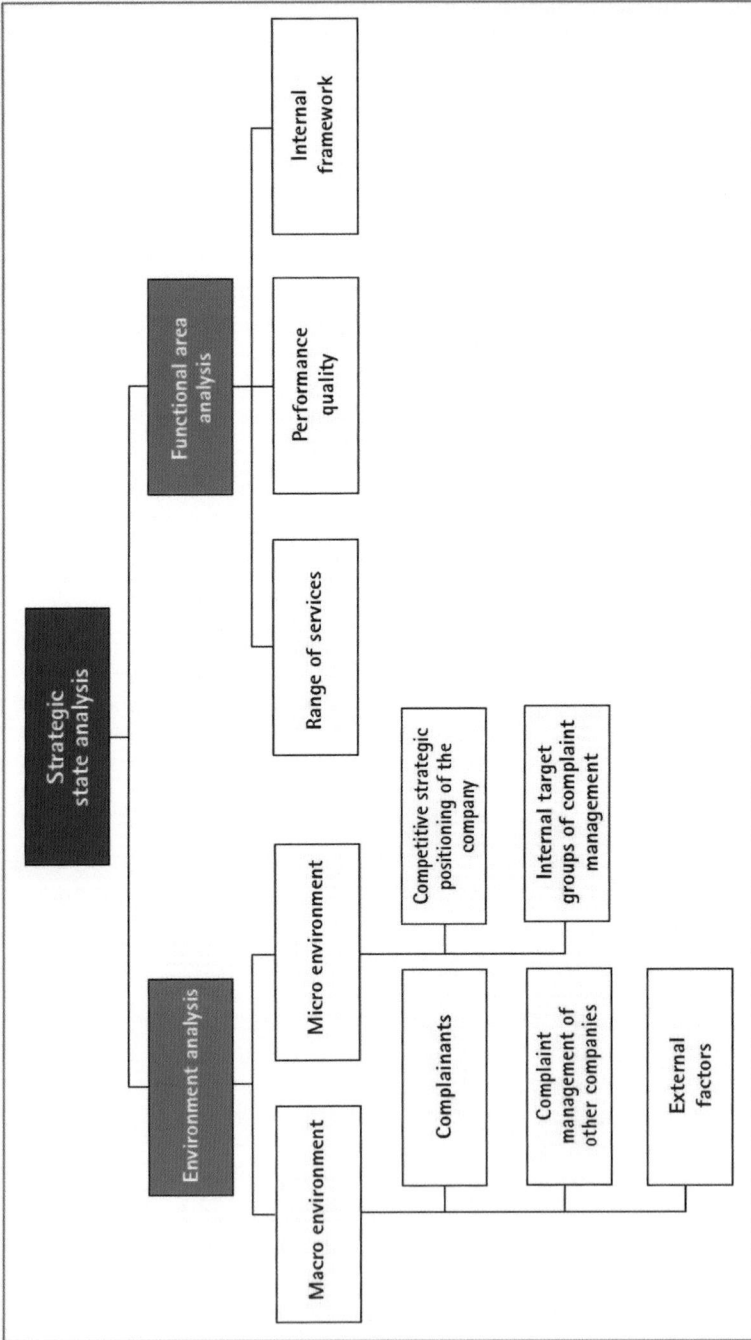

Fig. 5.1 Fields of the strategic state analysis

Furthermore, it is useful to get an idea of the *complaint management of other companies*. Dissatisfied customers experience the complaint handling of various companies and form their general expectations toward complaint management based on this experience. Therefore, it is essential to gain knowledge about the complaint management practice of companies of the same industry as well of companies with a similar strategic positioning.

In addition, those *external factors* must be identified and investigated that affect the complaint management activities. These influencing factors can be political or legal, social, economic or technological (Mende 2006). The analysis of these factors focuses on the question of what impact they have on the complaining behavior of customers and the resulting consequences for the direct complaint management process. This is always the case if external factors lead to quantitative shifts in the complaints volume or a qualitative change of the complainants' expectations and interaction behavior. It is also necessary to analyze whether the external influences enable new possibilities for efficient task fulfillment in the direct and indirect complaint management process, e.g. by allowing better forms of processing and evaluation of complaints.

With regard to the *political and legal dimension*, the influences of the legislator and the jurisdiction must be considered. What is particularly relevant here is the political significance of consumer policy and how this is reflected in legal regulations, e.g. regarding warranty claims, producer liability or disclosure obligations to regulatory authorities.

With respect to the *social dimension*, changes in the society's values are of particular interest, as far as this is reflected in an increased sensitivity to certain issues (such as ecology or security). Also relevant are general behavioral tendencies that may have an impact on the complaint behavior of customers, such as trends toward rising aspiration levels, lower tolerance thresholds or a decreasing willingness to engage in long-term commitments.

Aspects of the *economic dimension* can be significant, too. In particular, it should be observed how economic influences, such as reduced labor incomes or increased unemployment, affect buying behavior as well as forms of communication and the loyalty of the customers. Of still greater importance are the intensity and dynamics of the competition in the markets, as they determine the extent of the relevance of a company's customer-oriented behavior. For example, the stronger the competition, the more intense the fight for customers, the more expensive the acquisition of new customers, and the greater the importance of relationship-oriented complaint management.

In *technological terms*, of particular relevance are developments in the fields of new information and communication technologies that provide new media for the communication between complainant and company (such as Internet, e-mail, social networks, etc.). With a view to the direct complaint management process they must be checked with regard to their expected future dissemination and their suitability for the customer dialog and their suitability for customer self-services. For the indirect complaint management process mainly the development of specific software solutions has to be monitored. This means that it is constantly necessary to check whether there are cheaper and/or better possibilities for the evaluation of complaints, fast internal communication, the use of complaint information, as well as the implementation of controlling activities.

Analysis of the Internal Environment of Complaint Management (Micro Environment)

Complaint management is embedded in a specific internal environment. That is why it is necessary to identify the internal stakeholder groups and their needs and requirements, as well as to examine the central internal influencing factors with regard to their relevance to complaint management. Concerning this matter, the basic competitive strategy of the company plays a decisive role, as it determines the significance of the areas for action for which complaint management can make substantial contributions: customer relationship management and quality management. The expectations and requirements of the internal target groups can also be understood only in the light of the general strategic orientation.

According to Porter's (1998) widely accepted concept, two basic *competitive strategic positions* can be distinguished that can enable companies to gain lasting competitive advantages. On the one hand, customers can be offered a price advantage. In this case, the company succeeds in producing more cost-effectively than the competitors (*cost leadership*). On the other hand, the company can offer a unique product of higher quality that provides the customer with an added value in comparison to competitive offerings (*differentiation strategy*). The competitive strategy chosen by the company has important consequences for the alignment of customer relation management and quality management. Also, it has a decisive influence on the strategic options that are appropriate for complaint management (see Sect. 5.2.2).

The tasks of the direct complaint management process are performed for external customers, while those of the indirect complaint management are performed for internal customers. Therefore, a systematic analysis of the *internal customers* is necessary for target-oriented development of the internal services of the indirect complaint management process.

In principle, a large number of *internal customer groups* can be differentiated. A key customer group is the top company management that must be informed about the status and development of customer dissatisfaction. In addition, the areas affected by customer criticism must be considered as internal customer groups. Among these are business units (such as individual divisions), organizational units (such as subsidiaries) and functional areas (such as marketing, sales, service or quality management). Various staff groups, interest groups and temporary teams have to be considered, too. Also business partners who are involved in the performance chain can be regarded as an internal customer group; the term "internal" in this case refers not to the company, but to the business network (see Fig. 5.2).

Two particularly important internal customer groups will now be considered more closely: the company's top management on the one hand and business and functional areas on the other.

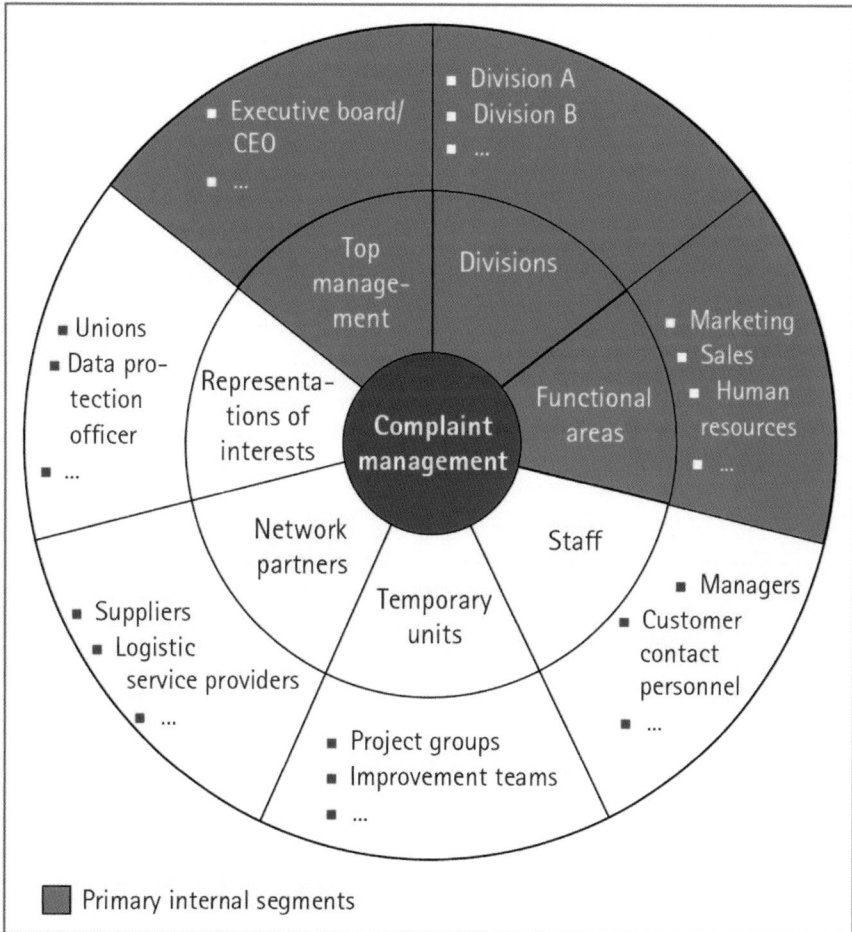

Fig. 5.2 Internal target groups of complaint management

The company's *top management* establishes the complaint management area, provides the budget and formulates the primary goals. Therefore, top management represents the most significant internal customer of complaint management.

The analysis must first examine what importance the top management attaches to customer relationship management and quality management, what specific targets it sets and which concrete expectations can be derived from these aspects for complaint management. With respect to customer relationship management, the contributions of complaint management to increase customer satisfaction and loyalty, to generate additional revenues from cross-selling activities and to avoid negative word-of-mouth communication are particularly relevant. Regarding quality management, it is important to identify which quality objectives are set, which organizational units and processes are controlled on the basis of customer data, and what information needs result from these analyses.

The second major internal customer groups are business units (such as individual divisions, subsidiaries or functional areas), here summarized under the term "*other departments*".

Direct and indirect relationships can exist between complaint management and other departments. There are direct relationships, for example, if complaint management provides information services, which enable internal customers to fulfill their duties more effectively. This is the case if the information is used to eliminate product defects, create customer-oriented offers, accelerate internal processes or avoid failure costs. If these information services should be charged internally, the relevant customer groups must be identified and the services must be priced. Regarding indirect relationships, other departments—in particular divisions— benefit from successful complaint management because secured revenues and profit contributions, as well as additional cross-selling effects, are attributed to them, without them needing to contribute to the costs of complaint management.

5.2.1.2 Functional Area Analyses

After considering the macro and micro environment with their stakeholders and influencing factors, it is important to focus on the analysis of the functional area of complaint management itself. Three fields of analysis are of interest here: the range of services, the quality of the performance and the internal framework conditions.

Range of Services

Initially, it is important to analyze which services complaint management offers and how these services can be combined into bundles, so that independent strategies can be developed for them analogous to strategic business units (Mende 2006). In principle, the most relevant service bundles are external problem solution services, internal information services, consulting services and training (see Fig. 5.3).

The direct complaint management process offers services to *external customers* by creating an easily accessible way for the articulation of complaints, the acceptance and processing of the complaints and the offering of solutions. Accordingly, the core of these services is the assistance with customer problems, so they can be characterized as *external problem solution services*.

For the *top management as internal customer*, complaint management provides information to support corporate decision-making because complaint evaluation can show what quality deficiencies the customers perceive and how great the risk of customer losses is. This information is primarily used for the customer- and quality-oriented control of internal processes and organizational units. Complaint management thus provides an *internal information service* by obtaining, evaluating and communicating complaint information. This general internal information service can be differentiated depending on the information content in terms of special services, such as customer problem analysis, analysis of customer losses, failure cost analysis, etc.

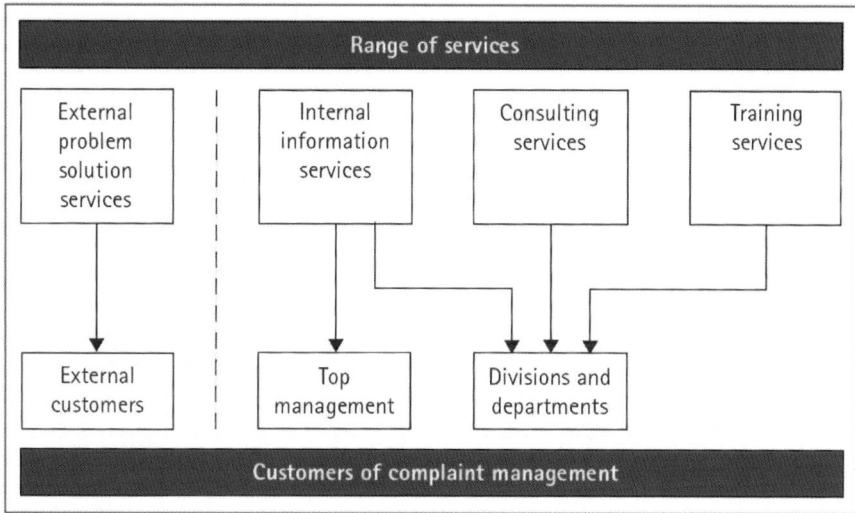

Fig. 5.3 Range of services and customers of complaint management

Complaint management also provides *internal information services* for *other departments*. The benefits for these departments are basically similar to those for the top management. The information describes specific risk potential such as quality defects, customer losses or failure costs, and gives hints on market opportunities through customer-oriented offerings and efficiency increases. However, it must be considered that complaint information is rarely actively requested by departments because of its critical content.

If divisions and departments are interested in complaint information and ask for it actively, it is possible to supplement it with more extensive services, namely consulting and training services. In *consulting services*, the complaint management function independently interprets and processes the information, for example, by performing a root cause analysis. It then gives recommendations for action and assists the department with the implementation of the proposed improvements. In addition, *training services* are conceivable. With these services employees can be taught about the relevance of customer orientation, essential aspects of customer satisfaction, dealing with dissatisfied customers, basic principles of complaint management and similar topics.

Performance Quality

The state analysis also includes the task of getting an accurate picture of the current status of complaint management, i.e. the performance quality of the direct and indirect complaint management processes. To this end, relevant quality dimensions and quality indicators must be identified for all task areas, and appropriate measurements must be taken. This is the essence of *task controlling*, which is an integral part of complaint management controlling (see Sect. 11.2).

Comparisons must be made in order to obtain clues for the evaluation of the current status. For this purpose, information about the complaint management of other companies can be used as a benchmark. Particularly valuable is information about "best practices" of companies with a comparable strategic profile.

Based on the analyses of the range of services on the one hand and of the performance quality on the other hand, a *service portfolio* can be developed. In analogy to known portfolio concepts of strategic planning of business units, the dimensions "service attractiveness" and "service strength" can be selected as axes of the portfolio matrix. *Service attractiveness* is determined on the basis of the external and internal environment analysis, by assessing factors such as the level of expectations of external customers, the influence of consumer policy and the nature of the internal demand.

Service strength is assessed based on data about the service evaluations of external and internal customers and on benchmarking data collected in the context of the functional area analysis. Figure 5.4 presents a fictitious application example. It

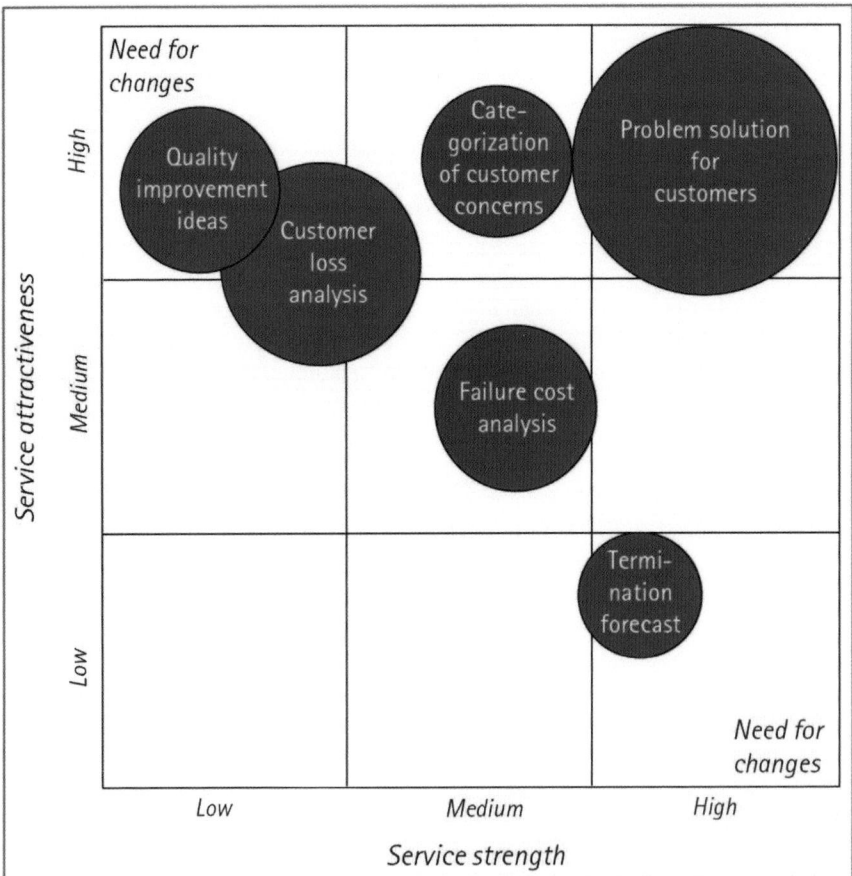

Fig. 5.4 Example of a service portfolio of complaint management

shows that there is a great need for changes with regard to the services "Quality improvement ideas" and "Customer loss analysis", since these services are highly attractive for customers, but considerable performance deficits exist. In addition, the portfolio suggests examining to what extent the offer of "Termination forecast" services is justified, because the service attractiveness is poor, although the service strength is assessed as high.

Internal Framework Conditions

The complete analysis also includes careful examination of the internal framework conditions. The task fulfillment in the fields of the direct and indirect complaint management essentially depends on the number, motivation and qualification of the available staff, the information technology infrastructure and the size of the allocated budget. Therefore, a quantitative and qualitative inventory of *the human, technological and financial resources* is required. Furthermore, scenarios for the future development of resources need to be developed in order to obtain a realistic view of the strategic options of complaint management. The *organizational integration* of complaint management and the existing communication structure also have to be investigated. Moreover, *corporate culture* aspects have to be included, in particular the relevance of customer orientation as corporate value as well as how the company deals with criticism and errors (error culture).

These internal framework conditions should be accepted in the short-term as fixed restrictions. However, the subsequent strategy evaluation must also reflect on what changes in resource allocation or organizational design are required in order to implement an intended strategy successfully. At the end of the strategic planning process, top management must be informed not only about the strategic concept, but also about the necessary changes to the internal framework conditions.

5.2.2   Strategy Options

5.2.2.1 Basic Strategies

Basic strategic alternatives of complaint management can be described and distinguished from each other on the basis of two criteria (Stauss 2008). First, they can be distinguished according to whether it is their primary aim to achieve customer retention (focus customer) or cost-efficient processing of complaints (focus efficiency). Second, they can be distinguished by a different focus on the tasks to be performed, either on the tasks of dealing with external customers (external focus) or on internal processes (internal focus). These distinctions result in the following four basic strategy types: complaint factory, relationship amplifier, quality control and customer satisfaction lab (see Fig. 5.5).

Complaint Factory   A complaint management of the type 'Complaint factory' has the primary task of processing the articulated customer complaints as cost-effectively as possible. Complaint handling is considered less as a customer retention tool than as a necessary administrative process, in particular in the cases of warranty

	External focus	Internal focus
Focus efficiency	Complaint factory	Quality control
Focus customer	Relationship amplifier	Customer satisfaction lab

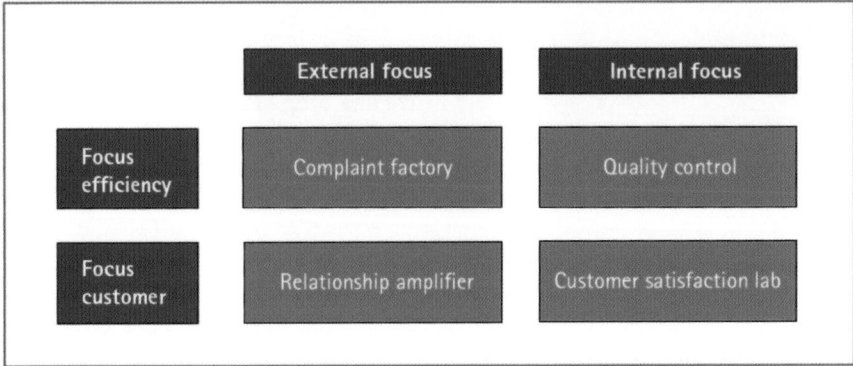

Fig. 5.5 Basic complaint management strategies

and guarantee claims. Therefore, dissatisfied customers are not encouraged to complain; on the contrary, there is a tendency to create complaint barriers, for example, by establishing only one complaint channel that is difficult to use for customers and cost-effective for the company. With regard to complaint acceptance, self-service components are widely used; detailed recording and categorizing of information are waived or the customers have to make a simple categorization themselves. A major focus of attention is the complaint processing procedures, particularly the implementation of efficient, and preferably (semi-) automated standard processes, such as the waiving of individual case examinations for specific complaint categories. Also, with respect to complaint reaction, standard responses dominate, restricted to a few low-cost alternatives and geared to what is legally required. The indirect complaint management process is of secondary importance. Only simple evaluations are carried out and brief standard reports are submitted to a limited number of internal customers. Complaint information is only used if lasting negative cost effects are otherwise to be expected due to conspicuous problem accumulations. Complaint management-controlling is performed only in respect to cost control aspects.

Relationship Amplifier The focus of the complaint management type 'Relationship amplifier' is not on the cost-efficient complaint handling, but on securing the relationships with the complainants. Of vital importance are the goals of maintaining customer loyalty and securing future margin contributions by restoring customer satisfaction. Accordingly, complaint stimulation plays an important role because as many of the dissatisfied customers as possible must be retained. With respect to the acceptance of complaints, easily accessible complaint channels are offered and customer data as well as problem-related information are documented in detail, in order to be able to respond in a differentiated and customer-individual manner. Regarding the indirect complaint management process, no clear statements can be made, but it is obvious that an external perspective easily dominates. In order to restore customer satisfaction sustainably, it is essential to analyze the main problem categories, inform the respective decision-makers and initiate correction and innovation processes. In addition, customer-specific complaint evaluations can be used not only to solve and correct problems, but also to provide the basis for the analysis of customer preferences and the development of customized offerings. Complaint-management controlling has a high priority. Above all, the determination of complaint satisfaction is relevant since it serves not only to ensure high quality complaint handling, but also represents a central target on the way to the desired emotional customer loyalty. Furthermore, data on complaint satisfaction and loyalty effects form the basis for assessment of the profitability of complaint management in the context of cost-benefit controlling.

Quality Control Complaint management of the type 'Quality control' must also interact with the complainants; however, the attention is not focused on the customer relationship, but on the internal quality assurance. Complaints are primarily considered as a complementary source of information on quality defects. Accordingly, the direct complaint management process does not have priority. Therefore, no significant efforts are made in the areas of complaint stimulation, complaint processing and complaint reaction. It is only of interest that detailed information about product and service defects is collected in the phase of complaint acceptance. Much more importance is attached to the indirect complaint management process. Here, differentiated analyses are made with respect to quality deficiencies, which are communicated to quality management. Complaint-management controlling plays a subordinate role. Of significance is only the assessment of the economic benefits that result from the use of complaint information for quality improvements and cost reductions.

Satisfaction Lab The complaint management type 'Satisfaction lab' takes on a mainly internal perspective, too. However, this perspective differs significantly from that of the 'quality control' type. Its primary function is to generate innovative impulses from the customer knowledge contained in complaint information and to use it actively for initiating change processes within the company. In this respect, the focus here, too, is not on the direct, but on the indirect complaint management process. But its responsibility is much more extensive and sophisticated. Complaint evaluation, reporting and utilization of complaint information are by no means restricted to quality assurance targets. Instead, they aim to stimulate customer-oriented ideas by extensive and complex evaluations, versatile and target group-oriented reporting as well as the integration of complaint information in development and innovation processes. Thereby, complaint management also initiates measures for the acquisition of further customer feedback (e.g. from customer forums) or integrates findings from other sources (such as satisfaction surveys). In this way, this type has the function of a 'satisfaction lab' of permanently bringing the critical customer view into the company, breaking up the routines and making a significant contribution to the customer-oriented alignment of the company as a whole.

5.2.2.2 Hybrid Strategies

The basic strategies are always based on the assumption that the focus is either on the internal or external performance of tasks. For example, the types 'complaint factory' and 'relationship amplifier' focus on the processes of dealing with external customers—the direct complaint management process—while the types 'quality control' and 'satisfaction lab' take the internal perspective and thus put more emphasis on the indirect complaint management process. However, companies have more options for their strategic orientation of complaint management. They can attach equal importance to the external and internal tasks. In this case, hybrid strategies exist that represent combinations of one external and one internal strategy type. Here, two combinations appear realistic, in which the efficiency-oriented and customer-oriented basic strategies are linked (see Fig. 5.6).

The hybrid *'efficiency first strategy'* combines cost-efficient complaint handling with utilization of complaint information that is restricted to quality assurance issues. The problem-solving and information services are offered only at minimum quality and at the lowest possible costs.

If customer satisfaction is the main goal of a company, the *'customer first strategy'* is appropriate. Complaint management within this hybrid strategic concept is not only responsible for restoring satisfaction with the help of the direct complaint management process; it also has the task of giving essential impulses for customer-oriented alignment of the company by the indirect complaint management process.

5.2.3   Strategy Evaluation and Selection

In the final stage of the strategic planning process, the strategic options must be evaluated and a specific option selected. This must be done on the basis of the strategic state analysis. This is briefly explained using the example of the basic complaint management strategies.

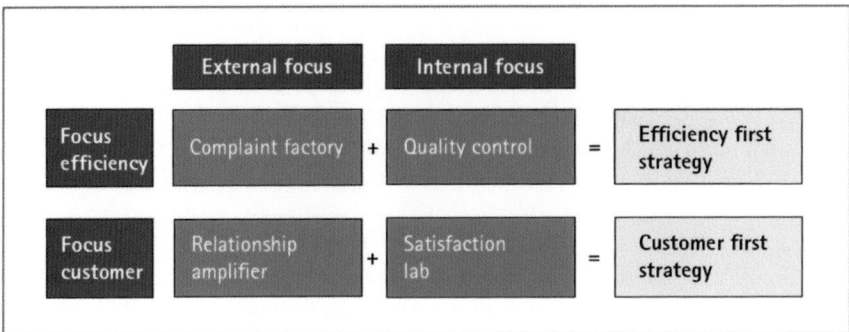

Fig. 5.6 Hybrid strategy options of complaint management

The results of the external environment analysis are of particular importance for the basic strategies with an external focus. The *'relationship amplifier'* strategy has proved to be superior in an environment characterized by high customer expectations and customer sensitivity, intense competition on the markets, and the existence of important competitors with the same complaint management strategy and an active consumer policy. In addition, the fundamental competitive strategy is crucial. If the company pursues a differentiation strategy to achieve a unique positioning through superior product quality and customized services, there is every reason to choose this strategy option. If the company pursues instead a cost leadership strategy, striving for a position in the market based solely on low prices, the *'complaint factory'* strategy is useful. This is not only the most cost-efficient solution, but in this case lower customer expectations can also be assumed.

With regard to the basic strategies with an internal focus, the results of the internal functional area analysis are particularly relevant. A *'satisfaction lab'* strategy gains great importance if the company pursues a differentiation strategy through superior, customer-oriented products and services. Such a complaint management type will also be able to meet the differentiated information requirements of various internal customer groups. However, the *'quality control'* strategy is especially suited if it is the primary goal of the company to ensure the consistent quality of standardized products by means of a cost leadership strategy. That is why this strategy variant of complaint management meets above all the information needs of quality management.

Once a basic (or hybrid) strategy option has been selected, it is important to investigate whether the complaint management in its current state is able to meet the current and future strategic requirements. The results of the functional area analysis should be used for this purpose. They provide information to answer the question of whether the service range offered and the quality of the current task fulfillment correspond to the desired strategic profile.

If the actual strategic profile differs from the target profile, there is an urgent need for action. If it turns out, for example, that the complaint management is currently operated as a 'complaint factory', but the strategy of the 'satisfaction lab' is to be pursued in future, comprehensive change management efforts are necessary. To this end, the required changes in the tasks of the direct and indirect complaint management have to be determined. Then the consequences for the staff-related, information technological, organizational and financial framework conditions must be fixed and temporal "milestones" have to be defined along the road to the planned implementation of the strategy. This strategic development path is the basis for discussions with the superordinate management level and the top management that is responsible for the change management process.

Chapter 5 in Brief
- Strategic planning is needed to exploit the potential of complaint management.
- The strategic planning process comprises three steps: strategic state analysis, development of strategy options, and strategy evaluation and selection.
- Within the context of the state analysis the essential external and internal demands and influencing factors must be identified and examined (environment analysis). In addition, the range of services of the complaint management, the quality of these services and the internal framework conditions must be investigated (functional area analysis).
- Depending on the selected focus, four basic strategic options can be distinguished: 'complaint factory', 'relationship amplifier', 'quality control' and 'satisfaction lab'.
- The options 'complaint factory' and 'quality control' can be combined into an 'efficiency first strategy'; the options 'relationship amplifier' and 'satisfaction lab' into the 'customer first strategy'.
- The company-specific choice of the appropriate strategy option is based on the results of the strategic analysis.

References

Mende M (2006) Strategische Planung im Beschwerdemanagement. Deutscher Universitäts-Verlag, Wiesbaden

Porter ME (1998) Competetive strategy. The Free Press, New York

Stauss B (2008) Strategisches Beschwerdemanagement. In: Stadelmann M et al (eds) Customer relationship management. Verlag Industrielle Organisation, Zürich, pp 155–170

B. Stauss, W. Seidel, *Effective Complaint Management*, Management for Professionals,
https://doi.org/10.1007/978-3-319-98705-7_6

Issues Raised
- Why does the maxim of minimizing complaints not make sense?
- Why is it right to encourage as many dissatisfied customers as possible to complain ('complaint maximizing')?
- What possibilities exist to stimulate verbal, written, telephone and electronic complaints in a targeted way?
- How can the existence of complaint channels be communicated successfully?
- What aspects must be taken into account in the implementation of complaint-stimulating measures?

6.1 Complaint Stimulation Rather Than Complaint Minimization

6.1.1 The Problem of "Unvoiced Complaints"

The goal of many firms is to *minimize the number of incoming complaints*. This goal only makes sense, however, if one proceeds based on the assumption that all dissatisfied customers complain, which in turn would mean that a low number of complaints was a clear indicator of a low level of customer dissatisfaction.

Empirical complaint research has shown, however, that this is not the case. The majority of dissatisfied customers do not complain. It is true that the respective percentages of unvoiced complaints vary depending on the product segment and the type of problem, but it is also the case that often more than 50% of dissatisfied customers do not complain. Instead of complaining, dissatisfied customers choose to react in a different way. They talk about their negative experiences with friends, relatives or co-workers, or they immediately switch to another provider. A low number of complaints should not, therefore, be interpreted as an expression of a high level of customer satisfaction. It could rather be the result of the fact that customers have a resigned attitude because in their experience, complaining is not "worth it". A low number of complaints may also be the result of defensive measures implemented by the firm that make complaints expensive, difficult and uncomfortable for customers.

If a firm really takes the goal of achieving customer satisfaction and customer loyalty seriously, it is more rational for them not to pursue an across-the-board minimization of complaints, but rather a *minimization of customer dissatisfaction and annoyance*. This requires that the firm be informed as extensively as possible as to the type, extent and causes of customer dissatisfaction. Only then can meaningful starting points for quality improvements be identified. Moreover, complaint management can only develop its retention goals with respect to customers who complain. It is thus necessary to maximize the percentage of those dissatisfied customers who choose the "complaint alternative".

6.1.2 Complaint Maximization as the Goal of Complaint Stimulation

Complaint stimulation includes the complaint management task area that is concerned with encouraging dissatisfied customers and making it easier for them to express dissatisfaction in a complaint. Accordingly, the central goal of complaint stimulation could be described using the—often misunderstood—term "*Complaint Maximization*". Complaint maximization in this sense does not somehow mean that customers should be given greater cause for complaint. Complaint maximization means rather that the greatest possible percentage of dissatisfied customers should be encouraged to come directly to the firm when they have a complaint.

Firms are thus faced with the challenge of *removing the barriers* that would prevent annoyed customers from filing a complaint. Important tasks here include the reduction of the customer's material, time and psychological costs, as well as the establishment and communication of proper channels of complaint. Firms must unmistakably signal the fact that they are willing to take responsibility for all the causes that could give rise to dissatisfaction, as well as their desire to eliminate these causes to the customer's satisfaction.

In particular, customers must be motivated to bring forward any type of dissatisfaction they might have experienced, not merely instances in which a problem has occurred and customers could invoke a legally enforceable solution. As has been proved, it is not only serious performance deficits that cause customers to be irritated and to switch to another provider; rather, it is often "*smaller*" *incidents*: an unfriendly remark, an arrogant gesture, insufficient or false information, etc. Incidents such as these only rarely become the subject of complaints, with the result that the firm hears nothing about these problems and does not have the chance to retain the dissatisfied customer or to eliminate the cause of the problem.

With the help of *complaint stimulation*, as many dissatisfied customers as possible should be prompted to come to the firm with all their problems. In this way, the proportion of unvoiced complaints will be minimized or, stated another way, the proportion of complaints of dissatisfied customers will be maximized. On the basis of the acquired complaint information, the firm can subsequently carry out a careful diagnosis of the problem and eliminate its cause.

Thus, two complementary objectives must be pursued: the goal of *maximizing complaints* from dissatisfied customers with the aid of complaint stimulation and the goal of *minimizing dissatisfaction* by introducing improvement measures. The success of complaint stimulation measures is the number of customers who complain, expressed as a percentage of the total number of dissatisfied customers. The success of complaint management itself can be seen primarily in the avoidance of mistakes and in the reduction of customer annoyance, as well as in the resulting decline in the number of complaints.

6.2   Measures to Stimulate Complaints

6.2.1   Establishment of Complaint Channels

The fundamental task of complaint stimulation is the establishment of complaint channels that make it easy for the customers to express their dissatisfaction. Basically, customers have verbal, written, telephonic and electronic *complaint channels* at their disposal. The establishment of complaint channels implies that *organizational units* for each complaint channel are clearly defined and communicated to the customer. In this context, complaint stimulation has two interconnected functions that must be performed: it must make it possible for the customers to articulate their complaint in the way that they desire, and it must make sure that the processes and responsibilities specific to each complaint channel are internally defined and established.

6.2.1.1 The Verbal Complaint Channel

The verbal complaint channel is primarily relevant for *service companies* that create their "product" in the presence of the customer (e.g., hotels or auto-repair shops). A similar situation exists for companies that market their products via wholesalers and retailers or through their own sales representatives.

Since customers communicate directly with employees, the barriers to complaints are especially low here, and dissatisfied customers are able to articulate their dissatisfaction immediately during the interaction. However, customers take advantage of the chance to express their complaints verbally to varying degrees, depending on the reaction they expect and how they perceive their own role in relation to the person with whom they are interacting. In particular, customers will choose to forego a verbal complaint and instead switch to another provider when they dread an uncomfortable argument that they do not feel psychically or rhetorically up to facing. The same applies to situations in which customers feel that they are in an inferior position of power, relative to the respective contact partner (for example, toward health care workers or physicians in hospitals), and even worry about negative sanctions if they were to make a complaint.

In order to reduce barriers to complaints such as the above, firms must communicate clearly and unmistakably that *critical expressions from customers are desired*. An excellent example of such communication is the saying that is posted in many small customer service firms: "When you are satisfied, tell your friends. When you are dissatisfied, please tell us!". It is further necessary to ensure that there are a sufficient number of employees available who will react positively and encouragingly to complainants. In particular, they must be capable of demonstrating cooperative behavior and not evoking feelings of inferiority.

Setting up a service or information area ("*Customer Relations Desk*") as a specific contact point for customer concerns—as, for example, in hotels or retail establishments—constitutes a facilitation of verbal complaint articulations. In this way, customers receive a clear signal from the firm that they have the chance to clear up any questions or problems in a personal conversation, and they are informed as to whom they can turn with their concerns.

Another possible way that the firm can use verbal communication as a feedback instrument for customer dissatisfaction is to *inquire actively about problems* that have been experienced, as opposed to waiting passively for complaints. Instead of hoping that customers will take the initiative, it is worthwhile for the firm itself to become active and to approach customers. After each transaction, a simple question can be asked: "Was everything okay?" and information about the customer's perception of quality can be obtained. A variation of the above has, however, proven to be a better way to phrase the question: "Could we have done anything better?" or "What should we do better in the future?" These questions make it easier for customers to answer candidly because they are able to disguise their criticism in the form of a suggestion for improvement. Moreover, the answers can be more easily used for specific corrective measures.

6.2.1.2 The Written Complaint Channel

Letters (including faxes) represent the classic form of written complaints. The written, formally correct presentation of the case demands much time and effort on the part of the customer. For this reason, many customers take the firm up on its offer of registering their complaints via telephone or the Internet. There are, however, situations in which the *customers prefer to make their complaint in writing*. Such is primarily the case when it is a question of liability, or when the complainants would like to approach management personally or to establish a permanent proof of their articulation. A complaint-stimulating effect for letters and faxes can be achieved when the firm clearly communicates to the customers to whom they should direct their written complaint.

A specific form of written complaint stimulation are *comment cards*, which are used especially in the customer service sector (e.g., hotels, restaurants, banks). These comment cards are pre-printed answer cards, on which customers can describe in their own words either what has upset them or what they have found to be positive.

The more comment cards offer the customers the possibility describe their problems in own words, the more they have a *direct complaint-stimulating effect*. But comment card that leave only little or no room for problem descriptions and instead primarily contain satisfaction scales have at most an *indirect complaint-stimulating character*.

Comment cards can either be placed in a *"feedback box"* at the firm itself or sent off to a specifically named person or department. If the firm intends for the cards to be mailed, it should provide addressed and postage-paid cards in order to avoid time and financial barriers for the customer.

6.2.1.3 The Telephone Complaint Channel

The telephone complaint channel exhibits substantial *advantages* when compared with the written complaint method, both from the customer's and from the firm's point of view.

For the customer, these advantages are primarily the reduced complaint costs and faster resolution of the problem; for the firm, they consist mainly of the cost advantages and the possibility of addressing the customer individually:

- Reduced complaint costs for the customer: By choosing the telephone channel of complaint, the customers usually reduce their costs. This is especially true with regard to financial costs when the firm establishes a toll-free phone number for complaints. In addition, it is usually much easier for the customers to express their problem verbally than in writing, so that their time and psychological costs are also reduced.
- Faster resolution of problems: It is frequently possible to reduce customer dissatisfaction with the implementation of complaint telephones. The firm is able to react immediately and in many cases can solve the problem over the phone or to transfer the customer directly to the person responsible and initiate the complaint processing procedure without delay.
- Reduced complaint-processing costs for the firm: In comparison to the written method of complaint, the firm can save substantial processing costs by using the telephone method, because the average processing costs for a typical phone conversation are considerably lower than those for the written response to a request.
- Addressing customers individually: Communication with customers can be conducted better and more thoroughly. The associate conducting the conversation has the opportunity to clarify the circumstances immediately, to provide explanations and to apologize personally. At the same time, the associates can also make a realistic assessment of the extent of the customer's irritation. In a telephone conversation, the emotions—such as irritation or bitterness—that the problem elicits in the customer become clear. The associates can take this into account in the way they conduct the conversation and thus bring about a calming of the situation. In addition, they learn details about the customers' expectations and can work with them to find an appropriate solution.

Before measures to stimulate telephonic complaints are introduced, a number of conditions have to be created. In particular, it is important to ensure that the necessary technical resources and sufficiently qualified personnel are available.

Regarding system technology, it is essential that the installed telephone system has mechanisms to ensure that callers do not have to wait and so become even more frustrated. These mechanisms include ACD, IVR and CTI systems.

An *ACD* (automatic call distribution) system enables an efficient distribution of the call volume. It connects the caller to the next available agent and organizes, among other things, the incoming call-load of the call center agents and the number of calls on hold. Such a system can lead to a sustainable reduction in waiting times but only if accurate revenue forecasting, as well as careful capacity planning and a correspondingly high service level exist. An ACD system is usually combined with

CTI (computer telephony integration) components that integrate telephone and computer systems, such as the customer database. Because of this integration, call center agents have automatic access to relevant data of the calling customer on a screen pop-up, and are able to save the new information in the database. ACDs often also integrate an *IVR* (interactive voice response) system. This enables the customers, through the use of voice or the input of data on the telephone keypad, to pre-structure their concern, so that the call center agent can be automatically assigned to the specific issue.

However, the IVR technology must be viewed in a critical light if it offers a multitude of alternatives, but the customers cannot clearly identify which of them is intended for the complaint articulation. Dissatisfied customers want to express their annoyance to a person and not be forced to master complex navigation processes. Therefore, if the alternative 'complaint' is not offered, the use of IVR may deter rather than stimulate complaints, as well as increase dissatisfaction and foster customer migration.

Employees in complaint management must be informed about processing standards, responsibilities within the company and action alternatives. In particular, they must be trained in dealing with dissatisfied customers and have the appropriate professional, methodological social and emotional competence. Moreover, they must be given decision-making powers so that they are able to respond appropriately to the articulated problems and to satisfy the complainants.

6.2.1.4 The Electronic Complaint Channel

The category of electronic complaint channel includes communication by e-mail or the Internet, including social media channels such as Facebook and Twitter, as well as the use of interactive kiosk systems with touch screens.

The articulation of complaints via *e-mail* has established for years as an important complaint channel. The reason is that the use of e-mail has a number of advantages, both for customers and for the firm.

From the *customer's point of view*, it is primarily the following aspects that are important: e-mail is an asynchronous medium—that is, the sender and the receiver of a message do not have to be present at the same time—so that the problem of accessibility is reduced in comparison to the telephone. Moreover, e-mail is a rapid medium, and even transfers of information that take place over great geographic distances do not take more than a few seconds. Since e-mail communications can be sent online, very little monetary cost exists for the customers, and the amount of effort and time they must expend is much less than it would be in the case of a letter. Customers also experience less psychological cost, because they do not expose themselves to a direct, critical conversation. Thus, e-mail provides low dialog barriers and promotes additional complaints that would not otherwise be articulated.

One *advantage for the firm* can be found in this stimulating effect itself, but there are others as well. With regard to costs, it should be noted that complaint information can be more easily collected and recorded because complaints exists as a file and can be immediately processed. Furthermore, the asynchronism of an electronic conversation means that it is not necessary to maintain processing capacity for short-term peaks in demand, so that there are lower idle time costs for unused personnel capacity. E-mails also offer the firm a low-cost way to react to frequently occurring customer concerns in a standardized or automated way.

Two *forms of access or communication* for the articulation of customer complaints can be differentiated:

1. The customers know the e-mail address for the business location that is responsible for handling complaints, and they make a complaint directly from their *e-mail system* (e.g., MS Outlook). In this case, complaint stimulation can only occur through the communication of the complaint-management e-mail address in other media.
2. The customer go to the firm's *homepage*, which then contains a link to a special "complaint site". In order to achieve a complaint-stimulating effect, the link to the complaint site must be conspicuously placed on the homepage and must also be available on the firm's other Internet sites if possible. In addition, the "complaint site" must be uncomplicated—that is, it must be reachable with one click. Such a form gives the company also the opportunity to collect information from customers which facilitates internal routing purposes, as well as the categorization and analysis of complaints.

In addition, many companies are active on social media platforms, for example, by opening their own *Facebook site, Twitter account or weblog* for the company or special brands. These interactive platforms offer customers communication opportunities. Thereby, they provide new complaint channels, regardless of whether this was originally planned or not. The intensity with which social media stimulate complaints depends, among other things, on the extent to which the possibilities of dialog are expanded. It makes a substantial difference whether companies only allow users to comment on their own posts or set up specific customer care accounts. In the latter case, a very clear signal is sent out that the company wants a dialog with the critical customer. Accordingly, a considerable increase in critical comments is to be expected, especially as there are hardly any material, psychological or temporal complaint barriers. Since social media represents a particular challenge for complaint management, this complaint channel will be discussed separately in Chap. 17.

The use of *touchscreens* opens another dimension of electronic complaint stimulation, especially for branches where transactions can be executed using kiosk systems, such as in banks. The same applies for services that customers use at the place where the service is provided, such as in hotels. Also *mobile devices*—smartphones and tablets—can be used for complaint stimulation, especially by the use of QR codes (see *Spotlight 6.1*).

Spotlight 6.1

Using iFEEDBACK® as a Mobile Complaint Management Tool to Increase Customer Satisfaction

It is essential to react to a customer's complaint to make sure the customer relationship stays intact. The faster a reaction follows a complaint the higher is the likelihood that the customer can be satisfied. With iFEEDBACK®, companies have the innovative opportunity to use mobile devices (e.g. smartphones or tablets) to reduce the reaction time to a minimum and thereby offer a special service experience to the customers.

Customer satisfaction is especially important in the hotel industry where a constant price battle prevails and customers have low brand loyalty. iFEEDBACK® offers hotels the chance to give their customers an opportunity to express their complaints with any Internet-ready device so that a reaction during their stay is ensured (see Fig. 6.1).

Every guest receives a card with a QR code at the check-in reminding him that compliments, complaints or suggestions are always welcome.

Furthermore, the QR codes are displayed via other channels (e.g. flyers, stickers or table cards) as well as stationary iPad Terminals. The terminals give customers without smartphones the opportunity to submit a rating. When guests scan the QR code they will be redirected to the hotel's individual questionnaire without having to sign up or register. Now they can submit a star-rating (from 1 star = very unsatisfied to 5 stars = very satisfied) via the hotel's predefined questionnaire, and they can also write a comment with each rating. If the guests submit a negative review (e.g. ≤ 2 stars), they are obligated to leave a comment so that the hotel knows the reason for the negative rating. Moreover, the customers can leave their contact data voluntarily so that the hotel is able to contact them if they express a wish for this to happen.

The generated feedback will be automatically sent to different hotel departments (e.g. reception, room service, management) via e-mail. In this way, the party concerned will be informed immediately and is able to react if needed. If the guests leave their contact data they will also receive an automated e-mail which has a different content depending on the rating. If they submit a bad rating they could receive a voucher as an excuse, and if they leave a good rating they could receive a link to the hotel's social media channels for customer retention.

In addition, the iFEEDBACK® software backend collects all the ratings and evaluates them. Employees can now prioritize and work on the complaints using the iFEEDBACK® helpdesk so that the management is able to monitor the steps taken to solve the problem. The reporting feature allows different locations and departments to be compared so that long-term optimization potentials are detected and the development of the satisfaction index can be checked without further evaluation effort. Since the guests are not obligated to rate each question, the reporting feature offers the possibility to show only specific KPIs. One side shows the relevance of a specific point (e.g. for 75% of the guests, cleanliness is relevant) while the other side shows the satisfaction

(continued)

Spotlight 6.1 (continued)

with this specific point (e.g. average rating on cleanliness: 2.5 stars). This analysis is especially important for strategic planning since complaints with a high priority need to be taken care of immediately.

As an example of a special customer experience, one feedback can be highlighted at this point. A guest finds a coffee machine in his room but the guest actually prefers tea, so he writes a comment ("Great coffee machine but I'm a tea lover"). Three hours later the guest submits another review saying "Wow, I have never experienced such great service before!" and he even goes to the reception desk to thank the hotel staff personally. While the customer was at the spa, the hotel changed the coffee machine to a tea service. Experiences like that can only be realized when complaints and reactions to them happen in real time, and they also have a lasting effect on customer satisfaction.

It is not only the hotel industry that is using feedback opportunities but also other branches with a high service awareness (e.g. gastronomy, automotive, retail). Usually those industries have major feedback barriers (e.g. unclear contact persons, or high expenditure of time). By using the iFEEDBACK® system those barriers can be removed and a vision becomes clear that every company will be able to manage their complaints in real time in the future.

Julia Kostovic
Business Development Manager
BHM Group—The Customer Engagement Company
http://www.bhmms.com

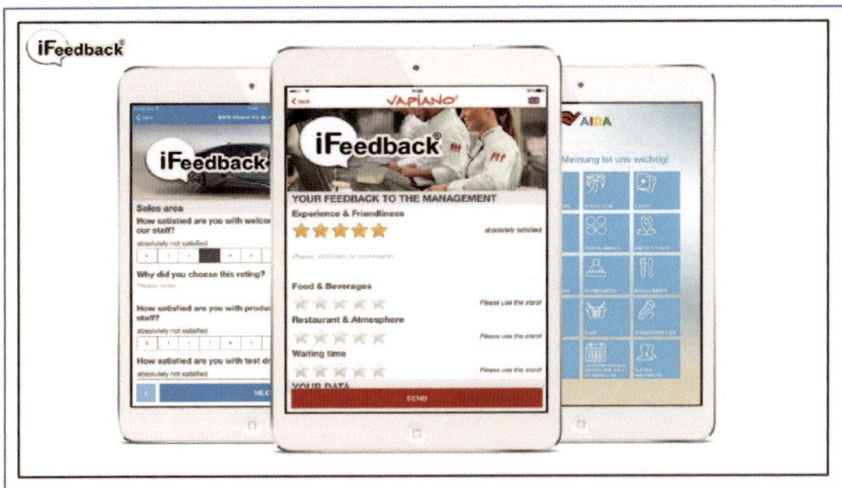

Fig. 6.1 Customer feedback using mobile devices

6.2.2   Active Communication of Complaint Channels

The complaint methods that are established in order to bring about complaint stimulation must be actively communicated to the customer. Only with this type of *"Complaint Marketing"* can it be guaranteed that customers will use one of these methods when they have a problem and that the volume of complaints of dissatisfied customers will increase.

The invitation to customers to make their complaints to the firm and the information about the complaint channel can be communicated in various ways:

1. *Existing means of correspondence and communication* such as form letters, informational brochures or catalogs can be used to target complaint stimulation in the context of direct customer communication.
2. A means *of communication that is specially developed for complaint management*—for example, business or comment cards that are used as inserts as part of a direct marketing campaign or conspicuously placed and communicated in sales and service locations. Figure 6.2 shows a business card from the Hannover utility company in Germany that was specifically conceptualized for the communication of the telephone and fax complaint hotline.

    Furthermore, *media with a higher level of information use*, such as specific informational brochures or websites, give the firm the chance to explain the principles of its complaint policy. Here, details of the information requested by the complainants should be presented as well as essential elements of the complaint process procedure (deadlines, forms of feedback) and action alternatives in case of continuing dissatisfaction. In this way the credibility of the firm as "complaint-friendly" is underscored.

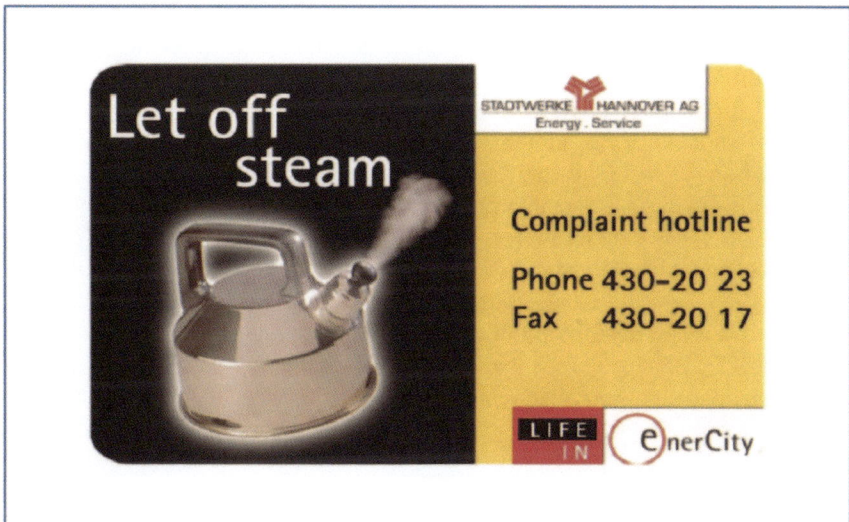

Fig. 6.2 "Business card" for a complaint hotline: Stadtwerke Hannover (enerCity)

Dialog cards can also be used as an active communication tool to facilitate dialog with customers. For example, SAS Airline distributed a dialog card ("Let's talk") at airports a few years ago (SAS 2014). This card gave customers the chance to articulate their wish for a conversation in a way that is convenient for them. The customers entered their name, address, phone number and/or e-mail address on the card and put it in the feedback box provided by the company. To find out the customer's exact reason for concern, the company had to take action and contact the passengers in the manner they wanted.

3. Firms can also carry out complaint stimulation through the *mass media*, such as when they request customer feedback in newspaper ads and radio and TV-spots and communicate the complaint management phone number, e-mail address, Internet address or mailing address. In their former "We try harder" campaign, Avis asks businesspeople to make a complaint if the ashtrays in their rental cars are dirty: "If you find a cigarette butt in an Avis car, complain. It's for our own good" (Demut et al. 1984, p. 60).

4. *Corporate web sites* offer excellent possibilities to stimulate complaints. Customers use them in particular if they are easily identifiable, contain concrete information about the processing procedure and give hints about further options for action.

5. An increasingly widespread form of complaint stimulation is the *printing of Internet addresses on invoices, receipts or advertising material*. In the accompanying text, customers are asked to visit this web site and provide feedback on their latest consumption experience. One example is the receipts that customers of fast food chains like Burger King or McDonald's get. When customers visit the web site, they are first asked to enter a restaurant or survey code printed on the receipt and then answer a series of questions about their satisfaction with the specific food and service experience. The survey usually includes the question of whether the customers experienced a problem during the visit, and gives them the opportunity to specify the nature of the problem. After answering all the questions, the customers receive a voucher, which they can redeem for a special product the next time they visit a restaurant. Such a feedback incentive not only promotes the willingness to participate in a satisfaction survey, but also serves as an instrument for collecting complaints and channeling customer dissatisfaction in a targeted manner.

Another interesting example represents the 'Happy Cards' of Anker Technology, the industry leader in mobile charging and accessories, that sells its products directly via web shops and Amazon Marketplace. The online buyers receive the Happy Card (see Fig. 6.3) with the ordered product. In the case of satisfaction ("Happy?"), the customers are asked to submit online a positive assessment, for example, via the Amazon account or on Facebook and Twitter. In case of dissatisfaction ("Not happy?") various contact possibilities (phone, e-mail, web) are provided "for a quick solution".

6. In addition to the previous methods, the addresses of complaint departments and the telephone number for complaint calls can, for instance, also be clearly noted on *packaging materials, user manuals* or *instructional leaflets*. Several companies place their 800-number directly on all their packaged goods and ask customers experiencing problems to contact the company directly. Brief

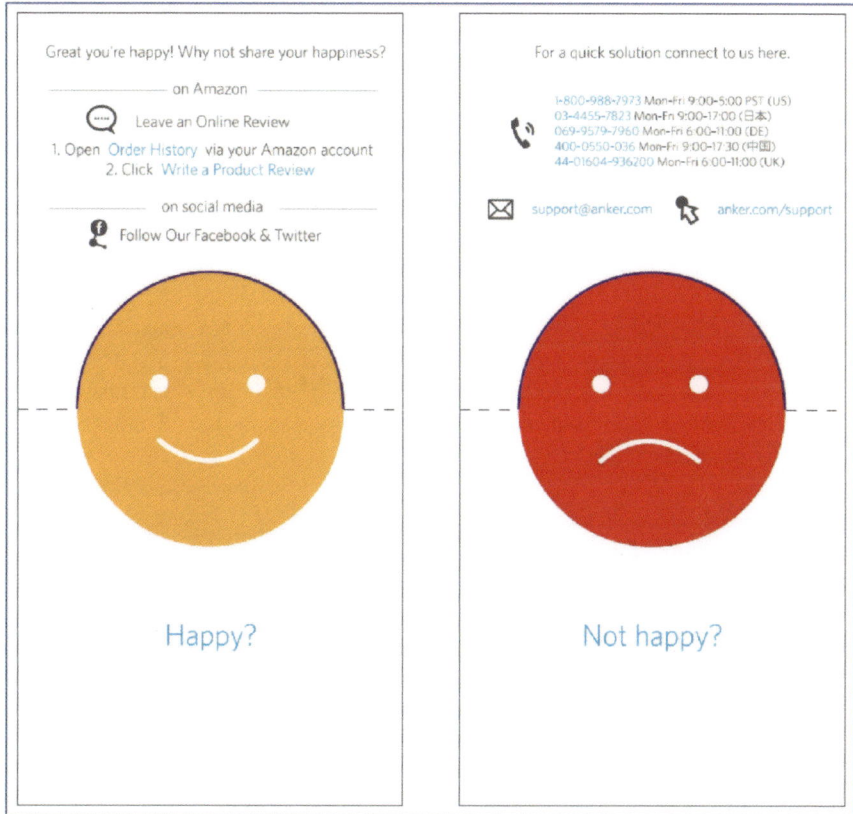

Fig. 6.3 Anker technology's "Happy Card"

addresses and easy-to-remember telephone numbers can also be displayed on *company vehicles*.

Spotlight 6.2 shows how a large university hospital uses complaint stimulating measures and at the same time transforms critical patient feedback from anonymous satisfaction surveys into active complaint management.

Spotlight 6.2
Patient Satisfaction Feedbacks and Complaints—Channeling the Voice of Patients at Charité—University Medicine Berlin
Patient satisfaction surveys are a well-established method of measuring quality perception in hospitals. Most of them—as is the case with the in- and outpatient satisfaction surveys of Charité—University Medicine Berlin—are

(continued)

Spotlight 6.2 (continued)

anonymous. Charité—University Medicine Berlin is Germany's largest hospital (130,000 inpatients per year, 800,000 ambulatory patient contacts per year) and has measured patient satisfaction with a pencil-and-paper-based survey on a continuous basis since 2006 (approx. 30,000 to 35,000 feedback forms per year). A noticeable percentage of patients communicate critical incidents and complaint-worthy experiences inside the free text fields of these surveys. However, the handling of the reported critical incidents is either impossible or delayed for two reasons. On the one hand, the survey is anonymous; no names or contact data are requested. On the other hand, the process from the physical data collection to the digitalization or processing of the data takes about 4–6 weeks due to the time-consuming data processing logistics. This leads to additional frustration of already dissatisfied patients. To channel the critical patient feedback from the anonymous satisfaction surveys directly into the active complaint management process, the responsible department of clinical quality and risk management undertook a number of complaint stimulation measures and interventions, as follows:

- Anonymous paper-based inpatient satisfaction surveys now clearly and actively guide the (dissatisfied) patient to the personalized complaint management team. An e-mail address is provided as the preferred contact medium; this allows for timely complaint replies and reactions.
- Anonymous paper-based ambulatory satisfaction surveys now provide a smartphone scanner code (QR code) to guide (dissatisfied) patients directly to the website-based complaint form.
- An internal communication campaign for hospital staff was launched to explain the different established patient feedback instruments and their differences.
- The mandatory input fields of the website-based complaint form were reduced (now only name, surname, e-mail and written complaint description are mandatory).

Shortly after being implemented, these measures started to have a considerable impact. Unsurprisingly the level of received personal complaints increased, see Fig. 6.4:

The intended change in the communication channels used by patients mainly explains this increase. Before the described interventions, many "complaints" (hidden in the written patient satisfaction feedback) remained unnoticed by the central complaint management team. After the interventions, more dissatisfied patients used the intended complaint articulation channels, resulting in a decline of critical feedback in the anonymous patient satisfaction surveys.

(continued)

> **Spotlight 6.2** (continued)
>
>   Thanks to the communicated, preferred reception channels for complaints (either e-mail or the workflow-integrated website-based complaint form) and the use of automatic first replies, the increased complaint level was still manageable by the established complaint management team.
>
> Dr. Nils Löber
> Director Clinical Quality and Risk Management
> Charité—University Medicine Berlin, Germany

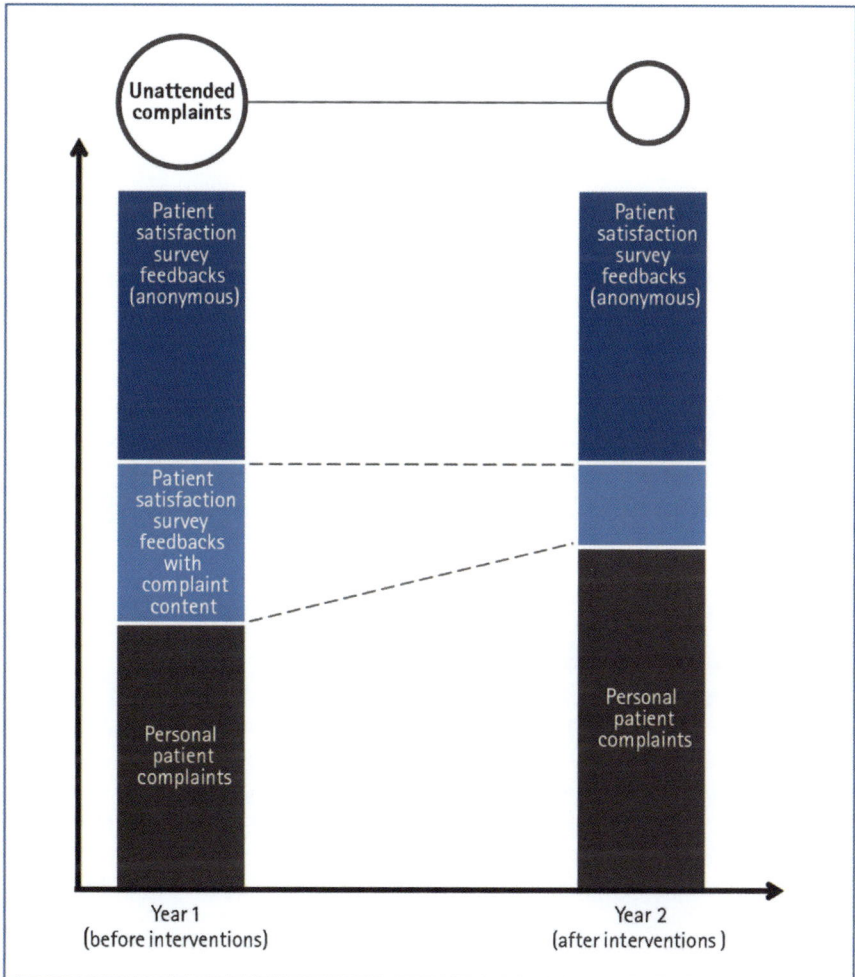

Fig. 6.4 Change in the communication channels after the implementation of complaint stimulation measures

6.2.3   Accompanying Measures to Remove Complaint Barriers

Companies stimulate complaints directly if they establish complaint channels and communicate the access options actively. These activities can be supported by measures aimed *indirectly* at complaint stimulation by breaking down complaint barriers. Some of the factors that determine the willingness of dissatisfied customers to choose the complaint option can be *specifically influenced* by the company. This applies in particular to the perceived probability that the complaint will succeed, and to the costs of complaining.

The establishment of easily usable complaint channels in itself reduces the psychological, financial and temporal costs of complaining. Further cost reduction is achieved when companies *simplify the problem-solving processes.* Customers refrain from complaining if complicated proofs are required of them. This is the case, for example, when companies base the examination of the articulated problem on certain conditions, such as the submission of the products in question, the invoices or other documents. Accordingly, an important complaint-stimulating measure is to dispense with extensive proofs and, as a rule, to rely on the testimony of the customers. In addition, it must be ensured that the customers are not involved in a multi-stage examination procedure, but preferably receive a problem solution in the first contact. Customer contact employees therefore need decision-making authority, which they can use flexibly for the development of individual solutions.

Customer satisfaction surveys also represent an indirect form of complaint stimulation because they reduce the customer complaint costs. Such a survey signals that the company has a strong interest in the customers' satisfaction and actively seeks to identify dissatisfaction potential. If the questionnaire contains open questions, the customers have the opportunity to describe the cause of their dissatisfaction, even if they previously did not articulate a complaint. Often, the respondents can revoke their anonymity by giving contact information, enabling companies to integrate these cases into their complaint handling processes.

Complaint satisfaction surveys also have a stimulating effect. If complainants are dissatisfied with the solution received or with another aspect of the complaint response, this survey offers a good opportunity for the customers to express their dissatisfaction in a follow-up complaint.

Firms can also achieve complaint-stimulation effects by increasing the utility of complaints or the perceived probability that the complaint will succeed. Product, service and satisfaction *guarantees* are the main tools that can be employed here. They contain promises about what the firm will do if certain performance promises cannot be kept, products or services fall short of defined quality standards or customer satisfaction is not achieved. Explicit promises such as 'money back', 'return if not satisfied', etc., substantially increase the perceived success probability of a complaint. They also make it simple for the customers to perform a cost-benefit calculation of their complaint. When these guarantees are unlimited and can be invoked with no problem, the complaint costs are also reduced. An impressive example is the unconditional guarantee that the big American clothing retailer Lands' End offers for over 50 years (see Fig. 6.5).

GUARANTEED. PERIOD. ●:
WE WANT NOTHING LESS THAN YOUR ABSOLUTE SATISFACTION.

The Lands' End guarantee has always been an unconditional one. It reads: „If you're not satisfied with any item, simply return it to us any time for an exchange or refund of its purchase price." We mean every word of it. Whatever. Whenever. Always. But to make sure this is perfectly clear, we've decided to simplify it further: Guaranteed. Period.®

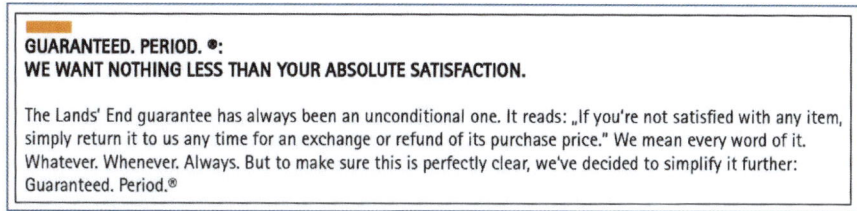

Fig. 6.5 Lands end's unconditional guarantee (Source: Lands' End 2017)

6.3   The Implementation of Complaint-Stimulating Measures

Before the firm introduces measures for the stimulation of complaints, it must make sure that an "avalanche of complaints" that would overextend the complaint management system is not set in motion. The results of this failure are longer processing times and unsatisfactory answers for customers, whose dissatisfaction is thereby increased even further. In order to avoid this danger, it makes sense to implement complaint-stimulation measures *gradually* and to adjust the required dimensions of the resource endowment accordingly.

During the introduction of complaint-stimulation measures, a series of several activities must be carried out: an actual state analyses of the complaint volume and the current processing times, a determination of the projected availability and speed of reaction, a prognosis of the prospective complaint volume, planning and provision of the technological and personnel resources required and the measured implementation and communication.

6.3.1   Actual State Analysis of the Complaint Volume

The first step in the introduction of complaint-stimulation measures is an analysis of the *current complaint volume*. The number of complaints that have come in and the channels over which they arrived must be documented exactly. Furthermore, the *processing times* must be determined, in order to acquire clear-cut data as to the length of time required for the acceptance and processing of complaints.

6.3.2   Determination of the Projected Accessibility and Speed of Reaction

The next step of the process is to determine what *service level* and which reaction times should be targeted. Complaint-stimulation measures only make sense if customers can immediately find a contact partner when they have a complaint and when they do not have to wait long for a solution to their problem.

A high level of accessibility must, therefore, be ensured for all the complaint channels. This statement applies primarily to complaints that are articulated verbally and by telephone, for which the shortest possible wait times should be planned. With respect to written and electronic complaints, customer-appropriate *standards* for reaction times—that is, for the final answer or for confirmations of receipt and intermediate notifications—must be established.

6.3.3 Prognosis of the Prospective Complaint Volume

Companies with active complaint management and intensive cultivation of customer dialog often experience that the number of complaints *can increase very quickly*. In order to prevent the capacities that are set up being insufficient, causing dissatisfied customers to experience another negative situation due to a lack of accessibility, careful forecasts regarding the expected future volume of complaints are necessary.

An important approach for estimating the number of complaints that can be expected from stimulating measures is to conduct a representative market research study among annoyed customers regarding their complaint behavior: "*annoyance iceberg survey*" (see Sect. 11.1). Customers are asked whether they have had cause for annoyance within a specified period of time and whether they have complained to the company. This provides information on the proportion of annoyed customers ("annoyance rate") and the proportion of annoyed people who have not complained ("non-articulation rate"). If these percentages are extrapolated to the total population of all customers, a rough estimate is obtained of the number of "non-complainants". This is an important indication of the additional volume of complaints that can be expected if appropriate stimulating measures are implemented.

Such a survey also provides *further insights into the behavior of the non-complainants*. They are also asked about the reasons they did not complain despite their anger. A detailed analysis shows whether inadequate channels of complaint constitute a decisive barrier to complaints or whether there are other obstacles that must be removed.

A market research study can, however, only provide a *rough prognosis* of the expected complaint volume. This is because, first, customers are not in a position to predict their future behavior completely. Second, even complaint-stimulating measures will not induce all annoyed customers to articulate a complaint. Third, the customers' complaint willingness is also dependent on external factors that cannot usually be influenced, such as a generally increasing aspiration level or technical media developments.

Therefore, there is every reason to *benchmark* the rough data obtained from the study against the results of firms that have already implemented comparable processes of stimulation. An even more precise prognosis can then be made as part of the gradual implementation of complaint stimulation based on experiences in *test markets*.

6.3.4   The Planning and Provision of Technological and Personnel Resources

The results of the prognosis form the basis for the estimation of any additional technological or personnel resources that may be required. As far as *technological matters* are concerned, the primary task is to provide the infrastructure that will ensure the projected accessibility and reaction speed. With respect to the telephone complaint channel, for example, this requires a *telephone system* in the call center that can automatically distribute the incoming calls to employees via ACD-linking (Automatic Call Distribution) and uses CTI (Computer Telephone Integration) to guarantee that employees have immediate, direct access to the customer database as well as to the firm's product and process databases. What is important with respect to the written complaint channel is, among other things, the presence of a *document management system* based on complaint letters that have been scanned into the system. As far as electronic complaints are concerned, the existence of a proper e-mail management system is of vital importance. In addition, *complaint management software* with the corresponding *hardware* must be available, as it will aid in the efficient fulfillment of all the specific tasks that have been defined as part of the firm's system of complaint management.

The necessary *employee capacity* must be planned at the same time so that the firm will be able to deal with the expected future volume of complaints in accordance with the standards that it has defined. The bases for establishing the necessary capacity come from data about the amount of time required for handling a complaint—differentiated according to complaint channel—as well as from data relevant to the yearly productive capacity of each employee. Dividing the yearly capacity per employee by the estimated processing time per complaint for each complaint channel yields the complaint volume that can be handled per employee per year. The next step is to divide the projected complaint volume per year by the above figure, and the resulting figure is the number of employees required per complaint channel.

6.3.5   Stepwise Implementation and Communication

Despite careful preparation of complaint-stimulating measures, a degree of *uncertainty in the planning* remains. The additional complaint volume cannot be predicted with 100 percent accuracy. In addition, the supposed processing times are simply projected values based on actual experiences, which could deviate from the real values when new complaint-stimulating structures are introduced. It is also conceivable that new tasks will be introduced in the context of complaint management for which no values based on experience exist.

To avoid the danger of falsely dimensioning the capacity, a *testing phase* in which the stimulation measure are implemented to a limited extent should first be carried out. If customer data is available the existence of a new complaint channel can be communicated to specific customer groups. Furthermore, it is possible to test the acceptance of the channel in a *regional test market* where information about the complaint channel is disseminated within a limited area. In each case, the test results serve as the basis for the prognosis of the total volume for all customer groups, or for the entire geographic collection area. This allows for a demand-oriented adjustment of the necessary capacity according to the required magnitudes. *Spotlight 6.3* shows practical examples of a stepwise implementation of complaint stimulation measures.

Spotlight 6.3
Complaint Stimulation in Small Doses

The Deutsche Post AG, a large German postal service and international courier service company, has set a goal of creating a central communication channel for its customers that is easily accessible for all kinds of customer feedback: requests—complaints as well as suggestions and compliments.

Since it was not initially possible to predict how many calls were expected and since the introduction of the hotline number was not meant to trigger an avalanche of customer requests and complaints, it was gradually activated over a period of 7 months for certain area codes: only callers from the activated areas were able to reach the hotline. Accordingly, the service phone number was only communicated in the local media in the activated areas and at the same time it was pointed out that only Post customers with the appropriate area code would be able to contact the customer phone line. With the constant expansion of the communication of this service channel proceeding in small doses, the number of calls gradually increased as well. However, the slow rise made it possible to steadily increase the number of personnel required (Anton 2002).

In a large German telecommunications company, the traditional complaint channels (telephone, letter and fax) were supplemented by a specific complaint site on the Internet. At first, this site was placed rather defensively in order to gauge how frequently it would be used. This was done by introducing the complaint site only for billing problems, making it available to customers who had clicked on a button 'bill-related questions'. During the implementation process, the complaint site was gradually made accessible by creating more and more corresponding links for various customer concerns. This gradual introduction and communication ensured that the necessary technical and personnel capacities could be provided. In addition, it was possible to introduce an ambitious complaint management concept. This included the implementation of a specific complaint management software tool, an extended competence framework for the customer contact employees, optimized temporal response standards, callbacks at the times desired by customers, and follow-up calls after the completion of the complaint handling process (Bordt 2007).

Chapter 6 in Brief

- Only a fraction of dissatisfied customers complain. Therefore, a low number of complaints does not give a realistic picture of the extent of customer dissatisfaction. Therefore, it is not rational to pursue minimization of the incoming complaints, but rather minimization of customer dissatisfaction and annoyance.
- Minimizing customer dissatisfaction is only possible if a company knows the underlying problems and gets the chance to restore customer satisfaction. To this end, it is necessary that the greatest possible percentage of dissatisfied customers articulate a complaint. In this sense, the maxim of 'complaint maximizing' should be understood.
- Complaints can be stimulated in many ways. These include inter alia oral requests, comment cards, telephone hotlines, touch screens or complaint forms on the corporate website.
- The establishment of complaint channels must be actively communicated. A wide range of media is available for this purpose.
- In order to provide the necessary resources for coping with an increased complaint volume, complaint-stimulating measures must implemented in small doses.

References

Anton R (2002) Dosierte Beschwerdestimulierung bei der Deutschen post AG. In: Stauss B, Seidel W (eds) Beschwerdemanagement, 3rd edn. Hanser, Munich, pp 122–123

Bordt J (2007) Dosierte Beschwerdestimulierung im Internet bei T-Online. In: Stauss B, Seidel W (eds) Beschwerdemanagement, 4th edn. Hanser, Munich, pp 138–139

Demuth A et al (1984) Unternehmenswerbung: corporate advertising. Spiegel-Verlag, Hamburg

Lands' End (2017) Guarantee. Period.®. https://www.landsend.com/aboutus/values/?values=guaranteed&cm_re=glb-_-global-_-ft-guaranteedperiod-_-20160316-_-txt. Accessed 26 Oct 2017

SAS (2014) 'Let's talk' dialog card. In: Stauss B, Seidel W (eds) Beschwerdemanagement, 5th edn. Hanser, Munich, p 113

© Springer Nature Switzerland AG 2019

B. Stauss, W. Seidel, *Effective Complaint Management*, Management for Professionals,
https://doi.org/10.1007/978-3-319-98705-7_7

Issues Raised
- Why is the initial contact with the complainant so important?
- What role does the principle of 'complaint ownership' play in the initial contact?
- How should the complaint acceptance process be organized?
- What complaint information should be documented?
- What aspects must be taken into account when developing a category scheme for complaint information?
- What possibilities exist to collect complaint information efficiently?
- How can the quality of the documentation process be ensured?

When dissatisfied customers come to the firm with a complaint, there are two fundamental tasks that must be accomplished in the context of *complaint* acceptance:

- *Organization of the receipt of the complaint:* The receipt of the complaint within the firm must be organized. Clear structures of responsibility must be established, and the associates who will have to take complaints during the course of their contact with customers must be prepared for the situations they will encounter (Sect. 7.1).
- *Documentation of complaint information:* All the relevant information contained in complaints must be documented (Sect. 7.2). In doing so, special attention must be paid to three groups of problems: the development of an appropriate system of categorization (Sect. 7.3), the determination of the forms with which the complaint information is to be documented (Sect. 7.4) and the quality assurance of the documented complaint information (Sect. 7.5).

7.1   Organization of the Complaint Receipt Process

7.1.1   The Crucial Experience of the Initial Contact

For customers who complain to the firm after a disappointing experience with a product, the initial contact with the firm that takes place during the articulation of their complaint often constitutes a *crucial experience*. Depending upon whether they experience sympathy or indifference and refusal, their pronounced dissatisfaction will be either reduced or increased to a substantial degree.

From the service-related satisfaction research it is known that upstream contact situations have an impact on the perception of downstream contacts (Stauss and Seidel 2006). Therefore, the experience of the initial complaint contact influences the customers' perception of the further contact points of complaint management—there is a *satisfaction dynamics of complaint handling*.

In view of the importance of this initial contact, all employees that accept *complaints in person or over the phone* face special challenges. They are confronted with the task of listening to the customer sympathetically, seeing to a calming of the situation and objectively explaining the incident described. Furthermore, they must attempt to resolve the problem immediately if possible, but at the very least, they should initiate a suitable process for handling the complaint. Since complaint receipt and complaint reaction coincide in this case, the corresponding rules of behavior for the receipt of and the response to verbal complaints will be treated in greater detail in Sect. 9.1.

7.1.2   The Principle of Complaint Ownership

First of all, the responsibility that falls on the employees to whom complaints are articulated must be clarified. Here is where the principle of *complaint ownership* has proved itself. According to this principle, the person in the firm who is the first to be informed by a customer about a problem or is the first to perceive a customer problem is responsible from that time on for the recognition, documentation and processing of this problem as a complaint. This person has consequently acquired *"ownership" of the complaint.*

The *complaint owners* then have the task either of solving the problem immediately, if it falls within their area of professional competence, or bringing in other employees who have the expertise and decision-making authority needed to resolve the issue.

The concept of complaint ownership has been impressively implemented by the hotel chain "The Ritz-Carlton". It is unequivocally anchored in the "Ritz-Carlton Values", a synopsis of the most relevant guidelines for expected employee behavior. One of the values reads "I own and immediately resolve guest problems" (Michelli 2008, p. 110). All employees who receive a complaint are then the "owner" of the problem and responsible for a thorough and rapid problem solution. In this way, the hotel aims to achieve the goal of resolving all guest complaints before the guests have departed and to make the dissatisfied customer an enthusiastic customer again.

An important aspect of the complaint ownership principle concerns the question of *how long* the "ownership of a complaint" should be maintained. For complaints that arise in the context of contact-intensive service interactions (e.g., a hotel stay, a restaurant visit or a bank visit) as well as for (product) complaints, which can be solved immediately during direct customer contact, complaint ownership lasts until the problem is solved. For complaints that are not immediately solvable and entail a corresponding processing procedure, on the other hand, the "ownership of the complaint" expires when the further processing of the complaint is ensured by the "complaint owner". This also applies to those cases in which the customers direct their complaint in writing, over the phone or in person to an associate who is not *"actually" responsible.*

It is essential that everybody in the company feels obliged to accept customer problems and to take care of everything that is necessary to solve the problems. That means, with regard to verbal or telephone complaints, for example, that the employees accepting the complaints themselves contact the responsible office and arrange for a callback. Written complaints must be immediately forwarded to the complaint management department, regardless of the addressee. It is crucial to ensure that the company takes the initiative and contacts the customers, so that complainants do not have to make attempts to find a responsible contact person. An essential prerequisite for the realization of this principle is that all employees are precisely informed about the complaint processes and responsibilities within the company.

Closely associated with the principle of "complaint ownership" is the *decentralization of decision-making authority* to the employees who engage in customer contact ("Empowerment"). Every associate at the Ritz-Carlton, for instance, can spend up to $2000 per day to pacify a guest who has complained without asking for permission from a supervisor (Michelli 2008, p. 110). The specific design of empowerment in the context of the initial contact with a dissatisfied customer will be addressed thoroughly in Sect. 14.3.5.

7.1.3 Complaint Receipt Processes

Customers do not always choose the channel intended by the firm when they make their complaint. Therefore, clear controls for the *complaint input processes*—that is, for the paths that complaints that are not directed to the responsible position (for example, the customer care department) should take—are needed.

Against this background of targeting consistent and timely complaint handling, it must be noted that all complaints first of all should be transferred to the person responsible, and from there the processing procedure should be *coordinated as far as content and time are concerned*. This demands that all employees of the firm be informed as to where the *central responsibility* lies, and especially employees in the incoming mail department must be trained to recognize complaint letters. For complaints received by e-mail or web form, the assignment to responsible teams or employees can be software-controlled and automated (see Sect. 16.3).

7.2 Documentation of Complaint Information

In the initial contact phase, it is not only important to behave in a way that is appropriate to the dissatisfied customer's situation; rather, all the relevant information about the complaint case must be documented. General criteria for the documentation of complaints will be introduced below (Sect. 7.2.1), after which the fundamental contents of documentation and possible ways of structuring them will be addressed (Sect. 7.2.2).

7.2.1 Criteria for Complaint Documentation

The three main criteria for the documentation of information that is contained in complaints are completeness, good structure and speed.

Completeness It is most important that *all relevant complaint information* be recorded. The focus here is on information about the complainants, the experience they had as a customer that gave rise to the complaint and the object of the complaint. Moreover, information that is important for the rapid and customer-oriented processing and resolution of the complaint must be thoroughly documented during the acceptance process. Information on the measures undertaken by the firm during this initial contact with the customer must also be recorded. Indeed, this information has a documentary character, but it also forms the basis for later complaint management controlling analyses.

Good Structure of the Documentation Categories The criterion of the structured recording of the customer's problem demands that the complaint information be ascertained in a certain *logical content structure*, in order to ensure that all the essential information is in fact documented. It must also be guaranteed that the *customers' way of telling the story* can be easily followed and that they be interrupted as little as possible during their account. The forms and software masks used must therefore allow for easy access to the documentation criteria.

Speed It is important to make sure that the thorough recording of information *proceeds quickly* when complaint documentation takes place during direct contact between the customer and the associate, which is necessary for reasons of efficiency. In addition, however, it must be recognized that the situation in which a complaint is articulated is an especially sensitive one, and the customer must not be expected to endure a complicated and time-consuming process.

7.2.2 Basic Contents of Documentation

As a basic principle, we can distinguish between complaint-content information and complaint-handling information. *Complaint-content information* is related to the complaint incident experienced by the customer and provides answers to the question: *"For whom did which problem with which object occur?"* Accordingly, the complaint-content information can be further subdivided into complainant, complaint-problem and complaint-object information.

Complaint-handling information refers not to the incident described in the complaint, but rather to the internal process of dealing with the complaint. This information provides answers to the question: *"How was the complaint accepted, processed and resolved?"* Consequently, complaint acceptance, complaint processing and complaint reaction must be differentiated from one another here.

For the recording and storing of all kinds of complaint information it must be generally ensured that the legal data protection regulations are observed.

7.2.2.1 Complaint-Content Information
Table 7.1 gives an overview of the informational details and the individual characteristics of complaint-content information.

Complainant Information

Complainant information pertains to the identity of the complainants, their role in the complaint process and the consequences they have considered for their future conduct in the business relationship, based on the appearance of the problem.

In the context of complaint documentation, data about the person who is articulating the problem to the firm is the first information that must be recorded.

Person All the specific details about the complainant's person and/or organization that are useful for the processing, resolution and analysis of the complaint itself fall into this category. Important details include the customers' name, their customer number (if available), their affiliation with a particular customer group or line of business (e.g., individual or business customer, membership in a preferred customer group) and other personal information, such as the date of birth.

Accessibility In addition, the customers' address, as well as the telephone/fax number and the e-mail address where they can be reached, must be recorded. With regard to complaints in business-to-business relations, the extension of the complainant must be collected in order to ensure a trouble-free communication during the complaint processing. It is also useful to note the times at which the customers

Table 7.1 Overview of the complaint-content information

Complainant information
- Identity of the complainant
  - Details about the complainant's person/organization of the complainant
  - Accessibility of the complainant
  - Internal or external customer
- Complainant's role in the complaint process
- Degree of annoyance and behavioral consequences
  - Extent of annoyance
  - Intentions to act or behavioral consequences

Complaint-problem information
- Type of problem
- Exact conditions of the complaint incident
  - Affected organizational unit
  - Date of problem occurence
  - Specific situation of the incident
- Cause of the problem
- Initial or follow-up complaint

Complaint-object information
- Products and/or services
- Marketing aspects
- Sociopolitical behavior

can be reached at each address or number, so that they can be contacted immediately in case further inquiries are necessary.

Internal or External Customer For the most part, complainants are not members of the firm itself, but rather customers who purchase the firm's products or services in the marketplace (external customers). In recent years, however, more and more internal processes have been modeled as customer-supplier relationships and implemented using internal performance standards. In a manufacturing company, for example, the production department can be the (internal) customer of the research and development department and evaluate its performance in relation to defined objectives for quality, costs and throughput times. The stronger the principle of internal customer orientation is upheld and implemented with the help of internal performance standards and service level agreements, the more an increase in complaints from internal customers can be expected. For this reason, then, there must be a way to identify the complainant as an internal customer during the complaint acceptance process, so that the processing routines that were specially developed for such cases can be initiated.

Relationship to the Complaint Incident As a rule, the person making the complaint is the same person who is actually affected by the problem. It sometimes happens, however, that complaints are brought *forward vicariously*, for instance when a son comes to the firm on behalf of his mother or attorneys approach the company on behalf of their client. In cases such as these, the name and contact information of the person making the complaint, as well as of the person actually affected by the problem, should be recorded. The communication during the processing procedure naturally takes place with the complainant; it may, however, be advisable to get in touch with the affected person as well, in order to apologize directly, for example.

Extent of Annoyance In order to react appropriately, to estimate the risk of losing the customer and to obtain an informational basis for the prioritization of any corrective measures that may be required, it is necessary to determine the importance that the dissatisfied customer attaches to the incident in question. This may take place *during the acceptance* of the complaint when the complainants use wording of their choosing to express the extent of their annoyance about the problem. Typical examples are as follows: "That sort of thing does happen sometimes, but I hope that this won't come up again in the future!" or "I'm furious!". In order to facilitate later analysis, it makes sense to utilize a *scale of annoyance* and to assign the most appropriate scale value to the respective verbalizations used by customers (see Fig. 7.1). This assignment of values demands a high degree of empathy on the part of the employees accepting the complaint, since they must perform the evaluation themselves and cannot ask the customer to do it.

One alternative is to include the scale of annoyance in a *satisfaction survey* and ask customers who complained to indicate the degree of their annoyance themselves. Such a scale can also be integrated into a *complaint web form*.

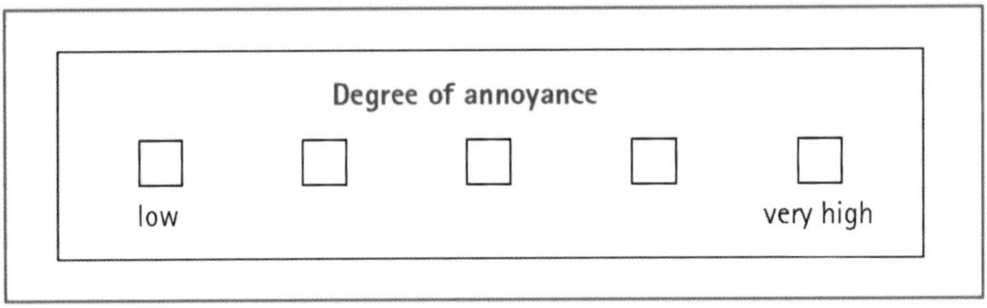

Fig. 7.1 Scale for recording the complainant's degree of annoyance

Intentions to Act or Behavioral Consequences There are a number of future intentions to act that can be taken from customer statements. On the one hand, the customers may make threats related to the business relationship ("You won't see me here again!"). On the other hand they may announce their intention to carry out other activities, by which they are attempting to assert their rights—for example, bringing in the media or consumer-rights organizations as well as communicating the incident in social networks. It is equally possible that they will point out decisions and consequences that have already taken place ("That's the reason I gave notice").

Information on the extent of the subjectively experienced irritation and the intentions to act that result from it constitute an indication of the *urgency of removing the problem* from the customer's perspective. Another indicator is the frequency with which these problems actually occur. In Sect. 10.2 tools are presented that use this information about the perceived urgency and the frequency of the problem to prioritize corrective actions as part of the continuous improvement process.

Complaint-Problem Information

Complaint-problem information is concerned with the type of problem, the exact conditions of the complaint incident (place, time, situational aspects), the cause of the problem and the classification of the complaint as a first or follow-up complaint.

Type of Problem The exact documentation of the problem that represents the actual content of the complaint is of decisive importance for the successful accomplishment of complaint-management tasks. Table 7.2 provides an exemplary classification of basic problem types. Each individual error must be assigned to one of the defined complaint objects (e.g., to a product or a service) during the complaint acceptance phase of each specific case.

Exact Conditions of the Complaint Incident In order to have an exact explanation of the circumstances, a deeper causal analysis and a differentiated evaluation of the frequency of the problem, the *location of the incident* or *the affected organizational unit* must be recorded. This is especially necessary in the case of a decentrally organized firm with multiple business locations (for instance, branch offices or franchise partners). If complaints about unfriendly behavior on the part of employees

Table 7.2 Typical types of problems that are articulated in complaints

Mistakes/Failures
- False price: incorrect price level, non-consideration of discount
- False product: delivery of another product that was not ordered
- False bill: charging of not-delivered services, double invoicing

Deficiencies in delivered services
- Lack of product quality: non-functional or damaged product
- Lack of service quality: poor fulfillment in the service process (e.g. slowness), insufficient service result (non-elimination of a repair problem)

Non-compliance of agreements
- Non-compliance with time promises (e.g. belated delivery)
- Non-compliance with service promises (e.g. reservations)

Interaction problems
- Interaction problems due to the inability of employees (language problems, incompetence)
- Interaction problems due to the unwillingness of employees (unfriendliness, lack of helpfulness)

Limited accessibility of service
- Limited accessibility due to incomprehensible instructions (instruction manuals that are not understandable)
- Limited accessibility due to absence of consultancy (not enough personnel, insufficiently competent personnel)
- Limited accessibility due to delivery problems (product is not in stock)
- Limited accessibility due to restriction of contact acceptance (inaccessible by telephone, non-customer-friendly opening hours)

Unfairness
- Unfair business practices (disclaimer of warranty in general terms and conditions)
- Unfair individual treatment (price discrimination, subordinate delivery)
- Unfair communication (false, misleading or deceptive advertising)

Inactivity
- No reaction whatsoever to customer inquiries, desires or claims

are more common for one particular branch office, discussions about combating the causes of the unfriendliness and eliminating the problem can be held with that particular unit of the organization.

The same principle applies to the recording of the *date* on which the problem appeared. This is important, for example, for the clarification of warranty questions, the determination of the cause of the problem and the discovery of the frequency of occurrence of the problem per unit of time (day, week, month, season, year).

It is also useful to record the *specific situation of the incident* when it has led to especially problematic experiences for the customers. For instance, the situation may be perceived differently by the customers if a problem with their car came up while they were on the way to a long-awaited vacation with the entire family, what is more, in the middle of a cold and rainy night, or whether the incident occurred under less dramatic circumstances. Such information is very valuable in order to be able to design an individualized complaint reaction.

Cause of the Problem If the customer's descriptions of the problem contain statements or speculations about possible causes of the problem, they should be recorded, as they may contain important indications for later internal analysis processes.

Initial or Follow-up Complaint It frequently happens that customers who lodge a complaint must broach the subject several times and in doing so, express their irritation about certain aspects of the complaint acceptance and complaint processing procedures. The original dissatisfaction they had that was based on the actual problem then escalates as a result of the unsatisfactory handling of their complaint. As this mishandling represents further grounds for complaint, it is important to differentiate between an initial complaint and a follow-up complaint. While the *initial complaint* is related to a specific problem with a product or a service, a *follow-up complaint* is always a complaint about how an original complaint was handled (see Table 7.3).

Even if follow-up complaints represent a specific, additional problem, they are also directly *related to the initial complaint*, since the customers see the new negative experience in the context of the original problem and their annoyance results from the combined effects of the both incidents. Therefore, the process of problem-solving or compensation must take into account the entire complaint history.

Table 7.3 Examples for articulated problems in the context of a follow-up complaint

About the complaint outcome ■ Refusal of the customer's wish ■ Compensation too low ■ Costs for error search and removal are charged to the customer ■ No excuse **About the complaint interaction** ■ Customer problem not taken seriously ■ Too little effort to resolve the problem ■ Assignment of blame to the customer ■ Unfriendly treatment **About the complaint process** ■ Poor accessibility ■ Varying information from different departments ■ Waiting too long for a solution

Complaint-Object Information

The subject of the problem articulated by the customer is the complaint object. As a rule, this object is a product or service offered by the firm. In addition to these firm offerings, other aspects of the market offering (e.g., the price) or the firm's overall social-political behavior (e.g., measures that are harmful to the environment) may also be the object of complaints.

Products and/or Services   For cause analysis and corrective measures, it is necessary that the *object* affected by the complaint (product or service) be clearly identified and recorded. The categorization that is applied should be fundamentally oriented toward the standard product classification (in the form of product lines or model ranges) used by the marketing and sales departments.

As far as services are concerned, the possible *customer-contact situations* should be described in more detail in order to be able to substantiate better the problem that has arisen. The customers experience many services as a sequence of situations in which they come into contact with some aspect of the service offering and gain an impression of the quality of the service. In the case of a hotel stay, for instance, this contact may include the check-in, the room stay, the restaurant visit and the check-out. Therefore, it is not only important for hotel management to find out that the customers are complaining about unfriendly behavior on the part of an associate, but rather also at what customer-contact point (check-in, room service, restaurant, etc.) they experienced this behavior. Only on the basis of such information can targeted corrective actions be introduced.

Marketing Aspects   Customer dissatisfaction can also result from the use of marketing instruments. For instance, customers may complain about the fact that the provider's products are too expensive, that an advertisement was misleading or the website is confusing. Such information contains indications on weaknesses in marketing planning and implementation or changes in customer preferences. These can be important for a customer-oriented modification of the marketing mix. For systematic recording of this information, it may be convenient to use the traditional catalog of marketing instruments as a basis (for example, the "4 P's" of marketing: Product, Place, Price and Promotion). With regard to services the areas of activity the so-called "4 Service P's" (Personnel, Processes, Physical Environment and Participating Customers) have to be taken into account.

Socio-political Behavior   Consumers do not restrict expressions of their opinion to the firm's market offerings, but rather take up social-political topics as well and criticize corporate behavior that violates *ethical norms or social-political positions* (breach of weapons-export restrictions, violations of environmental laws, discriminatory treatment of women, etc.). A firm can recognize consumer- and social-politically relevant problems in a timely manner and take them into consideration in its organizational planning if it undertakes a targeted documentation of critical statements such as these. Socio-political problem areas can be predefined as categories. However, a possibility to complement the category list is particularly needed in order to be able to react flexibly to new issues that arise.

7.2.2.2 Complaint-Handling Information

Complaint-handling information is not derived from the depiction of the case, but rather is related to the internal handling of complaint acceptance, processing and reply (see Table 7.4). With regard to *complaint acceptance*, the most relevant information is the time of receipt, the complaint channel chosen by the customer, the person or department that has received the complaint and the particular addressee of the complaint. Regarding *complaint processing*, it is especially important to record data on the initiated processing procedure, the responsibility for processing and already introduced processing steps. Regarding *complaint reaction*, the implications for the problem solution are of greatest importance. These include the customers' expectations regarding the corporate response, the classification as a warranty or goodwill case, and the urgency of the reaction. In addition, information about the commitments made to the customers and the actually realized problem solution need to be collected. All such information must be continually updated during the complaint handling process until the completion of the procedure.

Table 7.4 Overview of the complaint-handling information to be gathered

Complaint–Acceptance Information
- Time of receipt
  - Articulation date
  - Time of receipt in the firm
  - Time of receipt in complaint management
  - Date of record
- Complaint channel
- Employee accepting the complaint
- Addressee of the complaint

Complaint–Process Information
- Processing procedures
- Responsibility for processing
- Processing steps

Complaint–Reaction Information
- Aspects significant for the firm's response
  - Expectations of the customer with regard to the response
  - Classification of the complaint as warranty or goodwill case
  - Urgency of reaction
- Information about the corporate reaction
  - Promises of the complainant
  - Implemented problem-solving/payment of compensation

Complaint-Acceptance Information

Complaint-acceptance information documents the time of complaint receipt from various perspectives, the complaint channel selected by the complainant, the employee who took the complaint and the addressee chosen by the complainant.

Time of Receipt   The date of the complaint receipt in the firm is the *basis point* in terms of complaint settlement. From this point on, the firm is aware of the fact that it has dissatisfied customers who is awaiting an answer and a solution to their problem.

In order to be able to verify the observance of reaction times and to follow the time needed for the processing procedure within the firm, it is necessary to document the receipt of the complaint by the *different organizational units* that deal with that complaint. If the complaints are addressed to the complaint department this is the '*time of receipt complaint management*'; if complaint letters contain no specific or an incompetent address it is the '*time of receipt company*'. In the latter case, *idle and transfer times* occur, which must be measurable across the various points of entry if *standard reaction times* should be met—such as: "Initial contact with the dissatisfied customer in the case of written complaints within 48 hours".

Furthermore, the postmark of the letter (*articulation date*) should be recorded separately in the case of written complaints, because the customer has been waiting for a reaction since that point in time. When complaint-management software is being used, the date on which the complaint was entered into the system (*date of record*) must also be documented. Between the time at which a complaint case reaches the appropriate department and the time at which the case is entered into the system for processing, a period of days can elapse, due, for example, to lower entry capacity compared to the incoming complaint volume.

On the basis of differentiated documentation of the various receipt times, the firm can carry out, in the context of *complaint analysis* and *complaint management controlling*, a targeted analysis of which stations a written complaint in particular passes through, what processing times are associated with the complaint's path through the firm and what in the end stands in the way of a quick reaction to customer complaints. Based on this information, external and internal measures to channel complaints can be initiated and the processing times between the acceptance and the completion of the complaint can be minimized. For customers, this leads to a faster response to the complaint, and for the company to more efficient processing.

Complaint Channels   For each complaint, the *communication channel* chosen by the customer (in person, in writing, by telephone) should be recorded. On the one hand, indications as to the type of answer the complainant might desire can be drawn from the above information; on the other hand, familiarity with and acceptance of the established complaint channels can be verified.

Employee Accepting the Complaint   The employee accepting the complaint is the person who is the first to be informed by the customers about their dissatisfaction. The name of this employee should be documented so that the first person who talked to the customer can be asked follow-up questions in case anything in the complaint case is unclear, or so that this employee can be immediately named as a contact partner in case of further inquiries by the customer.

Addressee of the Complaint Dissatisfied customers either direct their complaints to the firm in general or name a specific person or department as the addressee. This information is important in monitoring the utilization of complaint-entry channels. If complainants frequently select complaint channels that were not intended by the firm, this is an indication of the fact that the established channels are not sufficiently well-known to customers or are inappropriate.

Complaint-Processing Information

Complaint-processing information includes information about the processing procedures put in motion by a complaint incident and about those in charge of the complaint case, as well as specific information about the individual processing steps.

Processing Procedures The various processing procedures are defined based upon the object of the complaint, the type of problem and the urgency of the reaction. The employees taking down the complaint must note which processing procedure they have initiated and to which person or department they have forwarded the case. This information is required for monitoring and optimizing complaint processing.

Responsibility for Processing For complaint cases that cannot be resolved during the initial direct contact with the customers, the employees responsible must be specified in the complaint-acceptance phase. The persons accepting the complaint must then record the name of the responsible associate and at the same time, forward the complaint case directly to that person.

Processing Steps If processing steps are introduced or carried out during the acceptance process, these steps should be documented so that transparency in processing is maintained at all times.

Complaint-Reaction Information

Complaint-reaction information refers to clues for response decisions and information about the solution to the problem that the firm promised or that it actually implemented.

Information About Aspects Significant for the Response Decision If certain aspects that will be significant for the firm's response are recognized during the acceptance of the complaint, they should be documented at this time. The following items are included in this group in increasing level of importance: The expectations of the customer with regard to the firm's reaction, the classification of the complaint as a warranty or goodwill case and the urgency of the reaction.

Expectations of the Customer with Regard to the Response The complainants frequently associate theirs depiction of the problem with a specific idea of the resolution to the problem or the reparation they desire. These *expectations* should be recorded during the acceptance process, as they facilitate the search for a need-oriented response by the firm.

Classification of the Complaint as Warranty or Goodwill Case   For legal-liability and process-technical reasons, it must also be recorded during the complaint acceptance whether this is a *warranty or goodwill* case. If it is clearly a warranty case, the solution to the problem—according to the guidelines of the warranty—is already decided, so that the necessary processing steps can be introduced immediately. If it is evident that the warranty period has just expired or a goodwill solution comes into play for other reasons, this must also be documented in order to introduce an appropriate processing routine.

Urgency of Reaction   Fundamentally, all customer complaints are equally important for a firm and should also be handled equally. The preferred processing and resolution of a complaint then appears to be justified, or necessary, for two reasons: first, if massive problems that have negative effects on a large number of customers can be uncovered via complaints—perhaps even effects that would carry a high risk of damage to health or property—*(Problem Risk);* or second, if the "usual" handling of complaints is associated with the danger of substantial economic losses or damage to the firm's image *(Customer Risk).*

Examples in the first case *(Problem Risk)* would be complaints that indicate defects in the product that are so grave that the affected firm feels compelled to *recall its products*. Car makers thus might request drivers of a particular model to bring their vehicles in for inspection or food manufacturers ask their customers to refrain from the consumption of certain foods. In the case of complaints whose content provides evidence of serious product defects such as these, the firm must deviate from the normal processing procedure so that the problem can be eliminated and possible damages can be limited immediately.

In the second case *(Customer Risk)*, it may be a question of complaints in which the complainants link their depiction of a serious incident with a *believable threat* to introduce legal or public measures if there is no reaction from the firm or if the firm does not react in a satisfactory manner. The same applies if they communicate on social networks and receive considerable reactions on the web. A comparable situation exists when the complainant is a customer that is of *extraordinary importance* for the existence and success of the firm. Here again, a greater urgency of reaction and preferred treatment of the complaint may be justified.

Promises to the Complainant   It may be practical to make the customer promises regarding time deadlines and content during the complaint-acceptance phase. In the case of *promises regarding deadlines*, an exact date is perhaps named, by which time the company will contact the complainant again or the case should be closed. In the case of an unequivocal case diagnosis, *promises regarding content* are also possible, with a view toward the resolution of the problem or an exact compensation amount.

In order to avoid further irritation later on, all promises made to the customers must be recorded. At the same time, all the firm's efforts must be directed toward making sure that these *promises are kept*. The customers' doubt in the reliability of the corporate service performance that was triggered by the product defect or service deficit must not be strengthened further in the course of processing the complaint. In case keeping the promise is not possible, contact must be made with the customers immediately, and the circumstances must be explained to them.

Implemented Problem-Solving/Payment of Compensation If the problem can be resolved right away during the complaint-acceptance phase, this response should be documented. In the case of problems that entail further processing, generally held proposed solutions should first be documented with an *increasing degree of specification* in the course of the processing.

Using the documentation of the solutions, a database can be established, which makes it possible for everyone in a firm that participates in the resolution of customers' problems to react consistently and quickly. Especially with regard to technical product complaints, an *expert system* for the generation of differentiated answers and suggestions for solutions can be developed based on the documented solutions.

The solutions implemented should not only be documented with respect to content (e.g., money back, exchange, apology), but the *costs* must also be recorded in order to allow for a permanent analysis of the operational efficiency of the reaction policy.

7.3   Categorization of Complaint Information

7.3.1 Development of a Categorization Scheme

The documentation of complaint information demands a unique and specific assignment to designated categories. A corresponding system of categories must, therefore, be developed.

The development of these categories is *one of the most fundamental tasks of complaint management* for two reasons: (1) The more precisely the categories reproduce the structure of the problem from the customer's point of view, and the more thoroughly all customer complaints can be unambiguously assigned to these groups, the more the information can be implemented for the *continuous improvement* of organizational processes. (2) As will be shown later, the correct definition of problem categories is a prerequisite for the differentiated and efficient *derivation of corresponding complaint-management processes*.

7.3.1.1 Requirements of a Category Scheme
So that the goals that are pursued through complaint documentation can be achieved, a series of requirements must be fulfilled by the categorization scheme. A good and efficient scheme for the classification of complaints is characterized primarily by action orientation, clear-cut demarcation, completeness, customer orientation and easy manageability.

- *Action orientation:* Each classification attribute and each problem category in particular must be action-oriented in the sense that it permits immediate conclusions to be drawn for complaint processing, cause analysis and the introduction of corrective measures.
- *Clear-cut demarcation:* Each category must be clearly demarcated from the others, which permits an unambiguous assignment of complaints. Only in this way can it be guaranteed that different employees will classify complaints in the same way.
- *Completeness:* The category system must make it possible for all customer complaints to be documented. An unspecific category called "Miscellaneous Problems" is of little use, as it provides no informational content for follow-up measures. If the firm does not wish to eliminate this category, it must be reviewed at regular intervals, and new categories must be created when the need arises.
- *Customer orientation:* The problem categories must be formulated from the customers' perspectives and not from the internal point of view. Many companies tend to use technical product features or an internal perspective for the categorization of problems. The focus is usually on quality and not on the customers. But to avoid misinterpretation, it is primarily necessary to understand the problem as it is perceived by the customers. The translation of the customer problems into the "internal" language of the firm should take place in a second step in which technical construction attributes or internally applied error classifications are logically associated with the categories of customer problems.
- *Easy manageability:* The system of categorization must be easily understandable and manageable so that employees can find the correct category when they are documenting the complaint. This requires restricting the categories to a limited number in the case of manual recording on documentary forms. In the case of software-supported documentation, a considerably greater complexity of category systems is fundamentally possible, although a simple introduction for users must be ensured.

It is obvious that the fulfillment of these criteria can lead to *conflicts*. The requirements of action orientation, clear-cut demarcation, completeness and customer orientation would seem to indicate a very differentiated system of categories, while the criterion of easy manageability would seem to indicate a simpler system. Accordingly, high demands on the informational content of the collected data often conflict with the wishes of customer contact employees and cost calculators, who are interested in a fast data entry process and reject a category system with a multitude of classification characteristics. In this situation, compromise solutions with abstract formulations of customer problems are often tolerated, even though they do not permit exact conclusions to be drawn as to the specific problem and its cause or to corrective measures. For a hotel company, for example, it is not sufficient to learn that customers experienced a problem with the room; it is also essential to know whether it was a problem with aspects such as size, comfort, cleanliness, technical equipment etc. A general complaint category 'room' prevents the hotel company from identifying the root cause of the problem. If, however, the criterion of action orientation is violated, it would appear to be more financially viable and efficient to forego documentation completely, since the recorded information cannot lead to any sort of targeted utilization. For this reason, it is part of the specific challenges of software-technical supports both to provide the required number of classification criteria and to ensure easy manageability on the part of the user.

7.3.1.2 Hierarchical Structuring of Category Schemes

The requirement for an action-oriented category system can lead to a very *detailed catalog of categories*, especially in large firms. These categories must be brought into some kind of order that provides for *increasing specification over different levels*.

The highest demands are placed on the *categorization of those complaint objects and complaint problems* that constitute the core of complaint information. When firms offer a large number of different products and services in a multitude of variations, and when very different problems may arise in each case, then complex structures for the clear-cut assignment of mistakes to the appropriate category develop very quickly.

In order to keep this complexity under control, a *hierarchical structuring of categories* is needed so that definite groups and subgroups of characteristics can be set up. Thus, several articles may be assigned to a particular product group or certain problems (e.g., lack of product knowledge) placed in an overarching problem category (e.g., lack of competence).

Figure 7.2 shows an *example* of the categorization of problems at a car dealership. The category of "service problem" has been chosen from among all the problems listed, and the two service problem subcategories "readiness/willingness to take action" and "competence" are hierarchically subdivided and specified.

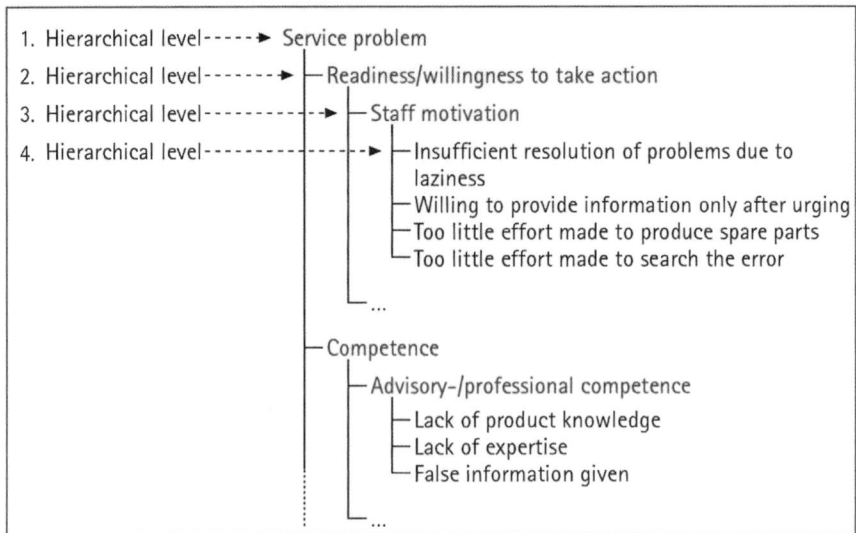

```
1. Hierarchical level -----► Service problem
2. Hierarchical level ------► ├─Readiness/willingness to take action
3. Hierarchical level --------├-► ├─Staff motivation
4. Hierarchical level --------├----├-► ├─Insufficient resolution of problems due to
                                        laziness
                                      ├─Willing to provide information only after urging
                                      ├─Too little effort made to produce spare parts
                                      └─Too little effort made to search the error
                                    └ …

                              ├─Competence
                                ├─Advisory-/professional competence
                                  ├─Lack of product knowledge
                                  ├─Lack of expertise
                                  └─False information given
                                └ …
```

Fig. 7.2 Hierarchical categorization of problem categories using automobile service complaints as an example

Spotlight 7.1 shows an innovative example of a multi-level categorization consistently focusing on customer-contact situations, which enables integration of all customer feedback about customer problems and contact point-oriented management of improvement measures.

Spotlight 7.1

Development of a Touchpoint-Oriented Categorization System

EOS is the world's leading technology provider in industrial 3D printing of metals and polymers. Founded in 1989, the independent company is a pioneer and innovator for integrated solutions in additive manufacturing. With the product portfolio of EOS systems, materials and process parameters, customers achieve decisive competitive advantages with regard to the quality and future viability of their production. Worldwide service and comprehensive consulting offers round off the portfolio.

Current status

As part of the company's continued customer-centric orientation, it was recognized that complaint management plays an important role. Thus, it was decided to optimize the existing complaint management processes. Among the central task blocks of complaint management are the acceptance and in particular the detailed recording of customer complaints. To ensure a high quality of the fulfillment of these tasks, a categorization system was developed, which will be explained in more detail in the following sections.

Problem definition

The central challenge generally consists of the fact that usually hardly any information on the subject of complaint management and customer satisfaction is available that can be used for customer-oriented management of a company. Often it is not possible to make a well-founded statement about how many customer complaints are received and which problems occur how frequently. This means that there is no basis for reliably identifying problem areas and deriving systematic and continuous improvement measures for quality assurance. Similarly, there is usually no information available on the complainants' satisfaction with the handling of their complaint and whether it has been possible to stabilize endangered customer relationships and prevent customers from migrating to competition. In addition, available customer feedback from the general customer surveys is not bundled with the information from the customer complaints received.

Objective

One of the strategic goals of EOS is the customer-centric orientation of the company. In order to further promote this goal the "Customer Experience Management Program (CEM)" was initiated. Among other things, this program includes the "Touchpoint Management" project to optimize the individual customer touchpoints. A customer touchpoint is defined as any occasion on

---

(continued)

Spotlight 7.1 (continued)

which the customer can come into contact with EOS. The second project, which is an integral part of the CEM program, concerns "complaint management". Its goal is to implement a company-wide process for dealing with customer complaints.

In order to record the customer's voice in a structured manner and to measure the performance of the customer touchpoints, a detailed and action-oriented categorization system for classifying customer problems was developed. This is based on the identified touchpoints and the information sources "customer complaint" and "proactive customer survey". It maps all customer touchpoints as well as the individual departments and thus enables customer feedback to be recorded in a targeted manner and assigned to the relevant specialist departments. This means that everyone in the company is informed at all times which problem has occurred at which point of contact and can react accordingly immediately.

Procedure for the development of the categorization system

Two dimensions play a role in the development of the categorization system: the reference areas and the problem categories. To define the reference areas all touchpoints at which the client comes into contact with EOS were identified and combined into a so-called "Customer Journey". These touchpoints were further hierarchically subdivided, resulting in a detailed reference area system that provides information on exactly where customer problems can occur. In a second step, the exact customer problems that could arise were determined for each individual reference area. In order to create appropriate transparency here too, the customer problems were also structured hierarchically on two levels and assigned to the individual reference areas. The two dimensions reference areas (where did the problem occur?) and problem categories (what was the problem?) can be linked and evaluated with the help of intelligent software support to ensure meaningful reporting.

One example of this is arranging an appointment—by telephone or e-mail—for a commissioning date for an EOS system at the customer's premises. A complaint relating to this would be categorized as follows: first level: "Installation & Training", second level: "System installation", third level: "Scheduling the visit of the service technician", fourth level: "System installation appointment". The customer problem "My desired date was not met" is recorded in the second dimension of the categorization system (problem category): "first level: "Date problems", second level: "Desired date not possible". At the same time, specific information about the desired date can be documented in a structured manner. Figure 7.3 shows this section of the categorization system.

(continued)

Spotlight 7.1 (continued)

Outlook

The categorization system is the basis for internal, target group-specific integrated complaint and annoyance reporting. With the help of the analyses provided, conclusions can be taken on how the performance turns out at which customer touchpoints with regard to customer orientation and at which touchpoints which problems how often occurred. Due to the high level of detail—the category system comprises a total of 1052 categories—targeted quality improvement measures can be taken in order to eliminate problem areas.

The touchpoint-oriented category system developed records not only the reasons for complaints, but also all feedback on customer problems—such as the reasons for annoyance raised in the rolling annoyance and complainant surveys. This creates the possibility to interpret customer problems from a holistic perspective and to derive customer-centered improvement measures. At the same time, a customer-centered, touchpoint-oriented control is guaranteed.

Alexander Lutter
Program Manager Customer Experience
EOS GmbH Electro Optical Systems

7.3.1.3 Monitoring of Category Schemes

A good category scheme is characterized by the fact that certain complaint information is *always assigned to the same categories*, regardless of which associate is entrusted with the documentation. Ensuring this consistency means that greater importance is attached to the monitoring of the category scheme with respect to the freedom to overlap, meaningfulness and reliability.

In the course of developing the system of categories, the assignment of specific complaints to the individual classification schemes must be carried out by at least two people independent of one another during a *test phase*. The quality of the categorization results from the degree of consensus between the two assignment processes and is then reflected in the percentage of complaints that are assigned to the same category classes according to both grouping processes. In addition, the proportion of complaints that are classified consistently for each type of complaint information that must be categorized is divided by the total number of complaints for each hierarchical level. The closer the result is to 1, the greater is the level of consensus. If a percentage of at least 80% is not reached, Hayes (2008) suggests verifying and modifying the categories at the respective levels.

The scheme developed must be *constantly enhanced*, since new products and services are offered, for instance, or previously unexpected errors arise. The scheme of categorization must therefore undergo a thorough verification process at regular intervals and be adjusted to the changed situation. Only in this way can it be ensured that meaningful results are targeted in the context of complaint analysis and that bad investments in the use of complaint information are avoided.

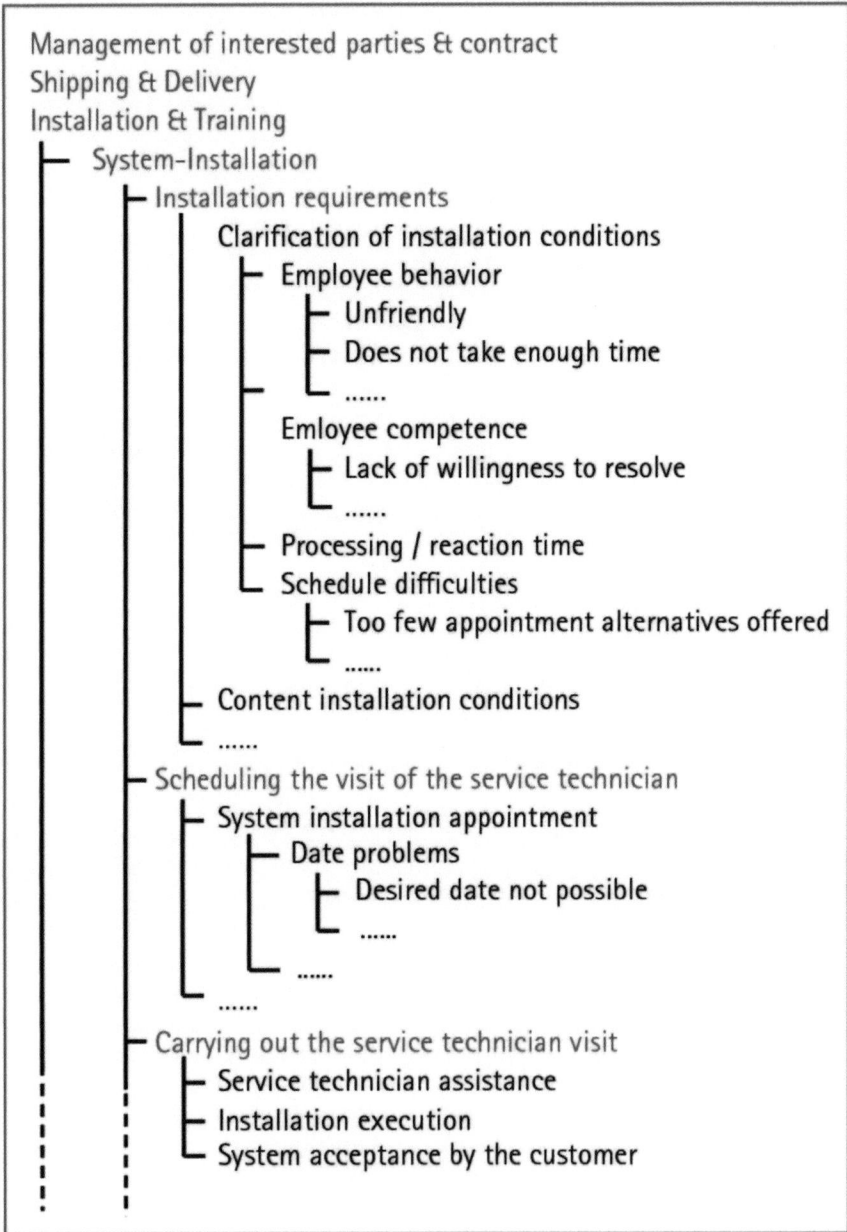

Fig. 7.3 Hierarchical categorization system (section)

7.3.2 Supplementation of Categorical Documentation Through a Clear Description of the Case

Each categorization represents a *simplification of complex circumstances*. The danger of losing information that could provide basic details about the causes of problems and the reasons for customer dissatisfaction thus exists. Hence it is important to record the complaint as thoroughly as possible as a *narrative of the case*. This is relatively easy to guarantee when complaints exist *in writing*, especially when it is possible to refer to a software-supported archival system. With the aid of systems such as these, complaint cases that are articulated in writing can be scanned in and administered. If, in addition, complaint-management software that is equipped with a corresponding interface to the archival software is implemented, the entire "complaint history" is immediately available and does not have to be documented again separately. In the case of complaints that are taken *over the phone or in person*, one must manage to record information about specific conditions in the form of *key words*.

7.4 Form of Documentation

The documentation of the contents of a complaint may be carried either by employees of the firm or by customers themselves. In the first instance, either standardized forms or input masks in complaint-management software systems are utilized. Customer documentation takes place in the form of opinion cards or documentation masks located on the complaint sites provided on the Internet.

7.4.1 Corporate Complaint Documentation by Means of Forms and PC-Supported Input Masks

7.4.1.1 Documentation Using Standardized Forms

Using standardized forms should put the employees accepting complaints in a position to document the complaint information in a thorough, structured and rapid manner. An *example* of such a form is reproduced in Fig. 7.4. This example takes into consideration complaint-content information (person of the complainant, product as complaint object, type of problem), as well as complaint handling information (type and date of complaint input, data on the resolution/reparation, measures taken and processing steps).

The categories of documentation are highlighted and furnished with alternative answers, or hints, as to which specific information must be recorded in detail. In this way, rapid and thorough recording of data can be guaranteed.

Standardized forms such as these are primarily suited to the documentation of complaint information that takes place *during direct contact* with the customer—that is, when the customer makes a complaint verbally or over the telephone. Such forms

Complaint acceptance

Associate who accepts the complaint: _____   Date of receipt: _____

Complaint channel
☐ Phone   ☐ Letter   ☐ E-Mail   ☐ Web form

Addressee of the complaint
☐ Customer care   ☐ Sales   ☐ Management   ☐ _____

Complainant

Basic data

Title: _____

First name: _____

Firm/last name: _____

Contact person: _____

Address: _____

City/zip code: _____

State: _____

Internal/external customer
☐ Internal customer   ☐ External customer

Affected person
☐ Complainant her-/himself
☐ Employee of the complainant
☐ Supervisor of the complainant
☐ Relative of the complainant

Annoyance
☐   ☐   ☐   ☐   ☐
low   very high

Complaint object

Product/service
☐ _____   ☐ _____   ☐ _____   ☐ _____

Market offering/marketing-mix
☐ Product   ☐ Price   ☐ Distribution   ☐ Communication
☐ Personnel   ☐ Process   ☐ Physical environ-   ☐ _____
                               ment
Sociopolitical behavior
☐ _____   ☐ _____   ☐ _____   ☐ _____

Complaint problem

Case depiction

_____

_____

_____

_____

_____

_____

Initial/follow-up complaint
☐ Initial complaint   ☐ Follow-up complaint

Case resolution desired by the customer

_____

_____

_____

Type of problem
☐ Problem 1   ☐ Problem 2
☐ Problem 3   ☐ Problem 4

Location of the problem occurrence

_____

Date of the problem occurrence

_____

Reaction urgency
☐ Urgency level 1
☐ Urgency level 2
☐ Normal processing

Warranty/goodwill
☐ Warranty
☐ Goodwill

Fig. 7.4 Example of a complaint documentation form

Complaint resolution

Resolution of the problem that was actually realized

_____

_____

Promises made to the customer

_____

_____

Time promises
☐ Immediately resolved ☐ Intermediate reply by _____
☐ Problem solution/compensation by _____

Complaint processing

Complaint owner   Complaint processing procedure
☐ Complaint owner 1 ☐ Complaint owner 2 ☐ Process 1   ☐ Process 2
☐ Complaint owner 3 ☐ Complaint owner 4 ☐ Process 3   ☐ Process 4

Fig. 7.4 (continued)

can be reasonably implemented by customer-contact personnel in retail locations, hotels or banks, for example.

If necessary, complaint information may also be recorded *after direct contact* with the customer. To take one example, when a hotel guest complains to a maid about a dirty bathroom, the focus then becomes the immediate restoration of the customer's satisfaction. The belated documentation of the complaint information remains important, however, so that they are later available for assessment and controlling purposes and thus also for continual process improvements.

7.4.1.2 Documentation Using Software-Supported Complaint Management Systems

As a rule, firms employ *software-supported complaint management systems* for the systematic documentation and processing of written and telephone complaints in particular. The distinct advantage of these systems is that the criteria of thorough, structured and rapid documentation of the complaint information can be easily met. Program configuration and control ensure that no fundamental complaint information is omitted. However, the use of these systems presupposes appropriate training for firm employees, in dealing not only with the complaint-management software, but also with the individual documentation contents.

Additional *manual complaint-documentation forms* must also be utilized when software-supported complaint management systems are put in place if not all subsidiaries or customer-contact personnel have a workstation equipped with the software system or cannot refer to it while a complaint is being made (e.g., in a retail location). The information recorded on the form can subsequently be entered into the complaint-management system and thus made centrally available for further processing. The firm may also be plan for the forms to be scanned into the system, which minimizes the amount of subsequent documentation required.

7.4.2 Customer Complaint Documentation Using Opinion Cards and Internet Complaint Sites

The use of opinion cards, touch screens or Internet complaint sites causes part of the information recording to be transferred to the customer *(customer complaint documentation)*.

The *design of opinion cards* or complaint sites may range from a single text field, to the free articulation of the complaint story, to a structured layout with predetermined entry fields. In designing the opinion cards and/or complaint sites, the firm must be careful to use the predefined fields to inquire only about information that the customer can easily provide. Auto makers or dealerships should, for example, avoid insisting that the customer provide the Vehicle Identification Number, since many customers do not have this information handy. Furthermore, default categories must be worded in such a way that the customer can easily understand them. The following data especially can be requested of customers with no difficulty: address, type of problem, complaint object, location where the problem arose, date when the problem arose, description of the incident as free text and expected attitude toward the resolution of the problem.

On Internet sites, *categories* which are consistently part of a complaint can be provided as classification criteria, so that customers get the possibility to choose complaint information from the corresponding lists appropriate to them, for example, the complaint object from the range of products or the location where the problem occurred from all bank offices. Thereby, it facilitates the input of the customer's statements and at the same time supports a consistent documentation. Furthermore, part of the effort to document the complaint is transferred to the customer, and information can be processed directly, if an interface between e-mails and complaint management software exists. Similar effects can also be achieved with the use of scanning technology on opinion cards or touch screens. An example of the extensive collection of complaint information by customers using a web form is shown in *Spotlight 7.2*.

Spotlight 7.2
Complaint Recording With the Help of Customers at Thomas Cook AG
    Thomas Cook is Europe's second largest tour operator. It has sold holidays for over 175 years and invented the packaged holiday. It all started with a train ride from Leicester to Loughborough in the UK. Today, some of the most well-known brands that belong to Thomas Cook are Thomas Cook,

(continued)

Spotlight 7.2 (continued)

Neckermann Reisen, Öger Tours and Bucher Reisen in Germany. Additionally, the Condor airline and hotel chains such as Casa Cook, Sentido Hotels, Sunwing, Sunprime, SunConnect and Smartline Hotels belong to Thomas Cook.

The complaint volume varies greatly throughout the year. The majority of complaints have to be handled after the summer travel season. Thomas Cook claims to work on each complaint in due time and to a very high standard since effectively dealing with a guest's complaint is a real chance to win back the guest's trust and loyalty. The complaint management department is centrally located in Oberursel, the headquarters of Thomas Cook Germany. Complaints are mainly received via e-mail (approx. 65%), followed by letter and our online tool (for screenshot see Fig. 7.5). Since complaints are closely linked with travel regulations where written statements, pictures etc. are necessary, other channels such as phone, SMS or WhatsApp are used very rarely. The main channel (e-mail) is on the one hand a very smart solution since a complaint can be handled quickly, loaded into the systems and can be worked on effectively. On the other hand, the "easy-way-to-handle" also results in an increasing number of responses from guests and the process time can go up. Ideally, the guest uses the online tool, where all necessary and required information needs to be filled in. Attachments such as pictures can be also uploaded. The tool can be used by the guest him/herself or by the travel agent who took over the complaint handling on behalf of the guest. To promote the usage of the online tool Thomas Cook offers a quicker response time. The complaint will automatically be forwarded to the responsible staff member and can be categorized immediately due to the internal tagging in the systems. Complaints made via e-mail or letter need to be reviewed and categorized manually, which is more time-consuming and results in a longer response time. The online form can be accessed through various websites as well as through the Thomas Cook Travelguide-app—a personalized travel app that every guest can use to monitor, check and adjust a confirmed booking.

Automation plays nowadays a leading role in complaint management since the guest's expectation is not only a short response time but also a high standard of service. So the main challenge and development field today as well as in the near future will be to enhance the current system landscape with the necessary tools to ensure a smooth and quick complaint handling process. Especially clear cases such as flight delays can be easily handled in an automated way. All complaints where statements from partners (hotels, agents, etc.) or Thomas Cook in-destination staff are required, as well as where a certain goodwill is needed the expertise of an experienced staff member will always be necessary.

(continued)

Spotlight 7.2 (continued)
Heidrun Steidle
Managing Director Thomas Cook Airport Service GmbH & Head of Complaint Management
Thomas Cook Touristik GmbH

Another *example* of a detailed and structured inquiry of relevant complaint information on the Internet is shown in Fig. 7.6. This is the complaint form of Taxi & Limousine Commission (TLC) of New York City. If you click on the menu item "I want to make a complaint" on the public services page of the city, this complaint page appears. Here the customer is first offered various complaint topics. A short explanation is given in each case where problems can be articulated. If you click on a complaint topic—as in our example "Yellow Taxi Complaint"—you get information about the rights of taxi customers. At the same time, concrete points are specified to which the "taxi complaint" can refer, differentiating between a complaint about the taxi driver (e.g. denied request, discourteous, refusal to accept credit card or unsafe driving) or the taxi itself (e.g. dirty condition, broken or missing equipment or not displaying a license). A click on the relevant problem leads to the next page, on which the complainant is guided step by step through the registration process. Here the complainant can provide detailed information on what exactly happened ("What"), where the incident happened ("Where"), who the complainant is ("Who") and how to submit the complaint ("Submit").

Fields that must be entered are marked separately and brief explanations are provided for important and possibly misleading information. In the section "Who" the customers are informed that they can also insert video, image, audio or text files and will receive an automatic confirmation e-mail as soon as they have sent the complaint. Furthermore, a summary of the information collected is provided before the complaint is sent, which can be corrected if necessary. Figure 7.6 shows the web forms for "What"—for a complaint about the driver—and "Where".

The categorization of possible customer problems, which is very well illustrated in this example, helps customers to quickly find and articulate the problems that have affected them. In addition, the structured query of the relevant information ensures that all the necessary information is immediately and efficiently available for further processing and evaluation.

7.5 Ensuring the Quality of the Complaint Information Collected

Recorded complaint information—especially on complaint objects and problems—forms the basis for the initiation of improvement processes. Therefore, special attention must be paid to the quality of the documentation. This is particularly true if a variety of employees—for example in an inbound customer care center are

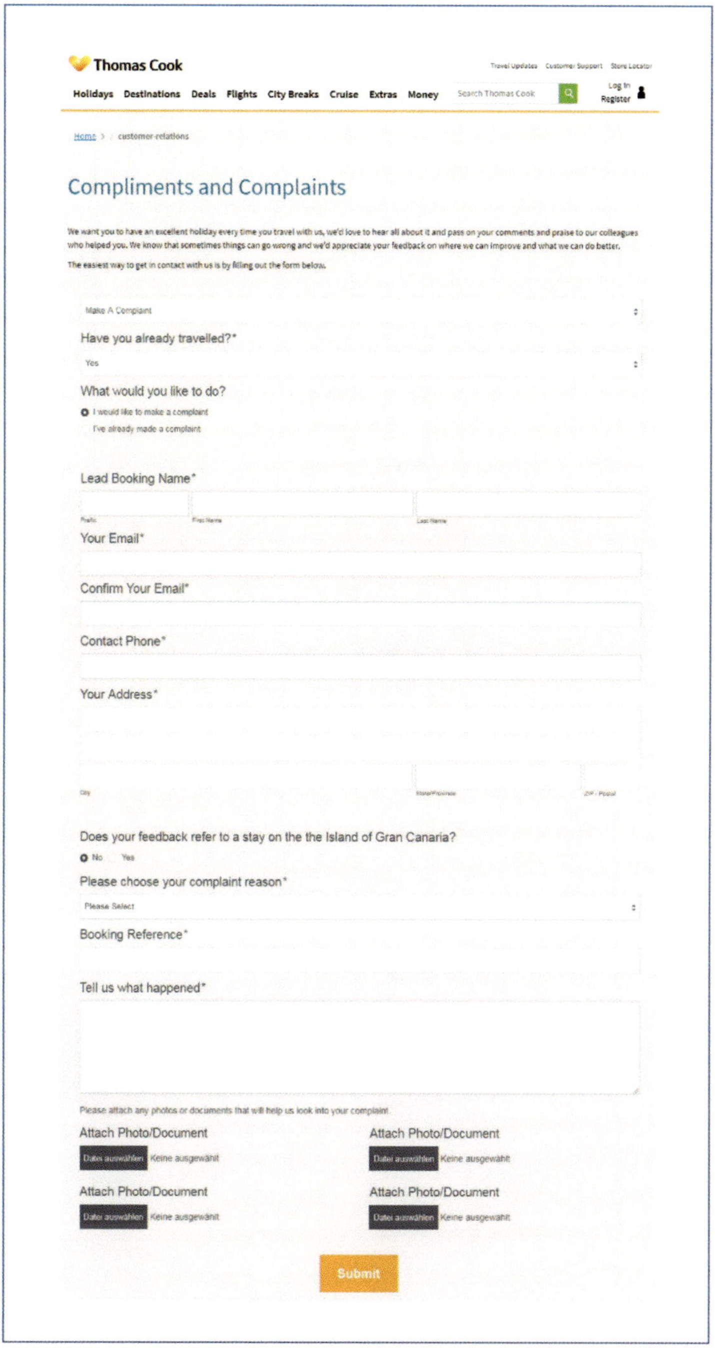

Fig. 7.5 Online feedback form

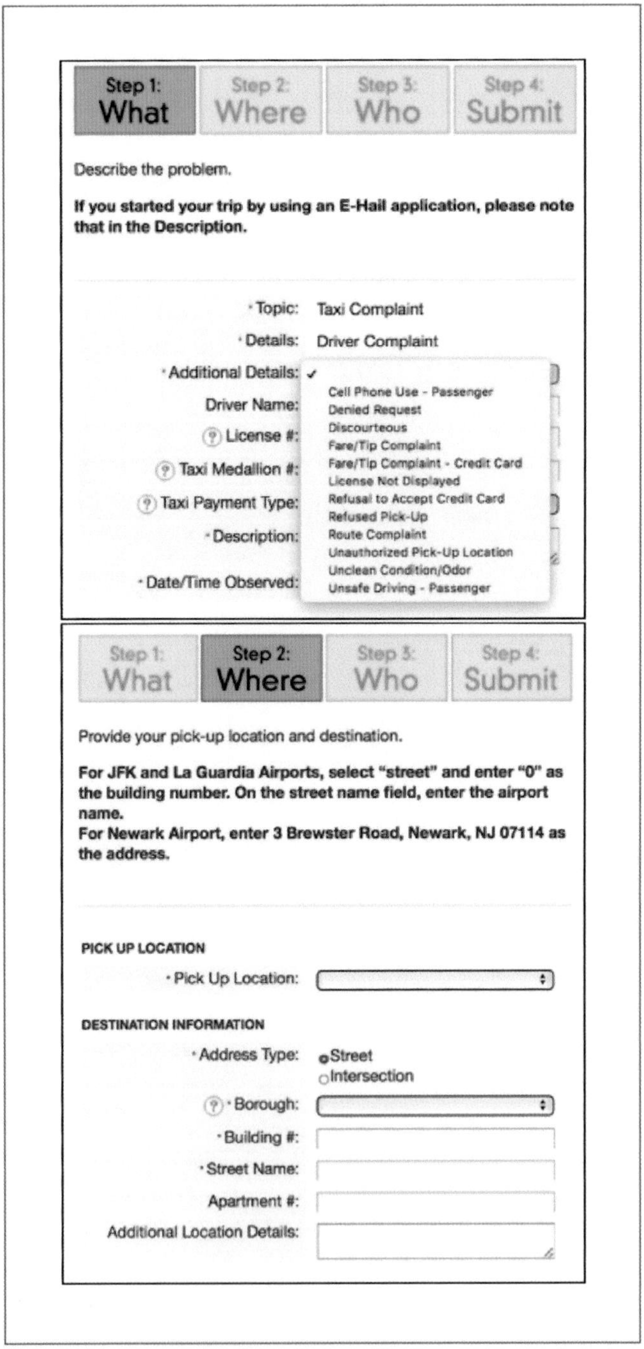

Step 1: What | Step 2: Where | Step 3: Who | Step 4: Submit

Describe the problem.

If you started your trip by using an E-Hail application, please note that in the Description.

·Topic: Taxi Complaint
·Details: Driver Complaint
·Additional Details: ✓
Driver Name:
License #:
Taxi Medallion #:
Taxi Payment Type:
·Description:
·Date/Time Observed:

Cell Phone Use - Passenger
Denied Request
Discourteous
Fare/Tip Complaint
Fare/Tip Complaint - Credit Card
License Not Displayed
Refusal to Accept Credit Card
Refused Pick-Up
Route Complaint
Unauthorized Pick-Up Location
Unclean Condition/Odor
Unsafe Driving - Passenger

Step 1: What | Step 2: Where | Step 3: Who | Step 4: Submit

Provide your pick-up location and destination.

For JFK and La Guardia Airports, select "street" and enter "0" as the building number. On the street name field, enter the airport name.
For Newark Airport, enter 3 Brewster Road, Newark, NJ 07114 as the address.

PICK UP LOCATION
·Pick Up Location:

DESTINATION INFORMATION
·Address Type: Street / Intersection
·Borough:
·Building #:
·Street Name:
Apartment #:
Additional Location Details:

Fig. 7.6 Example of the recording of complaint information by taxi customers on the internet (TLC 2018; TLC on-line complaint form used with permission of the City of New York; © 2018, City of New York. All rights reserved) entrusted with the receipt of telephone complaints and the task of recording complaint information. Two quality criteria must be taken into account: completeness and accuracy of documentation.

Completeness of Documentation In a first step, it is necessary to check whether all the information of a complaint that should be collected—such as complaint channel, complaint addressee, complaint object and type of the problem—has actually been documented. Since customers can articulate several problems in a complaint, it is also necessary to check, simultaneously, whether the employees have identified and recorded all problems raised.

Accuracy of Documentation This criterion refers to the correctness of the recording. Correctness has a multitude of aspects. These include orthographically correct spelling of the complainant's name as well as an accurate description of the case or the appropriate categorization of the problem. Errors in data entry usually lead to difficulties in the complaint processing and can cause further customer dissatisfaction and follow-up complaints. Furthermore, if the documentation of the articulated problems is incomplete or incorrect, false conclusions may be drawn regarding the need for improvement measures.

In the case of *written complaints*, the completeness and accuracy of the documentation can easily be examined by comparing the information in the customers' letters with the recorded information. Regarding *telephone complaints*, an analogous approach is applicable if the conversations are recorded.

The two documentation criteria are evaluated by comparing the number of incompletely or incorrectly recorded operations with the total number of examined operations. These comparisons result in *non-compliance rates* for both the completeness and the accuracy of the documentation.

The completeness and accuracy of the documentation should be checked *regularly*—in the case of a high number of complaints, at monthly intervals. Ideally, the rate should not only be determined with reference to departments or teams, but also for individual employees—insofar as it is legally permissible—in order to be able to provide specific feedback and to initiate adequate training measures.

The systematic and regular review of the completeness and accuracy of the complaint information recorded is often neglected in practice. As a consequence, employees in operational complaint management are not always aware of the importance of complete and correct documentation of complaint information. Another consequence is that the tasks of complaint evaluation, complaint reporting and in particular the usage of complaint information are based on an *insufficient or incorrect database*.

Chapter 7 in Brief

- The initial contact often determines whether or not it is possible to satisfy the complainant. In addition, immediate problem-solving is usually also the most cost-effective approach.
- According to the principle of complaint ownership, the employee who is the first to be confronted with a customer problem is responsible for the recording and processing of the complaint.
- Complaint receipt processes must be clearly defined.
- Complaint information must be captured completely, quickly and in a structured way.
- Information on the contents of the complaint and the complaint handling must be documented in detail.
- A good category scheme for complaint information is characterized by action orientation, clear-cut demarcation, completeness, customer orientation and easy manageability.
- For certain complaint information—in particular complaint objects and complaint problems—a hierarchical structuring of categories is needed.
- Complaint information can be collected by employees using standardized forms or templates in complaint-management software systems as well as by customers with the help of opinion cards and web forms.
- The completeness and accuracy of complaint information collected must be checked regularly.

References

Hayes BE (2008) Measuring customer satisfaction and loyalty: survey design, use, and statistical analysis, 3rd edn. ASQ Quality, Milwaukee
Michelli JA (2008) The new gold standard: 5 leadership principles for creating a legendary customer experience courtesy of the Ritz-Carlton Hotel Company. McGraw-Hill, New York
Stauss B, Seidel W (2006) Prozessuale Zufriedenheitsermittlung und Zufriedenheitsdynamik bei Dienstleistungen. In: Homburg C (ed) Kundenzufriedenheit, Konzepte—Methoden—Erfahrungen, 6th edn. Gabler, Wiesbaden, pp 171–195
TLC (2018) TLC on-line complaint form. https://www1.nyc.gov/apps/311universalintake/form.htm. Accessed 4 Jan 2018

Complaint Processing

8

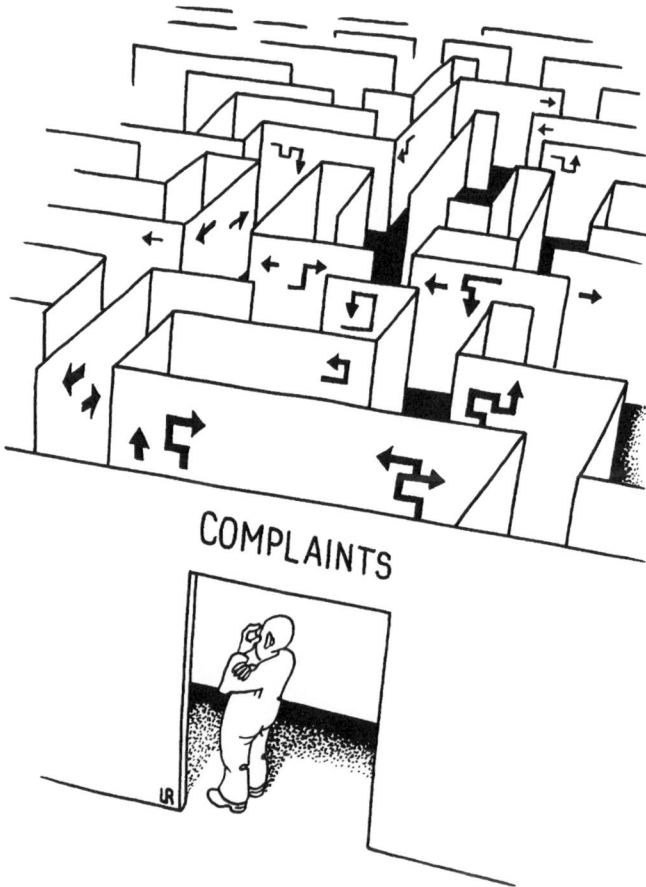

© Springer Nature Switzerland AG 2019

B. Stauss, W. Seidel, *Effective Complaint Management*, Management for Professionals,
https://doi.org/10.1007/978-3-319-98705-7_8

Issues Raised
- Which basic processing procedures should be distinguished?
- How should the current procedures be analyzed from the company's perspective of efficiency?
- How should the current procedures be analyzed from the customers' perspective?
- What responsibilities must be defined to ensure an effective and customer-oriented complaint handling process?
- How can realistic processing deadlines be specified?
- What aspects of the complaint processing must be documented?

At the center of complaint processing lies the question: *"Who does what, when, and in what order?"* To answer this question, the logical sequence of the processing procedures must be defined, the responsibilities at each step of complaint processing determined, the processing deadlines fixed, mechanisms for the monitoring of complaint processing installed, internal communication between the processing locations ensured and complaint processing documented in an appropriate history.

8.1   Definition of Complaint Processing Procedures

8.1.1   Identification of Various Complaint Processing Procedures

On a *rather abstract level*, the complaint processing procedures can be *uniformly defined* and the procedural limits clearly determined. The process begins with the documentation of complaints made either over the telephone or in person or after the receipt of written complaints in the firm. Complaint processing ends with the resolution of the problem and/or a written answer to the customer, or communication in person or by telephone that the complaint case has been closed and, when it is successful, creates a customer who is once again satisfied and loyal.

Upon closer observation, it becomes clear that complaints can be differentiated in many regards, so that one cannot proceed based on the assumption that complaint processing is more or less uniform. Some *examples* from the automotive industry will illustrate this point:

- Customers *complain in person to the owner of a car dealership* about the fact that they repeatedly had to wait for a long time when they brought their cars in for routine repairs. During the conversation, they could be satisfied with an apology and a small gift as compensation for the inconvenience they experienced.
- Customers *complain in writing to the manufacturer's central customer service department* that disturbing noises in the engine block have not been fixed, despite a number of trips to the garage. In this case, the responsible associate first informs dissatisfied customers that their complaint has been received, explain to them the

processing measures that will be introduced and forward the case to a sales unit for the final resolution of the problem. This unit then makes an appointment for the customers with the garage and attempts to eliminate the problem during a more thorough inspection by one of their experts.

- Customers *complain to the manufacturer by telephone* about a technical problem associated with a fundamental safety risk. Due to the potential danger of the situation, an immediate diagnosis of the problem must take place.
- In a *written complaint that is personally directed to the chairman of the board of the manufacturer*, large corporate customers threaten to break off the business relationship if a problem is not immediately solved to their satisfaction. First of all, care should be taken to ensure that the letters are answered by the board member to whom it was addressed; second, in view of the customers' importance to the firm, urgent processing of the case again appears to be called for here.
- Customers complain in *writing to their local garage* about damage that appeared after their warranty expired and demand a goodwill solution. The garage does not have the authority to decide on its own how to resolve a problem like this, so it must forward the case to the manufacturer, and the central customer service department may have to bring in other departments (the legal department) or sales and marketing units in order to resolve the goodwill case.

These examples *make three things clear*: (1) Every complaint received initiates an *internal processing procedure*. (2) The *requirements* of the processing procedure can be very different, depending on the product affected, the type of problem, the complaint channel, the addressee of the complaint or the urgency of the reaction. The measures taken and the persons or departments included in the process can also depend on whether it is a warranty or goodwill case, or a first or follow-up complaint. (3) It must therefore be determined which *basic processing procedures* must actually be differentiated and which *conditions* can be seen as comparable, so that a uniform definition of the process can take place.

8.1.1.1 Independent, Cooperative and Transfer Processes

At an *intermediate level of abstraction*, fundamental *key processes* of complaint processing can be differentiated.

The first classification takes place from the perspective of the department responsible for operative complaint processing. Depending on the extent to which the division responsible for complaint processing can manage the complaint processing *alone or requires the help of other organizational areas*, three basic types of complaint processing procedures can be differentiated:

(1) Independent Processes: the division that is responsible for operative complaint processing may process a complaint alone—that is, without including other divisions—all the way until its final stage.

(2) Cooperative Processes: in order to resolve the case completely, the complaint department must refer to information or to the expertise of other departments. These

departments will then be requested to take a stand on a certain circumstance or to clarify a legal position. The closure of the complaint case takes place through the complaint management department itself.

(3) Transfer Processes: in this case, it is necessary that the complaint case be transferred to another division. Here, the complaint ownership goes completely over to a new unit within the organization that then resolves the case with regard to the customer. However, the transfer process may also provide for the initial complaint owner to contact the complainants again at the end of the process and explain the result communicated to them by the downstream body.

The question of which of these processes should be chosen is dependent upon a series of *influencing factors*.

An important prerequisite for the creation of an independent processing procedure is the definition of a *maximum amount that can be spent to resolve the complaint*, up to which point an extensive investigation of the individual case is not required. Also decisive here is the *specific know-how* required to diagnose the problem. The more the employees who are responsible for the operative complaint processing have the appropriate expertise or the immediate access to the database of problem solutions, the more feasible become the independent processing procedures.

The decision between *first and follow-up complaint* is also relevant to the process, because the complaints are related to different types of problems. While first complaints deal with a product-related concern, follow-up complaints deal with an additional problem perceived by the customer in connection with the complaint processing. First complaints are thus to be processed with the inclusion of specialist departments, if the problem implies a certain cost amount or technical complexity, while follow-up complaints are mainly to be handled in the context of independent processing procedures by the complaint management department alone.

Warranty or goodwill cases are "classic" transfer or cooperative procedures, since the presence of legal or otherwise specified requirements usually has to be reviewed. It is also possible here, however, to make the review requirement dependent on the cost of the solution, so that an independent processing procedure for a clearly defined subset of these cases can be determined.

To a certain extent, the customers' articulation behavior also determines the necessary processing procedure. Complaints can reach the firm in very *different ways*. Organizational units that, from the firm's perspective, should not be the primarily units entrusted with this task are thus also included in the complaint-receipt process. In order to ensure rapid and correct processing, all locations that accept complaints must be recorded as process starting points. Furthermore, clearly defined transfer processes must be determined, and the organizational units receiving the complaints must be connected with the responsible processing stations via specific forwarding guidelines.

In articulating their complaints, customers may turn to a given *addressee* in the firm with their concern, perhaps to a member of company management that they know by name. In this case also, it is necessary to determine transfer procedures that will ensure that the incident is forwarded in a way that is appropriate to the problem. For such cases, cooperative procedures may also be defined through which the addressee is integrated in the response activities. In that case, they would, for example, sign the receipt confirmation or conclude the case with a personal answer.

The specific character of the processing procedures depends upon other factors as well. With respect to the cooperative procedures, it is highly dependent upon which *product or service* is affected as to which organizational units must be brought in, since different responsibilities in research and development or production, for instance, may be at issue in each case. Additionally, the *type of problem* often determines the processing requirements, because different technical expertise is required each time and because different organizational units are affected (e.g., the order acceptance department in the case of a delivery mistake and the deliverer in the case of shipping damages).

8.1.1.2 Routine and Non-routine Processes

A second classification of processing procedures is based on the criterion of *reaction urgency*, which suggests that a differentiation be made between routine and non-routine procedures.

The processes that can be characterized as *routine processes* are those that refer to the vast majority of "normal" complaints with no special sense of urgency. Complaints with a great sense of urgency, on the other hand, demand *non-routine processes*. For cases in which, for instance, the safety of customers is jeopardized or particularly high property losses could occur, preferred attention and handling are required. The same applies to the complaints of especially important customers, who threaten to switch to the competition or bring in official bodies or the media. In such cases, it is necessary to institute non-routine procedures that, for defined levels of urgency, provide for the immediate notification of specific decision-makers in the firm who have the professional competence to apply the case solution and processing that they deem necessary. This may occur by linking certain types of problems to different levels of reaction urgency through software. When such a problem arises, the processing employees receive a message on the screen that they must inform a particular person immediately. This person then handles the case individually and the situation appropriately. A comprehensive definition of the behavior is neither possible nor practical for these cases.

8.1.2   Analysis of Complaint Processing Procedures

The starting point for a systematic design of complaint processing procedures is an state analysis of how the current procedures are designed with respect to achieving both *efficiency* and *complaint satisfaction* among customers.

8.1.2.1 Analysis of the Current Complaint Processing Procedures from the Perspective of the Firm

The first step is *the analysis of the current organizational procedures of complaint processing* from the company's efficiency perspective. The basis for a differentiated as-is analysis is the consultation of a representative sample of complaint cases that were received within a certain time period (e.g., 1 year). These cases must be analyzed with differing degrees of detail. First, the *fundamental process phases* of each complaint processing case should be identified (for instance, internal transfers, case examination, intermediate reply, decision, final answer). Then, upon evaluating the available documents, it is important to determine which *organizational unit* has been active to what extent in the individual phases (for example, sales force, central customer service department, management). Moreover, the *length of time* spent by each organizational unit on each of the various activities must be recorded.

This view of the internal processes of complaint processing will be complemented by an analysis of the corresponding *customer processes of perceived complaint resolution.*

8.1.2.2 Analysis of the Complaint Processing Procedures from the Perspective of the Customer

This may occur by undertaking a *customer experience or contact point analysis* of the complaint processing procedure on the basis of representatively chosen complaint cases. In doing so, all customer contacts up to the final resolution of the problem are ascertained and visualized in a flowchart diagram, the intervals between the individual contact points are documented and interviews with complainants are carried out with respect to their experiences at the respective contact points.

In the context of the first process step, *contact point identification*, all the interactions must be documented: starting with the complaint articulation and continuing with the confirmation of receipt, intermediate reply and any follow-up inquiries by telephone or in writing, all the way until the final answer is provided.

A variation of the flowchart diagram representation, variously designated as *"Service Blueprinting"* (Shostack 1987) or *"Service Mapping"* (Kingman-Brundage 1992), provides a suitable instrument for the systematic visualization of the processing procedures as the customer experiences them. What is special about this technique is, on the one hand, the fact that the sequence of the experienced complaint case is documented from the perspective of the customer affected and, on the other hand, that it is made known via a *"line of complaint evidence"* which areas of the complaint management processes are visible to the customer ("onstage actions") and which take place "backstage" (see Fig. 8.1).

On the basis of this visualized customer process, former complainants can then be consulted with regard to their experiences at each contact point and about their assessment of the acceptability of the reaction time in the context of *contact-experience measurement*. In this way, important information is obtained with regard to a customer-oriented design of interactions, as well as the desired duration of the process.

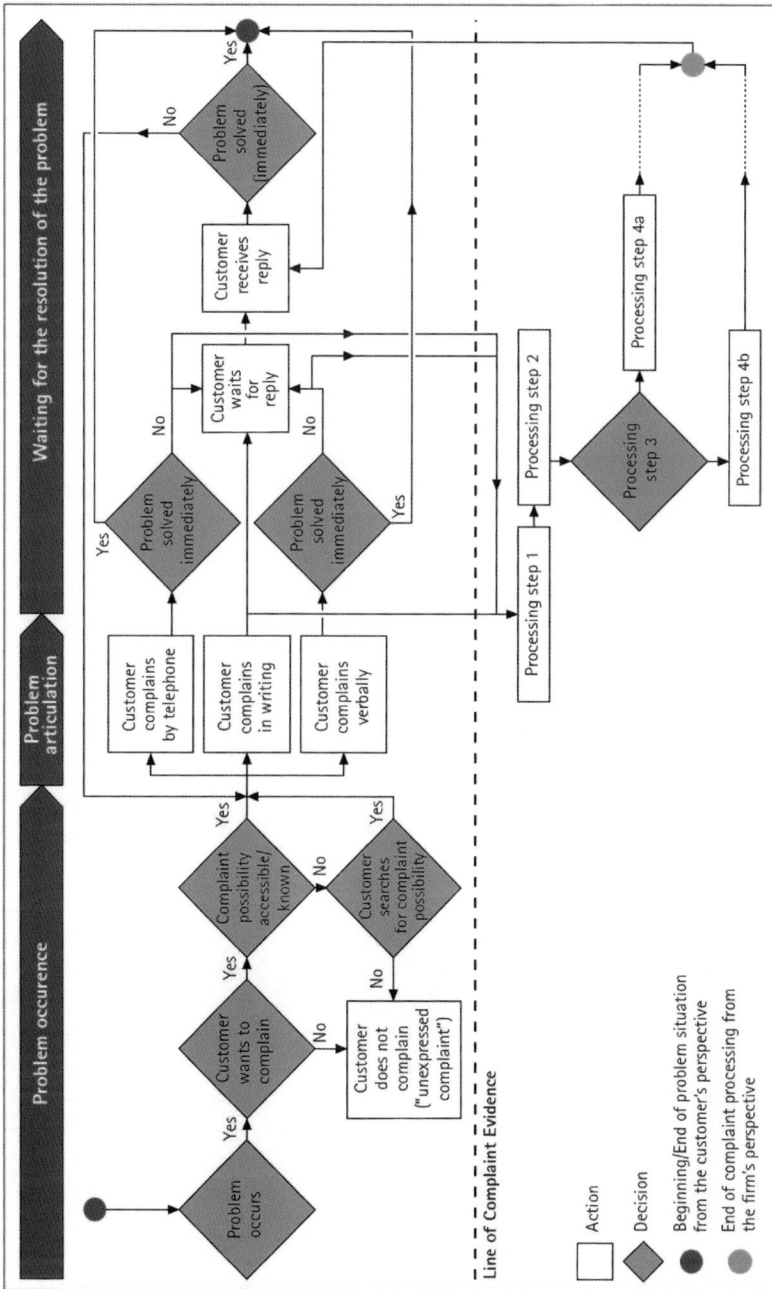

Fig. 8.1 Customer process of perceived complaint handling

The results of the contact-point analysis form the *starting point for the new conceptualization of the complaint processing procedures* from the perspective of the firm.

8.1.3 Specification and Visualization of Complaint Processing Procedures

The first level of specification in the complaint processing procedures is reached when the procedures are assigned to general classes of *participating organizational units* (independent, cooperative or transfer process) or to *levels of urgency* (routine or non-routine procedures).

Following this assignment of the procedures, the next level of specification consists of defining the *basic activities,* the *corresponding responsibilities* and the *processing times*. This involves processing steps such as "Prepare Confirmation of Receipt/Intermediate Reply" or "Forward for Comment" or decision nodes like "Resolution within X Hours Possible?" or "Comment Arrived?", upon which the different processing methods and their corresponding activities are dependent.

This process specification also includes the identification of *interfaces* at which the output of one organizational unit represents the input of another organizational unit at the same time. This determination should take place as much as possible in interdepartmental teams, whose members represent the participating business units. In this way, a consensus can be reached on a process sequence that is efficient and transparent and that takes into consideration the perspectives of those affected by that process.

In order to ensure a quick overview of the processing procedures, it is recommended that the processes be visualized in a *flowchart*. The phases of a process with the appropriate inputs and outputs, as well as the interfaces, can be immediately identified. In addition, one can recognize whether the subsequent activities can be dealt with simultaneously—process phases therefore run parallel to one another—or which phases are dependent upon preceding subprocesses and process steps. In this way, it is also possible to uncover sources of potential errors and to determine corresponding control points in the process. Furthermore, responsibilities as well as scheduled dates for individual processing steps can be determined and visualized.

Normally, it is necessary to depict special and detailed processes for complaints that reach the firm via different complaint channels, e.g., in person, over the telephone, in writing or electronically. Figure 8.2 shows an example of the processing procedure for a team that responds to complaints articulated by letter. In order to achieve a complete solution, it may be necessary to contact another organizational unit to clarify the facts and ask for specialized information. Upon receipt of the reply, the responsible member of the complaint team ("complaint owner") closes the complaint case in contact with the customer. For each individual process phase or activity, the departments involved must agree on time standards as well as on internal reminder and escalation systems that are triggered if the deadlines are exceeded.

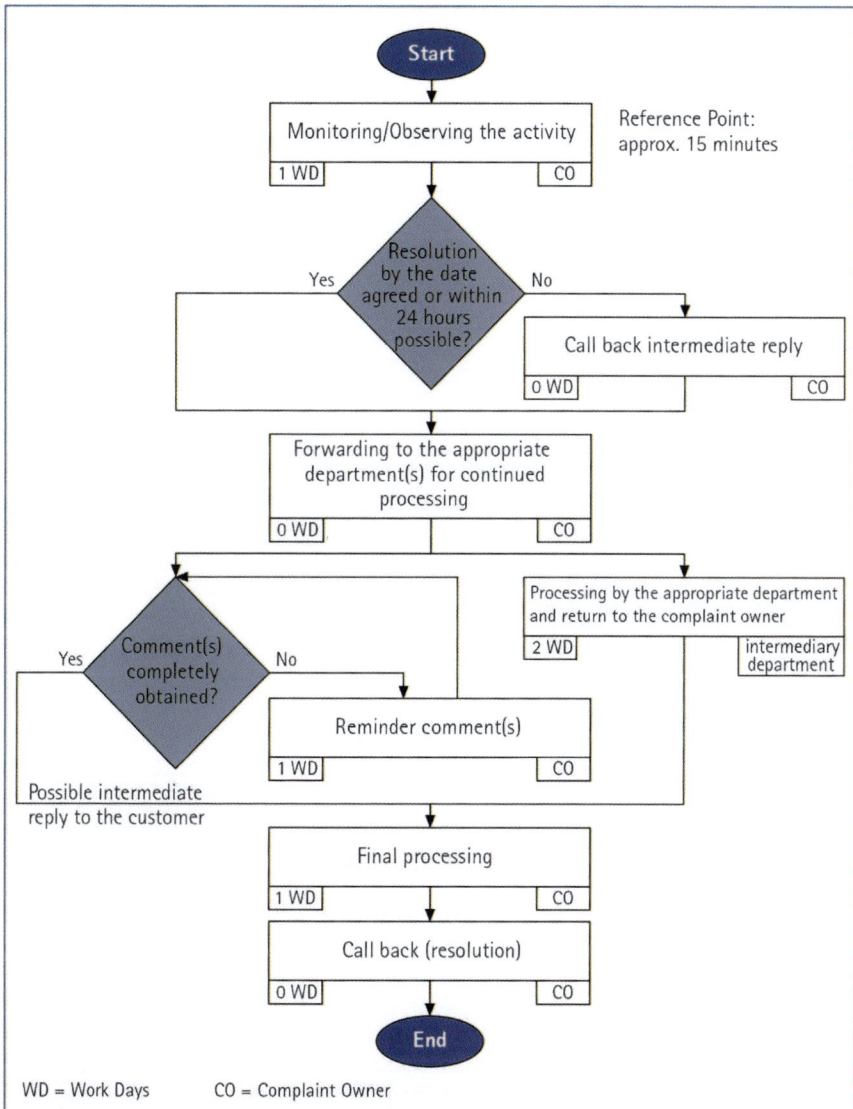

Fig. 8.2 Example of a complaint-processing procedure for written complaints

In the concrete planning of the complaint processes, the question arises of what level of detail should be chosen. This question cannot be answered in general, but only after consideration of various factors:

1. An important role is played by the *relevance of individual activities*. The more critical these are for the compliance with objective or subjective quality standards, the greater the importance of determining and describing them in detail.

2. It must be taken into account whether *personnel stability* in the handling of complaints can be ensured or whether new employees are repeatedly employed at short notice. If the latter is the case, detailed process documentation is required to facilitate the initial training.

3. The *perspective of the organizational unit* is another relevant factor. For example, the central customer care department of a large chain store, which acts as the main addressee for customer complaints, will be interested in determining those phases of the complaint handling process that it is responsible for finalizing. If, however, appropriate handling of the case requires a statement of a branch, it would appear sufficient from its point of view if this were documented by a sub-process 'processing by branch A'. It is only important for the central department that it receives the processing result of the branch in compliance with the defined time and quality requirements. From the branch's perspective, however, it is useful to break down the sub-process 'processing by branch A' into further process phases and to determine responsibilities and specific deadlines for each of them. For the branches it is of secondary relevance what measures the customer care center at the headquarter takes before or afterwards. All that is important for them is that the expectations of the customer care center are clearly communicated and that it receives a summary of the final result.

8.1.4 On the Standard Character of Complaint Processing Procedures

All defined processes represent standard processes insofar as a process sequence that takes place according to a *repeatable schema* can be determined for each type of case that may arise. This also applies to non-routine procedures, since they require that a specific processing path be taken—for example, a designated person must be informed, who is then responsible for the processing and case solution.

The term "Standard" thus refers to the *basic processing steps* but does not, however, imply that direct dealings with the customer exhibit a standard character. Each employee that participates in the processing of a customer complaint remains committed to putting the customers' individual concern at the center of the processing and using the available latitude to individualize the design of the process.

The sequences determined to be standard processes *do not represent rigid schemata* with instructions for handling that must be compulsively followed. Depending on the entire complaint history and the individuality of the problem, follow-up inquiries, comments or the inclusion of other departments may be necessary—which represents a deviation from the pattern of processing that was previously determined. If it turns out during processing that different causes are responsible for the problem than were originally supposed, for instance, other departments must be included in the processing of the case. It is also appropriate to inform the customers as to the change in circumstances, as when the deadlines or solutions promised to them cannot be kept. A similar situation exists when nonstandard activities become necessary due to follow-up inquiries on the part of the customer. Consequently, the dissatisfied customers and the elimination of their problem, not the strict observance of defined processes, must always remain in the forefront.

It is advisable, however, to observe the *deviations from standard processes* in a systematic manner, whether they arise by chance or follow a certain pattern. Such information may then form the basis for considerations of how the complaint processing procedures can be optimized from cost and time standpoints, as well as from the perspective of the customers and of the firm.

8.2 Responsibilities During Complaint Processing

From the standpoint of customer-oriented complaint processing, three *relevant responsibilities* result from the structure of the direct complaint management process (see Fig. 8.3):

- On the overall management process level: the *process owner.*
- On the individual case processing level: the *complaint owner.*
- On the level of the individual phases of complaint processing: the *task owner.*

8.2.1 The Process Owner

Complaints are frequently articulated to different persons or departments in the firm. Consequently, *employees from different departments* must be trained to deal with dissatisfied customers and must be informed as to whom the complaint should be forwarded. In many cases, one organizational unit—for example, the customer service department—cannot manage the processing of a complaint by itself. It is

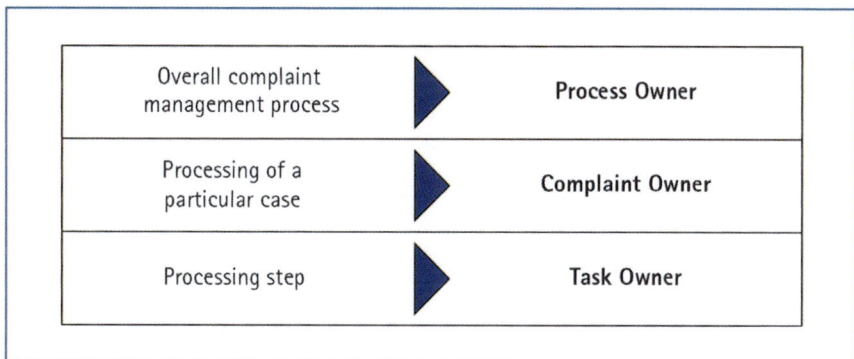

Fig. 8.3 Overview of the different responsibility levels during complaint handling

often necessary to include other departments or sales units in order to reach a targeted solution to the problem. In addition, interdepartmental management tasks arise from the dissemination and use of complaint analysis and controlling information.

The position within the firm that has the *inclusive responsibility and accountability for the procedures* that arise as part of complaint management, or the person that assumes this position, is designated as the *process owner*. This process owner directs and coordinates all the complaint-management task areas—across task-area and departmental boundaries. In firms that have a central "Complaint Management" or "Customer Care" department, the function of the process owner usually falls to the decision-maker responsible for this area.

8.2.2   The Complaint Owner

As has been previously described in connection with the complaint-acceptance procedure, the person who is first to be informed by a customer about a problem is responsible for recognizing, documenting and processing the problem as a complaint. This person has ownership of the complaint and is thus designated as the *complaint owner*.

It is principally the task of the complaint owners *to solve the problem immediately* if it lies within their area of competence. Should their competence be exceeded, but an immediate resolution is possible in principle, they have to inform the responsible party, introduce troubleshooting procedures and make certain that an arrangement desired by the customer takes place. Consequently, the complaint ownership in this case ends with the resolution of the problem.

In the case of complaints with problems that make the inclusion of other persons or departments necessary, the respective complaint owners are responsible for the smooth and timely *coordination and handling of the processing procedure*. As regards the customer, they must make sure that promises are kept or deviations from agreed-upon arrangements are communicated and elucidated without delay. As regards the line areas participating in the process, they perform a coordinating function and see to it that the measures that have been agreed on are observed properly and within the time limits. In addition, they also have the function of the "Team Leader" within the team of employees participating in the process and as such initiate common efforts toward continuous improvements in efficiency and effectiveness. In their relationship to the process owner, the tasks of the complaint owners consist of monitoring the outcomes of the processing procedures and presenting the results, as well as suggestions for improving the process.

In complaint cases that must be turned over to other units within the organization for processing and final replies, the question of *whether complaint ownership is also given up* may be asked. The situation can be regulated in this manner, but this solution cannot be recommended for all cases. If, for instance, bank customers complain to their account executive at the local branch, they do so because they expect that their addressee will assume responsibility for their case. In complaint cases in which the addressees turn the processing over to the central customer service department due to a lack of decision-making authority, they should remain informed as to how things are progressing, especially about the solution offered to the customer, and should maintain contact with the customer. At the same time, a complaint owner in the central complaint management department is then responsible on this organizational level for seeing to it that the procedures of complaint processing are carried out according to available principles and serves as the contact person for the complaint owner at the branch level.

8.2.3   The Task Owner

In addition to the structures of responsibility for the complete complaint-management process (process owner) and the respective individual case processing (complaint owner), the responsibilities for the *individual steps in the course of complaint processing* must likewise be determined.

Employees who are *occupied with carrying out the individual tasks* during the complaint processing (examination of the case, preparation of intermediate replies, etc.) are *task owners*. A corresponding task profile exists with specific case-handling instructions, time limits and clearly regulated competencies. The task owners must be informed as to which input the preliminary process step will provide them, what added value they contribute to the solution of the problem and which output is expected of them. At the same time, the determination of the task extent and authority will also regulate which problems necessitate that they get in touch with the complaint owner or when they can introduce measures independently. Task owners are also expected to take the initiative. Although they have only a limited decision area, they must feel fully responsible for the complainant and find the best possible solution to achieve complainant satisfaction.

8.3   Determination of Processing Deadlines

Empirical studies confirm that the speed with which firms react to a complaint *significantly* influences the satisfaction of the customer (Boshoff 1997; McDougall and Levesque 1999; Swanson and Kelley 2001; Liao 2007; Varela-Neira et al. 2010). If complainants have to wait a long time for a response from the company, they will become convinced that the firm does not care about its dissatisfied customers and does not treat them fairly. The dissatisfaction of the already dissatisfied customers increases significantly and a high percentage of them will intend to switch to a competitor in the future. The findings of the study of Wirtz and Mattila (2004) even suggest that an immediate reaction (and an apology) is the best complaint management strategy. It is likely to satisfy the customer and at the same time be cost-effective, as compensation is often not necessary in this case.

Customers' expectations of a fast response are high, and are rising with the increasing use of electronic media. However, many companies do not seem to meet these expectations. For example, the results of the German nationwide customer satisfaction survey reveal clear *deficits in the speed of complaint handling*: in seven of the 13 industries investigated, more than 40% of the complainants were disappointed by the speed with which the company reacted (Servicebarometer 2017).

These empirical results prove that active complaint management also means *deadline management*. Firms that take customer problems seriously must take care *to react to complaints immediately*, in that direct contact with the dissatisfied customer is sought—even if the problem itself cannot be resolved immediately. It is also important to ensure that the processing of the complaint takes place quickly and within a previously fixed time frame, and that contact with the customer is re-established, especially *in the case that deadlines are exceeded*. It is assumed, of course, that clear deadlines exist for all identified complaint processing procedures, as well as for their subprocesses and processing steps.

In order to schedule the deadlines, *two types of time indicators* must be determined and related to one another: (1) *Processing times that affect external customers* and thus exert a decisive influence on their complaint satisfaction. They apply to the entire time span from the complaint articulation to the final reply. Also included under this type of time indicator are time limits, by which time a confirmation of receipt or intermediate reply in the case of longer processing times must be sent to the customer. (2) *Processing times for individual process phases* as targets for the task owner.

The external, customer-oriented time targets depend to a great extent on the internal processing times. Therefore, *every scheduling* has to use them as a starting point. For the individual processing procedures, the entire processing time must be defined as the period of time from the receipt of the complaint in the firm up until the resolution of the problem. Then the amount of time must be calculated and assessed for the individual process phases ranging from handling times and idle times before and after processing up to internal transfer times associated with the handover of the complaint incident from one processing unit to another, respectively (see Fig. 8.4).

On the basis of this time analysis, the process owner and the complaint owner can engage in joint considerations about the reduction of ineffective time components and establish phase-related periods as *internal time standards*. In doing so, *various factors* must be taken into consideration: Besides the extent and complexity of the

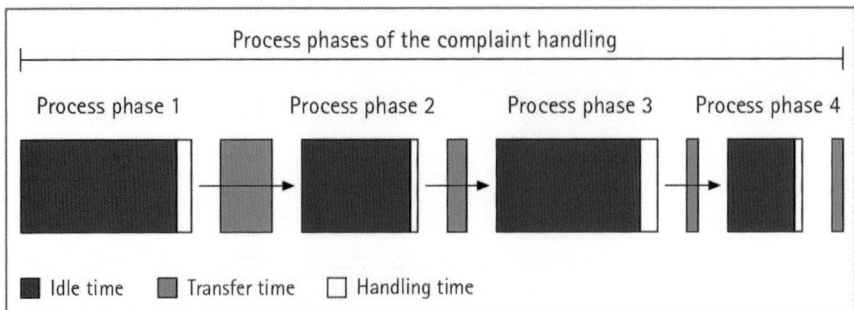

Fig. 8.4 Detailed analysis of the processing time

work to be carried out, these factors include the personnel and technological resources available, as well as the complaint volume and the expectations of the complainants regarding the firm's reaction speed. In any event, it depends on the fixing of time standards that represent *feasible targets* for employees and departments participating in the processing. If unrealistic processing times are set down, exactly the opposite of what should be achieved with time scheduling will occur. Delays in meeting deadlines that lie outside the immediate sphere of influence of the task owner become the rule. The standards set are not taken seriously. The employees become unmotivated. Furthermore, customers are promised unreliable deadlines, which contributes to an increase in their dissatisfaction.

When the planned processing times for all process steps have been defined from the internal perspective of the firm, the *customer-related time targets* for progress reports and final answers can be determined.

Another step is reached when time targets such as these are communicated to the customer as an *universal standard and promise of performance*, as for example: "We'll solve your problems within five days!". The indispensable prerequisite for an official publication of standards like these is the fact that they have proved their worth over a long period of time. If this is not the case and the standards are missed to a considerable extent, the firm can count on a massive increase in customer dissatisfaction and corresponding internal problems and de-motivation.

In determining internal standards as well as external temporal performance promises, it must be taken into account that usually *different measurement categories* are applied. The internal time targets are commonly given in *workdays*, while the customers base their understanding on *calendar days* when they are given temporal performance promises. For this reason, the internal targets that are calculated must be adjusted for external communication to consider non-work times (weekends, holidays).

8.4 Installation of Mechanisms for the Monitoring of Complaint Processing

Since the reaction speed and the observance of promised deadlines substantially influence the complaint satisfaction of the customer, the firm must install systems that ensure the *on-time processing of complaint cases* according to the standards that have been set and call attention to time delays that represent deviations from those standards: an employee-oriented reminder system and—coupled with it—an escalation system that may span several hierarchical levels.

8.4.1 The Employee-Oriented Reminder System

If the deadlines that have been set are *exceeded* during the course of processing a complaint, the respective task owner must be made aware of this fact and reminded of it. *Manual administration* of internal reminders hardly seems possible when the complaint volume is high, since the complaint owner cannot have a complete overview of the status of all the complaint cases and the respective deadlines that have been scheduled. The utilization of a software-supported complaint management system, in which the time standards are clearly set down and which allows for *automatic reminders*, thus proves to be nearly indispensable.

If the time delay can be attributed to their *own inattentiveness*, the reminded employees must then process the case immediately, or "preferentially". Reasons for exceeding the processing deadline may, however, also lie *outside the complaint owner's sphere of influence*. This is the case, for example, when a specific product defect leads to an unexpectedly large increase in complaint volume and causes the complaint capacity to be exceeded. The same applies if internal resources are temporarily are not fully available, for example due to a high level of sick leave or staff turnover. When such a development arises, the task owner should inform the complaint owner early, so that a remedy can be found via short-term corrective measures.

If, in the course of complaint analysis, it is discovered that *processing deadlines have been exceeded numerous times* by certain task owners or with respect to specific problem areas, the delays must be systematically analyzed as to their causes and appropriate measures must be devised, either in order to adjust the standards or to change the procedures so that the standards can be observed in the future.

8.4.2 The Hierarchy-Spanning Escalation System

In the case of a reminder system, the employees themselves are informed of the delays in their processing of complaints. In the context of an escalation system, however, the complaint cases for which the processing deadline has been exceeded are transferred to *higher levels in the hierarchy* at set time intervals.

Three main goals are associated with the establishment of this type of escalation system:

- Direct pressure is exerted on the *task owner* and the *complaint owner* to keep the performance promises that have been made to customers in terms of content and deadlines. For those affected, it is embarrassing to have to answer repeatedly to the next position up as to why the processing deadlines have been exceeded for no good reason. The escalation process thus serves as an internal medium for more discipline in complaint processing.
- Numerous messages regarding non-compliance with deadlines in the context of complaint processing force *process owners* to deal with the structural causes of process deficiencies and to develop appropriate corrective measures.
- *Managers at higher levels* of the hierarchy are immediately signaled through the escalation about the danger that existing customer dissatisfaction is substantially increasing. Immediate superiors can intervene, provide an accelerated processing of the case and check whether the customer has already been informed as to the delay and its causes. If executives are involved, they are personally confronted

with customers' problems and must take up the task of dealing with questions as to the proper handling of dissatisfied customers and the relevance of complaint management. This can lead to a greater sensitivity to customer problems and promote the willingness to accord complaint management the attention and support it requires.

In order to determine the specific design of the escalation process, the *number of reminder days* must first be generally determined, after which time the complaint case escalates. At the same time, it must also be determined: (1) the number of levels of escalation, (2) the persons responsible at each of those levels and (3) the number of days allowed before a complaint case is turned over to the next level of escalation. The practical execution of the escalation system presupposes the utilization of a software-supported complaint management system in the case of substantial complaint volume.

8.5   Design of the Internal Communication Between the Processing Units

Firms that practice active complaint management must determine to *which information* the processing units should refer, *which paths* the communication should take place and the timeframe within which the responsible units should respond. This responsibility lies with the process owner. He/she must also make these communication processes known within the firm in order to ensure smooth processing of complaints.

With respect to the *information required*, the specific data that are recorded for each individual case must be available at each step in the processing procedure to the extent required. In addition, the processors must receive information about the results of each preliminary step in the processing procedure. If new insights arise during the course of the complaint processing regarding the cause of the problem, for instance, or if the customer submits new documentation belatedly, the proper procedure for the forwarding of this information to the appropriate stations must be regulated.

The communication between the units can occur in writing, by telephone, in person or by e-mail. Principal consideration should be given to those *communication media* that ensure a rapid transmittal of information and minimize idle or transfer times. This is the case primarily with electronic mail systems, especially when they are integrated into a software-supported system of complaint management that directly assigns the mail messages to the appropriate case. If it is not possible to fall back on systems like these, contact in person or by telephone, as well as faxes, represent suitable media.

Independent of which media are used, all processing steps must be thoroughly documented, along with their results, and made accessible to the associates. This is quite possible in the context of a software-supported system of complaint management because the processing activities are entered into the system and the database is available to all those participating in the process.

If, in the course of complaint evaluation, it becomes apparent that certain task owners or specific problem areas have increasingly exceeded processing deadlines, the causes of the delays must be systematically examined. On the basis of this analysis, appropriate measures must be developed in order either to adapt the time standards or change the processes in such a way that the standards can be met in the future.

8.6   Documentation of Complaint Processing

8.6.1   Complaint Processing History

In order to maintain the transparency of the measures that have been implemented and carried out for the employees as well as for the complainants and to ensure target-oriented communication with the customer, the individual processing steps must be documented in the context of the *complaint processing history*, along with their results, for each individual complaint case. If all the associates who deal with customer complaints can refer to these histories, they are in a position to provide the customer or internal conversation counterparts with information as to the status of the processing. In this way, clarity is brought about and errors are avoided, such as would be the case if the customers perhaps received different information from different people about the status of their concern.

The following *information* in particular must be chronologically *documented*:

- *date/time*, on which the processing activity *should be completed* pursuant to the time standards defined
- *date/time*, on which the processing activity *is* actually *completed* pursuant to the time standards defined
- *going over/under* the time targets
- the *responsible employee* (task owner)
- the respective *processing result* (e.g., intermediate reply sent or result of a judicial assessment of the case)
- *processing status* of the activity (not yet in process, in process, completed)
- *type of reaction* to the complaint as well as the *individual case resolution.*

By disposing of the individual activities in accordance with the sequence defined in the processing procedures and recording the information and the processing status in each case, a complaint-processing history is *individually generated* for each particular case, as is clearly depicted in Table 8.1.

Table 8.1 Example of a complaint processing history

No.	Activity	Processing result	Responsible employee (Task Owner)	Planned deadline	Deadline for settlement	Remaining duration/exceeding/undershooting	Processing status
01	Distribution to the complaint team	Distribution of the complaint case to the complaint team	D. Walsh	01/10	01/10	0	done
02	Distribution to the responsible employee (Complaint Owner)	Assignment of the complaint case to K. Flynn	J. Bernstein	01/10	01/10	0	done
03	Distribution of a receipt confirmation	Form letter „A" + text module „B"	K. Flynn	01/11	01/11	0	done
04	Obtaining of a complaint from department A	E-mail-sample „M"	K. Flynn	01/14	01/16	-2	done
05	Reminder of the opinion from department A	E-mail-sample „O"	K. Flynn	01/15	01/15	0	done
06	Creation and forwarding of the final responses to the customer		K. Flynn	01/16			in process

8.6.2   Customer-Contact and Complaint History

Customers who make a complaint are, as a rule, actively doing business with the firm. A business relationship such as this is characterized by the purchase of products and services, the accompanying revenue and any complaints that lie in the past, as well as by other customer issues such as praise or requests. Furthermore, the firm actively approaches customers in the context of its direct marketing activities with special offers or surveys.

Table 8.2 Example of a customer-contact history

No.	Date	Customer concern/action	Responsible	Content/result	Concluded
01	10/31	Complaint	A. Jackson	Wrong booking	12/02
02	12/01	Information	Z. Bayles	Deposit administration	12/07
03	12/15	Brochure order	Z. Zeppelin	Brochure B	12/16
04	01/08	Cross Selling of product A	E. Thompson	No interest	01/27
05	02/13	Shipment of the Club-Magazine	D. Scott	Club-Magazine issue No. 1	02/13
06	03/31	This years vacation campaign	E. Thompson	Package A offered/portfolio opened	04/28

All these contacts between customers and firms denote the so-called *customer contact history*. Included in this history are all the contacts initiated by the customer, as well as all the actions initiated by the firm. *Customer contact* means any request or activity on the part of the customer, *not the individual contact* that is necessary for the handling of the requests and activities. In the case of complaints, the processing steps recorded in the context of the complaint processing history constitute the individual contacts, and the complaint itself represents the customer contact. For purposes of transparency in the individual business relationship, an overview of all customer contacts—issues and initiatives—as well as an overview of the individual activities in each case per customer contact in the form of a processing or settlement history should be provided—in the case of a complaint, this is the complaint-processing history. Table 8.2 shows an example of a customer-contact history.

If a customer has complained numerous times in the course of the business relationship, several customer-oriented complaint processes are available. The customer-individual, chronological preparation of these processes documents the *complaint-related experience of the customer* and reflects the *complaint history* as an excerpt of the entire customer-contact history.

Chapter 8 in Brief
- Depending on the extent of responsibility for the operative complaint processing, three basic types can be distinguished: independent processes, cooperative processes and transfer processes. A second classification according to the criterion of reaction urgency distinguishes between routine and non-routine processes.

(continued)

- The analysis of the current procedures of complaint processing must be performed from the company's perspective as well as from the customers' perspective to achieve both efficiency and complaint satisfaction among customers.
- Three relevant responsibilities for the complaint processing must be defined: the process owner for the entire management process, the complaint owner for the individual case processing and the task owner for individual phases of complaint processing.
- It is necessary to determine clear deadlines for all identified complaint processing procedures, as well as for their sub-processes and processing steps.
- The compliance with the deadlines must be reviewed with the aid of an employee-oriented reminder system and an associated escalation system that may span several hierarchical levels.
- With regard to cross-departmental processes, it is important to determine which information is to be provided between which units involved, on which paths and within what temporal service levels.
- The individual processing steps must be documented in the complaint-processing history as well as in the customer-contact and complaint history.

References

Boshoff C (1997) An experimental study of service recovery options. Int J Serv Ind Manag 8 (2):110–130

Kingman-Brundage J (1992) The ABC's of service system blueprinting. In: Lovelock C (ed) Managing services: marketing, operations, and human resources, 2nd edn. Prentice-Hall International, London, pp 96–102

Liao H (2007) Do it right this time: the role of employee service recovery performance in customer-perceived justice and customer loyalty after service failures. J Appl Psychol 92(2):475–489

McDougall GHG, Levesque TJ (1999) Waiting for service: the effectiveness of recovery strategies. Int J Contemp Hosp Manag 11(1):6–15

Servicebarometer (2017) Kundenmonitor Deutschland 2017. Servicebarometer, München

Shostack GL (1987) Service positioning through structural change. J Mark 51(1):34–43

Swanson SR, Kelley SW (2001) Service recovery attributions and word-of-mouth intentions. Eur J Mark 35(1/2):194–211

Varela-Neira C et al (2010) The effects of customer age and recovery strategies in a service failure setting. J Financ Serv Mark 15(1):32–48

Wirtz J, Mattila AS (2004) Consumer responses to compensation, speed of recovery and apology after a service failure. Int J Serv Ind Manag 15(2):150–166

Complaint Reaction

© Springer Nature Switzerland AG 2019

B. Stauss, W. Seidel, *Effective Complaint Management*, Management for Professionals,
https://doi.org/10.1007/978-3-319-98705-7_9

Issues Raised

- What rules of conduct must be observed in verbal, telephone and written contact situations with complainants?
- What must be considered when dealing with specific types of complainants such as repeat and multiple complainants as well as grumblers and grousers?
- How should special types of complaints (scattered complaints, complaints to top management, complaints about employees, threats) be dealt with?
- What are the basic solution options and what factors determine the choice of the appropriate reaction form for each case?
- Under what circumstances should the company forego an extensive investigation of the individual case?
- How should the company react in the case of 'unjustified' complaints?
- Should a complaint response be differentiated according to the customer value?
- What forms of communication are necessary in the context of complaint reaction?
- How should the communication be designed in temporal terms?
- How can the quality of complaint reaction be checked?

The term "Complaint Reaction" encompasses all the complaint management activities that the customer *perceives during the complaint handling process* and that thus have a direct effect on his/her complaint satisfaction. Among these activities are the immediate handling of complainants, the realized solution to the problem and all the communication with the customer during the processing of the complaint. All these aspects will be addressed in this chapter. In addition, it will be shown to what extent a differentiation of the complaint reaction that is based on the customer's value can prove useful and how the interaction with the complainant can be documented in the complaint history.

9.1   Basic Rules of Behavior for Handling Complainants

Many customers can completely sympathize with the fact that mistakes and errors can occur. This understanding very quickly changes to non-understanding and indignation, however, when firm employees show no willingness to eliminate the problem or make up for the damage. Customers are still turned away, put off, transferred or even suspected of wanting to cheat the firm. Typical statements by employees include the following: "I can't do anything about that, either!"; "I'm not responsible for that!"; "My colleague does that!"; "You must have used the product incorrectly!"; "Are you sure you purchased that from us?". Reactions like these are a sure way to drive away the customer for good.

In order to avoid this danger and ensure appropriate *behavior on the part of employees* during communication with the complainant, *fundamental rules of behavior* are required, both for the direct conversation and for the answering of written complaints.

9.1.1   Rules of Behavior for the Direct Conversation with Complainants

Situations involving a direct confrontation with complainants in person or on the telephone represent a great challenge for employees. Complainants frequently react emotionally and indignantly, exaggerate and confront the employees with personal reproaches. Under these conditions, it is difficult to control one's own emotions, have a reassuring effect and work out a constructive solution with the customer. Comprehensive explanation of the correct behavior and systematic training are thus required. For this, the following rules of behavior, which relate to five typical phases of a complaint conversation, can be used as a guideline (Haeske 2001; Dealing With Angry Customers 2016).

9.1.1.1 Greeting Phase

In the greeting phase, it is decided whether a destructive argument or a constructive conversation will develop. When employees receive a *complaint by phone*, their voice should sound friendly and open to signal their willingness to talk and make it difficult for the irritated customer to act rudely.

If employees receive *customer complaints in person*, they also must approach the customer in an open and friendly manner. The employee should maintain eye contact and focus his attention on the customer. It is especially important that the conversation be conducted in a calm environment if the problem is a difficult one. By retiring to appropriate premises and offering the customer a seat, the customer receives the message that the employee wants to take time for the problem and takes the complaint seriously. This shifting of the complaint dialog to a separate conversational area would seem to be especially necessary if extremely irritated customers attempt to use this opportunity to achieve effects with the other customers who are present by their behavior, by raising their voices as well as making certain statements.

9.1.1.2 Aggression-Reduction Phase

After the greeting, the customers should be given the opportunity to depict the incident from their point of view and to explain all reasons why they are angry. The employees must express their care and attentiveness through their facial expressions, eye contact and body language. What is important verbally is to express regret to the customer for the unpleasantness that has arisen or *to apologize officially*. This gesture is often difficult for employees, especially when they see the incident differently or have not caused the problem. Nevertheless, such an expression of regret or apology is necessary because it is perceived as the instrument through which understanding of the customer's annoyance is expressed and because it represents a key requirement for building a personal relationship with the customer that will be important as the conversation progresses.

In the aggression-reduction phase, what is of primary importance is to allow the complainants to have a chance to speak. They must be given the chance *to let off steam*. It is possible that an error caused by the firm has put them in a very uncomfortable situation, and strong resentment has been building up. Outbursts of anger during complaints lead to feelings of relief. Only when the customers have had the opportunity to express this irritation will it be possible to bring the conversation down to a factual level and to have a constructive discussion about possible solutions. Accordingly, the employees must first allow the customers *to have their say*—without interrupting them—and must *listen attentively* in order to be able to record the specific circumstances of the problem correctly. While they are doing so, they should make notes. The fact that the personal conversation is being recorded in writing pushes the customers to describe the incident more carefully and realistically. In the case of telephone conversations, short affirmative remarks should be made to demonstrate to the customers that they are being listened to attentively and that the problem has in fact been understood.

The *most common error* that is made in this phase consists of *interrupting the customers*, be it with counterclaims and instructions, or be it with hypotheses on the possible causes of the problem or hasty offers of solutions or compensation. The employee may be subjectively completely in the right, but in this phase, interruptions like these prevent reduction of the aggression and development of a constructive conversation. Instead, they cause the customers to react even more angrily, and the situation to escalate.

In this part of the complaint conversation, a situation may arise in which extremely annoyed customers *personally insult the employee*. Verbal attacks such as these are not to be taken personally, and certainly not to be answered in like fashion. It is, rather, necessary to maintain an inner distance from the criticism and react calmly to accusations of guilt, exaggerations and insults. This does not mean that all attacks have to be taken completely. Especially rude insults should be calmly rejected in the subsequent phases of the conversation.

9.1.1.3 Conflict-Settlement Phase

After the customer has been given the opportunity to express his annoyance and present the problem situation from his subjective point of view, it is then important to bring the conversation to a *factual level*. In order to do this, it is necessary to clarify the facts precisely by asking a series of specific questions. It is vital that all circumstances that are meaningful from the customer's point of view and for further processing are thoroughly addressed.

This factual dialog contributes to conflict reduction in the conversation. This applies especially when understanding of the customer's individual situation and for the extent of the irritation is expressed in a believable manner and with *empathy*. Even while showing sensitiveness toward the customer, however, the employees should avoid further admissions of guilt or assignments of guilt to other employees or departments in the firm.

9.1.1.4 Problem-Solution Phase

If the conversation can be successfully continued on a factual level and the situation explained clearly during the conflict-adjustment phase, the basis for talking about a *suitable problem solution* with the customer has been established. Demands articulated by the customer during the first phases may be seen in a different light and modified after the facts have been clarified. Solutions offered by the employees are now perceived as logical conclusions of the factual analysis and thus have a much greater chance of being accepted than would have been the case at the beginning of the conversation.

If the customers' expectations cannot be fulfilled or cannot be filled to the desired degree, it is the task of the employee to give the customer a *detailed justification*. The type and extent of this justification play a decisive role in arousing understanding of the firm's position in the customers and possibly causing them to hold onto the business relationship despite unfulfilled expectations.

Many times a suitable solution cannot be reached in the first conversation, since the causes and possible solutions must be investigated. Here it is advisable to offer the customer a *callback* or an *additional conversation*, making an exact promise as to the time of the call or conversation. It is imperative that the appointment given be kept. If this is not possible, despite every effort being made, the complainant is to be informed in a timely manner as to the reason.

As a matter of principle, the postponement of the immediate problem solution is not the best solution, neither for the customer nor for the firm, as other time- and cost-intensive steps must then be undertaken. If, however, such a postponement cannot be avoided, it at least has the positive effect that the search for a problem solution is *less stressful* than it would have been had it taken place in the presence of the customer, who leaves the provider with the feeling that someone is taking care of his problem now.

9.1.1.5 Conclusive Phase

In the conclusive phase of the conversation, the suggested solution is again repeated, and it must be ensured that the customer *has understood* it as well as *accepted* it. If the customer agrees with the stipulated approach or with the problem solution offered, the *farewell* to the customer takes place. The conversation should be ended with a positive verbalization, in which the employees express their satisfaction with the fact that they were able to solve the problem in accordance with the customer's wishes or to initiate the solution process.

Table 9.1 summarizes the *recommended activities for the direct conversation with complainants* in the form of a checklist.

Table 9.1 Checklist for dealing with dissatisfied customers [based on Brymer (1991) and Dealing with Angry Customers (2016)]

1. Understand complains as a **normal part of your job** and as a chance to reduce customer dissatisfaction and to ensure customer retention.
2. Look for a **quiet location** for the complaint conversation. Do not let other customers listen to the conversation. Offer the customer a seat. Address the customer by name.
3. Signal **willingness to talk** ("Let us talk about this calmly"). Use your gestures, eye contact and body language to convey that you are paying close attention.
4. Offer an **apology** or at least **regret** that the customer has had a bad experience. Use the **first person form** when formulating your responses. ("I am really sorry that you had this inconvenience" or "I apologize for the trouble caused").
5. **Listen carefully**. Do not interrupt the complainant. Let her/him speak first **without interruption** even though she/he may bring up unfounded statements.
6. Conduct the conversation in a **calm and courteous** manner. Respond even calmly to exaggerations and personal accusations. Don't take these personally.
7. **Do not argue** with the customer and do not engage in a power struggle. An argument with the customer is always won by the customer.
8. If the customer uses abusive language, make clear that this is not acceptable. Speak in a normal tone and bring the emotional conversation back to the **factual level**.
9. **Ask Questions** regarding the contents to focus the customer's mind on the facts and to clarify the situation completely. Pose questions in a courteous manner ("Thanks for the hint. One more thing I would like to know is...")
10. **Take notes.** The activity of writing down what she/he says demonstrates to the customer that you are taking the complaint seriously and encourages her/him to explain the circumstances more accurately. Furthermore, the notes are valuable in complaint handling and analysis.
11. **Avoid immediate diagnoses** and listen to all the information without confessing that you were at fault.
12. **Put yourself in the customer's place** ("I can easily imagine that you are annoyed"). Use positive statements whenever possible. Avoid wordings which increase the level of annoyance ("You've got that totally wrong!" or "But this is your fault!")
13. If a mistake actually happened, **do not blame** a colleague, other departments or the firm in general ("That happens all the time" or "They never get it right").
14. Initiate the handling of the complaint immediately. Offer a **fair solution.**
15. Ask if the customer **agrees** with the settlement.
16. If a prompt solution is not possible, promise the customer that the case will be **thoroughly reviewed** and indicate how long it will take before she/he receives a notice. Observe this deadline no matter what. If this is despite your best effords not possible, inform the complainant in a timely manner and explain the reasons.
17. If you are not responsible or you cannot do anything, **forward the complaint** and see to it that the receipt and handling process is continued according to the customer's wishes.
18. **Thank the complainant** for bringing the issue to your attention and giving the chance to improve.
19. Conclude the conversation **positively** ("I'm pleased that we could satisfy you like this").
20. **Analyze the complaint** case and notify the responsible manager so that the source of the error can be quickly eliminated.

9.1.2 Rules of Behavior for Responding to Written Complaints

In the case of written complaints, the reaction situation looks different. The *lack of direct customer contact* means that less pressure exists in this situation than in a direct conversational situation with a complainant. Where the causes of complaints lie and which problem solutions are suitable can be clarified in peace internally. This is, however, made more difficult by the fact that immediate follow-up enquiries to the customer are not possible.

With regard to the *response to written complaints*, rules of behavior similar to those presented for complaints made by telephone and in person also apply here.

9.1.2.1 Initial Wording

Just as in a complaint conversation conducted on the telephone or in person, it is also important in the case of written complaints to choose an *open and friendly introduction*. Bureaucratic, unemotional, legal or cold wordings such as, "We confirm the receipt of your complaint and advise you as follows", should be avoided. Sentences like this generate an inner resistance in the customer and reduce the likelihood that he will accept the subsequent approach taken. Positive examples are presented in Table 9.2.

9.1.2.2 Problem Repetition

It is important to communicate clearly to the customers that their problems have been *understood correctly* and to the fullest extent possible. In the next section of the response letter, therefore, the problems that the customers described in their complaint letter should be summarized again. This problem repetition is the foundation of the subsequent sections of the letter in which the conflict settlement takes place and the problem solution is explained (see Table 9.3).

9.1.2.3 Conflict Settlement

In a written response, it must be candidly signaled to the customer that one can *put himself in the customer's place*. In this respect, the individual case should be

Table 9.2 Examples of initial wordings [based on Brückner (2007), Haeske (2010) and Respond to a Complaint (2017)]

- "Thank you for taking the time to notify us of your problem with our product. We totally understand your annoyance and strongly agree to you: this sort of thing really should not happen."

- "Each customer complaint helps us to become better. Therefore, thank you very much for your help. We take your concern very seriously and addressed the problem immediately."

- "Thank you for informing me that you had problems with our service. I certainly understand your frustration."

Table 9.3 Examples of problem repetition [based on Brückner (2007), Haeske (2010) and Respond to a Complaint (2017)]

- "You are upset about the failure of the device."
- "We just received your mail regarding a broken touch screen."
- "I understand that you are dissatisfied with the performance of our customer care center, because your message was not forwarded."
- "In your letter to the management you complain about the long wait for the delivery of the product."

Table 9.4 Examples of formulations to settle the conflict [based on Brückner (2007), Haeske (2010) and Respond to a Complaint (2017)]

- "I apologize for our mistake. I understand how upset you are."
- "We are very sorry that you experienced this negative incident and received a bad impression of our company. The described behavior of our employee is of course not acceptable."
- "We understand your disappointment. Be sure: we will solve the problem as quickly as possible."
- "I am sorry that you have been subjected to such a frustrating event. We will make every effort to regain your confidence in our company."

addressed and understanding of the customer's irritation should be shown. Along with an *expression of regret* or an *explicit apology*, this make it possible to reduce negative emotions in a customer and to move the complainant to a factual level as he/she is reading the response letter, and the basis for a rational examination of the suggested solution is thereby created (see Table 9.4).

9.1.2.4 Problem Solution
The description of the problem solution that is offered to the customer lies on a factual level. It is important here that the customers can *understand this solution clearly* and can definitely *establish an immediate connection to their problems*. If the customers' expectations can be met or exceeded, the advantages and benefits that result from the solution should be emphasized. If the customer's expectations are not met or claims are denied, well-founded explanations must be provided (see Table 9.5).

Table 9.5 Examples for formulations regarding the problem solution [based on Brückner (2007), Haeske (2010) and Respond to a Complaint (2017)]

> - "The damage is now rectified. A defective spare part was replaced."
> - "Again we apologize for your inconvenience and reduce your bill by $ 40."
> - "We investigated what caused the mistake and took measures to prevent this problem from occuring again in the future."
> - "Of course, we bear the costs incurred. In addition we will give a 10% discount on your next order."

Table 9.6 Examples for positive concluding wordings [based on Brückner (2007), Haeske (2010) and Respond to a Complaint (2017)]

> - "We are glad that we could solve the problem and are convinced that you will have much pleasure with the product in the future."
> - "Thank you for bringing this problem to my attention. We make every effort to see that this will never happen again and hope for the opportunity to serve you again in the future."
> - "We hope that you are satisfied with the solution and will do everything to convince you of our performance in the future."

9.1.2.5 Concluding Wording

The concluding formulation depends upon whether the customer's problem has been solved in accordance with the customer's wishes, or whether a refusal must be communicated to the customer. In the case of a positive decision that corresponds to the expectations of the customer, reference can be made to the hoped-for reestablishment of the customer's satisfaction and the *continuation of the business relationship* (see Table 9.6).

In the case of refusals, it is advisable to express once again *regret about the incident* or to ask for *understanding of the decision*. Table 9.7 shows examples of formulations how you can say "no" in a friendly way.

9.1.2.6 Style of Language and Orthography

Basically, in the case of a written response, it must always be considered that the customers have no opportunity to pose follow-up questions directly if they have problems understanding. This means that escalating dissatisfaction can arise if text passages are worded incompletely, incomprehensibly or inconsistently. Exactly this *verbal quality* of written reactions to complaints is very commonly undervalued and neglected.

Table 9.7 Examples for negative concluding wordings [based on Brückner (2007), Haeske (2010) and Respond to a Complaint (2017)]

▪ "Please don't be disappointed that we cannot meet your demands. Thank you for your understanding."
▪ "It is always unpleasant to issue a negative reply, especially to a loyal customer like you. But we hope that you can accept the given reasons."
▪ "It is not easy to say "no". Also for us. But we hope that they can understand the submitted arguments."

The same applies to *spelling concerns* and aspects of grammar and punctuation. Errors of this kind are taken by the customers as indicators of careless handling of their concern. Therefore, great care should be taken with the automatic generation of confirmations of receipt, intermediate replies or final reply letters that the name and other details are written correctly in the address as well as in the salutation of the letter.

9.2 Application of the Rules of Behavior to Specific Types of Complainants and Complaints

The rules of behavior were previously presented as a function of the complaint channel chosen by the customer, without addressing the *specifics* that individual complainants or complaints may exhibit. Among the *special groups of complainants* are repeat or multiple complainants and grumblers or grousers. *Specific complaints* exist when customers take their complaints to different locations within the firm at the same time (scattered complaints), complain about individual employees or announce action consequences in their complaints (threats).

9.2.1 Special Types of Complainants

9.2.1.1 Repeat and Multiple Complainants

If customers complain about the same problem several times within a certain time period, one is dealing with *"Repeat Complainants"*. Such customers who have again experienced a problem about which they have already complained before, are obviously particularly upset and willing to migrate. This applies even if the customer received a satisfactory reaction to their first complaint. Maxham and Netemeyer (2002) investigated, for example, the effects of two service failures and recovery attempts during a 20-month span. The results show that for a single failure and satisfactory recovery, customers rated the firm paradoxically higher on satisfaction, word-of-mouth communication and repurchase intent ("recovery paradox"), but this was not the case after more than one failure.

This result seems plausible. Customers do not simply want to be treated appropriately in a complaint case; they also want to be able to assume that the firm is taking measures to preclude a repetition of the same occurrences in the future. If this is not the case, customers' trust in the seriousness of the firm's customer orientation will be significantly impaired.

Repeat complainants require special attention. The principles of listening and of sincere regret addressed under the rules of behavior apply here to an even greater extent. In addition, it must be explained to repeat complainants especially which measures were introduced, in order to ultimately eliminate the problem that has arisen. It is further recommended that they be contacted *after the complaint case has been closed* and informed as to the success of the measures that were carried out.

The same especially sensitive attention should be given to customers who have also complained repeatedly in a certain period of time, but about different problems. The business relationship with these *"Multiple Complainants"* is highly endangered, too, because they have multiple reasons to get annoyed about the company's products and services.

9.2.1.2 Follow-Up Complainants

Complaints can concern not only products or services, but also the complaint handling itself. This is the case if customers contact the company during or after the complaint processing and declare that they do not agree with the way in which their complaints are being handled.

These follow-up complaints need special treatment as long as they are not identified clearly as grumblers or grousers. Their annoyance is especially high because their expectations were disappointed for a second time within a short period, initially with regard to a specific product or service aspect and then in relation to the handling of their complaint (so-called 'double deviation').

As in the case of repeat and multiple complainants, the company should act very empathetically and a sincere apology should be made. An appropriate response is also needed in those cases in which the follow-up complaint relates to the complaint result, especially if a customer demand has been rejected. The company should express its understanding of the customers' frustration, assure them that their concerns have been carefully considered, and explain the negative reply with thorough information. If the follow-up complaint occurs during the handling of the initial complaint, all concerns must be addressed in the final response. If the follow-up complaint is articulated after the completion of the initial complaint, another final response is needed. Administratively, the follow-up complaint should be treated as an independent process, but should be linked to the initial complaint when using a complaint management software system.

9.2.1.3 Grumblers and Grousers

In principle, companies should assume that their customers are honest and that their claims are legitimate. Another basis assumption will take the company farther away from the customer. Nevertheless, there are also customers among the complainants who have no understandable reason for a complaint, present untenable demands or even consciously want to damage the firm with their complaints.

The *identification* of this small group that nevertheless frequently influences the internal organizational picture of complainants very negatively is not easy.

There is no generally valid characteristics by which a problem customer can be easily identified. It would be wrong to designate a customer who complained repeatedly within a certain time period as a grumbler. It would be equally wrong to regard someone as a grouser, simply because he doggedly insisted that his complaint case finally be processed after repeatedly broaching the subject.

However, several clues for identification can be found.

Grousers tend to

- *invent* problems
- *falsify* the facts considerably and to *dramatize*
- present demands that are *not related in any conceivable way* to the damage suffered
- make *serious threats* that go beyond the acceptable forms of action (switching, bringing in attorneys and the media).

Grumblers can be recognized by the fact that they

- choose even the *slightest cause* for detailed complaint articulations
- take a *(marginal) problem* as the occasion to criticize many aspects of the firm's range of products and services
- make realistic solutions *difficult* or *impossible* by objecting to every alternative
- derive obvious satisfaction from the *continuation of the conflict*.

The assessment of whether these circumstances are present in an individual case should, however, not be left to the personal opinion of the employee alone. The employees should, rather, accept each complaint in a basically impartial manner. If, however, they begin to have the impression that they are dealing with a grouser or a grumbler, they should undertake a *thorough examination of the case*. Along with his examination, they should investigate the occurrence of the problem in question and the associated consequences, as well as the previous complaint behavior of the customer, in the customer and complaint database.

If it turns out that definite deceptions on the part of the customer exist regarding the appearance of the problem and the damages, that the customer repeatedly presents extreme demands and that objective grounds for complaint are not present, then a case of an unjustified complaint exists. As a rule, such cases should be rejected matter-of-factly. In an extreme case, it may be perfectly reasonable to pursue an *active farewell to the customer*, in which the customer is politely but unmistakably advised that the firm is no longer interested in a continuation of the business relationship under the given conditions. This approach is consistent with strategies for terminating customer relationships (Helm et al. 2006; Butler 2009).

9.2.2 Special Types of Complaints

9.2.2.1 Scattered Complaints

Scattered complaints represent a form of complaints that is encountered again and again in practice. In this case, the customer turns to *different units in the firm simultaneously* with the same complaint—for example, to a regional subsidiary and to the executive board. This behavior can have *three causes*: (1) In the past, complainants have had bad experiences with making a complaint. In contacting several units simultaneously, they are counting on better chances for an appropriate reaction. (2) They would like to ensure that company management also acquires knowledge of the problem and in this way to lend emphasis to their demand. (3) They are attempting to obtain several compensation benefits for the same problem.

If complaint processing does not take place in a coordinated manner, the danger exists that the complaint will be *processed multiple times*. This is problematic because of the duplicated work alone. An additional problem arises when the complaint is processed by the different units with varying quality and/or different problem solutions are offered. The consequence is that the customers perceive the complaint processing to be unprofessional and at the same time are rewarded for their behavior.

The challenge thus consists of *identifying scattered complaints* such as these. One possibility is to collect all complaints in a central location and sift through them there, independent of who received them. If a decentralized access structure exists and a software solution for entering complaints is employed at the participating locations, the possibility exists for recognizing scattered complaints in the context of documentation by comparing them with processes that have not been closed out yet.

If *a complaint is identified as a scattered complaint* and it is conceivable that the processing will take up a longer time span, it should be communicated to the customers that their complaints have arrived at the various addressees, and the unit responsible for the coordinated processing must be given out to them at the same time. If the problem can be solved immediately, the processing is to be initiated and closed by the internally coordinating units, and in the final reply the fact has to be addressed that the individual complaints have arrived at the different addressees, but the processing was taken over by just one responsible unit.

9.2.2.2 Complaints to Top Management

Special attention must be given to complaints that are directly addressed to the firm's top management. *Two reasons* in particular are responsible for this treatment. First of all, customers *do not know who the competent contact person in the firm is.* Consequently, they turn to the head of the firm, hoping that the complaint will then be processed or forwarded to the correct department. Customers also deliberately write to management when they personally would like to *call attention to a serious problem*, or when they have *previously tried in vain* to achieve success in another way or were dissatisfied with the previous complaint handling (follow-up complaint).

The maxim that the *addressee of the complaint* should also answer the customer also applies to top management, even when the problem solution and case processing can or must be undertaken by another unit in many cases. Customers turn to executives because they expect that these will take personal care of their problem. If this is not the case, disappointment sets in, and the customer orientation and commitment to customer satisfaction that have been publicly proclaimed by firm management become unbelievable to the customer.

A special problem arises from the fact that customers turn to management with the request to review rebate or *goodwill demands* that have already been refused. In order not to undermine the credibility or decision-making authority of complaint management or of the customer-contact personnel, well-founded decisions made by the responsible employees should only be emended in exceptional cases. If this cannot be avoided, modified decisions should be passed on to the customer by the affected employee and not by the executive himself. The fact is that if customers perceive that they achieve more when they turn to top management, they will increasingly use this method in the future for their first complaints.

9.2.2.3 Complaints About Employees

A sensitive form of complaint—both for the customer and for the firm—are complaints about the behavior of individual employees. These may have various *causes*:

- there is a real misconduct on the part of an employee,
- the customer is difficult and has not behaved correctly toward the employee or
- the 'chemistry' is just not right.

Basically, the rules of behavior that have already been introduced are also to be applied in this case. Since it is not clear at the time of a personal articulation of such complaints who—the employee or the customer—has made an error, either admitting that the customer is right or standing up for the employee should be strictly avoided in the *first contact* with the complainant.

It is also necessary in this case to listen to the customer initially, to calm him down and to lead him over from an emotional conversational level to a factual one. Many times, it is advisable to offer the customer a *callback* or a *second conversation*, so that a consultation can first be held with the affected employee. In this consultation, the employee must be comprehensively informed about the incident and given the opportunity to present his/her perspective in detail. In addition, the responsible manager must maintain discretion and keep the employee informed during the further process.

If it turns out that the mistake is the *fault of the employee* and this employee must continue working with the customer, the employee should apologize to the customer personally with an appropriate offer of compensation. Internally, the situation must be used for feedback by discussing better ways of reacting with the employee. If similar cases accumulate with the same employee, an urgent need for training exists. If there are still no changes in behavior noticed, it should be reviewed as to whether the employee should be active in customer contact in the future, since the firm will have to accept uncontrollable customer losses otherwise.

If, on the other hand, it turns out that the mistake is clearly the *fault of the customer*, the supervisors should seek out a conversation with the customer and clarify the situation. It is also appropriate for the supervisors to explain the employee's position and give reasons for why they will also support appropriate patterns of behavior in the future. If there are repeated similar cases in which clear-cut misbehavior on the part of the customer is suggested, it stands to reason that consequences analogous to those presented earlier for employees—here, in the form of *active dissolution of the customer relationship*—should be contemplated. In doing so, however, the negative economic consequences of losing the customer must be weighed against the negative consequences that result from the conflicts and their accompanying de-motivating effects for employees if the relationship is retained.

9.2.2.4 Threats Associated with Complaints

Many customers associate the articulation of their complaints with the threat of consequences that they want to invoke if the complaints are not processed as the customers expect them to be. They announce the severance of the business relationship or the introduction of legal action or publicity measures. There can be several *reasons* for tactics like these. Customers threaten

- because they want to emphasize their demands
- when they have the feeling that their problem is not being taken seriously enough
- because they have the feeling that no one wants to help them further or
- when they have the feeling that they are being cheated.

Experience shows that a significant percentage of customers who threaten to *terminate the business relationship* at the next opportunity in fact carry out this reaction.

Customers who threaten to switch should therefore always be *openly confronted* and asked what exactly can be done in this particular situation to deter them from their intention. If realistic expectations are named, the firm must take advantage of the opportunity to bind them further to the firm. If customers who are willing to switch cannot be deterred from their intention, however, the business relationship is to be terminated with a positive farewell *(Goodbye Management)*. Doing so increases the chances that the customer can be won back to the firm after some time has passed.

A further threat made by dissatisfied customers is to introduce *legal means* or *bring in the media*. The rules of behavior are also to be applied in these cases. The firm should strive for conflict settlement, especially when the customers are candidly asked how the problem can be eliminated from their point of view. If the demands appear to be unrealistic upon assessing all the circumstances and the customers' value, the customers must be informed in a matter-of-fact way that the firm would like to have avoided the circumstances described, but is now prepared to advocate its position actively in court or in the media.

Another means of putting pressure on the firm that is often used by customers is the threat *to decrease the amount paid on current invoices* or *not to make upcoming payments*. This threat is mostly expressed when exaggerated performance promises are made by the firm that cannot be kept, and the customer feels *cheated* by this. If it turns out that the performance promise in fact is a substantial deviance from the performance rendered, rectifications should take place, or concessions to the customer in the form of rebates or goodwill benefits should be made. If performance deficits such as these are not discovered, this should be calmly explained to the customers, and their demand should be refused. It may be practical to deviate from this rule if specific circumstances exist or an otherwise successful customer relationship is in great danger.

9.3   Decision on the Case Solution

The decision on the case solution constitutes an essential part of the complaint reaction. Since this decision must take place on a *firm-specific and case-specific* basis, only rather rough guidelines for decision-making can be established here. In establishing these guidelines, *answers to the following questions* should first of all be found:

- Which solution possibilities are available?
- Which factors determine the choice of the appropriate reaction form for each case?
- Up to what amount demanded should the firm forego an extensive investigation of the individual case?
- How should one behave in the case of unjustified complaints?

9.3.1   Solution Possibilities and Influencing Factors for the Choice of Reaction Form

9.3.1.1 Basic Solution Possibilities

There are three groups of measures that are available as basic solution possibilities: financial, tangible or intangible reactions (Fig. 9.1). Among the *financial reaction forms* are money back, price reduction and compensation for damages. In the case of *tangible solutions*, the compensation takes place in the form of a payment in kind (exchange, repair, another product, gift). All customer-oriented forms of communication that target a decrease in the complainant's dissatisfaction (information, explanation, apology) are numbered among the *intangible reactions*.

The *choice of the reaction form in each case* is restricted by goods-specific conditions and led by cost considerations. *Exchange* and *repair* are thus not available as options where services are concerned. Repairs lend themselves primarily to durable consumer goods, whereas exchange and money back are especially suited for low-value consumer goods, for which an individual case investigation would be too costly. The offer of a *replacement product* is only possible when it offers

Financial	Tangible	Intangible
▼	▼	▼
▪ Money back ▪ Price reduction ▪ Compensation for damages	▪ Exchange ▪ Repair ▪ A different product ▪ Gift	▪ Explanation/ Information ▪ Apology

Fig. 9.1 Different forms of complaint reaction for solving the problem and compensating the customer

customers the same benefit as the product that they originally desired. In contrast to exchange, repair and the offer of a replacement product, *gifts* as a tangible reaction form represent not a real solution of the initial problem, but rather a gesture of compensation. For this reason, they are primarily considered when—as is frequently the case in the service sector—later elimination of the problem is not possible. Moreover, they can be used in addition to the other alternatives in order to increase the complaint satisfaction by providing a positive surprise. *Intangible reactions* are always advisable, regardless of whether the actual problem solution makes yet another reaction form necessary. With an apology, the firm takes on the responsibility for the problem that has arisen and contributes to the reduction of dissatisfaction on an emotional level. Through targeted information and explanations, many problems can be solved immediately, misunderstandings cleared up or future problems prevented.

The choice between financial or tangible reaction forms on the one hand and intangible reaction forms on the other hand is also determined by the type of error. Chase and Dasu (2001) thus recommend that *behavior-oriented intangible reactions* like apologies should be applied to process-based behavioral problems and *outcome-based financial or tangible reactions* should be applied to outcome-based errors and problems (see *Spotlight 9.1*).

Spotlight 9.1
The Right Remedy

How do you make up for a service encounter error? Research on what customers perceive as fair remedy suggests that the answer depends on whether it is an outcome error or a process error. A botched task calls for tangible compensation, while poor treatment from a server calls for an apology. Reversing these recovery actions is unlikely to be effective.

Imagine being a copy store manager faced with two complaining customers. One says that the job was done right but the clerk was surly. The

(continued)

Spotlight 9.1 (continued)
other says that the clerk was pleasant but when he got home, he realized that
his report was missing two pages, and he had to take it to a competitor near his
house to get the job done right. What should you do?

In the case of the rude clerk, don't give the customer some tangible
compensation, such as a coupon for his next visit. All the customer really
wants is a *sincere apology* from the clerk and the manager. In the case of the
botched job, you can apologize all over the place, but that won't satisfy the
customer. He wants the job done right, and he wants some *compensation for
his inconvenience*. Thus, while apologies are appropriate in both situations,
behavioral research clearly indicates that process-based remedies should be
applied to process-based problems and outcome-based remedies should be
applied to outcome-based problems.

(Adapted from: Chase and Dasu 2001, p. 84)

9.3.1.2 Reaction Forms and Their Influence on Complaint Satisfaction

When choosing the appropriate reaction form, one should pay attention to whether
the solution offered will be *judged to be adequate* by the customer, and the goal of
high complaint satisfaction can actually be reached. Estelami (2000) analyzed
consumer reports of delightful and disappointing complaint solutions. In goods
markets, the customers desired most a replacement of the product and a prompt
response. Also expressions of empathy, "no questions asked", and politeness by the
employees handling the complaint were among the top mentioned categories.
Goodwin and Ross (1990) investigated which forms of compensation are favored
by dissatisfied service customers and found, too, that the complaint dissatisfaction
depends not only on the form of solution (tangible or intangible compensation), but
also on the experience of the total processing procedure.

Generally customers prefer *tangible and financial compensations*. Even when
they are of relatively low value, they have a substantial positive influence on the
complaint satisfaction. However, the degree of complaint satisfaction varies with the
extent to which the complaint process is perceived as fair.

Complaint dissatisfaction is greatest when the demander's perspective is *blatantly
disregarded in the complaint processing* and the customer is put off with just an
apology. But even the customer who is initially listened to with understanding is
dissatisfied or even very dissatisfied with the complaint situation when he has the
impression, based on an *absent tangible and financial problem solution*, that the firm
simply gave him the opportunity "to let off steam", without taking him or his
concern seriously.

It thus becomes clear to what degree the customer's complaint satisfaction is
dependent upon the extent to which the complainants have the feeling that they are

being treated fairly. The *fairness* or *unfairness* of the treatment is judged by the customer on the basis of various aspects of the firm's reaction (Goodwin and Ross 1990):

- First, the *complaint processing procedure* must fulfill certain conditions so that is perceived as fair. Among these conditions is the fact that the customers can present their view of things and that they also have the impression that the special conditions of their case are fully appreciated. The perceived fairness in the procedure also includes the fact that they are not treated in an unfriendly manner when making their complaint, that no bad intentions are attributed to them and that they are not made responsible for the occurrence of the problem.
- Second, the *outcome of the complaint procedure* must be considered to be fair. From the customers' point of view, their own performance and the counter-performance of the firm must be balanced against the solution offered. In this respect, overly generous financial compensations or gifts are neither necessary nor reasonable. They will no doubt be accepted, but regarded as inappropriate and consequently as a blatant attempt to influence the customer and engender reactance—that is, psychological resistance—rather than enthusiasm. What matters is not wanting to buy the customer's satisfaction with exaggerated gifts, but rather solving the problem brought forward by the customer.

If the problem solution is missing, the assessment of this negative result is dependent upon whether the customer is of the opinion that the provider does not want to and/or cannot solve the problem. These connections are clarified in Fig. 9.2 with a *"Ability—Willingness Matrix" of complaint reaction* (Cottle 1990).

Willingness Ability	Yes	No
Yes	Case 1 **Able and willing** (hight complaint satisfaction)	Case 3 **Able but unwilling** (high complaint dissatisfaction)
No	Case 2 **Willing but unable** (low complaint dissatisfaction)	Case 4 **Unable and unwilling** (high complaint dissatisfaction)

Fig. 9.2 Ability-willingness-matrix of complaint reaction [adapted with changes from Cottle (1990, p. 247)]

Case 1 is unproblematic ("Able and willing"). Since firms are both prepared to solve the customer's problem and in a position to do so, complaint satisfaction is achieved. High complaint dissatisfaction is to be expected in *Case 4* ("Unable and unwilling"), since firms express an attitude with their reaction that is received by the customer in the following way: "I can't help you, but even if I could, I wouldn't."

Cases 2 and 3 are more interesting. In *Case 2* ("Willing but unable"), the provider recognizes the problem and tries to solve it, but is not in a position to do so, either at all or at the present time. It is thus conceivable that hotel guests complain about chilly room temperatures or noisy fellow guests, but it is not possible for the hotelier to see to it that the heat is repaired immediately or that the guests keep the noise down. In cases of this type, complaint dissatisfaction turns out to be relatively low, despite the inadequate problem solution, if the provider makes it clear that he is seriously trying hard to eliminate the problem and searching for creative alternative solutions.

The situation is different for *Case 3* ("Able but unwilling"). Here, the provider could solve the problem but is not prepared to do so. The hotelier, for example, declines to get actively involved with respect to the noisy group of guests. Insufficient willingness to strive for a problem solution leads directly to higher complaint dissatisfaction. Customers experience particularly negative emotions such as frustration or anger (McColl-Kennedy and Sparks 2003).

These insights make it clear that from the customer's perspective, the actual problem solution ("what" the complaining customer receives) is *not* judged *independently* from the way the firm treats the customer in case of a complaint ("how" the customer is treated). Therefore, throughout the entire complaint handling process, the customers must be given the credible impression that they are being respected and that the company is seriously seeking an appropriate solution.

9.3.2   Case Solution With or Without an Individual Case Examination

Many firms are only prepared to offer compensation, even of an insignificant kind, after they have subjected the case to a *thorough examination*. While they are thus extremely sensitive with regard to the possible compensation costs, they neglect the costs of the extensive case investigation. As a simple *arithmetic example* shows, this behavior is hardly rational.

For the following example, it is assumed that it costs 100 € to satisfy a customer who is complaining, and a careful examination of the facts, as well as the activities associated with that examination, result in costs in the amount of 50 € per complaint.

If the individual case examination results in the recognition of 80 out of the 100 complaints received as justified, a *cost comparison* comes to the following conclusion: *Without the examination*, reaction costs alone in the amount of 10,000 €

would have accrued. *With an examination of the facts*, the reaction costs on the one hand for 80 cases (8000 €) and the additional examination costs of 5000 € accrue. The "success" of the refusal of 20% of the demands as unjustified was purchased with *additional costs* in the amount of 3000 €. Moreover, there is the loss of the positive effects with respect to the firm's image and to customer satisfaction that would have occurred if the customers had experienced an unbureaucratic problem solution.

Naturally, the consequence of this arithmetic example is not that qualifying examinations should be renounced on principle. Nevertheless, the question must be answered as to the compensation amount up to which the firm *can forego an individual case examination*.

The starting point is the experience that a majority of the expenditures that accrue for problem solutions are allotted to a relatively small proportion of complaints. Conversely, this means that the majority of complaints only take up a minor proportion of the total settlement expenditures. Accordingly, it seems reasonable to *restrict* the detailed individual case examinations *to the few cost-intensive cases*.

In order to do this, Blanding (1991) suggests applying the *80-20 Rule* to complaint management. He proceeds from the assumption that 80% of the amount of money that must be expended for problem solutions is allotted for 20% of the complaints. Accordingly, 80% of the complaint cases account for only 20% of the total expenditure. On the basis of this assumption, he suggests subjecting only those complaints that account for 80% of the total expenditure to an individual case examination, or foregoing an extra examination for those complaints that account for 20% of the total expenditures. The outcome of this process is an Immediate Reaction Amount, up to which the solution desired by the customer can be offered without a further examination. The process includes the following steps (see also the example in Table 9.8):

1. Determination of the total amount of money that will be spent on problem solutions in the time period under consideration *(Total Reaction Amount)*.
2. Calculation of 20% of the Total Reaction Amount *(Non-Investigation Share)*.
3. Determination of the *complaint volume* during the period.
4. *Arrangement of the complaints* according to the respective reaction costs in increasing order and determination of the number of complaints until the Non-Investigation Share (20% of the total reaction costs) is reached.
5. Determination of the *Immediate Reaction Amount* as the highest amount of reaction costs for one of these complaints. All complaints with reaction costs up to this amount can be resolved without further examination in accordance with the customer's wishes. This only applies, however, if the proportion of the included complaints accounts for 80% of the total number of complaints.
6. Calculation of the *proportion of the included complaints* of the total complaint volume.
7. *Verification of the 80-20 Rule*. One can abide by the Immediate Reaction Amount even when the rule is not completely confirmed; however, the 20% of the total reaction costs should be allotted to at least 50% of the complaint cases.

Table 9.8 Example of how to determine the Immediate Reaction Amount [adapted from: Blanding (1991)]

1. Total reaction amount / year
$ 60,000

2. Non-investigation share = 20%
$ 12,000

3. Complaint volume / year
40 Complaints

4. Ordering of the complaints according to their reaction costs and determination ot the number of complaints that can be processed before non-investigation share is reached.

20 complaints	at	$ 100	=	$ 2,000	
10 complaints	at	$ 400	=	$ 4,000	
2 complaints	at	$ 3,000	=	$ 6,000	
32 complaints			=	$ 12,000	= non-investigation share (20%)

5. Determination of the immediate reaction amount

= highest amount of reaction costs of a complaint included in the non-investigation share (20%)
= $ 3,000

6. Calculation of the share of complaints included in the non-investigation share (20%) of the total complaint volume

$$\frac{32 \text{ complaints}}{40 \text{ complaints}} = 80\%$$

7. Verification of the 80-20 rule

Confirmed

In the example depicted in Table 9.8, 80% of the complaint cases that cause individual reaction costs of up to 3000 € account for 20% of the total reaction costs. The 80-20 Rule thus applies in this example, so that complaints up to the amount of the determined Immediate Reaction Amount of 3000 € can be settled without individual case investigation.

This approach is associated with *three advantages* for the firm. (1) 80% of all complainants can be satisfied immediately. (2) In 80% of the cases, the customer-contact personnel can decide the problem solution immediately, which brings about motivational effects. (3) For 80% of complaints, no internal processing costs accrue.

However, this method should not be applied schematically. If, for example, the Immediate Reaction Amount is comparatively high—as in the example of Table 9.8—and only rarely must be paid out, it can be useful to choose in the next lower amount (400 € instead of 3000 €).

9.3.3 Dealing with "Unjustified" Complaints

Many times the question is raised as to how one should react to unjustified customer demands. This question demands, however, an explanation of when a complaint should be viewed as *unjustified*.

9.3.3.1 The Subjective Justification of Customer Complaints

The question of the justification of a complaint should be primarily posed *from the customers' perspective*. Here, one can proceed from the assumption that the vast majority of complainants are subjectively fully convinced that their concerns are justified. There are no reliable figures about the proportion of customers who knowingly articulate an 'illegitimate' or 'fraudulent' complaint. This is due to the fact that there are only a few empirical studies on this topic (Piron and Young 2000; Harris and Reynolds 2004; Reynolds and Harris 2005; Plein 2016). Although managers report an increasing number of unjustified complaints, it is reasonable to conclude that only a small percentage of complainants can be assigned to the group of those who complain to the firm with intent to defraud and thus have no reason for complaint from their subjective point of view.

For this reason, it makes sense for companies to *accept this customer perspective*, independent of whether a later investigation reveals that the firm cannot objectively be held responsible for the problem. Regardless of whether the problematic can be attributed to a lack of information or a misunderstanding on the part of the customer, annoyance and disappointment are present for the customer in every case and have their causes. To prove to these customers that they are in the wrong only increases their annoyance and dissatisfaction.

The central requirement of complaint reaction is, therefore, *never to doubt the justification of the customer's complaint*. Nevertheless, this primary acceptance of all complaints does not mean that all of the customer's demands should be fulfilled. An *objective examination* of the facts may show a *different picture*. It may turn out, for example, that the customer has depicted the circumstances incompletely or incorrectly, or that he/she has either caused the problem or contributed to its cause. Consequently, in these situations, the subjective justification from the customer's point of view and the objective justification from the firm's point of view fall apart.

From the firm's perspective, it is sensible to ascertain the extent of these "unjustified" complaints because they provide important indications of the *necessity of corrective measures*. They might show where information deficits exist for the customer or where operating instructions are unclear. However, it must be ensured that the classification as 'unjustified' is based on objective criteria. If the classification is left to the subjective judgment of the staff, this normally leads to a greatly overestimated number of unjustified complaints.

9.3.3.2 Reactions to "Unjustified" Complaints

Accommodating Reaction to "Unjustified Complaints"

As far as the *firm's reaction to objectively unjustified complaints* is concerned, it is necessary to differentiate. While the subjective reason for the complaint may not be questioned in the answer to the customer, the decision as to *voluntary rebate and goodwill payments* depends on various factors. The tendency to fulfill the customer's expectations despite the fact that objective reasons for complaint do not exist is thus greater, the more the customer's perspective is understandable—for instance, due to the *especially unlucky conditions* of the case. An analogous situation exists when the *examination costs* for a complete clarification of the incident turn out to be higher than the reaction costs. Additionally, a refusal of the customer's wishes and an insistence on an "objective" point of view would seem to be absurd if a long-lasting, successful and profitable *business relationship were endangered* by such actions.

For this reason, there is much to be said for considering the problem of objectively unjustified complaints from an *economic perspective*. In accordance with Sewell and Brown (2002), the following *pragmatic approach* is recommended for deciding on voluntary rebate and goodwill payments:

- First, determine the *costs* that arise from the fulfillment of the (unjustified) customer demand.
- Cases whose reaction costs are below the individual case examination costs should be immediately resolved according to the customer's wishes *without restrictions* or expressions of mistrust of any kind.
- If the reaction costs are more than the examination costs and the obvious nonjustification of the complaint comes out during the examination, a customer-individual treatment *depending on the customer's value* should occur. If the customer's value is substantially more than the reaction costs, even an unjustified complaint should be solved in accordance with the customer's wishes. Negotiations with the customer about a reduction of his demands are not recommended, since then the settlement will not cause positive effects. Sewell and Brown (2002, p. 65) express it as follows: "If you want to keep their business, give customers exactly what they ask for—or even more—without any hesitation. If you do anything less, you might as well offer them nothing, because you'll have lost their good will". However, the customer's unjustified demand and the type of the firm's reaction should be recorded in the customer database in order to be able to make a different decision, if need be, should the situation repeat itself.
- If, based on the individual case examination, it turns out that the demand of a *less attractive customer* is unjustified or that this same customer has already attracted attention for his *deceitful behavior*, the demands should be refused in a clear but friendly manner. Sewell, a successful car dealer, says laconically: "Sometimes we even give them directions to our ‚favorite' competitor" (Sewell and Brown 2002, p. 68).

Independent of the terms under which rebate and goodwill decisions occur, these decisions must be *made very carefully* in every case. Rash promises made during the initial contact should be avoided, as these can rarely be taken back. In addition, goodwill and rebate payments are very *cost-intensive* and are among the largest cost pools in complaint management in many industries—as for example in the automobile or tourism industry. A further reason in favor of a cautious approval of monetary demands has to do with the fact that word of generously granted goodwill payments gets around quickly, so that a lasting *influence on the expectations* of other complainants follows. If the rebate or goodwill policy is later changed, it can lead to great irritation, since customers with similar or identical problems are not granted a commensurate payment.

Refusal of "Unjustified" Complaints

If *neither an objective nor a subjective complaint cause* exists, the complaint is to be rejected. However, the judgment of whether the complaint has a subjective complaint cause must be undertaken on the basis of "hard" data, not on the basis of employee assessments. This requires that the firm has clear evidence that the complainant belongs to the small group of grumblers, grousers and crooks ("customers from hell").

Moreover, all complaints that have no *objective foundation* and for which no specific reason to comply with the customer's subjectively based demands exists, should also be denied. This is the case when no special problem is discernable and the value of the customer is deemed to be slight. These reasons, however, are only to be applied if the reaction costs are relatively high, such that the absence of an objective complaint cause was proven in an individual case examination.

If the customer's complaint expectations are not fulfilled due to clear-cut and understandable facts, then this decision must be explained to the customer matter-of-factly and without doctrinaire instructions. Table 9.9 summarizes the recommended reactions.

9.4   Differentiation of Complaint Reaction According to the Customer's Value

The fact that reaction forms can be undertaken in a differentiated fashion according to the customer's value, if necessary, has already been addressed. The basis of this consideration is that the complaint reactions can be initiated for customer retention purposes, but at the same time, the maxim that *"not all customers are worth attracting and keeping"* (Rust et al. 2000, p. 187) applies. This chapter first introduces basic aspects of customer evaluation (Sect. 9.4.1). Subsequently, it is discussed to what extent differentiation according to customer value makes sense in the context of complaint management (Sect. 9.4.2).

Table 9.9 Reactions to justified and unjustified complaints from the customer's and the company's perspective

Company perspective / Customer perspective	Objective cause for complaint	No objective cause for complaint
Subjective cause for complaint	• **Recognition** of the subjective justification • **Complete fulfillment** of the customer's expectations	• **Recognition** ot the subjective justification • Complete or partial **accomodating** fulfillment of the customer's expectations depending on the specific circumstances of the case, the reaction costs and other factors (such as intensity and value of the customer relationship)
No subjective cause for complaint (e.g. fraudulent complaint)		• **Rejection** of the customer's demand

9.4.1   Foundations of Customer Valuation

The valuation of customer relationships occupies an important role, especially in the context of *Customer Relationship Management (CRM)*. In many CRM publications, a focus on *worthwhile customer relationships* is demanded (Rust et al. 2000; Gupta et al. 2004; Fader 2012; Helm et al. 2017). Accordingly, attention must be paid to the fact that the costs of customer care are justified by the customer's contribution to the economic value added. In a static perspective, normally the customer's revenue or net profit are the main criteria for the evaluation of the value of customer relations. In a dynamic perspective, primarily the concept of Customer Lifetime Value is used (see for example Kumar 2008; Malthouse 2013; Kumar and Pansari 2015).

9.4.1.1 Revenue-Related Evaluation of Customers

An *evaluation of customers based on revenue* and a differentiation as A-, B-, or C-customers according to their purchases is often the dominant approach. A-customers are those with the highest revenues, C-customers are those with the lowest. The revenue classes can be selected company-specifically. Such customer rankings reflect a company's dependency on specific customers and often show that a large proportion of the sales can be attributed to a small percentage of the customers. It is not unusual for the so-called *80-20 Rule* to be applied with regard to the customer-related concentration of sales, according to which 20% of all customers are responsible for 80% of the total sales.

In applying the ABC analysis, the value of customers depends on their assignment to a specific revenue class. Accordingly, it seems justified that A-customers generally receive more intensive support than customers of other sales classes. However, this conclusion can lead to *wrong decisions*, since customers with high sales do not necessarily provide the firm with a high profit contribution, for example, because they are able to enforce significant price reductions due to their market power.

9.4.1.2 Contribution Margin-Related Evaluation of Customers

The contribution margin analysis explicitly considers the *costs for maintaining the customer relationship* that are neglected in the revenue-related customer evaluation. For each customer, the direct cost is deducted from the sales to this customer. If a positive contribution remains to cover the fixed costs, this represents the *profit contribution* of the specific customer. This is a much *more meaningful criterion* for the economic evaluation of a customer relationship than revenues.

As with the revenue-related customer evaluation, a *classification of A-, B- and C-customers* can be made in the context of the contribution margin-related evaluation. If this classification is applied as the basis for decisions about the customer-specific service level, customers belonging to the best contribution margin class A receive the highest quality of care and support and a further differentiation is carried out according to the respective lower contribution margin classes.

The *precondition* for the implementation of customer margin contribution analyses is that the direct costs and sales associated with individual customers can be precisely assigned—a requirement that many companies cannot satisfy because the accounting system is designed in a product-oriented and not customer-oriented manner. In this respect, many companies are faced with the task of creating the basis for the application of customer contribution margin-oriented care concepts by introducing consistent process cost accounting.

9.4.1.3 Evaluation of the Customer Relationship Over the Entire Duration of the Customer Relationship

Customer valuations relating to sales and contribution margins are based on *historical values*. However, the decision as to whether a certain action or measure is worthwhile for a customer relationship from an economic point of view should not be made based only on a retrospective database. The decisive factor is how the customer relationship will develop *in the future* and whether the customer relationship will generate earnings in the future that justify the current investment. For this purpose, it is necessary to estimate how revenues and costs will develop over the expected duration of the relationship.

One method that examines the entire customer relationship from its beginning to its end is the calculation of *Customer Lifetime Value (CLTV)*. Here, the value of a customer over the average duration of a business relationship is considered to be desirable if the expected customer-related incoming payments (customer revenues) exceed the expected customer-related outgoing payments (costs caused by the customer relationship).

This means that the customer contribution margin is implicitly the reference value of the CLTV. Therefore, the prerequisites described above must be fulfilled. In addition, it must also be possible to estimate the potential a customer has for the future business relationship. Future incoming and outgoing payments are discounted to the respective time of consideration using the principles of the *dynamic investment calculation*.

The *(CLTV)* is the net present value of all profits that can be expected from the business relationship. To determine the customer lifetime value, various approaches exist (Günter and Helm 2011; Krafft and Bues 2017). The basic idea behind these approaches is to discount the periodic profits during the expected life of the business relationship and to calculate the net present value of the relationship.

Of all approaches to customer evaluation, the CLTV approach appears to be the most convincing. From the point of view of the desired focus on profitable customer relationships, it would be desirable to calculate the CLTV for each individual customer relationship in order to determine economically adequate measures. However, the use of this approach faces *considerable difficulties* in practice. In particular, it frequently proves to be exceedingly problematic to reliably predict the prospective customer-specific incoming and outcoming payments as well as the prospective loyalty period.

Only firms with excellently maintained customer databases and long-term customer relationships are in a position to address these problems by applying complex analytical methods. Other firms refrain from implementing the investment theory approach. They take up the *correct basic idea of the concept* that the value of a customer arises from the future expected net profit. However, they are content to make rough estimations of the customer-specific sales and cost development for a manageable time period and to differentiate customer service according to this medium-term-oriented calculation of the customer's net profit.

9.4.2   The Use of Customer Valuation in Complaint Management

The utilization of information about the customer's value for a differentiated complaint reaction are limited due to the calculation problem described. Also from a conceptual point of view it seems advisable to critically examine the question of a customer value-based differentiation in complaint management. Two facts are significant here. On the one hand it must be taken into account that active complaint management itself represents an important lever for increasing long-term customer value; and on the other hand, the consequences that arise from the inbound character of articulated customer complains must be considered.

9.4.2.1 Complaint Management as a Central Lever for the Sustainable Increase of the CLTV

The central objective target of complaint management—to stabilize business relationships with dissatisfied customers and retain them long-term for the firm—represents in itself a *central lever for the sustainable increase of long-term customer value*. With convincing complaint processing, customer relationships—even previously not very profitable business relationships—can be positively influenced in the sense of rising economic attractiveness. It is thus conceivable that customers build up trust based on their positive experience in complaint cases and increase their volume of business. Accordingly, it makes less sense to interpret the value of the customer relationship as the determinant of the complaint reaction than the reverse—namely, to see in the complaint reaction an investment in a more profitable customer relationship in the future.

This basic assessment is not contradicted by the fact that a differentiation with regard to the problem solution takes place, such as when the room for maneuvering toward especially profitable long-term customers for questions of goodwill is completely exhausted to the customer's advantage. In no way, however, may a differentiation be carried out in direct contact with the customer. In this regard, complaint management should treat each customer complaint equally, *irrespective of customer profitability*.

While a betterment of especially attractive regular customers can be rational in the context of complaint reaction, a conscious worsened treatment of less profitable customers is always to be avoided. The general expectation of a customer *to be heard* and to gain his rights should always be fulfilled. This is valid simply for ethical reasons, but it is also sensible in terms of an economic calculation, since otherwise

- *high complaint dissatisfaction* is provoked
- the potential *leverage effect on long-term customer value* in the form of increased net profit and longer-term retention are lost, and what is more, at the same time
- the probability increases that carelessly handled customer complaints are passed on to *attorneys or the media*, which is always associated with the risk of cost effects and loss of image.

9.4.2.2 The Inbound Character of Articulated Customer Complaints

A *further restriction* regarding customer valuation in complaint management results from the inbound character of complaints. In the usual *CRM-outbound activities initiated by the firm*—for instance, in campaign management—customers who have adequate customer value for the firm can be selected in a targeted and systematic manner. In the case of complaint management, however, a different situation exists. It is not the firm that decides which customers it wants to contact, but rather the customers who seek out contact to the firm of their own accord in order to get their problem solved. This then is an *inbound activity*, which means that the firm has only limited possibilities for customer-value-oriented differentiation at its disposal

(Stauss and Seidel 2009). The contact by the customer *can rarely be controlled* by the firm. Even when the employee accepting a complaint—for example, in a customer care center—recognizes in the context of the complaint dialog, based on customer database information, that the case involves a less profitable customer, it is not justifiable not to act on the concern or to handle it in a cold manner because it lacks significance.

Based on the positive influence of complaint management on the duration, the intensity and the profitability of the business relationship and because of the inbound character of complaints, the frequently stated requirement that customers be treated in a differentiated fashion can *only be carried over to complaint management within certain limits.*

9.4.2.3 Customer-Value-Oriented Complaint Acceptance and Processing

With regard to complaint acceptance and processing, there are only a few possibilities for a differentiation according to the customer value. It would thus appear to be problematic to *establish special access channels* for the complaints of valuable customers—the *status customers*. Since steps like these cannot be kept secretly, this measure would lead to irritation on the part of the remaining customer base. This applies especially when customers who do not fulfill the value requirements of the firm call the customer care phone number provided for status customers and are rebuffed. It can be assumed, therefore, that approaches such as these will be taken up by the media and lead to a loss of image.

The situation is somewhat different if the specific access channel is not directly established for complaints, but rather is part of an exclusive *customer-value-oriented service program*. A phone number, address and/or e-mail address is then communicated to the participating status customers, which they can use to claim specific benefits. This channel of communication can then also be used by customers for the articulation of complaints. Priority acceptance and processing is consequently an implied component of the specific service program, without being expressly communicated. Thus, the firm also rules out the possibility that customers who do not fulfill the requirements of customer profitability can purposefully use the communication channels provided for the service program to complain.

Another basic possibility for the differentiation of complaint acceptance is in designing the *length of the conversation* to be subject to the customer value—that is, for instance, to instruct the telephone agents in the call center to handle complaint conversations with less valuable customers more quickly than conversations with valuable customers. This way of handling the issue should, however, be rejected. The establishment of a complaint management system only makes sense if the goal of taking care of all customer problems is pursued. As soon as a customer conversation has begun, it is primarily the complexity of the customer's problem and the information requirements that determine the requisite length of the conversation, but not customer-value-oriented time targets.

A useful *differentiation of the access concept* for complainants from the perspective of the economic importance of the customer relationship consists, however, of making the rapidity of the acceptance of *telephone complaints* dependent on the telephone number dialed. As soon as the ACD (Automatic Call Distribution) system identifies a telephone number as the connection to a valuable customer relationship, this customer is ensured faster accessibility than other customers. In this way, it can be determined that for customers classified as valuable, a service level of 90/10 (that is, 90% of all callers will be put through to a telephone agent within 10 seconds) will be provided, and for all other customers, a service level of 80/20 will be provided. This approach avoids the problems of the other alternatives. On the one hand, there is a preference shown for valuable customers, but there is no discrimination of less attractive customers in the sense of below-average treatment. On the other hand, the preference is not communicated and thus is also not transparent.

The processing of *written complaints* can also be controlled similarly. The reaction times for confirmations of receipt, for intermediate replies or for the entire processing period can thus be determined subject to customer value. The corresponding levels for less valuable customers may, however, not be set so low that dissatisfaction develops for these customers.

9.4.2.4 The Customer-Value-Oriented Problem Solution

Reservations against customer-value-oriented differentiation also apply with respect to the problem solution. What is crucial for a complainant is that *his individual case is resolved* and that measures are implemented that ensure that a *recurrence of the problem in the future will be avoided*. If complaint management is taken seriously, then these expectations on the customers' part will be met regardless of the customer value.

Many times, however, problems cannot be completely undone, and it is necessary to make restitution to the customer for his unpleasant experiences with a reimbursement or compensation benefit (e.g., gifts). Or greater room for maneuvering exists with regard to goodwill questions because the customer's complaint indeed seems to be justified subjectively, but from an objective perspective is unfounded. In these cases, it is not only possible, but also absolutely advisable, to *accommodate* especially valuable customers *more* than less profitable customer relationships.

In a similar way, the customer valuation can be consulted as a criterion when it has to be decided which complainant should be contacted in the context of *individual follow-up measures*. The goal of such measures is above all to ensure after the complaint case has been closed that everything was settled to the complete satisfaction of the complainant and the business relationship is not jeopardized. These measures that tie up additional resources should especially be directed toward customer relationships that generate an adequate profit contribution for the firm.

9.5   Communication with the Complainant During Complaint Processing

As soon as the complainants have articulated their complaints, they begin to wait for the answer. The longer this waiting time lasts, the more impatient and dissatisfied they become. Therefore, what matters is to avoid the creation of this type of dissatisfaction by means of communicative measures. Basically, the following forms of communications come under consideration here: The *confirmation of the receipt of the complaint* in the case of written complaints, the notification as to where the processing stands in *intermediate replies* and the communication of the problem solution in a final reply. Furthermore, all intermediate *enquiries* by the customers must be answered.

9.5.1 Forms of Communication

9.5.1.1 Confirmation of Receipt
In the case of *written complaints* that cannot be solved immediately, it is necessary to confirm to the customers that their complaint has been received. It may also be sensible to confirm *complaints that have been made verbally* by the customers, for example, if the complaint is simply accepted and the customers are promised that it will be forwarded to the responsible department.

In cases for which the processing will take up a longer period of time, the confirmation of receipt should contain the following information in terms of content:

- the *thank-you* for the complaint
- the *date* the complaint *was received* in the firm
- a *summary* of the customer's problem
- an honest and sincere *regret* about the inconvenience experienced by the customer
- the *measures* implemented and
- an *expected settlement deadline* or, if this is not possible, a date (day or week) by which the customer will be informed once more about his case.

The customers is thereby *given the security* of knowing that their complaint has arrived at the appropriate unit and their problems have been understood properly. They know, furthermore, that measures to eliminate the problem have been introduced, and they are informed about the duration of the processing. In doing this, the firm signals them that their problems are in the right hands and that one is at pains to find a solution.

The firm can *forego a confirmation of receipt* if the time span expected by the customer with regard to the reaction to complaints will not be exceeded by the (expected) closure of the complaint process.

Confirmations of receipt can take place in writing or over the telephone. The *telephone reaction form* often proves to be the better way. On the one hand, the respective employee can record the customer's problem and the expected solution more exactly during the conversation; and on the other hand, he/she can explain to the customer why certain expectations cannot be fulfilled. In addition, the firm can apologize in a—desired by many customers–personal way.

Limits are, however, *placed* on telephone reaction forms when the written complaint volume reaches such an extent that the individual complaints can only be confirmed in the form of a standard letter. In using letters like these, however, the firm must avoid giving the impression that no individual case examination will take place. This can be achieved by making reference to the particular circumstances of the case and providing the name of a contact person for possible follow-up questions. In cases with a high level of urgency, telephone contact should occur even when the complaint volume is high, in order to accelerate the processing and solution procedure.

For complaints by e-mail, it is advisable to send the customer an automatic reply. However, this answer should only indicate that the customer's e-mail has arrived at the company technically correct. Regardless of this, e-mail complaints should also be answered by an individual acknowledgment of receipt with the contents described above.

9.5.1.2 Intermediate Replies
Sending out intermediate replies is always *necessary* when

- *no settlement date* can be given to the customer in the confirmation of receipt
- the *intermediate deadlines agreed on* with the customer in the confirmation of receipt or the *settlement deadline cannot be kept*
- *deviations* from the problem solution about which the customer has been notified or from other promises made in the context of the complaint processing crop up or
- such a *long period of time* lies between the confirmation of receipt and the final problem solution that the customer could get the impression that his complaint was neglected or has been forgotten.

Of crucial importance for the re-establishment of the complainant's satisfaction is the fact that the firm proves the effort it is putting into a problem solution and creates *transparency* in the case examination and the current state of the processing. Consents and promises to the customer in the context of the complaint case must also be kept. Should this not be possible for particular reasons, the firm must inform the customer about the respective deviations without delay. For processing procedures of longer duration, temporal standards should be fixed, within which an intermediate reply must be produced and sent. In the context of PC-supported complaint management systems, this process can be largely automated.

In choosing between *telephone and written methods of communicating* with the customer, the telephone is also preferred in the case of progress reports. In this way, the customer is informed in a more individual and detailed way about where things stand. Moreover, the customer has a stronger impression that someone is dealing with his problem and does not want to lose him as a customer. If a written form of the intermediate cannot be avoided due to a high number of complaints, the same applies as for the confirmation of receipt: an individual approach to the customers with regard to their specific problems must be chosen and a contact person must be appointed for any queries.

9.5.1.3 Final Reply

Final replies contain the problem solution developed by the firm and the communication that the complaint case is *closed for good*. As far as content is concerned, the answer should contain the following points:

- the *thank-you* for the complaint
- a *short*, repeated *summary* of the problem
- the *expression of regret* for the harm suffered by the customer
- the *result* of the problem analysis
- the *suggested solution*
- and—for customer-oriented problem solutions—the request to *have confidence* in the firm again in the future.

As a rule, the final reply should occur *in writing* in order to prevent possible discrepancies with respect to the actual result of the problem solution later on. This must happen independent of whether the firm was able to solve the customer's problem completely, partially or not at all in accordance with the customer's wishes. In cases which had no solution or an inadequate solution from the customer's point of view, it is further recommended that the reasons for the lacking or partial solution be explained to the customer and that the firm's good intentions be stressed once again.

9.5.1.4 Follow-Up Survey

In order to determine whether the complaint reaction actually led to the desired complaint satisfaction of the customer, it is advisable to carry out follow-up surveys—that is, *to contact the complainant immediately after the closure of the complaint process*.

Figure 9.3 illustrates the basic idea of this measure and its integration into the direct complaint management process. The customer receives a faulty product or service, which leads to dissatisfaction and a complaint. Immediately after completion of the complaint processing, a follow-up contact is made—usually no later than five working days after completion of the process. The central objective is to determine the complainant's satisfaction with the company and to ensure that the complaint process is *classified as closed* not only from the perspective of the firm, but *also from the complainant's point of view*. If action is required, the process is either concluded immediately by a new decision or an arrangement of a further contact with the customer to find a mutual solution.

In contrast to the performance measurements for complaint satisfaction introduced in Sect. 11.2.1, the primary target of follow-up surveys does not consist of deriving average data about the quality of the perceived complaint processing, but rather of ensuring that a complaint was actually closed to the *individual satisfaction* of the customer and the business relationship was *truly stabilized*. The survey thus has to take place in an immediate temporal reference to the complaint reaction and has a *direct effect on customer retention*, since the firm demonstrates genuine interest in the customer relationship. At the same time, a quality assurance effect is also achieved for the complaint processing and reaction, as it ensures that handling of the

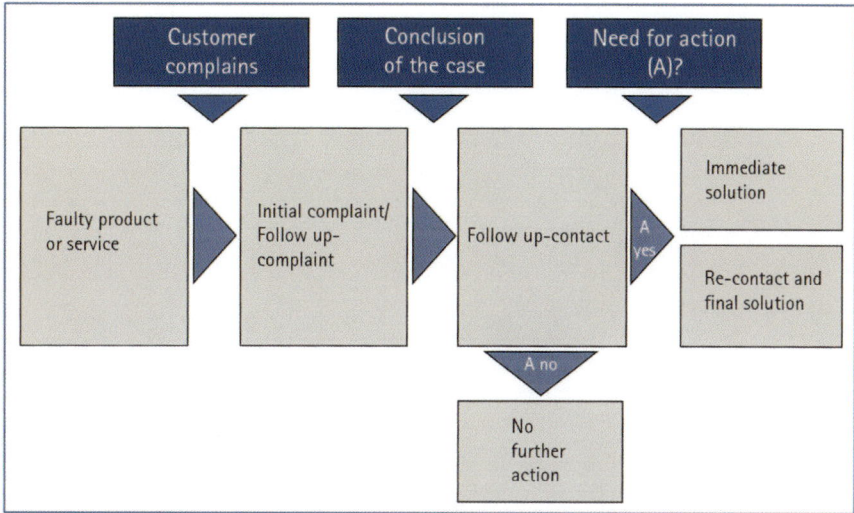

Fig. 9.3 Assignment of follow-up contacts in the direct complaint management process

complaint is actually completed. *Spotlight 9.2* illustrates this customer retention effect by an example from the energy industry.

Spotlight 9.2
Success of Follow-Up Contacts

The success of follow-up contacts was examined in an empirical study in an energy services company. All customers who had complained within 12 months were contacted by telephone. Telephone contact was chosen because it was expected that the complainants would be far more willing to participate in a telephone conversation than to fill in a questionnaire. In fact, a participation rate of around 85% was achieved.

A key finding of the study was that there was a large discrepancy between the assessment of companies and customers as to whether the complaint case was closed. While, from the company's perspective, only customers with a closed complaint were contacted, 25% of the initial complainants and 37% of the follow-up complainants stated that they did not consider the case to be closed and that they saw a need for further action. This feedback led not only to renewed examinations of complaints and solutions offered, but also to an analysis of the differences in perception and to corrective measures in complaint management, which were supported uncompromisingly by the top management. These measures included, among other things, that each individual complaint was documented, and that fixed temporal service levels were adhered to, especially in the intermediate communication with complainants.

(continued)

Spotlight 9.2 (continued)
In addition, intensive workshops were held to address the problems identified in the follow-up contacts and a task force for escalated cases was established.

In this way, the original need for action rates of 25% and 37% for initial and follow-up complaints respectively could be reduced to approximately 10% within 12 months. Thus, the follow-up survey has proven to be an excellent instrument for achieving quality assurance and improvement in complaint management. The Fig. 9.4 shows the development of the need for action rates over the entire project period.

Important findings were also gained with regard to the retention effect of complaint satisfaction. Of those customers who were less satisfied or dissatisfied with the settlement of the complaint, 7% of the initial and 10% of the follow-up complainants indicated their intention to terminate their business relationship. The prompt reaction during the follow-up contact or the immediate initiation of new problem-solving processes enabled more than three-quarters of these highly endangered business relationships to be maintained. In this respect, the follow-up contacts also proved to be an effective instrument of customer retention.
Source: servmark (2009)

In the *case of dissatisfaction*, customers will take this contact as the occasion to bring up their criticism, address unresolved questions or point out further demands that exist. They then expect specific answers to these articulations. In this way, follow-up complaints are stimulated by follow-up contacts if need be. Thus, it is necessary that the surveying employee have immediate access to the complaint case in order to bring about a solution immediately, if necessary. When planning follow-up contacts, it is also necessary to take into account the processing and reaction costs associated with follow-up complaints.

Follow-up contacts are basically meaningful after every complaint procedure. However, in the case of *complaints completed by telephone*, the follow-up contact should not be carried out by the same person who finally dealt with the complaint, but by a person who is not involved in the process in order to signal neutrality and to detect problems as objectively as possible. In the case of *written procedures*, follow-up contacts are particularly useful, since these can be used to determine whether the customer understands the written argumentation and agrees to the proposed solution. Rejections of customer demands can also be explained here again if necessary. Practical experiences with follow-up contacts show that a repeated telephone contact rarely leads to irritation or further annoyance on the part of the customer, but rather that such conversations help to bring even difficult, initially written operations to a satisfactory end for both sides.

Furthermore, follow-up contacts should be used if the company is *organized decentrally* and complaints are also processed in local branches. These contacts should be carried out by a central or independent body. It must be ensured that this

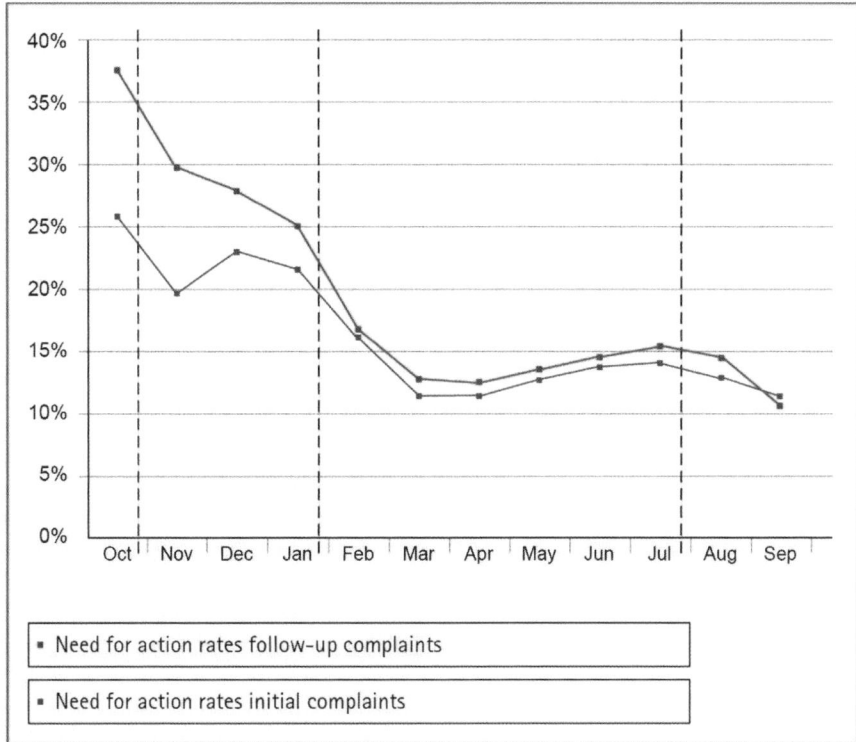

Fig. 9.4 Development of the need for action rates

activity is understood by the decentralized units not as a control measure but rather as a supportive measure to improve quality and to strengthen customer loyalty. This is because it aims to make sure that complaint management is carried out in accordance with the same quality standards throughout the company and that customer relationships at risk are stabilized. Finally, follow-up contacts can also be used as *a specific service* for very valuable or important customers in order to convey special appreciation of their business and to prevent the risk of customer loss.

If a survey of all complainants is impossible for capacity reasons, a *sample* can be defined, and it can be determined in accordance with the sample size that the complainant from every third, fifth or tenth complaint process will be surveyed. In doing so, the requirement of *random selection* is fulfilled, since the selection is oriented on the time of receipt in the firm and each complaint case has the same probability of being considered for the survey.

Since the primary point of follow-up measurements is not, however, to obtain representative results, but rather to ensure customer retention, it also makes sense to carry out a *methodic selection* of the complainants to be surveyed subject to customer value or the type of problem.

9.5.2 Temporal Design of the Forms of Communication

For the complainants' satisfaction it is not only important that they always are informed, but rather that they receive this information *within appropriate time limits*. Therefore, temporal standards for the sending out of official notices must be fixed and, in the context of the subjective task controlling, it must be monitored whether the standards are met and assessed as appropriate by the complainant.

For the confirmation of receipt and the intermediate reply it should be determined *as of which total processing time* they are necessary at all and at which point in time they should be mailed.

A *confirmation of receipt* is only necessary when the problem cannot be conclusively resolved within a very short time span (e.g., 5 days for written complaints). This confirmation should then follow as quickly as possible to the customer (for example, 48 hours after the arrival of a written complaint at the latest, or up to 24 hours after the receipt of an electronic complaint). *Intermediate replies* should in principle be produced when the processing drags on for a longer period of time (for instance, more than 2 weeks). They should be sent out when the length of the processing time can be foreseen (e.g., after 8 days). If the case cannot be resolved in the presumed processing time, the customer must be provided an explanation for the delay in an additional intermediate reply after a short time (for example, after further 8 days) and here at the latest be given a definitive deadline for the final clarification of the case. If the customer sends documents that are still needed during the processing of the complaint case, the receipt must be confirmed as soon as possible (for instance, within 2 days). The *final reply* with the solution suggested by the firm should be mailed out immediately after the decision about the case solution has been made.

When planning these communicative activities, it is advisable to mark the contacts made or to be met on a *timeline* in order to obtain a better overview of the actual or intended time structure (see Fig. 9.5).

9.5.3 Answers to Customer Requests During the Complaint Processing

Active complaint management implies that after the receipt of a complaint all the activities start *from the part of the firm* and no further contact is demanded from the customer.

If the customers deem it necessary to *make follow-up requests* or if they hands in *additional information* later, the employee addressed in each case must be in a position to provide them with the name of the responsible department, or they must see to it that the customers are contacted directly.

If the intermediate customer articulation reaches the responsible employees, they must decide whether it is actually a matter of a *further inquiry* or a *follow-up complaint*. The fact is that it frequently happens that the customers are ostensibly asking about the status of the handling of the case but in reality would like to express

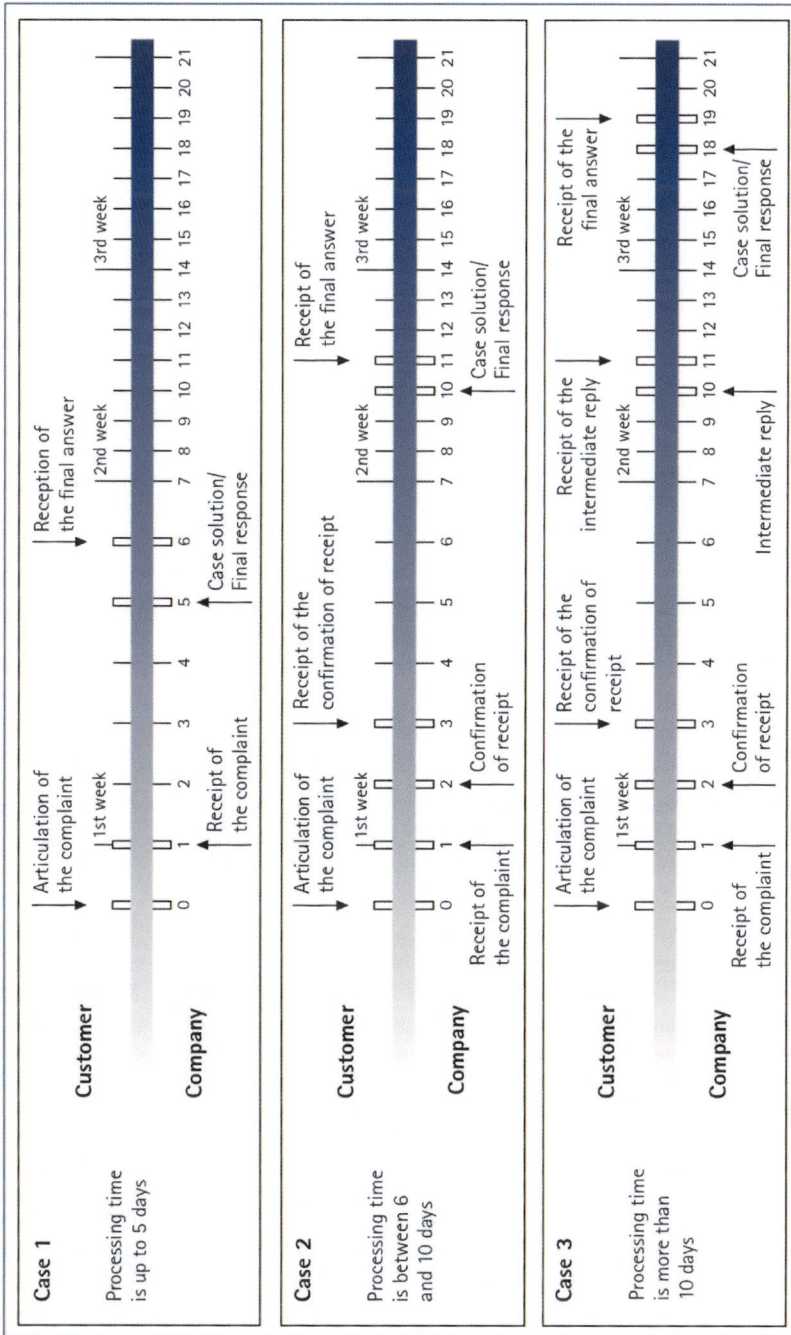

Fig. 9.5   The timing of external communication using written complaints as an example

their dissatisfaction with particular aspects of the complaint processing at the same time. This is the case, for example, if they point out that a promised callback did not take place or the promised intermediate reply did not arrive by the deadline they were given. In such cases, the accepting employees should respond to these points and record the follow-up complaint. This complaint can then be considered in the wording of the final reply. Moreover, information exists that can be used for the improvement of the complaint processing procedures.

Requests and follow-up complaints of the customer during the processing of complaints must be recorded in the complaint-processing history, as well as confirmations of receipt, intermediate replies, final replies and all internally oriented activities.

9.5.4 Ensuring the Quality of Correspondence and Telephone Calls

Customer-oriented communication is the key to achieving a high level of complaint satisfaction. This applies to all communication channels, but systematic quality assurance measures can only be implemented for written and telephone communications.

9.5.4.1 Ensuring the Correspondence Quality

The complete and systematic checking of the correspondence quality concerns all letters sent by the company to the customer (receipts, intermediate replies, final replies), regardless of whether they are sent as letters, faxes or e-mails. In each case, the quality of content and form must be checked against various quality criteria and the correct use of text modules:

Content Quality The quality criteria 'professional competence in responding to customer concerns', 'comprehensibility of the argumentation' as well as 'offering a solution' or 'adequate rejection of a customer demand' are examined here. If necessary, sub-criteria can be created for the individual criteria. It is conceivable, for example, that the criterion 'professional competence in responding to customer's concerns' will be substantiated by the sub-criteria 'concerns raised at the beginning', 'all problems addressed' and 'addressed problems correctly understood'. Another aspect of the content quality concerns the *tonality*, that is the emotional language style, with sub-criteria such as 'understanding of customer annoyance' and 'responding to the individual case (empathy)'.

Formal Quality This aspect includes the quality criteria 'orthography and punctuation' as well as 'other formalities', such as the correct spelling of the customer's name or the correct temporal reference to the customer letter or call.

Correct Use of Text Modules If text modules are used, their correct use is checked.

If each quality criterion for a sample of letters, faxes or e-mails is examined by an independent person for compliance or non-compliance, it is possible to obtain a very

Table 9.10   Review of written correspondence quality in the form of non-compliance rates

| Team | Quality dimension 'Content quality' | | | |
	Professional competence in responding to customer's concerns	Comprehensibility of the argumentation	Responding to the individual case (empathy)	Offering a solution
Team 1	55.0 %	35.0 %	55.0 %	44.0 %
Team 2	58.8 %	5.9 %	35.3 %	33.9 %
Team 3	65.0 %	10.0 %	40.0 %	27.0 %
Team 4	60.0 %	10.0 %	65.0 %	59.5 %
Total	**59.7 %**	**15.2 %**	**48.8 %**	**41.1 %**

| Team | Quality dimension 'Professional competence in responding to customer's concerns' | | |
	Concerns raised at the beginning	All problems addressed	Addressed problems understood correctly
Team 1	45.0 %	45.0 %	15.0 %
Team 2	35.3 %	47.1 %	3.0 %
Team 3	55.0 %	35.0 %	17.2 %
Team 4	25.0 %	55.0 %	22.4 %
Total	**40.1 %**	**45.5 %**	**14.4 %**

Explanatory note (for >Team 1):
In 55% of the replies, the standard 'professional competence in responding to customer concerns' was not fulfilled. This is due to the fact that the standards for the sub criteria listed have not been achieved either individually or collectively.

good overview of the quality achieved per quality criterion, per quality dimension, as well as for the complete written correspondence.

Table 9.10 shows as an example the results of a review of the written correspondence quality for four teams. The results concern the quality dimension 'content quality' with the quality criteria 'professional competence in responding to customer's concerns', 'comprehensibility of the argumentation', 'responding to the individual case/empathy' and 'offering a solution'. For the quality criterion 'professional competence in responding to customer's concerns', the three sub-criteria 'concerns raised at the beginning', 'all problems addressed' and 'addressed problems understood correctly' are also used.

In this example, it is assumed that the same number of complaints was reviewed per team. The reported results represent non-compliance rates, so that the need for action or training becomes immediately apparent. For example, the particular weakness in responding professionally to customer concerns is obvious: in all teams the quality requirements were not fulfilled in more than half of the written replies to complaints.

Such sampling should be carried out on a regular basis. Ideally, the correspondence quality should be reviewed not only at team level, but also at employee level—if it is legally admissible—so that individual feedback can be provided and effective improvements can be achieved.

9.5.4.2 Ensuring the Call Quality

The regular review of the quality of communication with the customer during complaint handling should not only be carried out for correspondence but also for customer conversations, although this is only possible in the case of telephone contacts. Telephone calls can be recorded, taking into account the legal requirements. If no recording of telephone conversations is planned, appropriate samples should be taken within the framework of employee coaching.

The quality criteria specified for correspondence are largely valid for call quality. Only a few communication-specific adjustments are required:

Content Quality The quality criteria 'professional competence in responding to the customer's concerns', 'comprehensibility of the argumentation' as well as 'offering a solution' or 'adequate refusal of a customer demand' are the focus here too. With regard to the emotional tone of the conversation (*tonality*), the criteria 'understanding of customer annoyance' and 'responding to the individual case (empathy)' can also be used again.

Formal Quality In formal terms, quality criteria such as 'correct greeting' and 'correct farewell' should be especially checked.

Only by consistently reviewing the quality of correspondence and calls is it possible to ensure that the company's complaint reaction policy is implemented in every interaction with the complainant.

> **Chapter 9 in Brief**
> - In direct conversations with complainants, five typical phases must be observed: the greeting phase, aggression-reduction phase, conflict-settlement phase, problem-solution and conclusive phase.
> - When responding in writing to complaints, the following content-related aspects must be taken into account: initial wording, problem repetition, conflict settlement, problem solution, concluding wording.
> - Repeat, multiple and follow-up complainants require particularly sensitive treatment.
> - If grumblers and grousers are identified, their complaints must be subjected to a special review.

(continued)

- Scattered complaints, complaints to top management, complaints about employees and threats associated with complaints require special treatment.
- There are three groups of measures that are available as basic solution options: financial, tangible and intangible.
- Financial, tangible and intangible compensations have different consequences for the satisfaction of complainants.
- Under certain conditions, an individual case examination can be waived.
- Most complaints are considered justified from the customer's perspective; even in the case of objectively unjustified complaints, it can make economic sense to react in a fair manner.
- A differentiation of the complaint reaction according to customer value should only be considered with regard to the kind of compensation but not regarding the behavior in the customer contact situation.
- Confirmation of receipt, intermediate replies, final replies and follow-up contacts should be used as forms of communication.
- The timing of the forms of communication must be carefully planned.
- The quality of the complaint correspondence and telephone calls must be reviewed systematically and regularly.

References

Blanding W (1991) Customer service operations: the complete guide. AMACOM, New York

Brückner M (2007) Beschwerdemanagement, 2nd edn. Redline Wirtschaft, Heidelberg

Brymer RA (1991) Employee empowerment: a guest-driven leadership strategy. Cornell Rest Admin Qual 32(1):58–68

Butler F (2009) Customer relationship management: concepts and technologies, 2nd edn. Routledge, Abington

Chase RB, Dasu S (2001) Want to perfect your company's service? Use behavioral science. Harv Bus Rev 79(6):78–84

Cottle DW (1990) Client-centered service: how to keep them coming back for more. Wiley, New York

Dealing with Angry Customers (2016) https://callcentrehelper.com/dealing-with-angry-customers-152.htm. Accessed 8 Nov 2017

Estelami H (2000) Competitive and procedural determinants of delight and disappointment in consumer complaint outcomes. J Serv Res 2(3):285–300

Fader P (2012) Customer centricity: focus on the right customers for strategic advantage, 2nd edn. Wharton Digital Press, Philadelphia

Goodwin C, Ross I (1990) Consumer evaluations of responses to complaints: what's fair and why. J Cons Mark 7(2):39–47

Günter B, Helm S (2011) Kundenbewertung im Rahmen des CRM. In: Hippner H et al (eds) Grundlagen des CRM, 3rd edn. Springer, Wiesbaden, pp 271–292

Gupta S et al (2004) Valuing customers. J Mark Res 41(1):7–18

Haeske U (2001) Beschwerden und Reklamationen managen: Kritische Kunden Sind gute Kunden! Beltz Verlag, Weinheim and Basel

Haeske U (2010) Kommunikation mit Kunden, 3rd edn. Cornelsen Verlag, Berlin

Harris LC, Reynolds KL (2004) Jaycustomer behavior: an exploration of types and motives in the hospitality industry. J Serv Mark 18(5):339–357

Helm S et al (2006) Suppliers' willingness to end unprofitable customer relationships: an exploratory investigation in the German mechanical engineering sector. Eur J Mark 40(3–4):366–383

Helm S et al (2017) Kundenwert—Eine Einführung in die theoretischen und praktischen Herausforderungen der Bewertung von Kundenbeziehungen. In: Helm S et al (eds) Kundenwert: Grundlagen—innovative Konzepte—Praktische Umsetzungen, 4th edn. Wiesbaden, Springer Gabler, pp 3–34

Krafft M, Bues M (2017) Aktuelle Konzepte zur Messung des ökonomischen Kundenwerts. In: Helm S et al (eds) Kundenwert: Grundlagen—innovative Konzepte—Praktische Umsetzungen, 4th edn. Wiesbaden, Springer Gabler, pp 237–253

Kumar V (2008) A customer lifetime value. Now Publishers, Hanover

Kumar V, Pansari A (2015) Aggregate and individual-level customer lifetime value. In: Kumar V, Shah D (eds) Handbook on research on customer equity in marketing. Edward Elgar, Cheltenham, pp 44–75

Malthouse CE (2013) Segmentation and lifetime value models using SAS. SAS Institute, Cary

Maxham JG, Netemeyer RG (2002) A longitudinal study of complaining customers' evaluations of multiple service failures and recovery efforts. J Mark 66(4):57–71

McColl-Kennedy JR, Sparks BA (2003) Application of fairness theory to service failures and service recovery. J Serv Res 5(3):251–266

Piron F, Young M (2000) Retail borrowing: Insights and implications on returning used merchandise. Int J Retail Distrib Manag 28(1):27–36

Plein K (2016) Dysfunktionales Beschwerdeverhalten: Ausprägungen, Entstehung, Auswirkungen und management-Implikationen. Springer Gabler, Wiesbaden

Respond to a Complaint (2017) http://www.writeexpress.com/compla05.html. Accessed 20 Nov 2017

Reynolds KL, Harris LC (2005) When service failure is not service failure: an exploration of the forms and motives of "illegitimate" customer complaining. J Serv Mark 19(5):321–335

Rust RT et al (2000) Driving customer equity: how customer lifetime value is reshaping corporate strategy. The Free Press, New York

Servmark (2009) Interne Studie zu Beschwerdeführer follow up-Kontakten. Servmark, München

Sewell C, Brown PB (2002) Customer for life. Doubleday, New York

Stauss B, Seidel W (2009) Customer care—Wertschöpfung durch inbound marketing, Thexis. Fachzeitschrift für Marketing 26(6):18–23

Issues Raised
- How can the quantitative distribution of complaints be determined?
- Which location parameters should be calculated?
- How can the correlations between the variables be investigated?
- Which more differentiated frequency analyses in terms of quantity and time make sense?
- How can data from complaint analysis be used to prioritize customer problems and necessary corrective measures by urgency?

The area of complaint evaluation is the *first building block of indirect complaint management*, whose measures can be carried out without direct customer contact. What is important here is systematically exploiting the information potential that is contained in the critical customer statements. The more precisely the complaint analysis captures the "voice of the customer", the more the firm is in a position to move from problem diagnosis to effective *problem prevention*. Basically, it can be distinguished between *complaint analysis* (Sect. 10.1) and *prioritization of problems (Sect. 10.2)*.

10.1   Complaint Analysis

In order to utilize effectively the indications of operational weaknesses and market opportunities that are found in complaints, it is essential that the entire complaint volume be analyzed quantitatively with respect to certain important characteristics.

Regarding the methods to be used one must distinguish between univariate and bivariate techniques. *Univariate techniques* analyze just one variable. They include absolute and relative frequency distributions, as well as location parameters (such as arithmetic mean and median). *Bivariate methods* (such as cross-tabulations) permit the examination of correlations between two variables. These methods will be addressed in greater detail below, using the example of the *complaint analysis of a car dealer*.

10.1.1 Frequency Distributions

Absolute and relative frequency distributions provide an overview of the quantitative distribution of the complaint volume—that is how the number of complaints is distributed across different categories. The absolute frequency refers to the number of complaints per category. The relative frequency is the result of dividing the absolute frequency of a complaint category by the total number of complaints.

In the following *example*, a car dealer is interested in knowing how the annual volume of 300 total complaints is distributed across five defined problem categories: Work not agreed on, Incomprehensible invoice, Faulty execution of the order, Unfriendly handling and Long waiting time. Table 10.1 provides a corresponding

Table 10.1 Absolute and relative frequency distribution of complaints by type of problem

Type of problem	Absolute frequency	Relative frequency
Work not agreed on	60	20 %
Incomprehensible invoice	75	25 %
Faulty execution of the order	45	15 %
Unfriendly handling	30	10 %
Long waiting time	90	30 %
Total	300	100 %

overview; it shows that complaints about long waiting times appear most frequently (absolute: 90; relative: 30%).

The *histogram* gives a quick overview of the frequency distribution (see Fig. 10.1). In this graphic representation, the individual criteria (here: problem categories) are plotted on the horizontal axis, while the relative complaint frequencies are plotted on the vertical axis. The height of each bar corresponds to the percentage frequency of a problem category.

The quantitative distribution becomes even more straightforward when it is presented in the form of a *Pareto diagram*, since such a diagram clearly visualizes a potential concentration of the complaint volume in a few categories. The first step in constructing a Pareto diagram is to put the relative frequencies of the individual problem categories into a hierarchy. These categories then are distributed from left to

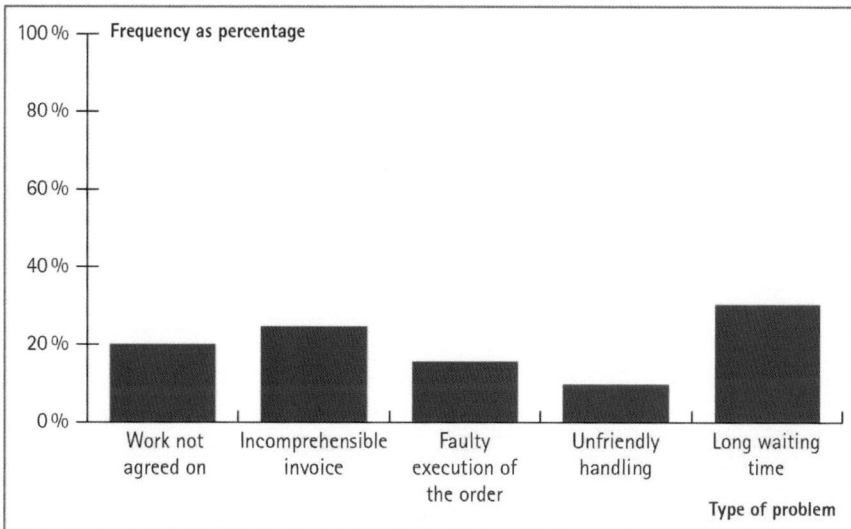

Fig. 10.1 Graphic representation of the frequency distribution as histogram

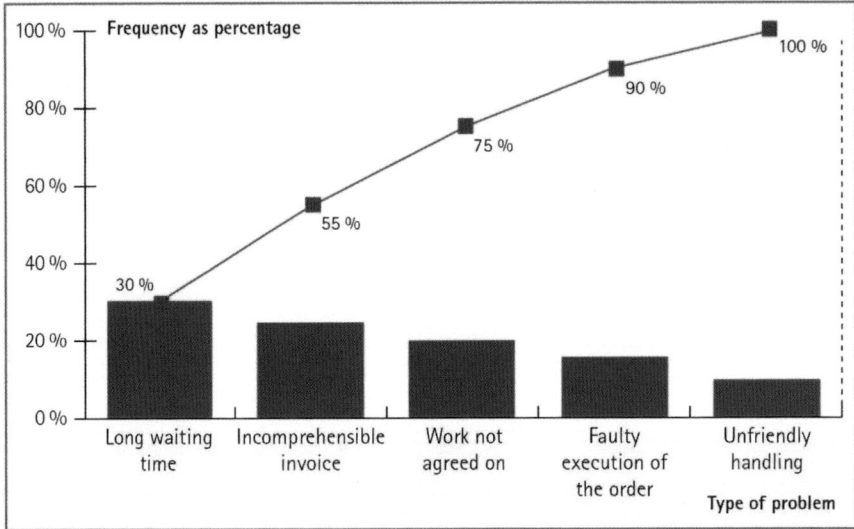

Fig. 10.2 Example of a Pareto diagram (type of problem)

right in descending order; the height of the bar indicates the relative frequency. In addition, the cumulative relative frequencies are plotted as a line diagram. From the Pareto diagram in Fig. 10.2, it immediately becomes apparent that the main problems are found in the categories of "Long waiting time" and "Incomprehensible invoice", which are collectively responsible for 55% of the customer complaints.

In principle, univariate frequency analyses, as they are presented here in an example citing problem categories, make sense *for all complaint information*. Tables 10.2 and 10.3 make this clear for complaint content and complaint processing information and provide indications as to which questions can be answered with the respective frequency distribution and for which individual tasks of complaint and retention management the answers provide an informational basis.

It is often advisable to calculate location parameters, in particular *arithmetic mean* and *median*, for the frequency distributions.

These measures are explained on the basis of complaint figures received last month by various car dealers of an automobile manufacturer. These dealers belong to the same size group and are either assigned to Region North or Region South. If you divide the sum of all complaints for Region North (516) by the number of car dealers (12), you get the arithmetic mean, i.e. the average number of complaints per dealership (43). A corresponding calculation for Region South yields a value of 54 and thus indicates that the average number of complaints at car dealers in this region is considerably higher (see Table 10.4).

However, the arithmetic mean for Region South does not make it clear that the value is distorted upwards by the unusually high number of complaints at the Southampton car dealer (142). In such cases it is advisable to use the *median* instead of the arithmetic mean. This is the value that appears in the middle position when you sort the values by size (see Table 10.5).

Table 10.2 Frequency distributions of complaint-content information

Complaint-content information	Questions in the context of frequency analysis	Relevance of analysis result
Complainant		
Internal or external complainant	▪ How many internal complaints were there in the reporting period? ▪ What is the share of internal complaints in relation to the total number of complaints?	▪ Internal process monitoring ▪ Cause analysis
Individual complainant (master data)	▪ How many complainants were there in the reporting period? ▪ How many times did an individual customer complain during this period? ▪ How many customers complained several times? ▪ How is the total number of complaints distributed across different customer groups?	▪ Complaint management controlling (calculation of articulation rate) ▪ Identification of repeat complainants and of gumblers ▪ Determination of customer group-specific problem perceptions ▪ Development of customer group-specific stimulation measures
Complainant's connection to the complaint case	▪ To what extent did the person who was directly affected by the problem take the initiative and complain in person? ▪ Which other persons/institutions did complain on behalf of the person affected?	▪ Detection of complaint barriers ▪ Complaint stimulation ▪ Development of sender-specific forms of reaction
Complainant's degree of annoyance	▪ How often were the customers annoyed and to what extent? ▪ What is the mean value on the annoyance scale?	▪ Evaluation of the relevance of the problems from the customer's perspective ▪ Basis for the implementation of the FRAC
Complainant's behavioral intentions	▪ Which behavioral intentions have the complaining customers expressed and how many times? ▪ What is the number of customers who threaten to switch? ▪ What is the number of customers who engage third-party institutions (media, consumer organizations)?	▪ Evaluation of the relevance of the problems from customer's perspective ▪ Clues for identifying jeopardized customer potential ▪ Development of reaction forms and dialog instruments directed towards third-party institutions
Complaint problem		
Type of problem	▪ Which problems led to complaints and how often?	▪ Priorities in the context of the continuous improvement process ▪ Cause analysis
Place where the problem occurred	▪ How many complaints were there per sales region (sales district, subsidiary) in the report period?	▪ Monitoring and controlling of decentralized units ▪ Detection of major problem areas specific to each organizational unit ▪ Cause analysis
Date and, if applicable, time of the problem occurence	▪ Are there particular times when more problems occur (time of day, week day, month etc.)?	▪ Cause analysis

(continued)

Table 10.2 (continued)

Initial or follow-up complaint	• How many initial complaints were addressed to the firm during the reporting period? • How many follow-up complaints were addressed to the firm during the reporting period? • What is the share of follow-up complaints in relation to the total number of complaints?	• Cofiguration of complaint management capacity and process • Calculation of performance figures in the context of complaint management controlling (follow-up rate) • Monitoring of the degree of goal achievement in complaint stimulation and problem minimization
Case solution desired by the customer	• Which solutions/compensations were expected by the complainants and how often?	• Clues to customer expectations in problem situations • Indications of desired reactions • Indications of adjustments needed in the existing problem solution/compensation policy
Warranty or goodwill case	• In how many complaint cases were warranty claims asserted? • In how many cases did the customer request a goodwill solution? • What are the respective shares of the above cases in relation to the total number of complaints?	• Monitoring of the warranty policy • Monitoring of the goodwill policy • Problem analysis in R&D and manufacturing
Urgency of reaction	• In how many complaint cases did the defined urgency levels have to be activated and how often in each case?	• Identification of serious problems • Monitoring of non-routine processes
Complaint object		
Product and/or service	• How many times during the reporting period did the customer perceive a product/service as problematic? • Which products/services were most frequently addressed in complaints (in aboslute and in relative terms)?	• Cause analysis • Indications of the setting of priorities in improvement measures • Assesment of the potential dangers with respect to product-related sales decreases, image losses or cross-selling losses
Other aspects of the market offering	• To what extent are other aspects of marketing made the subject of complaints? • What is the share of complaints that are related to pricing (promotional, etc.) measures?	• Indications of weaknesses in the strategic and operative marketing planning • Evaluation of the urgency of marketing-related corrective measures
Sociopolitical behavior	• To what extent are sociopolitical topics addressed in complaints? • How are sociopolitical complaints distributed across the specific subject areas?	• Indications of percieved weaknesses in the firm's sociopolitical engagement • Evaluation of the urgency to make modifications in the basic corporate strategies with social reference

Table 10.3 Frequency distributions of complaint-handling information

Complaint-handling information	Questions in the context of frequency distributions	Relevance of the analysis results
Complaint acceptance		
Date of acceptance	▪ How many complaints reached the firm at different times or in different periods of time?	▪ Basis of the capacity planning in the area of complaint management (particularly for the complaint center)
Complaint channels	▪ Which complaint channels were used by dissatisfied customers and how often?	▪ Monitoring of complaint stimulating measures ▪ Resource planning
Addressee of the complaint	▪ How many complaints were adressed to which persons/ departments? ▪ How many complaints were directly addressed to the top management?	▪ Monitoring of complaint stimulating measures
Complaint accepting employee	▪ Who or which department has accepted how many complaints and in which period?	▪ Monitoring of the adherence of the principle of complaint ownership ▪ Resource planning ▪ Indications of the targeted use of personnel-oriented measures
Complaint processing		
Complaint owner	▪ Which employee was involved in which processing procedures and how often?	▪ Monitoring of the adherence of the principle of complaint ownership
Complaint processing procedure	▪ Which processing prodedures were initiated and how often? ▪ How many written complaints were processed in how many days?	▪ Monitoring of the complaint processing procedure ▪ Monitoring of the processing speed
Complaint reaction		
Communication with the complainant	▪ How many written complaints got an acknowledgement of receipt within how many days?	▪ Monitoring of time standards for the communication with the complainant
Actually realized solution	▪ Which problem solutions/ compensations were realized and how often?	▪ Monitoring of the reaction policy
Promises made to the customer	▪ Which promises were already made during the acceptance and how often?	▪ Monitoring of the complaint acceptance ▪ Basis for trainings

The median of complaints in Region North is 41, which means that half of the car dealers in this region have fewer than 41 complaints, while the other half have received more than 41 complaints. The median for Region South is 47, which means

Table 10.4 Arithmetic mean of complaint figures in car dealers of two regions

Complaints			
Region North		**Region South**	
Dealer York	37	Dealer Plymouth	33
Dealer Manchester	40	Dealer Exeter	39
Dealer Sheffield	58	Dealer Portsmouth	32
Dealer Nottingham	54	Dealer Bristol	52
Dealer Blackpool	54	Dealer Southampton	142
Dealer Liverpool	48	Dealer London, Croydon	44
Dealer Lincoln	39	Dealer London, Enfield	34
Dealer Leeds	27	Dealer Oxford	46
Dealer Middlesbrough	29	Dealer Ipswitch	63
Dealer Huddersfield	42	Dealer Bath	60
Dealer Bradford	49	Dealer Reading	48
Dealer Newcastle upon Tyne	39	Dealer Canterbury	55
Total	**516**	**Total**	**648**
Arithmetic mean	516/12 = **43**	**Arithmetic mean**	648/12 = **54**

Table 10.5 Median of complaint figures in car dealers of two regions

Complaints			
Region North		**Region South**	
Dealer York	27	Dealer Plymouth	32
Dealer Manchester	29	Dealer Exeter	33
Dealer Sheffield	37	Dealer Portsmouth	34
Dealer Nottingham	39	Dealer Bristol	39
Dealer Blackpool	39	Dealer Southampton	44
Dealer Liverpool	**40**	**Dealer London, Croydon**	**46**
Dealer Lincoln	**42**	**Dealer London, Enfield**	**48**
Dealer Leeds	48	Dealer Oxford	52
Dealer Middlesbrough	49	Dealer Ipswich	55
Dealer Huddersfield	54	Dealer Bath	60
Dealer Bradford	54	Dealer Reading	63
Dealer Newcastle upon Tyne	58	Dealer Canterbury	142
Total	**516**	**Total**	**648**
Median*	(40+42)/2 = **41**	**Median***	(46+48)/2 = **47**

* Since this is an even number of car dealers, the median must be determined by calculating the average of the two mean values

Table 10.6 Cross-tabulation of "type of product" and "type of problem"

Type of product \ Type of problem	Work not agreed on	Incomprehensible invoice	Faulty execution of the order	Unfriendly handling	Long waiting time	Total
Brand A	24 (20 %)	15 (12.5 %)	30 (25 %)	24 (20 %)	27 (22.5 %)	120 (100 %)
Brand B	36 (20 %)	60 (33.3 %)	15 (8.4 %)	6 (3.3 %)	63 (35 %)	180 (100 %)
Total	60	75	45	30	90	300

that the 'outlier value' of the Southampton car dealer—which is a major contributor to the arithmetic mean of 54—has a lesser impact. The determination of the median thus contributes significantly to a better understanding of the frequency distribution and helps to avoid false conclusions that are possible when relying on 'distorted' arithmetic means.

10.1.2 Cross-Tabulations

Univariate frequency analyses provide a good overview of the distribution of the total complaint volume across the important criteria. Based on such an analysis, it can be established, for example, how often a particular problem appeared and to what extent various products are affected by it. However, whether a systematic correlation exists between problem appearance and complaint object (product) can only be determined with *bivariate* methods that *simultaneously* include *two criteria*—for example, problem category and complaint object—in the analysis.

Cross-tabulation should be regarded as the most important bivariate technique. Here the characteristic values of two variables are arranged in a matrix—*the cross table*—, and the frequency with which each combination occurs is recorded.

An *example* of a cross-tabulation in the context of complaint analysis is reproduced in Table 10.6.

This cross-tabulation links the criteria "Type of Product" and "Type of Problem" and provides an answer to the question: *"What relationship exists between the type of product/service on the one hand the problem occurred on the other hand?"* In the example presented, it is assumed that the car dealer offers two different brands

("Brand A" and "Brand B") and examines the correlation between the brands and the number of received complaints.

The *absolute and relative frequencies* indicate that for "Brand A" it is primarily the problem of "Faulty execution of the order" that crops up (25%) and for "Brand B" there is especially the problem "Long waiting time" (35%) that appears.

When using cross tables in practice, there is often a lack of a systematic analysis of the relationships between the combined criteria. Therefore, three essential aspects of the *procedure for creating and interpreting cross tables* are discussed here: the selection of the combined criteria, the arrangement of the criteria in the matrix, and the statistical testing to determine the strength of the relationship.

With the help of a cross table, it is investigated how two complaint criteria are related to each other. In principle, it is possible to combine all recorded criteria with each other. However, this does not make any sense at all, but often only produces data without an explanatory value. Therefore, at the beginning of every cross-tabulation the *choice must be made as to which criteria* will be combined. The solution of this task requires considerations of meaningful relationships between the individual variables. For example, it is conceivable that the nature of the problem experienced could influence the extent of customer annoyance, or that customers belonging to different customer groups might perceive different problems. Cross-tabulation is only recommended if such a *logical connection* can be made. Table 10.7 contains an overview of especially meaningful relationships among categories of complaint information.

Considerations of the relationships between the variables are directly associated with assumptions about which *variable* can be *used as a predictor of another variable*. The variable used as a predictor is designated as the "Predictor Variable", the variable to be forecast as the "Response Variable". In our example, we assume that the problems that occur depend on the product type. So the variable "Type of product" is the independent variable and "Type of problem" is the dependent variable.

This is taken into account in the corresponding *arrangement of the criteria in the matrix*: The attributes of the response variable are shown in the columns, whereas the predictor variables are arranged in the rows. The percentage values are always calculated in the direction of the independent variable (that is, row by row). In the example cited, we assume that whichever problems appear depend on the type of product. Therefore, the variable "Type of Product" is the predictor variable, and "Type of Problem" is the response variable.

In Table 10.8 *cross-tabulations with important conclusions for complaint management* are characterized. In the figure, the observed variables are always given in the order of the predictor variable followed by the response variable.

The next step is to pose the question of *how unambiguous the results of the cross-tabulation are*. This occurs in the context of a contingency analysis, which helps clarify whether the variables are independent of one another and how strong the association between the predictor and the response variable is.

Cross-tabulations should be used continuously as part of the complaint analysis. It is advisable to use *supporting software*—either special complaint management

Table 10.7 Particular reasonable relationships between variables of complaint information

	1. Type of problem	2. Place	3. Warranty or goodwill case	4. Urgency of reaction	5. Customer group	6. Extent of annoyance/behavioral intention	7. Product and/or service	8. Complaint channel	9. Addressee of the complaint	10. Actually realized solution
1. Type of problem	▩					●				●
2. Place	●	▩								
3. Warranty or goodwill case			▩							
4. Urgency of reaction				▩						●
5. Customer group	●				▩		●	●	●	
6. Extent of annoyance/ behavioral intention						▩				
7. Product and/or service	●		●				▩			
8. Complaint channel								▩		
9. Addressee of the complaint									▩	●
10. Actually realized solution										▩

programs, in which this analysis tool is integrated, or spreadsheet programs such as Microsoft Excel, in which cross-tabulation and the corresponding tests can be carried out automatically.

10.1.3 The Quantitative and Temporal Dimensions of Complaint Analysis

Within the scope of the complaint analysis, it must also be decided whether the analysis should refer to all complaints or to partial quantities. In addition, the temporal reference of the analysis must be determined.

Table 10.8 Explanation of important cross-tabulations

Considered variables	Relationship	Relevance of the relationship
Type of problem and degree of annoyance/ behavioral intention	The customer's degree of annoyance and his/her behavioral intention depend on the problem type.	▪ Problem priorization from the customer's perspective ▪ Access to problems that induce the customer to switch
Type of problem and actually realized solution	The actually realized solution depends on the problem type.	▪ Indications of consistency and appropriateness of complaint solutions
Place of problem occurrence and type of problem	Different problems occur more often at certain places (subsidiaries, branch offices).	▪ Indication of subsidiary-specific problem focus
Urgency of reaction and actually realized solution	The actually realized solution depends on the reaction urgency of the complaint, above all on the customer's threaten potential.	▪ Indication of the compliance with guidelines for the treatment of special cases
Customer group and type of problem	The articulated problem types depend on the complainant's affiliation to a certain customer group.	▪ Segment-specific problem identification ▪ Segment-specific urgency to eliminate problems
Customer group and product/ service	Members of different customer groups complain about problems regarding different products/ services.	▪ Segment-specific identification of problem afflicted products/ services
Customer group and complaint channel	Members of different customer groups use different complaint channels.	▪ Segment-specific stimulation measures
Customer group and addressee of the complaint	The addressing of a complaint depends on the complainant's affiliation to a customer group.	▪ Segment-specific stimulation and channelling
Product/service and type of problem	The occurence of problems depends on the particular complaint object (product/service).	▪ Indications of product- and service-related causes of the articulated problems ▪ Setting of priorities in the context of improvement measures
Product/service and warranty or goodwill case	The occurence of warranty or goodwill cases depends on the particular complaint object (product/service).	▪ Setting of priorities in the context of improvement measures in order to reduce warranty costs and goodwill costs
Addressee of the complaint and actually realized solution	The actually realized solution depends on the addressee of the complaint.	▪ Indication of the consistency of the complaint reaction

10.1.3.1 Analysis of Subsets of the Complaint Volume

In order to provide detailed information, it makes sense to apply univariate frequency distributions and bivariate methods for the analysis of relations between variables not only to the total complaint volume, but also to subsets of complaints. For example it may be of interest to managers who are responsible for "Brand A" in the mentioned car dealership to determine how often cars of this business segment were affected by the five problem categories recorded, without the same assessment being undertaken simultaneously for the "Brand B" division.

It may also be important to know whether complainants were offered different solutions to the same problem, depending on the addressees in the firm to whom they directed their complaints. In this case, it is advisable to relate the cross-tabulation with the characteristics "Addressee of the complaint" and "Actual realized solution" to individual problem categories, and not to the total complaint volume. A further refinement would be to restrict the analysis only to the most annoyed customers. In principle, each complaint criteria can serve as basis for a further differentiation of the analysis.

10.1.3.2 Temporal Analyses

In addition to the content dimension, the *temporal dimension* of the complaint analysis must also be considered. In doing so, one must differentiate between time-period analyses and time series analyses.

In *time-period analyses*, the facts to be examined are considered for a specific time period—e.g. for a year. From this analysis, one obtains a status report about the time period under consideration. The car dealer in question is, for instance, interested in knowing how often the five problem categories have given the customers of "Brand A" reason to complain during the current business year. The corresponding frequency distribution is then specifically created for the time period of this year (see Fig. 10.3). Depending upon the degree of time detail desired, other relevant time periods, say, a day, a week, a month or a quarter, can be selected.

If frequency distributions and cross-tabulations are performed for different points in time (e.g. days, weeks or months) that follow one another chronologically within a certain time period, one can speak of *time series analyses*. They make clear the temporal development of the analyzed contents over the time period under consideration. Figure 10.4 shows the development of complaint figures about long waiting times at the car dealer for a 6-month period.

Time series analyses are particularly important for resource planning in complaint management as well as for cause-and-effect analyses.

Complainants do not articulate their problems, e.g. by telephone, in an evenly distributed pattern over the day or week; peak hours may occur, which can lead to an overload of the telephone system and/or staff. In this context, it is important not only to evaluate the number of complaints for the period of 1 week, but also to record their development over the course of the day for half-hour periods. With the help of such time series analyses it is possible to *plan resources* appropriately, and in particular to adapt the personnel capacities of call centers to peak times or times with few calls.

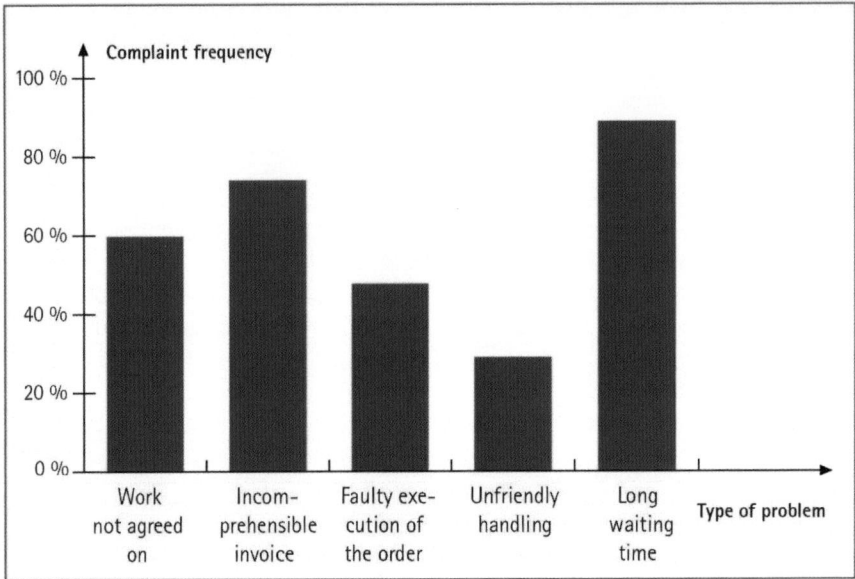

Fig. 10.3 Time-period analysis

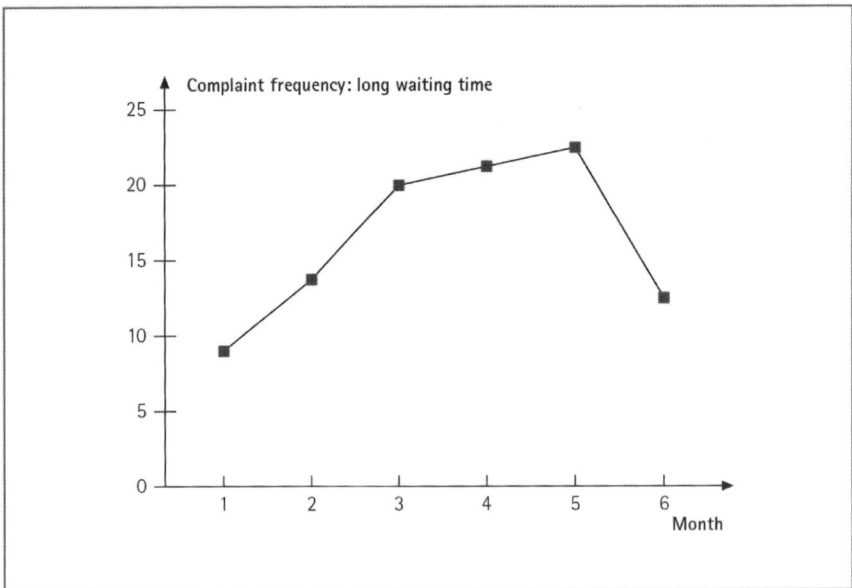

Fig. 10.4 Time series analysis

In addition, time series analyses are necessary to examine the impact of complaint management and quality management measures. For example, if a complaint telephone is set up to channel complaints, it is advisable to check the distribution of the complaints across the individual complaint channels for each month and compare the numbers over time. In this way, it quickly becomes clear whether the newly established procedure of a complaint telephone is more often used by dissatisfied customers and whether less suitable complaint channels (such as written complaints to various departments in the company) are actually used to a lesser extent. The same applies to the assessment of the effectiveness of quality management measures.

If time periods and time series from different periods are contrasted with each other in the complaint analyses shown here, one can speak of *period comparisons*. Here, the results for a particular time period or time series are compared with the results of a corresponding time period or time series. Again, the goal of this comparison is to track certain developments, although it is not the chronological progression that is the focus, but rather the comparison of the results from corresponding points in time from different periods. Figure 10.5 shows the development of complaint figures about long waiting times at the car dealer for 6 months of two periods.

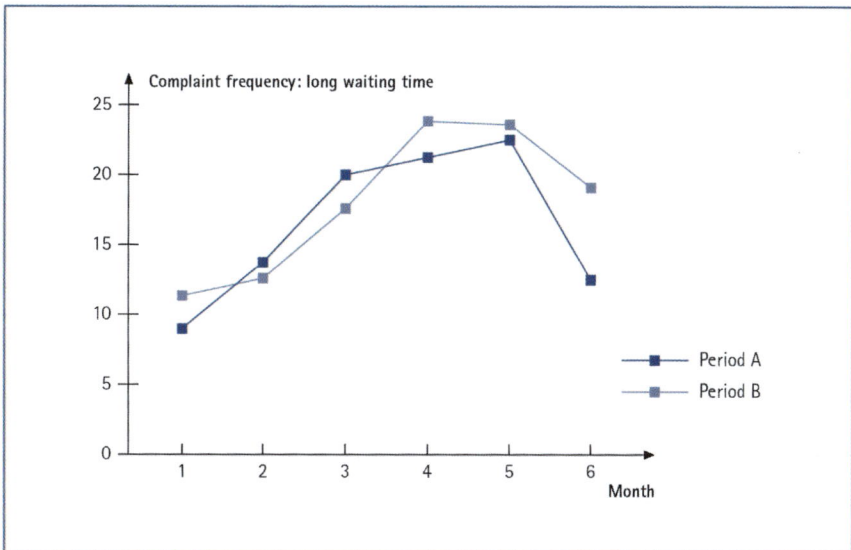

Fig. 10.5 Period comparison

10.2   Approaches for the Prioritization of Problems

What is important in the next step of the analysis is *to prioritize the problems* articulated in the complaints *from the customer's point of view* and consequently to make the "voice of the customer" the maxim for the continual improvement process. This prioritization is not based exclusively on the frequency with which a certain problem is made the object of a complaint, but also on the subjective importance that the customer attaches to a problem. Here, there are different ways of linking the collected data on frequency and perceived relevance in customer-oriented frequency-relevance analyses, thus creating a ranking of the urgency of corrective measures (Sect. 10.2.1).

However, it is also conceivable that companies, irrespective of the current complaint situation, can identify problems that must be absolutely avoided because they massively violate the quality promise to customers, greatly endanger customer relationships and lead to high warranty or guarantee costs. In these cases, the particularly problematic errors and problems can be defined and weighted *from the company's point of view*. Taking into account the frequency, company-oriented frequency-relevance analyses can then be used to determine the most serious quality deficiencies and therefore the most urgent quality improvement measures (Sect. 10.2.2).

10.2.1 Customer-Oriented Frequency-Relevance Analysis of Complaints (FRAC)

The *Frequency-Relevance Analysis of Complaints (FRAC)* is based on the fundamental consideration that the more frequently a problem occurs and the more annoying or significant the customer finds its occurrence, the more urgently the problem requires the attention of management. Accordingly, two types of information are necessary in each case with respect to the problems experienced by customers: on the one hand, data on the *frequency of the problem occurrence* are required; on the other hand, information is also necessary on *how significant* the customers consider this problem to be *(relevance)*.

10.2.1.1 Determination of the Frequency and Relevance of Customer Problems

Frequency analysis provides unambiguous and objective values concerning the *frequency* with which customers articulate a particular problem. In contrast, to determine the relevance of the problem from the customer's point of view, indicators must be used.

Three different *indicators* for the problem relevance perceived by customers are presented below: (1) the extent of the customer annoyance triggered by the problem, (2) serious consequences that customers announce, and (3) the actual migration of customers as a result of the annoyance.

1. A key indicator of the perceived relevance of the problem is the *degree of annoyance* of the complainant. In principle, this can be measured with the aid of an annoyance scale, as presented in the context of the documentation of complaint information (see Fig. 7.1). However, its use is only possible to a limited extent, because customers cannot be directly requested to indicate the extent of their annoyance on a scale. An application is only possible in the case of Internet complaints, if the complaint mask provides an appropriate field. Consequently, an external evaluation of the problem relevance *by employees in complaint contact* must take place. These evaluations must follow an appropriate classification based on the complainant's wording and pattern of behavior. Since there are no fully unambiguous criteria for this, and the evaluations by various employees can also turn out differently, values derived in this way should be interpreted with a certain degree of caution.

   An alternative to this external evaluation is to survey the customers immediately after the closure of the complaint process in the context of *follow-up interviews* as to the extent of their annoyance and the steps they have taken or consider taking. Consequently, a corresponding scale for the measurement of the perceived relevance is to be integrated in the survey instrument. Indeed, these results also involve some distortion, since a certain period of time has already elapsed and additional complaint experiences now exist. However, the degree of the annoyance is assessed *by the customers themselves*—and not by the employees. By comparing the subsequent customer information with the direct employee estimates, the *extent of agreement* can be determined, which provides an initial indication of the accuracy of the employees' evaluation.

2. A second way of assessing the perceived problem relevance is to draw on the particularly *serious consequences* threatened by complainants in the context of their complaints. This includes, in particular, the threat of migration/termination and the announcement that they will involve the media, lawyers or third-party institutions (such as consumer organizations or regulatory authorities). However, the prerequisite for this procedure is that these intended consequences are recorded during the acceptance of the complaint.

3. In the first two variants mentioned above, either an emotional state of the complainants (annoyance) or their behavioral intentions (e.g. planned migration) are used as a criterion of relevance. The third alternative takes into account the *actual migration behavior*, i.e. the extent to which the problems have actually caused customers to terminate the business relationship. This can be done within the framework of a *lost-customer survey*, which is particularly applicable to contractual customer relationships (Stauss and Seidel 2005).

   In a survey of lost customers, either all migrants or a representative sample of them are asked to state which concrete causes led to the termination of the business relationship. It is obvious that problems that cause terminations are particularly relevant to customers.

   Depending on which method is used to assess the relevance of the problem, there is also a different variant of customer-oriented frequency-relevance analyses: the Annoyance-FRAC, the Intention-FRAC and the Lost-Customer-

FRAC. However, since the logic of the linkage between frequency and relevance is similar in all three cases, only the Annoyance-FRAC is described in detail below, while the description of the Intention-FRAC and the Customer-Loss-FRAC is limited to necessary additions.

10.2.1.2 The Annoyance-FRAC

In order to carry out the frequency-relevance analysis of complaints based on information on the extent of the annoyance (*Annoyance-FRAC*), data must be available on the frequency of the problems addressed in customer complaints and on the annoyance caused by the respective problems.

Calculation of Problem-Value Indices

To illustrate the methodological approach, reference is again made to the example of a car dealer's complaint volume. The analysis of the complaints received during the observation period shows the *frequency* with which the respective problems occurred. In addition, follow-up interviews provide data on the perceived relevance of these problems. The average value calculated using the annoyance scale expresses the *relevance of the problem from the customer's point of view.*

By multiplying the frequency and the average relevance, the *problem-related relevance values* can be obtained. By subsequently dividing the problem-related relevance values by the total sum of all relevance values, the respective *Problem-Value Indices (PVI)* are obtained. They express the percentage proportion of each problem with regard to the total customer dissatisfaction articulated in complaints.

It is obvious that problems with the greatest PVI also have the *highest priority* and thus take precedence in being systematically analyzed and solved. In our example it becomes clear that, from the customer's point of view, it is not the most frequently mentioned problem 'long waiting time', but the problem 'work not agreed on' that is of particular urgency (see Table 10.9).

Table 10.9 Calculation of problem-value indices (PVI)

Customer problem	Frequency	Ø Relevance	Relevance value	PVI[a]	Rank
Unfriendly handling	30	2.5	75	7.9	⑤
Faulty execution of the order	45	4.4	198	20.9	③
Work not agreed on	60	4.5	270	28.5	①
Incomprehensible invoice	75	3.0	225	23.7	②
Long waiting time	90	2.0	180	19.0	④
Total	300	–	948	100.0	–

[a]Problem Value Index (PVI) $= \frac{\text{Relevance value} \times 100}{\text{Sum of relevance values}}$

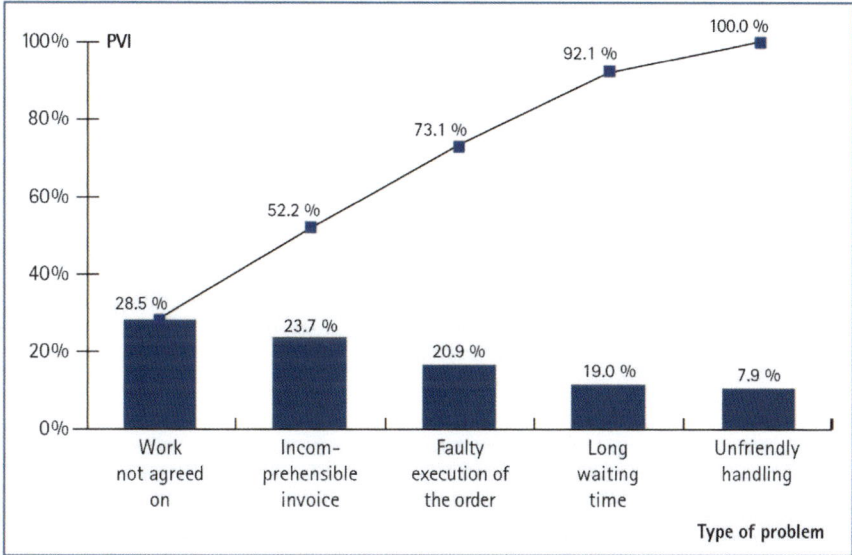

Fig. 10.6   Pareto diagram of the problem-value indices (FRAC diagram)

The FRAC Diagram

In order to *visualize the urgency of troubleshooting measures*, it now makes sense to depict the PVI graphically in the form of a *Pareto diagram* (see Fig. 10.6). On the abscissa, the problems—arranged in descending order according to their PVIs—are represented as bars, and their cumulative sums are subsequently drawn in as a line plot. In our example, it can be seen that the first two problem categories account for about 50% of the total problem.

The FRAC Matrix

A different form of prioritization of customer problems on the basis of the frequency and relevance values can take place with the help of a two-dimensional diagram that shows the *complaint frequency* (in percent) on the horizontal axis and the *average relevance per problem* on the vertical axis. Each problem can then be exactly placed in the diagram according to the (percentage) frequency of its occurrence and the perceived average relevance. By plotting dividing lines, one can obtain a *FRAC matrix* in which the problems are assigned to one of four fields according to their respective frequency-relevance combination (see Fig. 10.7).

Naturally, the problems found in the *upper right quadrant* ("Work not agreed on" and "Incomprehensible invoice") take first priority. After that, it has to be asked whether the problems that are perceived as having low relevance by many customers (*lower right quadrant*) should be solved first, or whether one should primarily eliminate those problems that actually appear less often, but are rated as more relevant (*upper left quadrant*). There is no general recommendation for making this decision, but there is a lot to be said for first addressing the problem with the

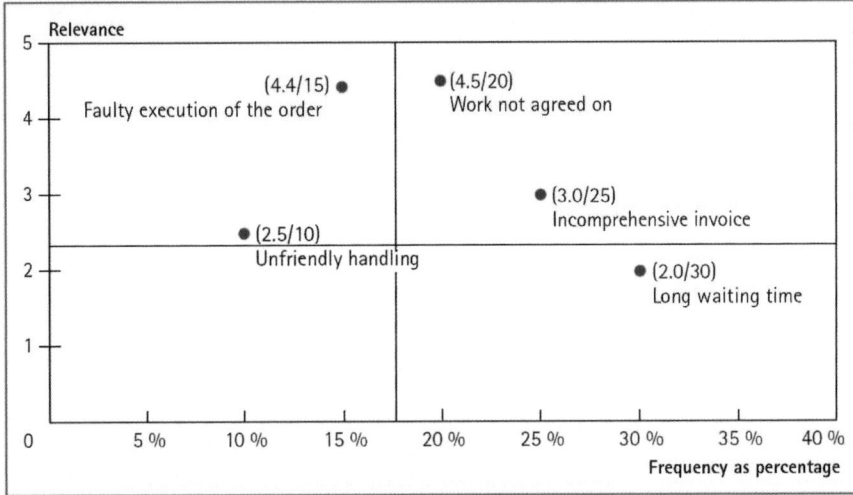

Fig. 10.7 FRAC matrix

greater relevance. This is especially necessary if one comes to the conclusion that this problem will increasingly appear in the future or that customers who are extremely annoyed will threaten to take serious sanctions. If, however, one deems the negative effects of the problems that are located in the upper left or the lower right quadrant to be equally serious, then the decision as to which should be addressed first should be made according to what is the quickest, easiest and most cost-effective solution. The problems shown in the *lower left quadrant* that have low relevance and occur with low relative frequency have, of course, the lowest priority.

The FRAC in a Time Series
With respect to the *analysis over several periods*, there are two possibilities imaginable: FRAC with a variable problem set and FRAC with a constant problem set.

1. As a rule, the FRAC has a dynamic character in that the problems recorded vary according to their respective appearance and their perceived importance *(FRAC with a variable problem set)*. This version consequently takes into consideration that new problems may occur or that customers may assess problems differently over time.
2. In contrast to the above version, it may be advisable for purposes of analyzing the effectiveness of certain measures to carry out a *FRAC with a constant problem set*. Here, the PVI is calculated at regular intervals for a fixed number of relevant problems, although whereby *restricting* the analysis *to the main problems* is sensible. From this time-period comparison of the problem-value indices, one obtains an instrument of control over whether the measures that are introduced to eliminate a particular problem have in fact led to the desired result. These

problems would have to fall into the lower rankings of the "Top five" or "Top 10" problem lists, taking into account the expenses for the elimination of the problem's cause(s). One must verify at regular intervals, however, whether the constant problem set still records the key problem categories and make an appropriate adjustment, if necessary.

10.2.1.3 The Intention-FRAC

In the second type of FRAC analysis from the customer's point of view, the customers' serious behavioral intentions expressed in the complaint articulation are used as an indicator of relevance. In the simplest variant, all documented behavioral announcements—such as termination or involvement of third parties—are considered equally relevant and their respective frequencies are recorded.

Table 10.10 illustrates an example of an Intention-FRAC which again refers to complaints from customers of a car dealer. The outer left column contains a list of the problems considered ("work not agreed on", "incomprehensible invoice" etc.). For

Table 10.10 Intention-FRAC

Consequence / Type of problem	Migration/Termination	Involvement of third-party institutions	Involvement of media	Involvement of lawyers	Total	Rank
Work not agreed on	12	3	4	4	23	①
Faulty execution of the order	10	4	1	5	20	②
Incomprehensible invoice	14	2	2	1	19	③
Unfriendly handling	8		2		10	④
Long waiting time	9				9	⑤

each problem, the number of serious behavioral consequences is indicated in the following columns (migration/termination, involvement of third-party institutions, media or lawyers). The sum of the respective serious consequences results in the ranking position for the priority of initiating quality improvement measures. Problems for which none of the above-mentioned consequences were articulated in complaints are not taken into account in this analysis.

10.2.1.4 Lost-Customer-FRAC

In the first two variants of the FRAC analysis, the extent of the annoyance and the announced behavioral intentions were used as indicators of the potential damage that could occur in the future as a result of the mentioned problems. The Lost-Customer-FRAC, on the other hand, takes into account the actual loss of customers that has already occurred. In a special lost-customer survey, the migrated customers are asked about the reasons for their decision to terminate the business relationship. Of interest are the cases in which customers have quit due to an experienced problem. These problems must be recorded and it is important to document how often these problems have caused migration.

If not all lost customers, but only a sample are surveyed, it is necessary to determine the percentage of the respondents that have terminated the relationship due to the respective problem. Afterwards, the total number of customers who terminated due to the different problems can be extrapolated on the basis of the total number of terminations. For example, if 7% of all respondents stated in the sample that they had given notice of termination due to unfriendly handling, and there are 10,000 terminations per year, the company lost 700 customers because of this problem.

If there are no contractual relationships and therefore no cancellations, it must be decided with the help of other parameters when a customer is to be regarded as lost. For a car dealer, for example, this can be a defined period of time in which the customer has no longer requested any services. Table 10.11 shows the fictitious

Table 10.11   Lost-customer-FRAC

Type of problem	Number of lost customers	Contribution margin loss[a]	Rank
Work not agreed on	98	17,640	②
Long waiting time	48	8,640	⑤
Incomprehensible invoice	82	14,760	③
Faulty execution of the order	116	20,880	①
Unfriendly handling	65	11,700	④

[a]Contribution margin loss = Number of lost customers × average contribution margin of customers (180 €)

result of a lost-customer survey of a car dealer, prepared in the form of a Lost-Customer-FRAC. Since information on average customer sales and contribution margins is also available internally, the losses caused by the different problems can also be clarified. It is the amount of these contribution margin losses that determines the ranking of problems.

The examples presented above show that it is quite possible that the rankings may differ according to the individual FRAC variants. This is due to the different indicators used for problem relevance and the different methodological approaches. Above all, however, it should be borne in mind that data from complaint analysis about customer annoyance and behavioral intentions are not reliable indicators of the actual behavior of disappointed customers. Only a proportion of those customers who quit due to annoyance about a problem will have articulated their annoyance in a complaint. In a survey of lost insurance customers, 82% of those who had terminated the contract due to perceived problems stated that they had not complained (Stauss and Seidel 2005). Therefore, if the necessary data is available, it is recommended to choose the Lost-Customer-FRAC since this is not based on the customers' information about psychological constructs (annoyance) or behavioral intentions (e.g. intention to terminate) but rather on the negative economic consequences that have already occurred.

The described procedures are not only analytical methods, but also *control instruments in the improvement process*. Problem-Value Indices of the Annoyance-FRAC, the ranking places of the Intention-FRAC and the contribution margin losses of the Lost-Customer-FRAC provide important information for the decision on the priority of product and process improvement measures. In addition, they are also key parameters for monitoring the success of corrective measures. In a time comparison, lower measured values provide important indications that quality improvement measures have actually led to improvements perceived by the customer.

10.2.2 Company-Oriented Frequency-Relevance Analyses of Complaints (FRAC)

Company-oriented frequency-relevance analyses are available if the most urgent problems are not identified anew with every complaint evaluation, but are determined on the basis of experience values for a longer period of time. The term "company-oriented" should not be misunderstood to mean that customer perceptions are neglected here. In most cases, the definition of particularly relevant problems will also be based on findings about customer annoyance, intentions to act or loss of customers. However, they are supplemented by further internal considerations. These can refer, for example, to safety standards, government regulatory requirements, cost considerations or estimates of the controllability of the problem. Three variants used in practice are presented below, which use different criteria and weight them in different ways: (1) no-go lists, (2) weighted problem lists and (3) lists of controllable causes.

(1) No-Go Lists On so-called no-go lists, companies list the errors that should be avoided under all circumstances. These are usually objective errors that can cause high physical or material damage, result in claims for damages or customer losses, cause the intervention of regulatory authorities or lead to high costs due to other circumstances. The frequency-relevance analysis determines the frequency with which the errors listed in the no-go list are the subject of the complaints and creates a corresponding ranking.

(2) Weighted Problem Lists These usually contain errors that occur again and again despite all quality efforts in the usual production or service processes and thus lead to complaints. These errors are weighted according to their seriousness. In this case, the priority results from multiplying the number of errors by the specific weighting factor. One application example is the "Service Quality Indicator (SQI)" of the logistics service provider FedEx, which is presented in *Spotlight 10.1*.

Spotlight 10.1
The Service Quality Indicator (SQI) at FedEx

For quality-oriented control of the freight deliverer's worldwide activities, FedEx has been using a *"Service Quality Indicator"* since the late 1980s. This firm-wide quality index comprises the key quality dimension that determines customer dissatisfaction. Twelve failure point categories are included in this indicator, such as "lost packages" or "missed pickups", and are weighted according to their importance to the customer. Thus, for example, a lost package is weighted at 10 points, whereas a package arriving late on the right day is weighted at 1 point (see Table 10.12).

The absolute numbers of the failures of each category are multiplied by the responding weight, resulting in a point value per category. The sum of the points across all categories yields the Service Quality Indicator.

Categories and weightings were chosen on the basis of a thorough analysis of customer complaints and ranked in a *"Hierarchy of Horrors"*. Therefore, this company-oriented frequency-relevance index is based on the customers' assessments of the significance of problems experienced. That ensures that FedEx focuses on the issues that matter most to customers.

Federal Ex uses the SQI as an instrument to guide the systematic *development of corrective measures*, as an *instrument of motivation* and as a *warning system*. Based on the sum of the worldwide SQI, *standard targets* are developed on a monthly basis at the beginning of each business year, whereupon the continental management allocates these standard targets among the countries for which it is responsible. Those responsible for the various countries in turn allocate their targets to the individual departments so that the company can ensure that all those participating in the process of improvement—initiated by the standard targets of the SQI—are equally involved. SQI failure points are

---

(continued)

Spotlight 10.1 (continued)

calculated daily and communicated to all those in charge, who in turn intensively analyze the causes of the problems for each category and make decisions to reduce the occurrence of the failures in future. The importance of the SQI as a central element of the continuous improvement process is further enhanced by the fact that it provides the basis for financial incentives.

Sources: Cooper (2011) and Birla (2013)

(3) Lists of Controllable Causes All company-oriented variants of FRAC are based on the consideration of naming relevant customer problems for which the company is clearly responsible and which could therefore have been prevented. However, the ability to influence the causes of the problem is not always completely clear. For this reason, some companies map the degree of controllability on a scale and weight the number of problems encountered with the respective scale value. A corresponding example of this is the variant of a company-oriented frequency-relevance analysis used by a German health insurance company (see *Spotlight 10.2*).

Table 10.12 The elements of the SQI and their weights

Elements of the SQI	Weights
Abandoned calls	1
Missed pickups	10
Right–day late–service failures	1
Wrong–day late–service failures	5
Overgoods	5
Lost packages	10
Damaged packages	10
Invoice adjustments required	1
Missing Proof of delivery	1
Complaints reopened by customers	5
Traces (incomplete scan data)	1
International SQI indicator	1

Spotlight 10.2

The Application of Frequency-Relevance Analysis at the Gmünder ErsatzKasse (GEK)

The Gmünder ErsatzKasse (GEK) was the fifth-largest German health insurance company and offered its services in a difficult environment.[1] On the one hand, the health insurance benefits were almost entirely regulated by law. On the other hand, the ongoing public debate about deficits in the health care system as well as about benefit restrictions and additional payments, led to uncertainty among customers. In this situation, GEK decided to strategically position itself by consistently focusing on customers through an outstanding range of services.

Consequently, GEK had a long history of a professional complaint management system. For example, customers had an easily accessible complaint channel at their disposal and it was explicitly promised to the complainants that their concerns would be dealt with within 24 hours. In addition, complaints were systematically analyzed in terms of their causes and used to improve services and processes as well as for behavioral control.

An essential basis for this was the *frequency-relevance analysis of complaints*. It captured the quantity and importance of customer criticism and made it possible to express the need for modification measures in a company-wide recognized value.

The *frequency* expressed the number of customer complaints per problem. The *relevance* was assessed on the basis of whether the causes of the articulated problem could be influenced by GEK. This aspect was particularly important because the company had limited room for maneuver in a highly regulated environment. The weighting of the problems differed depending on GEK's ability to control the problem (see Fig. 10.8). For example, controllable causes such as "bad advice" were weighted with a factor of six, while non-controllable causes such as "error caused by customer" were weighted by a factor of one only. Totally unindebted problems were included in the analysis because it had turned out that even such criticism could often have been avoided by comprehensive advice. Customer errors or unrealizable expectations pointed to shortcomings in the provision of information, and errors caused by third parties indicated improvement potentials with partners. By taking these problems into account, it was ensured that these hints were used to improve the service quality.

Based on the frequency (number) and weighting (relevance), a value was calculated within the framework of the frequency-relevance analysis, which

(continued)

---

[1]Gmünder ErsatzKasse merged with Barmer Ersatzkasse to form BARMER. The spotlight describes the pre-merger process.

Spotlight 10.2 (continued)

expressed the importance of the respective problem as a proportion of all weighted problems:

$$\frac{\text{Number of criticism of a problem} \times \text{weight}}{\text{Total number of criticisms} \times \text{average weight}} \times 100$$

In this way, it was possible to immediately identify which processes and which services the customers considered to be particularly problematic in the period under review. In this respect, the value calculation provided a clear overview of the ranking of the problems perceived by the customers and which could be controlled by GEK. For example, if it turned out that the topic of "sick pay" received the highest value across all departments it became clear that improvements were required here from the customer's point of view. If necessary, more detailed analyses were carried out in order to initiate the right change measures.

In addition, appropriate calculations could be made to assess the *quality of the performance of various business units (e.g. branches)*. In this case, a value was calculated that expressed the proportion of criticism of a branch in the overall criticism. The different "probability of criticism", e. g. depending on the number of customers or business transactions per branch, was taken into account.

A low value (or even a value of zero) proved the low occurrence of controllable customer problems and thus the high service quality of this branch. A high value indicated branch-related quality deficits, so that there was a need for action, e. g. for training courses. The evaluation according to problem contents as well as business units/branches was carried out continuously, so that the developments and effects of measures could be read off from the time series.

GEK successfully used frequency-relevance analysis for many years for analyses and controlling purposes. Targets were agreed on an annual basis with regard to the number of complaints, the controllability of problems, overall customer satisfaction and complaint satisfaction. Also, bonuses were paid to employees for achieving the targets. In this way, the management goal of customer satisfaction was consistently pursued internally. The fact that this was crowned with success is shown by the fact that the company was able to show both very high satisfaction levels and strong growth rates.

Jochen Zondler
(former) Head of Quality Management
Gmünder ErsatzKasse (GEK)

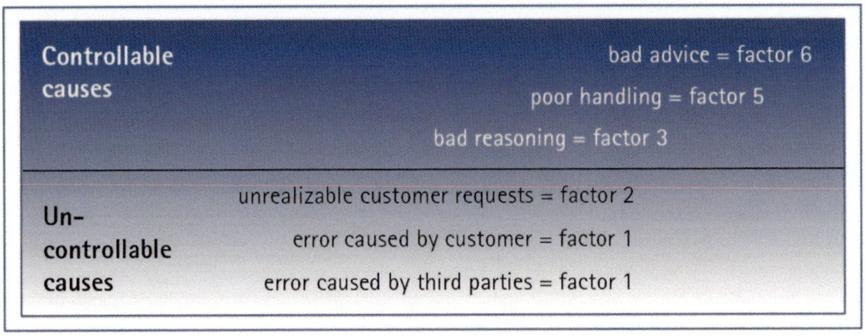

Controllable causes	bad advice = factor 6
	poor handling = factor 5
	bad reasoning = factor 3
Un-controllable causes	unrealizable customer requests = factor 2
	error caused by customer = factor 1
	error caused by third parties = factor 1

Fig. 10.8 Controllable and uncontrollable causes

In this way, companies have various methodological approaches at their disposal to prioritize the problems articulated in complaints and to take corrective measures on this basis. Which methodical variant is to be used in a concrete case must be decided on the basis of company-specific considerations with regard to data availability, manageability and cost efficiency.

Chapter 10 in Brief
- Complaint evaluation serves to systematically exploit the information potential that is contained in complaints. Basically, it comprises two areas: complaint analysis and prioritization of problems.
- The task of complaint analysis is to investigate the total complaint volume quantitatively with respect to certain important characteristics. For this purpose, univariate and bivariate methods can be used.
- The univariate methods include absolute and relative frequency distributions, as well as location parameters such as arithmetic mean and median.
- Bivariate methods such as cross-tabulations permit the examination of correlations between two variables.
- In order to provide detailed information, it makes sense to apply univariate frequency distributions and bivariate methods also to subsets of complaints (such as complaints about specific problems or complaints of a special customer group).
- In addition, the temporal dimension of the complaint analysis must also be considered (time-period and time series analyses).
- For the prioritization of problems, customer-oriented and company-oriented frequency-relevance analyses (FRAC) are available.
- The customer-oriented variants link the frequency of problems that have occurred with the importance that the customer attaches to the problem.

(continued)

There are three different variants: Annoyance-FRAC, Intention-FRAC and Lost-Customer-FRAC.

- Company-oriented frequency-relevance analyses are available if the most urgent problems are determined by the company on the basis of experience values for a longer period of time. In practice, three variants are applied which use different criteria and weight them in different ways: (1) no-go lists, (2) weighted problem lists and (3) lists of controllable causes.
- The selection of the FRAC-variant must be decided on the basis of company-specific considerations with regard to data availability, manageability and cost efficiency.
- In order to prioritize the problems raised in the complaint analysis, various variants of the customer-oriented and company-oriented frequency-relevance analysis are available.

References

Birla M (2013) FedEx delivers: how the world's leading shipping company keeps innovating and outperforming the competition. Wiley, Hoboken

Cooper M (2011) From architecture to action: the FedEx service quality journey. http://www.transportation.northwestern.edu/docs/2011/2011.10.25.FedEx_UE.pdf. Accessed 2 Dec 2017

Stauss B, Seidel W (2005) Non-complaining behavior of lost service customers. In: Paper presented at SERVSIG research conference, University of Singapore, Singapore 2–4 Jun 2005

© Springer Nature Switzerland AG 2019
B. Stauss, W. Seidel, *Effective Complaint Management*, Management for Professionals,
https://doi.org/10.1007/978-3-319-98705-7_11

Issues Raised
- What are the basic areas of complaint management controlling?
- How can evidence controlling determine to what extent complaint management is able to correctly record customer dissatisfaction?
- How is the quality of task fulfillment measured from the customer's point of view in subjective task controlling?
- How are the quality and productivity of task fulfillment measured in objective task controlling?
- How should the costs of complaint management be recorded in cost controlling?
- How can the information benefit be assessed in monetary terms within the scope of benefit controlling?
- What options exist in benefit controlling to calculate the retention benefit of complaint management?
- How can the communication benefit be quantified in benefit controlling?
- How can the profitability of complaint management be assessed?

Complaint management is a complex area of activity that must be controlled in a planned fashion with respect to corporate goals. It therefore requires systematic controlling that puts complaint managers in a position to set specific goals and constantly monitor the extent to which those goals have been reached and—if necessary—develop corrective actions.

Basically, one must differentiate between evidence controlling, task controlling and cost-benefit controlling in the context of complaint management controlling:

- The central issue in *evidence controlling* is the study of the extent to which customer dissatisfaction is expressed in complaints and the degree to which the complaints registered in the firm reflect the complaints actually articulated by customers. In addition, evidence controlling also monitors the extent to which the dissatisfaction of complainants is reflected in follow-up complaints (Sect. 11.1).
- The focus of *task controlling* is the specification and monitoring of quality and productivity indicators and standards for all complaint management activities. In the context of *objective task controlling*, compliance with performance standards in all the task areas of complaint management is monitored via objective measurement categories. In the course of *subjective task controlling*, the satisfaction of the complainant with the direct complaint management process (complaint satisfaction) is documented. The Complaint Management Index is a useful tool for controlling the fulfillment of all tasks (Sect. 11.2).
- In *cost-benefit controlling*, the costs arising from complaint management are systematically processed, and the benefit components of complaint management are operationalized. The most important benefit component, the retention benefit, is quantified in monetary terms. By comparing costs and monetary benefits, the profitability of complaint management can be calculated (Sect. 11.3).

11.1 Evidence Controlling

The fundamental *task of evidence controlling* is the determination of the extent to which complaint management is in a position to make the degree of dissatisfaction of the firm's customers evident to management. This task is so important because many studies have shown that customer dissatisfaction is often not adequately reflected in the complaints documented in the company. On the one hand, not all dissatisfied customers complain, and on the other hand some of the complaints that customers express are not recorded in the company. This is referred to as the *iceberg phenomenon of complaint management*. The resulting knowledge deficit is extraordinarily problematic because it can lead to a misinterpretation of the type, scope and perceived urgency of customer dissatisfaction and to a misallocation of resources invested in corrective and improvement measures.

In this respect, evidence controlling has two main tasks. Firstly, it is important to *identify the unvoiced complaints of dissatisfied customers*. Secondly, it is necessary to determine the extent of those complaints and follow-up complaints that are *indeed articulated, but not registered in the firm*—in other words, hidden complaints.

11.1.1 The Annoyance Iceberg

11.1.1.1 Non-articulated Complaints

It has been a well-known phenomenon that only a proportion of the dissatisfied customers complain—that there are non-articulated (unvoiced) complaints. For companies, this *non-articulation* implies that the number of complaints received, processed and analyzed does not adequately reflect the actual extent of customer dissatisfaction. This is called the annoyance iceberg (Stauss and Seidel 2008).

The small part of the iceberg that is visible indicates the percentage of dissatisfied customers who complain; the very much larger part that is "underwater" shows the percentage of dissatisfied customers who do not complain (Fig. 11.1).

Empirical studies indicate the size of the invisible part of the iceberg. Goodman et al. (2000) estimate for the USA that an average of approximately 50–80% of dissatisfied customers across all industries do not complain. The results of the German national satisfaction survey (Servicebarometer 2017) show that the proportion of non-articulation varies considerably across industries: it ranges from 26% (opticians) to 83.5% (post offices) and 93.5% (social networks). In any case, it must be expected that the complaints documented in the company do not adequately express the extent of customer dissatisfaction and do not adequately record the experience of dissatisfied customers with regard to the types and frequency of problems.

11.1.1.2 Non-registered Complaints

In addition to non-articulated complaints, non-registered—hidden—complaints are also part of the invisible segment of the iceberg. A portion of the articulated complaints remains hidden to the directors of complaint management. For these

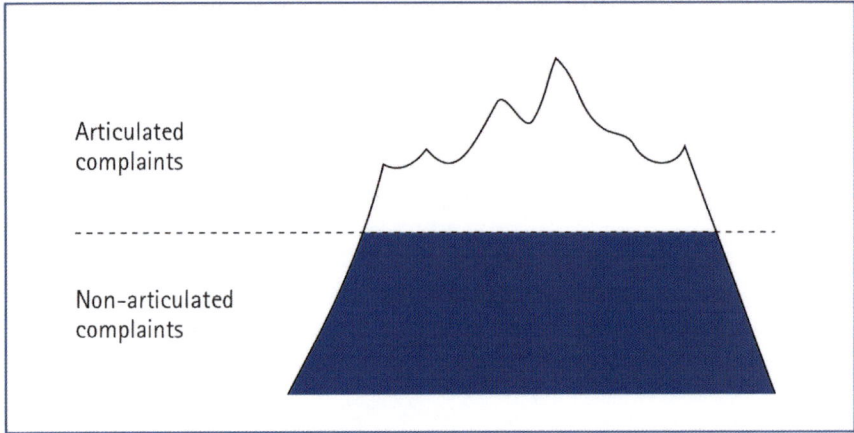

Fig. 11.1 The iceberg phenomenon considering non-articulated complaints, adapted (with changes) from: Heskett et al. (1997, p. 179)

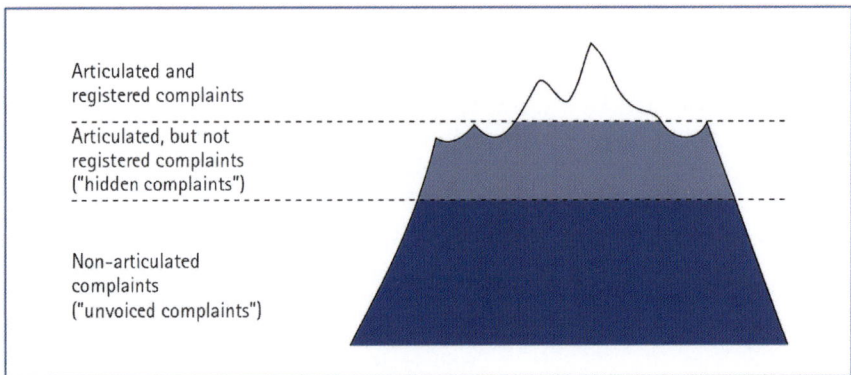

Fig. 11.2 The iceberg phenomenon considering non-articulated and non-registered complaints, adapted (with changes) from: Heskett et al. (1997, p. 179)

complaints are not directly submitted to the complaint department and usually are not documented either, so that their existence is not obvious. This applies primarily to all complaints that are expressed to *customer-contact personnel*. The associates accepting the complaints are oftentimes unprepared for complaint situations or are afraid of negative consequences and thus record only a *fraction* of the complaints. Studies show that—depending upon the industry and the extent of the problem— only about *10–60%* of the customer complaints that are articulated in decentralized customer-contact locations are registered and are therefore known to the central customer care department (Goodman et al. 2000).

Figure 11.2 illustrates this by distinguishing between articulated and registered complaints on the one hand and non-registered and non-articulated complaints on

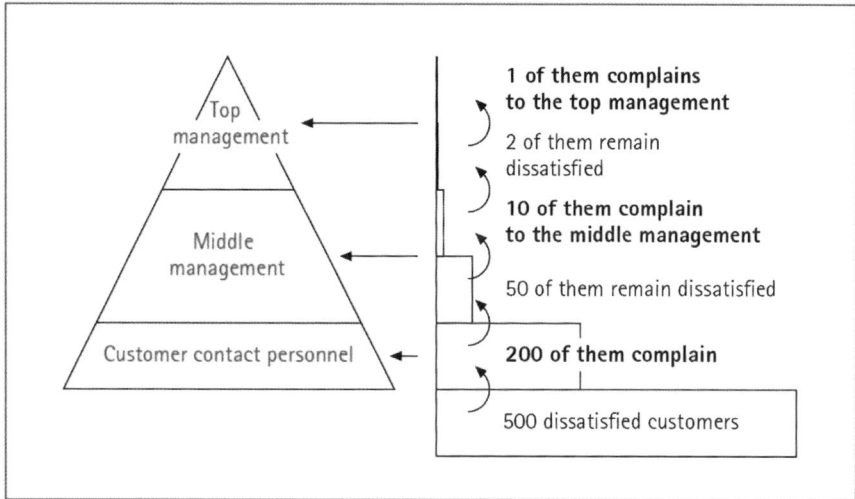

Fig. 11.3 Example of the extent of hidden complaints in the company, adapted (with changes) from: Heskett et al. (1997, p. 181)

the other. This figure shows that the *part of the iceberg that is visible* to management *shrinks considerably* when one takes the "hidden" complaints into consideration. At the same time, it becomes clear that a larger part of the iceberg can be made visible not only via complaint stimulation measures, but also via internal measures for the improvement of complaint acceptance and transfer.

A high proportion of hidden complaints also implies that inexact knowledge exists in management as to the reactions of the decentralized units and the level of complaint satisfaction that is reached. A small part of the dissatisfaction that still exists becomes clear when dissatisfied complainants themselves approach the *next higher level of authority* in each case. Since only relatively few complainants take this route, however, these follow-up complaints also represent merely a *tip of the complaint dissatisfaction iceberg*, which furthermore becomes smaller and smaller, the more hierarchical levels are added. Figure 11.3 gives an example and shows that it is quite possible that of 500 dissatisfied customers, in the end only one complaint is visible to the central complaint unit or to top management.

11.1.1.3 Key Figures of the Annoyance Iceberg

In order to be able to make concrete statements about the extent to which complaint management succeeds in uncovering customer dissatisfaction and recording the complaints articulated, meaningful key figures are required. These are used to control and monitor the success of complaint management measures that aim to increase the number of complaints from dissatisfied customers (such as stimulation measures) or to increase the proportion of complaints registered in the company (such as measures in the areas of complaint acceptance and processing).

The Problematic Complaint Rate

Before the key figures of the evidence controlling are presented, it is first necessary to address briefly a figure that firms frequently use as an indicator when estimating the relevance of the complaint volume, but whose use is extraordinarily problematic: the complaint rate.

The *complaint rate (CR)* represents the proportion of all customers who complain to the firm, in relation to the total customer base. The CR is expressed as the quotient of the total number of complainants on one hand and the total number of customers on the other hand. If the firm in question receives 5000 complaints, then the complaint quote with a customer base of 100,000 amounts to 5%. This figure is calculated by many firms and—when it turns out to be low—interpreted as proof of high customer satisfaction. Accordingly, efforts are being made to minimize the number of complaints. However, this approach is questionable.

Since not all dissatisfied customers complain, a low complaint rate cannot be interpreted as a high level of satisfaction. The control effect of this key figure is also problematic. Managers may consider themselves compelled to discourage dissatisfied customers by building barriers, avoiding the establishment and communication of easily accessible complaint channels or increasing the financial and psychological burden on complainants. In this case, they will be able to achieve the required reduction of the complaint rate, while customer dissatisfaction and customer churn may increase. Similarly critical is the fact that any internal suppression of complaints, such as non-registration or omitting forwarding of complaints has a positive effect on the complaint rate. In this respect, it is recommended to dispense with the complaint rate and instead to look for more meaningful key figures that make the extent of customer dissatisfaction evident to management.

Selection of Relevant Variables

For the development of meaningful key figures in evidence controlling, decisions must first be made on relevant variables that are included in these key figures. First, it has to be clarified whether the number of complaints or the number of complainants should be recorded. Then it is necessary to answer the question of how customer dissatisfaction is to be precisely operationalized: either defined by the number of customers who clearly state in a survey that they are dissatisfied (dissatisfied customers), or by the number of customers who state that they have experienced problems that caused annoyance (annoyed customers), regardless of whether or not they are still satisfied with the offer as a whole.

Number of Complainants or Number of Complaints

The "iceberg phenomenon" can either be investigated in relation to non-articulated and non-registered *complaints*, or in relation to dissatisfied/annoyed customers who do not lodge a complaint and the *complainants* whose complaints are "lost" in the course of processing.

There are good reasons for both approaches. However, it is recommended to use the person-related variable "complainants". With regard to the objective of making non-articulation of complaints transparent, this is primarily a matter of finding out how many dissatisfied or annoyed customers do not complain. The aim is to identify the group of non-complainants, to find out their motives and to draw consequences for complaint stimulation.

In addition, the number of non-complainants—and not the number of complaints received— is the basis for further consideration of the economic consequences that result if dissatisfied/annoyed customers react in another way, e.g. migrate immediately and/or engage in negative word-of-mouth communication. Thus, from an economic perspective, there is much to be said for choosing this variable. Another advantage is that the data is more readily available, as the customers' complaining behavior must not be recorded in a differentiated manner. However, the disadvantage is that multiple complaints of a customer are not taken into account, and the actual occurrence of non-articulated and non-registered complaints will be somewhat higher than the identified complaint volume.

Dissatisfied Customers or Customers with Reason for Complaint (Annoyed Customers)

Another question is to which variable the number of non-complainants should be related. At first it seems obvious to choose the total number of *dissatisfied customers*, since the proportion of dissatisfied customers can be easily determined within the framework of the usual satisfaction survey. However, it is conceivable that this approach may lead to an underestimation of negative customer experiences. When customers are questioned about their overall satisfaction, they make an average assessment, balancing positive and negative experiences in terms of frequency and relevance. In view of the fact that unproblematic transactions usually dominate strongly, many customers will claim to be satisfied, even if they have occasionally had cause for annoyance (Stauss and Hentschel 1992). Accordingly, it can be assumed that even among satisfied customers there are people who have been annoyed at some point but did not complain. Therefore, it makes sense not to choose the number of dissatisfied customers as a variable, but the number of *annoyed customers*. These are customers who indicated in a survey that they had a reason to complain during the period under review. This variable is therefore used in the following.

Figure 11.4 lists the alternatives once again, highlighting the variables used in the following (number of complainants, number of annoyed customers).

The Most Important Key Figures

The most important key figures of evidence controlling are the annoyance rate, the articulation/non-articulation rate, the registration/non-registration rate and the evidence rate.

Annoyance Rate The annoyance rate refers to the proportion of customers who, during the period under review, were annoyed by a product, service or corporate activity.

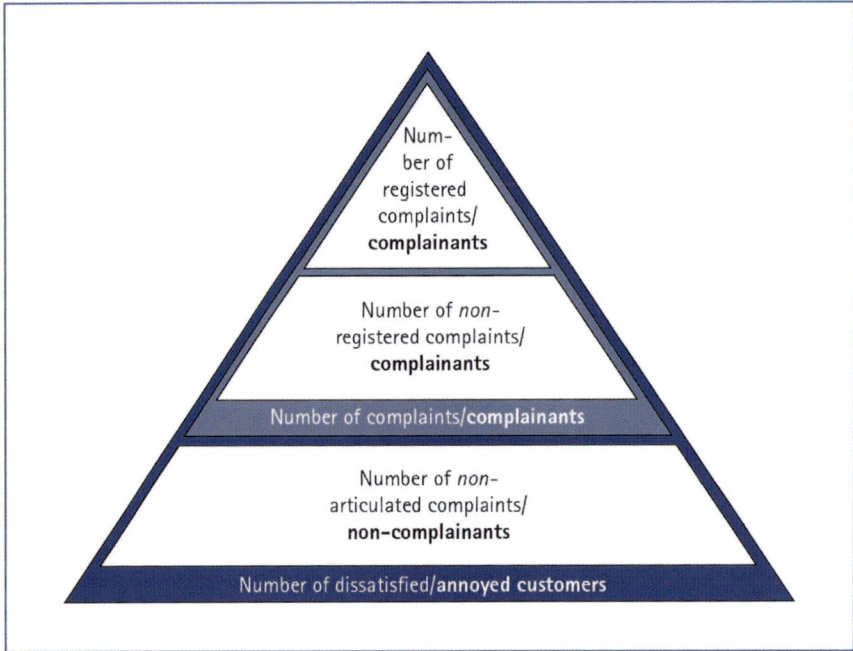

Fig. 11.4 Relevant variables of evidence controlling

$$\text{Annoyance rate} = \frac{\text{Number of annoyed customers}}{\text{Total number of customers}}$$

If the annoyance rate is determined from a representative satisfaction survey, the number of annoyed customers of the company can be extrapolated on this basis.

Articulation Rate/Non-articulation Rate Another important key figure is the articulation rate, which expresses the extent of the complaint articulation of annoyed customers. However, since the non-articulation of complaints is at the center of evidence controlling, the focus of the examination must be on the reciprocal value of the articulation rate—the *non-articulation rate*. This key figure represents the ratio of the number of customers who do not express their annoyance in a complaint to the total number of annoyed customers:

$$\text{Non-articulation rate} = \frac{\text{Number of non-complainants among annoyed customers}}{\text{Total number of annoyed customers}}$$

The non-articulation rate shows to what extent annoyed customers refrain from complaining. Since the goals of complaint management can only be achieved if annoyed customers actually turn to the company with their concerns, it must be the target of companies with a proactive complaint management *to minimize the non-articulation rate.*

Registration Rate/Non-Registration Rate The registration and non-registration rates are relevant for determining the extent of hidden complaints. While the *registration rate* provides information on the percentage of complaints that have been registered in the company, the *non-registration rate* expresses the ratio of complainants whose complaints are not registered in the company to the total number of complainants. This key figure is a measure of the percentage of complaints expressed to any part of the company that are lost and therefore not available to complaint management for analysis and information usage.

$$\text{Non-registration rate} = \frac{\text{Number of non-registered complainants}}{\text{Total number of complainants}}$$

In principle, it would be advisable to *minimize the non-registration* rate, too, because the discovery of hidden complaints increases the transparency regarding the number of complaints and the experiences of customers as complainants. However, with regard to the hidden complaints, it is not always economically justifiable or feasible to expect employees to completely record every critical remark in customer contacts. This applies in particular to smaller issues that can be solved directly to the customer's satisfaction. In this respect, a minimization of the non-registration rate should only be aimed at if it can be proven that the economic benefit of complete registration exceeds the resulting costs. Otherwise, *company-specific minimum standards* must be defined. The non-registration rate provides the company with realistic information about the actual number of complaints. On this basis, decisions on the priority of measures to improve internal processes must be taken.

Evidence Rate The evidence rate expresses the peak of the "annoyance iceberg". It is formed by the quotient of the number of registered complainants and the total number of annoyed customers.

$$\text{Evidence rate} = \frac{\text{Number of registered complainants}}{\text{Total number of annoyed customers}}$$

The evidence rate is a measure of the ability of complaint management to capture the annoyance among the company's customers in the course of complaint evaluation and thus to take it into account in complaint reporting and utilization of complaint information.

The evidence rate shows to what extent the data considered in complaint evaluation is representative of customer experiences or requires correction. If we assume that the distribution of the problems in the recorded and non-recorded complaints is equal and that the evidence rate, for example, is 50%, the documented number of complaints must be multiplied by a factor of two in order to be able to draw conclusions about the actual extent of annoyed customers. This factor can be called the "*evidence factor*", because it is only with its application that it becomes evident how serious customer problems and customer dissatisfaction in the customer base really are. Also problem-related evidence ratios should be calculated and corrected by differentiated evidence factors. Only in this way can complaint management get a realistic idea of the customers' experiences and ensure that the improvement processes are controlled according to the priorities actually perceived by customers. *Spotlight 11.1* illustrates the corresponding procedure.

Spotlight 11.1
Determination and Application of Evidence Factors in an Insurance Company

Complaint information is not representative of the problems perceived by customers, as usually only a fraction of the annoyed customers complain. An insurance company conducted an *empirical study* to check the *representativeness of the complaint information*, i.e. to determine whether the problem areas identified in the complaint analysis actually corresponded to the problem experiences of all customers. In the following, the practically relevant percentage results from the study are displayed precisely, whereas the absolute figures are alienated to ensure anonymity. The necessary calculation steps are summarized in Table 11.1.

Within the framework of a customer satisfaction survey, customers were asked to indicate whether they had been annoyed about the insurance company within the last year and what caused their annoyance. The percentages of the named annoyance causes (column 1) were now been multiplied by the absolute number of customers, resulting in the total number of annoyed customers per problem category (column 2). Column 3 shows the number

(continued)

Spotlight 11.1 (continued)

of complaints registered per cause of annoyance. A comparison of the problem-specific complaint figures (column 3) with the number of annoyed customers (column 2) reveals *problem-related evidence rates* (column 4). It becomes clear that the problems perceived by customers are visible to a very different extent in the registered complaints. For example, while 80% of the annoyance about "employees in the head office" becomes evident, this is only 18% in the case of the problem "processing of contract amendments". Accordingly, the evidence factors (column 5) are very different. For example, the number of registered complaints about "employees in the head office" must only be multiplied by an evidence factor of 1.25, while the documented number of complaints about "processing of contract amendments" must be multiplied by a factor of 5.55 in order to determine the real extent of annoyance.

Exemplary Determination of Key Figures of Evidence Controlling

The procedure for determining the key figures is explained in Fig. 11.5 using a simple example:

1. **Identification of customers with cause for complaint:** In a customer satisfaction survey, 10% of all customers state that they have had cause for complaint

Table 11.1 Problems of annoyed customers and evidence rates

Cause of Annoyance	Annoyed customers		Registered complaints	Evidence rate	Evidence factor
Annoyed about...	Percentage (1)	Extrapolated number of customers (2)	(3)	(4)	(5)
Employees in the head office	5.3 %	265,000	212,343	80.1 %	1.25
Field staff	17.1 %	855,000	321,212	37.6 %	2.66
Amount of disbursement for claims settlement	10.0 %	500,000	456,722	91.3 %	1.09
Handling of claims settlement	19.5 %	975,000	187,191	19.2 %	5.21
Processing of contract amendments	13.7 %	685,000	123,432	18.0 %	5.55
Letter from insurance company	17.2 %	860,000	432,101	50.2 %	1.99
Pricing	5.0 %	250,000	198,363	79.3 %	1.26
Assistance with the new insurance contract	3.3 %	165,000	65,312	39.6 %	2.53
Change of insurance agent	2.0 %	100,000	24,672	24.7 %	4.05

Customer base: 5,000,000

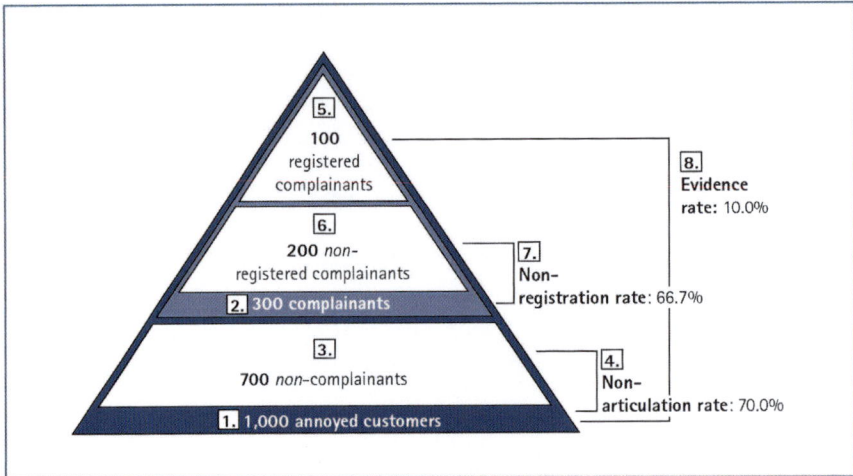

Fig. 11.5 Exemplary determination of key figures of evidence controlling

(annoyance rate). With a customer base of 10,000 customers, the number of customers with a complaint reason ("annoyed customers") is 1000.

2. **Determining the number of complainants:** In the survey, 30% of customers with a reason for complaint state that they have complained. The number of complainants is thus 300.

3. **Determination of the number of non-complainants:** The number of non-complainants is calculated as the difference between the number of customers with a complaint reason (1000) and the number of complainants (300). The number of non-complainants is thus 700.

4. **Determination of the non-articulation rate:** If the number of non-complainants (700) is related to the number of annoyed customers (1000), the non-articulation rate is 70%.

5. **Determining the number of registered complainants:** Complaint evaluation shows that 100 complainants have been registered.

6. **Determining the number of unregistered complainants:** Subtracting the number of registered complainants (100) from the number of complainants (300) yields the number of non-registered complainants (200).

7. **Determining the non-registration rate:** Relating the number of non-registered complainants (200) to the number of complainants (300), results in a non-registration rate of 66.7%.

8. **Determining the evidence rate**: Now the number of registered complainants (100) can be set in relation to the number of annoyed customers (1.000). This results in an evidence rate of 10%. This means that 90% of the annoyance iceberg was hidden and is now made evident.

11.1.1.4 Informational Basis for Determining the Key Figures

The data for the calculation of annoyance rate, non-articulation rate, non-registration rate and evidence rate can be taken from *complaint evaluation* or determined by *customer surveys*. This does not require an independent survey, but only a supplement to the traditional regular customer satisfaction survey with questions relating to complaint behavior.

The *annoyance rate* in the denominator takes into account the total number of current customers (full customer base). The counter shows the total number of customers with cause for complaint. This figure is derived directly from the customer satisfaction survey, in which customers are asked to answer the question of whether they had perceived a problem or had cause for complaint in the period under review.

The *non-articulation rate* includes in the denominator the total number of customers with cause for complaint. To determine this size, customers are surveyed in customer satisfaction surveys to indicate whether they have been confronted with a problem that would actually be an occasion for a complaint. The number of customers who answer "yes" is the denominator. The counter records the number of non-complainants among annoyed customers, which can also be determined in a satisfaction survey. Customers who have confirmed they have had a cause for complaint are asked to provide information on whether they have actually complained. The sum of all customers who answer in the negative to this question represents the total number of non-complainants among the annoyed customers.

The denominator of the *non-registration rate* is the total number of complainants. This is the number of all customers who stated in a satisfaction survey that they had complained. It is set in relation to the number of non-registered complainants (counter). This figure is the difference between the number of customers who said in the survey that they had articulated a complaint and the number of complainants registered in the complaint management process.

With regard to the *evidence rate*, the number of registered complainants (counter) is available in complaint management, as it is recorded within the scope of complaint analysis. The total number of annoyed customers (denominator) is determined by the satisfaction survey. In this survey, customers who report that they have not complained despite their dissatisfaction may also be asked to provide information about the perceived complaint barriers. This is an important input for complaint stimulation, since it shows starting points for measures to improve the cost-benefit ratio of complaints from the customers' perspective.

Table 11.2 shows an example of the *questions* that must be posed *as part of a general satisfaction survey* so that evidence controlling can then provide the information shown.

By including a number of further questions in the customer and complaint satisfaction survey, it is also possible to gain clues for the *economic risk potential of unvoiced and hidden complaints*. Customers must only be asked whether they have left or will leave because of the problem. On the basis of the answers, churn rates can be calculated for customers who have not complained. If the company has data relating to the average turnover or contribution margin of customers, it is possible to calculate the corresponding risk potential.

Table 11.2 Excerpt from a customer satisfaction questionnaire relating to complaint behavior as a basis for the calculation of evidence controlling rates

---

Did you experience a problem that gives reason to complain?

☐ Yes   Namely: _____

☐ No

If yes: Did you complain?

☐ Yes   To whom did you complain? (If you complained repeatedly and to
          different departments about this problem, please specify!)

          Namely: _____

☐ No   What were the reasons for waiving a complaint?

          ☐ Correct address unknown

          ☐ Correct phone number unknown

          ☐ Too circumstancial

          ☐ Lack of employee's competence

          ☐ Does not lead to a result, anyway

          ☐ Not worthwhile

          ☐ Problem difficult to explain

          ☐ Other, namely: _____

11.1.2 The Complaint Annoyance Iceberg

A significant indicator that complaint management has not succeeded in achieving complaint satisfaction is the fact that follow-up complaints have been made. These are particularly relevant to complaint management for several reasons. Firstly, they contain clear indications of perceived weaknesses in complaint management, which must be used for quality improvements. Secondly, the complaint has not yet been closed from a customer's perspective, so there is still a (last) chance of stabilizing the business relationship. Thirdly, the dissatisfaction among follow-up complainants accumulates, as the (primary) dissatisfaction with the product/service is massively increased by the (secondary) dissatisfaction with the complaint handling. Accordingly, dissatisfied complainants have an especially high risk of migration (Stauss and Seidel 2013).

It is therefore urgently necessary for complaint management that the dissatisfied complainants articulate a follow-up complaint and do not immediately terminate the business relationship. However, it is very likely that only some of the dissatisfied complainants will make a follow-up complaint. It is also likely that only some of the articulated follow-up complaints will be recorded by the company, especially if they can be interpreted as massive criticism of the employee who is processing them. Accordingly, there are *non-articulated and non-registered follow-up complaints*. It

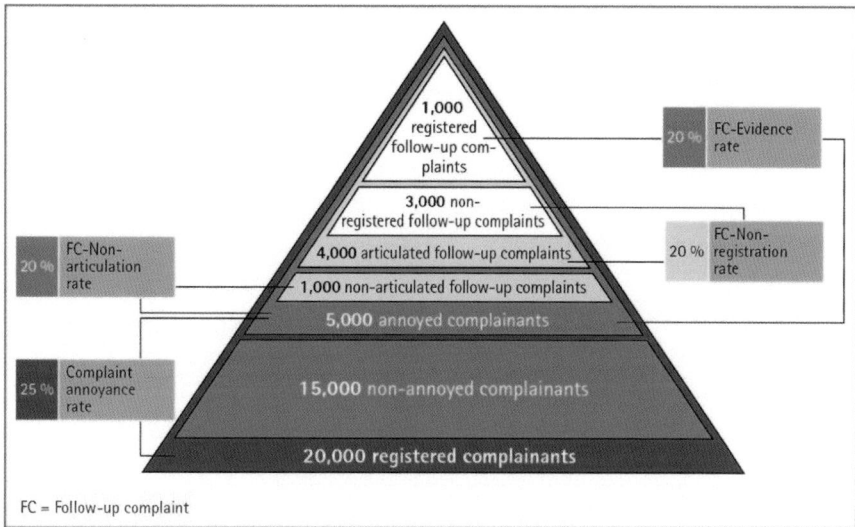

Fig. 11.6 The complaint annoyance iceberg (Stauss and Seidel 2013, p. 58)

is necessary to analyze the *complaint annoyance iceberg* precisely in order to obtain a realistic picture of the degree of dissatisfaction with the complaint.

The procedure is analogous to that presented for the determination of the annoyance iceberg. A valid sample of complainants will be asked whether there was cause for dissatisfaction with the handling of the complaint and whether they articulated their annoyance in a follow-up complaint (FC). Thus, the number of annoyed complainants as well as the number of non-articulated follow-up complaints are available. The difference between the number of articulated and registered follow-up complaints results in the number of non-registered follow-up complaints. Thus, various parameters can be calculated which show the proportion of annoyed complainants (complaint annoyance rate), the proportion of non-articulated follow-up complaints (FC non-articulation rate) and the proportion of non-registered follow-up complaints (FC non-registration rate). In addition, it becomes apparent to what extent the number of follow-up complaints registered in the company—as the tip of the iceberg— actually makes the extent of annoyance evident among the complainants (FC evidence rate) (see Fig. 11.6).

11.2 Task Controlling

In the context of task controlling, the quality of complaint management task fulfillment is to be monitored via meaningful standards. In order to establish these standards, *three activities* must be carried out:

- selection of *quality dimensions*

Table 11.3 Quality dimensions of complaint management

Task	Quality dimensions
Complaint stimulation	▪ Complaint volume of dissatisfied customers ▪ Correct addressing of customer complaints ▪ Use of existing complaint channels ▪ Easy accessibility
Complaint acceptance	▪ Customer-oriented design ot the initial contact ▪ Prompt forwarding of complaint cases ▪ Correct forwarding of complaint cases ▪ Complete registration of complaint information ▪ Correct registration of complaint information
Complaint processing	▪ Promptness of complaint processing ▪ Adherance to commitments ▪ Processing on time ▪ Active approach to the customer ▪ Individual treatment of the complaint
Complaint reaction	▪ High correspondence quality ▪ High conversation quality ▪ Complete solution ▪ Fair solution
Complaint evaluation	▪ User-oriented accomplishment of quantitative analyses ▪ Precision of cause analysis
Complaint reporting	▪ User-oriented provision of information ▪ On time provision of information ▪ Adherence to scheduled reporting dates
Complaint information utilization	▪ Use of complaint information for quality improvements ▪ Use of complaint information for the development of new products/services

- determination of *quality indicators* and
- determination of *target figures*.

The first step of the planning is to determine *quality dimensions* for the various tasks on the basis of complaint management goals. For example, timeliness, keeping of promises and on time execution represent quality dimensions of the "complaint processing" task module. Table 11.3 provides an overview of the quality dimensions of all the tasks in the complaint management process.

While these quality dimensions can, for the most part, be easily described in general terminology, the next step in the process is to tackle the difficult task of finding *quality indicators* for these quality dimensions. Here we can distinguish between subjective and objective indicators. In the case of the *subjective quality indicators*, the satisfaction of the complainant is chosen as the benchmark—for instance, satisfaction with the promptness of the complaint processing. In the case of the *objective quality indicators*, the quality dimensions are specified independent of the opinion of the affected person (for example, the time frame for complaint processing). Since subjective and objective quality indicators make different demands on controlling, it makes sense to distinguish between subjective and objective task controlling.

If the quality indicators have been defined, the *desired targets* must be determined, meaning that target values must be fixed on a measurement scale. For example, an average satisfaction level of 90% or a time frame of 5 days for complaint processing could thus be established as target values for the promptness of the complaint processing.

Combining quality indicators with desired targets results in *standards* that are the target figures upon which planning and monitoring are based. The performance expectations of management are reflected in the standards. They are, therefore, task specifications and benchmarks at the same time, based on which the employees can evaluate themselves and management can evaluate the performance of the employees and of the firm. In establishing the objective standards, one must keep in mind that they are based on the expectations of the customers, which ensures that the processes are consistently directed toward the complaint satisfaction being targeted. Furthermore, all standards must be realistic in order to avoid discouraging the employees. Therefore and to ensure the acceptance of the standards, it is necessary that employees are involved in the determination of the standards.

The focus of subjective and objective task controlling is the *monitoring of the standards*. A discrepancy between the actual values of a current measurement and the target values of the standards must lead to a verification of the causes and to the introduction of corrective measures.

11.2.1 Subjective Task Controlling

Within the framework of subjective task controlling, the firm determines how the quality of task fulfillment in the context of complaint management is assessed by the persons concerned. With respect to the tasks of the direct complaint management processes, the persons concerned are the *complainants*; with regard to the tasks of the indirect complaint management process, the persons concerned are the *internal customers of complaint management*.

11.2.1.1 Measurement of Complaint Satisfaction

A fundamental criterion for the successful execution of complaint management tasks is the satisfaction of the complainant. Customers associate their complaint articulation with certain expectations as to the accessibility of the firm, the processing of the case and the resolution of the problem. They then take this complaint expectation as a benchmark that they use to compare their actual experience with the corporate reaction. Depending on whether their expectations were fulfilled or exceeded, or else were not fulfilled, they experience *complaint satisfaction or complaint dissatisfaction*. The extent of this feeling of (dis-)satisfaction has an extraordinarily large influence on the *attitude* as well as on the *communication and purchase behavior* of the complainant. Satisfied customers thus develop an especially positive attitude toward the firm, talk about their good experiences within their social sphere and are characterized by particularly high loyalty (see Sect. 11.3.3). What is important, therefore, is to determine complaint satisfaction regularly for purposes of *performance measurement* and to identify the strengths and weaknesses of complaint management that are perceived by customers.

Complaint satisfaction measurement involves decisions about the content of the questionnaire, the date of the survey, the survey intervals, the choice of respondents and the use of the survey results for the derivation and monitoring of standards.

Design of the Contents of the Survey

With respect to the *contents of the survey*, the firm can fall back on insights of complaint satisfaction research into the fundamental dimensions and attributes of complaint satisfaction. According to this research, customers primarily evaluate corporate complaint management on the basis of the following *quality dimensions*:

- *Complaint Outcome*
  - Adequacy/Fairness of the Solution
- *Complaint Interaction*
  - Friendliness/Politeness
  - Empathy/Understanding
  - Effort/Helpfulness
  - Activity/Initiative
  - Reliability
- *Complaint Process*
  - Accessibility
  - Promptness of Reaction

Satisfaction values should be defined as subjective quality indicators for these *quality dimensions of complaint management* (see Table 11.4).

The determination of complaint satisfaction occurs via a standardized questionnaire that is either mailed within the context of a written survey or that forms the basis for a telephone interview. Table 11.5 shows a corresponding *questionnaire used to determine complaint satisfaction*.

- The customer is initially (in Question 1) asked about the *problem* that gave rise to the complaint.
- In Questions 2 through 4, the customers are asked to describe and to assess the *process of complaint articulation*. After the factual questions as to the chosen complaint method and the addressee, the complainants have the opportunity to make statements about the firm's accessibility and to describe access problems more exactly.

Table 11.4 Complaint satisfaction values as subjective quality indicators of complaint management

Task	Quality dimensions	Subjective quality indicators (Complaint satisfaction)
Complaint stimulation	• Easy Accessibility	• Satisfaction with accessibility
Complaint acceptance	• Customer-oriented design of the initial contact	• Satisfaction with friendliness/ politeness • Satisfaction with understanding • Satisfaction with helpfulness/ empathy
Complaint processing	• Promptness of complaint processing	• Satisfaction with promptness of processing
	• Adherence to commitments	• Satisfaction with reliability
	• Active approach to the customers	• Satisfaction with the activity/ initiative regarding the approach
	• Individual treatment of the complaint	• Satisfaction with the individual treatment of the complaint
Complaint reaction	• Complete solution	• Satisfaction with the completeness of the solution
	• Fair solution	• Satisfaction with the fairness of the solution
	• Solution as a whole	• Satisfaction with the overall solution

- The perceived thoroughness and fairness of the *solution*, as well as the overall satisfaction with the solution, is verified in Questions 5 through 7. The respondents are requested to specify both their expectations and the actual solution and to provide the degree of their satisfaction based on a comparison of these two items.
- Question complex 8 registers the assessment of the *interactions during acceptance and interim communications* with respect to competence, friendliness, understanding, effort, activity and reliability.
- The *promptness of the processing* is taken into consideration with one factual question regarding the duration of the processing on the one hand and another regarding the assessment of this time period on the other (Questions 9 and 10).
- *Global satisfaction* with the entire complaint handling process is then surveyed (Question 11). In this way, the influence of the various dimensions on the global judgment can be calculated in the context of a regression analysis. In addition, customers are provided the opportunity to make specific suggestions that point to shortcomings they might have experienced or *opportunities for improvement* they might have seen (Question 12).

Table 11.5 Complaint satisfaction questionnaire

1. **In the past months you were annoyed with our firm and you did complain. What was the exact reason for the complaint?**
   ☐ Problem A   ☐ Problem B   ☐ Problem C   ☐ Problem D   ☐ _____

2. **Through which channel did you articulate your complaint?**
   ☐ in writing ☐ in person ☐ by phone ☐ via website ☐ by e-mail ☐ _____

3. **To which person/department did you address your complaint?**
   _____

4. **Was it easy for you to complain to us?**
   ☐   ☐   ☐   ☐   ☐
   very easy   rather easy   neither nor   rather difficult   very difficult
   If difficulties arose: What were they about?
   _____

5. **Which solution did you want to achieve by articulating your complaint?**
   _____
   _____
   _____

6. **Which solution was offered to you?**
   _____
   _____
   _____

7. **How satisfied were you with the solution?**
   ☐   ☐   ☐   ☐   ☐
   completely satisfied   very satisfied   satisfied   less satisfied   dissatisfied

8. **How do you rate our reaction to your complaint (concerning the acceptance, inquiry calls, our reply) relating to:**

	completely satisfied	very satisfied	satisfied	less satisfied	dissatisfied
Professional competence	☐	☐	☐	☐	☐
Friendliness	☐	☐	☐	☐	☐
Understanding for your situation	☐	☐	☐	☐	☐
Individual treatment of your case	☐	☐	☐	☐	☐
Helpfulness	☐	☐	☐	☐	☐
Active approach to you	☐	☐	☐	☐	☐
Adherence to commitments	☐	☐	☐	☐	☐

9. **How long did it take until the case was closed (span from filing the complaint to the final answer)?**
   _____

(continued)

Table 11.5 (continued)

10. How satisfied were you with the promptness of the overall complaint processing?

☐	☐	☐	☐	☐
completely satisfied	very satisfied	satisfied	less satisfied	dissatisfied

11. If you consider your overall experience with this complaint, how satisfied are you with the handling of your complaint case?

☐	☐	☐	☐	☐
completely satisfied	very satisfied	satisfied	less satisfied	dissatisfied

12. What could we have done better regarding the handling of your complaint?

_____

_____

_____

13. Did you recommend to other persons (friends, relatives, colleagues) to buy products/services of our firm due to your complaint experience?

☐ Yes ☐ No   If "Yes": To how many persons?

Approx. _____ persons

14. Did you discourage from buying products/services of our firm due to your complaint experience?

☐ Yes ☐ No   If "Yes": To how many persons?

Approx. _____ persons

15. Did you purchase a product or a service from our firm or did you continue the business relationship respectively since the day you articulated your complaint?

☐ Yes ☐ No

15.1 If "Yes": Which impact has the complaint experience for the continuance of the business relationship?

☐ Crucially or great impact
☐ Low or no impact

15.2 If "No": Which impact has the complaint experience for your decision?

☐ Crucial or great impact
☐ Low or no impact

- In the concluding block of questions, the *effects of the complaint experience* on the attitudes and behavior of the customer are surveyed. First, the customers' *communication behavior* is documented in terms of how they related the complaint experience and with respect to any specific recommendations for or against the product or firm (Questions 13 to 14). Finally, Question 15 helps to determine whether the complainant has *maintained the business relationship* since the time the complaint was made and how *important complaint handling* was in this regard.

This questionnaire must, of course, be *modified* for specific purposes. Changes arise based on the product's purchase frequency and relevant specific analysis goals.

In addition, it makes sense to acquire socio-demographic data (age, gender, customer group, etc.)

Survey Intervals

There is a great deal to be said for carrying out the complaint satisfaction survey at fixed intervals. In small and medium-sized businesses with a low complaint volume, an *annual survey* may suffice. In large firms with a high complaint volume, a *continual survey at monthly intervals* would appear to be wise. On the one hand, the period of time that elapses before the final complaint reaction is always short and of approximately the same duration, which means that customers' immediate impressions are measured in a uniform way. On the other hand, the firm constantly has current data at its disposal, which also puts it in a position to react quickly to problems that are looming.

Selection of the Complainants to Be Surveyed

Only when the complaint volume is relatively low is it possible to survey all the complainants. When the complaint volume is high (for example, more than 1000 complaints a year), a representative sample should be drawn from the total population of complainants. Commonly used sampling procedures include quota sampling and random sampling. In *quota sampling*, a sample that is representative of the total population with respect to the relevant attributes (e.g. socio-economic data) is developed. If the distribution of these characteristics in the general population is unknown, random sampling is the only method that can be used to select a representative sample.

The application of *simple random sampling* involves identifying the complainants who should be surveyed according to a randomization process, such as, for example, selecting every third, fifth or tenth complaint from a list of closed complaint cases. The sample must always contain a sufficient number of cases to permit meaningful statistical analysis.

If the activities of complaint management are supported by *software systems*, the complaints to be investigated can be automatically displayed on the basis of appropriate random statistical methods. Once the required questionnaires have been integrated into the system, they can be printed out automatically at the predefined time together with the reply letter, or displayed on the screen for telephone interviews. Provided that the customers cancel their anonymity, the complaint satisfaction data can be stored in the customer database, so that in the context of cost-benefit controlling, analyses are possible with regard to the *conformity of the complainant's expressed and actual market behavior.*

Satisfaction Standards

The results of the complaint satisfaction survey serve as the basis for the *formulation of subjective quality standards* for the tasks of the direct complaint management process.

In the following section, we will proceed on the assumption that—as in the questionnaire in Table 11.5—complaint satisfaction is measured on a *five-point scale* that ranges from "fully satisfied" to "dissatisfied".

Table 11.6 Satisfaction values as subjective quality standards

Subjective quality indicators	Minimum-standard „convinced complainants"	Maximum-standard „disappointed complainants"
Overall complaint satisfaction	65 %	15 %
Satisfaction with the promptness of the complaint processing	90 %	5 %
Satisfaction with the reliability	80 %	8 %
Satisfaction with the active approach to the customer	60 %	5 %
Satisfaction with the individual treatment of the case	65 %	15 %
Satisfaction with the solution	85 %	5 %

For the analysis of the results, the values of this scale are assigned to *three groups*. Customers who marked the response category "fully satisfied" and "very satisfied" make up the first group of *convinced complainants*. The *satisfied complainants* are those customers who marked the response category "satisfied". All the customers who answered "less satisfied" or "dissatisfied" belong to the group of *disappointed complainants*.

For standard formation, only the convinced and disappointed complainants are considered, because the strongest consequences of behavior should be expected here. Convinced complainants generally prove to be loyal, while disappointed complainants are highly susceptible to migration. For this reason, it is important to achieve the greatest possible proportion of convinced complainants and the lowest possible proportion of disappointed complainants.

Once the current status of complaint satisfaction is known, *standards* must be established *as targets*. Table 11.6 shows an exemplary example of this *use of complaint satisfaction values as subjective quality standards*. Here, minimum standards for "convinced complainants" and maximum standards for "disappointed complainants" are established for global complaint satisfaction and the various individual characteristics. The fact that *different targets* are created for individual characteristics can be traced back to the fact that the current status indicates a different level in each case and is of differing importance for global complaint satisfaction. Furthermore, the goals may also be achievable to different degrees. This is the case, for example, when the requirements for rapid processing of complaints are already established; but measures for improving customer contact, such as the establishment of a hotline, are not planned until a later date. Accordingly, the standard values in our example of the indicators "satisfaction with the activity/

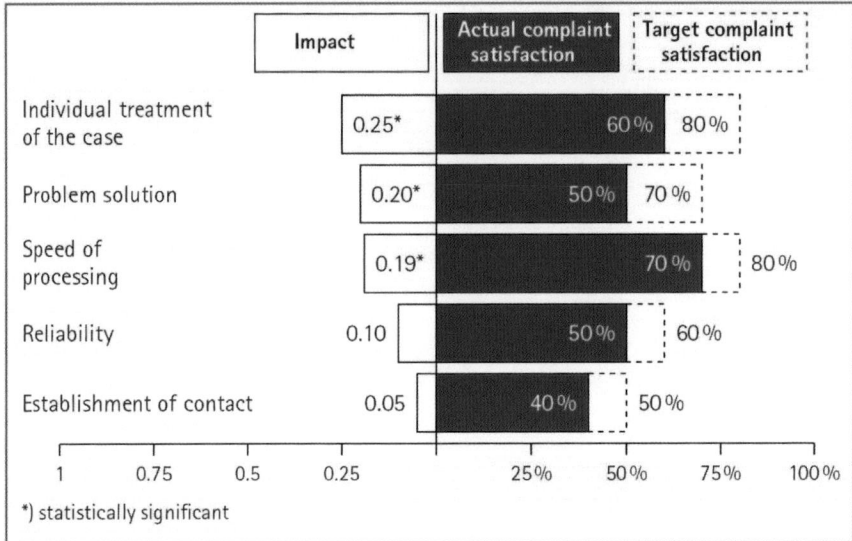

Fig. 11.7 Example of complaint satisfaction results and standards (based on Anton 2007, p. 48)

initiative in making contact" are lower than for the indicator "satisfaction with the promptness of complaint processing."

If the results of the complaint satisfaction survey are available, a multiple regression analysis can be used to determine the *impact of the complainants' satisfaction with individual attributes* on their overall complaint satisfaction. The results can, for example, be displayed in a two-sided bar chart so that, at a glance, the achieved complaint satisfaction values and their significance can be recognized (see Fig. 11.7). On the basis of such results, standards can be formulated which aim to achieve an improvement in satisfaction levels, with particular importance attached to quality attributes with a significant influence on overall complaint satisfaction. In Fig. 11.7 these are marked by an asterisk (*).

By comparing the actual value reached in a current complaint satisfaction survey with the defined target values, the firm can analyze the extent to which the *standards were met*. The results can then be presented in the form of degrees of fulfillment (performance indices). If performance standards are not met, thorough causal analyses must be performed in order to introduce appropriate *improvements in task fulfillment*. Such measures may refer, among other things, to

- a—from the customer's perspective—more efficient flow of processing procedures
- socio-psychological training and recommendations for dealing directly with dissatisfied customers
- time standards for communication with dissatisfied customers during the processing of their cases or
- the fundamental revision of the problem solution or compensation policy.

By comparing the values over time, one can follow developments and thus obtain insights about the *effectiveness of the measures introduced*.

Loyalty Standards

In the survey of complainants, they are not only asked about their satisfaction with the company's reaction, but also about the consequences with regard to their communication and repurchase behavior. Key figures and target standards must also be formulated for these aspects.

The positive impact of complaint management on *communication behavior* can be measured using two key figures. Firstly, *the recommendation rate* is relevant, i.e. the proportion of complainants who communicate about their positive complaint experiences with their friends, relatives or colleagues and recommend the company and its products and services. The aim is to achieve the highest possible value for this key figure.

In contrast, the *warning rate* reflects the proportion of complainants who report their negative complaint experience in their social environment and issue a purchase warning. This key figure should be minimized.

With regard to the *repurchase behavior*, it should be determined to what extent the complainants' experience was responsible for maintaining or terminating the business relationship. Question 15 of the Complaint Satisfaction Questionnaire covers the number of complainants who have opted for or against repurchase on the basis of their complaint experience. If these figures are put in relation to the total number of complainants, the repurchase or churn rate is obtained (see Table 11.7).

Loyalty indicators, in particular those for repurchase behavior, are crucial for assessing whether complaint management achieves the main objective of avoiding

Table 11.7 Loyalty indicators

Loyality dimension	Loyality indicators	
Communication behavior	Recommendation rate	$= \dfrac{\text{Number of complainants with purchase recommendations}}{\text{Total number of complainants}}$
	Waring rate	$= \dfrac{\text{Number of complainants with purchase warnings}}{\text{Total number of complainants}}$
Repurchase behavior	Repurchase rate	$= \dfrac{\text{Number of complainants who buy again because of their complaint experience}}{\text{Total number of complainants}}$
	Churn rate	$= \dfrac{\text{Number of complainants who do not buy again because of their complaint experience}}{\text{Total number of complainants}}$

customer losses. It is therefore referred to again in the context of cost-benefit controlling (Sect. 11.3.2).

Distinction Between Complaint Satisfaction Survey and Follow-Up Contacts
Both in a complaint satisfaction survey and in follow-up contacts, complainants are asked about their experience with the handling of their complaints. However, the objectives of the two instruments are different. The complaint satisfaction survey serves the purpose of gathering information about the quality of the complaint management process perceived by customers. This information is used to ensure and improve the quality of complaint management. In contrast, the follow-up contact investigates whether the case is actually closed from the customer's point of view or whether there is still a need for action. The information gathered here is used primarily to solve problems and satisfy the customer. Therefore, follow-up contact is an instrument of complaint reaction and not complaint management controlling.

11.2.1.2 Measuring the Satisfaction of the Internal Customers of Complaint Management
The quality of task fulfillment in the indirect complaint management process is relevant not for the complainant, but rather for *internal target groups* such as top management, quality management or marketing. For this reason, these internal customers of complaint management are likewise to be surveyed with respect to their satisfaction. Table 11.8 repeats the relevant quality dimensions for complaint

Table 11.8 The satisfaction of internal customers as a subjective quality indicator of complaint management

Task	Quality dimensions	Subjective quality indicators (internal target groups)
Complaint evaluation	▪ User-oriented accomplishment of quantitative analyses	▪ Satisfaction of internal customers with the quantitative analyses
	▪ Precision of cause analysis	▪ Satisfaction of internal customers with the precision of the provided data regarding the cause analysis
Complaint reporting	▪ User-oriented provision of information	▪ Satisfaction of internal customers with the benefit from the provided information
	▪ On time provision of information	▪ Satisfaction of internal customers with the time availability of the provided information
Complaint information utilization	▪ Use of complaint information for quality improvements	▪ Satisfaction of internal customers with the utilization potential of complaint information for quality improvements
	▪ Use of complaint information for the development of new products/services	▪ Satisfaction of internal customers with the utilization potential of complaint information for the development of new products/services

analysis, complaint reporting and complaint information utilization and exemplarily labels the satisfaction ratings of internal customers as subjective quality indicators.

With regard to measuring the satisfaction of internal customers, the same basic problems arise as in the case of complaint satisfaction measurement. *As far as content is concerned*, the relevant dimensions and attributes of quality should be determined from complaint analysis and complaint reporting. The attributes named in Table 11.8 can serve as a starting point here. For the firm-specific development of the questionnaire, however, it is recommended that extensive discussions be held with the internal customers in order to make sure that all the quality attributes that are relevant to them are in fact documented. *As far as time is concerned*, there is a great deal to be said for measuring performance on a yearly basis. At this interval, the assessment takes place on a sufficiently large experience basis. Also, the burden placed on the internal customers by the survey is limited to a reasonable level. Regarding the *selection of respondents*, it is usually possible to include all internal customers in the study. This would also appear to be desirable, because these customers often belong to different internal target groups that have different information needs and expectations.

11.2.2 Objective Task Controlling

In objective task controlling, objective standards that can be verified *independent of the judgments of external and internal customers* should be established for all complaint management tasks. Here we can roughly differentiate between objective quality standards and objective productivity standards. *Quality standards* represent target figures in which expectations related to the quality dimensions and attributes relevant from the customers' point of view are determined. *Productivity standards* refer to output-input ratios that measure the efficiency of the performance.

11.2.2.1 Objective Quality Standards
A comprehensive concepts of task controlling has to find objective quality indicators for as many complaint management tasks as possible and to establish standards for these indicators.

Complaint Stimulation
The goal of complaint stimulation is that the largest possible proportion of customer dissatisfaction *be expressed in complaints*. This goal is to be achieved by establishing and actively communicating a complaint channel that is easily accessible (for example, a central complaint center as addressee).

In order to verify accessibility, a series of objective indicators is to be used. In this way, the quality of telephone access can be measured by the *offered call answered rate (OCAR)* and the *immediate phone acceptance rate (service level)*. The former performance figure relates the number of telephone calls accepted to the total number of calls attempted by customers; the immediate telephone acceptance indicates the number of telephone calls compared to the total number of all attempted calls that were accepted within the defined target specifications (e.g. three rings). The immediate telephone acceptance rate is often defined as a service level in call centers—for example, as an 80:20 ratio that indicates that 80% of the calls should be taken within 20 seconds.

In order to verify the extent to which customer complaints were addressed to the right corporate department and were received via the desired complaint channel, two other performance figures may be used. If, for example, the firm is striving to have as many complaints as possible addressed directly to the central complaint center, then the *addressee rate (ADR) (Complaint Center)* indicates the percentage of complaints that were addressed by complainants in the desired manner. In a similar fashion, complaint stimulating activities can be designed in such a way that dissatisfied customers use the written complaint channel less and instead submit their concern by telephone to the employees of a newly established customer care center. The *complaint channel rate (CCR) (Telephone)* can be regarded as a quality indicator here, in that it again provides the percentage of the total complaint volume represented by those complaints that were received via the complaint channel preferred by the firm.

For these objective quality indicators, defined target specifications that establish the desired degree of achievement and thus constitute the basis for the monitoring of task fulfillment in the area of complaint stimulation must now be defined (for an example, see Table 11.9).

Complaint Acceptance

The *objective quality of complaint acceptance* can be seen in the proper and efficient transfer of complaint cases, as well as in the complete and accurate documentation of complaint information.

The *speedy transfer of complaints* can be verified with the aid of the *on time transfer rate (OTR)*, which records the proportion of the total number of transferred complaints represented by complaints that are transferred within defined processing times. It may be useful here to define various on-time transfer rates, depending on the department that received the complaint (for instance, firm management or branch), since communication channels vary in terms of how time-intensive they are. The

Table 11.9 Objective quality standards for complaint stimulation

Offered calls answered rate (OCAR):   "At least 90% of all calls should be answered."
Service level (SL):   "80% of all complaints should be answered within 20 seconds."
Addressee rate (ADR) (Complaint center):   "80% of all complaints should arrive at the complaint center directly."
Complaint channel rate (CCR) (telephone):   "At least 75% of all complaints should arrive by telephone."

accurate transfer rate (ATR) measures the accuracy of the transfer by providing the proportion of the total number of transferred complaints represented by the complaints directly received by the department responsible in each case.

In addition, what is important in the context of complaint acceptance is that the information is *completely and accurately* taken down, so that as little work as possible is repeated during the remainder of the process. The extent to which the respective goals are achieved can be expressed by the *information completeness rate (ICR)* and the *information accuracy rate (IAR)*. They should particularly be used when the number of complaints in which the information is not completely or accurately documented initially can be quickly determined on the basis of software-supported documentation of complaint processes.

Table 11.10 summarizes the objective performance standards for complaint acceptance.

Complaint Processing

The primary objective of complaint processing is to process the incoming complaints *quickly and on schedule*.

The *promptness of complaint processing* is primarily measured by the indicator of the *total duration of the process* from the receipt of the complaint until the final decision. This total duration is shortest when, in the case of complaints lodged in person or over the telephone, the firm is successful in conclusively solving customers' problems to their satisfaction during the initial contact. The proportion of the total number of complaints represented by these cases is designated the *first-time fix rate (FFR)*. A low first-time fix rate can be an indication of the fact that the customer contact personnel either do not have the necessary professional background or do not have sufficient decision-making authority.

Standards with respect to the *total process duration* of all complaint cases can only be established on the basis of a detailed time-related analysis of the various complaint processing procedures. In view of the fact that these processing procedures have different requirements with regard to time, it makes sense to define

Table 11.10 Objective quality standards for complaint acceptance

---

On time transfer rate (OTR) (Top management):
"90% of all complaints addressed to the top management have to be available in the responsible department after three work days at the latest."

Accurate transfer rate (ATR):
"90% of all complaints should reach the responsible department by the first forwarding."

Information completeness rate (ICR):
"In 85% of all cases the complaint information should be registered completely."

Information accuracy rate (IAR):
"In 90% of all cases the complaint information should be registered flawlessly."

different time standards in each case. If the results of a lengthy test phase show that almost all complaints were solved within a specified time frame (e.g. in five days), it is possible to make this period a standard that applies to all the procedures and potentially to communicate it to customers as a time-related service guarantee ("We'll solve your problems within five days").

In order to be able to comply with the total processing duration, it is advisable to establish time standards for important internal subprocesses. This applies primarily with respect to *maximal idle times and transfer times*. Accordingly, the maximum amount of time that incidents can remain unprocessed *(idle time)* or how much time can be spent for an internal transfer *(transfer time)* is to be fixed respectively as a time period variable (days, hours).

Other quality standards should be formulated with regard to complaint cases in which *reminders* have been made or that are in the *escalation process*. Here, it is necessary to use the *reminder rate (RR)* and the *escalation rate (ER)* to determine the maximum percentage of complaint cases that should even reach the reminder or escalation process.

Table 11.11 contains an overview of the essential objective performance standards for complaint processing and reaction.

Table 11.11 Objective quality standards for complaint processing and reaction

First–time fix rate (FFR): "85% of all complaints that are articulated verbally or by telephone should be solved and completed to the customer's satisfaction within the initial contact so that no following steps need to be initiated."
Total process duration: "90% of all complaints of complaint process A should be completed within 14 working days and 90% of all complaints of complaint process B should be completed within 20 working days."
Total handling time: "95% of all complaints should be completed within ten working days."
Idle time: "In 95% of all cases the maximum idle time should not exceed one day."
Transfer time: "In 95% of all cases the maximum transfer time to the next processing level should not exceed one day."
Reminder rate (RR): "Reminders should be required for no more than 5% of all complaint cases."
Escalation rate (ER): "The escalation process should be initiated for no more than 2% of all complaint cases."

Complaint Reaction

The central goal of the complaint reaction task module is to process customer complaints *actively, reliably and giving due consideration to the individual circumstances of the case*, and to offer the customers complete and fair solutions to their problems.

Active contact applies to the *external communication with the dissatisfied customer* by means of receipt confirmations, intermediate and final replies. Here, the firm must determine the maximum number of days that can elapse before the receipt of a complaint is confirmed, or by what date intermediate replies and the final reply must be mailed.

When customers make a follow-up complaint about the complaint processing or the solution offered to them, an objective indication exists that the firm has fallen short of achieving the goal of complaint reaction, which is to re-establish customer satisfaction. Therefore, the *follow-up complaint rate (FCR)*, which expresses the proportion of total complaints represented by follow-up complaints, must be noted and minimized. The higher the follow-up complaint rate is, the higher is the number of customers whose dissatisfaction increases during the process. Table 11.12 shows the formulation of a standard for the follow-up complaint rate.

Complaint Reporting and Complaint Information Utilization

We will refrain from providing performance target figures for complaint management controlling and complaint analysis as far as objective task controlling in the context of the indirect complaint management process is concerned. The verification of the goal orientation of complaint management controlling should take place more in the context of an audit and less on the basis of performance figures. The controlling of the complaint analysis is done by means of evaluating the complaint reporting as well as the complaint information utilization, as this is where the quality of the recorded and analyzed complaint information is reflected.

In the context of *complaint reporting*, it is imperative to supply internal customers with information in a way that is user-friendly and timely, and to observe established reporting deadlines. The adequacy of the reports for the individual target groups can be measured primarily by subjective indicators. However, an objective quality indicator should also be used with regard to the temporal aspect. If deadline targets are established for regular reporting (for example, weekly, monthly, yearly reports),

Table 11.12 Objective quality standards for complaint reaction

> **Adherence to deadlines:**
> "Deadlines for external communication (acknowledgement of receipt, intermediate notices, final reply) are kept to 90%."
>
> **Follow-up complaint rate (FQR)**
> "Follow-up complaints should occur in a maximum of 5% of all complaints."

the extent to which these activity standards are being observed can be determined with the aid of the *on-time report rate (ORR)*, which is the quotient of the number of timely reports and the total number of reports.

The *usage rate (UR)*, which indicates the proportion of information used by addressees for quality improvement measures or in the development of new products, can be used as an objective indicator of the target group orientation of complaint analysis. However, determining this rate causes a number of difficulties, because a clear-cut classification of informational units and definition of "usage" can rarely be made successfully. In this respect, warranty and guarantee figures should be used as indicators of the extent to which defects that have been the subject of complaints have been remedied.

In complaints with a legal claim, often objective errors are reported that lead to payments due to statutory liability for defects or voluntarily guarantees. If the complaint information is used to remedy defects, this must be reflected in reduced *problem-specific warranty and guarantee rates*, which put the number of problem-specific warranties or guarantee cases in relation to the number of products. If warranties and guarantees do not play a major role—which is especially the case with services—the subjective indicator of the (reduced) problem-specific annoyance rate must be used instead of these objective indicators.

Table 11.13 shows examples of objective standards relating to complaint reporting and complaint information utilization.

In Table 11.14 the objective performance indicators that are most important for the quality dimensions of complaint management are presented in summary.

With respect to all the objective standards defined, regular analyses should be carried out—similar to subjective task controlling—and the actual values determined should be compared to the target values of the standards. In this way, *standard-specific discrepancies or degrees of goal achievement* can be determined (Table 11.15).

Table 11.13 Objective standards for complaint reporting and complaint information utilization

---

On time report rate (ORR):
"At least 95% of all reports should be received on time."

Problem–specific warranty rate (WR):
"Maximum of 1 in 10,000 products to be covered by warranty for problem x."

Problem–specific guarantee rate (GR):
"Maximum of 1 in 20,000 products to be covered by guarantee for problem x."

Table 11.14 Objective indicators of complaint management

Task	Quality dimensions	Objective quality indicators
Complaint stimulation	Easy accessibility	Offered calls answered rate (OCAR) $= \dfrac{\text{Number of calls answered}}{\text{Number of calls offered}}$
		Service Level (SL) $= \dfrac{\text{Number of immediately answered calls}}{\text{Number of calls offered}}$
	Correct addresing of customer complaints	Addressee rate (AR) (Complaint center) $= \dfrac{\text{Number of complaints arrived at the complaint center}}{\text{Total number of complaints}}$
	Utilization of existing complaint channels	Complaint channel rate (CCR) (telephone) $= \dfrac{\text{Number of complaints arrived by phone}}{\text{Total number of complaints}}$
Complaint acceptance	Prompt tansfer of complaint cases	On time transfer rate (OTR) $= \dfrac{\text{Number of complaints transferred within defined cycle times}}{\text{Total number of transferred complaints}}$
	Correct tansfer of complaint cases	Accurate transfer rate (ATR) $= \dfrac{\text{Number of complaints arrived at the responsible department by the first forwarding}}{\text{Total number of transferred complaints}}$
	Complete documentation of complaint information	Information completeness rate (ICR) $= \dfrac{\text{Number of complaints with completely recorded information}}{\text{Total number of transferred complaints}}$
	Correct documentation of complaint information	Information accuracy rate (IAR) $= \dfrac{\text{Number of complaints with correctly recorded information}}{\text{Total number of registered complaints}}$
Complaint processing	Promptness of complaint processing	First-time fix rate (FFR) $= \dfrac{\text{Number of problems solved and closed within the first contact}}{\text{Total number of registered complaints}}$
		Duration of particular complaint process in days.
		Total process time in days.
	On time processing	Idle time
		Transfer time
		Reminder rate (RR) $= \dfrac{\text{Number of complaints within the reminder process}}{\text{Total number of complaints}}$
		Escalation rate (ER) $= \dfrac{\text{Number of complaints within the escalation process}}{\text{Total number of complaints}}$
Complaint reaction	Active approach to the customer	Deadlines for the shipping of external communication (receipt confirmation, intermediate replies, final answer)
	Complete solution Fair solution	Follow-up complaint rate (FCR) $= \dfrac{\text{Number of follow-up complaints}}{\text{Total number of complaints}}$
Complaint reporting	On time provision of information	On time report rate (ORR) $= \dfrac{\text{Number of reports on time}}{\text{Total number of complaints}}$
Complaint information utilization	Usage of complaint information for quality improvements and for the development of new products/services	Problem-specific warranty rate (WR) $= \dfrac{\text{Number of warranties for problem x}}{\text{Total number of products}}$
		Problem-specific guarantee rate (GR) $= \dfrac{\text{Number of guarantees payments}}{\text{Total number of products}}$

Table 11.15 Discrepancy calculation considering complaint stimulation as an example

Quality indicator	Target value	Actual value	Discrepancy (percentage points)	Realization degree (=actual/target)
Addressee rate	80%	95%	+15%	119%
Complaint channel rate	75%	60%	−15%	80%
Offered calls answered rate	90%	85%	−5%	94%
First-time fix rate	80%	55%	−25%	69%

11.2.2.2 Objective Productivity Standards

There is often great confusion in literature and practice about the use of the terms 'quality' and 'productivity'. Frequently, the same metrics are used for both quality and productivity. However, a clear conceptual distinction is made here.

Productivity does not refer to the result of a production process—like quality— but to the production itself. It is a measurement that relates the quantitative output of production to the quantity of the input factors (for example, the number of employees) utilized. Such a measurement makes it possible to assess the efficiency of the production process. As applied to complaint management, the measurement of productivity therefore serves to measure the efficiency of the production factors used in this process. The essential basis of this measurement is the definition of *appropriate output and input parameters*.

The key output parameter for performance in the context of the direct complaint management process is the *number of complaints*, whereby a task-specific differentiation is to be made. In the case of complaint stimulation, the number of additional complaint articulations stimulated is the relevant figure. In the case of complaint acceptance, it is the number of articulations received or registered, and in the case of complaint processing and reaction, it is the number of processed complaints. With respect to complaint analysis and complaint reporting as tasks of the indirect complaint management process, the *number of analyses performed and reports produced* is to be used.

Since the results of complaint management can only be generated using various *input factors* (employee, telephone system, software system, etc.), there is a possibility of relating the output generated to various input factors. It would, however, seem to be sensible to *concentrate on the employee input factor*, because it is usually the greatest cost factor. Accordingly, in the following section only the *labor productivity* will be considered, in which the output is compared to the labor input. To that end, the quantity of labor employed or the amount of the working time used can be

Table 11.16 Productivity ratios regarding complaint acceptance and complaint processing

Task	Productivity dimension	Productivity indicator	Productivity standards
Complaint acceptance	Number of complaints accepted	Number of accepted complaint calls / Number of employees	▪ At least 70 accepted complaints per employee and day
		Number of accepted complaint calls / Number of working hours	▪ At least 9 accepted complaints per employee and hour
Complaint processing	Number of complaints processed	Number of written complaints processed / Number of emplyees	▪ At least 20 written complaints processed per employee and day
		Number of written complaints processed / Number of working hours	▪ At least 3 written complaints processed per employee and hour

selected as the input. Typical productivity ratios would then be the number of complaints processed per employee or working hour.

Productivity ratios such as these make statements about the *efficiency of task fulfillment* achieved by the employees in complaint management. They can also be defined as standards in terms of target figures, such as, for instance, determining the number of telephone calls accepted per hour or a percentage increase in the next period. Table 11.16 provides several examples of possible productivity ratios and standards for complaint acceptance and complaint processing.

When using productivity standards, however, the following must be observed: productivity ratios make no statements about the quality of the output. High productivity with regard to the acceptance and processing of complaints may be associated with a high number of failures and intense customer dissatisfaction. Empirical studies in the service sector also confirm a significant negative relationship between productivity and customer satisfaction (Anderson et al. 1997). In addition, it has repeatedly been demonstrated that in cases in which they experience a conflict between quality and quantity goals, employees tend to focus more on the productivity targets because these targets are more easily controlled for and in many cases are the basis of their performance assessments (Singh 2000). For this reason, productivity ratios should never be used alone, but rather only *in connection with subjective and objective quality standards*. It is also necessary that management *set clear priorities* with respect to the weighting of quality and productivity goals.

11.2.3 Excursus: Objective Quality and Productivity Standards in Complaint Centers

In a complaint center, whose nucleus is usually the call center that is responsible for customer contact over the telephone, the ACD (Automatic Call Distribution) system offers the firm the opportunity to have all calls registered in a detailed manner and to have a wealth of data supplied for the formulation of other objective quality and productivity standards.

Table 11.17 provides an overview of frequently used ratios and their possible application as standards. A classification of these ratios as measurements of productivity or quality is only possible in a selective way. The ratios mentioned first are primarily quality indicators that point out whether customers' expectations in terms of the accessibility of a conversation partner and an immediate solution are fulfilled (e.g. first-time fix rate) or not (e.g. lost call rate or time in queue). The measurements for absolute times (e.g. communication time) that were subsequently presented provide the basis for productivity considerations. At the bottom of the list are productivity ratios that primarily provide information about the workload of the employees.

In using these ratios for *controlling purposes*, the following also applies: The productivity ratios provide starting points for efficient utilization of personnel, but should *not be interpreted as measurement categories for quality*. This applies especially to the productivity measurement "Calls Per Hour" that is commonly used in call centers. An increase in this productivity can be associated with a decline in quality. Furthermore, many factors that can influence this ratio are outside the employees' control (for example, the number and type of calls or the caller's ability to communicate). The fact remains that the data supplied by the ACD system indeed have the advantage of being objective, but *reveal nothing about the quality perception of the customer*. These ratios must, therefore, always be integrated into a complete system that also contains subjective quality standards.

11.2.4 The Linking of Quality and Productivity Standards in a Complaint Management Index (CMI)

In order to be able to give equal consideration to the subjective and the objective standards, the development of a *Complaint Management Index (CMI)* is recommended here. This is a flexible instrument that has to be designed individually for each company, depending on the initial situation and the challenges of the respective complaint management. The managers of this area must select the assessment dimensions and attributes that are relevant for them, weight the selected dimensions and attributes and establish standards. However, the resulting index concept is not static, but has to be *dynamically adjusted* to the concrete requirements and problems.

Table 11.17 Objective performance standards in a call center

Quality and productivity ratios	Definition	„Best Practice"- standard
First-time fix rate (first-time final)	$\dfrac{\text{Number of calls that do not require an additional call to the call center or return calls by the agent}}{\text{Number of calls answered}} \times 100$	70% – 75%
Average speed of answer	$\dfrac{\text{Total time in queue}}{\text{Number of calls answered}} \times 100$	31 seconds
Service level	$\dfrac{\text{Calls answered in less than x seconds}}{\text{Number of calls offered}} \times 100$	80% within 20 seconds
Calls transferred	$\dfrac{\text{Number of calls transferred from the original agent to someone else}}{\text{Number of calls answered}} \times 100$	1% – 3%
Calls blocked	$\dfrac{\text{Number of callers who received a busy signal}}{\text{Number of calls offered}} \times 100$	1% – 3%
Lost calls (abandonment rate)	$\dfrac{\text{Number of calls that are abandoned}}{\text{Number of calls offered}} \times 100$	3% – 5%
Time in queue	Average number of seconds that a caller spends waiting for an agent to answer the telephone after being placed in the queue by the ACD system.	30 – 90 seconds
Communication time	Total number of seconds the caller was connected to an agent.	Depending on type of call and industry: 210 – 580 seconds (Ø 254 seconds)
After call work time	Time after a call is completed that the agent needs to complete administrative work related to the call.	Depending on type of call and industry: 30 – 180 seconds
Average handling time	Sum of talk time and after-call work time.	Depending on type of call and industry: 240 – 760 seconds
Calls per hour	$\dfrac{\text{Total number of handled calls during one dayshift}}{\text{Total time logged into the telephone system}}$	Depending on type of call and industry: 5 – 100 calls
Calls per shift / agent	Accepted calls per agent during a dayshift.	66 calls

Its development consists of *five steps* that are introduced in an example below:

(1) Selection of the Relevant Assessment Dimensions and Attributes The first step is to select the relevant assessment dimensions and attributes. In our example, attributes for all the relevant quality dimensions are recorded, while the labor productivity of complaint acceptance and processing is considered in terms of productivity (see columns 1 and 3 in Table 11.18).

(2) Weighting of the Assessment Dimensions and Attributes Subsequently, management must weight the dimensions and attributes. On the one hand, the significance assigned to quality in relation to productivity is expressed in this weighting. On the other hand, a weighting of the individual quality and productivity attributes also takes place. Pragmatically speaking, the approach taken is to distribute a point total of 1.0 across the dimensions and attributes (see column 2 in Table 11.18).

(3) Establishment of Standards A standard must now be defined for each attribute, as was described in the previous chapters. Accordingly, subjective and objective quality indicators must be selected for the quality attributes, and the target level must be established as a quality standard in each case. A similar principle applies to the productivity attributes (see columns 4 and 5 in Table 11.18).

(4) Verification of the Fulfillment of Standards In the context of a periodic verification, the firm must now investigate whether the required target standard was actually reached. If this is the case, it is expressed by assigning a value of 1. If the standard was missed, this attribute is assigned a value of 0. The reason for using a 0/1 variable such as this is the fact that only those attributes should go into the index for which the quality and productivity goals were achieved (see column 6 in Table 11.18).

(5) Calculation of the Complaint Management Index The last step is to multiply the respective attribute weights (column 2) by the value of the 0/1 variable (column 6) and add up the respective results (column 7). In the example presented, the firm would obtain a value of 0.64 for the Complaint Management Index (maximum value = 1.00).

The process presented here is characterized by simplicity, transparency, flexibility and feasibility. It requires only *very little methodical effort* and can easily be adjusted to the specific situation in every firm. Each firm must decide individually which assessment attributes should be recorded and how they should be weighted. During this process, it is made transparent at the same time, where the firm's priorities lie with respect to quality and productivity and what significance is given to particular attributes. Moreover, the system is very flexible, since the recording of new attributes and new weightings make it possible for the firm to react immediately when action is required.

Table 11.18 Complaint management index (example calculation)

1 Assessment dimensions	2 Weight	Partial weight	3 Assessment attributes	4 Key figure	5 Standard	6 Standard fulfilled (yes=1 no=0)	7 Score (6 × 2)
Accessibility	0.10	0.04	Easy accessibility	Articulation rate	> 30%	1	0.04
		0.06		convinced complainants disappointed complainants	> 35% < 25%	1	0.06
Availability	0.15	0.15	Easy availability	Offered calls answered rate	> 80%	0	0.00
		0.05		Service level	> 80%	0	0.00
Interaction quality	0.30	0.08	Friendliness	convinced complainants disappointed complainants	> 80% < 5%	1	0.08
		0.07	Empathy	convinced complainants disappointed complainants	> 75% < 12%	1	0.07
		0.08	Helpfulness	convinced complainants disappointed complainants	> 90% < 5%	0	0.00
		0.07	Reliability	convinced complainants disappointed complainants	> 80% < 10%	1	0.07
Promptness of reaction	0.10	0.03	Promptness of complaint processing	First-time fix rate	> 70%	1	0.03
		0.03		Duration of the handling process	< 3 days	0	0.00

(continued)

Table 11.18 (continued)

1	2	3	4	5	6	7
Promptness of reaction	0.10	0.04	*Promptness of complaint processing*	convinced complainants / disappointed complainants	> 50% / < 25%	1	0.04
Problem solution	0.10	0.05	Fairness of solution	convinced complainants / disappointed complainants	> 50% / < 30%	1	0.05
		0.05	Completeness of solution	Follow-up complaint rate	< 5%	0	0.00
Quality of complaint processing	0.15		Prompt transfer of complaint cases	On time transfer rate	> 90%	1	0.15
Quality of complaint analysis	0.05	0.02	Usage-oriented information provision	Usage rate	> 10%	1	0.02
		0.03		Internal customers satisfaction with the quality of complaint analysis	> 70%	1	0.03
Quality of complaint reporting	0.05		On time information provision	On time report rate	> 95%	0	0.00
Customer loyalty	0.10		Repurchase intention	Willingness to buy	> 40%	1	0.00
Productivity of complaint acceptance	0.05		Accepted complaints	Number of answered complaint calls per day / number of employees	> 70	0	0.10
Productivity of complaint processing	0.05		Handled complaints	Number of written complaints processed / number of employees	> 40	1	0.05
Total	1.00	1.00					CMI = 0.64

Of course, this simple procedure can be modified and further developed in many different ways, for example by defining *tolerance limits* for the standards. If the tolerance limit is exceeded, the quality attribute could be weighted higher (for example, 1.25 instead of 1.0) and a failure of the standard could be weighted lower (for example, −0.25 instead of 0). However, with these and other refinements, it should always be ensured that the system remains manageable for everyone, because this is an essential prerequisite for its acceptance.

The Complaint Management Index can be regarded as the *key aggregate measurement of task controlling*. It makes clear at a glance the extent to which the defined quality and productivity goals have been reached. A more exact analysis of the calculation then reveals very quickly which measures will be necessary for goal fulfillment in the future or whether a *revision of the goals* is advisable.

11.3   Cost-Benefit Controlling

Another of the main tasks of complaint management controlling is to assess the *profitability of complaint management* and its contribution to the success of the firm.

Profitability is a measurement category that indicates whether the revenues exceed costs. The extent of the profitability targeted is expressed in the performance goals, which primarily include profit and rate of return.

In order to be able to assess the extent to which the complaint management process is designed in a profitable manner, it is first necessary to evaluate in monetary terms the resources that were employed and the results that were achieved. The *monetary evaluation of the resources employed*—for example, the personnel and physical resources—is expressed through the costs that arose from the use of those resources. The *monetary evaluation of the results achieved* is expressed through the sales and profit contributions that were secured or additionally brought about through complaint management.

In the following sections, the requirements and approaches for the detailed recording of the *costs relevant for complaint management* will first be described (Sect. 11.3.1). Section 11.3.2 deals with the operationalization and quantification of the *benefits* of complaint management. The cost and benefit measurements will be combined for purposes of *profitability controlling*, where the "Return on Complaint Management (RoC)" will be calculated (Sect. 11.3.3).

11.3.1 Cost Controlling

11.3.1.1 Cost Controlling from the Perspective of Traditional Cost Accounting

Managers who work in complaint management usually have very little to do with cost accounting. They also will not be the ones who will be engaged in cost-accounting activities. However, in order for them to be able to request the relevant analyses from the cost-accounting department and to interpret the results, it is essential that they be familiar with some of the main concepts and methods that are relevant in cost controlling.

The main tasks of cost accounting include the differentiated documentation of the costs incurred (cost-type accounting), the analysis of their internal development (cost-center accounting) and the assignment to the products and services offered for purposes of price calculation (cost-unit accounting). These are briefly described below with specific reference to complaint management.

Cost-Type Accounting

Cost-type accounting answers the question *"Which costs were incurred?"* Personnel costs, administrative costs, communication costs and reaction costs are designated *relevant cost types of complaint management.*

- *Personnel costs* arise from the salaries (including employee benefit costs) of the *employees working in a firm's complaint management dep*artment.
- *Administrative costs* (office supplies, costs of the office space itself and depreciation of the office equipment) make up another pool of costs.
- *IT costs* should be considered separately if information technology (hardware, software) is used to a considerable extent in complaint management.
- *Communication costs* include all the costs that are incurred in the context of the communication that takes place during the process of solving the customer's problem (e.g. telephone, fax and postage costs).
- Included among the *reaction costs* are all the costs that arise from the solution offered—for instance, when the customer is granted a price reduction, provided a new product or presented a gift. They are *compensation or goodwill costs* when they arise based on voluntary payments by a firm to which the customer has no legal claim. *Warrantee costs* arise in the case of solutions to which the customer has a legal or contractual right.

It is important to *document compensation and warrantee costs separately*, since only then is differentiated cost control possible. While a reduction of the compensation costs is possible immediately—albeit with negative consequences for complaint satisfaction—a cut in the warrantee costs can have grave consequences, since the firm must take into account the costs of judicial disputes and greater damage to its image, in addition to an increase in complaint dissatisfaction.

Cost-Center Accounting

Cost-center accounting analyzes the operational areas to which the costs can be assigned. It answers the question, *"Where were the costs incurred?"*

If a complaint management department has been established as an independent organizational unit, it represents the relevant cost center.

Only the *common costs* that cannot be assigned to an individual product—for instance, the personnel costs, administrative costs and communication costs—are assigned to the cost center. The reaction costs are, for the most part, related to very specific products and services and are thus of a direct-cost nature. For this reason,

Table 11.19 Ideal-typically structure of a complaint management cost center

Cost position	Complaint management department	Complaint center	Regional complaint units			Total
			North	South	Total	
Personnel costs	78,000 €	165,000 €	20,000 €	20,000 €	40,000 €	**283,000 €**
Administration costs	15,000 €	77,400 €	6,550 €	6,550 €	13,100 €	**105,500 €**
Communication costs	2,200 €	23,000 €	3,150 €	3,150 €	6,300 €	**31,500 €**
Total	**95,200 €**	**265,400 €**	**29,700 €**	**29,700 €**	**59,400 €**	**420,000 €**

they are directly assigned to the respective products and services (cost units) in the context of cost-unit accounting.

Table 11.19 shows a simple *example* of an ideal type of complaint management cost center, in which there is a differentiated documentation of the costs for a complaint management department consisting of a complaint management director, a complaint center with employees who receive and process customer complaints directly, and two complaint management departments in regional subsidiaries.

Cost-Unit Accounting

Cost-unit accounting assigns the costs to the respective causative products and services. It thus answers the question, *"For what were the (documented) costs incurred?"*

In corporate practice, this allocation normally takes place using overhead allocation. This means that the common costs of complaint management are allotted to the cost units on the basis of production cost. The presented approach leads to the situation that costs are not allocated to products fairly according to input involved, meaning that flawless products have to bear the costs of defective products, while the latter are disburdened with regard to costs. This represents a malfunction with regard to cost accounting, which requires rethinking. This is starting point of activity-based costing, which allows for a fair allocation of costs according to input involved.

11.3.1.2 Cost Controlling from the Perspective of Activity-Based Costing

Activity-Based Costing (ABC) avoids this problem by allocating common costs to individual items based on the resources they actually consume.

The basic principle of activity-based costing consists of *four steps:* (1) First, the business processes that generate the common costs must be defined. (2) Next, the cost drivers that generate these common costs must be identified. (3) These results then form the basis for the calculation of the process costs and process cost rates.

(4) Using these figures, it is possible to charge the cost objects (products and services) with costs according to the processes they consume, which in turn allows for targeted planning and control of the common costs. The application of these fundamental steps to complaint management will now be presented.

Process Identification The first step is to define the *business processes that generate the common costs*. This leads to a differentiation between core processes and support processes. *Core processes* deliver the output directly to external customers, whereas *support processes* deliver the output directly to internal customers. The classification of the overall complaint management process into direct and indirect complaint management processes reflects this differentiated perspective: *(1)* The *direct complaint management process* is a core process that is aligned to external customers, since "complaint satisfaction" or "reestablishing customer satisfaction" and thus achieving higher customer retention should be the result. *(2)* In contrast, the *indirect complaint management process* is a support process that supplies information to internal customers (e.g. other departments) in the form of complaint evaluations and analyses, as well as targeted reports.

A *detailed process analysis* is carried out for the direct and the indirect complaint processes, whereby the different activities (= subprocesses) are identified for each cost center that participates in a process. For the *direct complaint management process*, these could be the cost center "General Administration" that handles the incoming mail and the switchboard, the cost center "Complaint Management" and the cost centers of the departments that participate in complaint acceptance and complaint processing. *Activities or sub-processes* are, for instance, the opening and sorting of letters, the receipt or transfer of telephone calls, the structured documentation of complaint information or the generation of receipt confirmations or reply letters. Such activity lists should be produced for all the departments within the firm that are integrated into the complaint management process. If there is a central unit—a complaint center, for example—in which all the operational activities of the complaint contact process are united, the majority of the relevant sub-processes will occur here.

A similar identification of cost centers and activities also takes place for the *indirect complaint management process*. Here, the cost center in question is either the complaint management department itself or another functional area in which activities such as the performance of analyses or the moderation of quality circles takes place.

Figure 11.8 gives an exemplary overview of a possible *systematization of the processes and activities of complaint management* as the basis for the application of activity-based costing.

Determination of Cost Drivers Activity-based costing also differentiates between direct and common costs. *Direct costs* are immediately allocated to the cost object; *common costs* are recorded at the place where they arise and a differentiation is made whether those costs are activity-driven or activity-neutral. For the *activity-driven costs* so-called *cost drivers* are defined that determine the usage of the corresponding

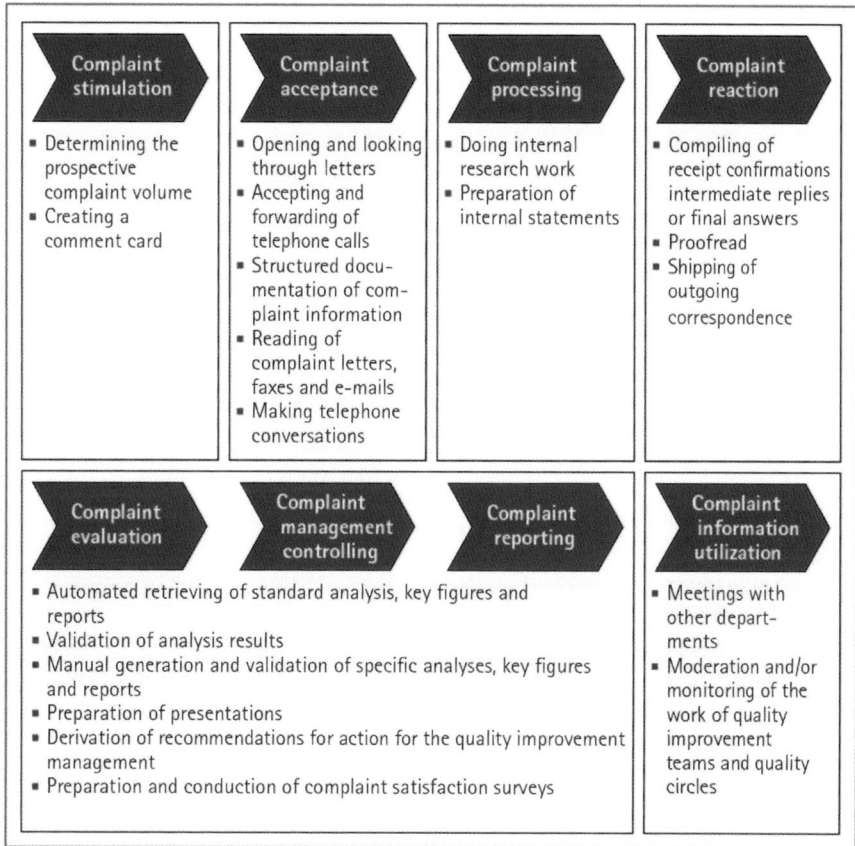

Fig. 11.8 Systemization of the processes and activities of complaint management

activities. For the direct complaint management process, these drivers are the articulated and documented, or processed, complaints; for the indirect complaint management process, they are the business activities that should be fulfilled—for example, analyses to be performed or reports to be produced. If the costs arising from a process—such as the costs for the executive in charge of complaint management—are not in direct proportion to the cost driver—e.g. the complaint volume—then we are dealing with *activity-neutral costs*.

Determination of the Activity-Based Costs and Process Cost Rates Based on the cost drivers, a *process cost rate (PCR)* is calculated as the quotient of the costs determined for a process and the process quantity—e.g. the complaint volume. It is thus possible to account for the per-complaint costs immediately. In addition, the process cost rate provides precise insight into the cost structure of complaint management because it also takes into consideration all complaint management activities in participating interface departments.

Table 11.20 Exemplary determination of process cost rates

Sub-process		Cost driver	Planned process quantity	Planned process costs	Process cost rate (ad)	Appor-tionment rate (an)	Total process cost rate
Accept and process customer complaints	ad	Articulated complaints	50,000	850,000 €	17.00 €	1.70 €	18.70 €
Analyze, prepare and provide complaint information	an	Requested analyses and reports	750	150,000 €	200.00 €	20.00 €	220.00 €
Manage department	an	–	–	100,000 €	-.--	-.--	-.--
Total				1,100,000 €			

ad = activity-driven;   **an** = activity-neutral

The process cost rate may either be calculated *globally* across all the activity-based costs of complaint management or in a *differentiated fashion for the direct and indirect complaint management processes*. The latter is especially advisable when an internal allocation of the services of the indirect complaint management process is planned. At the same time, this approach brings about greater transparency with regard to the cost structure of complaint management.

Table 11.20 shows an exemplary method of *determining process cost rates*. For the overall complaint management process, *total costs* in the amount of 1,100,000 € are projected for an estimated annual volume of 50,000 complaints. Of this total, 100,000 € is incurred by departmental management as activity-neutral costs, 850,000 € is incurred as activity-driven costs for the direct complaint management process (accepting and processing customer complaints) and 150,000 € is incurred for the indirect complaint management process (analyzing, preparing and supplying complaint information). The *process cost rates for the activity-driven costs* are determined by dividing the planned activity-based costs by the respective planned process quantities. The two process cost rates that result from this process are in the amounts of 17 € for the acceptance and processing of a complaint and of 200 € for complaint analysis and reporting. In order to calculate the *apportionment rates for the activity-neutral costs*, these costs (100,000 €) are divided by the sum of the activity-driven costs of the two sub-processes (1000,000 €). From this, we obtain a ratio coefficient (0.10), which is multiplied by the respective process cost rate. For the subprocess "Accepting and Processing Customer Complaints", we thus obtain an apportionment rate for the activity-neutral costs of 1.70 € for the direct complaint management process and 20 € for the indirect complaint management process. If we then add the process cost rate per sub-process for the activity-driven costs to the respective apportionment rate, the result is the *total process cost rate* per sub-process. For the subprocess "Accept and process customer complaints", this rate is 18.70 € and for the subprocess "Analyze, prepare and provide complaint information" it is 220 €.

Determination of the Costs for Cost Objects The activity-based costs of complaint management *are allocated to the cost objects* according to their usage of the two sub-processes "Accept and process customer complaints" and "Analyze, prepare and provide complaint information".

To *continue with our example*, we assume that of the volume of 50,000 complaints anticipated for the next accounting period, a total of four products (A, B, C and D) are affected, and that 40,000 complaints with the following distribution were received in the previous accounting period: 10% were allotted to Product A, 35% to Product B, 40% to Product C and 15% to Product D. If the same distribution is also assumed for the planning period, this means that Product A will cause the activation of the direct complaint process 5000 times, Product B 17500 times, Product C 20,000 times and Product D 7500 times. By using the process cost rate of 18.70 € that was ascertained for the direct complaint management process, 93,500 € (= 5000 × 18.70 €) is assigned to Product A, 327,250 € to Product B, 374,000 € to Product C and 140,250 € to Product D, and subsequently taken into account in the calculation of their respective prices.

The internal allocation of the performances of the indirect complaint management process is carried out in a similar way. In a parallel process, it is possible, in terms of a *realistic customer valuation,* to assign to complainants the costs that they generated.

11.3.1.3 Key Figures of Cost Controlling

The most important cost-controlling performance figures can be *considered on various levels.* On the one hand, it must be decided whether the costs for the entire scope of complaint management or for the two subprocesses of direct and indirect complaint management will be considered. In addition, one must differentiate according to whether absolute cost measurements will be collected, or whether ratios will be calculated. Furthermore, one must look for performance figures that provide insight into cost-oriented relationships with other operational departments. The most important cost-controlling key figures from complaint management are exemplarily summarized in Table 11.21.

With respect to the *entire scope of complaint management,* the *absolute measurements* of cost are of primary interest. A specific examination of the total costs with and without reaction costs is advisable here. In many firms, reaction costs indeed represent one of the largest cost blocks of complaint management, although they do not permit conclusions to be drawn as to how profitably tasks are executed. It is therefore recommended that, in addition to the absolute amount of the total complaint management costs, the total costs are also shown without the reaction costs.

Table 11.21 Selected key figures of cost controlling

Referred to the total area of complaint management

- **Absolute cost**
  - **Total costs of complaint management**
    - Total complaint management costs
    - Complaint management costs without reaction costs
  - **Reaction costs of complaint management**
    - Total reaction costs
    - Compensation costs
    - Guarantee costs
- **Relative cost**
  - **Costs per employee (without reaction costs)**
    - Costs per employee
  - **Costs per complaint**
    - Total costs per complaint
    - Costs per complaint without reaction costs

Referred to sub-processes of complaint management

- **Absolute cost**
  - Total costs of the direct complaint management process
  - Costs of the direct complaint management process without reaction costs
  - Costs of the indirect complaint management process

- **Relative cost**
  - **Costs per employee (without reaction costs)**
    - Costs of the direct complaint management process per employee
    - Costs of the indirect complaint management process per employee
  - **Costs per complaint**
    - Complaint management costs of the direct complaint process per complaint including reaction costs
    - Complaint management costs of the direct complaint process per complaint without reaction costs
    - Complaint management costs of the indirect complaint process per complaint
  - **Costs per activity (without reaction costs)**
    - Costs of the indirect complaint management per complaint report
    - Costs of the indirect complaint management per complaint satisfaction measurement

Referred to the linkage with other departments

- Relation of the costs caused by the complaint management department and the costs that are allocated to other departments

- Relation of the costs caused by the complaint management department and the costs that are allocated by other departments to complaint management

- Relation of the costs that are allocated to the complaint management by other departments and the costs that are allocated to other departments by the complaint management department

In the case of a *relative evaluation*, the complaint management costs are related to the number of complaints processed. This performance figure provides details about the costs resulting from the processing of a complaint. Here again, the total costs with and without the inclusion of the reaction costs are used as a basis. The first variation indicates which costs overall are triggered by a single complaint. The second variation is primarily relevant for the cost-related monitoring and controlling of complaint handling. If the information is available, the costs per complaint (excluding reaction costs) should also be displayed separately for each communication channel or complaint center team.

If an organizational separation exists with regard to the perception of the tasks of the direct and the indirect complaint management processes, it is obvious that absolute and relative cost performance figures should also be collected for these *subprocesses* in order to obtain detailed control measurements. In addition, *other reference figures* must be used for a specific analysis of the costs in the *indirect complaint management process*, such as determining the costs per complaint report generated or per complaint satisfaction survey conducted.

If the costs of complaint management are further allocated between individual cost centers or process groups in the context of *internal cost allocation*, performance figures should be calculated that also provide information on ratios between the costs that are caused and those that are allocated further.

The calculations presented, using either the traditional overhead costs calculation method or activity-based costing, make the costs of complaint management transparent. This may have the effect that managers who are solely focused on the goal of reducing costs hastily intensify their efforts to *minimize complaint management costs* in order to keep the price-increasing effects that accompany their allocation as low as possible. This attitude is *dangerous* because it can lead to a situation in which not only complaint management costs are reduced, but also the firm's opportunities to achieve financially relevant goals related to customer retention and quality. In order to avoid this danger, complaint management must also successfully quantify the specific contributions to the company's value creation in the context of *benefit controlling*.

11.3.2   Benefit Controlling

While complaint costs are recorded in many firms, only a relative few make an effort to identify and to quantify the *benefit components* of complaint management.

These benefits relate to the economically relevant effects of complaint management on both customers and the company itself.

As far as customers are concerned, the main objective of complaint management is to prevent customer switching—that is, the assurance of the customer's loyalty. Therefore, the *retention benefit*, which shows how the success of complaint management is reflected in secured revenues and profits, is of particular importance.

In addition to the purchasing behavior of the complainants, their communication behavior is also of economic importance, as their word-of-mouth communication influences the buying decisions of third parties. Thus, a *communication* benefit arises when, on the basis of recommendations from satisfied complainants, their interlocutors become new customers.

Within the company there is an economically significant effect of complaint management, if companies use the information provided by complainants to eliminate errors, to reduce costs and to improve the quality of products, services and processes. The more this is the case, the greater the *information benefit* of complaint management.

The challenge for complaint management is thus to *quantify the benefit components* mentioned and to compare them to the cost components. The methodical difficulties associated with these tasks are great. This is certainly one reason for the fact that so far, only sporadic systematic attempts of this type have been made (Goodman et al. 2000). A critical look at these approaches reveals that most of them are theoretically comprehensible, but in practice hardly feasible. As a rule, the required data is not available or can only be collected at disproportionately high expense. In addition, the calculations must be based on assumptions that are so uncertain that it is not responsible to relate the calculated benefit values to the costs.

Therefore, only relatively simple methodological approaches based on easily accessible information are presented below. These can only partially capture the benefit. It can therefore be assumed that the actual benefit of complaint management is greater than that calculated benefit.

11.3.2.1 Information Benefit Controlling

If the information contained in complaints is systematically documented, edited in the context of complaint analysis and regularly made available in complaint reports to the business units concerned, benefits accrue to the firm in many respects: On the one hand, one can expect that complaint information will bring about *cost savings*. This is the case when complaint information leads to an optimization of the internal processes, to time savings and to increases in productivity, and when settlement costs in terms of warrantee and product-liability payments can be reduced with the help of such information. Furthermore, *revenue increases* can be expected, provided that product variations and product innovations that prove to be marketable result from complaint analysis. Moreover, complaint information can be used to *prevent sales decreases*. Critical customer assessments with respect to all aspects of marketing and of the firm's perceived socio-political behavior give the firm the opportunity to optimize for example the implementation of the marketing mix and to adapt to new socio-political trends.

It will not always be possible to assess all of these effects. However, some easily available data can be used. These are above all the warranty and guarantee claims of the complaining customers. On the one hand, these should be recorded in terms of quantity using the warranty rate (number of warranties/number of products) or the guarantee rate (number of guarantee cases/number of products), and on the other hand, they should be evaluated internally with regard to their economic consequences. *Warranty and guarantee costs* are essential categories of failure costs due to quality defects. In this respect, the decrease in these failure costs provides an important indication of quality improvements, although these costs

Table 11.22 Information benefit in terms of reduced warranty and guarantee costs

Number of products year 1	80,000
Warranty costs year 1	4,000 €
Warranty unit costs year 1	0.05 €
Guarantee costs year 1	3,200 €
Guarantee unit costs year 1	0.04 €
Number of products year 2	100,000
Warranty costs year 2	4,000 €
Warranty unit costs year 2	0.04 €
Guarantee costs year 2	3,000 €
Guarantee unit costs year 2	0.03 €
Fictitious warranty costs year 2 without quality improvements	0.05 x 100,000 = 5,000 €
Fictitious guarantee costs year 2 without quality improvements	0.04 x 100,000 = 4,000 €
Σ Fictitious warranty and guarantee costs year 2	9,000 €
Σ Actual warranty and guarantee costs year 2	7,000 €
Difference between Σ fictitious and Σ actual costs year 2	9,000 € - 7,000 € = 2,000 €
Information benefit	**2,000 €**

must be set in relation to the respective number of products. Accordingly, *warranty and guarantee unit costs* form the basis for the economic evaluation of quality improvements initiated by complaint management. The information benefit of complaint management can then be seen from the amount of warranty and guarantee costs avoided. Table 11.22 shows how to proceed.

If in year 1, for 80,000 sold products there are warranty costs of 4000 € and guarantee costs of 3200 €, the unit warranty costs amount to 0.05 € and the unit guarantee costs amount to 0.04 €. For year 2, it is assumed that the number of products sold will increase to 100,000, with warranty costs of 4000 € and guarantee costs of 3000 € being incurred. The average costs are now lower: the unit warranty costs decrease to 0.04 € and the unit guarantee costs to 0.03 €. This reduction in unit costs can be interpreted as a result of quality improvements due to the use of complaint information.

In order to determine the overall effect of the reduction of failure costs, a calculation is made of which warranty and guarantee costs would have been incurred without quality improvements. For this purpose, the product number of year 2 is multiplied by the unit costs of year 1. This amount (9000 €) would have been incurred if the average warranty and guarantee costs had not been reduced by using complaint information. If you subtract from this amount the actual costs in year 2 (7000 €), you get a value for avoided failure costs of 2000 €. This amount represents a monetary value of the information benefit of complaint management.

It is conceivable that specialist departments will refuse to remedy the deficiencies identified by complaint management, so that warranty and guarantee unit costs will not decrease, but may even increase. This is an indication of the lack of assertiveness of complaint management, but this area cannot be held responsible for the undesirable development. Therefore, the reporting of any increased defect costs serves primarily to prove and communicate the *costs of missed quality improvements* within the company. The responsibility for increased defect costs can be clearly determined if the complaint management proves which indications of defects and possible problem solutions were given and how the problem-specific annoyance, warranty and guarantee rates have developed.

11.3.2.2 Retention Benefit Controlling

The *retention benefit* denotes the loyalty effect and is regarded as the key monetary measurement of the success of complaint management. The basis of the calculation is the number of customers who, in spite of their negative experiences with the product or service, have not moved away but continue the business relationship due to their positive complaint experience. However, this number of retained customers must be adjusted by the number of complainants who justify their decision to migrate with their negative complaint experience. The retention benefit is therefore the difference between the revenues or contribution margins saved by complaint management and the loss of revenues or contribution margins due to complaint management.

The *calculation of the retention benefit* is carried out in two steps: firstly, the net number of customers kept by the complaint management has to be determined. This results from the difference between the number of customers who stick to the business relationship due to their positive complaint experience and the number of customers who terminate the business relationship due to their negative complaint experience. This net number of customers kept by complaint management is then multiplied by revenues or contribution margins.

Determining the Net Number of Repurchasers/Migrants

In order to determine the net number of complainants retained through complaint management, it is necessary to have information about the *complaint behavior*, the *purchase behavior of the complainant* and the *importance of complaint management* in the continuation of the business relationship.

All this information can be collected in a complaint satisfaction survey. As shown in the complaint satisfaction questionnaire (Table 11.5), the complainants are asked whether they have bought products or services from the company or have continued the business relationship since the time of their complaint. By answering this yes/no question, the number of loyal or migrated complainants has already been determined. The subsequent question asks whether the complaint experience was responsible for the decision to continue or terminate the business relationship. This results in figures of customers who have been retained or "driven-away" by complaint management. Their difference is the *net number of repurchasers*.

Monetary Evaluation of the Retention Benefit

The monetary quantification of the retention benefit is based on the *revenues and profit margins* of those customers who were retained by complaint management. The calculation can be carried out for a period of one year (*annual analysis*) or by considering the value of the customer over the total duration of the business relationship (*Customer Lifetime Value analysis*).The procedure for the calculation is different, depending on whether customer-specific or only average data is available. If data is lacking on the retention effect of complaint management, the monetary evaluation must be based on a market loss calculation.

Monetary Quantification in the Form of Annual Values on the Basis of Customer-Specific Data

If the firm has a customer database with information about the *individual turnover and profit* of customers, the retention benefit can be easily calculated. For all the customers retained through complaint management, the customer-specific turnover or profits over the duration of the business relationship to date are determined as an average annual value. The same procedure must be followed for customers who have left the company due to their complaint experience. A comparison of the retained and lost revenues and contribution margins yields the monetary retention benefit on an annual basis. Table 11.23 illustrates this procedure using a *simple example* with

Table 11.23 Example of the calculation of the retention benefit for one year on the basis of customer-specific revenues

Customers retained due to complaint management	Customer-specific annual revenue	Customers migrated due to complaint management	Customer-specific annual revenue
Complainant A	1,239 €	Complainant Z	1,852 €
Complainant B	2,134 €	Complainant Y	3,044 €
Complainant C	3,343 €		
Complainant D	2,156 €		
Complainant E	3,121 €		
Sum	11,993 €		4,896 €
Retention benefit (revenue/year)		11,993 € – 4,896 € = 7,097 €	

customer-specific sales values; the calculation with contribution margin values is carried out analogously.

Monetary Quantification in the Form of Relationship Duration Values on the Basis of Customer-Specific Data

In many cases, however, annual observation is insufficient. A significant proportion of customers prove to be brand loyal and remain loyal for more than one year. In such cases, the *Customer Lifetime Value*—that is, the value of the customer over the total duration of the customer relationship—should be used. This is described below, although it is more practical for many companies to carry out the annual analysis and be aware that the retention benefit is only a minimum value.

The Customer Lifetime Value is defined as the net present value of all profits that can be expected from a business relationship during the remaining duration of the relationship. Accordingly, the profits for the accounting period of the likely remaining relationship duration are discounted back to the point of time in question, thus yielding the present value of the relationship. In practice, this approach usually proves to be either *unworkable or highly problematic*, because neither meaningful data about the in-payments and out-payments of future periods nor clear rules for the decision regarding the adequate internal rate of discount exist. For this reason, a greatly simplified and more practical approach, which settles for using *rougher estimates*, is recommended here. According to this approach, the Customer Lifetime Value is obtained by multiplying the number of periods remaining in the relationship duration by the customer's average revenue or contribution margin during the relationship duration to date.

When referring to the *remaining relationship duration*, we mean the difference between the average total relationship duration for all customers and the previously realized relationship duration of customers who have been influenced in their behavior by complaint management. If we multiply the individual turnover or profits (annual values) with the respective number of periods remaining in the relationship duration for these customers, we obtain the *Customer Lifetime Value of the retention benefit*.

Table 11.24 illustrates the *calculation of the remaining relationship duration*, as well as the determination of the retention benefit as the Customer Lifetime Value on the basis of customer revenues. This includes not only the *average annual revenue* generated during the previous relationship for the retained (column 1) and migrated customers (column 5), but also the respective previous relationship duration (columns 2 and 6). In addition, it is known that the average relationship duration for all customers is 5 years (60 months). By subtracting the customer-specific relationship duration from this value, the customer-specific remaining relationship periods are obtained (columns 3 and 7). By multiplying the values of the remaining period and the average revenues, the *customer lifetime values* of the revenues are calculated (columns 4 and 8). If one compares the cumulative lifetime values of the retained and lost customers due to complaint management, the monetary retention benefit is obtained for the duration of the business relationship.

The calculation described represents only a simple variant. The literature introduces more complex methods which are, however, often bound to requirements

Table 11.24 Example of the calculation of the retention benefit for the duration of the business relationship on the basis of customer-specific revenues

Customers retained due to complaint management	Customer-specific annual revenue in € (1)	Previous relationship duration in months (2)	Customer-specific remaining relationship period (3)	Customer Lifetime Value in € (4)	Customers migrated due to complaint management	Customer-specific annual revenue in € (5)	Previous relationship duration in months (6)	Customer-specific remaining relationship period (7)	Customer Lifetime Value in € (8)
Complainant A	1,239	36	24	29,736	Complainant Z	1,852	22	38	70,376
Complainant B	2,134	24	36	76,824	Complainant Y	3,044	40	20	60,880
Complainant C	3,343	20	40	133,720					
Complainant D	2,156	32	28	60,368					
Complainant E	3,121	12	48	149,808					
Sum				450,456	Sum				131,256
Retention benefit (revenue/year)						450,456 € – 131,256 € = 319,200 €			

that can hardly be fulfilled in reality (see for example Kumar 2008; Malthouse 2013; Kumar and Pansari 2015).

Monetary Quantification in the Form of Annual and Relationship Duration Values Based on Averages

If there is *no customer-specific data* on revenues and contribution margins, one must assume *average revenues and contribution margins* per period for all customers, and presume that these values are also valid for the customers retained by complaint management. The average remaining relationship period must be estimated on the basis of the company's own or third-party experience.

The following exemplary calculation (see Table 11.25) assumes that the net number of repurchasers is 5031. This means that the number of customers held by complaint management exceeds the number of customers who have migrated due to negative complaint experiences by 5031. Presuming that these customers have an average monthly revenue of 200 €, this results in a secured annual revenue of 12,074,400 €. With a return on sales of 8%, this corresponds to a secured annual profit of 965,952 €. Assuming an estimated remaining period of 20 months, a secured turnover of 20,124,000 € or a secured profit contribution of 1,609,920 € can be expected for the entire remaining period (Table 11.25).

Table 11.25   Example of the calculation of the retention benefit on the basis of averages

Annual calculation	
Net number of repurchasers	5,031
× Ø Monthly revenue	200 €
× 12 Months	12
= Secured revenue on a yearly basis	12,074,400 €
× Ø Return on revenues	8%
= Secured profit margin on a yearly basis	965,952 €

Relationship duration calculation on basis of relationship duration	
Net number of repurchasers	5,031
× Ø Monthly revenue	200 €
× Estimated remaining relationship duration in months	20
= Secured revenue on basis of relationship duration	20,124,000 €
× Ø Return on revenues	8%
= Secured profit margin on basis of relationship duration	1,609,920 €

Monetary Assessment When Data Regarding the Retention Effects of Complaint Management Are Missing (Market Loss Calculation)

If there is no data whatsoever available regarding the retention effects of complaint management, the retention benefit obviously cannot be calculated. In such cases, one has to be content with an estimation of the potential benefit by determining the loss potential of annoyed customers and its reduction by complaint management for different scenarios. This is based on assumptions about the extent to which disappointed customers will migrate if there was no complaint management. Taking into account the average customer revenue and the average customer return, it is possible to calculate the market loss for different observation periods, which results from the customer losses of disappointed customers. These values form the basis for estimating the benefits that complaint management can deliver by avoiding customer losses.

For this analysis, the firm must have at its disposal information regarding the customer base, the average revenue per customer and the average profit margin. Basically, it can be assumed that these data come from controlling. The information about the percentage of disappointed customers should be taken from a customer satisfaction survey. If even this information is not available, an alternative would be to refer to estimates—for example, the results of corresponding industry analyses.

Table 11.26 Matrix for the calculation of the economic effects of possible customer switching due to dissatisfaction

Customer base	100,000 customers			Ø revenue per customer p.a.: 1,000 €		
				Ø profit margin p.a.: 10 %		
Share and number of disappointed customers	30 % (30,000 customers)					
Share and number of disappointed and potentially lost customers	0.003% (1 customer)	0.50% (150 customers)	1.00% (300 customers)	5.00% (1,500 customers)	10.00% (3,000 customers)	20.00% (6,000 customers)
6 months	500 €	75 k€	150 k€	750 k€	1,500 k€	3,000 k€
	50 €	8 k€	15 k€	75 k€	150 k€	300 k€
1 year	1,000 €	150 k€	300 k€	1,500 k€	3,000 k€	6,000 k€
	100 €	15 k€	30 k€	150 k€	300 k€	600 k€
2 years	2,000 €	300 k€	600 k€	3,000 k€	6,000 k€	12,000 k€
	200 €	30 k€	60 k€	300 k€	600 k€	1,200 k€
3 years	3,000 €	450 k€	900 k€	4,500 k€	9,000 k€	18,000 k€
	300 €	45 k€	90 k€	450 k€	900 k€	1,800 k€
4 years	4,000 €	600 k€	1,200 k€	6,000 k€	12,000 k€	24,000 k€
	400 €	60 k€	120 k€	600 k€	1,200 k€	2,400 k€
5 years	5,000 €	750 k€	1,500 k€	7,500 k€	15,000 k€	30,000 k€
	500 €	75 k€	150 k€	750 k€	1,500 k€	3,000 k€

(Left axis label: Ø lost relationship duration)

4,500 k€	← **Upper cell:** lost repurchase benefit (revenue)
450 k€	← **Lower cell:** lost repurchase benefit (profit)

On the basis of this information, the market damage due to customer losses can then be calculated.

Table 11.26 shows a corresponding *matrix for the calculation of the lost repurchase benefit* that can arise when dissatisfied customers switch. The basis for this calculation are internal data regarding the customer base (100,000), the percentage of disappointed customers (30%), the average annual revenue per customer (1000 €) and the average profit margin (10%). The *vertical axis* of the matrix indicates different values for the length of the possible remaining relationship duration; the *horizontal axis* indicates different percentages of disappointed customers who will switch because of their dissatisfaction with a product or service. The corresponding values in the matrix indicate the market loss as well as the lost revenue and profit that the firm will suffer due to customer dissatisfaction.

The firm must then make assumptions—based on the estimates of experts in marketing, sales, service and controlling—about the potential probable remaining relationship duration and the percentage of disappointed customers who will switch. The corresponding amount of market losses can then be taken directly from the matrix. If, for example, the experts come to the conclusion that *5% of 30,000 disappointed customers* (= 1500 customers) will switch to the competition because of their annoyance and further assume that these customers would have remained in the business relationship for *another three years*, the result is a market loss of 4,500,000 € in terms of *lost turnover*, and of 450,000 € in terms of *lost profits*.

Based on the values determined for the lost repurchase benefit due to customer dissatisfaction, the firm can consider whether it is possible to achieve *retention effects* that will lead to a reduction of the customer losses indicated by introducing or optimizing complaint management. If we assume in the sample calculation above that the firm could have kept 30% of the 1500 lost customers with adequate complaint management, the result is a *potential realized repurchase benefit of complaint management* in the amount of 1,350,000 € (turnover) and 135,000 € (profit).

The calculation of the lost repurchase benefit is based on assumptions and thus does not provide a secure foundation for more wide-ranging conclusions. Nevertheless, it does provide an impression of the *lost turnover and profits* that the firm will have to accept in the absence of professional complaint management and the *retention benefits* that could be realized. Calculations such as these are also helpful in making an initial assessment about whether investments in complaint management are economically justified.

11.3.2.3 Communication Benefit Controlling

The *communication benefit* is closely related to the retention benefit. Based on their experiences with complaint handling, customers not only draw consequences for their repurchase behavior, but also make their experiences the topic of conversations with friends, relatives or colleagues. Depending on whether they assess their complaint experience as positive or negative, they *recommend* the firm to others or *advise* them *against* purchasing from it. This action also strongly influences the attitudes and behavior of other current and potential customers. Empirical studies prove that personal communication has a substantially greater impact than does advertising that is initiated by the firm itself. The reason for this lies in the fact that the communicant is not viewed as being commercially motivated, but rather as a neutral source of information, an advisor or a referee.

In order to determine the value of the communication benefit, the net number of referring complainants must first be determined, i.e. the difference between referrals and warners; then the number of newly acquired customers must be assessed in monetary terms.

Determination of the Net Number of Recommenders/Warners

With regard to the determination of the net number of recommenders/warners, it must first be decided whether the probable or actual communication behavior of the complainants is to be recorded.

Measurement of the Probable Recommendation ("Net Promoter Score")

In recent years, Reichheld (2003, 2006, 2011) in particular has drawn attention to the economic relevance of word-of-mouth communication. Triggered by growing skepticism about the meaningfulness of complex satisfaction surveys, he started looking

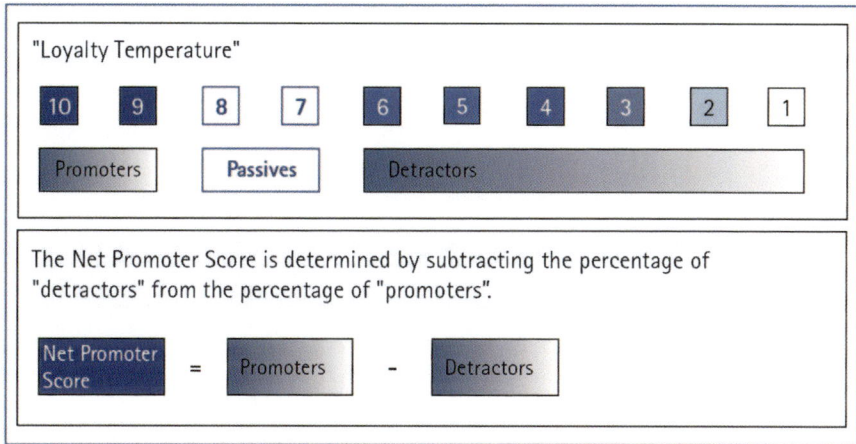

Fig. 11.9 Reichheld's net promoter score (following Reichheld 2006)

for the specific question that best predicted the customers' loyalty behavior. He conducted a wealth of empirical studies in various industries and came to a clear conclusion: the best indicator of future customer loyalty and thus of the relative growth strength in competition is the customers' recommendation behavior: "If growth is what you're after, you won't learn much from complex measurements of customer satisfaction or retention. You simply need to know what your customers tell their friends about you" (Reichheld 2003, p. 46). Based on this knowledge, the so-called NPS (Net Promoter Score) approach was developed..

It is based on a single question for customers: 'How likely is it that you would recommend X to a friend or colleague?' Respondents are asked to indicate the likelihood of recommendation on a scale of 0 to 10. Customers who choose the 9 or 10 are referred to as "promoters", customers who answer the question with a scale value of 8 or 7 belong to the group called "passives" and customers who choose a scale value of 6 to 0 are referred to as "detractors".

The decisive factor for the company's growth strength is its share of "net promoters", i.e. the percentage of promoters minus the percentage of detractors. Accordingly, the percentages for "promoters" and "detractors" are calculated, and their difference results in the *"Net Promoter Score"*. The larger the NPS, the more positive profit and growth should develop. Figure 11.9 summarizes the classification into the segments "Promoters", "Passives" and "Detractors" as well as the determination of the NPS.

The methodological approach of the Net Promoter Score could easily also be used to determine the net number of recommending complainants. In this case, the complainants would be asked to indicate the likelihood of their willingness to recommend the company on the basis of their complainant experience. The responses could then be used to determine the number of complaint-promoters and complaint-detractors and thereby, the number of net complaint-promoters. But the use of the NPS approach for complaint management is not recommended here. The fact that the Net Promoter Score is highly controversial as a loyalty indicator

(Keiningham et al. 2007; Ruf 2007; Kristensen and Eskildsen 2014) plays a less important role here. Rather, the skepticism in this context relates primarily to the fact that the probability of the customer's recommendation is queried. The likelihood of future communication behavior assumed by the customer at the time of the survey does not necessarily have to coincide with the actual behavior. In this respect, it appears to make much more sense to determine the net number of complainants who have actually recommended the company to others.

Measurement of the Actual Recommendation

The communication behavior of complainants cannot be observed directly; therefore, it is also necessary to rely on the statements of the complainants when determining the actual recommendation behavior. But experience shows that the answers are far more realistic than the probability assumptions.

The survey can be carried out as part of the complaint satisfaction survey. The complainants are asked whether they have recommended products or services of the company to other persons (friends, relatives, colleagues) or dissuaded them from buying on the basis of their complaint experience. They are also asked how many people they have recommended or warned (questions 13 and 14 in the questionnaire Table 11.5). In this way, the number of recommenders and warners is obtained immediately. If you calculate the difference, you get the net number of recommenders/warners. Similarly, the figures for the persons reached through communication are fixed. If you now calculate the difference between the recommendations and warnings made, you get the net number of recommendations/ warnings.

Monetary Quantification of the Communication Benefit

To what extent recommendations actually lead to purchases by third parties or purchase warnings to decisions not to buy cannot be ascertained with certainty in reality. Therefore, it is not possible to make a precise assessment of the communication benefit of complaints management. However, there is a practicable proposal for monetary evaluation, which at least provides a rough estimate.

This proposal is based on an approach of the American management consultancy TARP (TARP 1979; Goodman et al. 2000), which only takes into account the positive recommendations. If purchase warnings are taken into consideration, the modified procedure described below results.

The numbers of persons addressed by complainants in the form of recommendations and warnings are known from the complaint satisfaction survey. These form the basis for calculating the number of people who actually orientate their *purchasing behavior* toward the content of word-of-mouth communication. Empirical results of the consulting firm TARP from more than 1000 projects and studies prove in the case of positive oral communication that approx. 1% of the persons addressed actually establish a business relationship. There is no comparable experience with regard to purchase warnings. In this respect, in the absence of better data, it must be assumed in a simplistic manner that also 1% of the persons warned by complainants refrain from making purchases.

Table 11.27 Example of the calculation of the communication benefit (annual analysis)

Number of complainants with purchase recommendation	10,000	
Ø Number of persons addressed	15	
Recommendations		**15,000**
Number of complainants with purchase warning	6,000	
Ø Number of persons addressed	20	
Warnings		**12,000**
Recommendations - Warnings (net recommendations)		3,000
Percentage of persons whose purchasing behaviour was influenced	1 %	
Number of persons whose purchase behaviour was influenced		300
Ø Annual revenue per customer	2,400 €	
Communication benefit (revenue/year)		**720,000 €**
Return on sales	8 %	
Communication benefit (contribution margin/year)		**57,600 €**

Assuming this "1% formula", the economic value of the communication effect can be calculated. This is done by multiplying the number of affected customers by the *average revenue or contribution margin* of customers from the existing customer base.

Table 11.27 shows an example of the procedure. It is assumed that 10,000 complainants make a recommendation on average to 15 persons, and 6000 complainants warn an average of 20 persons. Assuming an average annual revenue of 2400 € and a return on sales of 8%, the monetary communication benefit of complaints management amounts to a revenue of 720,000 € and a contribution margin of 57,600 € on an annual basis.

Of course, the evaluation of the communication benefit can be carried out not only on an annual basis, but also from the perspective of the *duration of the relationship*. In this case, for all initiated or intensified customer relationships, the average relationship duration of the current customers is used as a basis. However, such a calculation makes the application of this method even more problematic.

The main problem lies in the assumption about the percentage of persons whose purchase decision was actually influenced. Although the one-percent variable specified by TARP is indeed based on the evaluation of a large number of empirical studies, there is no guarantee that this variable would also apply to an individual case or to purchase warnings. Therefore, if firms do not want to rely on this estimated variable, they must attempt to conduct an *independent survey* among their current customers to determine the extent to which word-of-mouth communication by complainants directly influences the decision to establish or avoid a business relationship. Such surveys are, however, not only costly, but also difficult, because customers are rarely in a position to understand and to report their own purchase decision-making processes. For this reason, it is more practical to forego a separate survey and calculate using the one-percent rule of thumb. In this case, however, one must be aware of the fact that the value determined for the realized communication benefit represents only a rough starting point, and not an exact variable.

11.3.3 Profitability Controlling

In order to be able to judge the success of complaint management from an *economic point of view*, it is necessary to compare the monetary benefits achieved with the costs involved and consequently to obtain insights into the *profitability of complaint management*. This applies to the overall domain of complaint management, as well as to individual sub-projects or measures planned to optimize complaint management processes.

11.3.3.1 Profitability of the Complaint Management Department

One of the key approaches to calculating the profitability of the complaint management department is to compare the monetary market success determined for complaint management with the costs caused by this department and thus to determine the *profit or loss* earned by complaint management in the period.

Profit Calculation
Table 11.28 exemplarily shows the *structure of a profit calculation for complaint management*. In this table, the monetary values for information benefit, retention benefit and communication benefit are added first. From this market success of complaint management the personnel costs are subtracted. The result is the gross profit of complaint management, from which—in a next step—the administrative, communication and reaction costs are deducted, which yields the profit of complaint management.

In our sample calculation, we refer to the monetary quantification of the information benefit (Table 11.22), the retention benefit (Table 11.25, revenue/year) and the communication benefit (Table 11.27).

With regard to costs, the values are taken from Table 11.19. After deducting personnel costs from the market success of complaint management, the gross profit of complaint management amounts to 1,025,552 €. After further subtraction of the administrative, communication and reaction costs, the profit of the complaint management amounts to 365,552 €. Even if the problematic determination of the values for information and communication benefits were not taken into account, there would still be a considerable gain on the basis of the retention benefit of 305,952 €.

Table 11.28 Profit calculation for complaint management

Position	Monetary benefits/costs
Information benefit	2,000 €
+ Retention benefit	965,952 €
+ Communication benefit	57,600 €
= Market success of complaint management	**1,025,552 €**
- Personnel costs	283,000 €
= Gross profit of complaint management	**742,552 €**
- Administration costs	105,500 €
- Communication costs	31,500 €
- Reaction costs	240,000 €
= Complaint management profit	**365,552 €**

Table 11.29 Return on complaint management

$$\text{Return on Complaint Management} = \frac{\text{Complaint management profit}}{\text{Investments in complaint management}} = \frac{365,552\ €}{660,000\ €} = 55.39\ \%$$

Return on Complaint Management
The variables underlying the profit calculation form the basis for the calculation of a relevant profitability figure of complaint management: the Return on Complaint Management.

This performance figure is calculated by dividing the profit earned by the "capital invested". If the costs incurred by complaint management in the accounting period are interpreted as "capital invested", the performance measurement of the *"Return on Complaint Management"* is the result of the quotient of the profit of complaint management and its costs in the same period. Table 11.29 shows an example of the calculation of the Return on Complaint Management based on the numerical values from the profit calculation above. In this sample calculation, complaint management has earned a return of 369.09 percent.

11.3.3.2 Profitability of Measures Intended to Optimize Complaint Management

Profitability calculations should also be performed to assess *investments in projects intended to optimize complaint management*, such as introducing a complaint management software system or conducting a training program. Investments such as these are always associated with out-payments and are made in order to earn the largest possible profit in terms of an in-payment surplus. Evaluating whether and to what extent the projected investment satisfies goals such as these is the *task of investment calculation*. At the same time, investment calculation methods provide decision rules to select the optimal alternative when several possible measures are at choice.

In the following sections, the evaluation of investments in complaint management will be described using a simple *example* in which techniques from the cost comparison, profit comparison and return comparison methods are applied.

We assume an *initial situation* of a firm that has a customer base of 100,000 customers, 48,000 of whom have cause for a complaint. Half of them have actually articulated a complaint (24,000).

Definition of Measures

In this situation, consideration is made as to which specific measures should be taken in order to retain more dissatisfied customers for the firm in the future. Basically, there are *three key drivers of customer retention*:

- *Reducing annoyance rate:* The fewer customers are confronted with a problem that gives rise to a complaint, the smaller the probability that customers will switch providers because of the problem.
- *Increasing the articulation rate:* The more dissatisfied customers who complain, the more complaint management can influence the elimination of the dissatisfaction and prevent intended switching.
- *Increasing complaint satisfaction:* The more satisfied complainants are with the processing of their complaints, the smaller is the probability that they will terminate the relationship.

These drivers of customer retention point simultaneously to specific starting points for the *establishment of measures* designed to maximize the number of customers retained through complaint management and minimize the loss of customers.

This will be demonstrated in the following *example case*. In order to illustrate the different impacts of the three drivers of customer retention described, an appropriate measure is envisaged in each case: The first, *Measure A*, includes a sensitivity training program for all customer-contact employees in order to improve the satisfaction level of complainants. *Measure B* is intended to increase the articulation rate by increasing the communication of a central telephone complaint channel. *Measure C* has to do with the implementation of a quality improvement program for a problem area and thus targets the goal of reducing the annoyance rate.

Table 11.30 Example of the assessment of investments in complaint management using comparative calculations

	Initial situation		Measure A		Measure B		Measure C	
	Current complaint management		Training program for customer contact staff		Intensified communication of the central telephone complaint channel		Implementation of a quality improvement program	
Assumptions regarding the expected customer retention effects								
Annoyance rate	48 %	48,000	48 %	48,000	48 %	48,000	41 %	41,000
Articulation rate	50 %	24,000	50 %	24,000	60 %	28,800	50 %	20,500
Complaint satisfaction	15 %	3,600	20 %	4,800	15 %	4,320	20 %	3,075
Retention benefit								
Customers retained by complaint management	20 %	4,800	25 %	6,000	20 %	5,760	20 %	4,100
Customers 'driven away' by complaint management	5 %	1,200	3 %	720	5 %	1,440	5 %	1,025
Net number of repurchasers		3,600		5,280		4,320		3,075
Effects of measures A and B								
Additional net number of re-purchasers (in comparison to the initial situation)				1,680		720		
Additional revenue (annual revenue: 2,400 €)				4,032,000 €		1,728,000 €		
Additional gross profit (return on sales: 8%; excluding the costs of the measure)				322,560 €		138,240 €		
Costs of measures								
Costs p.a.				120,000 €		40,000 €		
Evaluation of the profitability of the individual measures								
Cost comparison calculation (costs per additional purchaser)				71.43 €		55.56 €		
Profit comparison calculation								
Profit per measure				202,560 €		98,240 €		
Profit per additional repurchaser				120.57 €		136.44 €		
Return calculation (return on investment per measure)				168.80 %		245.60 %		

Customer base: 100,000

Planning the Customer Retention Effects per Measure and Calculating the Results Achieved

The first step is to make specific *assumptions regarding the expected impact* with respect to the individual drivers of customer retention—annoyance rate, articulation rate and complaint satisfaction. Table 11.30 shows that *the sensitivity training program (Measure A)* is intended to increase the percentage of satisfied complainants from 15 to 20%, to increase the number of customers retained by complaint management from 20 to 25% or to reduce the number of customers driven away by complaint management from 5 to 3%. This means that $(5280 - 3600 =)$ 1680 additional repurchasers are gained.

Increased communication of the central telephone complaint channel (Measure B) is intended to increase the articulation rate from 50 to 60%, thereby increasing the number of customers contacting the company's complaint management. If the quality of complaint handling is maintained, a retention rate of 20% and a churn rate of 5% will continue to be achieved. In this way $(4320 - 3600 =)$ 720 additional repurchasers can be retained through the increased number of complainants.

The quality improvement program (Measure C) aims to reduce the number of customers who have cause for complaint from 48 to 41%. As fewer customers are now complaining, the net number of repeat customers will also decrease (from 3600 in the initial situation to 3075). But the economic success of measures to reduce the annoyance rate cannot be measured by the number of retained customers, but rather from the following effects: (1) First of all, a quality improvement program can lead to lower warranty and guarantee costs. (2) In the long term, the *costs of complaint management* may decrease as fewer resources are needed to deal with complaints. (3) Furthermore, a reduction in the annoyance rate also ensures that *fewer customers* have cause *to terminate the business relationship*.

Due to the complexity of the calculation of the monetary effects of quality improvement measures, only the calculation of the economic success for Measures A and B is illustrated below. The economic success is measured by the amount of the retention benefit. If you multiply the number of additional retained repurchasers by an average annual turnover of 2400 € per customer and an average return on sales of 8%, you will get an additional retention benefit of 322,560 € for Measure A and 138,240 € for Measure B. This means that all the data required for economic efficiency analyses is available.

Evaluating the Efficiency of the Individual Measures

In the context of the *cost comparison*, preference is given to the alternative that incurs the least costs. If we use the absolute values based on the *average annual costs* as an assessment criterion, the decision falls in favor of *Measure B (40,000 €)*. If the average costs are calculated per additionally secured customer relationship, preference will be also given to *Measure B (71,43 €)*. Only when the latter decision-making criterion is applied it is guaranteed that the firm will choose the measure with which the preventable customer losses in each case can be achieved in the most cost-effective way.

The overall goal, however, is to cover the costs incurred by a measure through the profits initiated by this measure. For this reason, it is advisable to apply the *profit comparison method*. This approach allows to determine and to select the alternative that will earn the highest profit. The profit per measure is computed by subtracting the annual costs from the additional gross profit.

In our example, the decision falls in favor of *Measure A*, which shows the highest profit value *overall* with $(322,560 € - 120,000 € =) 202,560 €$.

Since even the amount of profit does not allow conclusive statements to be made regarding which investment is most profitable, it is advisable to perform a *return on investment calculation* as the last step. The return on investment that is calculated here provides information as to how much the capital yields that is invested in the different measures. Thus, it is calculated as ratio of the annual profit per measure and the costs involved. For example, applied to Measure B, this means that the profit of 98.240 € will be divided by the cost of 40,000 €. Multiplying the result by 100 gives a value of 245.60 per cent. This is the highest rate of return and therefore is Alternative B preferable from a profitability point of view.

Weighing the Decision

It would be erroneous to make decisions regarding measures for the optimization of complaint management based exclusively on profitability. In our sample calculation, everything in this regard would speak for Alternative B. Solely on the basis of the rate of return, however, it would be overlooked that with the implementation of Measure A, a substantially greater effect with respect to the additionally secured customer relationships or with respect to the additionally generated retention benefit can be achieved. At the same time, the profit values determined for each additional repurchaser for the Measures A and B are relatively close to one another.

In a case like this, the *basic goals that are being pursued* must be weighed out: If the firm is exclusively focusing its attention on *cost efficiency aspects*, the decision should be made in favor of Measure B. If the firm is striving for a clear increase in the *absolute number of additionally retained customers*, preference should be given to Version A. Furthermore, the effects with respect to a measure's *external and internal impacts* should be kept in mind. Measure A underlines the seriousness of the subject and has a direct announcement effect for all employees. At the same time, the firm's endeavors are also visible and comprehensible to all its customers. The latter also applies to Measure B, which presents the firm as customer-oriented, especially in problem situations. Measure C, however, has probably the least external and internal impact.

This evaluation shows that a firm should *by no means confine itself* to calculating only the return on investment of individual measures when upcoming investments in complaint management should be made. Since it is always necessary to determine the respective cost and profit variables in order to calculate this rate of return, it is fundamentally advisable to use the approaches of the cost comparison and profit comparison methods for well-founded decision-making. Measures that are identified as being inefficient should basically not be pursued any further. Profitable measures should be evaluated in comparison to one another with respect to the aspects shown above.

After the selected measure has been implemented, the firm should verify, after an appropriate period of time, the extent to which the projected improvement was achieved and whether the profitability calculated in advance was *actually attained*. Here, it is necessary to collect anew the data upon which the profitability calculation is based, and to calculate the amount of projected costs that were actually incurred and the extent to which the lost repurchase benefit was actually reduced.

Chapter 11 in Brief

- Complaint management controlling consists of three areas: evidence controlling, task controlling and cost-benefit controlling.
- Evidence controlling determines the extent to which customer dissatisfaction is expressed in complaints. It reveals the extent of non-articulated ("unvoiced") and non-registered ("hidden") complaints and thus makes the real size of the annoyance iceberg visible.
- The focus of task controlling is the specification and monitoring of quality and productivity standards.
- In the course of subjective task controlling the quality of task fulfillment is measured and monitored from the complainants' point of view by satisfaction and loyalty indicators.
- Objective task controlling defines objective quality and productivity standards for all task modules of complaint management.
- The operational control of complaint management tasks can be carried out using the Complaint Management Index (BMI).
- Cost-benefit controlling serves to assess the profitability of complaint management.
- The costs of complaint management are recorded in cost controlling, either according to traditional cost accounting or by means of activity-based costing.
- The purpose of benefit controlling is the monetary evaluation of the information benefit, the retention benefit and the communication benefit of complaint management.
- The assessment of the information benefit can primarily be based on the reduction of warranty and guarantee costs resulting from the use of complaint information.
- The retention benefit consists of the revenues and profits generated by those customers who could be retained by complaint management.
- The communication benefit lies in the revenues and profits generated by those customers, who could be won by positive word-of-mouth communication of satisfied complainants.
- The Return on Complaint Management (RoCM) can be used as a measure of the economic efficiency of complaint management.

References

Anderson EW et al (1997) Customer satisfaction, productivity, and profitability: differences between goods and services. Mark Sci 16(2):129–145

Anton J (2007) Call center management by the numbers. Perdue University Press, West Lafayette

Goodman JA et al (2000) Turning CFOs into quality champions. Qual Prog 33(3):47–54

Heskett JL et al (1997) The service profit chain. The Free Press, New York

Keiningham TL et al (2007) A longitudinal examination of net promoter and firm revenue growth. J Mark 71(3):39–51

Kristensen K, Eskildsen J (2014) Is the NPS a trustworthy performance measure? TQM J 26 (2):202–214

Kumar V (2008) A customer lifetime value. Now Publishers, Hanover

Kumar V, Pansari A (2015) Aggregate and individual-level customer lifetime value. In: Kumar V, Shah D (eds) Handbook on research on customer equity in marketing. Edward Elgar, Cheltenham, pp 44–75

Malthouse CE (2013) Segmentation and lifetime value models using SAS. SAS Institute, Cary

Reichheld FF (2003) The one number you need to grow. Harv Bus Rev 81(12):46–54

Reichheld FF (2006) The ultimate question: driving good profits and true growth. Harvard Business, Boston

Reichheld FF (2011) The ultimate question 2.0: how net promoter companies thrive in a customer-driven world. Harvard Business, Boston

Ruf S (2007) Würden Sie diese Methode einem Freund empfehlen? In: Verband Schweizer Markt- und Sozialforscher (ed) Jahrbuch 2007. vsms Alpnach, Switzerland, pp 38–40

Servicebarometer (2017) Kundenmonitor 2017. Servicebarometer, München

Singh J (2000) Performance productivity and quality of frontline employees in service organizations. J Mark 64(2):15–34

Stauss B, Hentschel B (1992) Messung von Kundenzufriedenheit. Marktforschung and Management 36(3):115–122

Stauss B, Seidel W (2008) Discovering the "customer annoyance iceberg" through evidence controlling. Serv Bus 2(1):33–45

Stauss B, Seidel W (2013) Zur Notwendigkeit eines Follow Up-Beschwerdemanagements. Mark Rev St Gallen 30(3):54–62

TARP (1979) Consumer complaint handling in America: final report. U.S. Office of Consumer Affairs, Washington

© Springer Nature Switzerland AG 2019

B. Stauss, W. Seidel, *Effective Complaint Management*, Management for Professionals,
https://doi.org/10.1007/978-3-319-98705-7_12

Issues Raised
- What types of complaint management reports are available?
- Which contents should be considered in complaint reports?
- How should the reports be formally designed?
- At what intervals should reports be provided?
- For which internal target groups should complaint reports be prepared?
- What barriers hinder the active use of information provided in complaint reports?

Complaint reporting pertains to the active and regular reporting of to internal target groups. This process is primarily concerned with significant results from complaint analysis, but the focus is also on information from complaint management controlling about the efficiency and effectiveness of complaint management itself. In addition to this *active reporting (Information Push)*, other activities that belong to the task spectrum of complaint reporting are carrying out special analyses at the request of internal customers and *making available* all the complaint-relevant information so that authorized internal customers have direct access to it or are able to carry out independent analyses *(Information Pull)*.

12.1   Active Reporting of the Results of Complaint Analysis and Complaint Management Controlling (Information Push)

The first step is to determine which *contents* should be prepared *in which form* and actively transmitted at which time intervals (daily, monthly, weekly, etc.) for which internal customers (upper management, quality control, marketing department, etc.)

12.1.1 The Content Dimension of Complaint Reporting

First of all, it is to decide *which contents with which level of detail* must be made available to the respective internal target groups. In terms of content, one must distinguish between complaint-related and complaint management-related information.

12.1.1.1 Complaint-Related Information
Complaint-related information provides details about the complaint volume, the complainants, the complaint channels chosen by the complainants and the complaint objects and problems. The information required for this purpose is provided by the complaint analysis (Sect. 10.1).

Complainants	930
Complaints	1,100
Complaint problems	1,300

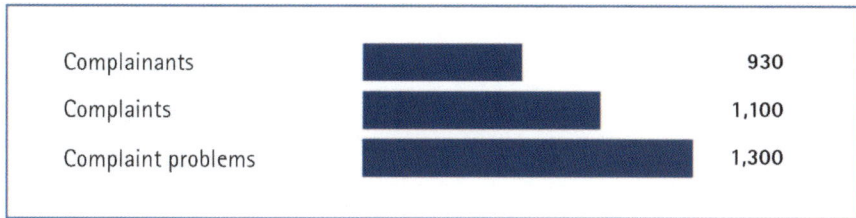

Fig. 12.1 Differentiated presentation of the complaint volume

Reporting Dimension "Complaint Volume"

As far as the complaint volume is concerned, primarily the overall number of complaints received and the development over time are of interest. For a differentiated view, it makes sense to document not only the number of complainants and complaints, but also the total number of articulated individual problems because their volume informs about the actual number of aspects addressed in complaints (Fig. 12.1).

When describing the development over time, it should be noted that an increased complaint volume does not necessarily mean that customers have become more dissatisfied. It is also conceivable that a higher proportion of annoyed customers have complained, which would be a positive development. Therefore, the number of complaints should always be assessed by taking into account the annoyance and articulation rate (Fig. 12.2).

Reporting Dimension "Complainant"

With regard to the complainants, an examination of the different types is of particular importance, i.e. it must be shown separately how many repeat, multiple and follow-up complainants are registered (Fig. 12.3).

In addition, it makes sense to illustrate how many times multiple complainants have approached the company (1-times, 2-times, x-times complainants) and how the number of complaints is distributed among different customer segments.

If companies have very different customer groups, it also makes sense to differentiate complaint reports by segment (see *Spotlight 12.1*).

Spotlight 12.1
Customer Segment-Specific Complaint Reporting at SOKA-BAU

SOKA-BAU provides the German construction industry with industry-specific services in which collective agreements are implemented, for example, on holiday pay, pensions and financing vocational training.

The areas of activity of quality management at SOKA-BAU also include the tasks of indirect complaint management. Within the scope of an optimization project, complaint reporting was identified and newly developed as a

(continued)

Spotlight 12.1 (continued)

nucleus for customer-driven quality improvement processes. In a first step, in customer complaints all information was identified that is relevant for the quality management processes and assigned to the central complaint reporting perspectives. These are listed below with the most important analysis dimensions:

Complaint volume

- Annoyance iceberg
- Number of complaints
- Types of complainants
- Complaint channels
- . . . . . .

Complaint reasons

- Frequencies
- Cross tabulations
- Further problem prioritization
- . . . . . .

Complaint handling from the customer's point of view

- Need for action rate
- Process/result satisfaction
- Rate of follow-up complaints
- Customer expectations for the handling of complaints
- . . . . . .

Complaint handling from the company's point of view

- Confirmation of receipt and interim notification rate
- Average total processing time
- Realized solutions (incl. costs)
- Processing backlogs
- . . . . . .

Effectiveness of quality improvement measures

- Quality improvement measures initiated for the prioritized reasons for complaint
- Development of the complaint volume of reasons for complaints with regard to which quality improvement measures were implemented
- . . . . . .

(continued)

Spotlight 12.1 (continued)

Among other things, the reporting of the analysis results is consistently geared to the individual stakeholder groups. These stakeholder groups include on the one hand the customers for whom SOKA-BAU provides services directly, e.g. employees, employers, pensioners or trainees. On the other hand, complaint information will in future also be recorded in a differentiated way for companies and institutions that are in a service relationship with the direct SOKA-BAU customers, but also have contact with SOKA-BAU, e.g. tax consultants, lawyers, labour courts or the Federal Employment Agency. These indirect customers are further differentiated as to whether they articulate problems of their customers or clients or their own problems in the form of a complaint. Figure 12.4 summarizes the described complaint reporting concept.

This differentiated view seems particularly relevant because the individual stakeholder groups differ considerably in their role, their interests, expectations and perceptions of problems. Accordingly, specific (problem) categorization systems, differentiated according to the stakeholder groups, are developed and made available for the recording of complaints. For each customer segment, an average of approximately 500 complaint reasons with corresponding reference areas were identified, which can be handled easily by the users with special complaint management software. In this way, the basis is created for providing not only "one" complaint report, but also different, specific complaint reports for the individual stakeholder groups. This has the advantage that those responsible in the company for the respective stakeholder groups are specifically informed and enabled to develop segment-specific improvement measures. On the one hand, this leads to a high level of acceptance among those responsible managers and, on the other, to a great effectiveness of initiated improvement measures.

Kerstin Mages
Head of Quality Management
SOKA-BAU
Urlaubs- und Lohnausgleichskasse der Bauwirtschaft
Zusatzversorgungskasse des Baugewerbes AG

Reporting Dimension "Complaint Channels"

The presentation of the complaint channels concerns the ways of communication and addressees chosen by the complainants, which can be viewed separately or combined in the form of a cross table (Table 12.1).

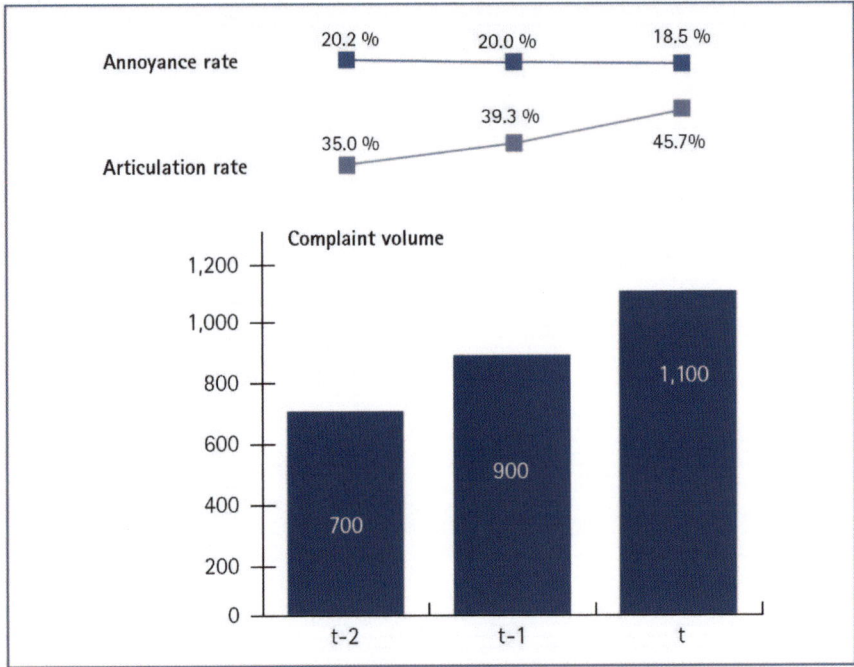

Fig. 12.2 Positive assessment of an increased number of complaints taking into account the annoyance and articulation rate

Fig. 12.3 Different types of complainants

Reporting Dimension "Complaint Problem" and "Complaint Object"

This *reporting dimension* refers to the errors perceived by the customers, in particular the frequency distributions of complaint objects and types of problems. The content structure in which the reasons for the complaint are presented depends very much on the type of problem categorization. If a hierarchical categorization is used,

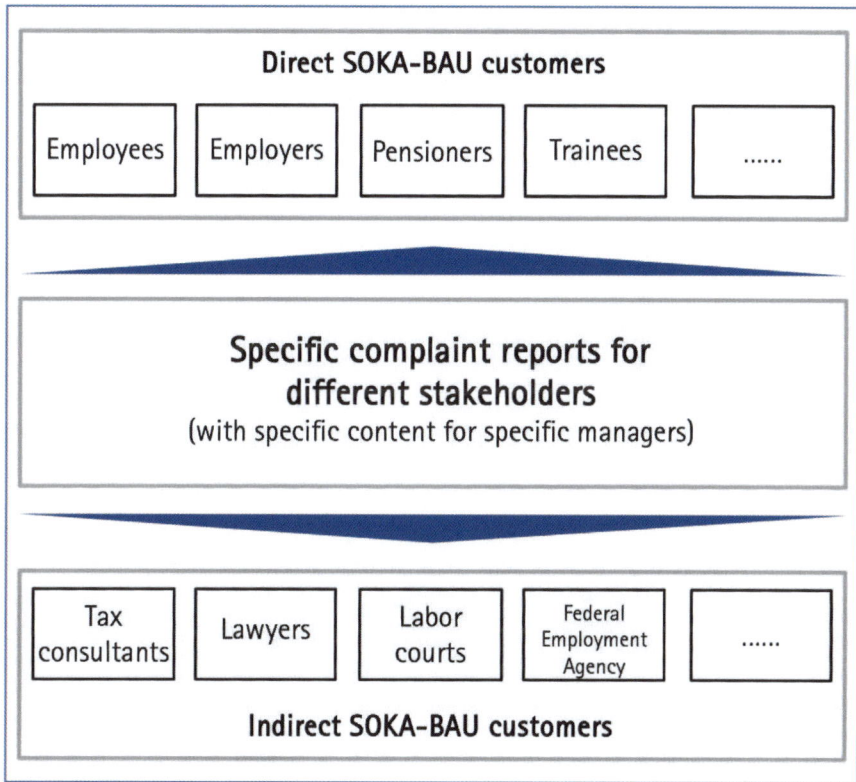

Fig. 12.4 Specific complaint reports for different stakeholders

Table 12.1 Ways of communication and addressees chosen by complainants

Ways of communication	Phone		E-Mail		Letter		Fax		Internet		Total	
Addressees	abs	%	abs	%	abs	%	abs	%	abs	%	abs	%
Complaint management	60	22 %	90	33 %	70	26 %	5	2 %	45	17 %	270	100 %
Complaint center	400	62 %	200	31 %	0	0 %	10	2 %	40	6 %	650	100 %
Departments	30	38 %	30	38 %	10	13 %	5	6 %	5	6 %	80	100 %
Senior management	0	0 %	20	20 %	80	80 %	0	0 %	0	0 %	100	100 %
Total	490	45 %	340	31 %	160	15 %	20	2 %	90	8 %	1,100	100 %

the reasons for the complaint can be processed from the abstract to the concrete level, so that a step-by-step focusing is possible. If complaint object and problem categories are recorded in separate but linked categorization trees, they can be analyzed not only in mutual dependency, but also separately.

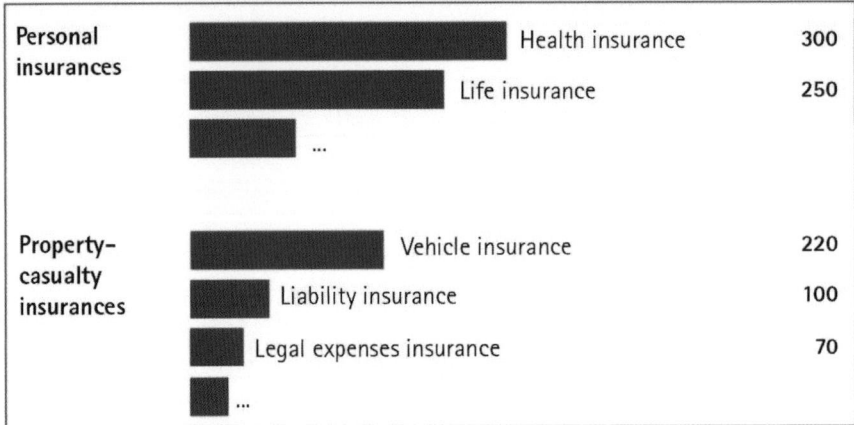

Fig. 12.5 Complaint objects affected by customer problems

The more concrete and action-oriented the categorization available, the better measures can be derived to eliminate errors and reduce the annoyance rate.

Figure 12.5 shows an exemplary presentation of the *complaint objects* affected by the customers' problems in hierarchical form. The first two hierarchy levels of the category tree are taken into account, giving a quick overview of the products that caused most of the problems.

Figure 12.6 shows the *cross-complaint object view of the articulated problems*, independent of the affected product. It provides an insight into which problems customers most often express in complaints.

The same statement is illustrated even better by presenting a list of the five most frequently encountered problems (*top five problems*), indicating the proportion of complaints that reflect the top problems—in our example 67% (see Table 12.2).

Table 12.3 shows the extent to which the individual problems have occurred with the respective products.

Even more meaningful information on complaint problems is available if the complaint evaluation not only records the frequency of the problem occurrence, but also their relevance, e.g. by applying the Lost-Customer-FRAC (see Sect. 10.2).

The diagram in Fig. 12.7 shows the required prioritization of problems for corrective actions.

Furthermore, *selected cross tables* should be provided showing relevant relationships between the variables, such as between the products concerned and the scope of warranty and guarantee cases. In addition to the numerical reporting, a selection of *representative customer complaints* should also be reproduced verbatim, because only these give a real impression of the customers' experience and the extent of their annoyance (e.g. "Top three complaint stories").

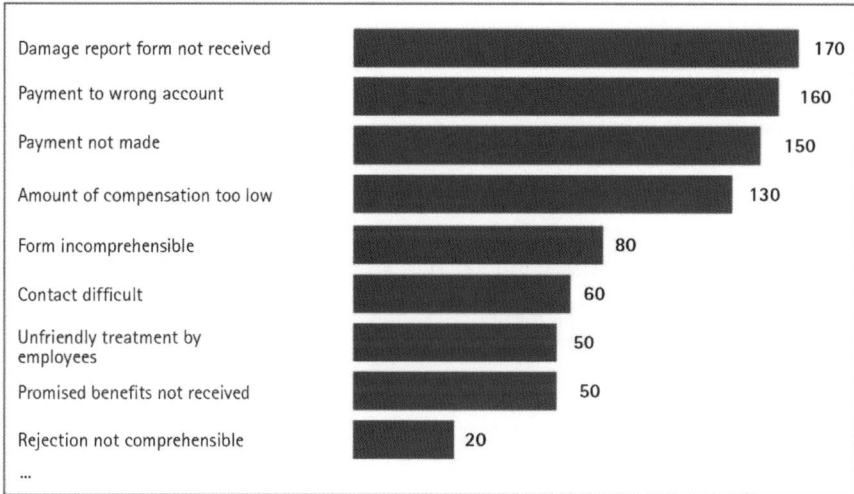

Damage report form not received	170
Payment to wrong account	160
Payment not made	150
Amount of compensation too low	130
Form incomprehensible	80
Contact difficult	60
Unfriendly treatment by employees	50
Promised benefits not received	50
Rejection not comprehensible	20
...	

Fig. 12.6 Cross-complaint object view of customer problems

Table 12.2 Top five problem view with year-on-year comparison

Top 5 problem categories (67%)	Jan – Jun	Deviation from previous year
Damage report form not received	170	−25.1 %
Payment to wrong account	160	−11.8 %
Payment not made	150	+29.9 %
Amount of compensation too low	130	−17.5 %
Form incomprehensible	80	+20.3 %

12.1.1.2 Complaint Management-Related Content

The complaint management-related contents refer to the complaint management itself, and provide information about the strengths and weaknesses of this area of activity and its economic contribution to success. The reports reflect three perspectives: strategic, operational and economic.

The Strategic Perspective: Key Performance Indicators

From a strategic point of view, it is important to demonstrate the extent to which complaint management has succeeded in achieving its goals of avoiding customer

Table 12.3 Problems encountered with the individual complaint objects

	Damage report form not received	Payment to wrong account	Payment not made	Amount of compensation too low	Form incompre-hensible	Sum
Personal insurances						
Health insurance	--	22.2 %	16.7 %	--	33.3 %	100 %
Life insurance	--	20.0 %	10.0 %	--	0.0 %	100 %
...	...	...	...	...	...	100 %
Property-casualty insurances						
Vehicle insurance	62.0 %	16.0 %	12.0 %	32.0 %	8.0 %	100 %
Liability insurance	38.0 %	25.0 %	20.0 %	15.0 %	10.0 %	100 %
Legal expenses insurance	38.0 %	10.0 %	20.0 %	10.0 %	5.0 %	100 %
...	...	...	...	...	...	100 %
Total	15.5 %	14.5 %	13.5 %	11.5 %	7.3 %	100 %

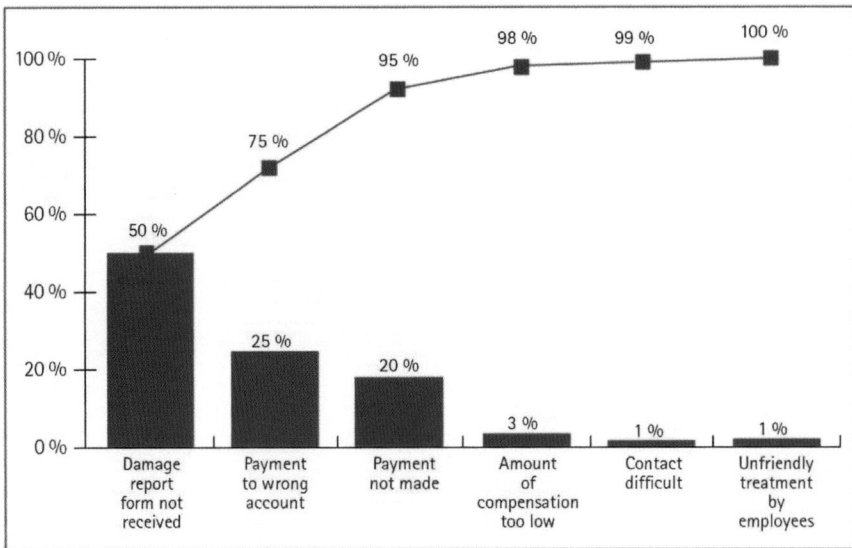

Fig. 12.7 Graphical representation of the Lost-Customer-Frac (frequency-relevance analysis of complaints)

losses, improving product quality and increasing productivity. For this purpose, the defined *key performance indicator*s must be used.

Customer Relationship-Related Key Performance Indicators As explained in Sect. 4.2, the most important key performance indicators relevant to customer relations refer to the articulation and registration of complaints on the one hand,

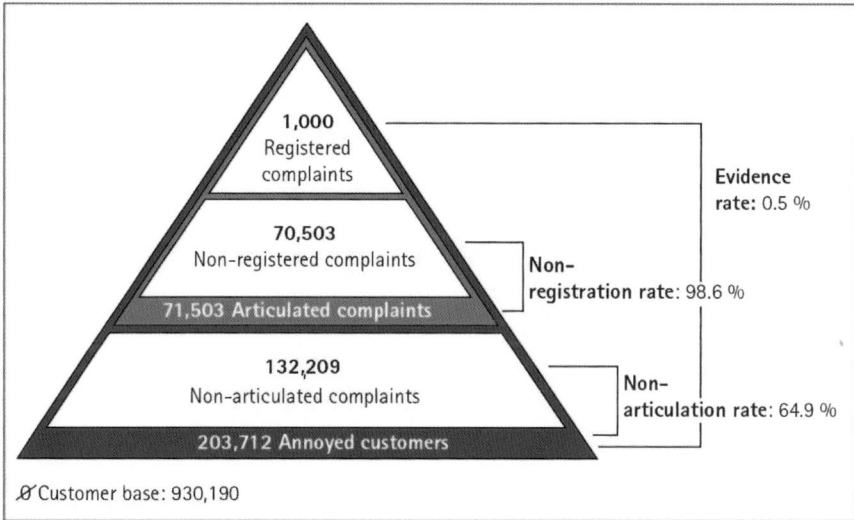

Fig. 12.8 Non-articulation rate, non-registration rate and evidence rate

Table 12.4 Proportions of convinced/disappointed complainants

Key performance indicator	Convinced complainants	Disappointed complainants
Complaint satisfaction	23 %	54 %

and the behavior of the complainants based on their complaint experience on the other.

With regard to *complaint articulation*, it must be documented to what extent complaint management actually records the customer annoyance. Two key performance indicators should be used for this purpose: *(1) KPI articulation rate/Non-articulation rate* indicating the proportion of annoyed customers who do (not) complain; *(2) KPI registration rate/Non-registration rate* expressing the proportion of complaints voiced by customers that are (not) documented in complaint management. These rates allow the *evidence rate* to be calculated, which shows to what extent the annoyance of customers is reflected in the number of registered complaints. Together, these key figures illustrate the annoyance iceberg (see Fig. 12.8).

The central customer relationship-related goal of complaint management is to avoid customer losses by stabilizing the endangered business relationships. A key indicator for the achievement of this goal is *complaint satisfaction (KPI: Percentage of convinced or disappointed complainants)* (Table 12.4).

Repurchase rate (share of customers re-tained by complaint management)		20.0 % 186
Churn rate (share of customers "driven away" by complaint management)		5.0 % 47
Net repurchase rate		15.0 % 139

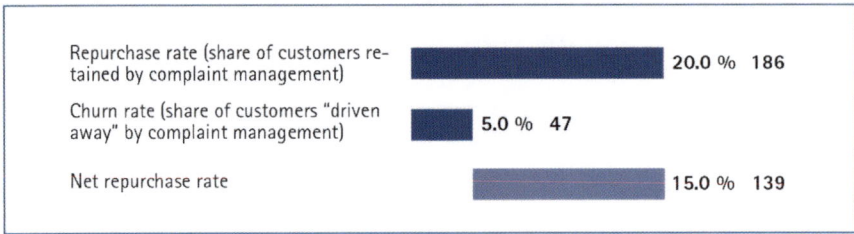

Fig. 12.9 Repurchase rates and churn rate

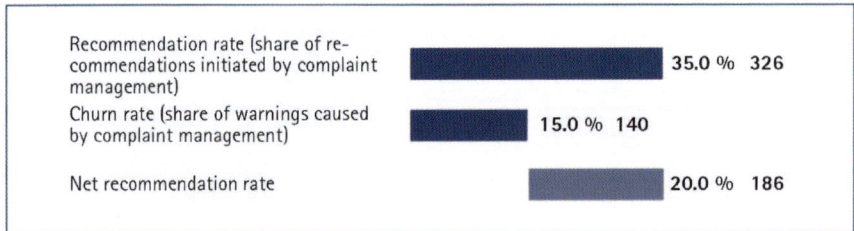

Recommendation rate (share of re-commendations initiated by complaint management)		35.0 % 326
Churn rate (share of warnings caused by complaint management)		15.0 % 140
Net recommendation rate		20.0 % 186

Fig. 12.10 Recommendation rates and warning rate

Even stronger indications of the customer loyalty caused by complaint manage-ment provide information on the *actual behavior* that complainants show based on their complaint experience: the *repurchase behavior (KPI: repurchase rate/churn rate)* on the one hand and the *communication behavior (KPI: recommendation rate/ warning rate)* on the other hand (Figs. 12.9 and 12.10).

Quality-Related Key Performance Indicators The main quality-related objective of complaint management is to eliminate sources of error by improving the quality of products and services. Whether and to what extent this succeeds is subjectively reflected in the changed extent of *customer annoyance* with regard to certain problems *(KPI: annoyance rate)*. Its development must be documented in the report, as well as the objective key figures for the numbers of *warranty and guarantee claims (KPI: warranty rate; guarantee rate)* (Fig. 12.11).

Productivity-Related Key Performance Indicator The productivity of complaint management is primarily reflected in the *efficiency of complaint handling*. Therefore, the report should include information on the development of efficiency, measured by the number of complaints processed per employee *(KPI: number of complaints processed per employee)* (Table 12.5).

The Operative Perspective: Standards of Task Controlling
A further focus of complain reporting is on achieving operational targets. In the context of subjective and objective task controlling, a large number of subjective and objective key figures were described, with the help of which the *quality of the*

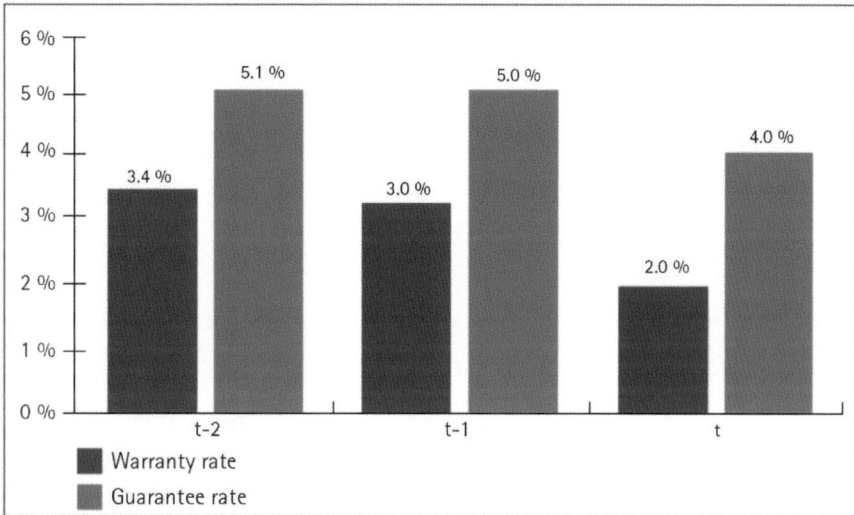

Fig. 12.11 Warranty rates and guarantee rates

Table 12.5 Number of complaints processed per employee

	t	t-1	t-2
Complaint volume	1,100	900	700
Number of employees in complaint handling (FTE)	2.00	1.75	1.50
Number of complaints processed per employee	550	514	467
FTE = Full-Time Equivalent			

fulfillment of individual tasks of the direct and indirect complaint management process can be measured. Here, a company-specific selection has to be made and target standards have to be defined. This can be based on the *Complaint Management Index (CMI)* as described in Sect. 11.2.4. The report should indicate the target and actual values and the deviations from the target values (Tables 12.6 and 12.7).

In addition, it is also necessary to document how the *Complaint Management Index* develops (Fig. 12.12).

The Economic Perspective: Profitability of Complaint Management

Cost-benefit controlling provides fundamental input for reporting on the profitability of complaint management. Regarding the *costs of complaint management* the reports

Table 12.6 Fulfillment of subjective standards

Subjective quality indicator in the Complaint Management Index	Minimum standard "convinced complainants"			Maximum standard "disappointed complainants"		
	Target value	Actual value	Deviations (percentage points)	Target value	Actual value	Deviations (percentage points)
Accessibility	35 %	20 %	-15	25 %	30 %	-5
Friendliness	80 %	85 %	+5	5 %	2 %	+3
Empathy	75 %	60 %	-15	12 %	15 %	-3
Helpfulness	90 %	90 %	0	5 %	2 %	+3
Reliability	80 %	77 %	-3	10 %	8 %	+2
Promptness of reaction	50 %	40 %	-10	25 %	20 %	+5
Adequacy of the solution	50 %	35 %	-15	30 %	45 %	-15

Table 12.7 Fulfillment of objective standards

Objective quality indicator in Complaint Management Index	Target value	Actual value	Degree of realization
Offered calls answered rate	80 %	78 %	98 %
Service level	80 %	73 %	91 %
First-time fix rate	75 %	60 %	80 %
Total handling time < 3 days	80 %	85 %	106 %

should include information about the total costs (with and without reaction costs) as well as the costs per employee and the costs per complaint (with and without reaction costs). Figure 12.13 shows an example of the quarterly development of reaction, processing and overall costs per complaint.

Cost-benefit controlling also provides data for determining the economic benefit of complaint management. With regard to the information benefit, it must be verified whether the complaint information is actually used and whether *warranty and guarantee costs* are reduced (see Fig. 12.14).

The *retention benefit* results from multiplying the number of net repurchasers/ migrants by the average turnover or contribution margin; the *communication benefit* results from a corresponding evaluation of the net new customers won on the basis of recommendations from satisfied complainants. The addition of all benefit categories constitutes the *overall benefit* of complaint management (see Fig. 12.15).

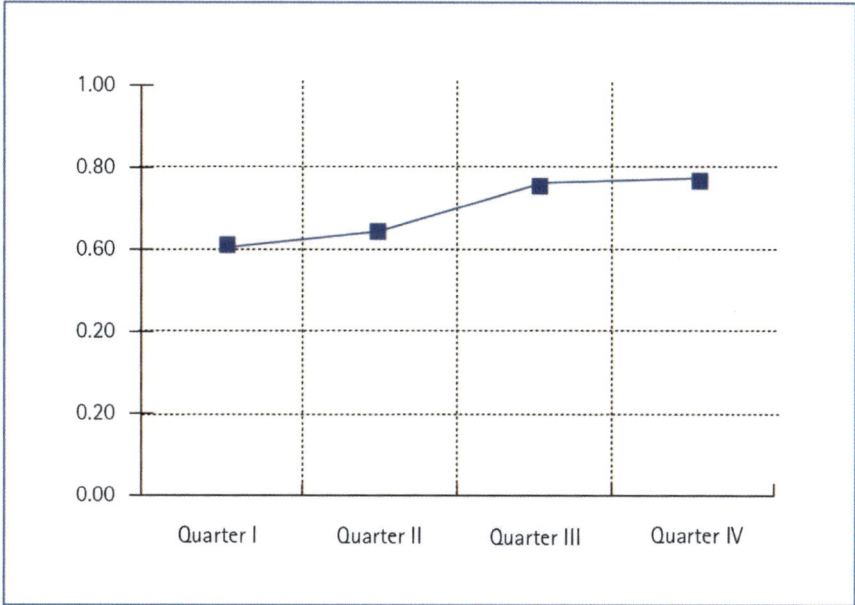

Fig. 12.12 Quarterly development of the complaint management index

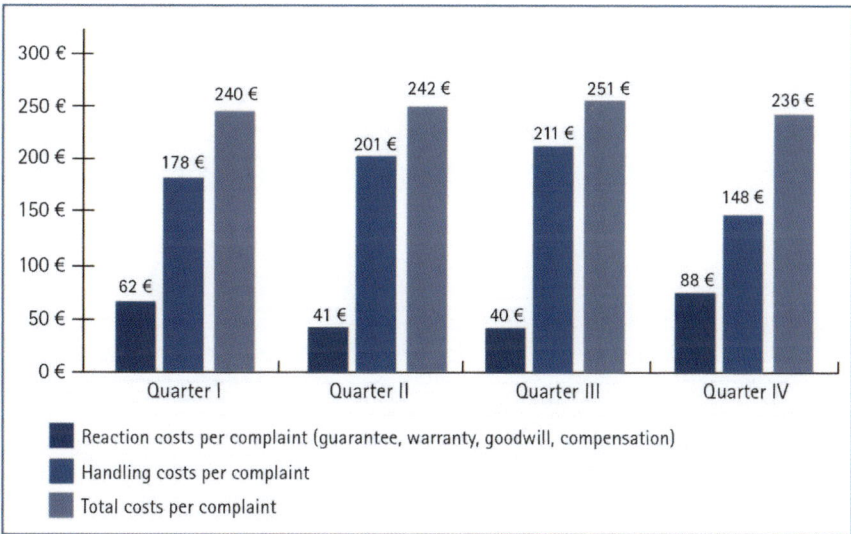

Fig. 12.13 Complaint unit costs

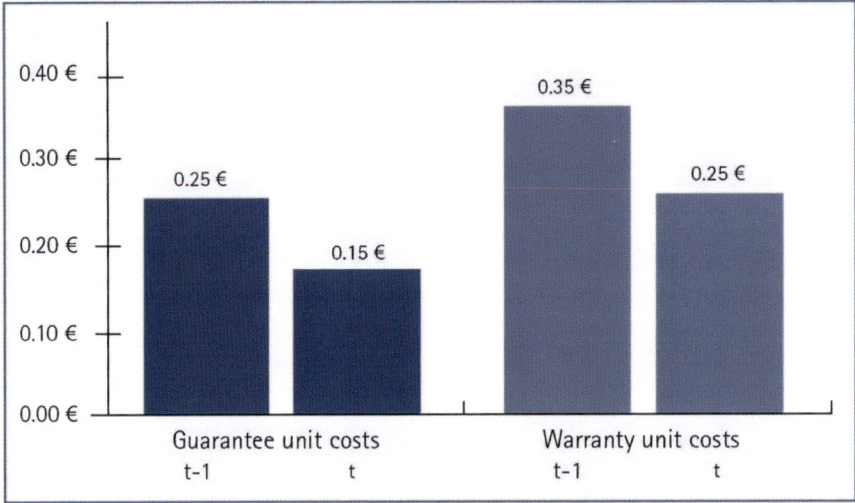

Fig. 12.14 Information benefit as reduced warranty and guarantee costs

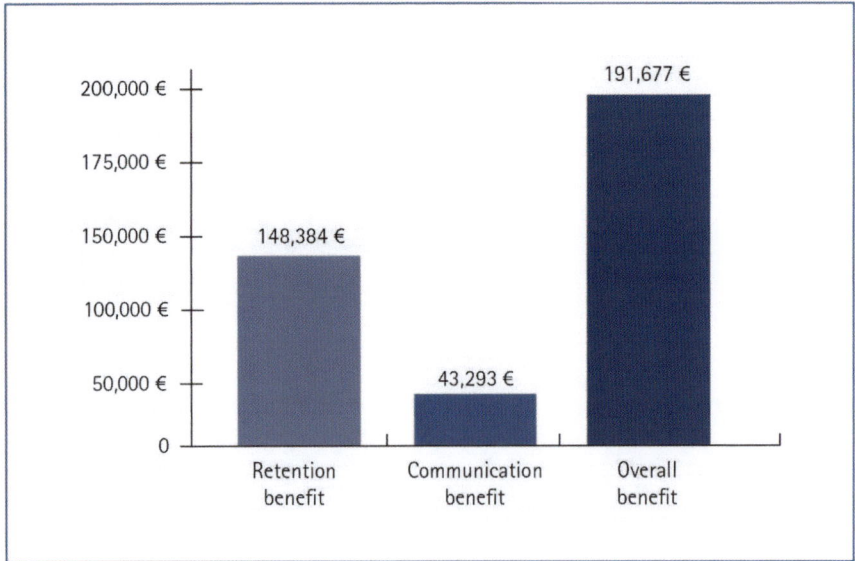

Fig. 12.15 Retention, communication and overall benefit of complaint management

By comparing the monetary costs and the benefits of complaint management, complaint management controlling provides information on profitability, so that the development of the *Return on Complaint Management* can be documented (see Fig. 12.16).

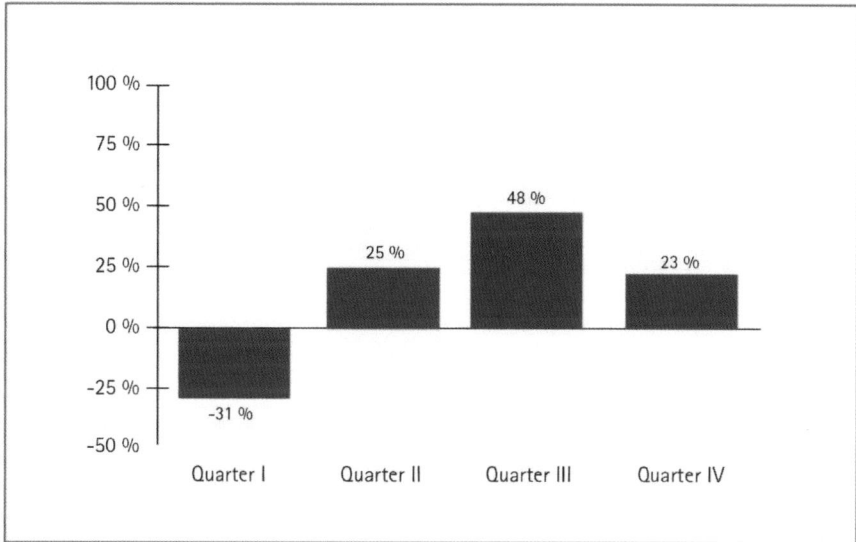

Fig. 12.16 Development of the return on complaint management

12.1.2 The Formal Dimension of Complaint Reporting

With respect to the *formal presentation*, we can distinguish between the following possibilities:

- Detailed lists and tables on the level of classification characteristics, standards/performance figures and complaint processes
- *Aggregate results and performance figures*, for example, at higher hierarchical levels or at the level of the respective overall results and
- *"Hit Lists"* that provide a concise summary of the key information (e.g. top complaint objects, top problem categories, top complaint methods, etc.). The extent of the hit lists depends upon the number of classification characteristics of the individual information concerned; however, care must be taken to ensure that the information remains easily comprehensible.

With regard to the format, one must also decide how the lists, tables and target figures contained in the complaint reports should be prepared. This applies to the structure of the contents of the tables and lists, the selection of the appropriate graphics and the way in which the results are communicated. Moreover, the report medium must be determined. Usually, reports are distributed in written form or sent electronically as data.

12.1.3 The Temporal Dimension of Complaint Reporting

With respect to the different reports, the frequency with which the defined contents are sent to the individual target groups (e.g. daily, weekly, monthly, quarterly or yearly report) must be established. The *reporting intervals* are dependent upon the complaint volume and the informational requirements of the internal customers. In addition, the contents of the analyses that should be presented suggest differing reporting intervals. Problems with especially high reaction urgency—for instance, serious health damage resulting from product use—require daily reporting. It is also advisable to generate frequency distributions and cross-tabulations of problem types and complaint objects more frequently (e.g. weekly) than corresponding analyses of first and follow-up complaints (e.g. monthly). A uniform recommendation cannot be provided. On the contrary, here again it is the responsibility of the process owner and the internal target group to determine what information must reasonably be made available at what intervals.

12.1.4 Target Group-Specific Dimension of Complaint Reporting

In principle, decisions must be made on the *persons or departments* to whom or to which complaint information should be made accessible. Basically, all those who are responsible for customer management, as well as departments that can derive direct benefits from the results, should be accommodated. A total of five reporting target groups can be identified: *(1)* The first addressee is the *executive management* of the company as the budget provider and central principal of complaint management. *(2)* A second important group of internal recipients are *business units* such as divisions or branches, in whose area of responsibility the customer problems have occurred, because they must be informed about weaknesses and corrective needs in order to be able to initiate appropriate improvement processes. *(3)* In addition, *functional areas* (such as controlling, human resources management, quality management, marketing, sales and service) must be informed if they depend on continuous customer feedback for the optimal fulfillment of their tasks. *(4) Complaint management* itself is a fourth important target group because it needs information for the continuous optimization of complaint management processes. Another decision concerns which results from complaint evaluation and complaint management controlling should be made accessible to *(5) all the employees* in the firm—for instance, in the context of specific, regular contributions to *employee magazines* or in specially designed *complaint management intranet pages*.

These decisions should be made in accordance with the *chosen basic complaint management strategy*. For example, in a complaint management system of the "Complaint Factory" type, which is primarily aimed at cost-efficient complaint handling, there will only be standard reports for a very limited number of internal customers. Quality management is the most important internal customer for information services of the "Quality Assurance" type, whereas in the case of the

Table 12.8 Level of detail of report content for different target groups

Reporting content	Executive manage-ment	Business unit	Functional area	Complaint manage-ment	All employees
Complaint-related contents					
- Complaint volume - Complainants - Complaint channels - Complaint objects and problems	Overview	Detailed report, tailored to the business divisions	Detailed report, tailored to the functional areas	Detailed report	Overview
Complaint management-related contents					
- Key Performance Indicators	Detailed report	Overview	Overview	Detailed report	Overview
- Standards of task controlling				Detailed report	
- Profitability of complaint management	Detailed report	Detailed report on retention benefit and communication benefit	Detailed report on information benefit	Detailed report	Overview

"Relationship Amplifier" type, this role is taken on by the market-related functional areas (such as marketing, sales or service).

In addition, depending on their function and the amount of potential benefits they can derive from complaint information, the individual internal target groups have *different requirements* on the reports, both in terms of content and the abstraction level of presentation.

It is not possible to make generally valid statements about the exact *content and form* of reports for the defined target groups. It is the responsibility of the process owner, together with the target group representatives, to determine the need of information and ensure that the required data is collected and forwarded in the desired form. However, a few rough guidelines can be given. Table 12.8 shows which report contents are generally relevant for which target groups and in what degree of detail.

12.2   Provision of Complaint-Related Information (Information Pull)

The scope of activity of complaint reporting includes not only the target group-oriented distribution of previously defined reports, but also the provision of complaint-oriented information for *special, irregular information wishes* of internal customers. Due to the initiative required from the internal customers with respect to the acquisition of information, we can speak of *information pull* here. From complaint management, relevant information from complaint analysis and complaint management controlling can be supplied in two ways—on-stock and on-demand:

On-stock supply of information is available when complaint management establishes a pool of information to which authorized internal customers have access. Firstly, this pool of information should include the original documents on the one hand, so that members of the departments involved can also gain insight into the complainants' original descriptions. Secondly, all the detailed analyses should be available, even when they are not part of the standard program of the reports. This makes it possible for the members of internal target groups to consolidate their activities using complaint information in a more detailed and extensive manner. Through the provision of simple tools of analysis, the information users also have the opportunity to generate their own analyses in an easily manageable way.

On-demand supply of information is provided when analyses are carried out based on the individual demands of internal customers. This is relevant if specific cases (for example, complaints with a high problem or customer risk) are investigated at request of internal target groups, or there are deviations from the stipulated frequency.

The supply of information on an on-stock and an on-demand basis is an *important internal service of complaint management* that contributes to increasing the use of complaint information and thus to achieving the goals of quality improvement and customer retention.

12.3   Barriers to Information Use

Active complaint reporting and the provision of complaint-relevant information is carried out with the aim of facilitating and initiating the intended use of information. However, empirical studies show that this rarely succeeds. As the results of an empirical study among German companies shows, an extensive consideration of complaints is usually not taken into account by executive management or other business units (Fig. 12.17). In addition, there is essentially a reactive use of information. For example, the majority of respondents use the complaint information to avoid future errors; 41.6% of respondents agree with the corresponding statement "completely", but far less use it in this way with process innovations (19.6%) or product innovation (6.8%).

In view of these results, the question arises as to the reasons for the comparatively low utilization of information from complaint reports. To answer this question, research on information behavior and information barriers in organizations provides important insights (Mende 2006; Schöler 2009).

In order to systematize the factors influencing the use of information, it is advisable to refer to the core elements of each communication: transmitter, medium and receiver. Accordingly, a differentiated analysis is made according to the influencing factors on the part of complaint management (transmitter), reports

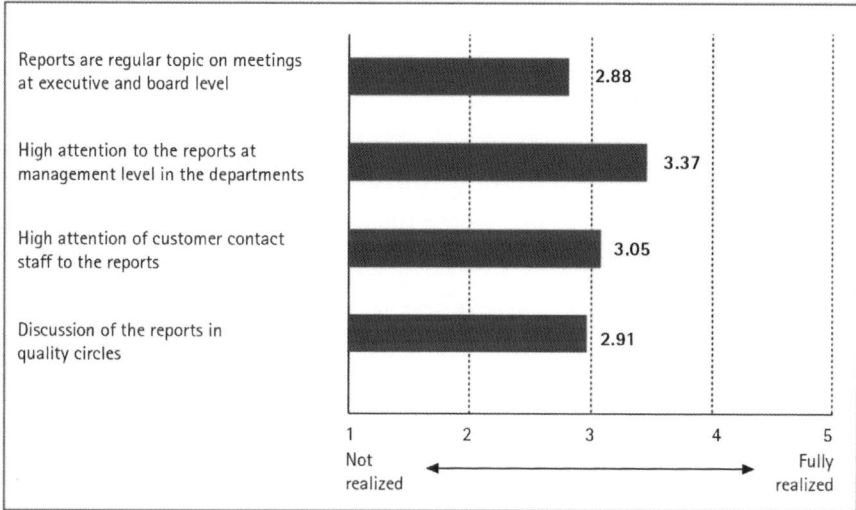

Fig. 12.17 Consideration of complaint reports by different business units (Stauss and Schöler 2003)

(medium) and internal customers (receivers). In addition, the corporate culture is addressed as a central framework for internal communication.

With reference to *complaint management as a transmitter*, its trustworthiness plays a major role (Moorman et al. 1992, 1993). An organizational unit is trusted as a provider of information services, especially when there is no doubt about the professional competence of the providers, its approach is perceived as fact-oriented and the provider has proved to be reliable, objective and largely error-free in the long run.

Accordingly, one of the tasks of complaint management is to build up a *reputation* as an internal information service provider by employing employees with a high level of expertise in the preparation of information. In addition, this competence as well as the well-founded and methodically clean approach must be demonstrated and proven to internal customers. In this context, it may also make sense to apply specific confidence-building measures. This can be done, for example, by pointing to successes achieved through the use of complaint information or positive comments from internal users (Mende 2006).

This characterization of a trustworthy transmitter already addresses important criteria that also play a major role in the perception of *reports as a medium* of information. The use of information by internal customers is largely determined by the perceived *quality of information* (Deshpandé and Zaltman 1982; Maltz and Kohli 1996). In this context, "information quality" encompasses a large number of features, including in particular relevance, completeness, objectivity, accuracy, comprehensibility and accessibility (Lee et al. 2002), see Table 12.9.

As regards *internal customers as recipients* of the information, it is particularly important that they know the existence of complaint reports, consider them as

Table 12.9 Dimensions of information quality

Relevancy	Interpretability
Completeness	Concise representation
Objectivity	Consistent representation
Free-of-error	Appropriate amount
Understandability	Reputation
Accessibility	Timeliness
Believability	Security
Ease of operation	

relevant information source and accept them cognitively and emotionally. Firstly, many internal customers do not or only insufficiently *know* which information service the complaint management system provides or could provide. Secondly, there is often a lack of understanding that this information service is *relevant* for fulfilling their own tasks. Thirdly, complaint information encounters *acceptance barriers* because it often contains notes on errors and criticism of those responsible for decisions in the past. It is also difficult for the addressees to accept these "negative news" in view of the fact that time and resources have to be used for the development and implementation of improvement measures that were not planned for this purpose. In this respect, it is obvious that the affected units tend to be reluctant to act, to repel complaint information emotionally and to use a lot of energy in doubting the justification of the customers' requests or the reliability of the data. Such practices lead to a reduction of cognitive dissonance on the part of the addressees, and at the same time establish the subjective right not to use complaint information (Fornell and Westbrook 1984).

Complaint management must be aware of these factors and act accordingly. First of all, by means of *internal marketing* it must make its range of information services known. It is also important to analyze the tasks of the internal customers in a differentiated way and to identify their specific objectives and personal preferences, as well as their potential need for complaint information. In this way, it is possible to create an *individual information offer* for each segment. In addition, with the support of the company's executive management, as many addressees as possible must be convinced that the purpose of complaint reports is not to look for guilty parties or assign criticism, but rather to *identify potential for improvements and opportunities*.

If the executive management acts accordingly, it will influence the *corporate culture as a framework* for internal communication. Fundamental corporate values and norms—in particular a low level of customer orientation and the interpretation of errors only as a risk—can prove to be serious barriers to the use of information (Schöler 2009). Lack of customer orientation causes managers to place little emphasis on customer-oriented information in comparison to other (e.g. cost-oriented) forms of information. If errors are only understood as risks and not also as chances and learning opportunities, the tendency increases to ward off and suppress complaints. Complaint management alone cannot change the cultural environment of a company, but it can identify corporate cultural barriers and urge executive management to take action to remove them. This will be particularly successful if complaint management can convincingly demonstrate how important the use of complaint information is for achieving the company's goals.

Chapter 12 in Brief
- Complaint reporting pertains to the regular reporting to internal target groups. It includes both the active provision of information on complaints received and on complaint management (Information Pull) as well as the internal service function of providing further specific information on internal demand (Information Pull).
- With regard to the content of the active reporting, a distinction must be made between complaint-related and complaintmanagement-related information. Complaint-related information provides details about the complaint volume, the complainants, the complaint channels chosen by the complainants and the complaint objects and problems. The complaint management-related contents provide information about the strengths and weaknesses of complaint management and its economic contribution to success (key performance indicators, standards of task controlling, profitability of complaint management).
- Formal aspects of complaint reporting concern detailed lists and tables, aggregated results and key figures as well as "hit lists" that provide a concise summary of the key information (e.g. top problem categories).
- The reporting intervals depend on complaint volume, the problem urgency and the informational requirements of the internal customers.
- Complaint reports should be prepared in a target group-specific way. The main target groups are the executive management, business units and functional areas that are affected by the reported customer problems, complaint management itself and all employees of the company.
- In order to ensure that the information from complaint reports is used, internal information barriers must be identified and removed. In addition, internal marketing measures must be applied to encourage the usage of information provided by complaint reports.

References

Deshpandé R, Zaltman G (1982) Factors affecting the use of market research information: a path analysis. J Mark Res 19(1):14–31

Fornell C, Westbrook RA (1984) The vicious circle of consumer complaints. J Mark 48(3):68–78

Lee YW et al (2002) AIMQ: a Methodology for information quality assessment. Inf Manag 40 (2):133–146

Maltz E, Kohli AJ (1996) Market intelligence dissemination across functional boundaries. J Mark Res 33(1):47–61

Mende M (2006) Strategische Planung im Beschwerdemanagement. Deutscher Universitäts-Verlag, Wiesbaden

Moorman C et al (1992) Relationships between providers and users of market research: the dynamics of trust within and between organizations. J Mark Res 29(3):314–328

Moorman C et al (1993) Factors affecting trust in market research relationships. J Mark 57 (1):81–101

Schöler A (2009) Beschwerdeinformationen und ihre Nutzung. Gabler, Wiesbaden

Stauss B, Schöler A (2003) Beschwerdemanagement Excellence, State-of-the-Art und Herausforderungen der Beschwerdemanagement-Praxis in Deutschland. Gabler, Wiesbaden

Utilization of Complaint Information

© Springer Nature Switzerland AG 2019

B. Stauss, W. Seidel, *Effective Complaint Management*, Management for Professionals,
https://doi.org/10.1007/978-3-319-98705-7_13

Issues Raised
- Which quality planning techniques are suitable for eliminating the causes of complaint problems?
- How can complaint information be used in quality improvement teams and quality circles?
- How can additional suggestions for improvement be obtained from complainants?
- How can complaint information and complaint management information be integrated into a comprehensive customer knowledge management system?

A key goal of complaint management is to make a *substantial contribution to quality management* by guaranteeing an active utilization of documented complaint information for measures of improvement. In this way, a recurrence of customers' problems will be avoided in the future, and customer retention will be realized by means of customer satisfaction. In order to reach this goal, specific *management measures and instruments* must be employed. Four relevant aspects will be considered in greater detail in the following chapter: the application of quality planning techniques to the development of problem solutions (Sect. 13.1), the use of complaint information in quality improvement teams and quality circles (Sect. 13.2), the leveraging of complainants' problem-solving competence (Sect. 13.3) and the integration of complaint information into a customer knowledge management system (Sect. 13.4).

13.1 Utilization of Complaint Information Through the Application of Quality Planning Techniques

For many years now, the application of planning techniques has been proven valuable in quality management. Among these techniques are base methods that can be unified under the term *"Seven Tools of Quality"*. They serve primarily in failure mode documentation and failure mode analysis (Tague 2005). Two important representatives of this group of methods, the histogram and the Pareto diagram, were already introduced in connection with quantitative complaint analysis. In addition, this chapter presents the Cause-and-Effect Analysis. It also shows how the more complex Failure Mode and Effects Analysis (FMEA) can be applied to use complaint information for quality improvement.

13.1.1 Cause-and-Effect Analysis

The complaint analysis reveals organizational weaknesses but as a rule cannot provide clear indications as to the actual causes of the deficiencies. Thus, the use

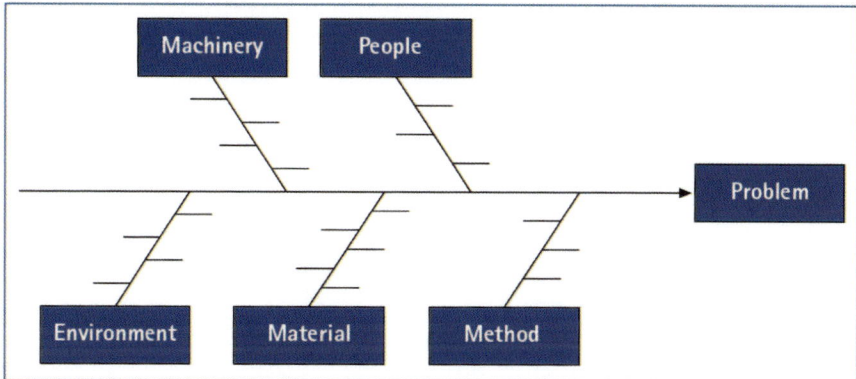

Fig. 13.1 Basic layout of Cause-and-Effect Diagrams

of instruments is required, whose purpose is to analyze the diagnosed problems *with regard to their exact causes* and from this to derive measures for improvement.

At the start of each causal analysis, it is necessary to undertake an exact definition of the problem. For this purpose, the individual cases within a problem category should be investigated in detail. In doing so, it usually turns out that indications of possible problem causes can be found in the detailed description of the problem's circumstances. In order, however, to avoid rash conclusions and uncover further causes and their interdependencies, the analysis must be carried out in a systematic manner. The *Cause-and-Effect Analysis* using the *Cause-and-Effect Diagram* (Ishikawa or Fishbone Diagram) is an graphic tool that is particularly well suited to this purpose.

Here, we are concerned with a process by which all the possible influencing variables (= Causes) are determined for each clearly defined problem (= Effect). These influencing variables and their relationships to one another are described in a structured manner in the Cause-and-Effect Diagram, and the goal of this process is to identify the causes that are *actually responsible for the occurrence of the problem* by tracing the chain of events back to its origin. Figure 13.1 shows the basic layout of a Cause-and-Effect Diagram.

The construction of Cause-Effect Diagrams usually involves *six* steps:

1. *Problem Formulation (Effect):* Based on the problem focuses shown in the complaint analysis, a specific problem is selected and defined. This problem is recorded on the right side of a chart in the "effect box", and a long horizontal arrow ("spine") is drawn from the left to the problem on the right.
2. *Identification of the Main Causes (Cause):* The Cause-and-Effect Diagram receives its structure from the identification of global causal dimensions. In order to uncover all the potential key influencing factors, it is advisable to fall back on generally accepted major categories like Method, Machinery, Material, People and Environment. The main causes identified are written in boxes above or below the spine, and the boxes are connected to the spine.

3. *Identification of Detailed Causes for the Global Causal Dimensions:* As a next step, all the possible detailed causes for each causal dimension are compiled during a brainstorming process. They appear in the diagram as branches within the bones, whereby each cause itself can again be described more exactly in the form of "smaller bones". At this point, it is important to consider only the causes of errors, and not possible solutions.

4. *Identification of the Most Likely Detailed Causes:* The detailed causes identified must be analyzed and evaluated as to which are probably most responsible for the occurrence of the problem. These causes are then visually highlighted in the diagram.

5. *Verification of the Detailed Causes Identified:* The causes identified are now subjected to a detailed examination in the order of their probable influence. This process is to be continued until a consensus is reached within the improvement team as to the key individual causes.

6. *Derivation and Introduction of the Problem Solution(s):* On the basis of this analysis, action plans are developed for how the problem can be eliminated in the long term. In developing these plans, both the advantages and the possible disadvantages associated with each potential problem solution should be brought out, so that a balanced decision can be made.

Before the measure on which the team has decided is implemented, it must be discussed by all the departments and people affected in the firm and modified if necessary. If a consensus is reached in the course of this feedback process, indicating that all those in charge support the suggested measures, then the solution is implemented. After the implementation of the measures for improvement, the firm must verify whether it was *in fact* able to *minimize* the occurrence of the problem, or that new and different problems were not created by the implementation of the problem solution. If the complaint volume with respect to a certain problem that had to be eliminated was very high before the initiation of the continuous improvement process, the measures introduced must be reflected in a lower complaint volume with regard to the observed problem in the short term.

Below, in *Spotlight 13.1* the procedure of the Cause-and-Effect Analysis will be made clear by means of an *example case*.

Spotlight 13.1
Cause-and-Effect Analysis of Problems with Telephone Accessibility
The *results of a firm's complaint analysis* showed that many customers complained about not being able to reach the firm by telephone. The phone often rang more than ten times before an employee answered. At times, it seemed that the firm was completely unreachable. Many customers were very annoyed and preferred not to call any more or conduct their business with a competitor.

(continued)

Spotlight 13.1 (continued)

Since neither technical errors nor low personnel capacity could account for the cause at first glance, an *improvement team* was given the task of uncovering the *actual cause*.

The problem of "Phone Not Answered" was first defined even more narrowly. A reaction was rated as "delayed" when callers heard more than three rings before they were greeted. The major categories (Machinery, People Method, Material, and Environment) were initially entered on the diagram as the main causes.

In order to specify the causes further, a *brainstorming* session was then held, which led to the identification of a series of individual causes (see Fig. 13.2).

In the discussion about the reasons for the excessively long waiting times, the team rated the factors "Away from Desk" and "Preoccupation with Other Tasks" *as especially likely*. The firm did not have a main switchboard. Instead, the receptionist who worked in the reception area out front took the incoming calls.

In order to verify whether these reasons were in fact responsible, the reception area and the telephone reaction behavior was carefully observed for five days. It turned out that the receptionist was not at her desk for an average of 65 min per day. She left her desk for breaks and when she accompanied important guests to the CEO of the firm. During this time, the firm received an average of 12 calls that were not answered. In addition to this problem, there was the fact that the employee took about eight calls per day only after the phone had rung numerous times because she was busy with other activities (receiving mail, greeting customers, providing information). The results of the observation confirmed the presumed problem causes (see Fig. 13.3).

The Cause-and-Effect Analysis provided the basis for the development of the following *specific suggestions for improvement*:

- A second employee, who primarily carries out paperwork, is made responsible for accepting telephone calls and trained for this task.
- During the receptionist's official break times, this employee completely takes over the reception desk and the telephone.
- If the receptionist briefly has to leave her desk for other reasons, she switches over the telephone system. The colleague is automatically informed by the system about this switchover.
- The receptionist no longer accompanies important customers to the CEO, but instead informs the secretary to pick up the guests in the reception area.
- If the employee at the reception desk is so busy with other tasks that she cannot attend to the telephone immediately, she transfers the call to the colleague by simply pressing a button.

(continued)

Spotlight 13.1 (continued)

When the firm attempted *to implement these suggestions*, it turned out that personnel (training), technical (telephone system) and organizational (workplace of the former typist) issues had to be solved, which required the cooperation of a number of affected employees.

The recommendations of the team were finalized by management and subsequently implemented. In order to be able to judge properly the *effectiveness of the measures introduced*, on the one hand a comparative observation was carried out, and on the other hand the number of related complaints was used as a comparison.

13.1.2 Failure Mode and Effects Analysis (FMEA)

Failure Mode and Effects Analysis (FMEA) is a formalized analytical method for the *systematic recording and prevention of potential failure modes* in the development of products and services. It was developed in the mid-1960s in the American aeronautics industry and since that time has been among the key methodological instruments in quality management (McDermott et al. 2009; Carlson 2012).

Basically, the FMEA is a method of *preventative quality assurance*, since it is concerned with the timely identification, rating and prevention of potential failure modes. For this reason, its use in the context of complaint management might at first appear to be unsuitable, because complaints contain information about failure modes that have already occurred and can no longer be prevented. Closer examination reveals, however, that very practical applications are nevertheless conceivable,

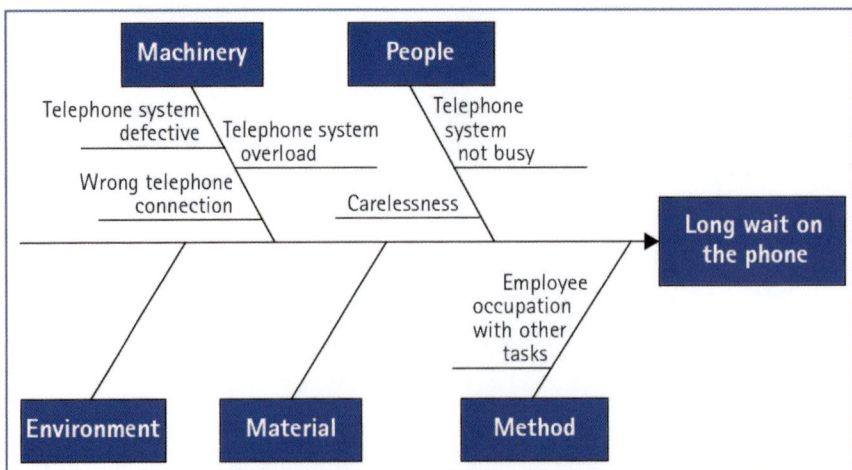

Fig. 13.2 Cause-and-Effect Diagram for the customer problem "Long Wait on the Phone"

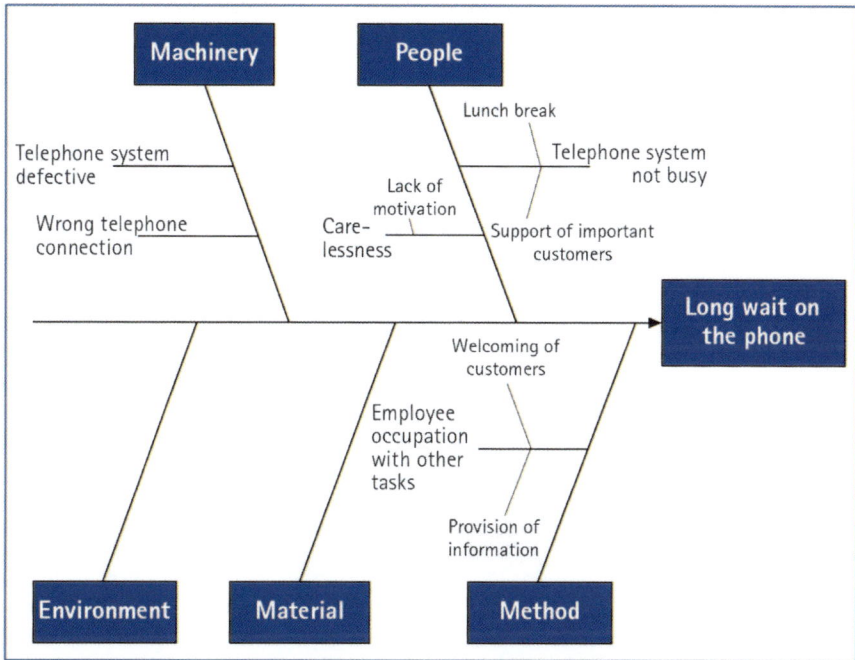

Fig. 13.3 Detailed Cause-and-Effect Diagram for the customer problem "Long Wait on Phone"

specifically through the supply of complaint information for use in the FMEA on the one hand, and the prevention of failure modes in complaint management itself on the other hand.

13.1.2.1 The Use of Complaint Information in the Context of the Traditional FMEA Application

An essential area of application for the FMEA is the *new development or modification of products and services*. Here it is necessary to recognize and reduce the risks of potential failure modes by taking a structured approach. This occurs when a team of experts from different departments carries out the discussion and assessment of failure modes using a specific form (Fig. 13.4).

The approach can be characterized in *ten steps*:

1. The initial discussion is about which failure modes could actually occur, and the potential failure modes identified are listed in the first column *"Potential Failure Modes"*.
2. For each potential failure mode, the problems that could result are recorded in the column *"Potential Effects of Failures"*.
3. Subsequently, for each failure mode, the *causes* that are responsible for its occurrence must be found.

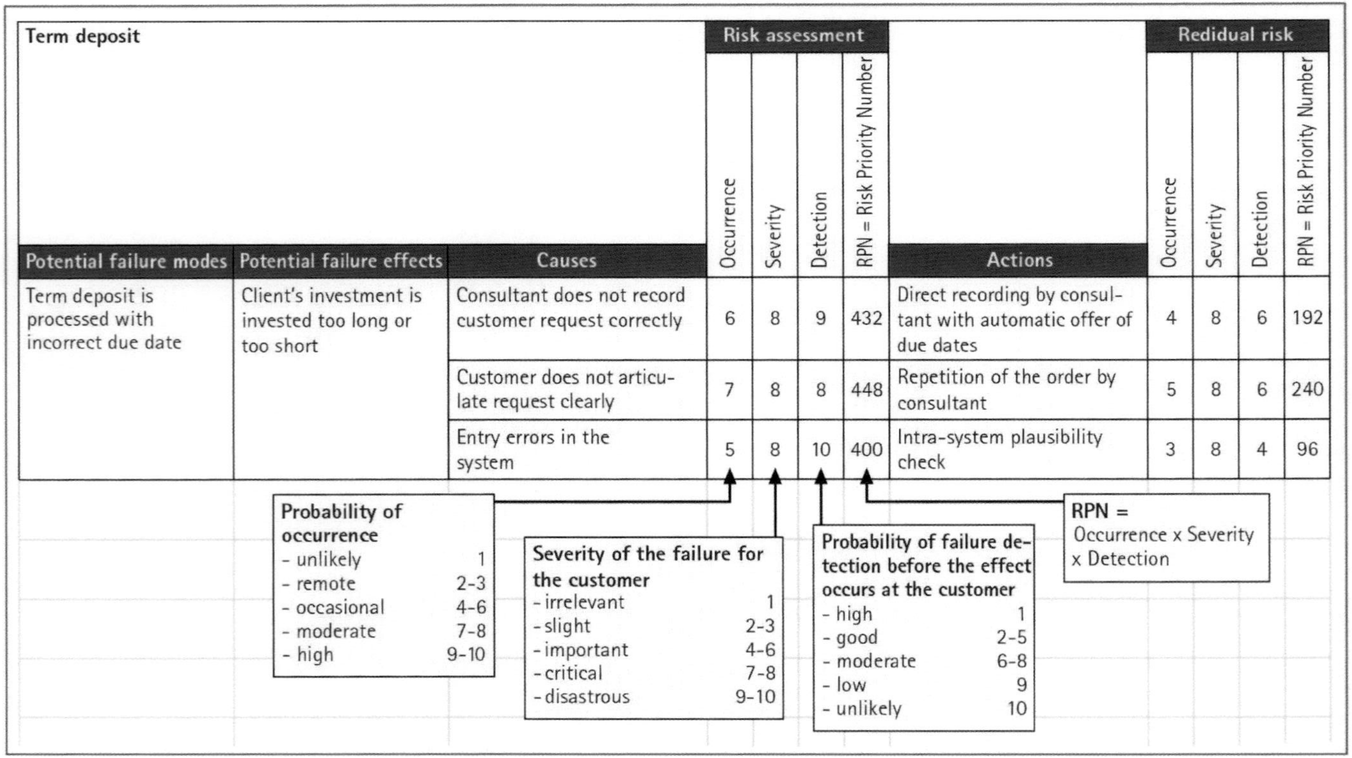

Term deposit

Potential failure modes	Potential failure effects	Causes	Risk assessment				Actions	Residual risk			
			Occurrence	Severity	Detection	RPN = Risk Priority Number		Occurrence	Severity	Detection	RPN = Risk Priority Number
Term deposit is processed with incorrect due date	Client's investment is invested too long or too short	Consultant does not record customer request correctly	6	8	9	432	Direct recording by consultant with automatic offer of due dates	4	8	6	192
		Customer does not articulate request clearly	7	8	8	448	Repetition of the order by consultant	5	8	6	240
		Entry errors in the system	5	8	10	400	Intra-system plausibility check	3	8	4	96

Probability of occurrence
- unlikely   1
- remote   2–3
- occasional   4–6
- moderate   7–8
- high   9–10

Severity of the failure for the customer
- irrelevant   1
- slight   2–3
- important   4–6
- critical   7–8
- disastrous   9–10

Probability of failure detection before the effect occurs at the customer
- high   1
- good   2–5
- moderate   6–8
- low   9
- unlikely   10

RPN = Occurrence x Severity x Detection

Fig. 13.4 FMEA form: example term deposit (based on Ruß 1999, p. 323)

4. Next, the risks associated with the failure modes are assessed on the basis of this information. For this purpose, it is first estimated in the column *"Occurrence"* how probable it is that this failure mode could occur. The rating is based on a scale that ranges from "unlikely" (= 1) to "highly likely" (= 10).
5. After that, the gravity of the effects of the failure mode is analyzed from the customer's perspective. The rating is again based on a ten-point scale that ranges from "hardly noticeable" (= 1) to "serious failure mode" (= 9 or 10). The respective value is entered in the column *"Severity"*.
6. The column *"Detection Ratings"* is used to express an estimate of how likely it is that the failure mode can be detected before the product reaches the customer. Since the risk of a failure mode is greater, the later it is detected, the rating scale ranges from "highly likely" (= 1) to "unlikely" (= 10).
7. The *Risk Priority Number (RPN)* is the result of multiplying the values for Severity, Occurrence and Probability of Detection. It is the standard that permits a comparison of the risks of various potential failure modes and thus is also an essential variable in prioritizing failure mode prevention measures.
8. The causal analysis is the basis for the recommendation of *actions* that should prevent the occurrence of the failure mode.
9. Subsequently, the *effect* of these measures is to be discussed and evaluated by making a new risk assessment. Taking the corrective measures into consideration, Occurrence, Severity and Probability of Detection are assessed anew, and the *residual risk* is expressed in a new Risk Priority Number.
10. A *comparison of the Risk Priority Numbers* before and after the planned measures is therefore possible, and in this way, measures with the greatest influence on the reduction of risk can be selected.

This approach shows on the one hand that the FMEA can be used not only for failure mode prevention, but also for the assessment of failure modes that are documented in complaints and for the development of corrective measures in the context of quality management. But even if one clings to the preferred FMEA application—in the context of new developments—the *recourse to information from complaint management* makes a great deal of sense.

As the presentation of the FMEA process has shown, the team must constantly make *valuing decisions*. They must determine the likelihood with which failure modes occur and are detected in a timely manner, and they must perform an assessment of the failure mode's consequences from the customers' point of view. There is a great danger here that the team members will rely on their personal evaluations and come to the wrong conclusions. The recourse to complaint information can reduce this danger by permitting a customer-oriented and factually supported assessment. This applies particularly in the vast majority of cases in which, instead of a completely new product being developed, a product re-launch is to be made:

- The complaint analysis provides a number of indications as to failure modes that have actually occurred and could recur in the changed product, or that contain *suggestions valuable* in the detection of other possible failure modes.
- The information from complaint management concerning complainants' intended actions and actual behavior after the failure mode has occurred provides specific insights into the *failure mode's consequences and relevance from the customer's perspective*. The severity of the failure can firstly be seen from the information provided by the customer during the acceptance of the complaint, secondly from the results of the complaint satisfaction survey, thirdly from a survey of the terminating customers and fourthly from the analysis of the complainant's loyalty behavior.
- Moreover, quantitative complaint analysis permits definite conclusions with respect to the *probability of occurrence* and the *probability of detection*. Failure modes that lead to complaints are obviously detected too late by the firm, and the failure mode statistic shows differences in the probability of occurrence. It makes sense to use this information in the risk assessment.
- In addition, the Cause-and-Effect Analysis offers valuable indications as to the *causes* of problems and possible *measures* that can be used to combat those causes.

It is therefore advisable to integrate information from complaint management systematically into the traditional failure mode and effects analysis.

13.1.2.2 Use of the FMEA for the Improvement of Complaint Management Processes

However, complaint management does not merely provide valuable input for the application of the FMEA planning instrument in the development process. It can also use this instrument to subject its own processes to a failure mode analysis. In this case, the FMEA serves to *prevent failure modes in complaint management.*

Gierl (2000) provides an *example* of this when he applies the FMEA to complaint stimulation, a task area of complaint management. He interprets a low number of dissatisfied customers that complain to the firm as a failure mode. Along the lines of the approach presented above, it is then recommended that a working group with members from the marketing, sales and customer service departments be established, so that this failure mode can be addressed more closely. Accordingly, the team describes the failure mode's consequences (high rates of customer switching and negative word-of-mouth communication) and analyzes the causes of the low complaint articulation. A survey of annoyed customers shows that this is mainly due to high perceived complaint costs and a low probability of success. The team performs a risk assessment and develops proposed solutions. Taking these measures into consideration, the new risk priority numbers are calculated. In view of the superior impact on risk reduction, the introduction of service guarantees is the chosen measure. Figure 13.5 shows an appropriate form for this hypothetical example.

The FMEA is a recognized systematic method whose general application can be improved *in its informational content* by the utilization of complaint information and furthermore can reasonably be used in the improvement of complaint management

Complaint stimulation			Risk assessment					Actions	Residual risk			
Potential failure modes	Potential effects of failures	Causes	Occurrence	Severity	Detection	RPN = Risk Priority Number			Occurrence	Severity	Detection	RPN = Risk Priority Number
Dissatisfied customers who do not complain	High rate of customer switching and negative word-of-mouth	High perceived complaint costs	4	9	10	360		Installation of a hotline	2	9	9	162
		Success probability assumed to be low	8	9	7	504		Introduction of service guarantees	2	9	6	108

Fig. 13.5 FMEA in the context of complaint stimulation, adapted (with changes) from Gierl (2000, p. 170)

processes. Nevertheless, one should always consider the following: What is essential is not the filling out of the form, but rather the structured guidance of preventative thinking, the inclusion of experts across departmental boundaries and the structured documentation of the problem solution process.

13.2   Use of Complaint Information in Quality Improvement Teams and Quality Circles

The systematic analysis and evaluation of complaint information and the development of possible solutions cannot be carried out by individual experts exclusively. The problems must be considered in all their various aspects, the causes must be analyzed in their complexity and the influencing variables must be completely understood. A similar principle applies to the generation of ideas for solutions and their assessment with respect to their ability to prevent future failure modes. Thus, one of the requirements for the comprehensive use of complaint information is the formation of *teams* that allow for the creative process and the use of diverse expert know-how.

Spotlight 13.2 describes how a large insurance company takes a team-oriented approach to using complaint information in the company's continuous improvement process.

Spotlight 13.2
The Role of Complaints as Part of the Continuous Improvement Process at Generali Health Insurance (Central Krankenversicherungs AG)

Generali Health Insurance (Central Krankenversicherungs AG) is one of the five largest private health insurance companies in Germany. Its back offices handle a large variety of different processes, ranging from underwriting over simple contract changes, to claims handling and complaint management. Complaint management is extremely important for keeping customers and distributors satisfied, and to continuously learn from their experiences.

A few years ago, Generali Health Insurance implemented a holistic continuous improvement process (CIP). The key objective of this process was to be able to routinely detect systematic issues in each team in order to quickly install specific improvement levers. A crucial element of the underlying project was to integrate input from three sources:

- Quality/error rates (inside-out)
- Customer and distributor satisfaction (outside-in)
- Complaints (outside-in)

This integration enabled systematic learning about service performance, from both an inside-out and an outside-in perspective.

(continued)

Spotlight 13.2 (continued)

Before the implementation of the CIP, the different back office departments did not have a common understanding of service quality. The existing quality reporting focused solely on error rate measurements. The range extended from 2% to 25%, which was not due to differences in the service quality of departments, but rather to different definitions and measurements of errors. An external perspective was not reflected in the reporting.

As a consequence of the shortcomings of the prior system, the key objective of the new quality management was to enable everyone within the organization to provide consistent, high quality processes and outcomes to all customers and distributors by systematically learning from mistakes and feeding a sustainable improvement process.

The Continuous Improvement Process (CIP)

There are five steps to the CIP (see Fig. 13.6). It begins with data collection and evaluation, proceeds to actual improvement, and then it repeats. More detail about each step is discussed below.

Step 1: Data Collection and Evaluation

In this first step, quality, satisfaction, and complaints are measured.

The CIP starts by measuring service quality. At Generali Health Insurance, service quality is defined as the sum of customer and distributor expectations. The definition covers four dimensions of quality:

- Technical accuracy
- Formal accuracy
- Friendliness & comprehensibility
- Process performance

The first three of these four quality dimensions are measured by means of random sample tests. These tests focus on the core processes of each operative team. For each business process, a maximum number of points can be achieved. Depending on the type and quantity of errors, this number is reduced according to a predefined checklist. Then, the remaining number of points are simply matched to a scale indicating three categories:

- Green: Customer demand completely fulfilled with no or only marginal deficits that do not affect the outcome (e.g. spelling errors). No corrections needed.
- Amber: Customer demand fulfilled only partially or with relevant deficits. Corrections needed to prevent customer or broker dissatisfaction/grievance.
- Red: Customer demand not fulfilled. Deficits led to wrong result. Corrections and apology needed.

Sample tests are performed by a central and independent service management team. This team is also responsible for providing monthly reports.

(continued)

Spotlight 13.2 (continued)

In order to obtain and report a complete picture, the team then gathers information from additional sources to validate and enrich the findings, and to check for further deficits. These additional sources include internal tests such as mystery calls, internal audits, process performance measurements, etc. They also include the outside-in perspective by means of customer and distributor interviews, Net Promoter Score (NPS), complaints, etc.

Satisfaction is measured by various means. At several customer and distributor contact points, the NPS is used to systematically detect specific needs for action. Both for the tests described above and the satisfaction scores, it is not the absolute number that is relevant, but rather the change over time.

Further insight is generated from a broad variety of surveys and other market research handled by other departments.

Complaints are processed in different departments in a multiple-level-structure. First level complaints cover the full range of topics and are usually not expressed as complaints but rather as questions or remarks. They are mostly received by phone or e-mail, and can be resolved immediately in a customer-oriented and efficient way, without having to involve other departments. These issues are recorded in a simple database structure, gathering information about the customer and topic according to a predefined list.

Some complaints require deeper knowledge, more detailed research, or a more elaborate solution, all of which involve routing to another team or department. These complaints are recorded in the complaints database, and include more detailed information about the specific issue and solution. First and second level issues cover more than 95% of all complaints.

Third level complaints are usually addressed to the executive board, the supervisory board, or an external ombudsman/auditor. Handling of these complaints requires in-depth and often legal knowledge, and is performed by highly skilled specialists. These issues are recorded in the complaint database in detail. This information is often used for in-depth root cause and further analyses, which lead to improvements of processes, training, tools etc.

The sum of all complaints delivers information about processes that have not been performed well over the period under consideration. In addition, the central service management team uses the more qualitative in-depth information to validate findings and to suggest improvement levers.

Step 2: Reporting on Team Level

Reports are delivered on a monthly basis and include the number of complaints as well as an interpretation of the results.

Step 3: Discussion of Report with Team

In the next step of the CIP, every team leader has the task of discussing the indications of the report with their teams (e.g. as part of a monthly team meeting).

(continued)

Spotlight 13.2 (continued)

For example, a team could show deficits regarding friendliness and comprehensibility in letters to customers. Possible improvement levers could be to raise awareness of these topics, train team members, install new text modules, switch from free-style texting to working with text blocks, or change to a more interactive way of corresponding with customers (e.g. by phone instead of letter), etc.

It is difficult to identify the right lever simply by analyzing numbers in reports. Furthermore, searching for the right lever by means of trial and error would possibly cause unnecessary trouble. Therefore, more detailed insights are required from other sources. It is crucial that the team itself is responsible for finding the best way to solve the deficits since they usually have expert knowledge of the relevant processes and tools. Furthermore, being involved ensures higher commitment to improving the situation.

Steps 4a & b: Definition of Improvement Activities, Feedback to Central Service Management Team, and Validation

In this step, the team has the obligation to define specific activities to improve the situation, including responsibilities, timing, and expected results. The team leader reports the action plan back to the central service management team.

Step 5: Actual Improvement

The operational team is required to improve its processes and tools according to its plan.

In this step, the continuous improvement circle merges with the next cycle. The service management team measures service quality as described above, and tracks implementation progress according to the delivered plans. By keeping track of not only input parameters, but also output parameters, Generali Health Insurance can track whether each activity was the right one to improve the situation. If there is no improvement, other levers have to be found—either by the responsible team working alone or in collaboration with the central service management team.

Furthermore, the service management team ensures continuous alignment through periodic customer centricity board meetings including the board and top management from operations, sales, organization, IT, and marketing.

It is important to mention that findings are never used to control the behavior or performance of individual employees. Instead, the goal is to learn and enable teams to systematically self-improve service quality. Furthermore, service quality has been established as an integral part of company results and the corresponding incentive bonus system.

Gunnar Klaming
Manager Business Development Kobold Systems
Vorwerk Deutschland Stiftung & Co. KG, Germany
Former Manager Complaints & Quality Management
Central Krankenversicherungs AG, Germany

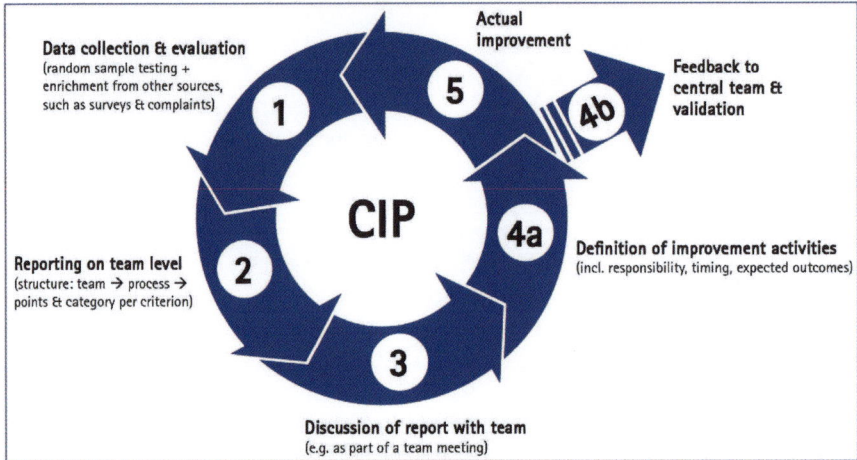

Fig. 13.6 Steps of the continuous improvement process

The teamwork in quality improvement utilizing complaint information may be designed differently, depending on the firm's situation and on the problem. Two different kinds of team concepts can be primarily differentiated with regard to the *permanence of their existence* and the *structure of their membership*: quality improvement teams and quality circles.

13.2.1 Quality Improvement Teams

Quality improvement teams are characterized by the fact that they are charged—*on a short-term basis*—with formulating a solution for a specific quality problem that has previously been clearly defined and are assembled across departmental boundaries. Accordingly, they can be identified by the following *characteristics*:

- *The task is clearly defined:* Depending upon which weak points are highlighted in the context of complaint analysis and complaint management controlling, a very specific problem becomes the focus of the work of an improvement team.
- *The improvement team is assembled from the standpoint of assembling those people with the highest potential for formulating solutions and implementing measures:* The crucial factor is that all the required expertise is represented, so that the problem that needs to be solved can be addressed effectively. Furthermore, all departments that may have contributed to the occurrence of the problem or can make a contribution to the solution should be represented. The involvement of all those concerned should reduce interdepartmental conflicts, and realistic solutions that can be supported by all those involved in the new process should be developed.

- *The work in improvement teams is an essential component of the work performed by employees:* Teams are only successful if their work is not perceived as disturbing by those involved, but as an important part of their own tasks. Many efforts to improve quality fail due to the fact that employees only grudgingly take part in the meetings, believing that the real work is being left undone. Not until this attitude that *"quality is outside the job"* is overcome and the efforts to improve quality are seen as part of the corporate performance requirement, and not as a burdensome additional task, can the firm count on successful teamwork and the necessary commitment from the employees.
- *Improvement teams disband after the problem is eliminated:* Improvement teams exist during the time in which the quality problem is being processed and are disbanded when it is solved. They are not a permanent structure.

13.2.2 Quality Circles

Quality circles are a special form of quality improvement teams. They are also dedicated to the systematic elimination of failure modes and the creative search for new solutions to problems. Their distinctiveness comes from the fact that they are designed for regular meetings *on a continuing basis*, operate on a *volunteer basis* and are principally concerned with *problems in the more immediate work environment.*

Quality circles have *proven* their worth in many companies as an important instrument for the improvement of product quality and process flow. Moreover, it has been shown that they can greatly contribute to increasing motivation, improving internal communication, continuing job-related training and strengthening employees' identification with their company. Furthermore, there are relatively few barriers to their implementation, since the establishment of quality circles is not associated with structural changes in terms of the operational and organizational structure of the firm.

So that quality circles can serve as an important committee for the use of complaint information, a series of requirements must be fulfilled:

- *The results of the complaint analysis* should be *forwarded* to all quality circles in the context of complaint reporting.
- Part of the *standard procedure of the work of quality circles* must be to analyze complaint reports with the objective of identifying possible causes within one's own field of activity and making these causes the object of improvement activities.
- If the Cause-and-Effect Analysis takes place *elsewhere* (for instance, in quality improvement teams), insights into possible sources and causes of problems should be forwarded immediately to the quality circles. Additionally, a *link* between the work of the quality circle and more comprehensive improvement activities should be established.

- For an exact analysis of the problem and a targeted development of solutions, members of quality circles must have *access to the complaint database,* and they must furthermore be trained to *work with problem solution techniques.*

Employees from complaint management play a key role in the fulfillment of these requirements. Not only must they carry out analyses and supply information in the context of reporting; they must also become active internally as stimulators of quality improvements by purposefully approaching the quality circles, supplying additional information on customers' problems and requests for change and providing training with regard to the application of customer-oriented methods of information use. This underlines not only the necessity of closely interlinking complaint management and quality management, but also the need to integrate these areas into the company through institutional solutions in such a way that the information potential of complaint information is actually fully exploited (see *Spotlight 13.3*).

Spotlight 13.3
Integration of Complaint Management and Quality Management at the KKH Kaufmännische Krankenkasse

KKH is one of the largest national health insurance companies, with 1.8 million policyholders. Approximately 3800 employees provide advice on all matters relating to health insurance issues at 110 advisory offices throughout Germany. The annual budget of the KKH amounts to 5.7 billion euros. The head office is in Hanover, Germany.

KKH is one of the more than 100 statutory health insurance (SHI) companies with which nine out of ten German citizens are insured. Unlike private health insurance, the SHI acts according to the solidarity principle, i.e. the healthy pay for sick people, high-income earners pay for low-income earners. Family members are also insured free of charge. In addition, more than 70 million people with statutory health insurance can rely on receiving quality assured services—without having to compare prices and worry about whether they can afford the treatment.

In addition to excellent health care, KKH has set itself the goal of offering the best possible service as a customer-oriented service provider. Complaint management plays a central role here, because it is important to learn from dissatisfaction and to use the findings from complaints for quality management and thus for improvements in the range of services and customer care.

To achieve this, complaint management at KKH has been consistently integrated into a pragmatic quality cycle (see Fig. 13.7). This ensures that complaint management brings the customers' perceived problems to the company's attention and controls their systematic handling and resolution.

(continued)

Spotlight 13.3 (continued)

Step A: Recognizing and communicating deviations from the customer's point of view

The first step is to identify deviations from customers' quality expectations. In complaint and quality management at KKH (a staff position of the executive board), the complaint data recorded are regularly evaluated quantitatively. Thereby, the volume of complaints, the reasons for complaints (specialist topics such as aids, medicines, rehabilitation measures, etc.) and the causes of complaints (dissatisfaction with e.g. processing time, reliability, advisory competence, range of services) are investigated. In addition, information from employees, escalated individual cases and complaints from customer Internet forums (Facebook, ciao. de, Krankenkassenforum, etc.) are evaluated.

Complaint evaluations are examined for abnormalities and hitherto unidentified problem areas. This examination also includes data and evaluations from customer surveys, cancellation analyses and objection management. The results are communicated to all executives once a quarter.

In order to remedy the quality defects identified from the customer's point of view, institutional dialogs are held with the individual departments and branches. "Controlling dialogs" serve as an exchange platform for this purpose. Here, abnormalities are discussed, corresponding needs for action are derived and necessary measures are developed, initiated and then followed up.

Step B: Evaluating risks and needs for action

If deficiencies cannot be remedied informally, i.e. without a formal decision-making process, or if the problem is very complex or urgent, quality circles are convened which vary according to the topic. For example, in addition to quality management and the specialist departments, the departments of law, process management, auditing and controlling as well as the branches concerned may also be involved. Quality management is responsible for the circle, i.e. it invites, moderates and documents the results.

The quality circles (participants are predominantly managers) assess the risks of the problems, evaluate the need for action and decide on measures. If necessary, immediate measures will be taken to prevent the problem from spreading further until a lasting solution is found.

If no agreement can be reached in the quality circle on the assessment of a problem or the implementation of measures, quality management escalates the problem to the higher management of KKH (to board level or the senior head of department, depending on the topic) with a precise indication of risks, costs and possible measures. The top management either directly commissions the

(continued)

Spotlight 13.3 (continued)

implementation of a solution or returns the problem to the quality circle with an assessment for further processing. Depending on the complexity of the topic or the need for information and decision-making, several cycles of the quality circle may be necessary until a solution is found.

Step C: Implementing measures/Controlling quality projects

If there is agreement in the quality circle, the measures to eliminate problems are commissioned directly from the circle. Depending on the scope of the measure, the improvement activities are carried out by the departments or cross-functional quality projects are started. In all cases, the effectiveness of the measures is checked by the quality management with the customer-oriented measuring methods used in the company (complaint analysis, objection analysis, customer surveys, etc.). If required, company-oriented measurements are also used by the controlling department.

In addition to the internal communication described above, which is supplemented by the regular reporting, "quality meetings" are held at all management levels and with the executive board. Here, the results of complaint and quality management are reported in compact form, abnormalities and observable changes are discussed and, if necessary, issues are prioritized.

Figure 13.8 shows an overview of the institutionalization of integrated complaint and quality management.

Two aspects of this solution are of particular importance: the integration of complaint and quality management and the involvement of all management levels, including the executive board. The integration of complaint and quality management and their merging into one organizational unit enables complaint information to be used in a targeted way for quality improvement, innovation and product development. The involvement of the executive board in the process illustrates the great importance that KKH attaches to customer satisfaction. It ensures that customer requests are processed with high priority and quality improvements are implemented quickly, thus demonstrating KKH's high standards as a premium health insurance company.

Uwe Schröder
Head of Complaint and Quality Management
KKH Kaufmännische Krankenkasse

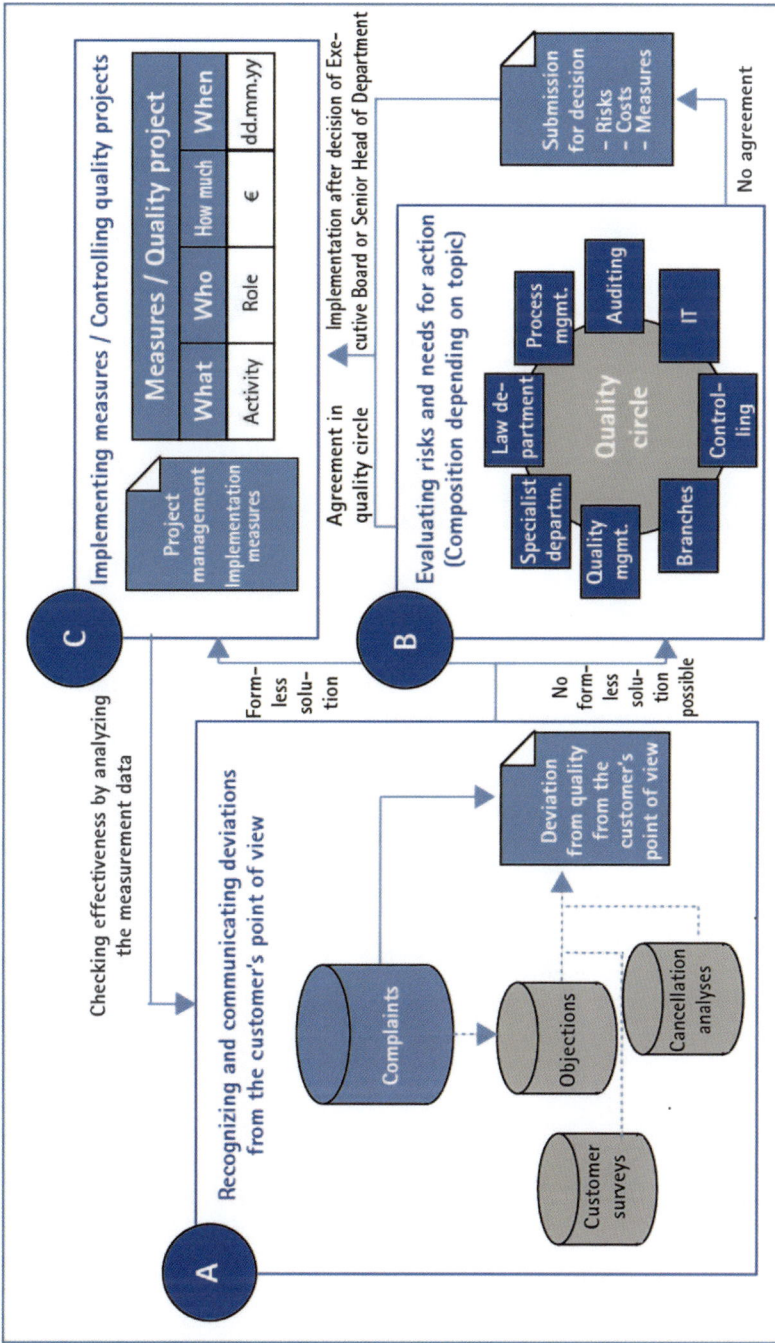

Fig. 13.7 The use of complaint information as a starting point for a pragmatic quality cycle

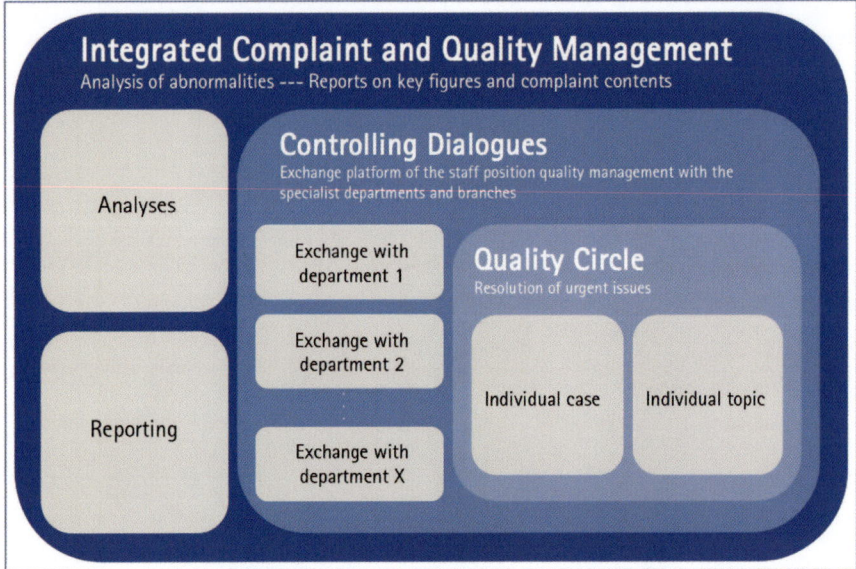

Fig. 13.8 Integrated complaint and quality management

13.3   Customer Panels with Complainants as an Instrument of Quality Improvement

Quality improvement teams and quality circles are forms of teamwork in which the creative potential of employees is used to arrive at solutions for problems. Another approach is to enlist the complainants themselves in developing these solutions.

Customer panels are an important instrument in this process. In the following section, the basic value of customer panels with complainants will be discussed first (Sect. 13.3.1). Subsequently, it will be shown how the creative potential of customers can be increased through the use of specific methods in customer panels (Sect. 13.3.2). In a third section, the advantages and disadvantages that result when the dialog with complainants takes place in virtual customer panels (online customer focus groups) will be demonstrated (Sect. 13.3.3).

13.3.1 General Goals of Customer Panels with Complainants

Customer panels—also known as customer conferences or customer focus groups— are group discussions with a circle of selected customers with whom *certain topics related to the business relationship* are *discussed* in detail.

Basically, customer panels are established in pursuit of the following goals:

- Gaining *deeper insights* into the desires, motives and assessments of customers
- Identifying *spontaneously* expressed criticism and suggestions for improvement
- Achieving a *greater understanding* of problems observed in the provider's behavior from the customer's point of view
- *Signaling* customer orientation
- *Enhancing* customer retention
- *Sensitizing* employees to customer concerns and supporting efforts directed toward customer-oriented change in the firm.

Experience shows that these goals can for the most part be reached when customer panels are used professionally. The group discussions give customers the opportunity to present their perspectives extensively. They are also stimulated by the contributions of other participants to reflect on their desires and to evaluate their experiences, so that the information gain is greater than it is in individual interviews, due to the *group dynamic*.

The opportunity to have an extensive discussion of the problems often makes it possible to obtain not only *detailed information about the problems observed*, but also about the *causes of the problems* and the *dynamic of annoyance in the customer's experience process*. In this way, valuable indications as to possible corrective actions and new solutions can be extracted.

This effect is particularly to be expected when *complainants* are invited to the customer panels. Complainants have already taken a critical look at the problem in their minds and frequently have developed ideas for alternative pathways. They prove, therefore, to be especially critical and valuable advisors. Customer panels thus not only have a *complaint stimulating function*, but also can be regarded as an important instrument for *using the creative potential* of customers in the improvement process.

13.3.2   Use of Methods in Customer Panels

The stimulation of creative processes among customers begins, when *joint deliberations on problem solutions* are started with them after the actual and extensive phase of criticism. This can already occur by requesting that customers speak out about the changes they would like to see in the future and the steps the firm should take in their opinion. The suggestions must then be collected and logged by the moderator. Additionally, at the end of the session the participants may be requested to weight the different suggestions in terms of their preferences.

An alternative to having this rather intuitive type of conversation in customer panels is to apply *simple creativity and planning techniques* for the generation of proposed solutions, which does, however, require adequate skill on the part of the moderator.

The first technique is the application of *brainstorming*, which usually produces a variety of ideas within a short period of time if specific rules are observed. Principal among these are the following:

- Criticism is *ruled out*. Adverse judgment of ideas must be withheld until later.
- *"Free-wheeling"* is welcomed. The wilder the idea, the better; it is easier to tame down than to think up.
- *Quantity* is wanted. The greater the number of ideas, the higher the likelihood of useful ideas.
- *Combination* and *improvement* of ideas are sought. In addition to contributing ideas of their own, participants should suggest how ideas of others can be turned into better ideas; or how two or more ideas can be joined into still another idea.

Sympathizing with the customer's experience once more during the group discussion and making it the cause for reflecting on new ideas can also stimulate the generation of creative ideas. This can take place with the aid of the *Sequential Incident Technique for Innovations (SITI)*, which itself is especially designed for extracting ideas for improvements in services or in the complaint process.

When using a service (e.g. that of a hotel), customers go through a sequence of individual episodes at a variety of contact points (e.g. arrival, check-in, stay in the room, restaurant visit, check-out). Their quality perceptions thus consist of a series of partial experiences. Quality perception takes place at each contact point, and the quality impression at the end of a transaction is the result of a cumulative process of perception. The *Sequential Incident Technique* takes this circumstance into account and has as its aim the collection of customers' positive and negative quality experiences on the basis of a visualized customer pathway in personal interviews. The basis and the main component of the method is the determination of the path customers typically take in using a service, as well as its graphical representation in a customer path or blueprint (Shostack 1987; Boughnim and Yannou 2005; Bitner et al. 2007; Zeithaml et al. 2017). On this basis, the customers are then requested to go through the process of the service experience in their minds and to describe the individual contact situations in detail (Stauss and Weinlich 1997).

This process can very reasonably be applied to customer panels and simultaneously developed further—with respect to exploiting the customer's creativity—into a *Sequential Incident Technique for Innovations (SITI)*. Decker and Meißner (1999) demonstrated this with an *example* of customer panels in car dealerships. In these panels, initially the typical customer path taken in having a car repaired was developed. The customers were not solely requested to describe their respective experiences with regard to each episode (for example, making an appointment, driving onto the premises, conversing with the customer service employee). In addition, they were asked to reflect on possible improvements or to describe whether they had noticed superior solutions in the case of other providers—even in different sectors. The result showed that customers are in an excellent position to make a number of very specific suggestions for improvement.

The application of these methods in customer panels with complainants is suitable above all for situations in which customers who have experienced their problems during a *similar customer process* are invited. This principle applies to a majority of purchase and service processes. In addition, the direct complaint management process experienced by the customer can itself be made the subject of the discussion when it is intended to improve this process and to increase the complaint satisfaction of the customer.

For this type of *application of the SITI* to the direct management process in the context of customer panels, one should proceed as follows (see Fig. 13.9):

- The complainants invited are each initially requested to list the *individual contact points* in the course of a normal service transaction with the firm in *chronological order.*
- In the joint discussion, the progression of a *typical customer path* is recorded and visualized.
- Based on this customer path, the customers describe what they experienced at each point and *evaluate* the experience they had.
- Finally, *suggestions for improvement* are developed and recorded for each contact point on the customer path.

The use of methods such as these not only improves the chances of using the creative potential of customers, but it also signals *the firm's earnest desire to learn from the customer.* As a rule, this even increases the willingness of very critical customers to work constructively with the firm after they articulate their criticism. In doing so, a sense of community actually develops in many cases during the discussion of the problem and the possible solutions, which includes not only the customer group, but also the employees and the firm collectively. One experiences the community of the efforts toward improvements for the customer, which stresses the firm's proximity to its customers and contributes to the development of a true customer relationship.

Customer panels thus have not only external functions directed toward customers, but also *internal functions.* The participation of employees gives them an immediate impression of the perceived quality experience of customers. Even employees that otherwise have no contact with customers now receive the complaint information directly, rather than in aggregate form and as a written document. In this way, they are directly confronted with the customers' opinion and trained by the customers themselves with respect to customer-oriented behavior. With adequate preparation and post-processing, customer panels thus represent an essential instrument of *employee coaching* and of *organizational change* toward customer orientation.

13.3.3 Virtual Customer Panels with Complainants: Online Focus Groups

The Internet has made new forms of customer dialog available. Among these is the possibility of hosting customer panels *virtually as chats (online focus groups)*, rather than in person (Sterne 2000; Reid and Reid 2005; Abrams and Gaiser 2017; Stewart and Shamdasani 2017).

Similar to the approach taken in "traditional" face-to-face customer panels, complainants are requested to participate in a dialog; this dialog, however, takes

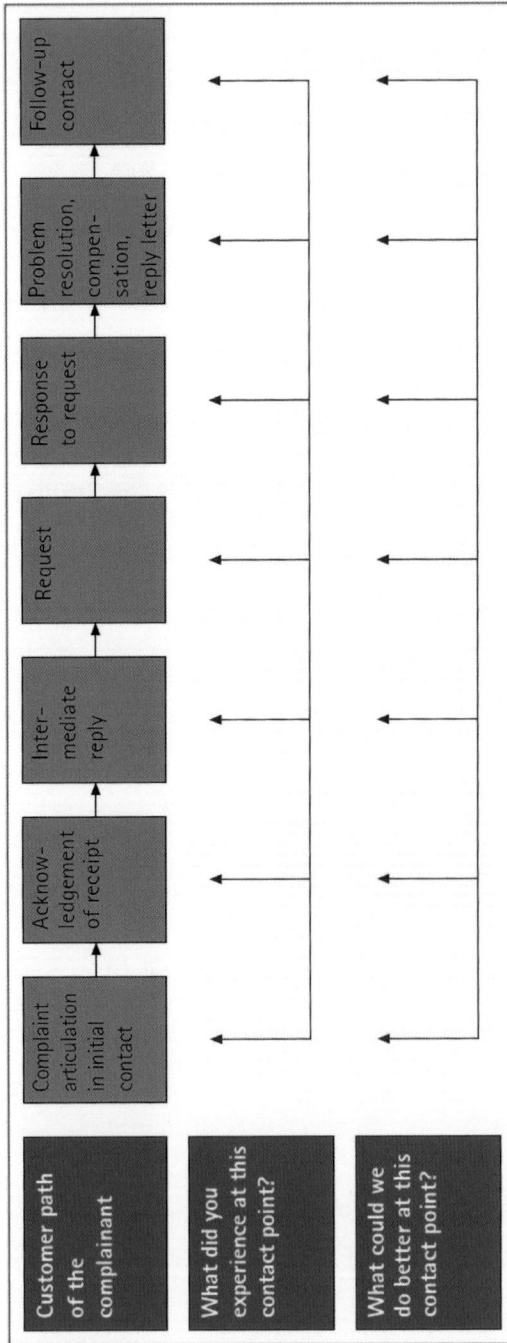

Fig. 13.9 The application of the Sequential Incident Technique for Innovations (SITI) to the direct complaint management process

place over the Internet and mostly in written—not in verbal—form. The participants interact with one another and with a moderator by sending and receiving messages. The following *sequence of events* is typical.

After logging in with the previously disclosed password, the participants arrive in the chat room. This is followed by an orientation phase, in which the participants are introduced to each other and may be asked by the moderator for a contribution. In the subsequent *discussion phase*, the moderator and the participants enter their contributions in the designated fields and these appear immediately on the screen, where the discussion process is recorded visibly for all to see. Participants can react spontaneously to the published messages. In the *final phase*, the moderator ends the discussion.

The *moderator* can direct the discussion in a number of ways. He/she can copy prepared questions from a text file. A *"whisper mode"* allows him/her to address individual participants without the other participants noticing, for example, in order to ask that dominant participants restrain themselves. *Live links* to other websites and the transmission of multimedia data files are also possible during the discussion. Since the time and sender of each answer and of the links to external sources are recorded, the entire chronicle of the customer panel is available as a *transcript* immediately after the conclusion of the "round of talks".

Compared to traditional focus groups, virtual focus groups have a number of *advantages* (Abrams and Gaiser 2017; Stewart and Shamdasani 2017). Participants can be recruited from a wider geographical spectrum and it is possible to form groups over a longer period of time instead of meeting once, as is usually the case with face-to-face groups. The participants do not spend a long time with the social processes of getting to know one another and exchanging pleasantries. They devote more time to the answer and give answers that are more thought-out. The greater anonymity of the situation also appears to promote a frank articulation of opinions. In this way, both the participants and the firm can realize significant savings in time and costs. Another advantage for the firm in terms of time and costs is the fact that the content of the dialog is immediately available as a data file and can be directly analyzed and entered in the customer database.

Nevertheless, these advantages are also somewhat balanced out by several *disadvantages*. The moderator and participating observers from the firm only have access to the written messages. Forms of nonverbal communication that can be observed in the context of traditional customer panels are not visible, which means that a related information loss is incurred. Moreover, the information exchange proceeds in a more controlled and less spontaneous fashion.

The use of customer panels with complainants shows, however, that even this less elaborate version of feedback is a good *instrument of information utilization*. The participating complainants give detailed information about their experiences and their ideas with regard to improvements. At the same time, they see the opportunity they are offered for feedback and cooperation as an expression of the firm's interest and appreciation, so that retention effects can be expected. This holds true even more when the firm informs them at a later time as to how the information has been used internally.

13.4   The Integration of Complaint and Complaint Management Information in Customer Knowledge Management

By knowledge management we mean the *targeted design of knowledge processes* in the firm. Knowledge is regarded as the central organizational resource. Therefore, one of the fundamental goals of managing this resource is to identify and to acquire relevant knowledge, to retain and to expand it within the firm, to make it available to the respective users in the firm and to ensure that it is used to add value (Davenport and Prusak 2000; Dalkir 2011; Hislop 2013). In this way, the company should gain learning ability, flexibility and capacity for innovation and realize competitive advantages on the market.

An analysis of the current discussion shows, however, a *strange reduction of the problem.* Although the knowledge should primarily be used to develop marketable—that is, customer-suited—products, customer-oriented knowledge is by no means the focus of consideration, and the importance of complaint information is underestimated in customer knowledge management.

Basically, *three forms of customer knowledge* can be distinguished: Knowledge about the customer, knowledge of the customer and knowledge for the customer.

Knowledge about the customer is the customer-oriented knowledge that is at the firm's disposal. This knowledge comes from information available within the firm that describes the customer, and represents the fundamental basis for individualized one-to-one marketing measures. Included here is information about the industry or legal structure of the company in the case of business-to-business customers, or key data such as age or gender in the case of end customers. In addition to this information, there is knowledge of the available product spectrum, the purchase history or the purchase times. Other areas include the customized actions of the firm, as well as the related customer reactions that are reflected in, among other things, customer sales and profit contributions.

In the case of *knowledge of the customer*, it is not the firm, but rather the customer, that is the knowledge carrier. Customers are experts with respect to themselves, their goals and strategies, their expectations and interests. In addition, customers have at their disposal knowledge concerning their experiences with the firm's product range and thus have clear ideas of strengths and weaknesses. As customers often have experience with competitive offerings, they are also able to compare the company's products and services with alternatives on the market. They also know how they have experienced the product emotionally and cognitively and the steps they want to take in their future purchase behavior. This knowledge of the customer can only become knowledge about the customer by means of targeted information procurement.

In the case of *knowledge for the customer*, the customer is the addressee of the knowledge. Knowledge is supplied in the firm with regard to the customer's knowledge deficits. The corresponding deficits may exist from the customer's and/or the firm's perspective:

A *knowledge deficit from the customers' point of view* exists when they believe they lack the knowledge to achieve their goals. This is the case, for example, when they lack information regarding the conditions of use and side effects of medications. A *customer knowledge deficit from the firm's point of view* exists when the customers' lack of knowledge results in the fact that corporate goals are jeopardized. As an example of this, we would refer to the dissatisfaction of a customer that is based on lack of knowledge about performance components or user instructions.

The *task of customer knowledge management* is then to collect the knowledge of the customer; to store, distribute and make the knowledge about the customer accessible for use within the firm; to identify the customer's knowledge deficits and to develop, provide and communicate knowledge for the customer. Since these tasks are not independent of one another, but rather represent steps in a continual process, we can also speak of a *customer knowledge management cycle* (Stauss 2002). Complaint information is extraordinarily important in this cycle (see Fig. 13.10).

Complaints contain a wealth of indications as to the *knowledge of the customer* that otherwise would not be available to the firm in this way. In complaints, customers provide details about their product-related experiences, the problems

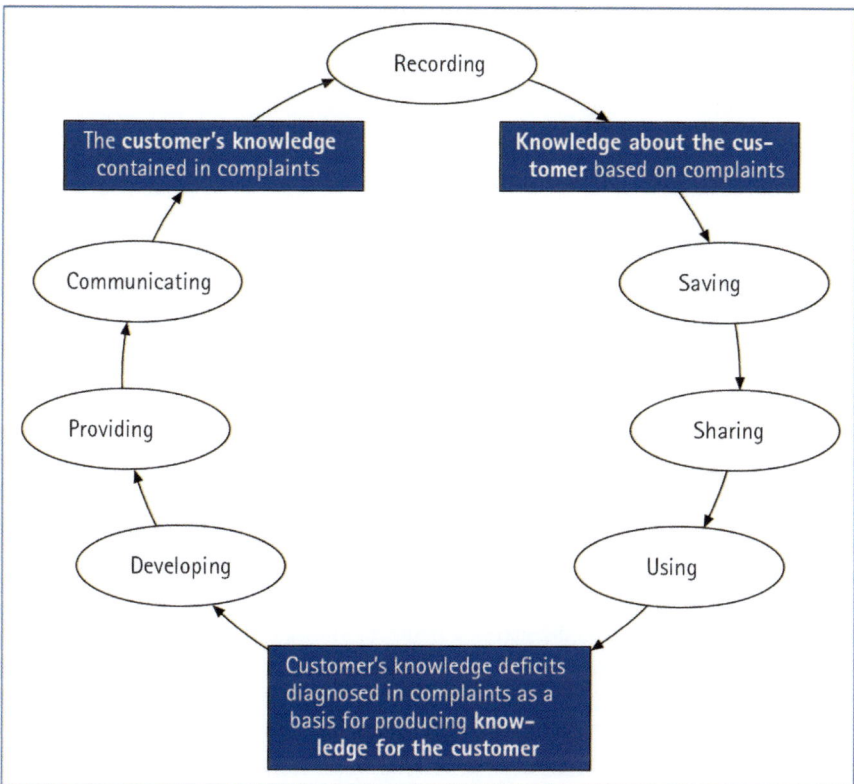

Fig. 13.10 Complaint information as essential part of the customer knowledge management cycle (based on Stauss 2002, p. 281)

they observe, their disappointed expectations, their desires for the firm and their future intended behavior. An essential task of complaint acceptance is, therefore, to *document* the information contained in complaints and *to store it as knowledge about the customer*. It is not only a matter of putting the complaint case itself into the customer database and make it part of the customer's contact history. In addition to this, the added knowledge generated in the context of complaint analysis and Cause-and-Effect Analysis must be likewise documented and archived. The *distribution and use of knowledge about the customer* takes place on the one hand in the context of complaint reporting, and on the other hand due to the fact that via the intranet and media such as "electronic yellow pages", integration of complaint information into the customer knowledge management system can take place. To achieve this integration, it is also necessary to *link* complaint information with the customer-related information available in marketing and sales, logistics and customer service as well as research and development.

Recording the indications of *customer knowledge deficits* that are contained in complaints is also part of complaint analysis. Many problems arise because customers do not feel that they are sufficiently informed, because corporate sources of information are unavailable or unknown or because the information is processed in such a way that it is not understood or used by the customer. For this reason, *complaints* represent one of the most important sources for the generation of *knowledge for the customer*. They provide specific assistance when it is important to develop knowledge for the customer with regard to content or to supply or communicate this knowledge via appropriate media.

The development of knowledge must occur in such a way that the contents precisely match the knowledge requirement of the target group and that the channels of communication are carefully aligned with the acceptance behavior and the media preferences of the customers. In terms of communication, the firm basically has *two options* available, namely the supply or the active communication of knowledge. The criterion for this differentiation is whether the firm or the customer takes the initiative for transporting the knowledge. *Knowledge supply* requires that the customers display initiative in order to attain the knowledge they desire; *knowledge communication* describes the initiative of the firm in closing the customers' unwanted knowledge gaps via active measures.

Complaint management is given a *key position* here. As an *expert on customer concerns*, it has the best information regarding the customers' perceived knowledge deficits at its disposal. Moreover, it is—especially when a customer care center is available to customers as a communication interface—also immediately in a position to close knowledge gaps on the part of customers during direct contact with them. A requirement for an adequate supply of relevant knowledge for customers is, however, that complaint management constantly discloses knowledge deficits and makes specific suggestions for reducing them. Furthermore, it must not only have direct access to customer databases, but also to expert or case-based reasoning (CBR) systems that are able to suggest problem solutions for current questions on the basis of analogous cases from the past (Richter and Weber 2013).

In many firms, customer knowledge management is *not yet a reality*. In the case of future implementations, complaint management will have to see to it that the importance of complaints in the extraction and use of customer knowledge is recognized and taken into account in the configuration of the system.

Chapter 13 in Brief

- With the help of cause-and-effect analysis and failure mode and effect analysis (FMEA) the causes of the problems mentioned in complaints can be systematically investigated and correction processes can be initiated.
- Proposals to eliminate the causes of problems should be developed in quality improvement teams and quality circles in order to exploit the competence and creativity of different experts.
- In order to involve the dissatisfied customers in the development of problem solutions, face-to-face or online focus groups with complainants can be set up.
- With complaint information, companies can refine their knowledge about the customer and increase their awareness of the customers' knowledge or knowledge deficits. For this reason, complaint and complaint management information must be integrated into corporate customer knowledge management.

References

Abrams KM, Gaiser TJ (2017) Online focus groups. In: Fielding NG et al (eds) The Sage handbook of online research methods, 2nd edn. Sage, London, pp 435–450

Bitner MJ et al (2007) Service blueprinting: a practical technique for service innovation, Working Paper. Center for Services Leadership, Arizona State University, Phoenix, AZ

Boughnim N, Yannou, B (2005) Using blueprinting method for developing product-service systems. In: Paper presented at the 15th international conference of engineering Design (ICED), Melbourne, Australia, 15–18 Aug 2005

Carlson CS (2012) Effective FMEAs: achieving safe, reliable, and economical products and processes using Failure Mode and Effect Analysis. Wiley, Hoboken, NJ

Dalkir K (2011) Knowledge management in theory and practice. MIT Press, Cambridge, MA

Davenport TH, Prusak L (2000) Working knowledge. Harvard Business School Press, Boston, MA

Decker A, Meißner H (1999) The Sequential Incident Technique for Innovations (SITI): a tool for generating improvements and ideas in service processes. In: Kunst P et al (eds) Service quality and management. Deutscher Universitäts-Verlag, Wiesbaden, pp 203–222

Gierl H (2000) Beschwerdemanagement als Bestandteil des Qualitätsmanagements. In: Helm R, Pasch H (eds) Kundenorientierung durch Qualitätsmanagement. Deutscher Fachverlag, Frankfurt/Main, pp 149–189

Hislop D (2013) Knowledge management in organizations: a critical introduction, 3rd edn. Oxford University Press, Oxford

McDermott RE et al (2009) The basics of FMEA, 3rd edn. Productivity Press, New York, NY

Reid DJ, Reid FMJ (2005) Online focus groups: an in-depth comparison of computer-mediated and conventional focus group discussions. Int J Mark Res 47(2):131–162

Richter MM, Weber RO (2013) Cased-based reasoning: a textbook. Springer, Berlin

Ruß T (1999) Qualitätsmanagement in der Bankunternehmung. Peter Lang Verlag, Frankfurt

Shostack GL (1987) Service positioning through structural change. J Mark 51(1):34–43

Stauss B (2002) Kundenwissens-Management (Customer Knowledge Management). In: Böhler H (ed) Marketing-Management und Unternehmensführung. Schäffer Poeschel, Stuttgart, pp 273–295

Stauss B, Weinlich B (1997) Process-oriented measurement of service quality: applying the sequential incident technique. Eur J Mark 31(1):33–55

Sterne J (2000) Customer service on the Internet, 2nd edn. Wiley, New York, NY

Stewart DW, Shamdasani P (2017) Online focus groups. J Advert 46(1):48–60

Tague NR (2005) The quality toolbox, 2nd edn. ASQ Quality Press, Milwaukee, WI

Zeithaml VA et al (2017) Services marketing. McGraw-Hill Education, New York, NY

Human Resource Aspects of Complaint Management

14

© Springer Nature Switzerland AG 2019

361

B. Stauss, W. Seidel, *Effective Complaint Management*, Management for Professionals,
https://doi.org/10.1007/978-3-319-98705-7_14

14.1   The Importance of Employee Behavior in Complaint Contact

The way employees react to customers' complaints plays a significant role in whether customers feel that they are being taken seriously, whether an consensual solution can be reached and whether complaint satisfaction is created. Practical experience shows that extreme customer irritation often arises *in the complaint acceptance and reaction process itself*: "Angry customers are created by the firm itself" (Blanding 1991, p. 94). The majority of customers state their concerns calmly and constructively; however, when they are simply turned away, put off with false information or constantly transferred to other departments within the firm, then irritation and anger are the results. The following example from corporate practice confirms this:

The manager of the R&D department of a large pharmaceutical corporation—chemist, prototype of the rational thinking man—orders an analysis device from a well-known manufacturer. About 3 months later, the device fails. But the defect is only due to a little part worth around three dollars. After sending a claim to the manufacturer, a letter comes back from the responsible engineer. In this letter, the engineer blames the researcher for not using the device properly and states that therefore his company is not responsible for the defect. The following return letter stays unanswered. Instead, three experts of the manufacturer behave arrogantly and insensitively in three subsequent telephone conversations. That is the last straw for the researcher. He gives the instruction, never to buy from this particular manufacturer again. Since then, 10 years have passed and the decision remained final (Scheerer 1994, p. 10).

A *study* by Bitner et al. (1990) provides additional insights into the relevance of the right employee response in problem situations. In their survey, they asked customers of hotels, restaurants and airlines about "critical incidents", i.e. service experiences that they had found to be extraordinarily positive or negative. The majority of the negative experiences (42.9%), which customers had kept in mind for a long time and which they recounted over and over, could be assigned to the category *"Employee response to service delivery system failures"*. A problem had occurred (a reserved hotel room was not available, the flight was unpunctual, etc.) and in this situation the respondents reacted wrongly. They gave no explanation, did not apologize, offered no compensation or even gave pathetic answers. On the other hand, almost a quarter (23.3%) of positive stories belonged to the same category. In this problematic situation, employees reacted sensitively and in a customer-oriented manner. They offered an apology, gave sufficient information, showed they were making a personal effort to eliminate the problem or at least to improve the situation of the customers as far as possible. This is an astonishing result: although a failure in the core service was the starting point of the narrated story, the experience is judged to be extraordinarily positive if employees behave properly. This impressively underlines the widely documented experience that customers tolerate the occurrence of problems—within certain limits—but react with great dissatisfaction if they are not heard.

Not only must the employees in customer care departments be aware of this, but also *all employees in contact with customers*, because the majority of complaints will be articulated to them. Only a proportion of customer dissatisfaction is reflected in written complaints. A large part of the criticism is brought forward personally—for instance, to salespeople or to other customer-contact employees. Only a few complainants who are not satisfied with the results of the first encounter demand to speak with a manager. Letters to the board of directors, the CEO or corporate headquarters are comparatively rare. Articulations to third-party institutions (consumer organizations, media, government agencies) represent the absolute exception. Usually, this method is only chosen when all other efforts have been in vain.

In view of these insights, the *central importance of customer-contact employees* for the implementation of active complaint management becomes clear:

- They have direct contact with customers who complain and thus the *first opportunity* to reduce dissatisfaction.
- They can potentially bring about an immediate solution to the problem and thus in many cases ensure especially *rapid and cost-effective processing*.
- They have an important function in accepting information about customer problems that are not made the *subject of written complaints*.
- In addition, they can significantly ease processing, solution and analysis by recording *additional information* (about the complaint case or the solution desired by customers).

Therefore, an *essential task of human resource management* is to prepare all customer-contact employees for complaint situations and provide them with the skills necessary for successfully coping with these contacts.

14.2 Necessary Employee Skills

The attributes that complainants use to evaluate the firm's reaction and determine significantly their complaint satisfaction provide important indications as to the skills that should be demanded of complaint-contact employees. Generally, what customers expect from the firm is a high degree of accessibility, friendliness/politeness, empathy/understanding, effort/helpfulness, activity/initiative, reliability, reaction speed and appropriateness/fairness of the solution offered. Accordingly, in the specific complaint situation, they must observe employee behavior that can be characterized by these attributes. There are, however, *essential requirements* that must be fulfilled so that employees will be able to display this behavior. First, employees must possess the adequate motivation toward service orientation, as well as social, emotional and professional competence. Second, using internal marketing measures, the firm must see to it that employees with appropriate skills are attracted and retained, and that employees are able to strengthen their competencies. Through these measures and the goal-oriented design of the corporate culture and the infrastructure, the firm must further guarantee that employees actually translate their skills into corresponding behavior. Figure 14.1 presents an overview of the relationships among the complainants' expectations, the necessary employee behavior and qualification, and the executives' tasks to design the general corporate conditions and to apply internal marketing instruments.

14.2.1 Service Orientation as the Basic Motivation

The basic requirement for any successful action by service-contact employees is distinct service orientation. What is meant here is the fundamental willingness to be a problem solver for customers and the desire to serve them (Coenen 2001, 2005; Cherbakov et al. 2005; Lytle and Timmerman 2006).

Service orientation has two motivational roots—motivation to help and achievement motivation. *Motivation to help* includes the desire and the willingness to take care of customers' problems. *Achievement motivation* refers to an inner drive to fulfill a task in an excellent way, to be involved and to learn in order to be able to meet the requirements even better in the future. In this sense, *service orientation* is the motivation to be a problem solver for customers to the best of one's ability and to serve them in an excellent way. Only employees who display this service orientation are also prepared to use their skills to find the best possible solution to the complaining customer's problem.

14.2.2 Social Competence

Social competence is the ability to pursue one's own goals during the interaction process, while also taking into account the goals of one's interaction partner. This type of competence primarily includes the abilities *to observe and to assess* the partner, the situation and one's own possible actions *correctly*. Employees who speak with complainants must be able to put themselves in the customers' place and to relate to their view of the situation. In addition, employees must keep an eye on the complaint situation and recognize factors that would have a disturbing influence, in order to be able to reduce or eliminate them. It is also necessary that they correctly recognize the impact of their own behavior on their conversation partners—that is, correctly pick up on the words, gestures and measures that would have a calming

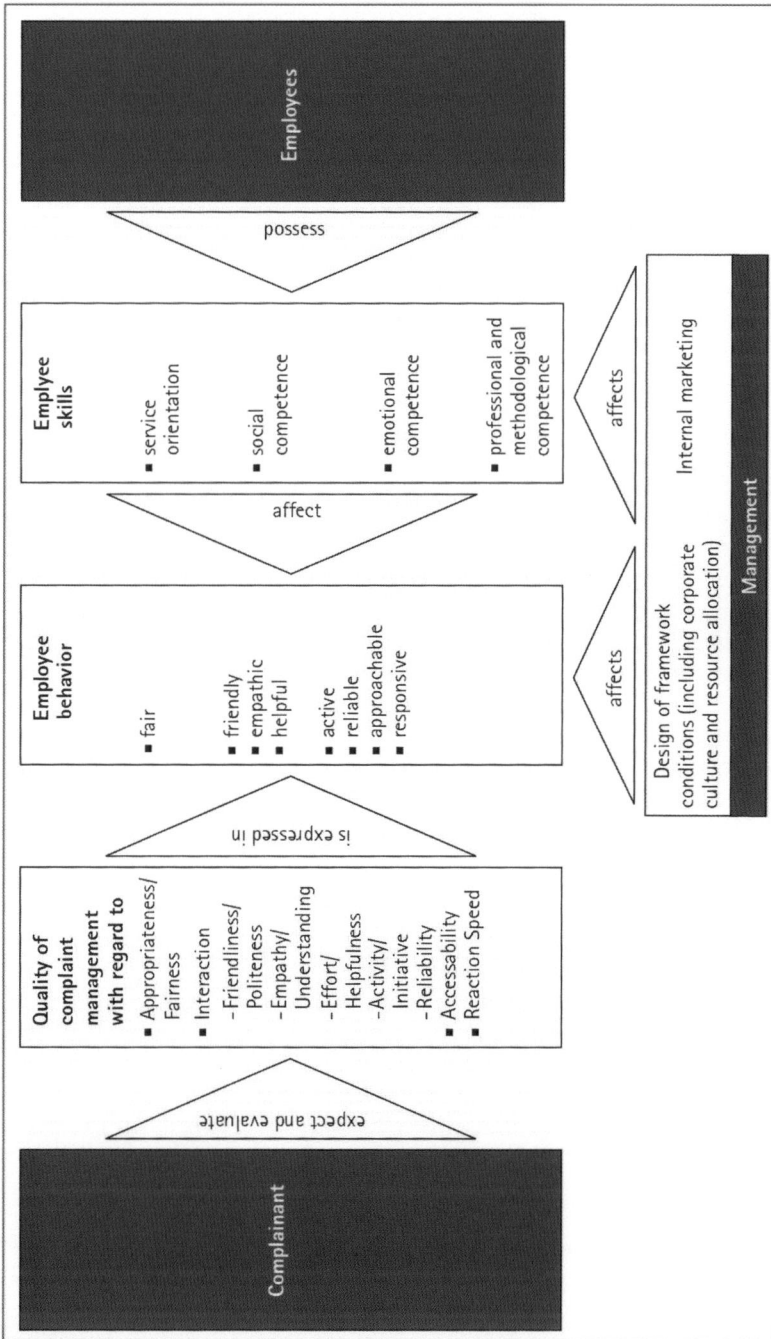

Fig. 14.1 Model of appropriate employee behavior in the complaint situation

effect on customers, or those that would annoy them even further. In order to be able to draw the right conclusions from these perceptions and act as a conflict solver, however, it is also necessary that employees possess *sophisticated communication abilities* (Fontana 1990). Only with the correct use of verbal and nonverbal instruments—such as wording, tone, facial expression and gestures—is the employee's social competence noticeable to and effective for the partner. A broader understanding of social competence also includes additional key skills such as *flexibility* and *creativity*, which permit employees to act in a way that is appropriate to the situation and fair to customers—that is, to be prepared for customers' different expectations and to develop problem solutions that correspond to those expectations.

14.2.3 Emotional Competence

To a certain extent, customers who complain experience strong negative emotions. They feel harmed and hurt, are annoyed and angry. These negative emotions are partly expressed by the type of complaint articulation, when customers "let off steam". But even when they express their concerns in a more composed manner customers are negatively affected. For this reason, dealing with complainants demands that employees perform not only a technically defined task, but also *"emotional labor"* at a particularly high level. Emotional labor is the modulation and control of feelings by service-contact employees with the goal of evoking those specific emotions that are desired by the firm and/or the customers (Guy 2008; Hochschild 2012).

Regarding the ability to fulfill these requirements, it is frequently referred to the concept of *"emotional intelligence"*, which means the ability of a person to perceive and express feelings, to comprehend and control their impact and consciously to influence them in oneself and in others. Goleman's publications in particular have made this concept known to a broad public (Goleman 1998, 2005; Goleman et al. 2013). He distinguishes five dimensions of emotional intelligence.

Two of these relate to interpersonal skills in dealing with other people:

- *Empathy:* the ability to understand the emotions of other people and take them into account when making decisions.
- *Social skill:* proficiency in managing relationships and building networks.

Three dimensions concern social self-management:

- *Self-awareness:* the ability to understand one's emotions, strengths, weaknesses, values and goals as well as their impact on others,
- *Self-regulation:* the ability to control or redirect one's disruptive impulses and moods,
- *Motivation:* the passion to work for reasons that go beyond money or status.

The interpersonal skills have already been taken into account in the context of social competence and the motivational dimension in the service orientation construct. For this reason, we will focus here only on the remaining "intrapersonal" competencies of self-awareness and self-regulation. They are summarized under the term *emotional competence*.

To a great extent, complaint-contact employees must perform emotional labor in the sense of *managing their own emotions, as well as the emotions of others*. They have to use their emotions to satisfactorily demonstrate empathy. They must be in a position to influence customers' emotional sensitivity—to reduce their annoyance, for example, and to put them at ease. This requires that employees be capable of emotional self-perception and able to influence the interaction systematically by employing their own feelings (Cook 2012). A high degree of emotional self-control is also required, so that they will not react aggressively to unjustified criticism, for instance, thus making the situation worse. It is exactly this emotional self-control that in many cases represents an especially high mental burden for the employee.

14.2.4 Professional and Methodological Competence

In the specific situation of complaint acceptance, the service orientation and the social and emotional competence of the employee accepting the complaint are indeed particularly critical. Nevertheless, an efficient and satisfactory solution will not be reached if employees do not also have the necessary *professional and methodological competence*. In order to be able to record the complaint contents precisely, employees must know which information to collect and in what way, and how the internal complaint processing procedures are organized. Moreover, precise knowledge of the products in question is necessary for accepting and processing complaints. Broader and more sophisticated professional and methodological competencies are required when the overall spectrum of complaint management tasks is taken into consideration. Employees in the customer care department must, for example, have detailed knowledge of the software that is being used, a good command of internal processes and methodological knowledge of complaint analysis, as well as be able to implement processes of complaint-management controlling.

Figure 14.2 provides a summary view of the requirements for employees in complaint management and reveals the *range of necessary skills*. It should be remembered that individual skills frequently encompass a whole array of requirements. Communication ability, for example, includes the ability to express oneself in a language that is appropriate to the addressee, to gather the necessary information using techniques of questioning and analytical reasoning, etc. The figure also shows that service orientation and social and emotional competence skills are more urgent, the more employees are occupied with tasks of direct complaint management—that is, the more they have direct contact with customers. In contrast, the proportion of professional and methodological competence required grows with respect to tasks of indirect complaint management, which in essence demand that methods be implemented within the firm. This should, however, only be understood as a rough assignment. Without professional competence, social and emotional

```
┌─────────────────────────────────────────────────────────────────────┐
│                        Service Orientation                            │
├───────────────────────────────────┬───────────────────────────────────┤
│ Professional and methodological    │    Social and emotional           │
│ competence                         │    competence                     │
├───────────────────────────────────┼───────────────────────────────────┤
│ • Expertise regarding the main     │ • Sensitivity                     │
│   features of complaint behavior   │ • Communication skills            │
│ • Knowledge of guidelines          │ • Flexibility and creativity      │
│ • Proficiency in communication     │ • Emotional self-awareness        │
│   techniques                       │ • Emotional self-control          │
│ • Knowledge of complaint processing│ • Coping with critisism           │
│   procedures and their steps       │ • Conflict resolution skills      │
│ • Proficiency in complaint         │ • Coping with pressure            │
│   management software              │                                   │
│ • Methodological skills regarding  │                                   │
│   complaint analysis and complaint │                                   │
│   management controlling           │                                   │
└───────────────────────────────────┴───────────────────────────────────┘
```

Direct complaint management process

Complaint stimulation → Complaint acceptance

Complaint processing → Complaint reaction

Complaint evaluation → Complaint management controlling

Complaint reporting → Complaint information utilization

Indirect complaint management process

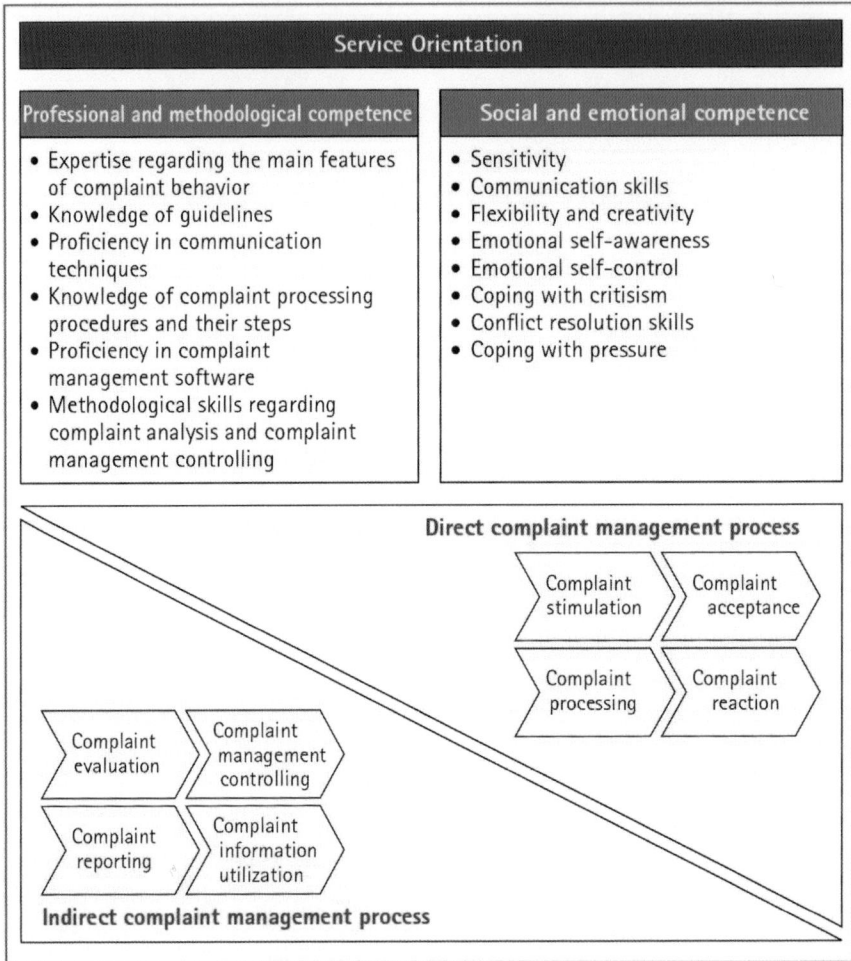

Fig. 14.2 Essential qualifications of employees for complaint management

competence do not lead to successful conduct, and even the highest professional and methodological competence of internal employees will not lead to the desired result if these employees are unable to configure the interactions with their internal partners in a socially and emotionally competent fashion.

14.3 Personnel-Oriented Internal Marketing as a Concept for Securing the Required Employee Skills

Fully aware of the fact that the quality perception of service customers is substantially determined by the behavior of service-contact employees, service firms have generally come to believe that customer-contact employees are a key internal customer group whose skills should be designed in a systematic manner. In order to highlight the similarity of this task to external marketing, we speak of internal marketing. The application of the internal marketing concept aims to ensure that employees conduct themselves in such a way that customers are acquired, satisfied and retained (Berry and Parasuraman 1992; Stauss 2000; Ahmed and Rafiq 2003). The target groups of *internal marketing* in the context of complaint management are managers and employees of all hierarchical levels on the one hand, and employees that are occupied specifically with complaint management tasks, particularly complaint acceptance, on the other hand.

First of all, *employees at all hierarchical levels*—that is, primarily also top management—must be convinced of the fact that complaints contain business opportunities and are not to be interpreted as dangers to be averted. This basic message should be disseminated via different instruments of internal communication. What is even more important, however, is that it is effectively supported and authenticated through an appropriate corporate culture, consistent actions and an appropriate incentive structure.

The introduction of professional complaint management is commonly associated with difficult learning processes, especially in the case of *managers*. They must

- be able to *acknowledge their own mistakes*
- make the importance of complaints clear by scheduling *personal management time* for reading and answering of complaint letters
- prove on an everyday basis that they are not interested primarily in naming culprits, but in *analyzing the causes of problems and developing solutions to those problems*
- *give employees responsibility* and *grant* them *decision-making autho*rity
- correct employees who made a mistake in their efforts to find a customer-oriented solution and help them with their future behavior, but *not "punish" t*hem
- *honor* exemplary reactions to customer complaints.

Learning processes such as these should be initiated and promoted with the aid of information, feedback and behavioral training.

For the personnel of the *complaint management department*, the goal of personnel-oriented internal marketing is to attract, develop and retain service-oriented employees for the firm—employees who demonstrate a high degree of service orientation, as well as emotional, professional and methodological competence, and thus are willing and able to fulfill the goals of complaint management and the expectations of complaining customers in the best possible way.

The entire *array of measures* that can help to influence the service orientation, the various skills and the behavior of employees are available for use as instruments of personnel-oriented marketing. In the following sections, we will address in more detail the instruments that are ascribed particular importance in the context of complaint management: the recruiting of service-oriented and qualified employees, employee communication and training, incentive systems, burnout prevention measures and empowerment.

14.3.1 Recruiting Service-Oriented and Qualified Employees

A fundamental goal of internal marketing is to select the most suitable candidates during the recruiting process. This requires a *systematic approach*, which in many cases is disregarded with respect to the recruiting of customer-contact employees. Special care is required when recruiting employees who will constantly be dealing with dissatisfied customers in customer care centers, for example, because the demands on the employee's social and emotional competence are especially high in these cases.

Among the crucial steps in a *systematic selection process* are task analysis, the resulting personal attributes analysis, the development and implementation of a selection system design strategy and the continuous validation of the recruiting process (Schneider and Schechter 1991).

In the context of *task analysis*, what is important is to describe in detail the specific tasks to be performed by the prospective employee. By surveying current employees and supervisors and by observing their work, the specific activities that applicants will have to perform in the future can be determined. For instance, for an *employee in a customer care center*, these activities may include the following:

• Greeting the customer in a friendly manner
• Asking questions designed to encourage the customer to describe the circumstances precisely
• Entering the complaint content and complaint processing information quickly and correctly in the system
• Calming distressed complainants
• Determining the solution desired by the customer
• Developing one's own suggestions for solutions
• Making independent decisions while keeping in mind both the customer's desire and the organizational rules
• Explaining to the customer the solution being offered
• Using the customer's name during the conversation
• Listening, accessing the available information in the database and entering new information during the conversation
• Initiating the appropriate processing procedure when an immediate solution is not possible
• Informing the customer as to the further procedures
• Thanking the customer and ending the conversation on a friendly note.

The insights from this task analysis form the basis for the *personal attributes analysis*—that is, the specific description of skills that employees must possess.

Basically, the approach is to ask employees and supervisors with appropriate experiences to indicate the characteristics that employees must possess in order to fulfill the requirements well, as far as the individual job tasks are concerned.

According to a study by Schneider and Schechter (1991, p. 223), a *specific telephone job with sales and service responsibilities* requires the following competencies:

- *Persuasion* = the ability to influence the opinions and attitudes of others through the skillful use of information.
- *Comprehension and memory* = the ability to understand the written and spoken language of others; skilled at listening; the ability to learn, understand and remember large amounts of facts, rules and procedures and codes.
- *Reasoning* = the ability to apply learned rules and procedures, use judgment, combine pieces and make decisions.
- *Social sensitivity* = the ability to act enthusiastically in interpersonal situations. Involves skillful adjusting of behavior to fit demands of a call and requires figuring out how others are likely to react. Involves the skillful use of control and assertion.
- *Understandability* = the ability to express oneself through written and/or spoken language so that others will understand.
- *Clerical speed and accuracy* = the ability to quickly and accurately look up, write down, and/or key in facts, codes, data, numbers and so forth that are heard, looked up, or already in memory.
- *Dealing with pressure* = the ability to act and react without losing effectiveness given the very strong requirements on rapid, efficient and courteous sales and service.

A list of characteristics generated in this manner must then be *evaluated in two respects*—first, with respect to the importance of the characteristics and second, with respect to the extent to which the employees must already possess these characteristics when they have their first day on the job.

Among the characteristics that *employees absolutely must possess when they are hired* are those that the employees must apply very quickly in order to fulfill their tasks and that are difficult to convey. Here, it is primarily the differing degrees of difficulty between conveying social and emotional competence, as compared to professional and methodological competence, that must be taken into account. Professional and methodological knowledge can be trained and learned much more easily when the employee possesses adequate apprehension than can basic aspects of social and emotional competence. Not least because of this reason, the American department store Nordstrom's basic principle when recruiting employees is that the important behavioral characteristics must be observed and technical deficits compensated for in on-the-job training: "Nordstrom hires the smile and trains the skill" (Spector and McCarthy 2000, p. 80).

If, based on the *assessment of the necessary characteristics*, the desired requirements are firmly established, the third step is to develop and implement *suitable selection methods*. The methods that should be regarded as suitable are those that measure the relevant characteristics, that can be easily applied by the selection team and that are insightful from the applicants' perspective with regard to their importance in the workplace.

For the characteristics of comprehension and memory, as well as understandability, speed and accuracy, which belong more to professional and methodological competencies, the firm should administer standardized *tests* that permit it to make a judgment as to the extent to which applicants possess the required cognitive abilities. In terms of the characteristics that are classified more under social and emotional competence, primarily interactive selection methods are suitable, which include interviews and work simulations. What is most important in the *interviews* is achieving clarity regarding the applicant's motivation, particularly the degree of service orientation. In *work simulations*, applicants are faced with a task whose accomplishment demands the required characteristics, without the applicants themselves having to be familiar with the specific job. Applicants are then confronted with a fictitious complainant on the telephone, for example, and are assigned the task of accepting the complaint, calming the caller down and correctly recording the circumstances in writing. In carrying out this task, the candidates obtain information about responsibilities, deadlines and decision rules. Using checklists, observers and evaluators can then perform an assessment of the applicant. Figure 14.3 shows an example of a checklist for the telephone contact and the written documentation of the complaint incident (Schneider and Schechter 1991).

Aided by methods such as these, the selection team is not dependent on the answers of applicants in the context of interviews, but rather can observe them in realistic scenarios in which they must actually apply the abilities relevant to the job.

Every recruiting process—to be developed on a firm-specific basis—must of course be *validated with regard to efficiency* on an ongoing basis. The combined implementation of three different methods is advisable here. Firstly, the firm must investigate the extent to which the recruited applicants actually fulfill the requirements as defined. For this purpose, supervisors should revaluate the employees after a certain period of time based on the criteria laid out when they were hired. Secondly, it makes sense to supplement the internal perspective with an external assessment from the customer's point of view. Analyses of customer satisfaction surveys, praise and complaint analyses and the use of professional testers, who monitor the observance of predefined standards as pseudo customers ("Silent Shoppers", "Mystery Callers"), are recommended here. Thirdly, it is a good idea to increase employee satisfaction and loyalty constantly, in order to have starting points for determining from the employees' perspective whether the general organizational conditions tend to encourage or to hinder them from applying their own skills in an appropriate fashion.

Behavioral characteristic	Indicator The candidate...	Evaluation true false
Comprehension and memory	... records all important aspects of the complaint incident	1 2 3 4 5
	... refers correctly to responsibilities, time standards and decision rules	1 2 3 4 5
Reasoning	... properly classifies the complaint as a routine case and initiates the adequate complaint process ... applies correctly the designated decision rule	1 2 3 4 5
Social sensitivity	... is able to put himself/herself in the complainant's position and to express his/her understanding ... expresses his/her regret for the customer's annoyance ... avoids rash problem diagnosis	1 2 3 4 5
Understandability	... clearly expresses himself/herself, provides clar-cut information about the corporate standards ... concentrates on the facts ... rarely makes verbal and orthographical mistakes	1 2 3 4 5
Clerical speed and accuracy	... needs few further enquiries to resolve the case ... assimilates quickly the facts of a case ... needs little revision	1 2 3 4 5
Persuasion skills	... is able to persuade the caller that the problem remains in good hands ... is able to argue the caller out of engaging the supervisor without the caller being dissatisfied	1 2 3 4 5
Coping with pressure	... reacts objective to customer reproaches ... maintains the performance level even during multiple consecutive conversations ... keeps calm even under time pressure	1 2 3 4 5

Fig. 14.3 Checklist with regard to behavioral characteristics of the candidate in the context of work simulation

Spotlight 14.1 shows the approach of the servmark consultancy in recruiting employees for its customer care center.

Spotlight 14.1
Hiring Tests for Recruiting Quality-Oriented Employees in a Customer Care Center

The servmark consultancy operates a customer care center which focuses on the operative handling of telephone and written contacts regarding critical customer relationships. Primarily, these are outbound-oriented activities of complaint and cancellation management, such as the processing of follow-up contacts with complainants or contacts with customers who cancelled the relationship. These activities consistently follow a clearly defined quality philosophy. According to this, each operation should be carried out faultlessly under the aspect of defined minimum qualities, i.e. "everyone's" basic performance requirements must be met without exception.

The quality and performance standards for the tasks to be carried out without error are geared to the subjective and objective requirements of the customers as well as to the performance levels defined by servmark.

In order to enable the employees of the customer care center to meet these requirements, a specific recruitment test has been developed, which is described below.

Typically, applicant days are organized for both student part-time assistants and full-time employees who apply for a job as call center agents or quality controllers, where the entry into the field of quality assurance is only possible through working as a telephone agent.

The selection process takes about six to seven hours, including the breaks, with an ideal group size of four to a maximum of six applicants.

The applicants must complete the following tasks as part of the selection process:

1. Observing customer conversations of experienced agents: In strict compliance with legal data protection regulations and after signing a confidentiality agreement, applicants are given the opportunity to observe the work of experienced agents for approximately 20–30 minutes and gain an authentic insight into the field of activity of the agents.
2. Dictation: A dictation is used to check the applicant's spelling skills. After an introduction to the task, an employee slowly reads a text of about 250 words to the participants, which describes a typical complaint situation that is recorded by call center agents every day. The individual text passages are repeated several times. The participants write down the dictation on the PC without having a spell-checker available. The evaluation of the dictation is based on the number of errors. The check includes among

(continued)

Spotlight 14.1 (continued)

other things the correct use of punctuation, use of upper and lower case letters, relevant foreign words and compound and separate spelling.

3. Fast writing: A particular challenge in an agent's everyday work life is the ability to record the facts of the case directly during the customer interview as skillfully and accurately as possible. If the agent is unable to do so, either unpleasant pauses in the call are caused by slow typing or the agent only captures rough key points, which can lead to long rework times and a loss of information. In order to check the speed of the documentation of texts, taking into account the correctness of the typed text, the participants receive a text that can be typed in, while the time required is simultaneously measured by the system. For efficiency reasons, the same text as for the dictation is used for this task. The participant decides for himself/herself what time he/she wants to invest in a (multiple) review of the text, and sets the final time stamp by saving the text. At the end, the system displays the time in which the text was written off and the number of errors.

4. Listening and documenting: It is of crucial importance for adequate problem solution that the underlying problem is correctly understood and documented by the agent. Therefore, listening and documenting is checked in another test section. A conversation is played to the candidates that was simulated and pre-recorded for data protection reasons. They are asked to write down the information heard in the form of a coherent story. In this exercise the following aspects are evaluated: the coherent documentation (transitions, description of cause-effect relationships) and the correct elaboration of the relevant individual information contained, where the evaluation is carried out on the basis of a sample solution developed in advance.

5. Standardized conversation: In order to get an idea of the candidates' suitability for standardized interviewing in general or for specific applications, the conversation process is checked by means of three fictitious customer interviews. After an introduction to the technology used (start of an online questionnaire, use of telephony software and headset) and a short explanation of the three study-specific questionnaires used, the applicants conduct the interviews with the employees and record the contents of the interviews directly in the respective online questionnaire. The employees, who have a detailed interview guide and an evaluation form, evaluate the conduct of the interview from three perspectives on the basis of defined criteria. From the customer's point of view, the following criteria are used: "friendliness", "comprehensibility of the statements", "pleasant voice", "confident demeanor", "responding to the customer's concerns" and "text capture in the interview without unpleasant breaks". From the servmark perspective, the evaluation is carried out according to the criteria "actively conducting or directing the conversation", "use of

(continued)

Spotlight 14.1 (continued)

appropriate questions" and "targeted enquiry or questioning". From a study perspective, which of the three study types the applicant can handle best from the start is analyzed.

6. Free conversation: In order to find out to what extent applicants are able to deal with non-standardized interview situations, they have to carry out a follow-up telephone contact without an interview guide, i.e. they only see a single input screen. In the explanation of the task, the interviewers are informed that they should ask whether the matter about which the customer had contacted the company has been settled. In addition, they should ask freely chosen questions about the complaint experience. Whether further action is still needed should also be clarified, irrespective of the complaint. The interlocutor is a quality assurance employee who takes on the customer's role and describes an individual complaint experience.

7. Hardware and software operation: The ability of the applicants to handle the used technology or to learn this handling quickly is checked by observation. An employee is entrusted with the task of recording, during the whole application day, how well the individual applicants are able to operate the technology used (computer, mouse, keyboard and software).

Tasks that have already been completed are evaluated in the background during the execution of other tasks and prepared for an immediate feedback discussion. Each applicant receives individual feedback on the day of the recruitment test. If the test is positive—taking into account the potential for improvement—the applicant is told that he/she will be contacted by the human resources department in the following days. In case of a negative test result, the application is rejected immediately with precise reasons on the basis of the test results.

Conclusion

Experience has shown that CVs only provide a very limited orientation when selecting personnel for interviewing in customer care—at most they can be used to screen out apparently unsuitable candidates. The selection procedure presented here appears to be quite complex and thus cost-intensive; however, according to the available experience, it pays off over time through a better quality of the interviews and thus through a higher achievement of objectives and less per capita supervision costs of in-house quality assurance.

Udo Körner
Consultant
servmark consultancy

14.3.2 Employee Communication and Training

Particular importance is ascribed to *employee communication* in the context of the internal implementation of complaint management. Everyone associated with the firm must be informed of the importance of customer satisfaction for customer loyalty, for corporate profits and last but not least, for their own job security. It is necessary—especially in the cases of customer-contact employees—to create acceptance with respect to the maxim of consistent orientation toward customers' wishes, to motivate the customers and to make them see themselves as problem-solvers for customers. In addition, the employees must be informed as to all the principles of a customer-oriented complaint policy, as well as the codes of behavior, and be in a position to fulfill these principles and standards.

Generally speaking, the firm's *internal communication policy* serves the following *purposes* here:

- Creating a *fundamental appreciation* of the importance of customer satisfaction for the economic success of the firm
- Conveying and increasing the awareness of the *potential opportunity* for achieving customer loyalty and improving performance quality that is found in complaints
- Illustrating the *significance* that top management ascribes to complaint acceptance in the corporate goal system
- Ensuring *the identification of employees* with their complaint tasks
- Increasing the *feeling of responsibility* for the accurate fulfillment of all complaint management tasks
- Contributing to a *corporate culture* that is characterized by customer orientation, error prevention and the constant search for better solutions for customers
- Pointing out *examples of excellent employee conduct* in complaint situations
- Conveying *factual information* in order to achieve complaint management tasks in the best possible way
- Systematic *informational promotion* of professional, methodological, social and emotional competence
- Providing *feedback information* with respect to specific employee behavior in complaint management.

A considerable *number of instruments* are available to help the firm achieve these goals. These instruments can be analyzed according to their focuses using *two criteria*. The first criterion pertains to the question of whether the communication predominantly takes place via the use of various media, or rather in the form of personal interactions. The second criterion makes a distinction based on whether the instrument is directed more toward conveying information or more broadly toward training certain skills (see Table 14.1).

Media-supported instruments of corporate mass communication are the primary instruments that serve to *convey information* regarding the fundamental importance of complaint management, to sensitize employees and to show the corporate

Table 14.1 Employee communication tools

	Communicating information	Communicating qualifications
Media communication	<ul><li>posters</li><li>contribution to employee magazine</li><li>circulars/brochures</li><li>handbooks</li><li>intranet</li></ul>	<ul><li>written learning materials</li><li>multimedia learning materials</li><li>e-Learning</li></ul>
Personal communication	<ul><li>information events</li><li>meetings</li><li>feedback sessions</li><li>employee surveys</li><li>ad hoc talks</li><li>team discussions</li></ul>	<ul><li>instruction at work</li><li>coaching</li><li>role plays</li><li>simulations</li></ul>

importance. Through *posters*, for example, the fundamental ideas of complaint management can be strikingly expressed, and prejudices can be reduced. In contributions to the *employee magazine*, top management can express its personal commitment to the goals of complaint management. Persuasive examples of exemplary employee behavior may also be presented here. *Circulars, brochures and handbooks* are suitable for the communication and documentation of behavioral rules and processes. Actuality, completeness and access to the appropriate information at any time are ensured when the information is placed on the *intranet*.

In addition to media-supported information, a great deal of importance is also placed on *direct personal* communication. Management can emphasize the importance of customer satisfaction for the firm in *specific information events*. *Meetings* provide an opportunity to obtain detailed information and exchange ideas on current developments and challenges in the area of complaint management. Even more important for the behavior of individual employees are *feedback sessions*. These sessions may concern either customer complaints about the employee's behavior or about the performance of complaint management tasks by the employee. *Customer complaints about a specific employee* should be discussed between the supervisor and the employee. In order to avoid jeopardizing the basic goals of complaint management, however, supervisors must observe important rules of conduct during such discussions. The type of approach they use must creditably demonstrate that they see the incident primarily as an opportunity for improvement and not simply as a chance to denounce the culprits. They must allow for a factual explanation of the case and, based on this explanation, develop ideas about future approaches in cooperation with the employee. These ideas may also include decisions regarding necessary qualification measures. A similar principle applies to feedback sessions that *pertain to the performance of given complaint management tasks*. In jointly conducted discussions between employers and employees, the parties must agree on goals, determine and analyze the level of achievement, perform deviation analyses and draw consequences for activities. These conversations must take place in an atmosphere of trust that is unmistakably supported by the common desire to improve performance for the customer. In the case of feedback like this, the line has been crossed from pure information to coaching, and thus to a guided and systematic improvement process.

While media communication is primarily used by management to propagate its own perspective in the firm in a type of top-down communication, the various forms of personal communication provide many more opportunities for a dialog in which employees can also bring in their perspectives. This perspective is explicitly requested when standardized methods of *employee surveys* are used as a form of bottom-up communication. As far as complaint management is concerned, what is important here is to survey the employees' expectations regarding active complaint management, their own roles as complaint managers and management's support. The results of the survey then form the basis for the collective identification of deficits and the development of problem solutions.

Even between the regularly administered surveys, however, the firm must ensure that the idea potential of customer-contact employees is utilized to analyze the current situation and to stimulate ideas for possible improvements. A possible consideration here would be the promotion of ad hoc *conversations* between customer-contact employees and management. These conversations may include, for example, establishing roundtable discussions with top management—e.g. a "breakfast with the boss". Furthermore, informal communication in terms of *"management by walking around"* or of *"open house" days or hours*, in which top managers are available to talk, should be initiated.

The personal forms of communication include not only the interactions between managers and employees, but also the interactions between the employees themselves. Employees need opportunities to exchange ideas with one another, to eliminate information deficits on a spontaneous basis and to pass on their own experiences and knowledge to others. It is therefore task of the management to give ample scope for informal employee contact and for formal *team meetings*. The latter also include the quality improvement teams and quality circles described in Sect. 13.2.

Training programs for all customer-contact employees and the employees in customer care departments are of special importance. Specific courses should be offered to all customer-contact employees in order to acquaint them with the philosophy of active complaint management, train the appropriate behavior during complaint acceptance and illustrate the function and mode of operation of a customer care department.

A broad spectrum of media and measures are also available for specific *training programs* designed to impart and increase professional, methodological, social and emotional competence. Written and especially multimedia *learning materials*, as well as forms of e-learning offered over the Internet and the intranet, can be made available in order to convey the specific content of the individual complaint management tasks in different modules and to provide opportunities to practice behavior patterns.

These media-supported practice opportunities should be supplemented by *forms of personal training*, in which employees have the opportunity to reflect on and to improve their behavior in actual or simulated situations. These training forms include *workplace instruction* by experienced colleagues and the employment of trainers who observe the behavior of employees and subsequently talk with them about their strengths and any adjustments that need to be made. If supervisors possess adequate qualifications, especially observational ability and intuition, it would even make sense to assign the *coaching* to them (Chow et al. 2006). They would then observe the behavior of their employees and help them with individual improvements by providing constructive feedback.

In order to test specific behavior and bring about permanent changes, however, it is necessary to create opportunities for practice independent of the "real world" situation at the workplace. Here, it is advisable to offer workshops using *simulations* and *role-plays* on specific topics, which make it possible to do away with reactions that are ingrained but ineffective and to practice the desired new behavior patterns.

14.3.3 Incentive Systems

Normally, it is not sufficient simply to nurture the desired competencies through information and training programs. The willingness of employees to utilize their competencies on a long-term and independent basis must also be supported by appropriate *incentive mechanisms*. Even if one is aware of the limits of any incentive-oriented employee motivation, it must be ensured that that goal-oriented behavior must be rewarded, and counterproductive incentive structures must be abolished.

The entire spectrum of *tangible and intangible incentives* can be used to reward excellent employee behavior in the fulfillment of complaint tasks. Employees might thus be rewarded individually or as a team for fulfilling or exceeding agreed objectives or when they have been especially successful—such as in solving an extraordinarily difficult complaint case—with financial bonuses or non-cash benefits, such as the occasional use of company vehicles. In addition, there are intangible incentives like certificates, public distinctions, complimentary portrayals in firm communications, membership in a "Best Service Club", and so on. In making a decision regarding the incentive system, it is necessary to verify the reward character of the individual incentives with the respective employee segment in advance and to leave the employees opportunities to choose their rewards where appropriate. Moreover, the firm must ensure that a direct connection exists between performance and reward, and that the practice of rewarding is transparent.

Just as important as the existence of a goal-oriented reward system is the *abolishment of counterproductive incentive structures*. What we mean here are actual incentives that lead employees in a direction other than the one desired. Firms frequently expose their employees to conflicting expectations by simultaneously demanding unequivocal customer orientation, strong turnover growth and consistent cost reductions, for instance. If the reward system only provides for bonuses that are dependent upon turnover growth or cost reductions, it is implicitly made clear to employees that these goals, and not customer satisfaction, are the only ones that really count; and they will behave themselves accordingly. Paying employees in telephone centers based solely on their productivity will lead to deterioration in quality (Singh 2000), for example, to a tendency to interrupt customers, not to clarify the facts thoroughly or to transfer the customer unnecessarily in order to stay within the time limits set. If firms want to remain true to the goals of active complaint management, they must design their incentive system in a way that such counterproductive conflicts are prevented.

14.3.4   Measures to Prevent Burnout

Specific personnel-related activities are needed in the case of customer-contact employees who not only accept complaints on an occasional basis, but constantly encounter complaint information in the course of their jobs in a customer care center or a telephone complaint department. The mental stress that is associated with managing conflict situations and uninterrupted "emotional labor" in terms of having to respond emphatically to another person's feelings while simultaneously suppressing one's own must be taken into account here. Especially these employees are in great danger of suffering from so-called *"burnout syndrome"* (Bährer-Kohler 2013). This syndrome is a form of emotional exhaustion that is expressed in an employee's reduced productivity and indifferent behavior toward the person receiving the service. This emotional exhaustion can be seen in the fact that these employees feel emotionally overwhelmed and inwardly burned out when dealing with customers. They have the feeling that their competence is decreasing, feel worn out and dispirited, and see themselves less and less in a position to provide the emotional care demanded by customers. Furthermore, they tend to perceive the customer relationship more anonymously and to find fault for most of the problems with the customers themselves (Humborstad et al. 2007). In order to avoid these serious consequences, management must proceed in an active and preventative manner.

Bowen and Johnston (1999) propose a type of *support concept* for employees involved in direct complaint acceptance, to which they apply the—somewhat misleading—term "internal service recovery". They emphatically point out the stresses and strains that are associated with negative experiences in complaint situations. Such experiences include not only discrepancies between one's own feelings and the feelings that must be expressed in a given situation, but also doubts in one's own abilities to satisfy customers completely and resentment for having to bear the consequences of mistakes for which the individual employee is not responsible. In order to cope with this situation, the authors recommend that managers take care of their employees and behave themselves the way that they would want employees to behave toward customers. Accordingly, they should take time for the employees, recognize that they have a difficult job and demonstrate a great deal of empathy and social support. In addition, they must ask employees how the management of complaint contacts can be improved from their perspective.

The firm must also make practical arrangements to ensure that the constant burden of stressful emotional labor is interrupted. Measures of *"job rotation"* are particularly suitable for this purpose. These may include, for example, directing employees in the complaint department to alternate the performance of complaint acceptance tasks and indirect complaint management activities—that is, without customer contact—such as in the areas of complaint analysis and controlling.

Furthermore, it is necessary to prevent feelings of helplessness and lack of control over the situation from emerging among employees. This can be achieved primarily by allowing them *more responsibility and decision-making authority* in solving customers' problems ("empowerment").

14.3.5 Empowerment

By "empowerment", we mean *shifting the right to make decisions* and transferring autonomy to employees at lower levels of the hierarchy (Brymer 1991; Bowen and Lawler 1992), an approach that has attracted great interest in the corporate world as the importance of customer-contact employees in complaint situations has increased.

The *basic idea* is that customer satisfaction can be re-established especially quickly when the first contact person has the ability and expertise to solve the problem without having to call in a supervisor. Customers should be spared the experience of having to deal with employees who claim not to be responsible and being referred to other persons without recognizing an immediate effort to handle the case.

For this reason, the *central goal of empowerment* is to increase customer satisfaction by solving the problem quickly and to improve the process and reduce costs by saving processing time (especially management time). Moreover, the firm can strive to increase motivation on the part of its personnel, based on increased responsibility and improved communication between customer-contact personnel and management (Brymer 1991; Bowen and Lawler 1995; Rafiq and Ahmed 1998; Chebat and Kollias 2000). Empirical studies show that these goals are actually achieved (Gazzoli et al. 2010).

Within the framework of the empowerment concept, a distinction must be made between two versions that differ with regard to the degree of autonomy given to employees and with respect to the breadth of discretion they are allowed—structured empowerment and flexible empowerment (Brymer 1991; Sparks et al. 1997; Cacioppe 1998). *Structured empowerment* refers to guidelines that are specified in a relatively clear manner and allows customer-contact personnel the opportunity to propose or select certain solutions independently or to decide between specified versions. Brymer (1991, p. 60) gives examples for such a structured empowerment by presenting sample guidelines developed by the Hilton Hotel at Walt Disney World Village. If a guest experienced a room-related problem (e.g. no hot water, bad television reception) and complains about it at check out, the front-desk clerk is

Table 14.2 Structured empowerment developed by Hilton Hotel at Walt Disney World Village

Guest complaints or problems	Actions front-desk clerk is authorized to take
A guest announces during check out that he or she experienced a room-related problem (e.g., no hot water, bad television reception, room was too noisy, lack of heat)	Offer an upgrade for next visit, or adjust current bill by as much as $100. Make logbook notation
At check out, a guest complains about something unrelated to his or her room, as follows: ■ The service in the café or dining room ■ The guest did not receive some item that he or she requested (extra towels, soap, blankets, etc.) ■ The maintenance department was slow to respond to some complaint ■ Luggage or parcels were delivered late ■ Mail or messages were not received	Adjust guest's current bill as indicated and make a logbook notation ■ $50, and advise supervisor ■ $50 ■ $50 ■ $100, and advise supervisor
A guest is charged an incorrect rate	The supervisor should make the room adjustment
Guest experiences a problem with the room key or lock	Offer an upgrade for next visit, or adjust current bill by as much as $100. Make a logbook notation
Guest reports that a complaint was passed from department to department	Offer an upgrade for next visit, or adjust current bill by as much as $100. Advise the supervisor
Guest insists that he or she did not incur any mini-bar charges	Make the adjustment
Guest disputes phone charges	Make the adjustment
Guest complains about a rude or insensitive employee	Refer problem to the assistant manager

Source: Brymer (1991, p. 60)

authorized to offer an upgrade for the next visit, or adjust the current bill by as much as $100. In case a guest complains about a something unrelated to his room (e.g. luggage was delivered late), the front-desk clerk is supposed to offer a compensation of $50 for the inconvenience. Table 14.2 provides an detailed overview.

There are also comparable examples known from the restaurant industry. A regulation at Satisfaction Guaranteed Eateries, for instance, stipulates that guests who have to wait between 10 and 20 minutes for their reserved table should be offered a free drink; but if they have to wait more than 20 minutes, the entire meal may be complimentary. Employees are nevertheless encouraged to decide for

Table 14.3 Guidelines for resolving a complaint during check-out

> "If the guest is uncertain how she or he would like the problem to be solved, the employee should ask if the guest is planning a return visit in the near future. If so, offer to her or him an upgrade at no additional charge. If the guest does not plan to return soon, the employee may ask again of the quest, 'What may I do to help make up for the inconvenience you experienced?' Follow through with the guest's suggestion or propose to the guest one of the company's approved adjustments, including making changes to the current room bill."

Source: Brymer (1991, p. 61)

themselves, based on what is appropriate in the situation, what they consider necessary in the interests of satisfying the customer, rather than to follow the rules blindly (Firnstahl 1989). An approach such as this marks the transition to a more flexible form of empowerment.

Flexible empowerment allows customer-contact personnel greater discretion in their behavior. The guidelines are established more broadly, and the employees are asked to react flexibly and creatively to customers' desires and demands. Not only should they have a standard repertoire of behavior ready to use in a given situation, but they should also increase customer satisfaction with customized reactions, whereas offers of price reductions represent only one of many action alternatives here. Even guidelines for flexible empowerment can be specified to differing degrees. Nordstrom, the American department store known for its service policy, simply formulates the general basic rule, "Use your good judgment in all situations" (Spector and McCarthy 2000, p. 180). In the majority of cases, however, the rules refer to specific problem situations. Table 14.3 shows an example of solving complaints upon check out from a hotel.

Guidelines and action alternatives may be *generated and put in concrete terms by the employees themselves*. This is—to some extent, at least—the case at the hotel group Marriott Corporation, where employees discuss typical complaint situations among themselves and come up with appropriate possible courses of action and the competencies associated with them (Furlong 1993).

The *"complaint ownership"* approach is also an integral part of the empowerment concept. Employees to whom a complaint is expressed or who even just accidentally find out about a customer problem then "own" this problem and must bring about a solution. They may not claim that they are not responsible for the problem. Instead, they should ask themselves, "What can I do for the customer in order to remedy this problem?" Within broad limits, they also have the expertise to solve the problem in the way the customer desires; otherwise, they must see to it that more qualified employees carry out a settlement that suits the customer. When, for instance, a guest dining in the hotel restaurant mentions that the television reception in his room is bad, the waiter must inform the repairman and attend to the problem until he is certain that it is actually solved (see Sect. 7.1).

Flexible empowerment and the "complaint ownership" approach place *increased demands* on employees. They must think and act more independently and creatively and, in doing so, keep an eye on customers' needs while also considering the corporate interests. Therefore, the granting of responsibilities and competencies is also associated with certain *risks* (Bowen and Lawler 1992). Implementing the empowerment concept demands greater investments in the personnel selection process and in employee training, may involve higher personnel costs and may lead to other cost-intensive consequences if employees make decisions and incorrectly assess the consequences of those decisions. Nevertheless, this latter risk should not be overestimated, either. Against the background of their many years of experience in complaint consulting with TARP, Goodman and Grimm (1990, p. 52) report that they have never encountered a case in which employees "have given away the store" while on the other hand a reduction of the processing costs by 30 to 50% through empowerment could be observed.

Furthermore, the risks can be avoided and the advantages realized when management ensures that the *necessary qualifications* are established with respect to leadership and organization. These qualifications include the following (Bhote 1991; Brymer 1991; Furlong 1993; Venkatesan 1993):

- A *basic trust* in employees that they will not exploit the demand for consistent customer orientation in a way that is irrational and damaging to the firm.
- The involving, informing and winning over of *middle management* at an early stage. These managers fear loss of power, competence and authority the most and may obstruct the introduction of empowerment. These managers must be won, for their support is imperative for the guidance and training of contact personnel.
- An *information system* that allows employees fast, direct access to all the data needed for their decisions.
- *The overcoming of reservations on the part of the employees* themselves, who indeed do gain a measure of responsibility but loose a certain amount of comfort, and only really use the new level of discretion they enjoy when they are convinced that the advantages associated with it outweigh the risks.
- The establishment of *empowerment teams* in which fundamental principles can be clarified, specific behavior patterns discussed and developed further, and barriers removed.

Thus we can see that empowerment is a *long-term oriented concept* for firms that consider themselves learning organizations (Venkatesan 1993). For this reason, it is also advisable to proceed with the implementation in manageable steps, while taking into account the situational conditions. Flexible empowerment is especially appropriate in the context of a corporate strategy that is geared toward differentiation and customized performance, whose goal is long-term business relationships, where complex and changing customer demands are typical and there are a large number of interactions between customers and employees (Bowen and Lawler 1995; Rafiq and Ahmed 1998). This means that flexible empowerment is primarily appropriate within a strategic concept of complaint management of the type *"Relationship Amplifier"*.

In situations that can be characterized by contrary characteristics (a cost-leadership strategy in bulk business, a short-term transactional relationship with customers, relatively rigid customer desires, no customer contact or temporary customer contact), it seems advisable to use a more structured form of empowerment and to regulate the respective courses of actions in a differentiated and detailed fashion. The success of the largest fast food chains is based at least partly on the fact that the employees are provided explicit scripts for everything from the greeting to the farewell and are monitored for compliance, all of which results in uniform performance and gives the customer a great deal of security regarding the expected service. In the context of the strategy options of complaint management, it is in particular the type *"Complaint Factory"* that provides the strategic framework for a structured empowerment.

14.4   Design of the Corporate Cultural Environment

The appropriate framework conditions must be created in firms so that employees can use their abilities. Above all, this includes a corporate culture that supports the chosen strategic orientation. This is illustrated by the example of the complaint management type "Relationship Amplifier", i.e. a complaint management that primarily aims at achieving complaint satisfaction and strengthening customer relations.

By *corporate culture*, we mean the entire range of ideals and ways of thinking and acting that are present in a firm and that shape the attitudes and the behavior of those affiliated with that firm. This corporate culture is expressed in various forms such as formal mission statements, unwritten rules, beliefs regarding corporate reference groups, patterns of success that have been passed down, and traditions (Kotter and Heskett 1992; Schein 2009).

Active complaint management of the *"Relationship Amplifier"* type is not compatible with every corporate value system, but instead demands a specific corporate culture (Bellou 2007). In public pronouncements, in internal statements and in actual behavior, it must be unmistakably clear that customer orientation is at the core of the value system. It is only when the firm does not simply proclaim customer satisfaction as a goal, but rather strives consistently to achieve it, that a climate develops in which complaints are seen as customers' natural right and as an opportunity for the firm. In a corporate culture like this, however, complaint management itself then becomes a symbol of customer-oriented goals. Top management underscores the strategic importance of complaint management through organizational closeness, informational involvement and the provision of the necessary resources.

In addition to consistent customer orientation, a specific way of dealing with failures—a type of *"no-blame culture"* (Johnston and Mehra 2002, p. 149) or *"organizational error management culture"* (van Dyck et al. 2005)—is also necessary for complaint management. First, in the context of preventative quality management, this culture involves making every attempt to prevent failures in the first place. Second, one must be realistic about the fact that a zero-defects concept represents a goal that is not fully achievable in the service sector, which means that it is necessary to correct these defects in the way that is best for the customer and to ensure that they do not recur in the future. Accordingly, errors that do arise are viewed with regard to their informational value for possible improvements, and not primarily as indicators of employee weaknesses.

Uncompromising customer orientation, even and especially when dealing with errors, must be implemented in everyday corporate actions and experienced by employees and customers. It should also be established in *official mission statements*, so that its significance can be documented and employees are given a solid basis for their actions. For an excellent example of this, we refer to the corporate philosophy of Avis Car Rental, in which exactly this can be found: the unconditional obligation to go to greater lengths for the customer ("We try harder"), the effort toward an error-free performance fulfillment ("Doing the job right the first time") and the anchoring of complaint management ("Effective complaint management") to ensure customer satisfaction and loyalty (Jackson 1997, p. 117; Meffert 1998, p. 127).

Chapter 14 in Brief
- Customer-contact employees are of central importance, as they have the first chance to reduce dissatisfaction, resolve problems quickly, and correctly gather complaint information.
- Employees who are in contact with complainants must have a strong service orientation as well as high social, emotional and professional competence.
- In order to ensure the necessary employee qualifications, internal marketing with a bundle of measures is required. These include the recruiting of service-oriented and qualified employees, employee communication and training, incentive systems, activities to avoid burnout effects, and empowerment.
- Through these measures and the goal-oriented design of corporate culture and infrastructure, the firm must further guarantee that employees actually translate their skills into corresponding behavior.

References

Ahmed PK, Rafiq M (2003) Internal marketing issues and challenges. Eur J Mark 37(9):1177–1186

Bährer-Kohler S (2013) Burnout for experts: prevention in the context of living and working. Springer Science + Business Media, New York, NY

Bellou V (2007) Achieving long-term customer satisfaction through organizational culture: evidence from the health care sector. Manag Serv Qual 17(5):510–522

Berry LL, Parasuraman A (1992) Services marketing starts from within. Mark Manag 1(1):24–34

Bhote KR (1991) Next operation as customer (NOAC). How to improve quality, cost and cycle time in service operations. American Management Association, New York, NY

Bitner MJ et al (1990) The service encounter: diagnosing favorable and unfavorable incidents. J Mark 54(1):71–84

Blanding W (1991) Customer service operations: the complete guide. AMACOM, New York, NY

Bowen DE, Johnston R (1999) Internal service recovery: developing a new construct. Int J Serv Ind Manag 10(2):118–131

Bowen DE, Lawler EE (1992) The empowerment of service workers: what, why, how, and when. Sloan Manag Rev 33(1):31–39

Bowen DE, Lawler EE (1995) Empowering service employees. Sloan Manag Rev 36(4):73–84

Brymer RA (1991) Employee empowerment: a guest-driven leadership strategy. Cornell Restaur Admin Q 32(1):58–68

Cacioppe R (1998) Structured empowerment: an award-winning program at the Burswood Resort Hotel. Leadersh Org Dev J 19(5):264–274

Chebat JC, Kollias P (2000) The impact of empowerment on customer contact employee's roles in service organizations. J Serv Res 3(1):66–81

Cherbakov L et al (2005) Impact of service orientation at the business level. IBM Syst J 44 (4):653–668

Chow IH et al (2006) The impact of developmental experience, empowerment, and organizational support on catering service staff performance. Hosp Manag 25(3):478–495

Coenen C (2001) Serviceorientierung und Servicekompetenz von Kundenkontakt-Mitarbeitern. In: Bruhn M, Stauss B (eds) Dienstleistungsmanagement Jahrbuch 2001. Gabler, Wiesbaden, pp 341–374

Coenen C (2005) Prosoziales Dienstleistungsverhalten im Kundenkontakt. Deutscher Universitäts-Verlag, Wiesbaden

Cook S (2012) Complaint management excellence. Kogan Page, London

Firnstahl TW (1989) My employees are my service guarantee. Harv Bus Rev 67(4):28–32

Fontana D (1990) Social skills at work. Routledge, London

Furlong CB (1993) Marketing for keeps: building your business by retaining your customers. Wiley, New York, NY

Gazzoli G et al (2010) The role and effect of job satisfaction and empowerment on customers' perception of service quality: a study in the restaurant industry. J Hosp Tour Res 34(1):56–77

Goleman D (1998) What makes a leader? Harv Bus Rev 76(6):93–102

Goleman D (2005) Emotional intelligence: why it can matter more than IQ, 10th anniversary edn. Bantam Books, New York

Goleman D et al (2013) Primal leadership: unleashing the power of emotional intelligence. Harvard Business Review Press, Boston, MA

Goodman JA, Grimm CJ (1990) A quantified case for improving quality now! J Qual Particip 13 (3):50–55

Guy ME (2008) Emotional labor: putting the service in public service. Routledge, Abingdon

Hochschild AR (2012) The managed heart: commercialization of human feelings. University California Press, Berkeley

Humborstad SIW et al (2007) Burnout and service employees' willingness to deliver quality service. J Hum Resour Hosp Tour 7(1):45–64

Jackson D (1997) Dynamic organisation: the challenge of change. Macmillan Press, Basingstoke, London

Johnston R, Mehra S (2002) Best-practice complaint management. Acad Manag Exec 16 (4):145–154

Kotter JP, Heskett JL (1992) Corporate culture and performance. Free Press, New York, NY

Lytle RS, Timmerman JE (2006) Service orientation and performance: an organizational perspective. J Serv Mark 20(2):136–147

Meffert H (1998) Dienstleistungsphilosophie und -kultur. In: Meyer A (ed) Handbuch Dienstleistungs-Marketing, Band 1. Schäffer-Poeschel, Stuttgart, pp 121–138

Rafiq M, Ahmed PK (1998) A customer-oriented framework for empowering service employees. J Serv Mark 12(5):379–396

Scheerer H (1994) Kundengefühle sind Tatsachen. Harvard Manager 16(2):9–13

Schein EE (2009) The corporate culture survival guide. Jossey-Bass, San Francisco, CA

Schneider B, Schechter D (1991) Development of a personnel selection system for service jobs. In: Brown S et al (eds) Service quality. Lexington Books, Lexington, KY, pp 217–235

Singh J (2000) Performance productivity and quality of frontline employees in service organizations. J Mark 64(2):15–34

Sparks BA et al (1997) The impact of staff empowerment and communication style on customer evaluations: the special case of service failure. Psychol Mark 14(5):475–493

Spector R, McCarthy PD (2000) The Nordstrom way: the inside story of America's #1 customer service company. Wiley, New York, NY

Stauss B (2000) Internes Marketing als personalorientierte Qualitätspolitik. In: Bruhn M, Stauss B (eds) Dienstleistungsqualität, 3rd edn. Gabler, Wiesbaden, pp 203–222

van Dyck C et al (2005) Organizational error management culture and its impact on performance: a two-study replication. J Appl Psychol 90(6):1228–1240

Venkatesan MV (1993) Empowering employees. In: Scheuing EE, Christopher WF (eds) The service quality handbook. AMACOM, New York, pp 259–266

Organizational Aspects of Complaint Management

15

© Springer Nature Switzerland AG 2019
B. Stauss, W. Seidel, *Effective Complaint Management*, Management for Professionals,
https://doi.org/10.1007/978-3-319-98705-7_15

Issues Raised

- Which factors determine whether centralized, decentralized or dual complaint management is chosen?
- Which organizational units should be distinguished in the complaint center and which tasks should be assigned to them in the operative handling of complaints?
- What tasks does the head of complaint management department perform in the conceptual control of complaint management?
- What are the advantages and disadvantages of different organizational forms (staff function, line function or matrix organization) for complaint management?
- Can complaint management be organized as a profit center?
- How should outsourcing of complaint management be assessed?

There are a number of *organizational questions* that must be clarified when an active complaint management system is established. With respect to the company's organizational structure, decisions must be made as to the assignment of responsibilities to particular organizational units (positions, departments, etc.). In this regard, the primary question that must be answered is related to the degree of centralization or decentralization of complaint management. If a complaint management department is established, the extent of conceptual-strategic control and operative tasks in the complaint center should be clarified. The firm must also decide how the complaint management department will be integrated into the corporate structure and whether it can be designed as a profit center. It is also necessary to reflect the extent to which tasks can be outsourced to external service providers.

15.1   Centralized, Decentralized or Dual Complaint Management

The alternative *organizational structures* are frequently limited to the extremes of centralized and decentralized complaint processing. In the case of purely *centralized complaint management*, a central complaint unit single-handedly administers all the tasks. This means that customers who complain to decentralized units—such as branch offices or subsidiaries—are consistently referred to the central complaint location, or that complaints received at decentralized locations are immediately forwarded to the head office. Purely *decentralized complaint management* implies that complaint cases are independently processed by the decentralized sales units, without the involvement of the head office. If complaints are received at the central level, they are forwarded to the proper organizational units, and the complainants are then referred to these units.

This ideal type of dichotomy however, unduly simplifies the complex decision problem, because for many firms it is either absolutely necessary or more efficient to establish a solution with centralized and decentralized elements—that is, a *dual complaint management system*.

The decision regarding the design of the organizational structure design of complaint management must be made in accordance with the specific corporate environment, which can vary widely from firm to firm. Consequently, for *small businesses* that market a limited product range directly to a small clientele, the problem is usually limited to determining the complaint-related responsibilities for customer-contact employees and for company management. *Large companies* that market a broad range of products via various distribution channels to a large number of geographical locations face the much more complex task of how to implement customer-oriented complaint management with the involvement of their distribution partners and/or via the establishment of a direct complaint channel. Franchise providers, for example, face a comparatively difficult problem because their uniformly structured offering is presented at several locations by different franchisees. They have a strong interest in the consistent implementation of the complaints policy in order to avoid negative effects on other system members.

Therefore, there is no one organizational solution that is optimal for all firms. Rather, the particular *situational factors*, which place different demands on the complaint management process, should be identified.

15.1.1 Factors Influencing the Choice of Centralized, Decentralized and Dual Complaint Management

A number of factors influence the choice of organizational form. Chief among these factors are the type of product, the number of customers, the type of distribution and the centrality of customer contact.

Type of Product The product essentially determines the categories of possible problems and the necessary actions resulting from those problems, which raise organizational questions of their own. As a rule, services (such as those of a restaurant or a hotel) are rendered in direct contact with the customer. Based on the customers' involvement in the production of services, they have the opportunity to voice complaints directly to customer-contact personnel; and in many cases, employees have the chance to eliminate problems immediately. Therefore, the possibility of a decentralized complaint solution must be envisioned for these problems. For problems related to technical problems, it is necessary to establish rapid access to technical information, as well as to service and repair facilities.

Number of Customer If a firm only has relatively few customers who are significant to its bottom line, each individual complaint becomes very important. For this reason, the firm must ensure that all complaints are handled immediately. This handling should take place either centrally or decentrally, in the same way that the customer contacts are organized. Regardless of whether sales and service employees or members of company management are involved, the person addressed by the customer in each case is the "complaint owner" and must see to it that the problem is solved. In order to put this complaint owner in a position to solve the problem quickly, it is most important that competencies are conferred and that direct paths of communication with top management are established. When the number of customers is very large, it makes sense for the firm to establish its own department for complaints and customer communication, which can professionally manage the large numbers of complaints according to a uniform principle.

Type of Distribution Different challenges must be met, depending on whether the firm is in direct contact with the customer or is distributing the products by means of other institutions—e.g. wholesale and retail distributors. In the case of direct distribution, the firm can design its complaint management system autonomously. In terms of indirect forms of distribution, on the other hand, there is a special situation. At the retail level, for example, additional services are created whose perceived quality also has an impact on the customer's assessment of the quality of the manufacturer and his products. This results in a variety of problems for the manufacturer's complaint management. In addition, the problem arises as to how to integrate the market partner in the firm's own complaint management system, in order to be able immediately to record and eliminate the customers' dissatisfaction with the product. Furthermore, the quality of retail services must also be influenced in order to avoid customer dissatisfaction with retail services. The integration in vertical distribution systems is more difficult, the more independent the partner are legally and financially, and the greater their market power is.

Centrality of Customer Contact Even in the case of firms that distribute their products directly, it frequently happens that customers have multiple decentralized contacts with the firm or with operational subsystems. For example, one may think about the hotels of an international chain, which are built in a multitude of different locations. Customers experience the quality decentrally in each hotel visited. It is thus extremely important for the management of the hotels to obtain information about the problems customers experience via their own complaint management systems. Nonetheless, the customers' perception of quality is not related to the individual hotel alone, but rather influences their assessment of the entire brand and other hotels of the chain. For this reason, it is necessary for the management of the hotel chain to be informed about customers' problems with all system units—in other words, to establish a dual complaint management system.

15.1.2 The Importance of These Factors for Selected Types of Firms

Depending on the products or product range offered, the category, segment and number of customers, the distribution structure and the existence of different customer contacts, a multitude of situations is conceivable, each of which places specific demands on the organizational design of the complaint management system. These

Table 15.1 Types of firms with different requirements for the organization of complaint management

	Type A	Type B	Type C	Type D
Type of Product	Tangible good (capital good)	Tangible good (consumer good)	Tangible good (consumer good)	Service
Number of customers	Small	Large	Large	Large
Type of distribution	Direct	Indirect[1]	Indirect[2]	Direct
Centrality of customer contact	Central	Decentral	Decentral	Decentral/ Central
Example	Mechanical engineering firm	Consumer goods manufacturer	Car manufacturer	Retail bank

[1]) Retail trade as distributor;   [2]) Retail trade with service functions

situations cannot be presented here in full detail. Instead, we restrict the discussion to *four typical cases* (see Table 15.1):

- For *Type A* firms, the criteria named above have the following characteristics: tangible good, low number of customers, direct distribution, centralized customer contact. Here, we will cite the example of a medium-sized manufacturer of durable goods that sells drilling machines to a relatively small group of well-known industrial customers via a centralized distribution network *(mechanical engineering firm)*.
- *Type B* firm has the following characteristics: tangible good, large number of customers, indirect distribution and decentralized customer contact. A representative of this type of firm is an industrial *consumer goods manufacturer* of packaged foods that distributes its products nationally via retailers to an anonymous mass market. The customers come into contact with the product in a multitude of different purchase locations that are distributed across a wide geographical area. The retailer only distributes the product; product-specific and customer-oriented services (such as consulting services) are not involved.
- *Type C* firms have the following characteristics: tangible good, large number of customers, distribution via retailers that perform additional services related to the particular tangible good, decentralized customer contact. As a prototypical of this type of firm, one may think of a *car manufacturer* whose products are sold via dealerships that are closely connected to the firm by contract. The dealers not only sell the automobiles, but also offer a number of product-relevant services, such as repairs, maintenance, leasing, parts sales, etc. Since the dealers also use the

manufacturer's brand name, the customers' perceptions of the quality of the product and the service are not independent from one another; rather, there are carry-over effects, which means that service failures can also lead to customers' switching from the manufacturer.

- The characteristic features of *Type D* firms are as follows: service offering, large number of customers, direct distribution and both central and decentralized customer contact. Representative of this type of firm is a *retail bank* that has direct business relationships with a large number of known customers. Customer contact is primarily maintained via local branches and the Internet.

The specific tasks of complaint management turn out to be *different*, depending on the *type of firm*, which gives rise to varying organizational consequences with respect to the question of centralization versus decentralization.

In *Type A firms (mechanical engineering firms)*, all employees must be aware of the fact that the firm's survival can depend on the consistent support of each individual customer. Customer orientation in this case therefore means individual customer care. It is necessary to maintain a permanent dialog with customers in order to notice changes in the structure of their needs and expectations, as well as the degree of their satisfaction or dissatisfaction. Every dialog partner in the organization—be it a sales associate, a customer service representative or a member of company management—thus has the task of encouraging customers to express their dissatisfaction and of accepting and forwarding complaints. As "complaint owners", they must ensure a rapid solution, which requires wide latitude to act, clear competencies and direct communication channels. Moreover, the complaint processing and complaint analysis tasks can be assigned to the customer-contact departments (sales or service). It is frequently advisable, however, to have a *central complaint management department* monitor the processing and analysis and take over essential controlling and reporting functions. In this way, the firm can ensure that those who are directly affected by complaint management become actively involved and that the management concept is internally enforced with the necessary emphasis.

Type B firms (manufacturers of packaged foods) do not have direct contact with customers, since the products are exclusively sold through retailers. When customers experience problems with a product, they do not have a strong incentive to complain. The items are usually sold at low prices, and it seems to be less effort for the customers to switch to a competitor when they make their next purchase than to take on the stress of an additional visit to their retailer just to make a complaint. This is particularly the case when they anticipate the difficulties of a complaint: they must return the opened package to the shop, find a responsible contact person and then prove the incident in a dispute without being sure that the small amount will be refunded.

Another factor is that discounters in particular, who sell based on very low prices, do not dispose of sufficient quantitative or qualitative resources for product information and customer service. Thus, they are hardly in a position to *take over complaint acceptance and processing functions, as manufacturers would like* them to do. Indeed, manufacturers usually work out an agreement with retailers to replace spoiled items that are returned. Nevertheless, the number of these exchanged products is usually the only information that the firm can expect from the retailer regarding customers' problems with the product. More detailed descriptions of the negative customer experience rarely become the subject of complaints with the retailer and are not usually forwarded to the manufacturer. Even specific efforts on the part of the manufacturer to implement systematic complaint acceptance at the retail level (by providing complaint forms, for instance) seem to be illusory, given the differing interests of the parties involved, the human resources policy in discount businesses and the market power of the retail chains (Stauss and Seidel 2012).

Consequently, the manufacturer must *centralize* all complaint management tasks in-house. This statement applies to complaint stimulation especially. Information requesting that customers seek direct contact with the manufacturer in case of a problem should be printed on the product packaging, and an easily accessible channel for that contact must also be communicated to them. In this way, all customer-initiated communication comes together at one location in the firm, and it is also advisable to assign tasks of complaint processing and reaction, complaint analysis, controlling and reporting here.

For *Type C firms (car manufacturers)*, the situation is similar to that presented in the preceding case, insofar as here also a tangible good is sold decentrally to a large number of customers via retailers. There is, however, one essential difference. The car dealers influence the quality perception of the customer because they themselves render their own automobile-related service. Accordingly, the car manufacturers are faced with the task of directing the members of their distribution network in such a way that the dealers ensure manufacturer- and retail-oriented customer satisfaction and loyalty.

The complaints that arise at car dealerships may cover different product- or service-related customer problems. For the dealers, the relevant questions are whether they themselves caused the problem or whether the manufacturers did, and who is responsible for the costs. The dealers' contracts obligate the retail businesses to accept complaints about car problems caused by the manufacturer, to process them on the basis of defined guarantee and goodwill guidelines and *to bring customer complaints to the attention of the car manufacturer*. This approach guarantees that the manufacturer at least receives information about customer problems that the retailer views as relevant and originated by the manufacturer. These problems encompass only a fraction of the automobile-related customer problems:

- Product-related problems that the retailer assesses as being irrelevant or that do not fall under the guarantee and goodwill conditions are either not forwarded to the manufacturer at all or are forwarded incompletely, so that the manufacturer only receives an extremely *imperfect view* of the product-related problems experienced by customers.
- In addition, it must be noted that complainants *predominantly* express their complaints to the dealer *in person*. Since the majority of these complaints are

not recorded as complaints, but rather are processed in the context of routine procedures, not even the dealership itself has a systematic overview of the articulated customer complaints.

- The manufacturer finds out about *dealer-related customer problems* if the customer informs them about these problems. As a rule, however, this only happens when the dealer, despite repeated efforts on the customer's part, fails to solve a serious incident satisfactorily. For this reason the manufacturer faces the problem that shortcomings in the dealer's complaint management system can lead to customer switching, without the manufacturer itself receiving any information about the causes of this switching.

For the *manufacturer*, a series of *difficult tasks* arise from this situation:

- With respect to *product-related complaints*, the dealer must be fully integrated in the complaint management system. That is, a uniform system of complaint stimulation, acceptance, processing and reaction is needed.
- Part of this system is that *complaints brought forward in person* are also documented as thoroughly as possible and forwarded from the dealer to the manufacturer.
- With regard to *dealer-related complaints*, the dealership should also be able to practice complaint management according to the manufacturer's conceptual understanding. This also includes training the customer-contact personnel appropriately. All dealer-related complaints must also be processed, categorized and analyzed according to a system approved by the manufacturer.
- The necessity of acknowledging great importance to *complaint stimulation* arises from the manufacturer's insufficient overview of customers' problems. A significant increase in product-related articulations is only to be expected if customers are provided an easily accessible (e.g. telephone or online) channel to the manufacturer. If, however, customers are requested to direct their complaints to a centralized customer care department of the manufacturer, an increased number of dealer-related articulations will also be received there. For the manufacturer, this has the advantage that the information level related to dealer-oriented customer problems will increase, and they can become active toward both the dissatisfied customer and dealerships that are reacting incorrectly. Nevertheless, this approach will encounter reservations and resistance from the dealers if they suspect that another instrument of control is being established.

Therefore, a certain amount of *fine-tuning with respect to the execution of tasks is required between the manufacturer and the dealership*, in terms of vertical cooperation. The focus of this version of complaint management, which is at the same time *dual and vertical*, is the determination as to

- which complaint stimulation measures should be implemented

- which type of complaint should be forwarded to which department
- which complaints should be resolved on site
- which alternative solutions are practical and acceptable
- how the information regarding complaints decided on site should be collected and forwarded
- how the dealerships should receive feedback from analysis and controlling of comparative information and information relevant to their operations
- how the system of incentives for the execution of tasks should be designed.

The situation for *Type D firms (banks)* is similar to that previously discussed, in that the question of controlling decentralized systems is also an issue here. There is, however, some difference in the fact that here the good in question is a service and the firm is set up as a branch operation, which facilitates the control of the decentralized units and generally also provides centralized customer contact via online banking.

Several banking services are performed decentrally in a multitude of branch offices that are scattered across a wide geographical area and in direct contact with known customers. Many bank customers only have contact with the employees at "their" branch bank and turn to these employees when they have a problem. The problem here is, however, that a number of the problems experienced by customers are also caused on site. The result of this fact is that many customers encounter *barriers to complaint articulation,* whereas bank employees encounter obstacles to complaint stimulation and forwarding. The fact is that if customers complain at the branch office, employees are frequently confronted with errors that they caused themselves, which brings about the danger of suppressing the facts of the complaint case.

In this situation, a *dual*—that is, both centralized and decentralized—complaint management system is required. In order to eliminate customer dissatisfaction immediately, the employees in the decentralized branch offices must be trained to deal with dissatisfied customers, equipped with competencies and directed to accept complaint information. In order to combat the tendency of contact personnel to suppress, distort or select complaints expressed by customers in person, branch managers must also be present on a regular basis during the service process and question the customers regarding their satisfaction. In addition, a central customer care department must be established, that allows each customer to articulate dissatisfaction centrally. This is necessary in any case if the bank offers its services online and, in this respect, there is also a central contact.

In a dual system like this one, both centralized and decentralized tasks of complaint stimulation, acceptance, processing and reaction come up. Moreover, analysis, reporting and complaint management controlling functions must—to differing extents—be carried out.

Spotlight 15.1 provides an insight into the dual complaint management of a bank, in which the central systematically supports the decentralized complaint processing complaint.

Spotlight 15.1

Strengthening of the Decentralized Complaint Processing as a Strategic Lever for Improving Service Quality at Baden-Württembergische Bank

Baden-Württembergische Bank (BW-Bank) is a customer-oriented and regional service provider. This self-concept results in high quality standards with regard to service and consulting, products and processes. In order to meet these standards in a difficult market environment and in view of increasing customer expectations, quality management as the driving force of the continuous improvement process has also aligned its complaint management strategy to a consistent "customer-focused" approach. In a learning organization with a positive culture of error and learning, strengthening decentralized complaint handling is the logical conclusion.

Macro Perspective

Dissatisfied BW-Bank customers usually address their requests to their trusted interlocutor in the branch offices—even in times of multi-channel banking. Therefore, a major success factor for the management of customer satisfaction is to build up target-oriented (problem-solving) competences at branch level. In principle, every sales representative becomes a complaint manager! The original strength of the sales force, to be very close to the customer, is thus meaningfully supplemented.

Micro Perspective

The initial situation for the sales staff is demanding: dissatisfaction is often associated with negative feelings such as worry, annoyance or disappointment. The satisfaction of complainants therefore depends to a large extent on the ability of the employees to react with understanding, competence and commitment; perhaps even more than on the solutions offered. This is because positive employee behavior gives the customers a good feeling. They can trust that their concern is in good hands. That is what intuition and experience say, but also what the results of market research prove.

Solution Approach

The consequence is to strengthen the communicative and complaint handling skills of the sales staff. In BW-Bank, an integrated approach has proven its worth, focusing on ongoing process optimization and freedom of decision-making for employees.

Decentralized complaint processing is conceptually embedded in the service initiative "110%—better than good!" Under this motto, BW-Bank has been promoting the continuous improvement of service quality for several years. This is because service excellence is essentially based on the professional handling of negative customer reactions. En passant, the "difficult" issue of dissatisfaction is thus integrated into a positive context and the acceptance among employees is promoted.

(continued)

Spotlight 15.1 (continued)

The direct complaint management process in the service initiative is entitled "professional handling of difficult conversational situations". In a toolbox, recommendations for dealing with dissatisfied customers in all contact phases are presented, along with the existing regulations, standards and instruments.

The decentralized recording and processing of "customer impulses", which has been IT-based for many years, also provides important procedural support. The complaint management software ensures the reliable and fast processing of customer articulations. In addition, these are an essential basis for bank-wide improvement processes.

Management support is important. This ranges from keynote speeches on the target process to ongoing "management awareness". Such support ensures that the managers on site work consistently on the topic.

In addition, the Personnel Development department is systematically involved in the initiative, from the training of new employees to seminars on decentralized complaint processing in sales.

In order to continue the service initiative with further targeted impulses, BW-Bank has been breaking new ground for some years now with branch visits to ensure the service quality. Branch teams take advantage of this quality management consulting and coaching offer in order to work specifically on improving service quality. An experienced quality coach observes the behavior of the employees during customer meetings as well as the interaction between the team members, and analyzes further the factors influencing the quality of service. A multi-level feedback process (employee, team, manager) ensures that the resulting recommendations are communicated directly on site, reflected upon and ideally implemented immediately. The recommendation repertoire ranges from practical tips and quick wins to systemic considerations with impulses for personnel and team development.

One success factor of this format is the distinction to existing controlling instruments. An evaluation of the branch-specific service quality is not performed, as this would be methodically questionable on the grounds that such a snapshot would hinder the learning process.

Conclusion

The sole focus on a central complaint management, which sometimes prevails in companies, carries the danger of working very professionally on the tip of the "dissatisfaction iceberg", but of neglecting the powerful "deep layers" below. For this reason, BW-Bank has embarked on the path of continuing to strengthen the decentralized complaint management competences on a sustainable basis. The main advantages of this strategy are:

- Efficiency, as it is a resource-saving procedure,
- Effectiveness, because it also invests in prevention and thus reduces dissatisfaction at an early stage, instead of having to rectify at high cost.

(continued)

Spotlight 15.1 (continued)

Wolfgang Falkinger
Quality and Sales Management
Baden-Württembergische Bank

15.1.3 Advantages and Disadvantages of the Organizational Alternatives

With respect to determining the proportion of centralized or decentralized elements, their respective advantages and disadvantages must be weighed out. If the *decentralized branch offices* are given increased complaint management responsibility, then a customer-oriented, often immediate solution to problems can be expected. On the other hand, from the perspective of the head office, the complaint contacts are more difficult to control, and there are great difficulties in terms of the internal processing and analysis of complaints. It is also more difficult to utilize complaints as controlling instruments for the branches, the less the central office can prompt the branch offices to document the cases of dissatisfaction and to forward the information to the head office.

If instead a *central solution* is chosen, the advantages and disadvantages are reversed. The establishment and clear communication of a central contact point for complaints results in a dismantling of complaint barriers, increases the complaint volume, prevents complaint suppressions by employees, permits controls and simplifies internal complaint paths. Empirical studies verify that central departments—such as customer care centers—really have advantages, because the firm avoids duplicate work, saves management time, reduces processing costs, improves the information level regarding the extent and structure of customer problems and above all, greatly increases customers' complaint satisfaction.

The precise extent of the task assignment in a *dual complaint management system* must be determined in each individual case. The range extends from a primarily centralized complaint management system that cedes only the complementary acceptance and processing functions to the decentralized units, all the way to a principally decentralized complaint management system that is supplemented by a head office that functions as a "safety net". In this last case, the central unit indeed takes over the relevant functions of analysis, reporting and controlling, but sees itself only as a "second line" in terms of acceptance and processing.

Table 15.2 gives an overview of the *focal task assignments* between centralized and decentralized units for the four types of firms presented.

In *Cases A and B*, only central complaint units are needed, whereby the organizational implementation for each type is still different. In the case of Type A firms (mechanical engineering firms), it is sufficient to concentrate the responsibility for complaints with management and the customer contact departments and to assign the fulfillment of specific tasks to the customer contact employees, due to the low

Table 15.2 Distribution of tasks between centralized and decentralized complaint management units for the different types of firms

	Type A (E.g. mechanical engineering firm)	Type B (E.g. consumer goods manufacturer)	Type C (E.g. car manufacturer)	Type D (E.g. retail bank)
Organizational form	Centralized complaint management	Centralized complaint management	Dual complaint management	Dual complaint management
Centralized responsibility	Executive management, sales or service department	Complaint management department/customer care	Complaint management department/customer care	Complaint management department/customer care
Decentralized units	---	---	Authorized dealers	Branches

number of customers and the low number of complaints. On the other hand, the establishment of a special department would be wise in the case of Type B firms (manufacturers of packaged foods). Here it would be logical that this unit not only deals with questions of complaint management, but rather be equipped as a customer care department with broader competencies with respect to customer information and the internal transfer of customer concerns.

In *Cases C and D*, a dual system of complaint management is necessary. In addition to responsibility for complaint management at a central level, the firm must see to it that essential tasks are also undertaken on the retail or branch level, respectively, and that employees are able to accept and process customer complaints correctly. The manufacturer or the head office of a service provider with a number of branch offices thus has the additional challenge of coordinating the procedures and allocation of roles, creating an incentive system that ensures role fulfillment and creating the organizational requirements for rapid communication between the head office and the decentralized units. Provided that the products are sold via indirect distribution, these tasks must be handled in the context of vertical complaint management keeping in mind the different interest structures of the parties involved.

A glance at Table 15.2 shows that a purely decentralized solution does not seem to be appropriate in any of the cases presented. Whether such a version makes sense at all is doubtful in principle. For regardless of the situational factors, it is reasonable to *perform* certain functions of complaint management *centrally*. Among these functions are the following:

- The conceptual integration of the complaint management system in the *strategic framework* of company-wide customer orientation.
- The monitoring of *compliance with principles* in the performance of complaint management tasks.
- Supporting the system by *providing resources* and *creating the necessary infrastructure*.

On the other hand, it is especially in the case of services with direct customer contact possible to ensure a fast and efficient restoration of customer satisfaction by a *decentralized* fulfillment of tasks of the direct complaint management process. *Spotlight 15.2* illustrates this impressively with the example of a tour operator.

Spotlight 15.2
Decentralized Complaint Handling at Thomas Cook

Every holiday is a personal and highly emotional experience, and expectations are usually very high. An unfortunate start to the holidays such as a flight delay, can often be the reason why the hotel or even the entire holiday experience is rated on a rather lower level. Therefore, it is of the utmost importance to assist the guest in case of a complaint as soon as possible while he or she is still at the destination. To fulfill the guest's expectations or even go beyond them is Thomas Cook's main goal. This means complaint handling can definitely start during travel and while the customer is still at the destination.

A packaged holiday cannot easily be substituted like any other physical product. A tour operator buys its services from third parties such as airlines and hotels, and bundles these into packages. However, ultimately, the tour operator is fully responsible for the fulfillment of the guaranteed services. Thus, it is essential for Thomas Cook to offer 24/7 assistance for every guest during their trip. This can take the form of either physical representation in the destinations or virtual assistance through Thomas Cook's Connected Service representatives. What is important is the continuous availability of assistance 24 hours per day and 365 days per year. Physical representation is offered in all popular "volume" destinations such as Spain, Greece, Turkey, the Dominican Republic, Cuba etc. The other destinations are covered through the Connected Service team. The Connected Service team can be reached via telephone but of course also through all established social media tools such as SMS, WhatsApp, Facebook, etc. (see screenshot in Fig. 15.1). All representatives (physical and virtual) receive regular training to ensure they are knowledgeable on products (hotels, airlines, etc.) as well as on the source market's travel laws. Frequent quality and service training sessions complement this. In each case of a complaint, the representative's aim is to immediately solve the problem. This might involve changing a hotel room or hotel in case a guest is not satisfied with the product. In some cases where all efforts have not been successful the representative is also allowed to compensate the customer with a voucher payment according to the respective regulation parameters. Quick and uncomplicated complaint handling on the spot not only results in a higher guest satisfaction rate but also reduces the volume of complaints sent to the complaint management department in the source markets. To monitor the development and to identify further training requirements, Thomas Cook has established various KPIs that are reported regularly. The number of complaints, the resolving rate, the amount of compensation payments and, very important, the guests' satisfaction rate are some of these.

(continued)

Spotlight 15.2 (continued)

   Thomas Cook has realized that the level of service is the only major differentiator-KPI in the tour operator industry, and to satisfy a guest even when there is a complaint is the only way to win back trust and convince the customer to book another holiday.

Heidrun Steidle
Managing Director Thomas Cook Airport Service GmbH & Head of Complaint Management
Thomas Cook Touristik GmbH

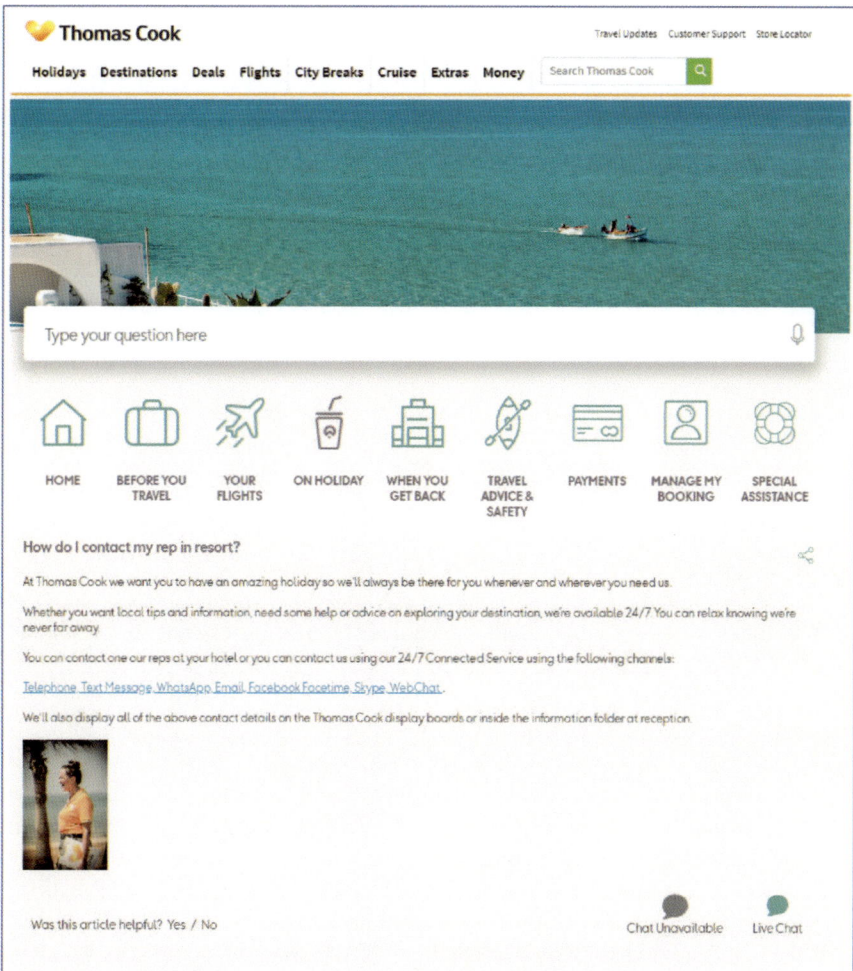

Fig. 15.1   Communication channels to contact the connected service team

15.2   The Complaint Management Department

If firms make the decision to integrate the centrally performed tasks in a specific organizational unit, it should be designated as the *complaint management department*. Often, however, it is not advisable in practice to limit the responsibility very narrowly to the complaint articulation form. The integration of the different customer-initiated forms of communication in one unit and the necessary coordination between the different measures in dealing with customer concerns makes it seem practical to expand the scope of responsibility to *all types of customer-initiated communication*—that is, to notices of amendment, praise, requests and ideas, or suggestions for improvement. If the organizational unit acquires such comprehensive competence for all the relationship-oriented customer articulations, it would seem appropriate to label it as a *customer care department*. For the following section, we will assume that firms have opted to establish a customer care department. Since the discussion here—as elsewhere in this book—is restricted to presentations of complaint management tasks, we subsequently will only speak of the *complaint management department*.

In order to implement the tasks of complaint management efficiently, this department should be divided into the operative component of contact handling *(complaint center)* and the conceptual controlling component *(direction of complaint management)*.

15.2.1 Responsibility for the Operative Processing of Complaints by the Complaint Center

The direct corporate interface with customers, in which the essential *operative tasks of the direct complaint management process* are accomplished—especially complaint acceptance, processing and reaction—, is the complaint center.

15.2.1.1 Complaint Center: Customer Care Center: Customer Interaction Center

In practice, different terms can be found for this operational organizational unit, such as "Customer Service Department", "Customer Interaction Center" or "Customer Care". In terms of the differentiation made in Sect. 1.2, it is advisable to *designate* this unit *in different ways*, depending on how broadly the fields of action and responsibility are set for this unit that accepts and processes customer concerns:

- If the range of activity consists primarily of accomplishing tasks of complaint management, then the term *"Complaint Center" (CC)* should be used. A Complaint Center focuses predominantly on complaint-related inbound activities and carries out outbound activities only insofar as they serve the goals of complaint management (e.g. follow-up surveys of complainants).
- If the unit is placed in charge of handling all the relationship-oriented forms of communication (notices of amendment, praise, complaints, requests), the

designation *"Customer Care Center" (CCC)* is appropriate. The emphasis of the
tasks here is also clearly on inbound activities; however, the scope of activities—
even in terms of potential outbound contacts—extends to customer concerns of
all kinds.
• If all customer-initiated inbound activities are included, regardless of whether
they are purchase- or relationship-relevant, and if marketing- and sales-oriented
outbound activities are also integrated, it is appropriate to speak of a *"Customer
Interaction Center" (CIC)* in the comprehensive sense.

The use of the term *"Center"* makes it clear that a *centralization of customer
communication* occurs in each case. A call center, where the customer contact that
takes place over the phone is centralized, is usually the heart of this centralization.
Complaint centers, customer care centers and customer interaction centers comprise
call centers, but complement the concept by consistently bundling all communication channels. Regardless of whether the customer contacts the firm by letter, fax,
e-mail or telephone, the customer articulations in each case arrive at a single
organizational unit. For the customers, this has the advantage that they only have
to contact a single department with all of their concerns. Consequently, the firm has
the chance to have the current status of all customer data at its disposal at all times
and thus to increase the quality of addressing those concerns. Furthermore, significant cost advantages can be realized, due to the synergy effects and the high degree
of professionalism achieved.

15.2.1.2   Operational Units of a Complaint Center
The organization of complaint centers is basically oriented to that of *call centers*.
Simply put, this means that all calls are taken by employees of the so-called *"Front
Office" (1st level)*. If customers' calls cannot be closed during the initial telephone
contact, they are turned over to employees at the *2nd level* for further processing by
experts. In addition to the customer contact units, which deal exclusively with the
processing of customer concerns by telephone, the *back office* takes responsibility
for customer concerns articulated in writing. In addition, this office takes over
extensive investigational activities and takes care of processing complex customer
concerns. For this purpose, it is also necessary to integrate the expertise of *specialist
departments or individual sales units (3rd Level)* in addressing and resolving
customer concerns.

In the following section, we will expand on this perspective, which is based on
traditional concepts of call centers, and briefly characterize the *individual operational units of a complaint center*.

Inbound Calls (1st Level)   This team is responsible for the direct acceptance of
customer complaints articulated by telephone.

2nd Level (for Inbound Calls)   Complaints articulated by telephone that exceed
the expertise and/or decision-making authority of the "Inbound Calls" (1st Level)
Team can be forwarded on a "stand-by" basis during direct contact with the customer

to a group of employees at the 2nd level (for inbound calls) that is equipped with adequate competencies and skills. The necessity of installing such a team primarily results from the complexity of the contents of the complaint and the urgency of resolving the problem. This approach also guarantees the continuous accessibility of the 1st level, since its employee resources are not tied up with time-consuming investigational activities. If it is not necessary to establish a 2nd level (for inbound calls), a callback is arranged with the customer if complaints are not resolved during the initial contact at the 1st level, and the concern is turned over to the back office, where appropriate investigations are carried out and contact is again made with the customer.

Inbound Mail (1st Level)   This function is not envisioned in conventional concepts of call centers. Traditionally, it is located in the back office. The establishment of an inbound-mail team (1st Level) becomes relevant, however, when the volume of written complaints is high, but a large percentage of these customer concerns do not require specific expert knowledge, and when these processes can be standardized. Keeping in mind that expensive know how regarding complex problem solutions is available in the back office, it is advisable from a financial standpoint to establish a 1st level for complaints that can be easily processed.

Inbound Social Media (1st Level)   The Social Media Team is responsible for the dialog in the social networks (especially Facebook and Twitter). Employees are generally responsible for responding to all forms of customer contact, whether inquiries, ideas, praise or complaints. However, they must be particularly sensitive to complaints for two reasons. On the one hand, they must not disseminate customer-specific information on the Internet, and on the other hand, when answering, they must be aware that the published answer is immediately enormously widespread and can therefore—in the case of an unfortunate choice of words or argumentation—trigger an escalation of criticism, even a storm of indignation (a "shitstorm"). It is therefore particularly important to ask the authors of customer reviews via Facebook or Twitter to contact the complaint center directly by e-mail in order to find an individual solution. For this to happen quickly, a close organizational and system-related connection between the inbound mail and the inbound social media team is required.

Back Office   This team is traditionally responsible for processing customer corre-spondence. If, however, an "Inbound Mail (1st Level)" unit exists, the back office is primarily responsible for customer complaints that cannot be processed at this level. The same applies to telephone complaints forwarded from "Inbound Calls" (1st level) or "2nd level (for Inbound Calls)". Accordingly, employees that are especially skilled should be available in the "back office".

Depending on how heterogeneous the expertise required in the back office is, it may be wise to compose this unit of several teams with differing emphases in terms of know-how. If the utilization of the telephone capacity is low, it is also conceivable that the back office also executes the 2nd level (for Inbound Calls). In this case, however, the firm must take into account that the employees should be systematically trained with respect to the different demands. This is necessary, too, if employees carry out not only customer-contact tasks but also indirect complaint management tasks as a consequence of a "job rotation" concept in order to reduce the employee's burden of permanent critical costumer contacts and to increase the task variety.

3rd Level (Specialist Departments) If the back office cannot solve the problem, it is necessary to involve specialist departments within the firm that possess detailed expertise (3rd level) in examining and resolving cases. Here the firm must be careful not to burden these departments with too many customer complaints, since the efficiency gains that would normally be achieved by establishing a customer care center are lost. In order to avoid this possible danger, it is recommended that the firm constantly monitor the quantitative volume of forwarded complaints and the employed resources of the specialist departments. If these departments reach the limits of their capacity, adequate capacity should be built up in the back office at the customer care center level.

Figure 15.2 illustrates the interrelationships among the various levels of processing. On the 1st level, the firm should employ generalists who can process and conclude a large number of uncomplicated complaint cases as rapidly as possible in ways that are largely standardized. The expensive expertise that is available in the other units is used to solve complex, special complaints that can be processed with a certain amount of delay.

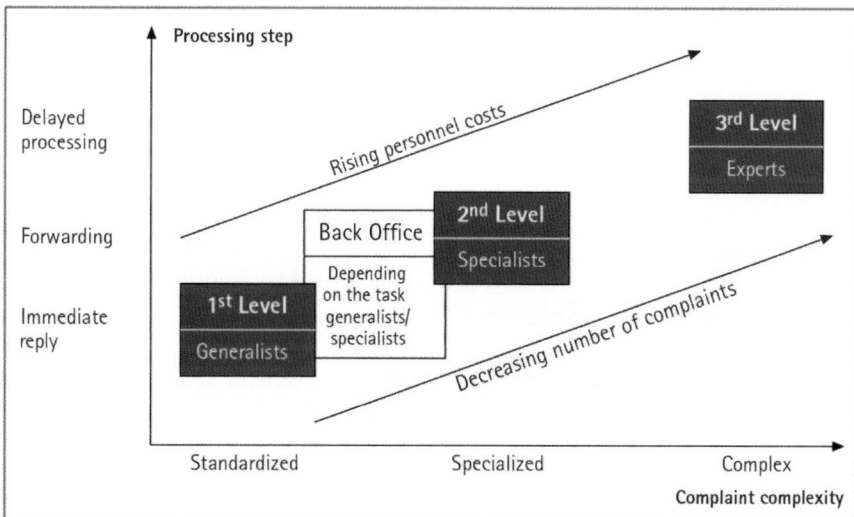

Fig. 15.2 Major operational inbound organizational units in the complaint center (Source: based on Fichte 2001, p. 34)

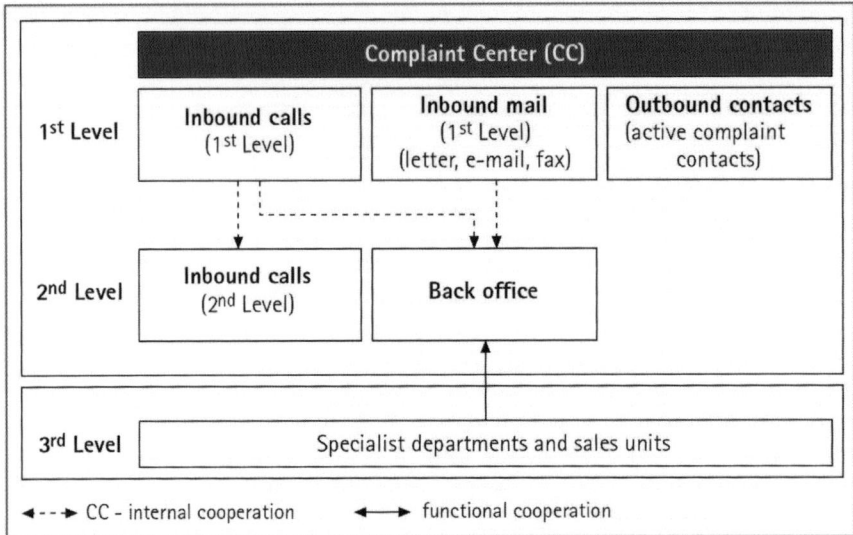

Fig. 15.3 Typical organizational structure of the operational units of a complaints center

Outbound Contacts: Active Complaint Contacts This unit, which is not envisioned in traditional concepts of call centers, takes responsibility for carrying out active complaint contacts. Actions and measures that serve the accomplishment of complaint management and are initiated by the firm take place here. Among these actions are the processing of follow-up complaints (Sect. 9.5) and the conducting of complaint satisfaction surveys in the context of performance measurement (Sect. 11.2).

Figure 15.3 presents a typical *organizational structure for the operational units of a complaint center* with its interfaces to the specialist departments and sales units of the firm.

15.2.1.3 The Management of the Complaint Center and Its Tasks

In order to guarantee and maintain operational complaint handling, the management of the complaint center has to perform a series of *executive and managerial functions*, specifically on a strategic and operational level, as well as on the personnel management level:

- *Strategic level:* overall responsibility for human resources, ensuring the operational process, budget preparation and accountability
- *Operational level:* project development, review of sales and service targets
- *Human resources management:* coordination/control of employee and team activities, disciplinary responsibility, employee information, motivation and assessment.

Referring specifically to complaint management, the following tasks are of primary importance:

Direct Complaint Management Process Here, the main responsibility is to implement the targets for complaint stimulation, acceptance, processing and reaction and to ensure the quality of task performance. To this end, the quality and productivity standards that have been defined must be communicated to the employees and must be measured. The Complaint Management Index described in Sect. 11.2.4 offers a suitable starting point.

In order to secure the competence of the operational complaint centers for the smooth handling of customer contacts, it is advisable to establish an *"Information Management"* unit. The central task of this team is to request and to process current information from other departments or branch offices—about new prices, products, services or corporate activities, for instance—and to ensure that the operational units of the complaint center have access to this information. In this way, the processing and problem-solving expertise of the complaint center can be increased and the activation of the 3rd level can be avoided.

Indirect Complaint Management Process In coordination with the direction of complaint management, which will be presented in the following section, some of the tasks of indirect complaint management can be assigned to the complaint center. These tasks may include sub-areas such as complaint analysis, complaint reporting and complaint management controlling. It is obvious, then, that significant key figures from evidence and task controlling, especially quality and productivity figures, must be collected directly in the Complaint Center. This applies especially to all the complaint department-related indicators such as length of conversations, lost calls or the observance of defined service levels.

Personnel Management The employees who accept complaints are the most valuable resource in every Complaint Center. That is why one of the essential tasks for the management of this unit is to implement important human resources-related aspects of complaint management. Among these aspects is recruiting the "right" employees with the needed social, emotional, methodological and professional competencies and ensuring that all employees continue to enhance their skills on the basis of profound training concepts. Another core task pertains to the planning, the calculation and the deployment of personnel that is needed to process the incoming customer concerns efficiently and to observe the agreed service level (workforce management).

Information Technology Apart from personnel resources, information technology represents the second key factor for complaint centers. Mastery of the technological aspects of complaint management is thus one of the requirements for the management of complaint centers. Directors must be able to guarantee the reliable performance of complex telephone systems, software systems and demanding hardware environments with adequate maintenance and support services. This also includes providing continuous information and training to the customer contact personnel with respect to user-related system-technical questions as well as implementing software-technical requirements in order to optimize operational complaint processing.

If complaint centers are operated by the firm itself, a *coordination of task performance* is required between the departmental leadership unit in complaint management and the management of the complaint center on the one hand, and between the departmental leadership unit in complaint management and other functional business areas such as IT management and human resources on the other hand. For reasons of efficiency, it thus proves advantageous to assign clearly defined personnel-related and information technology tasks to the appropriate internal departments by contract.

15.2.2 Responsibility for Conceptual Control by the Direction of Complaint Management

The departmental leadership in complaint management is the conceptual steering part of the complaint management department. Therefore, the *relationship between the departmental leadership in complaint management and the complaint center* is established in such a way that the departmental leadership in complaint management carries the expert responsibility for the entire complaint management process and its strategic anchoring in customer relationship management. The complaint center acts as an operational unit *in accordance with the guidelines of the departmental leadership in complaint management.* This applies in cases in which operational complaint handling is carried out in the firm itself or is outsourced to an external customer care center as well.

Strategic planning is a central responsibility of the departmental leadership in complaint management. In addition, it must ensure that the direct and indirect complaint management process is carried out in line with the strategy. The *conceptual control tasks* to be performed by the departmental leadership in complaint management will be briefly described below. This description follows the same structure as the presentation of the tasks of the complaint center management, which illustrates the division of tasks between these units:

Direct Complaint Management Process A key departmental leadership function is to develop and to optimize the task performance in the direct complaint management process on a continual basis. This includes the planning of complaint-stimulation campaigns, the development of guidelines and process descriptions for all aspects of complaint acceptance, as well as the constant monitoring of the complaint receipt concept and the resulting complaint input processes. This area of responsibility also includes the definition, development and software support of the concept for collecting complaint information.

Furthermore, the detailed and cross-functional development of the work flow for the processing of customer concerns, including the definition of the responsible departments and persons, the temporal standards for the reaction and the contents of communication—for confirmations of receipt or intermediate replies, for instance— also take place here. In addition, the employee behavior guidelines regarding complaint reaction must be defined.

All the guidelines and process descriptions for the handling of customer complaints together form the basis for the operational processing in the complaint center. They must be developed, discussed critically and implemented in coordination with the responsible units there.

Indirect Complaint Management Process A crucial task of the departmental leadership in complaint management is their responsibility for the indirect complaint management process, that is, for complaint evaluation, complaint management controlling, complaint reporting and utilization of complaint information. The departmental leadership must develop the relevant analytical concepts, make fundamental decisions on evidence-, task- and cost-benefit controlling, specify different report formats and plan the use of information. As part of complaint management controlling, the divisional management has the particularly important task of monitoring and steering the entire complaint management process. This is done using the key performance indicators (Sect. 4.2) and the Complaint Management Index (Sect. 11.4.2).

Personnel Management The departmental leadership in complaint management is responsible for continually providing, sensitizing, motivating and developing the employees in the complaint management department. Here—in cooperation with the corporate human resources department—concepts in personnel recruiting, instruction and training, the design of incentive systems and measures for the prevention of burnout should be developed, implemented and evaluated. Furthermore, the departmental leadership has to formulate and support initiatives that aim at the empowerment of all company employees to behave in a more customer-oriented manner.

Information Technology This task area falls within the scope of responsibility of the departmental leadership in complaint management in that the technical requirements for the implementation of the software and databases must be defined here. The departmental leadership thus represents an important interface to IT experts within the firm itself and—especially when an external service provider is engaged—to IT experts in the complaint center.

The departmental leadership's central instrument for the *direction and monitoring* of the operational processes are the quality and productivity standards, which were presented in Sect. 11.2. The departmental leadership in complaint management has to decide on the relevant assessment dimensions and attributes, weight them and define a standard for each attribute. The observance of these standards—and, where appropriate, a defined value from the Complaint Management Index—then becomes, in addition to the financial aspects, the subject of the agreement with the complaint center. The management of the complaint center bears responsibility for compliance with these standards. Pertinent agreements should not only be made in the case of outsourcing, but rather also when the complaint center is assigned internally to the complaint management department.

Figure 15.4 shows the *organization of the complaint management department* and the participation of various units in task performance.

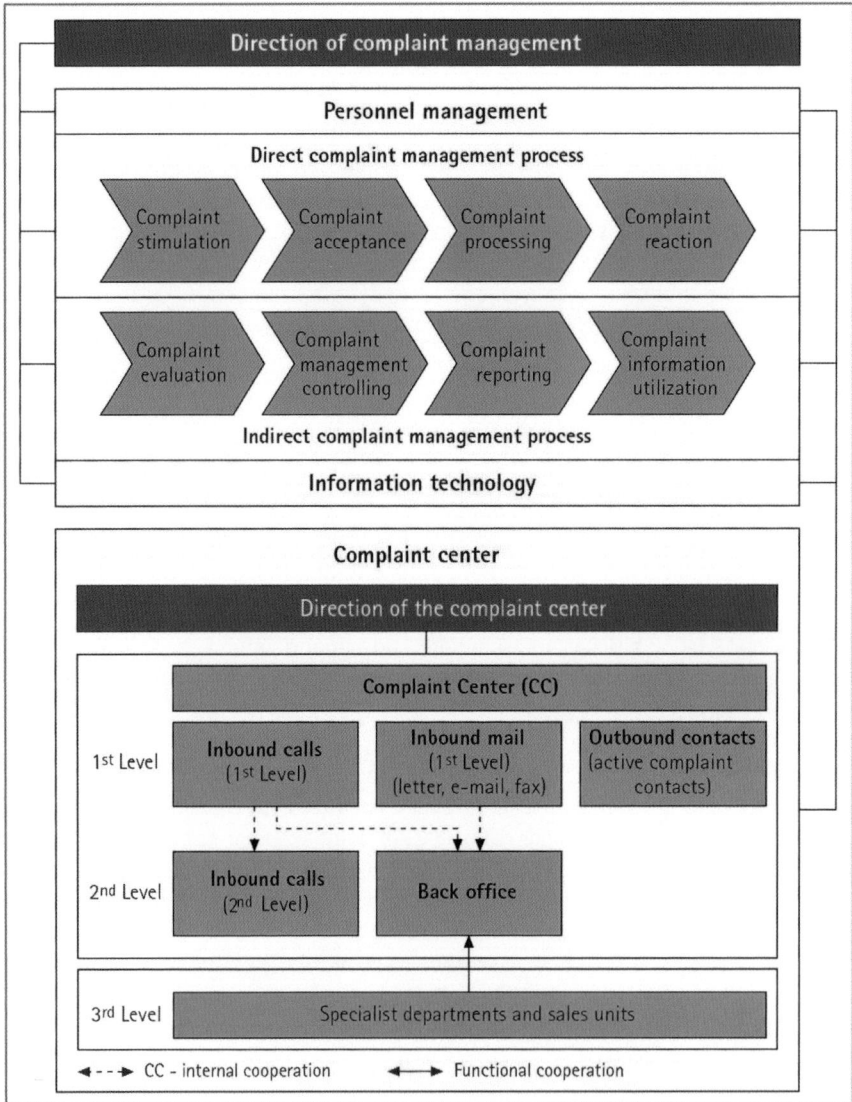

Fig. 15.4 Basic organizational structure of the complaint management department

Spotlight 15.3
Establishment of a Complaint Center

A large energy company recognized complaint management as an essential component of the company's orientation toward even more consistent customer orientation. In order to obtain well-founded starting points for its future development and positioning as well as for the identification of potential for improvement, both internal analyses and, in particular, an "annoyance iceberg" and termination survey were carried out. A number of organizational deficits were identified:

- There were no explicitly communicated complaint channels, so that complaints were articulated at all contact points, but processed in an unstructured manner.
- There were no dedicated complaint acceptance, processing and reaction processes and therefore no time and content obligations with regard to the creation of confirmations of receipt and interim notices.
- Complaint reporting was based on rudimentary complaint information, so its significance was very limited.
- Systematic quality improvement processes based on complaint information (therefore) did not exist.
- Whether or to what extent the complaint handling actually satisfied the complainants and prevented them from possibly terminating the contract was not monitored.
- More than half of the angry customers did not complain; the proportion of non-complainants was much higher among the terminators.
- Annoyed customers who complained were characterized by a high level of complaint dissatisfaction.
- A considerable proportion of the complainants terminated their contracts and switched to the competition.
- An equally not insignificant proportion of the cancellers could have been held with more empathic behavior.
- The CRM software used did not in any way support any functionalities that were technically necessary.

These results led to the reorientation of complaint management—in an uncompromising form, by establishing a *complaint center* consisting of different teams for telephone and written complaints as well as outbound contacts (see Fig. 15.5).

This complaint center is characterized in particular by the following features:

- All complaints are channeled to the Complaint Center through the offensive communication of complaints channels on all relevant communication media (including the provision of a specific complaint portal on the Internet).

(continued)

Spotlight 15.3 (continued)

- The Complaint Center is responsible for the "complaint ownership" of all complaints without exception. This means that every complaint process is completed by the Complaint Center. This is done either by preparing the complaint response—also on the basis of technical assistance requested by the specialist departments within the agreed timeframe and content—or by conducting a follow-up contact, provided that activities still have to be carried out by other departments within the scope of problem-solving or the complaint process is completed by other departments in exceptional cases.
- Cooperation with all departments involved in complaint handling—as well as active participation in quality improvement processes—is regulated in specific service level agreements, compliance with which is checked weekly and demanded by management.
- Complainant follow-up contacts by telephone are carried out systematically to ensure that the complaint process is completed not only from the company's point of view, but also from the customer's point of view.
- A specific complaint management software system is implemented, so that all technical issues are fully supported by the software.
- Employees with the "Complaint/Customer Care Gene" are recruited and developed in a targeted manner.

The Complaint Center itself will be controlled by a specific management unit, which is also responsible for fulfilling all strategic and operational KPIs. In particular, this unit (control unit) is to perform the following tasks:

- Professional development and continuous optimization of all relevant complaint management processes
- Continuous employee sensitization and development
- Provision of specific complaint reports for individual customer segments and all relevant internal target groups
- Initiation and coordination of quality improvement workshops with specialist departments affected by the identified problem areas
- Monitoring the effectiveness of implemented quality improvement measures on the basis of complaint, annoyance and termination information.

Consistent support of the management will be indispensable for the implementation as well as founding by a meaningful business case in which the costs incurred and in particular the economic benefits produced have to be shown in the form of targeted customer loss avoidance.

Wolfgang Seidel
Company owner and manager
servmark consultancy

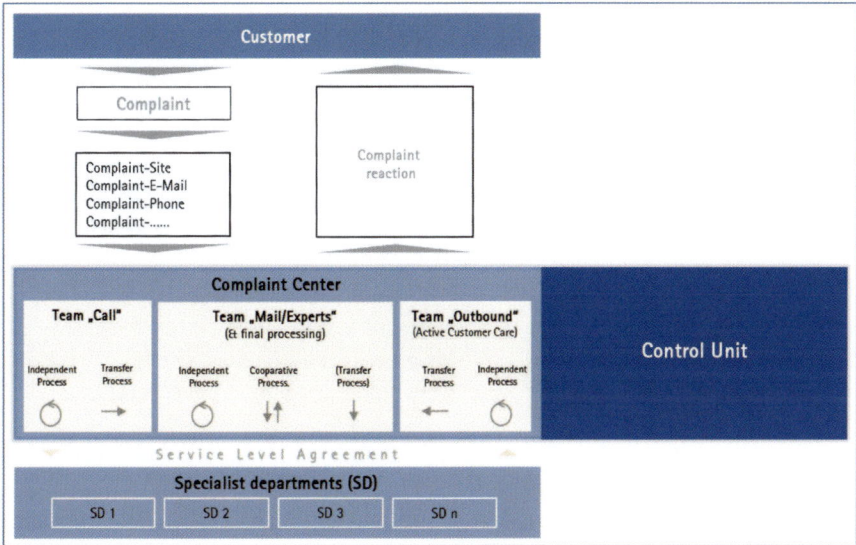

Fig. 15.5 Complaint center and control unit

15.3   Integration of the Complaint Management Department in the Organizational Structure of the Corporation

On a company-wide level the way has to be assessed how the complaint management process is linked with other corporate processes, which influence rights a complaint management area requires for the comprehensive fulfillment of its tasks and which consequences for the institutional anchoring of the department in the overall corporate organization result from these connections.

15.3.1 Responsibility and Linkage of the Complaint Management Processes with Other Corporate Processes

The complaint management department cannot fulfill its *function as a dialog interface* to the customer if its responsibility is limited to narrowly defined tasks. The targeted reduction of communication barriers is only achievable when the department is designed to accept all customer problems and when customers perceive that this is the case. Likewise, the elimination of individual customer dissatisfaction can only be fully accomplished when the complaint management department has the opportunity to receive and analyze all customer demands and problems and to insist on their solution.

Even when taking into account the *internal* function of making an important contribution to the customer-oriented direction of the firm, a limitation of the responsibility should be avoided. A sensitization of the firm through information, instruction and innovative impulses requires that the work of the complaint management department is not completely defined in terms of content. Customers and their complaints are also the starting point for the tasks of the indirect complaint management process. The articulated customer problems must be solved and signal the need for training and innovation. They also determine the spectrum of activities for the complaint management department.

If we accept this assessment of *comprehensive customer-related responsibility*, then the resulting *consequences for cooperation with a multitude of other internal fields of activity* and the integration of sub-processes with other corporate processes must be taken into consideration. Here, we would like to point out several *examples*:

- *Complaint stimulation* measures should be planned and implemented in cooperation with marketing, sales and service.
- *Complaint processing and reaction* demands an especially close relationship with the departments that are frequently the subject of customer concerns or that often implement problem solutions, such as billing or technical service.
- A *complaint reaction that is specific to a customer segment or that is individualized* requires that a classification of customers according to segment affiliation and customer value be carried out on an ongoing basis via CRM or database marketing.
- *Complaint evaluation* and *reporting* can only take place in a goal-oriented way when the relevant internal customers (e.g. research and development, production, quality management, marketing, sales, service) are identified, and the analyses and reports are geared toward their needs.
- The *utilization of complaint information* must be planned in close cooperation with quality management.
- *Complaint management controlling* is to be aligned with the firm's overall system of controlling.
- Provided that the complaint management system determines *failure costs* and assigns them to the departments that caused them, integration in the controlling system and intensive cooperation with the units in question is also necessary.
- Supporting and developing the *infrastructure of the information technology system* necessitates constant cooperation with the IT department.

Therefore, detailed *process definitions and documentation*, which also highlight the interfaces with other departments and the respective customer-supplier relationships, must be available for all the task modules of the complaint management process. Moreover, service levels for the quality of internal services and institutionalized forms of participation in decision-making processes must be agreed upon. In addition, consideration must be given to the equipment of the complaint management department with *rights to influence* that are necessary in order to fulfill its functions in an optimal fashion.

This is important because the implementation of a complaint management department leads to a *change in the internal company structure*, which is by no means welcomed by all of the affected internal partners. This applies in particular to comprehensive complaint management of the "satisfaction lab" type. It

- *confronts* other departments *with customer problems*, criticism and the demand to analyze the causes of problems and develop preventative measures,
- *demands problem solutions* in the customer's interest, which involve costs for other departments (e.g. a free repair),
- *allocates* possibly *failure costs* to the causing units,
- *develops* its *own analyses and suggestions for improvement*, which other departments may find undesirable or patronizing,
- *informs,* through complaint reporting, additional internal groups of people, in particular top management, about the type and extent of customer problems that have occurred.

In this respect, it is realistic to assume that there is internal skepticism toward complaint management, a lack of willingness to cooperate, frequent rejections of proposals and even resistance to its activities. In order to *prevent the complaint management department from failing*, it must have *effective influence rights*.

15.3.2 Equipping the Complaint Management Department With Influence Rights

If the complaint management department is responsible for all tasks of the direct and indirect complaint management process, it must also be endowed with influence rights in order to fulfill this responsibility. The term "right of influence" encompasses a *wide range of different rights*, ranging from the right to information to the right to make exclusive decisions.

The *right to information* affords the opportunity to forward information that has been accumulated to decision-makers. The *right to consultation* goes over and beyond the right to information and allows the processing of information for initiatives and alternative suggestions. The *right to control* bestows the power to review the decisions of others with reference to their compliance with agreed-upon principles. This right experiences an increase in the *right to veto*, which can help prevent the implementation of others' decisions, until a higher authority solves the conflict. The *right to co-decision* gives the opportunity to participate in intermediate and final decisions. The most far-reaching right, a *right to make exclusive decisions*, exists when a department can come to fully autonomous decisions.

The equipping of a complaint management department with rights to influence must take place on a *task-specific* basis. In addition, the requirements must be taken into account resulting from belonging to one of the strategic types of complaint management presented in Sect. 5.3.

In order to perform the *tasks of the direct complaint management process*, "strong" rights such as the right to participate in decision-making and the right to make independent decisions are necessary—regardless of the strategy type. This requires the principle of congruence between influence and responsibility. Moreover, only with such a set of rights is it possible to ensure that the customer relationship, quality and productivity-oriented goals can be pursued efficiently and flexibly in response to changing situations.

With regard to the tasks of the *indirect complaint management process*, the situation has to be considered differently, depending on the strategic type of complaint management.

The *"Complaint Factory"* type has the primary task of handling customer complaints as cost-effectively as possible. Since indirect complaint management is only of secondary importance here, simple *information rights* are sufficient in this respect.

Complaint management of the type *"Relationship Amplifier"* focuses on securing the relationship with the customer by restoring customer satisfaction. This means that the tasks of indirect complaint management are given a much higher priority than in the complaint factory: more extensive and detailed analyses must be carried out, suggestions for quality improvements made, and complaint satisfaction must be monitored, which is a central indicator of the relationship strength. In this respect, it is appropriate that complaint management areas of this type should not only have information rights within the company, but also at least *consulting rights*.

The primary interest of the *"Quality Control"* type is not strengthening customer relations but quality assurance. This clearly directs the focus of attention to the tasks of the indirect complaint management process: complaints must be carefully analyzed with regard to quality defects, correspondingly differentiated forms of reporting must be carried out and, above all, errors must be eliminated and failure costs reduced. This implies that complaint management of this type must have at least *co-decision* rights with regard to the evaluation of complaints and complaint reporting, but also the *right to control or veto* regarding the usage of complaint information.

Complaint management of the *"Satisfaction Lab"* type also takes a more internal perspective. However, in contrast to the quality control type, the customer knowledge generated by complaint management must be used actively and comprehensively for innovative impulses and the initiation of customer-oriented change processes. In this respect, the complaint management area must have a strong influence, which can only be guaranteed by the clear allocation of *co-decision rights*. Table 15.3 provides an overview of the relationship between the complaint management strategy type and the required minimum level of influence rights.

In practice, the enforcement of influence rights to ensure the *fulfillment of internal tasks* often proves to be problematic. There is the least resistance to the exercise of information rights because it provides other departments with additional information that improves their decision-making basis. The formal granting of consultation, control, veto or co-decision rights, on the other hand, is an *intervention in the autonomy* of other departments.

Table 15.3 Complaint management strategy type and required minimum level of influence rights

Complaint management strategy type	Minimum level of influence rights	
	Direct complaint management process	Indirect complaint management process
Complaint factory	Co-decision right	Information right
Relationship amplifier	Co-decision right	Consultation right
Quality control	Co-decision right	Control or veto right
Satisfaction lab	Co-decision right	Co-decision right

This is explained using the example of *control rights*. A major objective of complaint management is to identify problems with products and services perceived by customers and to prevent their future occurrence. In order to achieve this goal, complaint management can be granted a right to control with regard to the consideration of its information on product defects by specialist departments. This should be combined with the possibility of imposing consequences if it turns out that the responsible departments ignore the concrete indications and the meaningful evaluation data provided because they shy away from the costs of the corrective measures. Since the department's ignorance generates constantly high complaint management costs, it makes sense to allocate the relevant *failure costs* internally to the department areas causing them. These can be either the reaction costs only, but also the complete complaint handling costs for such problems. In the latter case, the control effect would be considerably greater, since it can be assumed that cost considerations now cause the department to take corrective measures.

The influence would be even greater if the complaint management department were granted *veto rights*. The purpose of this assignment of rights is also explained by the example of the unwillingness of departments to eliminate errors. In long-term business relationships, customers may experience the same problem several times, and therefore complain repeatedly (*repeat complainants*). If the results of the complaint analysis show that customers have terminated business relationships just because of the repeated occurrence of problems and despite a satisfactory complaint handling process, this means that the ignorance of the departments is causing customer churn and at the same time is preventing the complaint management from achieving its customer retention goals. In these cases, it is obvious to burden the departments with the *costs of dealing with repeat complainants*. More far-reaching, however, would be to give the complaint management department a *veto right with regard to the further sale* of the products affected by the problems. Such a veto requires a final decision at a higher management level.

By allocating a veto right to the complaint management department, top management makes it clear that it intends to make decisions on product variations, innovations and eliminations not only with regard to sales aspects but also taking into account customer loyalty goals and the securing of future sales potential. Thereby, complaints management is assigned an important role in the implementation of a consistent customer relationship management strategy.

In order to minimize the conflict potential in the event of internal differences of interest, all decision-relevant rights (right to control, right to veto, right to co-decision and exclusive decision) require formal and specified regulations. These should be understood as minimum forms of influence. The actual degree of influence depends on other factors, such as the expert power, i.e. a high level of *professional competence*. It is therefore necessary to fill management positions in complaint management with proven experts and respected personalities. In addition, it is important to strengthen *the understanding of the role of complaint management* in the company as a whole. This must be achieved by appropriate appreciation on the part of the company's top management, but can also be supported by other measures, e.g. personnel policy actions. It is conceivable that temporary work in the area of complaint management will be made obligatory for managers. This would not only provide insights into the department's basic concept and working methods, but would also make it clear that efforts to achieve customer satisfaction are a prerequisite for a career in the company. In addition to these supportive measures, the relevance and scope of complaint management is largely determined by the organizational classification in the company hierarchy.

15.3.3 The Establishment of the Complaint Management Department as a Staff Position, a Line Position or in a Matrix Organization

For the hierarchical arrangement and the equipping with influence rights, there are primarily *three basic alternatives* available, each of which can be found in various forms: staff position, line position or matrix organization.

15.3.3.1 The Establishment of the Complaint Management Department as a Staff Position

In many firms, the complaint management department is established as a *staff position* that is directly subordinate to top management (see Fig. 15.6).

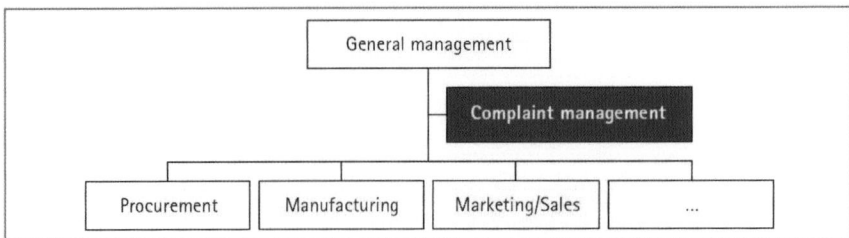

Fig. 15.6 Complaint management department as a staff position

The primary *advantages* of this solution are the department's functional independence and its closeness to top management. The *functional independence* makes it easier for the department to establish the necessary relationships with various functional areas and to carry out innovative suggestions and subsequent controls with the required autonomy and self-confidence. Its *direct subordination and closeness to top management* documents the high value that is attached to the complaint management department; and since the attitude of top management is perceived by organizational units, the documented positive assessment strengthens the informal authority of the department and increases its chances for effectiveness. Moreover, this organizational classification guarantees short paths of communication for the transfer of strategic information.

The *disadvantage* of the staff solution, however, is that staffs have *no rights of instruction and no decision-making rights* over the line and cannot force other corporate units make use of the customer-related expertise that is available here. Furthermore, if complaint management is understood in the sense presented here—as having a comprehensive field of activity—and especially if a complaint center is attached, the design as a staff no longer proves to be suitable. In this case, the work that is typical for a staff—to provide consultation to top management in its decision-making—is no longer the dominant work performed; rather, there are differentiated managerial functions to be performed, which also imply at least inner-departmental decision-making rights. Therefore, the alternative of institutionalizing complaint management as a line position should be considered.

15.3.3.2 The Establishment of the Complaint Management Department as a Line Position

If the complaint management department is conceived as a *line position*, the question arises as to assignment within the organization's hierarchy. In the first chapter, complaint management was characterized conceptually as a key component of customer care management and as the core of customer retention and customer relationship management. Accordingly, it stands to reason that the organizational classification follows along the lines of this conceptual consideration. In a functional organizational structure, it would thus be required that below the top management level, a customer relationship unit be established in addition to the key traditional organizational units such as purchasing, production or finance. Within this unit, the complaint management department could be institutionalized as a line position on the same level as marketing, sales and service (see Fig. 15.7).

The *advantages* of an organizational solution such as this one are that the responsibility for achieving the defined goals can clearly be assigned to the complaint management department and that the strategic anchoring in customer relationship management is institutionally secured. In this way, the customer-oriented integration of customer data from marketing, sales, service and customer care/complaint management can be achieved. Moreover, the maxim of "one face to the customer" can be realized if all customer-initiated communication is bundled in the customer care center/complaint center. A possible *disadvantage* of the line version is the loss of direct access to top management. It may be that the marketing and sales

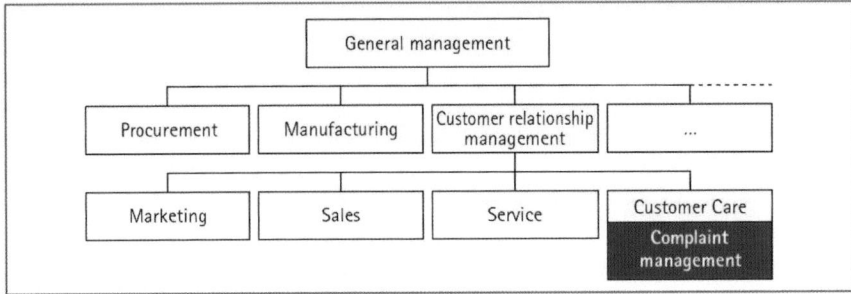

Fig. 15.7 Complaint management department as a line position

departments in particular gain a dominant influence in customer relationship management due to their importance for turnover and impede a complete fulfillment of the functions of the complaint management department. To reduce this danger, the complaint management department must be equipped with adequate power. This can be achieved by designing the area as a profit center (Sect. 15.3.4) and by assigning influence rights (Sect. 15.3.2).

15.3.3.3 The Complaint Management Department in a Customer-Oriented Matrix Organization

For firms that make not only a functional differentiation, but also *consistently implement* the perspective of *customer relationship management*, this means that the *primary organizational structuring is made according to customer groups*. Accordingly, varying organizational responsibilities are determined for different customer groups (for example, corporate customers/private customers or private customers with varying need profiles or values). The managers then have to coordinate all the transaction-oriented activities in the marketing, sales and service functions for these customer groups. Additionally, the relationship perspectives must be expressed in the fact that the responsibilities for relationship-relevant customer groups—e.g. acquisition, retention and regain management—are defined. For this reason, the customer relationship manager's task of coordination extends to these measures, the result of which is a type of *matrix organization* in which the complaint management department is responsible for all the complaints from all the customer groups (see Fig. 15.8).

For *complaint management*, the *advantage* lies in the extensive independence of this department from other functional departments. In this way, the internal significance is hardly determined by the marketing and sales functions, but rather by the interests of the customer relationship managers in maintaining jeopardized business relationships. A real gain in power can arise from this situation. A *disadvantage* results from the fact that the type of cooperation with other departments can scarcely be defined unequivocally, since the type and extent of task achievement depend to a significant degree upon the requirements of the different customer relationship managers, as well as upon their ability to be persuasive.

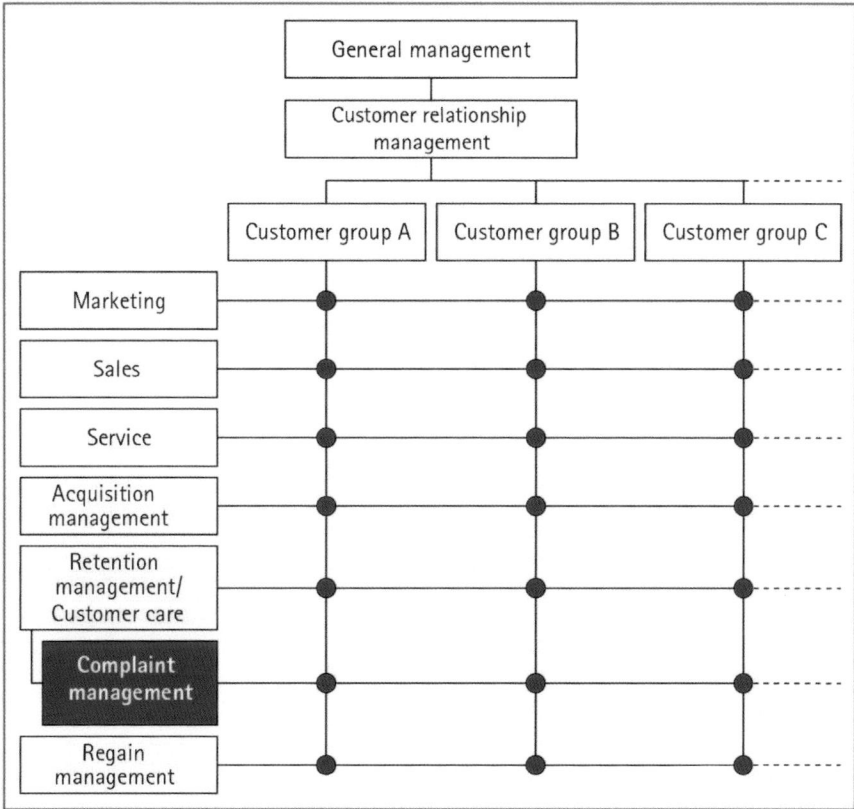

Fig. 15.8 Complaint management department in a customer-oriented matrix organization

15.3.4 The Complaint Management Department as a Profit Center?

The potential power of the complaint management department can be significantly increased internally if this department can successfully be designed as a profit center. The director of complaint management would then be responsible for the achievement of *defined profit goals*. In this way, the complaint management department could express the relevance of its work to the firm in the most effective internal language—namely, in its profit contribution.

Whether the profit center concept can be *applied* to the complaint management department *at all* is certainly a controversial question. Often, this question is answered in the negative, primarily with a notice that the success of complaint management is expressed essentially by non-financial target figures (customer satisfaction, loyalty), opportunity categories (sales losses prevented) and benefit figures that are difficult to quantify (information benefits, communication benefits). Moreover, in the case of the complaint management department, we are dealing with an internal service provider whose information services are not often actively demanded and even less often internally calculated. For this reason, specific revenues or profits are rarely available.

As well-founded as this argument is, it nevertheless also provides starting points that would lead to a *different conclusion*. According to this way of thinking, a profit center solution seems to be realistic if the complaint management system is successful in *verifying its real profit contribution*, supplying relevant internal services and allocating these services internally. There is every reason to believe that a professionally managed complaint management department is increasingly able to accomplish the above tasks.

The complaint management department is the central contact point within the firm for dissatisfied customers. If this department is successful in preventing dissatisfied customers from switching, it secures for the firm the scarce resource of customer loyalty and the sales revenue and profits that are associated with it. The comments made regarding complaint-related cost-benefit controlling (Sect. 11.3) showed that the economic retention benefit of customer complaints, which arises from the ongoing retention of dissatisfied customers, can be verified and thus provides a solid foundation for a *real profit and loss statement for complaint management*. By a targeted monitoring of the causes of potential customer losses the turnover and profit contributions can clearly be determined that complaint management actually secures for the firm. By periodically calculating these figures, the firm obtains the actual monetary profit contribution of complaint management.

The complaint management department essentially plays the role of an *internal service provider*. It takes over all the tasks of direct and indirect complaint management for the firm as a whole. Successful performance of the tasks of *direct complaint management*—such as accepting complaints, recording the complaint information and communicating with complainants—allows the firm to take advantage of the chance to preserve a jeopardized business relationship. It would make sense from a logical perspective, therefore, to allocate the costs arising from such activities—at market prices—to the respective departments that caused them. Nevertheless, the advantage expected to accompany this novel approach—i.e. creating a strong incentive for the responsible departments to eliminate the causes of those problems—must be checked against the problems associated with allocating the costs and the difficulty of making such an allocation acceptable.

In terms of the *tasks of indirect complaint management*, such as performing analyses and furnishing reports, which can lead to product and process improvements, the situation must be evaluated somewhat differently. If these services are only delivered at internal prices, it might be that they are not requested by all the relevant internal groups and/or are only procured occasionally, so that the advantage of information utilization is only partially realized. In order to prevent the occurrence of such a situation, it would seem to be wise to make the acceptance of a standard program of analysis and reporting obligatory for the relevant target groups, wherein content, frequency and price should be negotiated. For more extensive information and support services, the complaint management department has to make innovative proposals and market them internally.

If the firm is successful in establishing the conditions necessary to determine the actual profit and in internally allocating the costs of direct complaint management and information services in indirect complaint management, *organizing the complaint center department as a profit center would appear to be appropriate.*[1]

15.4 On the Question of Outsourcing Complaint Management

Many firms go on to source out at least a part of their complaint management to external service providers. An assessment of these *outsourcing* decisions cannot be made in general; rather, it requires a differentiated view. In particular, it is necessary to differentiate between the strategic-conceptual tasks and the operational tasks.

The responsibility for dissatisfied customers and the responsibility for the professional steering of the complaint management process as a whole, including its framework factors (human resources, organization and technology), cannot be delegated externally under any circumstances. It is a *fundamental task of every firm* to accept responsibility for problems and failures that occur, to create the appropriate conditions to satisfy the complainants and to introduce measures that prevent the future occurrence of problems. Another reason for arguing against outsourcing this responsibility is the fact that complaint management represents the core of customer relationship and customer retention management, and its philosophy must originate within the firm and be lived and supported by the employees there. It is incumbent upon the complaint management department to accept this responsibility and to create the appropriate basic conditions. It is a truism that core competencies cannot be outsourced. Firms that count their relationships with their customers among their core competencies cannot, therefore, delegate these corporate functions to external service providers *under any circumstances.* Accordingly, most firms limit themselves to reflections of whether and under what conditions the operational handling of contacts with complainants, can be outsourced.

This operational aspect affects the *complaint center,* with which the customers interact and where they experience customer orientation and quality, as the firm understands these concepts. If the firm wants to outsource the complaint center, it must *fulfill* a series of *requirements* and at the same time ensure that the risk associated with outsourcing—namely, that the firm would fail to achieve its complaint management goals—is minimized with the help of *Service Level Agreements (SLA):* (1) of central importance is the fact that the complaint management department leadership defines *detailed targets* for the procedures of processing telephone and written complaints. These targets include, for example, requirements with

---

[1] In science-fiction novels, this situation has already become a reality. In his book The Restaurant at the End of the Universe, Douglas Adams (1982: 10) writes of the hugely successful Sirius Cybernetics Corporation Complaint Division, "which now covers the major land masses of three medium-size planets and is the only part of the Corporation to have shown a consistent profit in recent years."

respect to the times for telephone conversations and reactions, the social skills of employees who come into contact with customers or problem solutions and compensatory benefits that are allowed. Furthermore, the firm must determine the conditions under which complaints should be forwarded to the 3rd level of the company. (2) at the same time, the subjective and objective quality and productivity standards described in task controlling should be implemented, in order to permit *continuous monitoring* with regard to compliance with the standards that have been defined. In this context, the strong focus of current service level agreements on productivity and objective quality standards must be changed. In order to make the goal of complaint satisfaction manageable, the satisfaction standards in particular must be taken into account. (3) in addition, the firm must see to it that *customer and service provider cooperate very closely*. Here, the firm should ensure that employees in the complaint center are not only trained in system-technical, conversation-tactical and socio-psychological matters, but also are familiar with the details of the organizational structure and the responsibilities of the client and possess specialized knowledge of products and how to eliminate errors. Moreover, the firm must create framework conditions that guarantee the necessary identification with the firm and its services and above all a high degree of willingness to accept responsibility for failures that have arisen on the part of the external service provider. (4) another important point pertains to the client's *constant access to customer information generated in the complaint center*, since it is precisely these data that in many firms represent an essential strategic resource for developing customer relationship management activities and realizing competitive advantages. Providing an adequate information technology infrastructure creates the necessary conditions for successful fulfillment of these tasks.

If the firm takes these cornerstones into account in the context of outsourcing its complaint center functions, the conditions are created for achieving the goals of complaint management, *even with the help of an external service provider*. At the same time, the *advantages* of such a delegation of operational task performance, which first and foremost relate to cost arguments, can be realized. These cost arguments involve on the one hand cost savings with respect to human resources and telephone technology, and on the other hand the conversion of fixed costs to variable costs and the higher degree of cost transparency that is associated with it. Furthermore, additional expert know-how can be utilized, since professional customer care/customer interaction center providers possess extensive experience in terms of the selection, training and directing of suitable employees.

If the external service provider does not simply feel responsible for supplying personnel and technological resources, but also sees itself in the role of *actively providing impulses* in areas of complaint management that have not yet been considered or that are innovative (e.g. preparation of complaint reports that are suited to the needs of particular target groups or development of new methods for complaint analysis), all the conditions exist for a successful design of the outsourcing of operational contact processing in the context of complaint management.

Chapter 15 in Brief

- The choice among centralized, decentralized and dual complaint management depends on a number of factors. These include above all the type of product, number of customers, type of distribution and the centrality of customer contact.
- The complaint center is mainly responsible for the operational tasks of the direct complaint management process. For this purpose, organizational units for inbound calls (first and second level), inbound e-mails, back office, third level (specialist departments) and outbound contacts are set up if the number of complaints is high.
- The management of the complaint center is responsible for personnel and budget, project development, monitoring of sales and service targets and staff deployment.
- The central responsibility of the head of complaint management lies in strategic planning and ensuring that the tasks of the direct and indirect complaint management process are carried out in line with the strategy chosen.
- For optimal task fulfillment, influence rights must be assigned to the complaint management department, the strength of which depends on the strategic type of complaint management.
- When choosing the organizational form for complaint management (staff department, line function or matrix organization), the respective advantages and disadvantages must be weighed up individually for each company.
- The complaint management department can be organized as a profit center if it is possible to prove the profit contribution from its own activities.
- In customer-focused companies, the fundamental responsibility for the entire complaint management process cannot be outsourced. However, it is possible to outsource operational activities if appropriate service level agreements ensure that the objectives of complaint management are achieved.

References

Adam D (1982) The restaurant at the end of the universe. Ballentine Books, New York, NY

Fichte M (2001) Organisation. In: Schmid C, Jendro L (eds) Call Center Compendium: Konzeption, Aufbau, Betrieb und Technik eines professionellen Kundenmanagements. Deutscher Wirtschaftsdienst, Köln, pp 31–49

Stauss B, Seidel W (2012) Complaint management in retailing. In: Kandampully J (ed) Service management, the new paradigm in retailing. Springer, New York, pp 207–230

Technological Aspects of Complaint Management

B. Stauss, W. Seidel, *Effective Complaint Management*, Management for Professionals,
https://doi.org/10.1007/978-3-319-98705-7_16

Issues Raised
- What are the prerequisites for using complaint management software?
- Which arguments speak in favor of special complaint management software; what are the advantages of an integrated CRM solution?
- Which core functionalities should complaint management software fulfill?
- How can Internet and intranet be used effectively in the context of a software-supported complaint management system?

Especially when there is a significant volume of complaints, the tasks of complaint management can only be efficiently realized with the use of software programs. Therefore, those in charge of complaint management must keep themselves informed about the functional performance of the programs currently offered in the marketplace and plan their implementation.

However, one must realize that appropriate programs can only be effective within the framework of a *consistent strategy of complaint management* and that they are not a replacement for a well thought-out management concept.

The latter point must be stressed because complaint management—primarily in the context of Customer Relationship Management Initiatives—has been *misinterpreted as a simple software project*, and in seeing it this way, firms overlook the fact that a *comprehensive management and leadership concept* is involved. However, only when such a concept exists and when it provides the strategic framework the great potential of complaint management software can be used to enhance efficiency and increase quality.

16.1 Fundamental Determinants for the Implementation of Complaint Management Software

First of all, the firm must review the conditions under which it would be advisable to support the processes of complaint management with a software solution. In order to answer this question, one should primarily refer to the following *determinants for implementing a software solution*: complaint volume, complexity of the processing procedures, extent of the product range offered by the firm and analysis and controlling requirements. Accordingly, software support becomes essential

- when the *complaint volume* is so high that accepting, processing and resolving all the complaints rapidly and efficiently is no longer possible without an software system
- when the *processing procedures* are complex, e.g. when different organizational units are integrated in the acceptance, processing and reaction procedures
- when the firm offers a *variety of products and services* that in turn can have *various problems*, meaning that very differentiated procedures for recording and processing complaint information are necessary

- when extensive, multi-level and regular *analyses and reports* must be performed and generated, respectively, and when the functions of *complaint management controlling* must be fulfilled.

In addition, if we take into consideration that complaint management is at the core of every system of customer relationship management, which usually requires the implementation of a software system, then we can emphasize that it is necessary and practical not just for all larger firms, but also for the vast majority of all medium-sized businesses, to fall back upon complaint management software.

16.2 Deciding Between Special Complaint Management Software and an Integrated CRM Solution

If the conditions named above exist in the firm, the fundamental decision that must be made is whether a *special complaint management software or an integrated CRM solution* should be implemented. The answer to this question mainly depends upon whether complaint management is interpreted as an independent management concept (or software project) or as an integrated component of CRM. If the former is the case, it would seem reasonable to decide in favor of a software system that is specifically developed to support the complaint management processes. However, even when the overall concept of customer relationship management is established with the aid of comprehensive software systems, the firm may decide to implement special complaint management software. This is always the case when a firm opts for the best possible software solution for each problem area of CRM—for example, on a special campaign management tool, a software solution for the targeted support of sales processes or even a specific solution for the implementation of active complaint management. This type of software strategy is also designated a *"best-of-breed" solution* in the context of CRM.

As an alternative to the "best-of-breed" strategy, a firm can opt for a *completely integrated solution*, in which all the relevant CRM requirements are taken into consideration. The basic *difference between these two software strategies* is that the integrated approach guarantees uniform software implementation and thus prevents the implementation of software systems from different providers. In particular, the problems associated with having different user interfaces, as well as different database interfaces, can thereby be limited and—from this standpoint—the costs reduced. Indeed, though, this advantage is frequently counteracted by the disadvantage of qualitative losses. As a rule, "best-of-breed" solutions are based on a better complaint management concept and feature a greater functional range, the result of which is that they may in part ensure more efficient processes and require fewer adjustments and often prove to be more cost-effective in the end. An obvious alternative, which combines the advantages of "best-of-breed" solutions and completely integrated solutions, can be achieved by mapping the basic functionalities of "best-of-breed" solutions in integrated complete solutions.

Whether and to what extent such possibilities exist should be verified during the phase in which the completely integrated solutions are evaluated.

A variant that is considered and often implemented by many firms is to *realize* the software-technical support of complaint management processes *with their own resources*. Usually, the primary reason for considering this perspective is the seamless technical integration of new software modules into the existing system landscape. As meaningful as this variant seems to be from this point of view, such a decision is often regretted for other obvious reasons, the further the implementation proceeds (Terentis et al. 2002): (1) Standard software systems include a series of functionalities for the support of the complaint management process, which are usually industry-independent and rely on diverse know-how and thus do not have to be reinvented from scratch. As a rule, this means that the expenses for firm-specific upgrades or changes in available functionalities can be reduced to a minimum. (2) Oftentimes, neither the necessary programming skills nor the corresponding capacity are available that would ensure a sound and prompt programming of the functional requirements. (3) Last but not least, the costs of in-house development usually exceed the licensing costs and the costs of the data-technical integration, service and support of standard systems to a not insignificant degree.

If in-house programming is still preferred for strategic IT considerations, it is advisable to fall back on external expertise with respect to the definition of the detailed functional requirements of such a system and the programming of individual system components.

The *general guideline* for the decision regarding the software-technical support of a software system of active complaint management should be shaped by *functional, economic and IT considerations*—in this order—regardless of whether a "pure" complaint management project or an integrated CRM project is chosen. The software must take into account the CRM approach described, which is oriented toward all the possible situations of a customer relationship, and be able to handle all the task modules of complaint management. Any concession made toward a minimum software-technical fulfillment of the functional requirements will later prove to be an *erroneous decision with serious consequences* that will be reflected both in additional expenditures for software adaptations and in jeopardized or lost customer relationships.

In any event, the *functional perspective must drive* the introduction of complaint management software systems. The software should not determine the action alternatives and thus the corporate value contribution of complaint management; rather, it must be able to fulfill the requirements of a complaint management concept that is strategically oriented and specifically defined for the individual firm in an optimal fashion.

16.3   Core Functionalities of Complaint Management Software Systems

In the context of *complaint acceptance*, the essential function of software solutions is to ensure that the goal of thorough, structured and rapid *complaint documentation* is reached.

16.3.1 Thorough Documentation of Complaint Information

The *thorough documentation* of complaint information on a software-supported basis is made possible by the fact that all the information to be documented in a complaint case is stated and predefined in specific masks of the software system, whereby the documentation of this information covers the entire complaint processing procedure. If a complaint incident cannot be resolved during the initial contact with the complainant, the documentation of the internal handling of the complaint takes place as the complaint processing and reaction progress.

Specific data fields can be defined as so-called *"required fields"* in order to support the process of documentation and to promote the discipline of documentation. Having such fields would mean that a complaint case normally could only be saved after all the information defined as "imperative" has been entered. If it is not possible for customers to provide the information essential for smooth complaint processing at the moment they are making the complaint, the program can provide for the possibility of reminding the users at the start or during the use of the application that individual data in certain complaint processes are not yet fully documented, so that they can introduce other measures to obtain the data that are still needed.

An essential requirement for the thorough documentation of all the relevant complaint information is the provision of appropriate fields, which are designed in a way that is logical in terms of content and which follow the complainants' narration of the incident.

16.3.2 Structured Documentation of Complaint Information

The *structured documentation of complaint information* is essentially determined by the provision of specific options for documenting individual complaint information and by the layout of the documentation masks. It is encouraged when the complaint content and complaint processing information are recorded in different masks, and the structure of the information to be recorded is consequentially arranged according to content and the basic flow of the complainants' conversation. At the same time, it should be possible to switch back and forth between the different masks easily and access the various input fields, so that the information can be entered as the complainants give their descriptions, especially in the case of complaints articulated over the telephone.

The fundamental *differentiation between the documentation of complaint-content and complaint-processing information* is important because complaint-content information must be directly taken from the customer's articulation, while complaint-processing information may (also) be recorded after the initial contact with the complainant. A good structuring of the relevant information in the context of complaint acceptance, processing and reaction is also the basic requirement for *rapid documentation* of that information.

16.3.3 Rapid Documentation of Complaint Information

Rapid documentation of complaint information can be ensured by implementing complaint management systems in which appropriate classification attributes for individual complaint data are simply and flexibly defined for like or similar circumstances and provided to employees in the form of predefined alternatives when they are in the process of recording the information. For instance, all the meaningful characteristics for customer groups, products or problem categories are given as single-level or hierarchical lists in the appropriate fields. During the documentation of a complaint case, the applicable items can be chosen with a simple mouse click from the respective lists, so that it is not necessary to enter the information manually.

This selection process may be supported by an *automated pre-selection* of the relevant alternatives. If, for example, processors are looking for the customer group "Private Customers" during the course of typologizing complainants with respect to their affiliation with a particular target group, they can type the first letter "P", which will take them to a pre-selection of possible customer groups beginning with that letter.

Moreover, *content relationships and dependencies* may exist between the complaint information to be recorded and the respective classification attributes. If, for instance, a complaint about a specific product is lodged, the problem types that are offered as possibilities for further documentation should exclusively be those that could be related to and have been defined for that product. Similar connections between the type of problem and the corresponding solution or between the type of problem and the corresponding processing procedures would also make sense. The mapping of such dependencies between the individual complaint data in a complain management system implies a *filter effect* with regard to the alternatives available for selection and also makes it possible to manage comprehensive and complex categorization structures. At the same time, such filter effects minimize the incorrect recording of complaint information, since only the relevant information is displayed as recording alternatives for each data entry field.

In the context of the software-technical implementation of the documentation process, the firm usually attempts to achieve rapid recording of information by including only the "really important" complaint information and/or providing the classification attributes on a very abstract level (e.g. "Product Errors" or "Employee Behavior"). When the firm does so, the quality of information suffers at the expense of rapid documentation, which limits the opportunities for customer-oriented complaint processing and for meaningful analyses and specific quality improvements. For this reason, rapid documentation such as that described above can be seen as problematic *"less documentation"*. Therefore, during the software-technical implementation of the documentation process, conditions must be created that will ensure not only rapid, but also differentiated and detailed recording of complaint information.

16.3.4 Documentation of Internal Complaint Handling

In the task areas of *complaint processing and complaint reaction*, software systems can be used primarily for steering the complaint processing procedures, for effectively managing deadlines and communication and for promoting a policy of rapid and consistent problem-solving.

Systematically steering the flow of complaint processing is possible insofar as the predefined complaint processing procedures can be initiated properly when a new case is entered in the system—either automatically, e.g. depending on the respective type of problem, or manually. The "complaint owner" for each complaint case can be determined at the same time. When a processing procedure is initiated, the person responsible for the first processing step (the "task owner") is immediately informed that a processing case has entered the system, and this person also receives the temporal targets for the completion of this step of the procedure.

After the respective subtasks are completed by the "task owners", the case is *automatically forwarded*, and *deadlines are set* for the next subphase and for the remainder of the whole processing procedure. In this way, the firm ensures that all the persons or departments involved in the processing act according to the procedures defined and within the framework of the deadlines that have been established. At the same time that the complaint incident is being processed, the *processing history* is generated in chronological order as each processing step is completed.

In order to be able to guarantee completely the performance of these functions, the firm must *integrate a workflow engine* in the process that will permit flexible modeling of the processes and ensure complete documentation and monitoring of deadlines, as well as ongoing status checks.

An important way to simplify the processing procedure, especially in the case of complaints articulated in writing, is to integrate a *document management system* into the complaint management software. Complaint letters, as well as additional documents submitted by the complainant, can be scanned into the system, classified under a specific complaint case and processed further by, for example, highlighting important text passages in a different color or attaching commentary and processing notes to the document. By forwarding the complaint cases in the network along with the scanned documents directly to the person responsible for the processing, the firm can eliminate sending out duplicate or delayed customer correspondence that is related to the case, and the processing procedure can be expedited.

As far as effective *deadline management* is concerned, the implementation of software has further advantages. The processing times associated with the individual processing steps are translated into specific target dates—starting with the date the complaint was received. If the deadlines that have been set are exceeded, an integrated *reminder system* can automatically inform responsible employees about their delays when the program starts up or while the application is running. If the delay of the complaint case continues, it is possible that the case will be automatically assigned to the *escalation system*. When the network is adequately integrated, the persons responsible (from the process owner and the complaint owner all the way up to the company management) are informed about the temporal delay at various escalation levels and can intervene to steer the process.

Software technology can also provide services valuable for managing communication between the persons or departments involved in complaint processing, and especially for managing communication with complainants. Firstly, it is possible to send notes and processing comments as e-mail messages or telefaxes automatically generated by the system in the course of forwarding the complaint incidents to the departments located downstream in the processing procedure. In this way, the firm will be successful in expediting the flow of information considerably and in optimizing the *internal communication* during the process.

Secondly, the firm can also significantly simplify *external communication* with complainants. If the communication intervals for receipt confirmations, intermediate replies and the final answer are stored in the software, it is possible to give the employees an automatic reminder when communication is necessary. Form letters and text elements that are regularly used in correspondence can also be managed by the program and made available, depending on the specific complaint information in the individual case. Establishing interfaces to popular word processing programs can further optimize written communication. Case-specific data (customer address, complainants' preferred form of address, the problem or the reference to the problematic product) can be incorporated in the letter to the customer and can aid the complaint-specific manipulation of text components. Likewise, the system should be linked to corresponding telephone software, which would make it possible for complaint management employees to establish an immediate telephone connection with customers.

Complaint management software can also be implemented with respect to the efficient and intelligent design of the firm's *problem-solving policy*. Linking problem solutions or compensatory payments to defined problem types for each complaint object gives employees the opportunity to see all the previous solutions for similar cases when they are processing complaints. This method allows for consistent reactions and the rapid elimination of customers' problems. Furthermore, if the costs incurred are allocated to the solutions or compensatory payments, the firm obtains a detailed overview of the costs of disputes and the external failure costs that result from dissatisfaction.

16.3.5 Analysis and Reporting of Complaint Information

The advantage of implementing a software-supported system of complaint management is not only that the relevant complaint information can be better registered and the processing procedure more efficiently steered, but also the fact that the documented information is available for use in *complaint analysis* and in *complaint management controlling*. At the same time, the firm can make sure that the program automatically initiates appropriate procedures for these task areas.

The frequency analyses and cross-tabulations that are part of the *complaint analysis* can be performed within the program or be supported by appropriate third software systems, such as MS Excel, business intelligence systems or even specific data mining software. In either case, it is important to see that the desired analyses can be defined, accessed and processed by *functional users* without a great deal of effort on their part and without specific statistical or system-technical knowledge. This statement applies both to the architecture of the tables and to the desired translation of the information in the tables into graphic form. In addition, it is important that special procedures, such as the Frequency-Relevance Analysis of Complaints (FRAC), can be performed, and that problems can be prioritized from the customers' perspective. The firm must also use the opportunity it has to link logical data selections with defined frequency analyses and cross-tabulations in order to specify analyses even further. In this way, an analysis of the complaint volume, for example, can be performed separately for written or telephone articulations.

The *cause-effect analysis* in the context of the utilization of complaint information can also be supported by the use of software, since the individual case descriptions and complaint histories can be accessed and planning instruments like the Failure Mode and Effect Analysis (FMEA) can be integrated. Ideally, the detailed analysis of individual case descriptions and complaint histories would also be directly initiated from complaint analysis. For instance, for each problem focus identified in a cross-tabulation for a particular product, one can go directly to the associated complainants with their respective individual case descriptions and complaint histories. On this basis, further cause analyses can be performed and/or specific follow-up measures defined for this group of complainants.

The definitions necessary for *complaint reporting*—in terms of the respective addressees, the analyses to be performed and the temporal rhythm at which the reports should be generated—can likewise be anchored in the system, so that analyses can automatically be performed by the program at the established times and sent out using the appropriate distribution list.

16.3.6 Monitoring of the Task Performance of Complaint Management

In the context of complaint management controlling, there are a number of other possibilities for using software. For *subjective task controlling*, a complaint satisfaction survey can be integrated into the software solution and, ideally, adapted and printed out as well. The data can then be entered online in the case of telephone surveys or recorded subsequently in the case of written surveys, so that they can be directly linked to other complainant or complaint management data. This process supports both regular *performance measurements* and *individual follow-up contacts* in particular. At the same time, standards for the individual complaint satisfaction dimensions can be formulated, and the fulfillment of those standards can be monitored automatically.

Using the example of the "b.better" complaint management system, *Spotlight 16.1* provides an excellent description of the software-supported administration of follow-up surveys to complainants.

Spotlight 16.1
Software-Supported Conduct of a Follow-Up Survey of Complainants

In the course of its subjective task controlling, the complaint management system of a sample firm has made a decision that complainants whose complaint case has been concluded in writing should be asked in the context of a follow-up survey about their satisfaction with the complaint processing one week after the answer letter is mailed.

For follow-up surveys, the users have a specific mask at their disposal, based on which they can select complainants to be interviewed on the basis of different customer characteristics (see Fig. 16.1).

In a next step, the survey contents relevant to the planned contacts are selected for the selected complainants in the form of follow-up questionnaires stored in the system. The system also provides an overview of previous and current surveys.

By selecting the relevant questionnaire, you branch to the questionnaire contents (see Figs. 16.2 and 16.3). The upper part of Fig. 16.2 shows which interviewer is contacting which customer at which date with which type of survey. Then the survey begins with the initial question to the customers as to whether, in their view, the problem that was the subject of the complaint has been solved or whether there is still a need for action.

Figure 16.3 shows part of the questions relevant to the upcoming follow-up survey, which can be flexibly defined by the system as well as the corresponding answer alternatives. The responses are saved individually for each customer so that the survey results are available in the customer's complaint history. At the same time, it is possible to carry out special analyses for the entire survey.

Udo Körner
Consultant
servmark consultancy
b.better® is a joint product of servmark consultancy, Ingolstadt, Germany, www.servmark.de, and CURSOR Software AG, Gießen, Germany, www.cursor.de

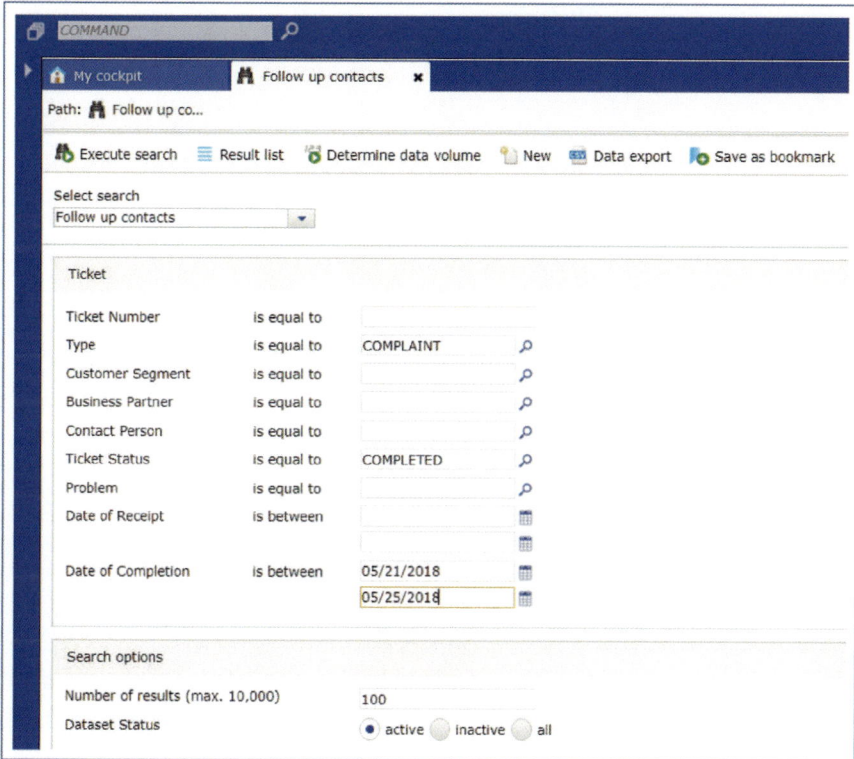

Fig. 16.1 Start mask

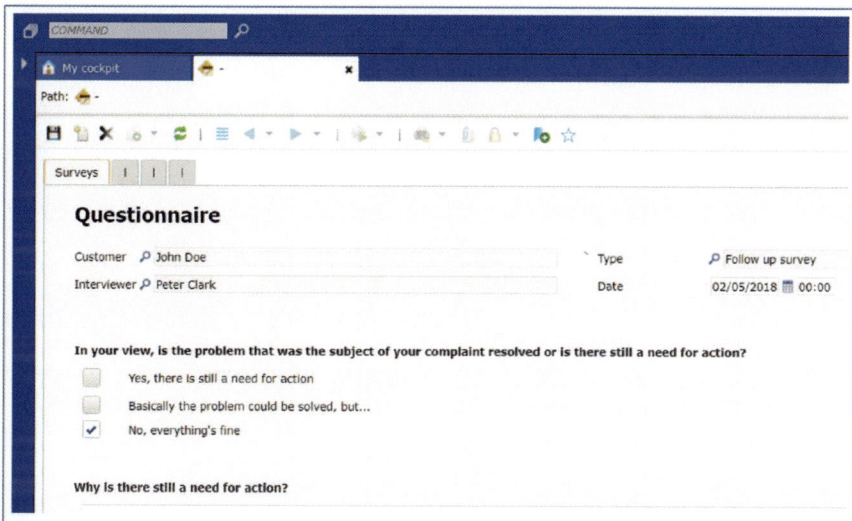

Fig. 16.2 Initial question

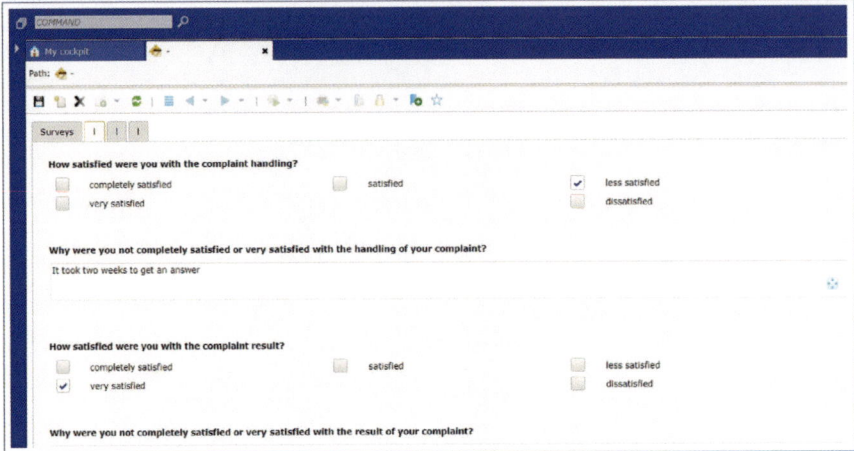

Fig. 16.3 Part of the questionnaire

The objective task controlling standards can be similarly stored and monitored by the system—in part automatically and in part by accessing other data. By revealing the discrepancies between actual values and target standards, the complaint management system also provides the basis for the cause analysis that can be used to improve complaint management, in that the system takes into account the results from subjective task controlling. For purposes of cost-benefit controlling, it is possible to incorporate the necessary calculation procedures—e.g. for ascertaining the costs of complaint management, the individual benefit components and the causes of customer switching—in a system such as this one.

Ideally, *data interfaces* to the databases would be created, which would then register customers' actual purchase behavior. Current information regarding customer sales and profit contributions would thus be made available in the complaint management system for purposes of cost-benefit controlling. At the same time, complainants whose purchase behavior changed significantly after a complaint could be specifically observed. In this way, it would be possible to calculate the "Return on Complaint Management" and to verify the profitability of various investments in complaint management.

Although the advantages of a software solution in performing the tasks of complaint management are undeniable, the *restriction* made at the beginning of this section is just as indisputable: Complaint management software is an instrument that can make a consistent complaint management concept significantly better and more efficient; however, it cannot replace efforts to develop and implement this concept.

16.4   The Integration of Internet, Intranet and E-Mail Communication

The Internet not only provides new communication and distribution channels, but also by new opportunities for the *software-technical support of complaint management processes*.

The *Internet* links individual networks that are independent of one another and consequently permits universal communication among all the computers that are connected to it. The goal of an *intranet* is similar. In this case, however, we are dealing not with an open system, but rather with an internal communication network that is related to the way the firm is set up, with its organizational units, departments and employees.

Since external communication with the complainant and internal communication between those involved in the complaint process are key factors in a system of active complaint management, it seems natural to use the Internet and the intranet for both these types of communication. While the Internet provides specific starting points for complaint stimulation and complaint acceptance, as well as for complaint processing and reaction in the area of external communication, the intranet provides similar potential for optimization, particularly for complaint reporting and for complaint information use (see Fig. 16.4).

We have previously addressed the opportunities that the WWW offers in the context of *complaint stimulation and complaint documentation* in Sects. 6.2.1 and 7.4.2. When complaints are stimulated via the Internet, the firm must ensure that the *organizational and personnel conditions* are fulfilled to process the induced complaint volume in a customer-oriented manner. Firms must be aware of the fact that more and more customers utilize the Internet as a communication medium and adjust their expectations to the possibilities that the Internet offers: In many cases, customers expect an e-mail answer to complaints articulated by e-mail, and they expect that answer within a timeframe that matches the speed with which the information is transferred via this medium.

In the area of *complaint acceptance*, targeted contact with the "right" contact person can be optimized with differing responsibilities for eliminating problems in either a decentralized or a dual complaint management system. When, for instance, a clear connection exists between the addressee responsible for a complaint and the

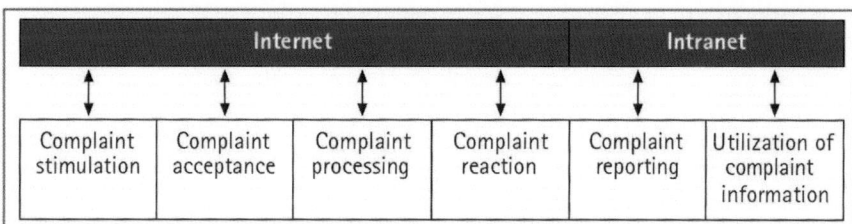

Internet				Intranet	
Complaint stimulation	Complaint acceptance	Complaint processing	Complaint reaction	Complaint reporting	Utilization of complaint information

Fig. 16.4 The connection between Internet/intranet and the task modules of complaint management

business location indicated by the complainant as being the one where the problem occurred, the firm can make sure that the complaint automatically reaches the proper "complaint owner" by e-mail. The prerequisite is that *structured possibilities for recording* the information that determines the distribution to the responsible locations—in this case, the place where the problem occurred—are provided on the Internet site. In this way, the firm excludes at the outset the possibility that complaints will take the wrong path. If the complaint management software has a corresponding interface to the Internet, the incidents entered by complainants on the "complaint site" can automatically be transferred to the complaint management software. At the same time, information that is recorded in a structured manner is automatically included in corresponding fields in the software. Entry errors and duplicate expenditures can thus be prevented.

When complaints are not sent directly via the Internet site, but rather directly by e-mail without adequate documentation structure, modern *methods of text recognition* offer the possibility of searching for certain key terms in the text of the e-mail and distributing it to the person responsible in each case on the basis of this search. Alternatively, an appropriate department must manually distribute such e-mails.

Many complaint management systems are also offering the possibility of connecting with so-called *"web clients"*. These web clients provide access to the basic functionalities for documentation and processing to all authorized employees in the firm that have PC work stations and an installed Internet browser. With this technological version, the firm can avoid having to configure specific networks for the complaint management system, use the Internet in a targeted fashion to process corresponding transactions and make it possible to integrate decentralized organizational units that have contact with complainants into the software in a rapid and cost-effective manner. The conditions are thus created for putting the registration of complaint information on a sturdy footing and above all for organizing complaint processing on a company-wide level. From this perspective, the Internet can be seen as the logical basis for constructing a comprehensive *network* of communication and thus *of complaint management*.

The intranet provides the main communication platform for *complaint processing*. If several persons or departments are involved in processing a complaint case, the *internal communication* and coordination between the organizational units can be accomplished quickly and thoroughly in accordance with predefined processing procedures via e-mail or via web clients, provided the organizational units participating in the processing have computers with Internet browsers at their disposal.

There are similar advantages as far as *communication with complainants* is concerned. Each complaint owner or task owner can contact the customers via e-mail and keep them up-to-date on their complaint cases or inform them of the answers to their complaints with the help of a receipt confirmation or an intermediate reply. The communication process can be designed efficiently when an interface exists between a word processing program and the e-mail functionality. The responsible employee generates the document to the customer in the usual manner with the help of a word processing program and initiates the e-mail communication at this point. If complaint management software is used, the e-mails sent out to the customer during the various processing procedures can be archived.

Using the example of Condor Flugdienst GmbH, *Spotlight 16.2* shows how comprehensive complaint handling processes can be automated by software.

Spotlight 16.2

Automated Complaint Management Processes at Condor Flugdienst GmbH—Part of Thomas Cook Group Airlines

Tourism is subject to rapid change. There are many competitors and the customer often decides on the basis of price. In order to stand out from the multitude of providers, good service is the best lever. However, this must not end with the provision of the service, but must continue, especially if the customer has reason to complain. After all, effective and rapid complaint handling creates a good overall experience, which makes the customer more likely to consider the company when planning the next holiday.

For many years, the airline Condor has had a complaint form for customers as part of the contact options on its website and has continuously developed it, tailoring it specifically to the underlying complaint management software. Each Condor customer-contact area is required to communicate only this contact method in the event of a complaint in order to achieve the best possible enforcement. This is important because logic and automation are behind it, which make the processing efficient.

The customer enters in the web form, which has mandatory fields, all information (differentiated by complaint reason) that the employee needs to process the complaint, including documents and/or images that can be uploaded. A first check takes place when the form is sent. The customer is informed of missing or incorrectly used fields.

When sent, the contact form entries are transferred to a structured XML e-mail and sent to a dedicated e-mail inbox. From there, the XML mail, including all attachments, is read by the complaint management software and transferred to the complaint management database.

An import workflow processes the imported information. First, the travel order number entered by the customer in the web form is used for a search in the central customer and travel order database, to which the complaint management software is linked via web services.

If the customer is found with his or her travel order in the database, the customer data record including the relevant travel order information is transferred to the complaint management software. If the customer has specified a different address and communication data via the web form, this information is added to the transferred customer data record.

If a search is not successful, the system automatically creates a new customer file with the data from the web form in the complaint management software. The customer data record is then also stored in the central customer database via a service call.

(continued)

Spotlight 16.2 (continued)

For this customer data record, a new complaint transaction is now created, controlled via the import workflow. All information from the web form is transferred to the transaction and the uploaded documents are added as attachments. In addition, the process is enriched with further information, such as the travel agency through which a customer has booked his or her trip.

If the complaint management software recognizes that the form sent is a follow-up letter for an existing process (for example, subsequent delivery of missing documents), it is automatically assigned to the original transaction. The import workflow then takes over the dispatch of an acknowledgment of receipt to the customer, informing him/her of the transaction number under which the customer request is being processed at Condor. Processing by the employee can start immediately.

If searches are necessary for the solution of a customer request and comments from other departments are required, this is not done separately by e-mail, but directly from the complaint management software. The incoming response is then automatically assigned to the transaction and a message is sent to an employee or a staff pool that the activity can now be processed further. Comments can also be automatically reminded after timeframes are set.

For travel agency partners, the Condor Extranet provides the same opportunity to pass on complaints from mutual customers. For this support, the partner is guaranteed a fixed processing time and receives a copy of the response letter to the customer—completely automatically—without the processing employee having to initiate this.

An upgrade to a modern stage of the complaint management software is currently being implemented in order to establish further automation and relieve the processing employees of administrative tasks. In the future, mails that do not come from the contact form (e.g. internal forwarding) will also be searched for address data and travel order number—with simultaneous checking of the customer database and easy indexing—and automatically processed by the system into transactions. If necessary, the employee only completes data before processing. Figure 16.5 shows the automated process.

In the case of complaints made via the website or e-mail, the allocation to a clerk or employee pool is made automatically by the complaint management software on the basis of complaint reasons and/or keywords, instead of manually by the supervisor. For this purpose, keywords and keyword combinations can be stored for searching the e-mail body. If corresponding keywords are identified, the system forwards the complaints to the defined employees/pools.

Of course, the system offers form letters and text modules, which can be easily used, because they are offered to the employee depending on the complaint reason and/or the keyword. Access to all text modules is retained.

In order to guarantee the service for the customers during the processing time, a special link can be generated with the dispatch of the acknowledgment

(continued)

Spotlight 16.2 (continued)

of receipt, which makes it possible for the customers to see the status of the processing at any time. Via the link, the guest is then shown the status of his or her complaint, e.g. whether a statement of a partner is still pending. This relieves Condor and the customer of the need to respond to /make inquiries by e-mail or phone, and the customer always feels informed.

A platform within the complaint management software that offers the customer a kind of "self-service" is conceivable in the medium term. For example, automatic processing of a classic flight delay would be conceivable. All relevant data (e.g. duration of the delay, customer's travel price) must be stored in the software, so that the reimbursement to which the customer is entitled can be calculated automatically. Ideally, the customer can choose between a travel voucher or a refund.

Of course, the employees should continue to treat customers humanely. Modern complaint management software offers the best chance to create time windows for this and still become much more efficient.

Heidi Schüritz
Head of Customer Contact Center
Condor Flugdienst GmbH

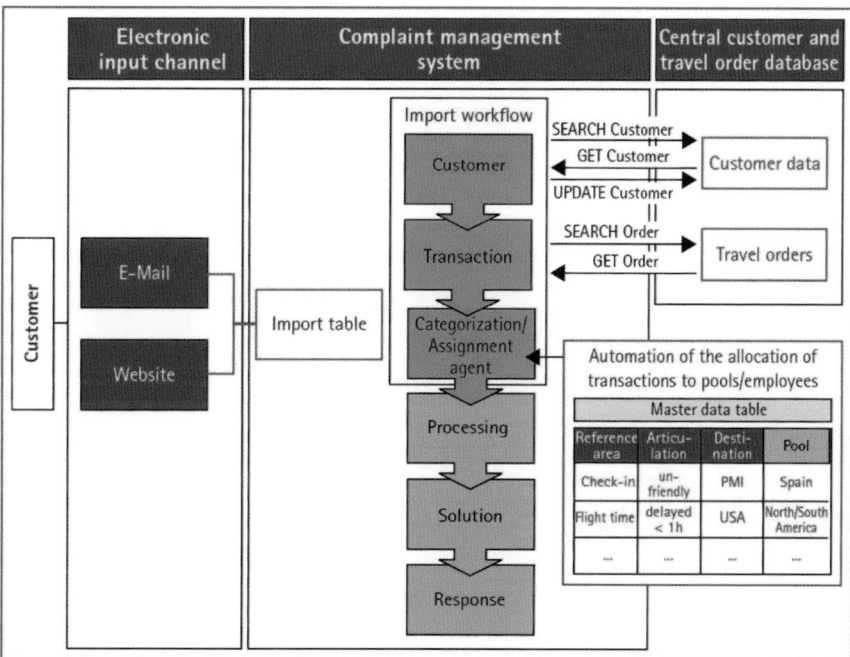

Fig. 16.5 Automated complaint management processes (Source: Rödl IT-Consulting, Nürnberg—Software Targenio, www.roedl.com)

While there are no direct starting points for the Internet or intranet in the case of *complaint analysis* and *complaint management controlling*—the focus here is not on communication, but rather on defining meaningful analysis contents—the possibilities, especially of the intranet, can be fully exploited in the context of *complaint reporting*. The department responsible for complaint analysis and complaint management controlling can put its own home page on the intranet, thus making itself known as the key broker for customer information and promoting its acceptance within the firm. Supplying the individual target groups for complaint reporting with specific passwords for logging in to the reporting platform gives them targeted access to the analyses and performance figures that have been defined and that are relevant for them. Moreover, if the analysis module has adequate functionalities, the target groups can also perform further analyses on the data sets released to them.

If the intranet is not available as a communication platform, analyses and performance figures can also be quickly forwarded *via e-mail* to the respective target groups at pre-arranged times.

The Internet and intranet also offer a sensible platform for the *utilization of complaint information*. On the intranet, employees can spontaneously put ideas for problem diagnosis and the prevention of future problems up for discussion. Additionally, interdepartmental and inter-location teams that communicate with another about problem solutions during electronic chats can be quickly formed. In this way, barriers of time and space can be bridged. Finally, the Internet offers new opportunities for customer dialogs with complainants, first and foremost among which are virtual customer forums—E-customer chats (see Sect. 13.3.3).

Chapter 16 in Brief
- The use of complaint management software is particularly necessary in the case of a high volume of complaints, complex processing procedures, an extensive product range, different types of problems or if there are high demands on complaint evaluation and controlling.
- The decision to use special complaint management software or an integrated CRM system depends in particular on the desired functional depth and the possibility to map special complaint management functionalities in CRM systems.
- The in-house development of complaint management software usually proves to be an inefficient alternative when realistic estimates are made of implementation costs and development time.
- The core functionalities of complaint management software primarily comprise the possibilities of the complete, structured and efficient recording of complaint information, the gapless documentation of the internal complaint handling, the detailed and flexible analysis of recorded complaint information as well as the automatic generation of key figures for subjective and objective task controlling.

(continued)

• The possibilities of the Internet and the intranet should be used effectively within the framework of software support for complaint management processes.

Reference

Terentis J et al (2002) Customer service, complaints management and regulatory compliance. J Financ Regul Compliance 10(1):37–54

Social Media Complaints

17

© Springer Nature Switzerland AG 2019
B. Stauss, W. Seidel, *Effective Complaint Management*, Management for Professionals,
https://doi.org/10.1007/978-3-319-98705-7_17

Issues Raised
- Why do social media have particular importance as a complaint channel?
- What types of complaints exist in customer-controlled and company-controlled social media?
- How can a social media strategy and a complaint management strategy be coordinated?
- What special requirements do social media make on the task modules of direct and indirect complaint management?
- Which personnel-related and organizational questions have to be considered with regard to social media?

Many companies are active in social networks, for example by setting up their own *Facebook or Twitter accounts or weblogs* for the entire company or their brands. These have an interactive character, offering customers the opportunity to express their criticism and dissatisfaction with the market offer or the socio-political behavior of companies. This turns social media into a new complaint channel, regardless of whether it was initially planned to do so. Due to this specific situation and its growing importance, social media are considered separately as a complaint channel in this chapter.

17.1   Relevance of Social Media as a Complaint Channel

The term *social media* (or Web 2.0) refers to Internet-based platforms that enable interaction and networking between the participants, who can simultaneously assume the roles of the information transmitter and receiver. The peculiarities of social media lie firstly in their fundamental *interactivity*, i.e. the reciprocity of the receiver and sender role, secondly, in the *potentially worldwide perceptibility* of articulations (posts) and thirdly, in the diversity of the *multimedia design possibilities*, since besides texts, photos, videos or voice recordings can also be used.

Social media is relevant for complaint management for a variety of reasons, which are mutually reinforcing:

(1) The Enormous Reach of Social Media In 2017, nearly 3.6 billion people worldwide used the Internet (statista 2018a). Social media, particularly social networks, are playing an increasingly important role. More than two billion people worldwide use Facebook: in India there are 250 million registered users, in the United States 230 million and in Brazil 130 million (statista 2018b). As a result, Internet customer-to-customer communication has an enormous potential reach and social media complaints can become widespread without companies having this under control (Safko 2012; Hadwich and Keller 2013).

(2) The Speed of Communication Dissemination The high use of the Internet and social media, networking and the immediate availability of web information results in the possibility of extraordinarily rapid dissemination of critical customer comments.

(3) Decreasing Complaint Costs Due to Uncomplicated Use Social media can be used anywhere, at any time and free of charge. This means that there are *no* monetary or physical and hardly any time *complaint costs* (van Noort and Willemsen 2012). For customers who do not expect individual problem-solving but only want to criticize, there are no psychological complaint costs because they can express their anger anonymously.

(4) The Increasing Use of Social Media as a Complaint Channel Customers see social media as a better opportunity to make their voice heard (Fishburn Hedges and Echo Research 2012), and are increasingly using this channel to voice complaints. Complaint sites are mainly used to protest after several poor complaint experiences, and are seen as a last chance to reach a solution to the problem by generating a public impact (Harrison-Walker 2001; Hadwich and Keller 2013). In contrast, dissatisfied customers are increasingly using Twitter and Facebook to describe problems that have occurred for the first time (Hogreve et al. 2013).

(5) The Complainants' High Degree of Annoyance and Their Migration Behavior The proportion of social media complaints from users with a very high degree of annoyance is large. Many customers who complain to social networks feel extremely strong negative emotions. They are not only dissatisfied, but *feel cheated, disappointed, annoyed and angry* (Tripp and Grégoire 2011; Hogreve et al. 2013). Although the intensity of the negative emotions decreases over time, the migration decision made by the disappointed customers remains and can hardly be revised. In addition, especially those customers who had the most intensive positive relationship with the company prior to the occurrence of a problem show the highest degree of anger and the most decisive migration behavior ("love-becomes-hate effect", Grégoire et al. 2009).

(6) The Potential Dynamics of Customer Criticism Due to the enormous reach of social media, the rapid dissemination of information and the high emotionality of articulation, even a single social media complaint can trigger an extraordinary dynamic of customer criticism. There are three dimensions of this dynamic that are closely interlinked (Stauss 2000):

The *first dynamic* is the *escalation of the number of communication participants*, with other users taking up the topic. Affected and/or interested readers of the message react, send replies and comments, and thus generate more public attention and resonance.

The *second dynamic* concerns the aggravation of the conflict by an *escalation of criticism* caused by a missing, inadequate or awkward reaction to an initially private or moderate customer complaint. If the company does not respond to the customers' concerns at all, the customers become even more annoyed, intensify their activities and receive more and more public support. At the same time, it becomes generally clear that the company is not ready to listen to its customers. This is a strong stimulus for the originally affected customers and for the readers of the "tales of woe" to look for measures that the company can no longer ignore or overlook.

The *third dynamic* comprises the *escalation of the communication object* by changing the thematic focus during the discussion process. For example, a complaint about deficiencies in an airline's in-flight catering is confirmed by another user and supplemented by further complaints about the behavior of employees at the check-in or during the flight, which can initiate a new phase in the discussion cycle. In addition, there are a number of examples where not only customers but also (former) *employees* take part in this discussion. From the company's perspective, it is particularly problematic if these contributions support the customer's point of view by providing insights into inadequate internal processes.

Such escalations have often occurred in in recent years, especially triggered by private blogs, watchdog blogs or hate sites (Stauss 2000; Sen and Lerman 2007; Kucuk 2008). However, social media are intensifying the escalation effects enormously, since the range and speed of information dissemination is increasing massively through the networking of groups.

(7) The Impact of Social Media Complaints on Corporate Image and Brand Value If a single customer complaint escalates on the Internet, a strong publicity effect is created. In the extreme case, mass indignation *(a "Shitstorm")* develops, in which it is hardly possible to react objectively due to the increasing aggressive, sarcastic and insulting contributions. In any case, however, a serious negative impact on corporate image and brand value is to be expected (Hogreve et al. 2013; Pfeffer et al. 2014).

(8) The Impact of Social Media Complaints on the Attitudes and Buying Behavior of Other Customers Complaint research shows that customers make their particularly negative consumer experiences the subject of personal communication in their social environment. A comparable but more massive effect occurs with social media complaints. Readers of customer criticism on social media consider the contributions to be reliable—in spite of repeatedly proven manipulations—and change their behavior. Already in the pre-purchase phase, many potential customers include the evaluations of other customers in their purchasing decisions and rank them among the most *credible sources* (Heinemann 2013). This applies to the evaluations of products and providers at general online merchants such as Amazon as well as to valuation portals that specialize in certain product or service categories, for example, travel services such as TripAdvisor (Xiang and Gretzel 2010; Muchazondida and Tribe 2017.).

Customer reviews on the Internet reach a potentially unlimited number of readers and thus have a significant influence on their attitudes and buying behavior (Chevalier and Mayzlin 2006; Hadwich and Keller 2013). This is especially the case with social media complaints, as they are spread among circles of friends who are at least partly personally acquainted with each other and therefore are considered trustworthy. In geographical terms, a double phenomenon is noteworthy. On the one hand, there is a huge geographical spread of critical information, limited solely by the language used. On the other hand, just a complaint about a local provider (restaurant or car repair shop) can have a massive negative impact if a large number of potential or current customers are among the networked readers. This effect is further exacerbated if the complainant experiences a negative reaction of the company to his complaint and puts it online.

17.2 Forms of Social Media Important for Complaint Management

With regard to complaint management, the abundance of different forms of social media can be differentiated primarily on the basis of whether the communication is controlled by customers or the company.

Customer-controlled communication occurs when the initiative for dialog with other participants in the network and/or with the company comes from the private user. This is always the case, for example, when customers set up their own Facebook or Twitter accounts and report on their experiences with products and companies or take part in an already ongoing discussion. In any case, there is no planned complaint stimulation by the company.

Forms of *company-controlled communication* occur when companies set up their own Facebook or Twitter accounts or weblogs for the entire company or their brands. In most cases, these forms are used for corporate and brand communication and market research purposes. However, the corporate social media presence—whether intended or not—also opens the door to customer comments. The new platform can be used by customers for social media complaints and therefore represents a new complaints channel and can be interpreted as a form of complaint stimulation.

A second criterion for the differentiation of social media is its occasional or regular use for complaints. Customers can use social media only in exceptional cases or permanently for critical comments. Similarly, companies can vary the use of social media for the complaint dialog and thus the extent of the complaint stimulation. Table 17.1 gives an overview of the social media important for complaint management.

17.2.1 Complaints in Customer-Controlled Social Media

17.2.1.1 Occasional Customer Criticism in Customer-Controlled Social Media

Occasional use of social media for complaints occurs when individuals use a medium for their public and private communication of all kinds of content, so that critical consumer comments are only one of many topics. This is the case, for

Table 17.1 Forms of social media important for complaint management

Social media complaints	Customer-controlled dialog	Company-controlled dialog
occasional	▪ Private Facebook account ▪ Private Twitter account ▪ Private Blog ▪ Private Video	▪ Brand Facebook account ▪ Brand Twitter account ▪ Brand Blog
regular	▪ Evaluation platforms ▪ Watchdog blogs and social media presence of watchdog organizations ▪ Complaint sites	▪ Customer care Facebook account ▪ Customer care Twitter account ▪ Customer care Blog

example, when individuals report negative product experiences in their personal Facebook or Twitter accounts or post a critical video in their private weblog.

Facebook is the world's largest social network and one of the most visited websites. Every user can post messages on the "wall" of his/her profile. Facebook is increasingly being used to describe negative consumer experiences.

The same applies to Twitter, which serves as a microblog for the distribution of short messages (tweets) with a maximum of 280 characters.

An empirical study shows that these private reports mention brand names very often, with over 22% of the ratings clearly being negative (Jansen et al. 2009). In the meantime, Twitter is also used for more extreme forms of customer criticism. For example, a customer bought an ad on British Airways' Twitter site to complain about baggage loss and poor service. He thus attracted enormous attention on the Internet and in the classical media. When the company tried to apologize for its late reaction with reference to the opening hours of its Twitter editorial office, it caused another wave of mockery (Jansen 2013).

Private blogs are dynamic websites on which people regularly make new entries using easy-to-use content management systems. They are thus, in a sense, online diaries that are frequently updated, with new entries at the top of the list and older ones arranged in reverse chronological order. Private weblogs are mostly personal recordings, which serve primarily for entertainment and personal self-portrayal on the Internet. Here too, however, the exchange of experiences with products and services is increasing. Complaints represent essential content, which is articulated in different ways and with differing intensity.

Usually a single negative experience is described in the complaint, sometimes supplemented by a request for support, advice and help. A step further is taken by those who address a complaint as an "open letter" to the company and at the same time send it—together with an explicit purchase warning—to consumer organizations, classic media as well as relatives, friends and acquaintances. The highest escalation level and the transition to regular customer criticism is achieved when the customers make their complaint the sole content of their weblogs and then link them to other weblogs.

It is becoming increasingly common for customers to record their negative consumer experiences as a *video* or even produce a criticism video and post them on a video platform such as *YouTube*. Some of these videos have a worldwide audience. An example of this is the video by the musician Dave Carroll, who described his service experiences with Airlines in a music video. Coincidentally, he saw his $3500 Taylor guitar being thrown into the cargo hold during loading, and he realized after the flight that it was severely damaged. After almost a year of trying in vain to get compensation from the airline for the repair, he wrote the song "United Breaks Guitars" and uploaded it to YouTube.

The video posted in July 2009 was an immediate success. After only one month it had five million views. The story was picked up by the classical media and even spread internationally. Carroll posted two more songs and later wrote a book with the same title. The original video was viewed almost 18 million times until 2018. This video complaint had not only caused considerable damage to the company's image, but also had a negative impact on the company's stock price (United Breaks Guitars 2009; Mandviwalla and Watson 2014; Li et al. 2017).

17.2.1.2 Regular Customer Criticism in Customer-Controlled Social Media

Customers can also place their experiences, opinions and problems on special websites, which have the evaluation of products and companies as the sole content or content focus. These include evaluation portals, watchdog blogs and hate sites. Social media complaints are regularly found on these media.

Many vendors, especially online dealers (such as Amazon) and service providers offer their customers the opportunity to evaluate the products or services they purchase. There are also independent *evaluation portals*. Such customer evaluations are playing an extremely important role in the purchase decision process of Internet users. In some industries, they have an almost market-changing effect. This applies, for example, to the travel industry. The independent evaluation portal TripAdvisor, the world's largest travel website, has over 400 million users, giving customers the opportunity to rate hotels, restaurants and attractions, upload photos and videos or provide travel tips. In 2017 there were 570 million reviews and opinions on TripAdvisor (Smith 2017). Empirical studies show that such user-generated content has a considerable influence on all phases of the travel decision of Internet users (Herzog and Luthe 2010; Schmeißer 2010; Mühlenbeck and Skibicki 2010), and it is proven that negative assessments have a stronger impact than positive ones (Schmeißer 2010).

Another variant of regular customer criticism is the social media presence of watchdog organizations, which critically accompany and control companies and their behavior and accordingly exercise a kind of public *watchdog* function. As a rule, bloggers and watchdog organizations are also active on Facebook and Twitter, where they can spread their criticism very effectively. One example is the consumer organization "foodwatch", which fights against problematic practices of the food industry. Its Facebook criticism of an advertising campaign for a glucose product led directly to a massive "shitstorm", that could hardly be stopped despite a prudent and cooperative reaction by the company (Bruns 2013).

In addition, for many years there has been an abundance of websites which deal exclusively with the criticism of a company and offer a complaint platform to all disappointed customers. These *complaint sites, hate sites or brandname.sucks sites* are often professionally designed. They bundle current customer criticism and reinforce it with a wealth of information. One example is the "allstateinsurancesucks. com" website, which serves as a complaint platform for all disappointed customers of the Allstate insurance company and is ranked among the best "Corporate Complaint Sites" by the business magazine Forbes (Wolrich 2005). Allstate-customers can express their anger and read other customers' complaints. They also receive differentiated information on a wide range of topics, such as the usual procedure and arguments of the insurance company or support options by lawyers and consumer organizations. In addition, the site offers a number of specialized discussion forums, for example for problems with different types of damages (Allstateinsurancesucks 2018).

Complaints of this kind have specific similarities (Ward and Ostrom 2006): (1) The escalation process almost always starts with an individual complaint to which the company does not respond at all or rejects without sufficient justification. This ignorance is perceived as disrespectful and offensive, as well as a violation of the norm of customer orientation propagated by the companies themselves. Due to the high negative emotions associated with this, there is a desire for retaliation and the intention to warn other customers of this company. (2) The experiences and their material and psychological consequences are described in dramatic form and are therefore often referred to as "horror stories". (3) The problems encountered are described less as the consequence of faulty processes or incompetence than as the result of malicious managers and employees who deliberately and routinely mistreat customers. (4) Initiators see public and mass criticism as an effective way of forcing companies that simply ignore individual customer complaints to change their behavior. (5) Organizers of the websites see themselves as "crusaders" fighting for the many victims of corporate machinations, and they are reinforced in this respect by the supportive comments of readers. (6) The complaint websites encourage dissatisfied customers to see themselves as a group that gains its identity through the opposition to the company. In this way, they unite the affected customers into virtual interest groups and this can lead to real initiatives, e.g. to the bundling of claims in class-action suits or extensive protest campaigns and boycott actions.

With regard to all forms of customer-controlled communication in social media, the main challenge for complaint management is to identify and analyze social media complaints and to participate in the discussion by explaining and providing information. In addition, the offer must be made to transfer the social media complaint to conventional complaint channels and then to find an individual solution to the problem.

17.2.2 Complaints in Company-Controlled Social Media

In company-controlled social media, customer criticism can only be expected *occasionally* if social media such as Facebook or Twitter accounts or corporate weblogs are primarily used for brand communication. This is especially true if the company restricts the possibilities for dialog and only allows users to comment on the company's postings.

Another situation exists if companies express credibly through their social media presence that they really want to address their customers' questions, problems and concerns. In this case, they set up their own customer care accounts or blogs in Facebook or Twitter and enter into an intensive dialog with critical customers. In this situation, complaints are part of the *regular* content of the dialogs and social media communication becomes a central part of a strategy of complaint stimulation.

The computer hardware manufacturer Dell is often regarded as the best practice in this respect. With its blogs—Direct2Dell (2018)—but also with the Facebook and Twitter accounts @DellCares—the company makes it clear that it listens to its customers and takes care of their concerns (Basic 2011; Wiedmann et al. 2013).

17.3 Complaint Management Strategy and Dealing with Social Media Complaints

In view of the high relevance of social media complaints, companies face a major challenge that requires a strategic approach. However, various empirical studies have shown that many companies do not proceed strategically in their social media use, but rather act spontaneously and are oriented toward external factors such as the approach of competitors (Wilson et al. 2011; Reinecke and Klautzsch 2013; Tsimonis and Dimitriadis 2014).

In a *communication strategy perspective*, two basic positions should be distinguished which can be called monitoring and dialog strategies. When pursuing a *monitoring strategy*, the company remains largely passive, monitors the critical discussion among customers and intervenes only in exceptional cases. With a *dialog strategy*, on the other hand, the company seeks to exchange information with users, actively participates in the various social media and stimulates dialog with and among customers.

The social media strategy must be consistently aligned with the *complaint management strategy* (see Chap. 5). A *monitoring strategy* makes sense when companies focus their complaint management on efficiency ("efficiency first strategy"). In the complaint management type "*complaint factory*", any incentive for complaint articulation is avoided, and for the purpose of quality assurance in the type "*quality control*" it is sufficient to record and correct the perceived quality defects. If escalation risks are identified, further measures will only be taken if their costs do not exceed the expected losses due to web criticism. However, a pure monitoring strategy is only possible if companies do not have their own independent social

Table 17.2 Complaint management strategy and social media strategy

Complaint management strategy		Social media strategy
Efficiency First	„Complaint factory"	Monitoring strategy (only passive monitoring)
	„Quality control"	
Customer First	„Relationship amplifier"	Dialogue strategy (monitoring plus active participation: customer care accounts in social media)
	„Satisfaction lab"	

media presence, because otherwise they open (unintentionally?) a complaint channel.

Monitoring social media interactions is of course also relevant for all companies that strategically orient their complaint management toward customer orientation and customer satisfaction ("customer first strategy"). However, they cannot confine themselves to this, but must take an active part in the discussion and thus adopt the *dialog strategy*. The complaint management type "*relationship amplifier*" is primarily aimed at maintaining customer loyalty and avoiding customer losses by restoring customer satisfaction. For this reason, the social media channel also plays an important role in the stimulation of complaints and it is advisable to set up separate social media platforms for the customer care area. Also for the complaint management type "satisfaction lab" only the dialog strategy is possible. This is because only through intensive dialog with the critical customers can the company obtain significant ideas for necessary change processes and the internal implementation of customer-oriented thinking and acting. Table 17.2 shows the allocation of the complaint management strategy and social media strategy.

17.4   Consequences for the Tasks of Complaint Management

If a company chooses a dialog strategy with regard to social media, this has a significant impact on the tasks of the direct and indirect complaint management process.

17.4.1 Direct Complaint Management

Regarding *complaint stimulation*, it can be assumed that with every active dialog offer in social media a complaint channel will be opened, so that the number of incoming complaints will increase considerably. Since the complaint barriers are also decreasing, it is not only to be expected that there will be a higher number of complaints, but also changes in content. Customers describe, for example, smaller problems without expecting an individual problem solution. In addition, the company's social media presence itself becomes a new object of customer criticism.

In view of the great and increasing importance of this complaint channel, it is usually necessary to establish a dedicated social media team for *complaint acceptance*. It is advisable to present this team in the social media with photos and names, so that a personalized approach is possible. Members of this team must be available 24 h a day if possible in order to be able to accept criticism and react immediately. According to an empirical study of Facebook complaints, the majority of customers articulate their complaints outside of traditional business hours, and complainants and other users react massively if no timely response occurs (Hogreve et al. 2013).

Regarding the collection of the complaint information it is necessary to observe and analyze the articulations in social networks systematically. This requires the application of specific social media monitoring software systems, which not only allow an analysis of trends and topics, moods or demographic and geographical distributions, but also provide a pragmatic interface for complaint management and CRM systems.

Provided that complaints are not articulated anonymously on the company's social media sites, the information on the complainant, the complaint problem and the object of the complaint can be categorized with the help of the existing complaint management system. However, it is expected that new problems will be addressed via the social media channel, so that a revision of the category system is necessary. In addition, it is important to ensure that the complaint information is collected in a differentiated manner across the various social media channels (such as Facebook or Twitter).

In the context of *complaint processing* the principle of complaint ownership must be applied consistently. This means that the social media complaint owner has "ownership" of this complaint and is responsible for the entire process of accepting and reacting to the complaint. He/she must not only take up the information and respond immediately, but also follow and respond to the further discussion. If the social media complaint reveals that the case has not yet been closed from the customer's point of view, the complainant must be asked to transfer the matter to a conventional complaint channel in order to allow an individual solution, taking data protection aspects into account. If internal research processes are required, the complaint owner must ensure that these are carried out smoothly and quickly, while maintaining a dialog with the customers and informing them of the process and the result. His/her tasks also include the publication of the final solution in social media, if possible.

With regard to *complaint reaction*, the rules of a professional response still apply to social media complaints, namely: take criticism seriously, show empathy and understanding, remain objective, offer problem solutions, give explanations. However, there is a need to adapt the language style, which should be more concise and informal. At the same time, however, the corresponding rules must be observed with particular attention, as the answer is publicly available on the Internet. Unfriendly or aggressive responses (even to very unfriendly and very aggressive complaints) usually lead to outrageous reactions from previously uninvolved parties. Therefore, clear guidelines are needed for all employees who communicate in social media. For example, the IBM Social Guideline states that participating employees must make it clear that they are speaking for themselves and not on behalf of IBM. Furthermore they should be respectful to others and their opinions, respect copyright, fair use and financial disclosure laws, should not provide confidential information and should not cite clients, partners or suppliers on business-related matters without their approval (IBM 2005). Comparable rules of conduct can also be formulated for respectful communication by complainants ("Netiquette"; Netiquette Guidelines 2013).

In terms of time, rapid reaction is crucial. If the social media complaint is more of a general criticism, an answer must be given immediately. However, if personalized complaint handling can be carried out, the reference to the initiation of the processing procedure must be published at the same time the complaint is accepted. It should also be noted that the reaction to social media complaints is not completed even when a satisfactory problem solution has been implemented. On the one hand, third parties can react to the case with a time delay. On the other hand, these third parties also expect information about the outcome of the case. In this respect, the employee must describe and justify the decision taken or ask the complainants to post the successful solution (Hogreve et al. 2013).

17.4.2 Indirect Complaint Management

As part of the *complaint evaluation*, a channel-specific complaint analysis for social media complaints should be prepared. It also makes sense to compare the frequency distribution of social media complaints with that of conventional complaint channels. In this way it is possible to gain insights into the extent to which certain products and problems are critically addressed in an above-average manner in social media.

Furthermore, consequences for prioritizing problems are conceivable. If social media complaints are generally given a higher priority due to their publicity impact, the articulated problems usually receive a high degree of urgency in the usual Frequency-Relevance Analysis of Complaints (FRAC). Accordingly, the ranking of problems in a corresponding analysis of social media complaints will deviate from the classic FRAC and will require preferential attention.

It also makes sense to differentiate the urgency of social media complaints and thus apply an independent variant. With regard to relevance, simple criteria for resonance in the network can be selected, such as the net number of supporting comments and visibility—the degree of dissemination—of the medium), see Table 17.3.

With regard *to complaint management controlling*, special features must be taken into account in task controlling. For *subjective task controlling*, all individually addressed complainants may be asked to indicate the degree of their complaint satisfaction on Facebook or Twitter. The questionnaire must be very brief, but it must contain all important quality aspects of complaint handling, namely the

Table 17.3 Frequency-relevance analysis for social media complaints

Customer problem	Frequency (A)	Relevance				Relevance value (A) x (D) x (E)	PVI* (%)	Rank
		Gross number of supporting comments (B)	Number of contradictory comments (C)	Net number of supporting comments B-C) (D)	Score for the visibility of the social medium (1 - 5) (E)			
Problem A	10	48	2	46	1	460	23.7	2
Problem B	15	21	5	16	3	720	37.1	1
Problem C	26	4	1	3	5	390	20.0	3
Problem D	9	8	-	8	4	288	14.8	4
Problem E	17	4	3	1	5	85	4.4	5
Total	77	85	11	74	-	1,943	100.0	-

* Problem Value Index (PVI) for social media complaints = $\dfrac{\text{Relevance value x 100}}{\text{Sum of relevance values}}$

adequacy of the outcome, the interaction (friendliness/politeness; empathy/understanding; effort/helpfulness; activity/initiative; reliability) and the process (accessibility, reaction speed). In addition, special objective quality standards for the processing of social media complaints have to be defined within the scope of *objective task controlling*, e.g. media-specific specifications for the first-time fix rate, the total processing duration and the follow-up complaint rate.

Complaint reporting also needs to be adapted. It is not only a matter of including social media complaints in the traditional reporting system, but also of defining a specific reporting process for web complaints. In terms of content, the results of permanent monitoring, social media complaint analysis and problem prioritization must be recorded in a differentiated manner. In addition, the regular social media reports must be produced and distributed at shorter intervals and, in the event of considerable publicity risks, they must be supplemented by early warning reports.

Social media complaints also create new opportunities for *the utilization of complaint information*. Firstly, a far greater amount of information is available. Secondly, this information can be enriched through the fast dialog and thirdly, the dialog between the customers themselves often contains a wealth of ideas and suggestions, so that improved opportunities arise to use customer criticism and creativity for quality improvements. However, it is also necessary to ensure that these opportunities are exploited through an appropriate internal interlinking of complaint management, marketing and quality management.

17.5   Consequences for Selected Frameworks of Complaint Management

With regard to the *frameworks of complaint management*, social media particularly raise questions around human resources and organization.

The high demands placed on customer contact employees in terms of service orientation, social and emotional competence as well as technical and methodological competence increase considerably when dealing with social media. The employees must communicate quickly and briefly, but at the same time they have to correctly recognize the problem and formulate it in such a way that their response is not only accurate but seen as appropriate by the addressee and, if possible, by all readers. In view of the often offensive and aggressive comments of anonymous critics, they must have emotional self-control and they have to possess advanced system and media knowledge. In terms of *human resources policy*, this results in complex tasks of personnel recruitment, employee communication and training.

Social media are important for companies, not only in terms of complaints, but also for corporate communications, marketing and service. This raises the question of the *organizational design*. With regard to the *organizational structure*, two prerequisites must be met: on the one hand, there must be consistent coordination of the various activities, and on the other hand, the specific competencies of various communicative units must be used (Fishburn Hedges and Echo Research 2012; Bruhn and Hadwich 2013).

Of the various organizational variants that meet these requirements to varying degrees, the following are of particular relevance: (1) a central social media team or (2) functional social media teams and their coordination (see Fig. 17.1).

(1) Central Social Media Team In this variant, all social media activities are combined in a central department of corporate communications. This allows for a uniform corporate web presence, but is associated with the risk that functional competencies may not be sufficiently available.

(2) Functional Social Media Teams In this alternative, decentralized organizational units—such as brand communication, market research and customer care—are entrusted with specific social media activities. Complete central control is therefore not possible, but coordination takes place via a social media center within the corporate communication department. This determines the guidelines and supports the decentralized social media units.

The second option is strongly recommended for complaint management. This is because the entire body of knowledge with respect to customer communication and complaint management is available in this area and only in this way is it possible to consistently integrate social media complaints into the complaint management processes.

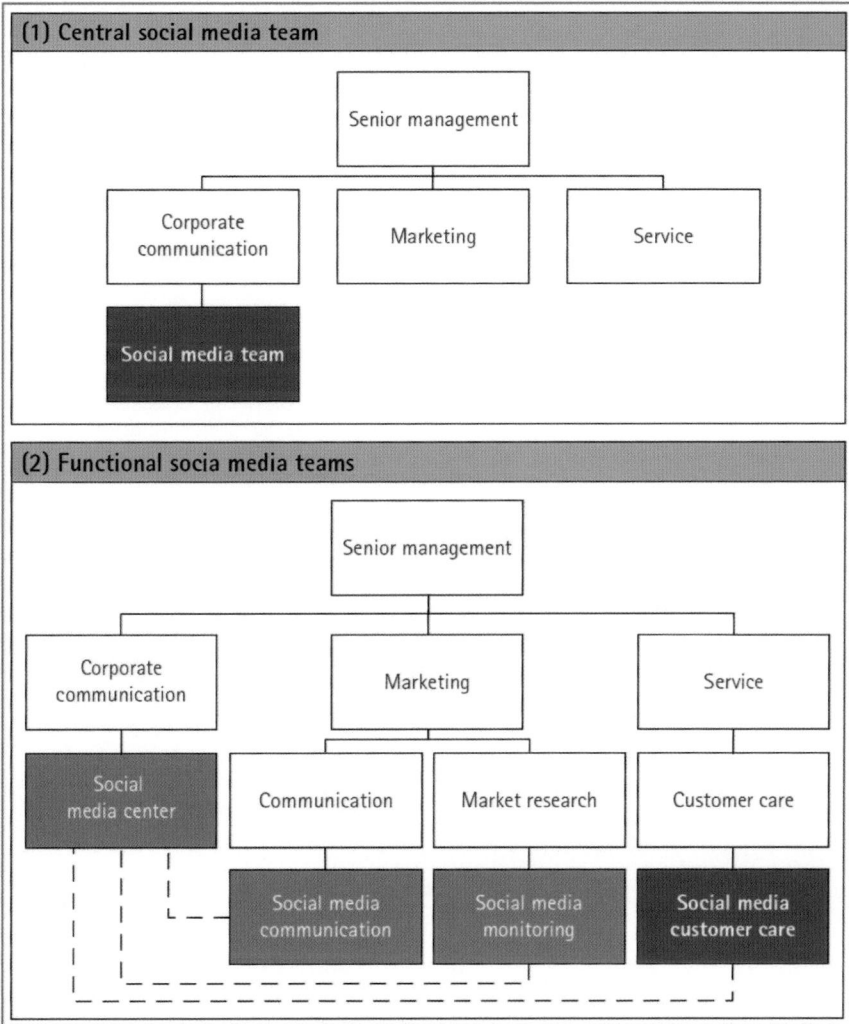

Fig. 17.1 Integration of social media into the organizational structure (based on Bruhn and Hadwich 2013)

In order to ensure a uniform appearance in social media and a fast reaction, *operational organizational consequences* must also be taken. These include clear responsibilities, the definition of standard codes of conduct, IT-specific integration, close coordination between the functional units and their permanent coordination by the Social Media Center.

Chapter 17 in Brief
- With regard to complaint management, the abundance of different forms of social media can be differentiated on the basis of two aspects: (1) whether the dialog is controlled by the customer or the company; (2) whether the social media is occasionally or regularly used for complaints.
- Essential customer-controlled social media with occasional customer criticism are private Facebook and Twitter accounts, private blogs and private videos. Regular customer criticism takes place on evaluation portals, social media platforms of watchdog organizations, and complaint sites.
- Corporate brand Facebook and Twitter accounts, as well as brand blogs, tend to have customer complaints occasionally, while customer care Facebook and Twitter accounts and customer care blogs regularly contain complaints.
- Social media are particularly relevant as a complaint channel because they have a high reach and allow for rapid escalation of complaint content. Accordingly, social media complaints potentially have a strong impact on the attitudes and behavior of other customers, as well as on corporate image and brand value.
- From a communication strategy perspective, two basic positions can be chosen: a passive monitoring strategy or an active dialog strategy. The choice between a monitoring or dialog strategy for social media must be consistently aligned with the respective complaint management strategy.
- Social media complaints place specific requirements on the task modules of the direct and indirect complaint management.
- The handling of social media complaints requires special human resource policy measures and the establishment of a specific organizational unit.

References

Allstateinsurancesucks (2018) http://www.allstateinsurancesucks.com. Accessed 2 Mar 2018
Basic R (2011) Dell: Wie man mit Kundenkritiken umgehen kann. http://www.robertbasic.de/2011/01/dell-wie-man-mit-kundenkritiken-umgehen-kann. Accessed 19 Nov 2017
Bruhn M, Hadwich K (2013) Dienstleistungsmanagement und Social Media – Eine Einführung in die theoretischen und praktischen Problemstellungen. In: Bruhn M, Hadwich K (eds) Dienstleistungsmanagement und Social Media: Potenziale, Strategien und Instrumente. SpringerGabler, Wiesbaden, pp 3–40
Bruns J (2013) Dextro Energy: Schulstoff sorgt für Facebook-Shitstorm. http://www.computerbild.de/artikel/cb-Aktuell-Internet-Shitstorm-bei-Dextro-Energy-8480039.html. Accessed 28 Feb 2018
Chevalier JA, Mayzlin D (2006) The effect of word of mouth on sales – online book reviews. J Mark Res 43(3):345–354
Direct2Dell (2018.) https://blog.dell.com/en-us/. Accessed 3 Mar 2018

Fishburn Hedges, Echo Research (2012) The social media customer. http://www. instituteofcustomerservice.com/files/The_social_media_customer_by_Fishburn_Hedges.pdf. Accessed 26 Nov 2017

Grégoire Y et al (2009) When customer love turns into lasting hate: the effects of relationship strength and time on customer revenge and avoidance. J Mark 73(6):18–32

Hadwich K, Keller C (2013) Einflussfaktoren und Auswirkungen der Beschwerdezufriedenheit im Social Media-Bereich – Eine empirische Untersuchung. In: Bruhn M, Hadwich K (eds) Dienstleistungsmanagement und social media: Potenziale, Strategien und Instrumente. SpringerGabler, Wiesbaden, pp 541–564

Harrison-Walker LJ (2001) E-complaining: a content analysis of an Internet complaint forum. J Serv Mark 15(5):397–412

Heinemann G (2013) Social Media als Spiegelbild des neuen Kaufverhaltens im Handel. In: Bruhn M, Hadwich K (eds) Dienstleistungsmanagement und Social Media: Potenziale, Strategien und Instrumente. SpringerGabler, Wiesbaden, pp 87–104

Herzog L, Luthe M (2010) Liebe auf den zweiten Blick – Vom souveränen Umgang mit Hotelbewertungen. In: Amersdorffer D et al (eds) Social Web im Tourismus. Springer, Berlin, pp 161–168

Hogreve J et al (2013) When the whole world is listening – an exploratory investigation of individual complaints on social media platforms. In: Bruhn M, Hadwich K (eds) Dienstleistungsmanagement und Social Media: Potenziale, Strategien und Instrumente. SpringerGabler, Wiesbaden, pp 515–540

IBM (2005) IBM social computing guidelines. https://www.ibm.com/blogs/zz/en/guidelines.html. Accessed 17 Feb 2018

Jansen J (2013) Ein Mann kämpft gegen British Airways. http://www.handelsblatt.com/ unternehmen/handel-dienstleister/werbeanzeige-gekauft-ein-mann-kaempft-gegen-british-airways/8732586.html. Accessed 18 Jan 2018

Jansen BJ et al (2009) Twitter power: tweets as electronic word of mouth. J Am Soc Inf Sci Technol 60(11):2169–2188

Kucuk US (2008) Negative double jeopardy: the role of anti-brand sites on the internet. Brand Manag 15(3):209–222

Li LP et al (2017) Dynamic multi-actor engagement in networks: the case of United Breaks Guitars. J Serv Theory Pract 27(4):738–760

Mandviwalla M, Watson R (2014) Generating capital from social media. MIS Q Exec 13(2):97–113

Muchazondida M, Tribe J (2017) Beyond reviewing – uncovering the multiple roles of tourism social media users. J Travel Res 56(3):287–298

Mühlenbeck F, Skibicki K (2010) Authentizität von Hotelbewertungsplattformen – wie mächtig und wie glaubwürdig ist User Generated Content? In: Amersdorffer D et al (eds) Social Web im Tourismus. Springer, Berlin, pp 57–70

Netiquette Guidelines (2013) http://tools.ietf.org/html/rfc1855. Accessed 17 Jan 2018

Pfeffer J et al (2014) Understanding online firestorms: negative word-of-mouth dynamics in social media networks. J Mark Commun 20(1–2):117–128

Reinecke S, Klautzsch E (2013) Social Media-Audit für Dienstleistungsunternehmen. In: Bruhn M, Hadwich K (eds) Dienstleistungsmanagement und Social Media: Potenziale, Strategien und Instrumente. SpringerGabler, Wiesbaden, pp 105–125

Safko L (2012) The social media bible – tactics, tools, and strategies for business success, 3rd edn. Wiley, Hoboken, NJ

Schmeißer DR (2010) Kundenbewertungen in der eTouristik – Segen oder Fluch? Psychologie der Reiseentscheidung im Social Web. In: Amersdorffer D et al (eds) Social Web im Tourismus. Springer, Berlin, pp 41–56

Sen S, Lerman D (2007) Why are you telling me this? An examination into negative consumer reviews on the Web. J Interact Mark 21(4):76–94

Smith C (2017) 34 amazing TripAdvisor statistics and facts – by the numbers. https:// expandedramblings.com/index.php/tripadvisor-statistics/. Accessed 2 Mar 2018

statista (2018a) Number of social media users worldwide from 2010 to 2021 (in billions).. https://
    www.statista.com/statistics/278414/number-of-worldwide-social-network-users/.   Accessed
    19 Feb 2018
statista (2018b) Most popular social networks worldwide as of January 2018, ranked by number of
    active users (in millions). https://www.statista.com/statistics/272014/global-social-networks-
    ranked-by-number-of-users/. Accessed 19 Feb 2018
Stauss B (2000) Using new media for customer interaction: a challenge for relationship marketing.
    In: Hennig-Thurau T, Hansen U (eds) Relationship marketing – gaining competitive advantage
    through customer satisfaction and customer retention. Springer, Berlin, pp 233–253
Tripp TM, Grégoire Y (2011) When unhappy customers strike back on the Internet. MIT Sloan
    Manag Rev 52(3):37–44
Tsimonis G, Dimitriadis S (2014) Brand strategies in social media. Mark Intell Plan 32(3):328–344
United Breaks Guitars (2009.) http://www.youtube.com/watch?v=5YGc4zOqozo.   Accessed
    27 Jan 2018
van Noort G, Willemsen LM (2012) Online damage control – the effects of proactive versus
    reactive webcare interventions in consumer-generated and brand-generated platforms. J Interact
    Mark 26(3):131–140
Ward JC, Ostrom AL (2006) Complaining to the masses: the role of protest framing in customer-
    created complaint web sites. J Consum Res 33(2):220–230
Wiedmann KP et al (2013) Social Media im Feld von Luxusmarken und -Services – Skizzen zu
    Gestaltungsansätzen und Best Practice-Beispiele. In: Bruhn M, Hadwich K (eds)
    Dienstleistungsmanagement und Social Media: Potenziale, Strategien und Instrumente.
    SpringerGabler, Wiesbaden, pp 153–170
Wilson HJ et al (2011) What's your social media strategy? Harv Bus Rev 89(7):23–25
Wolrich C (2005) Top corporate hate web sites. https://www.forbes.com/2005/03/07/cx_cw_
    0308hate.html#2b79f6194ed5. Accessed 24 Jan 2018
Xiang Z, Gretzel U (2010) Role of social media in online travel information search. Tour Manag 31
    (2):179–188

Implementing Active Complaint Management

18

© Springer Nature Switzerland AG 2019

469

B. Stauss, W. Seidel, *Effective Complaint Management*, Management for Professionals,
https://doi.org/10.1007/978-3-319-98705-7_18

Issues Raised
- Which phases should be distinguished in the implementation of complaint management and which activities should be carried out in each phase?
- What are the barriers to implementation and how can they be overcome?

The goal of implementation is to introduce a system of complaint management in the desired form quickly and without any major difficulties. In order to accomplish this goal, a series of measures must be *realized* in a *step-by-step* manner. Moreover, significant *barriers to implementation* must be overcome, so that a successful introduction is guaranteed.

18.1   Steps Toward Implementation

In the course of implementing complaint management, it is necessary to carry out a number of steps that can roughly be placed in a certain order, even if there are overlaps and interdependencies in the actual course of events. Table 18.1 provides an overview of an *ideal implementation cycle*.

18.1.1 Activities in the Decision Phase

The key starting point of any implementation process is the *top management decision*. This decision must be more than a general declaration of the intention to introduce a system of complaint management; rather, it is essential that already in this basic decision, the understanding of complaint management as the expression of consistent corporate customer orientation and as the core of customer relationship management is made clear. The relevance of this area of activity is thereby made explicit, and an important cornerstone of the company's values for dealing with complaints in the organization is laid. In order to obtain the absolute approval of top management, in a decision memo the necessity for action has to be elaborated clearly by (1) exposing the firm's actual status of complaint management and the deficits that result from it, (2) outlining the targeted status, including the expected consequences as far as the organization, personnel and information technology are concerned and (3) indicating the financial consequences. (4) In addition, it is necessary to present a rough schedule of the project in chronological order and to highlight important milestones.

Table 18.1 Implementation phases of an active complaint management (Source based on Gierl 2000, p.184)

Decision phase
- Preparation of the decision memo for the top management
  - Brief analysis of the actual state
  - Brief description of the target state
  - Representation of the economic consequences
  - Outline of the rough budget and time schedule
- Management decision

Project organization phase
- Establishment of the project organization including the steering committee, the core project team as well as specific work groups
- Information of all employees

Analysis phase
- Detailed analysis of the actual status of complaint handling
  - Analysis of the range of services
  - Analysis of the performance quality
  - Analysis of the human resource, organizational and information-technological framework
- Environment analysis
  - Analysis of the macro environment
  - Analysis of the micro environment

Conception phase
- Defining the objectives of complaint management
- Choice of the basic complaint management strategy
- Comparison of the strategic target profile with the actual profile of complaint management
- Preparation of detailed concept and process descriptions for all task modules of the direct and indirect complaint management
- Decicions on important human resource, organizational and information-technological changes
- Preparation of a handbook 'Complaint Management'
- Adoption of the budget and time schedule for the realization of the conceptual requirements

Introduction phase
- Implementation of modified processes with regard to the task components
- Realization of changes in the company's organizational structure
- Provision of the required IT-support
- Realization of an attitude changing process through sensitization and training events
- Execution of internal audits

18.1.2 Activities in the Organization Phase of the Project

Based on the decision by top management the *project organization*, which includes the core project team, the steering committee and working groups, is to be established.

The main task of the *core project team*—as a rule, this is also the group of people who prepared the presentation for top management—is to steer the entire project from an operational point of view and to install efficient project controlling. The team thus has to ensure that the project proceeds smoothly, on time and on budget, as well as in accordance with the complaint management concept. The *steering committee*, on the other hand, represents the body that is in charge of the project at the upper management level. It has to be informed about the progress of the project at regular intervals and makes fundamental decisions as the project unfolds—e.g. with respect to additional funds that might be needed or key conceptual alternatives.

As a rule, both project groups should be staffed with decision-makers from groups that will be most affected by the implementation process and the complaint management system that will be introduced, and these group members should be selected in a way that spans both *functional areas and vertical distribution levels*. These areas include groups that deal closely with customers, such as Customer Relationship Management, Marketing, Sales and Service, but also Quality Management and the IT department. Due to the central importance of complaint management to customer retention, it is natural that the organizational unit in charge of this topic has a responsible position on the planning group. In any event, the firm must see to it that the implementation is planned from a professional complaint management perspective, and not primarily from an information technology point of view. If the relevant know-how is not present in the company, experts from specialized consulting firms must be brought in to help.

The core project team must further ensure that *working groups* are formed with *members from various departments and vertical sales levels* in accordance with the project's conceptual and information technology focuses. These working groups will then be assigned specific sub-tasks in the analysis, conception and introduction phases.

With the transition to operational project work and the start of the analysis phase, *all the employees of the firm* should be *informed* for the first time about the planned introduction of complaint management. Here it is necessary to emphasize the importance of complaint management in achieving the goals of customer retention. The employees who are directly involved in the complaint management process are also to be surveyed with respect to the type and extent of their involvement in complaint-related activities. Their answers provide a basis for quantitative estimates of the gains in efficiency that can be achieved by implementing complaint management.

18.1.3 Activities in the Analysis Phase

A fundamental task of the core project team and primarily of the individual working groups is first of all to prepare an *analysis of the firm's current situation*. Complaints are received in the firm even before systematic complaint management is established. In many cases, however, firms have no idea about the extent of the complaint volume, nor do they have a precise overview of the complaint channels chosen by customers or of the number and sequence of actual processing procedures.

A detailed level of awareness of the firm's current situation is, however, a prerequisite for further planning.

In this respect, the field of action of complaint handling must be systematically investigated. In the first step, the *range of services* is analyzed, i.e. it is checked which services are provided for end customers (external problem-solving services) and which services are delivered to internal customers (internal information and consulting services). Then it is necessary to get an exact picture of the current *quality of task fulfillment* with regard to all aspects of complaint processing.

In a further step the inventory of the firm's situation applies to the *framework factors* of personnel, organization and information technology. Among other things, answers must be found to the questions of which employees come into direct contact with complainants, to what extent these employees possess the necessary skills, which organizational unit is currently in charge of complaint management, which organizational structure variant is established at present or whether and with which software system complaint information is documented and the processing procedures steered.

In addition to the current status of complaint processing, an environment analysis should be carried out to identify the main requirements and the relevant influencing factors outside and within the company. The analysis of the *macro environment* focuses on identifying end customers' expectations of the company's response, understanding how other companies handle complaints and investigating factors that can influence complaint management activities. These can be political-legal, social, economic or technological factors that either lead to changes in the customer's complaint behavior or enable new forms of task fulfillment.

The *micro environment* analysis examines the internal environment of the company's complaints management system. The main objective here is to identify the fundamental strategic competitive orientation of the company and the requirements of the various internal customer groups (such as top management, other functional areas or business units).

18.1.4 Activities in the Conception Phase

Based on the results of the as-is analysis, the main *goals and tasks of complaint management* can be specified. At the same time, the *basic complaint management strategy* must be chosen that corresponds to the company's competitive strategic positioning and meets the requirements of external and internal customers: Complaint Factory, Relationship Amplifier, Quality Control or Customer Satisfaction Lab—see Sect. 5.3.2.

The current status of complaint processing must be measured against the selected target strategy of complaint management. If the *strategic actual profile and the target profile differ*, the necessary changes in the direct and indirect complaint management process must be determined and the associated consequences for the design of the framework factors must be fixed.

The complaint management strategy chosen is the basis for generating detailed *concept and process descriptions* for the different task modules of complaint management. Taking into account the specific realities within the firm and using the results of the analysis of its current situation, the essential features of the *targeted process flows* can be developed and recorded. At the same time, the *documentation structure and content* should be determined for complaint content and complaint processing information.

The descriptions of the documentation and process structures that should result in optimal fulfillment of the goals of complaint management determine the fundamental demands placed on the *framework conditions* when the newly defined processes are introduced. These conditions are related firstly to the necessary process-oriented organizational changes, secondly to the required information technology support and thirdly to the number of employees utilized for complaint management and the skills of these employees. Accordingly, the decisions that must be made in this phase of the project concern organizational changes, hardware and software procurement and the necessary allocation of personnel, both in quantitative and in qualitative terms. The results of this conception phase should be documented in a *complaint management handbook* that contains a complete overview of the overall concept that will be implemented.

Furthermore, it is necessary to *set a* definite *deadline*, by which time the complaint management system should be working, by specifying milestones for the implementation process. The specific *budget* for the implementation of complaint management must also be approved.

18.1.5 Activities in the Introduction Phase

The focus of implementation is the *realization* of the defined processes and of the conceptual targets with respect to the individual task modules. At this point in time, the *organizational changes* should be made, the *complaint management software* customized and installed, and the *employees* hired and *trained* for the tasks they will have to perform in the future.

Internal audits must be performed not only after complaint management has been fully implemented, but also as the project progresses, in order to monitor the exact realization of the conceptual targets and their efficiency. The results of these audits may lead to changes in the planning process and in the details of the complaint management concepts, as well as to adjustments in the processes that have actually been introduced.

Table 18.2   Barriers of the implementation of an active complaint management

---

Acceptance barriers
- Lack of problem awareness
- Negative appreciation of complaints
- Doubts about the economic benefit of complaint management

Management barriers
- Missing commitment of the top management
- Resistance emerging from the corporate culture
- Lack of companywide sensitization
- Short-term perspective
- Misinterpretation of complaint management as an IT-problem

Organizational barriers
- Resistance against the impulses of complaint management toward correction and improvement
- Resistance against increasing influencing rights of complaint management

---

18.2   Barriers to Implementation and Measures to Overcome Them

There are frequently a number of *acceptance, management and organizational barriers* to the implementation of a comprehensive system of active complaint management. These barriers will be discussed in detail in the following section, along with possible countermeasures (see Table 18.2).

18.2.1   Acceptance Barriers

A *key obstacle to implementation* exists when a basic *acceptance* of complaint management is lacking in the firm.

The first reason for non-acceptance may be a *lack of awareness that there is a dissatisfaction problem*. Such is often the case when a low volume of complaints leads to a perception that customer satisfaction has been achieved, which would make an integrated system of complaint management unnecessary. This assessment can be changed if the firm looks first to the results of the analysis of its current situation, second to the results of a customer satisfaction survey and third to a survey of lost customers. Experience shows that a *careful analysis* of the number of complaints received in the firm as a whole will prove that the extent of the actual complaint volume is systematically underestimated. This statement is often confirmed by the results of *customer satisfaction surveys* in which data is collected regarding the extent to which customers have complained to the firm. A comparison of the stated number of articulated complaints with the number of documented complaints (usually only complaints in writing) may lead to a more realistic assessment of the situation. Oftentimes, however, *surveys of lost customers* contribute the most to creating the necessary awareness that a problem does indeed exist. Such surveys usually confirm that a majority of the lost customers terminated the business relationship because of dissatisfaction. If customer-specific turnover and profits for lost customers are available, these losses, which are generally preventable, can be quantified. It is a convincing argument to show losses on such a scale as potential gains that could be tapped in the future by employing specific measures of complaint management.

A particularly stubborn barrier to acceptance is the *negative opinion* people have *of complaints*. As stated in the first sentence of this book, "Everyone in the company hates complaints." For employees, they mean anger and criticism that may lead to further negative consequences; and managers see primarily the costs associated with processing complaints. A great deal of explanation is needed on this score. The opportunities for maintaining customer relationships, improving products and increasing process efficiency that are contained in complaints must be convincingly proven. Moreover, the firm must ensure that employees' negative experiences with complaints are not confirmed on an ongoing basis. This includes the introduction of an *open "culture of failure"*, which is expressed on the one hand by an effort to prevent failures and on the other hand by an understanding of failures that do occur as a source of learning and not as a reason to seek out and "punish" the "culprits". Not until employees tangibly experience the fact that they can improve and develop themselves on the basis of complaint feedback will they give credence to the sentence, "Complaints are opportunities."

As far as management is concerned, the principal barrier that must be overcome is their *doubt in the economic benefit* of complaint management. In this respect, the main challenge is to make it possible to calculate and to verify the benefits of complaint management—that is, its profitability. This is a difficult task, since there are no direct market exchanges in complaint management that would result in direct income. Nevertheless, there are promising approaches to calculating such figures, which were presented in the context of cost-benefit controlling (Sect. 11.3). These computations are based on the calculation of the retention and communication benefits—i.e. on the economic benefit that arises from the fact that dissatisfied customers continue to be loyal to the firm because of complaint management and at the same time are motivated to engage in positive word-of-mouth communication, thus initiating new customer relationships or strengthening existing ones. In order to make a reliable calculation of these benefit components, though, the firm must have appropriate data regarding customer and complaint satisfaction and customers' complaint, purchase and communication behavior. Since this data is usually not available when complaint management is first introduced, analogous calculations must be performed on the basis of assumptions that must be made with great care, so that the acceptance of the concept is not called into question at the outset. Experience tells us that it seems completely plausible, for example, to think that at least 25% of customers that would otherwise be lost can be retained with the help of complaint management. If we then base our calculation on the average customer turnover or profit and on just a short continuation of the business relationship (e.g. 3 years), then we usually obtain figures on a scale that would make investments in complaint management seem necessary from an economically rational perspective.

18.2.2 Management Barriers

Complaint management is a comprehensive management concept that, as the core of the firm's focus on customer orientation, does not simply affect one specific organizational unit, such as the customer care department; instead, it affects many employees in the most diverse departments and hierarchical levels that are involved in accepting, processing or resolving complaints and in utilizing complaint information. Furthermore, the introduction of complaint management alters customer-related processes, leads to changes in tasks and in many cases demands a modification of learned patterns of behavior. The importance of complaint management in the firm as a whole and the organizational changes associated with its introduction make a strong, visible *commitment* on the part *of top management* vital. If such a commitment is lacking, there is a danger that the implementation of complaint management will fail because of management barriers.

Accordingly, the highest management barrier is the *lack of commitment of top management.* A comprehensive system of complaint management is not an administrative task that can be fully delegated; it is the expression of a company philosophy that is consistently customer-oriented and that must be personified by management. If top management does not accord the complaint management project its full attention and highest priority, it signals to the rest of the firm that it views the customers and their problems as being secondary and that customer satisfaction is not really its main goal. Therefore, the deciding factor in the comprehensive success of the project and the anchoring of complaint management in the firm is that top management not only stands behind the project completely, but also that it is actively engaged in the process. The aim here is that executives on the steering committee are in charge of and also play an important role in the implementation process—one that is readily perceivable to the employees. The responsibilities of this role include appearing at information and sensitivity training events as contributors, personifying the commitment to resolving customer problems and rewarding employees who exhibit the desired conduct when dealing with complaining customers. It also has great symbolic meaning when executives seek out dialog with customers on a regular basis, such as by personally taking customer complaints in the call center or by participating in focus group interviews with complainants.

If the appropriate attitude and the willingness to engage in such conduct is lacking among executives, there must be an *active effort to convince* them of the importance of these matters. The president and CEO, as well as those in the firm who promote a customer-oriented corporate philosophy (e.g. the director of marketing or sales), play a special role here. They will be successful in convincing others the more they can refer to operational goals with respect to customer retention and quality improvement and the more they urge skeptics to answer the question of why the firm should consciously accept preventable customer losses.

If executives campaign intensively for complaint management and the concerns of dissatisfied customers, they will begin to reduce *possible resistance within the corporate culture*. In many firms, there is a great deal of talk about customer orientation, but the important realities in the corporate culture make it clear to the employees that other values dominate. In technologically oriented firms, there is a widespread conviction that only internal experts, and not customers, can properly assess the quality of the products. In other firms, cost considerations are most important by far, or employees are rewarded solely on the basis of short-term sales goals and not for achieving higher customer satisfaction and maintaining relationships with customers. It is imperative here that these existing cultural barriers be identified and removed, a process which involves the appropriate utilization of internal marketing, especially the internal communication policy and the incentive mechanisms, in addition to the example that the executives must set.

Another management failure in the implementation process is when *company-wide sensitivity for the topic of complaint management remains undone*. Indeed, many complaint management tasks can be assigned to a specific customer care department; however, as far as accepting and processing complaints and implementing quality improvement measures are concerned, employees from other organizational units must be involved in task performance. Every employee in the company is responsible for accepting complaints properly, for performing sub-tasks of complaint processing and particularly for eliminating the quality defects that have become evident in the complaints. Therefore, all employees must be notified about the goals of complaint management and informed and trained with respect to the behavior expected of them in this context. This is also especially true when we consider the widespread barriers to acceptance that were previously addressed and that exist in the minds of the employees. In this respect, it is not sufficient to attempt to sensitize employees simply by throwing a "kick-off" event for the complaint management project. Instead, this subject should be expanded on regularly and in a number of different ways in the context of internal communication.

Given the importance of complaint management for the company as a whole, it may also prove to be a barrier to introduction if a *short-term perspective marks* the thinking and actions of company management. Indeed, it is possible to define processes and translate them into procedural instructions in a very limited period of time. Even selecting and installing a suitable software solution and establishing a complaint center are possible within a clearly defined timeframe. Nevertheless, the process of change that must take place within the corporate culture, as well as the changes in attitude on the part of management and employees, cannot occur over the short term.

For this reason, it is important to understand the introduction of complaint management as a long-term concept and to recognize the implementation itself as an instrument of change within the company. To that end, the overall process of implementation should be broken down into individual *pragmatic implementation steps*, or realistic milestones, that make it possible to achieve immediate successes, have a motivating effect on all process participants and reinforce the overall process. The way to accomplish this goal is to define clear, manageable sub-projects that can be assessed and that are self-contained but build on each other at the same time. These sub-projects may include the introduction of complaint stimulation measures, the regular performance of complaint satisfaction measurements or the targeted initiation of quality improvement measures. Another approach, which can be applied along with the above, is to increase the level of realization of the complaint management tasks that should be performed in a step-by-step fashion. This process might begin, for example, with a single report based on simple analysis procedures and performance figures, and this process would not be expanded until a higher level of experience and knowledge is reached. In any event, it is necessary to link the "long wind" of the new conceptual orientation with a "policy of small steps" in the implementation process.

Another lasting management barrier that may come up is management's *misinterpretation of complaint management as an IT problem*. Particularly since the implementation of complaint management takes place in the context of CRM projects in many firms, some executives have a tendency not to see complaint management primarily as a managerial task, but rather as a problem of software implementation and database integration. As valuable as software support is to the efficient and qualitatively superior performance of complaint management tasks, the focus must nevertheless remain on the management concept. The firm must have a strategic concept for the management of customer relationships, at the core of which is complaint management. This strategic concept is the framework for the operative realization that takes place with the support of software. The goals of complaint management will only be achieved, however, if the strategic concept determines the significance of the technology, and not if the technology determines the scope of complaint management.

18.2.3 Organizational Barriers

The introduction of a system of complaint management does not take place in a vacuum but instead touches on a multitude of other fields of activity. Complaint management forces other departments to confront customer problems and the demands to solve and remedy those problems, requires problem solutions for which costs must be incurred, generates suggestions for improvement and makes clear through complaint reporting the nature and extent of the customer problems that have occurred. In this respect, therefore, *internal resistance to the impulses toward correction and improvement* that go along with complaint management is to be expected.

Experience from implementation processes shows that one of the greatest challenges is in fact persuading affected organizational units to actively use the results of complaint analysis for measures of improvement. In many cases, internal organizational units still have an image of the complaint management department as being only responsible for dialog with dissatisfied customers, but this image does not include granting the department a great deal of influence within the company.

The defensive mindset with respect to the utilization of complaint information is easy to explain. Departments in which *serious problems* are identified must *accept* their responsibility, have to invest *time and resources* in developing and implementing measures of improvement that they had not planned to use in this way. In light of these consequences, it is natural that the units in question tend to act in a rather reluctant manner and expend more of their energy in disputing whether customer concerns are in fact justified. In order to bring about a change here, various measures should be used in combination. The first requirement is an open culture of failure, which was addressed before, that emphasizes the possibility of learning from mistakes. Secondly, this possibility must be expressed in the fact that quality circles and quality improvement teams are permanently institutionalized and deal with customer problems from complaints and opportunities for improvement on a regular basis. In this way, the utilization of complaint information becomes an integral component of day-to-day work. Thirdly, it makes sense to design complaint reporting as a dialog. In this case, the complaint management system does not simply report the frequency and relevance of the identified problems to the various departments; rather, the departments are obliged on their part to report the corrective measures that they implemented to the director of complaint management and to top management.

The establishment of a system of complaint management also restricts the decision-making authority of others. Therefore, *resistance to complaint management's influence* on the decisions of other units can also to be expected. This resistance can only be overcome by making sure that the complaint management department is given sufficient power, which comes from awarding it a high position in the hierarchy—i.e., having it report directly to management. Yet another step is to have the view that complaint management should be established as a line position in the context of customer care. At the same time, and in order to strengthen the integration process as an "unfamiliar line position", rights of influence should be defined and implemented in coordination with other line departments. Moreover, the firm must ensure that the extent of functional authority that has been attained is reinforced by excellent competence in complaint management. Table 18.3 summarizes the significant barriers and the necessary countermeasures.

Table 18.3 Implementation barriers and possible counter measures

Implementation barriers		Counter measures
Acceptance barriers	Lack of problem awareness	▪ Generating and mediating information about problems experienced by the customers from - The analysis of the actual status - Customer satisfaction surveys - Surveys of lost customers
	Negative appreciation of complaints	▪ Communicating the opportunities for customer retention and quality improvement provided by complaints ▪ Implementation of an open failure culture
	Doubts about the economic benefit of complaint management	▪ Calculation of the number of lost customers as well as their turnovers and profit ▪ Calculation of the retention and communication benefit ▪ Calculation of the profitability of complaint management
Management barriers	Missing commitment of the top management	▪ Personal commitment of the executives in the implementation process ▪ Special commitment of the CEO ▪ Active convincing through promoters ▪ Formulation of operational customer retention and quality goals
	Resistance emerging from the corporate culture	▪ Credible exemplification through the executives ▪ Modification of the corporate principles, if necessary ▪ Use of instruments of internal marketing, especially of internal communication and targeted incentive mechanisms
	Lack of company-wide sensitization	▪ Companywide information events ▪ Complaint management as a topic within the scope of basic employee information and training programs
	Short-term perspective	▪ Fixing of realistic milestones ▪ Definition of sub-projects ▪ Gradual increase of the requirement level ▪ "Long wind" in relation to the objectives of changing corporate culture and employee attitudes ▪ Sustainment of motivation through a "policy of small steps"
	Misinterpretation of complaint management as an IT-problem	▪ Integration of complaint management into a strategic customer relationship management concept ▪ Derivation of the requirements of an IT-solution from the conceptual requirements
Organizational barriers	Resistance against the impulses of complaint management toward correction and improvement	▪ Adoption of an open failure culture ▪ Institutionalization of quality circles and quality improvement teams ▪ Realization of a "dialogical" complaint reporting
	Resistance against increasing influencing rights of complaint management	▪ High hierarchical establishment of complaint management or integration of complaint management within the framework of customer relationship management as a line department ▪ Targeted assignment and communication of influencing rights ▪ Securing of the high informal authority through excellent professional competence

Overcoming barriers in the implementation of complaint management is difficult. The experience report in *Spotlight 18.1* gives an impression of how long and arduous the journey to the desired destination is.

Spotlight 18.1

Implementation of Complaint Management: A Long and Arduous Journey

At the beginning of the 2000s, a large German financial services provider was confronted with great challenges in the face of increasingly intense competition in the markets. With declining customer loyalty and rising numbers of cancellations, the insight into the economic potential of existing customers grew and the goal of customer retention increasingly became the focus of strategic considerations.

First, the initial situation was analyzed. It turned out that the complaint management consisted only of rudimentary approaches. In essence, it was limited to recording the complaints addressed to the Board of Management and the complaints articulated to external institutions such as the industry ombudsman and the federal financial supervisory authority (Bundesanstalt für Finanzdienstleistungsaufsicht—BaFin). However, there was a lack of a complete overview of the considerable complaint volume, of efficient processes and of meaningful complaint reports.

The introduction of a software program was seen as an essential step on the way to professional complaint management. In the following intensive discussions with responsible departments, the perspective of information technology became increasingly established. The question of a seamless technical integration of new software modules into the existing system landscape became more important. This led to the decision preferred by IT to develop its own software solution.

However, this proved to be a step in the wrong direction. IT-driven and not sufficiently well-founded in terms of concept, new problems constantly arose when using the software to carry out the complaint management tasks, which again and again required lengthy adjustment processes.

Thus, the software introduction, intended as an implementation impulse, proved to be an obstacle to implementation in several respects. The constant application problems demotivated the employees and took away their belief in effective complaint management. Top management criticized the cost increases without any noticeable increase in benefits and did not provide any financial resources for the further development of complaint management.

This officially brought the implementation process to a standstill. However, those responsible for complaint management remained convinced of the relevance of the area of action, expanded their conceptual know-how and pushed ahead with improvements in content. This process included the development of a meaningful complaint report. About a decade after the first

(continued)

Spotlight 18.1 (continued)

implementation considerations began, this report received excellent marks from a neutral certification body, making it a breakthrough for complaint management. A project "Professional, active complaint management" was set up and the position of a person responsible for quality management/complaint management was created. However, the requirements of supervisory authorities also played a significant role here. The competent authority (BaFin)) implemented the Guidelines on Complaints-Handling by Insurance Undertakings (EIOPA-BoS-12/069) of the European Insurance and Occupational Pensions Authority (EIOPA) and ordered the establishment of complaint management functions.

With the institutionalization, the issue of complaint management increased in importance within the company again, even if significant obstacles to implementation still existed. The top management stuck to its assessment that there was no problem of lacking knowledge, but only a realization problem, which made the conceptual reorientation more difficult. There were also strong doubts about the economic benefits of complaint management because visible successes did not appear immediately. The levels of implementation already achieved were called into question and had to be maintained by those responsible for complaint management, against resistance.

Overall, the initiators of professional complaint management were confronted with a number of implementation barriers. Leadership and acceptance barriers proved to be the hardest to overcome. They included the doubts of top management about the economic relevance of complaint management, the resulting lack of support from above and the misinterpretation of complaint management as an IT problem. These factors have far-reaching consequences, which also prove to be high implementation barriers. These include, on the one hand, the inadequate organizational links between the actors involved, such as service, human resources development and quality management for complaint handling and the use of complaint information for improvements. On the other hand, a lack of management commitment and IT dominance leads to a lack of attention and appreciation of employees who are in contact with the complainants and represent the main pillar of complaint management. Successful complaint management is not possible without appropriate changes in these areas.

Complaint management alone cannot completely overcome these barriers due to its limited influence rights. However, it has been shown that important steps in the right direction can be taken through persistent further work, constant efforts to improve, and proof of success. This applies all the more, the stronger the market pressure, the more competitors professionalize their complaint management and the stricter the requirements of the state supervisory authorities for complaint management are.

(continued)

Spotlight 18.1 (continued)

The path to professional complaint management is difficult and involves detours. Also, the end of the journey is usually not foreseeable. Therefore, those responsible for complaint management must be prepared—with stamina, a high degree of frustration tolerance and a constant search for in-house supporters.

Michael Philipps
Former head of department of a large private health insurance company

Chapter 18 in Brief
- A complaint management system must be implemented in a systematic five-phase sequence, with decision, project organization, analysis, conception and introduction phases.
- When implementing a complaint management system, acceptance, management and organizational barriers can be expected to be overcome with specific activities.

Reference

Gierl H (2000) Beschwerdemanagement als Bestandteil des Qualitätsmanagements. In: Helm R, Pasch H (eds) Kundenorientierung durch Qualitätsmanagement. Deutscher Fachverlag, Frankfurt, pp 149–189

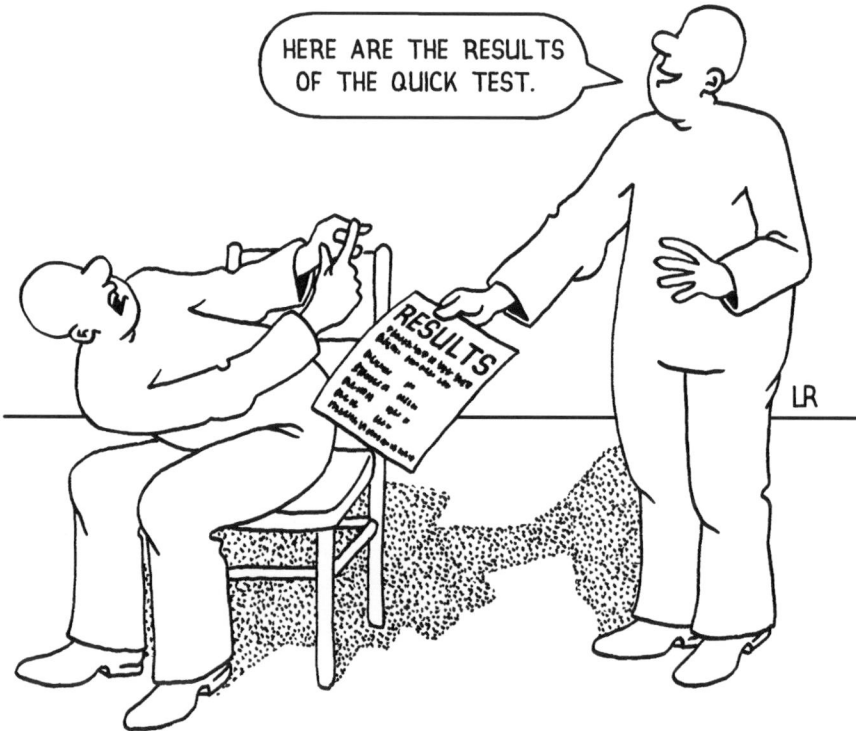

B. Stauss, W. Seidel, *Effective Complaint Management*, Management for Professionals,
https://doi.org/10.1007/978-3-319-98705-7_19

A list of statements regarding your complaint management is presented below. With this instrument, you can get a quick overview of the extent to which the basic principles of complaint management have *already been implemented* and where *deficits exist and action needs to be taken*.

The checklist is designed in *questionnaire* form and follows the structure of this book. First, there are statements concerning the general importance of complaint management in the firm (Part I) and the strategic planning (Part II). These are followed by statements related to the tasks of the direct (Parts III through VI) and indirect complaint management (Parts VII through X). Part XI contains statements on dealing with social media complaints. At the end, human resources-related, organizational and technological aspects of complaint management are addressed (Parts XII through XIV). For each topic, five statements are formulated and you will be asked to express your rejection or agreement on a scale of 1 ("does not apply at all") to 5 ("fully applies").

Specifications for analysis are provided below the checklist.

Quick Test Checklist

I	General Importance of Complaint Management	1	2	3	4	5
1	The goal of customer satisfaction is a top priority in our company.					
2	The managers and employees of our company see complaints as an opportunity.					
3	The goals and tasks of complaint management are clearly defined.					
4	Top management regularly takes time to read and answer complaints.					
5	Complaint reports are a high priority in board meetings.					
Σ	**Sum of scale values I**					

II	Strategic Planning of Complaint Management	1	2	3	4	5
6	We regularly carry out a strategic analysis of the external environment (e.g. changes in customer expectations, complaint management of other companies, socio-political and technological developments).					
7	We regularly carry out a strategic analysis of the internal environment (e.g., competitive strategic positioning of the company, internal target groups of complaint management).					
8	We regularly review the effectiveness and efficiency of the complaint management department (e.g. quality of task fulfillment, adequacy of resources available).					
9	We have a clearly defined complaint management strategy.					
10	There is strategic controlling of complaint management with the help of Key Performance Indicators.					
Σ	**Sum of scale values II**					

III	Complaint Stimulation	1	2	3	4	5
11	We want as many dissatisfied customers as possible to complain to us.					
12	We encourage customers to complain to us when they are dissatisfied.					
13	We make it easy for customers to complain (e.g. by offering a toll-free or low-cost service hotline).					
14	We actively communicate the existing complaint channels to our customers.					
15	The complaint management resources are designed to meet the communication requirements of our customers.					
Σ	Sum of scale values III					

IV	Complaint Acceptance	1	2	3	4	5
16	The complaint acceptance procedures are completely and clearly defined.					
17	All accepted complaints are forwarded to the responsible units quickly and accurately.					
18	During complaint acceptance, the necessary complaint information is recorded completely and accurately.					
19	There are well-structured software masks and/or standard forms for complaint recording.					
20	Information provided by customers on the feedback site of our website is immediately recorded and processed in the complaint management software system.					
Σ	Sum of scale values IV					

V	Complaint Processing	1	2	3	4	5
21	There are clear procedural definitions for complaint processing.					
22	Responsibilities for the overall complaint management process, as well as for individual sub-processes, are clearly defined.					
23	There are temporal standards for the processing of complaints.					
24	If processing deadlines are not met, an internal reminder is sent out.					
25	In the event of considerable delays in processing, complaints are automatically escalated to a special team or higher hierarchy level.					
Σ	**Sum of scale values V**					

VI	Complaint Reaction	1	2	3	4	5
26	All complainants receive a receipt confirmation and a final answer and – if necessary – intermediate replies.					
27	There are clear temporal standards for sending out the reply letters.					
28	The answers sent to customers take into account the individual circumstances of each case.					
29	Complainants receive a fair solution to their problems.					
30	The complaint process is completed by a follow-up contact.					
Σ	**Sum of scale values VI**					

VII	Complaint Evaluation	1	2	3	4	5
31	The complaint volume is analyzed on a regular basis with regard to quantitative criteria.					
32	The analyses performed are differentiated (e.g. according to customer groups, products or problems).					
33	The relationships between relevant criteria (such as products and problems) are systematically analyzed.					
34	There are methods used to prioritize problems.					
35	A time series analysis of the complaint volume is performed on a regular basis.					
Σ	**Sum of scale values VII**					

VIII	Complaint Management Controlling	1	2	3	4	5
36	Our company analyzes on a regular basis, how many dissatisfied customers do not complain and how many articulated complaints are not registered by the company.					
37	Complainants' satisfaction with complaint handling (complaint satisfaction) is surveyed regularly.					
38	Quality and productivity standards are defined and monitored in regard to he tasks of complaint management.					
39	The costs of complaint management are determined systematically.					
40	The benefits of complaint management are assessed monetarily and taken into consideration when the profitability of complaint management is calculated.					
Σ	**Sum of scale values VIII**					

IX	Complaint Reporting	1	2	3	4	5
41	The internal customer segments to whom complaint-relevant information should be forwarded are clearly defined					
42	There are clear definitions with regard to the contents, design and level of detail of the reports.					
43	In addition to the reports that are generated according to a clearly defined temporal rhythm, special reports are compiled if special circumstances (e.g. a serious increase in the number of important customer problems) require it.					
44	Special analyses and the reports corresponding to these analyses are made at the request of internal customers.					
45	Authorized internal customers have access to all the complaint information and to detailed analyses of that information.					
Σ	Sum of scale values IX					

X	Utilization of Complaint Information	1	2	3	4	5
46	The information gathered as part of the complaint management process is systematically used for quality improvements.					
47	Complaint information is utilized by employing specific methods (such as FMEA).					
48	Quality improvement teams and quality circles use complaint information for systematic failure prevention and continuous improvement.					
49	Our company uses customer panels with complainants to tap into the creative potential of criticizing customers.					
50	Complaint and complaint management information is an integral part of our system of corporate customer knowledge management.					
Σ	Sum of scale values X					

XI	Social Media Complaints	1	2	3	4	5
51	Social media complaints are monitored and processed by a specialized team.					
52	There is systematic monitoring of social media complaints.					
53	Social Media complaints are answered immediately.					
54	If individual problem solving is still possible, social media complainants are asked to contact the complaint management directly.					
55	There is specific complaint analysis and special complaint reporting for social media complaints.					
Σ	**Sum of scale values XI**					

XII	Human Resource Aspects of Complaint Management	1	2	3	4	5
56	Great value is placed upon the appropriate employee behavior in complaint contact situations.					
57	Employees are trained to handle complaint situations properly.					
58	Employees involved in complaint processing are extensively informed about the procedures, responsibilities and technology that are part of the complaint management system.					
59	Customer-contact employees have ample discretion in solving customer problems.					
60	Our incentive systems reward customer-oriented solution behavior.					
Σ	**Sum of scale values XII**					

XIII	Organizational Aspects of Complaint Management	1	2	3	4	5
61	A complaint management department exists.					
62	There is an efficient division of tasks between centralized and decentralized complaint handling.					
63	Competencies and responsibilities are clearly distributed between the head of the complaint management department and functional units (such as a Complaint Center or Customer Interaction Center).					
64	The competencies and responsibilities of the complaint management department are clearly regulated in relation to other organizational units.					
65	The complaint management department has clear targets and definite budget accountability.					
Σ	**Sum of scale values XIII**					

XIV	Technological Aspects of Complaint Management	1	2	3	4	5
66	A software-supported complaint management system has been implemented so that tasks are performed efficiently.					
67	The program implemented permits quick and structured recording of information during the customer's complaint articulation.					
68	The program implemented permits automatic control of the processing procedures.					
69	The program implemented contains comprehensive analysis and controlling elements.					
70	The technology used is consistently integrated into a comprehensive complaint management concept.					
Σ	**Sum of scale values XIV**					

Instructions for the Evaluation

1. Determine the *sum of scale values* for each of the 14 blocks of statements and enter the number in the box provided at the end of each block.
2. *Transfer* the results to the appropriate lines on the result form provided below.
3. Determine the respective *gap* between your results and the *maximum achievable result*.
4. Consider the results for the *"General Importance of Complaint Management"*. If deficits are found here, your efforts must initially focus on this basic level.
5. Determine the *block of statements for which the highest discrepancy value* exists. This is where corrective measures to optimize your system of complaint management should begin.

Quick Test Result Form

	Block of statements	Max. score	Achieved score	Gap	
				Absolute	%
I	General importance of complaint management	25			
II	Strategic planning of complaint management	25			
III	Complaint stimulation	25			
IV	Complaint acceptance	25			
V	Complaint processing	25			
VI	Complaint reaction	25			
VII	Complaint evaluation	25			
VIII	Complaint management controlling	25			
IX	Complaint reporting	25			
X	Utilization of complaint information	25			
XI	Social media complaints	25			
XII	Human resource aspects of complaint management	25			
XIII	Organizational aspects of complaint management	25			
XIV	Technological aspects of complaint management	25			

Σ	**Sum**	**350**			

Printed in Poland
by Amazon Fulfillment
Poland Sp. z o.o., Wrocław
23 March 2022

1745bce0-4d5d-4f20-8bcb-37a558647229R01